Cases on Chinese Corporate Giants and Global Expansion

Henni Appelgryn
Beijing Normal-Hong Kong Baptist University, China

Youssef Elhaoussine
Beijing Normal-Hong Kong Baptist University, China

IGI Global
Scientific Publishing
Publishing Tomorrow's Research Today

Vice President of Editorial | Melissa Wagner
Director of Acquisitions | Mikaela Felty
Director of Book Development | Jocelynn Hessler
Production Manager | Mike Brehm
Cover Design | Jose Rosado

Published in the United States of America by
IGI Global Scientific Publishing
701 East Chocolate Avenue
Hershey, PA, 17033, USA
Tel: 717-533-8845 | Fax: 717-533-7115
Website: https://www.igi-global.com E-mail: cust@igi-global.com

Library of Congress Cataloging-in-Publication Data

Names: Appelgryn, Hendrik Lodewyk, 1959- editor | Elhaoussine, Youssef, 1980- editor
Title: Cases on Chinese corporate giants and global expansion / [edited by] Henni Appelgryn, Youssef Elhaoussine.
Description: Hershey, PA : IGI Global Scientific Publishing, [2027] | Includes bibliographical references and index. | Summary: "This book explores the rise of a new generation of Chinese companies that are shaping the global economic landscape. It delves into how these enterprises--ranging from tech unicorns to consumer goods disruptors--leverage digital transformation, localization strategies, global capital, and policy alignment to compete with established multinational corporations"-- Provided by publisher.
Identifiers: LCCN 2025035289 (print) | LCCN 2025035290 (ebook) | ISBN 9798337343020 hardcover | ISBN 9798337343037 paperback | ISBN 9798337343044 ebook
Subjects: LCSH: International business enterprises--China | New business enterprises--China | Corporations--China--Growth
Classification: LCC HD9210 .C265 2026 (print) | LCC HD9210 (ebook) | DDC 338.0951--dc23/eng/20260123
LC record available at https://lccn.loc.gov/2025035289
LC ebook record available at https://lccn.loc.gov/2025035290

British Cataloguing in Publication Data
A Cataloguing in Publication record for this book is available from the British Library.

Table of Contents

Detailed Table of Contents

This chapter examines the globalization strategy of Air China, the nation's sole flag carrier, within the context of a saturated domestic market and intensifying international competition. The purpose is to analyse the airline's differentiated approach to overseas expansion, focusing on its non-acquisition growth model through strategic alliances, hub development, and membership ecosystems. Key themes discussed include target market selection in Asia and Europe, entry modes such as joint ventures and e-commerce, and competitive advantages derived from fleet scale and brand reputation. The chapter also addresses significant challenges, including geopolitical conflicts and trade wars, and details mitigation strategies like route network changes and supply chain diversification. The overall contribution provides strategic insights for aviation enterprises navigating global uncertainties, showing how leveraging national initiatives and alliance networks can transform external vulnerabilities into differentiated advantages while maintaining brand integrity.

This chapter examines the globalization strategy of SF Holding, China's leading comprehensive express and logistics company. The purpose is to analyse the motivations, market selection criteria, entry modes, and competitive advantages that have driven the firm's international expansion. Key themes include the saturation of the domestic market, the pull of cross-border e-commerce, and the supportive role of national policies like the Belt and Road Initiative. The chapter details SF Express's phased approach, prioritizing Southeast Asia before targeting Europe and the Middle East, and its hybrid entry strategy combining mergers and acquisitions, such as the acquisition of Kerry Logistics, with strategic partnerships. It also addresses the challenges faced, including cultural adaptation and regulatory compliance, and the mitigation strategies employed. The overall contribution is a comprehensive framework illustrating how a Chinese logistics firm builds a global network through technology-driven integration and localized operations, offering strategic insights for similar enterprises.

This chapter analyzes JD.com's globalization strategy, examining the Chinese e-commerce conglomerate's transition from domestic leader to international competitor. The purpose is to investigate strategic drivers, market selection, and entry modes shaping JD's overseas expansion. Key themes include the "dual-engine" strategy targeting Europe as a margin engine and Southeast Asia as a volume engine, tiered entry models balancing control with local partnerships, and implementation of a logistics-centric ecosystem abroad. To explores competitive advantages from self-operated logistics and authenticity governance, plus challenges including profitability pressures, brand positioning against price-focused competitors, and joint venture governance frictions. Through PESTEL and Porter's Five Forces frameworks, the analysis illuminates factors shaping JD's international trajectory. The case study of how an asset-heavy business model translates across contexts, highlighting adaptive governance, localized execution, and conversion of supply-chain into sustainable competitive advantage.

This chapter examines the global expansion strategy of Geely Auto Holding, tracing its evolution from a domestic Chinese manufacturer into a multinational automotive conglomerate. Key themes encompass the company's diversified market entry approaches across developed and emerging economies, its development of modular vehicle architectures for cost efficiency, and vertical integration in batteries and intelligent systems. Also addresses implementation challenges such as regulatory barriers, cultural integration, and geopolitical risks, alongside mitigation strategies involving institutional adaptation and sustained research and development investment. By applying SWOT analysis, the PESTEL framework, and Porter's Five Forces, provide a comprehensive evaluation of Geely's competitive positioning. The chapter contributes insights into how emerging-market multinationals can use acquisitions, localized production, and technological innovation to achieve global competitiveness while managing complex international environments.

This chapter examines JCET Group's strategic transformation from a domestic Chinese packaging provider into a top three global OSAT leader through its 2015 acquisition of STATS ChipPAC. The analysis explores the internal and external motivations for expansion, including domestic market saturation, China's Chip Replacement Initiative, and the need for advanced packaging technologies. Details of the sophisticated acquisition structure using a Special Purpose Vehicle and backing from China's National Integrated Circuit Industry Investment Fund (Big Fund) to execute a leveraged cross-border merger while navigating geopolitical sensitivities. The case shows how state-backed capital enabled rapid technological advancement and market access, though significant challenges emerged, including heightened debt burdens, complex post-merger integration, and exposure to Sino-U.S. trade tensions. Insights into how companies can gain an edge by making their global production the best it can be and by developing an array of technologies.

This chapter examines BGI Group's globalization strategy, tracing its evolution from a national research institute to a multinational life sciences corporation. Per the authors, the purpose is to analyse the dual drivers of international expansion: internal motivations for technological advancement and market diversification, alongside external support from Chinese industrial policies. Important things to think about are figuring out who the customers are, looking at different ways to do business like joining with others, and getting ahead by spending less or having new technology. The analysis covers implementation through overseas subsidiaries and Huo-Yan Laboratories, while assessing challenges such as regulatory scrutiny, geopolitical tensions exemplified by inclusion on the U.S. Entity List, and data sovereignty issues. The chapter contributes insights into the distinctive pathways and systemic challenges confronting Chinese high-technology firms operating in knowledge-intensive global markets.

This chapter examines the globalization strategy of WuXi AppTec "WuXi" is pronounced Woo-shee, a leading pharmaceutical outsourcing company, detailing its evolution into an integrated Contract Research, Development, and Manufacturing Organization (CRDMO). The purpose is to analyse the company's market entry, core strengths, and operational strategies across key regions, including the United States, Europe, and the Middle East. Key themes discussed encompass the end-to-end CRDMO model, strategic mergers and acquisitions, technological platforms, long-tail customer strategy, and resilience in global supply chains amid geopolitical challenges. The chapter also addresses significant obstacles such as the BIOSECURE Act and trade tensions, along with mitigation strategies like divestitures and expansion in Singapore. The contribution offers insights into how latecomer firms can achieve global leadership through strategic vision, localized operations, and adaptive responses to international dynamics.

This chapter examines the international expansion strategy of Hengrui Pharmaceutical, a leading Chinese innovative medicine enterprise. The purpose of the chapter is to analyse the company's motivations for globalization, including domestic market saturation and policy pressures from centralized procurement, alongside the allure of larger international markets. The key themes explored include Hengrui's market selection criteria, it's evolving entry modes such as license-out agreements and the novel NewCo model, and the competitive advantages derived from sustained research and development investment and a differentiated product pipeline. Notable challenges include regulatory obstacles with the US Food and Drug Administration and dependence on partnership income. The overall contribution provides a replicable framework for other Chinese pharmaceutical firms seeking global expansion, emphasizing the critical role of technological innovation, strategic partnerships, and robust regulatory preparedness in navigating geopolitical and competitive landscapes

This chapter examines Tsingshan Holding Group's expansion into Indonesia through the Indonesia Morowali Industrial Park (IMIP), analysing the complex interplay between industrial strategy, geopolitical alignment, and socio-environmental consequences. Using a PESTEL framework, the analysis reveals how Indonesia's downstream processing policies and China's Belt and Road Initiative enabled the world's largest nickel processing facility, yet one marked by debates. The movement of Moronene indigenous communities, uncertain conditions for migrant workers, environmental coal-powered operations, and risks for Tsingshan and its electric vehicle partners show that the company's competitive advantage derives from regulatory asymmetries rather than technological superiority alone. This contributes a critical perspective on extractive globalization, arguing that large-scale resource investments in the Global South must transition from enclave-based growth toward ethical, sharing industrialism to achieve long-term validity and sustainability in an increasingly values-oriented global economy.

This chapter examines Envision Group's evolution from a Chinese wind turbine manufacturer into a global green technology leader, analysing how the company strategically integrates external climate governance frameworks into its core business model. It presents the company's "resource-policy-demand" three-dimensional framework for global market selection across country, regional, and urban scales, detailing entry strategies including mergers and acquisitions, greenfield investment, co-construction models, and digital export of the EnOS™ platform. Through SWOT analysis and examination of zero-carbon industrial parks as replicable infrastructure, this shows how Envision transforms climate governance compliance into competitive advantage. The analysis contributes insights into the coupling effects between international rule systems and corporate strategy, offering a framework for understanding how energy enterprises can navigate geopolitics, secure green financing, and capture governance-driven premiums in the global energy transition.

Preface

The rapid rise of Chinese multinational enterprises has reshaped the dynamics of global business, technology, manufacturing, logistics, finance, healthcare, and sustainability. Once viewed primarily as domestic challengers or cost-driven manufacturers, many Chinese corporations have emerged as influential global actors capable of competing with established multinational giants through technological innovation, strategic adaptation, and increasingly sophisticated internationalization models. This volume, *Cases on Chinese Corporate Giants and Global Expansion*, explores the diverse pathways through which leading Chinese enterprises expand beyond national borders and navigate the complexities of international markets.

The cases assembled in this collection reflect the growing importance of Chinese firms in industries central to the twenty-first century global economy, including artificial intelligence, electric vehicles, batteries, biotechnology, pharmaceuticals, logistics, aviation, finance, energy, consumer electronics, and digital infrastructure. Across these sectors, the featured companies confront common challenges: geopolitical tensions, regulatory divergence, trade barriers, sustainability pressures, supply chain disruptions, cultural adaptation, and technological competition. Yet each organization demonstrates distinct approaches to market entry, localization, innovation, governance, and competitive positioning.

This book contributes to the broader understanding of international business by highlighting perspectives that are often underrepresented in traditional globalization literature. Rather than portraying globalization as a one-directional process led solely by Western multinational corporations, the cases illustrate how Chinese enterprises are actively shaping global markets through alternative business models, state-market coordination, open-source innovation, infrastructure-led expansion, strategic acquisitions, and technology-driven ecosystems. The chapters collectively reveal that successful internationalization increasingly depends not only on scale and capital, but also on adaptability, regulatory intelligence, stakeholder engagement, and cross-cultural strategic management.

The volume further demonstrates the diversity of Chinese globalization models. Some firms pursue aggressive acquisition strategies to accelerate technological upgrading and market access, while others emphasize localized manufacturing, strategic alliances, digital ecosystems, or sustainability-oriented expansion. Several cases illustrate how companies transform regulatory constraints and geopolitical pressures into strategic opportunities, building resilience through supply chain diversification, localized operations, and adaptive governance structures. At the same time, the collection critically examines tensions surrounding environmental accountability, data sovereignty, ethics, labor conditions, and national security concerns associated with global expansion.

Designed for scholars, students, business practitioners, policymakers, and international managers, this book offers both theoretical insight and practical relevance. The case studies employ analytical frameworks such as SWOT, PESTEL, Porter's Five Forces, VRIO, value chain analysis, and internationalization theory to evaluate strategic decision-making in real-world contexts. The volume therefore serves not only as a collection of corporate narratives but also as a teaching and research resource for courses in international business, strategic management, global marketing, political economy, and emerging-market multinationals.

CHAPTER OVERVIEW

1. The opening chapter investigates the rise of an emerging artificial intelligence company that challenged dominant global technology firms through open-source innovation, efficient architecture design, and strategic positioning across international markets while navigating geopolitical tensions and export restrictions.
2. The second chapter explores the international expansion of a major Chinese financial data provider, focusing on data sovereignty, compliance adaptation, institutional partnerships, and the transformation of regulatory complexity into competitive advantage.
3. The third chapter examines the global internationalization strategy of a leading electric vehicle manufacturer through the lens of the Kangaroo Theory, highlighting localization, technological innovation, and adaptive market entry strategies across developed and emerging economies.
4. The fourth chapter analyses the international growth trajectory of the world's largest lithium-ion battery producer, emphasizing regional expansion strategies, sustainability pressures, localization models, and operational resilience amid geopolitical uncertainty.
5. The fifth chapter focuses on the globalization strategy of a multinational electronics corporation, demonstrating how localized innovation, diversified man-

ufacturing, and global branding initiatives contribute to sustainable competitive positioning.

6. The sixth chapter presents a state-capitalist model of globalization through the international expansion of a major Chinese conglomerate, illustrating the interaction between policy support, institutional adaptation, finance, and diversified industrial operations.
7. The seventh chapter investigates the overseas expansion of a national airline carrier, examining alliance-based growth, route diversification, risk mitigation, and the strategic use of national branding in highly competitive aviation markets.
8. The eighth chapter analyses the globalization strategy of a leading logistics enterprise, emphasizing technology-driven integration, phased regional expansion, strategic acquisitions, and localized operational models.
9. The ninth chapter explores the internationalization of a major e-commerce conglomerate through supply chain integration, logistics ecosystems, localized governance structures, and differentiated regional market strategies.
10. The tenth chapter examines how a Chinese automotive manufacturer transformed into a multinational corporation through mergers, technology acquisition, vertical integration, and adaptive international market entry.
11. The eleventh chapter studies the strategic acquisition of a global semiconductor packaging company, illustrating how cross-border mergers, state-supported financing, and technological upgrading accelerated international competitiveness.
12. The twelfth chapter explores the globalization of a biotechnology enterprise operating in politically sensitive and knowledge-intensive markets, focusing on innovation, overseas laboratories, regulatory scrutiny, and data governance challenges.
13. The thirteenth chapter examines the rise of a pharmaceutical outsourcing company into a globally integrated CRDMO leader through mergers, technological platforms, localized operations, and adaptive supply chain strategies.
14. The fourteenth chapter analyses the transformation of a pharmaceutical company from a domestic generic producer into an innovation-driven international competitor through research and development, licensing partnerships, and evolving market entry models.
15. The fifteenth chapter critically examines the expansion of a major nickel producer into Indonesia, highlighting the intersections between industrial policy, environmental governance, labor conditions, geopolitical alignment, and sustainability debates.
16. The sixteenth chapter investigates a green technology company's integration of climate governance frameworks into global strategy, emphasizing zero-carbon infrastructure, renewable energy systems, and governance-driven competitive advantage.

17. The final chapter explores the globalization of a leading AIoT and surveillance technology company, focusing on technological leadership, localized manufacturing, regulatory adaptation, and strategic responses to sanctions and geopolitical pressures.

Collectively, these chapters offer a multifaceted examination of how Chinese corporations are redefining global expansion in an era characterized by technological disruption, geopolitical fragmentation, sustainability imperatives, and shifting economic power. The cases underscore the strategic complexity of internationalization while providing valuable lessons for organizations operating in increasingly interconnected yet contested global markets.

We hope this volume encourages further scholarly discussion and practical reflection on the evolving role of Chinese multinational enterprises in shaping the future of global business.

Acknowledgment

We are deeply grateful to all the authors who took part in this project and generously shared their valuable case studies. Their dedicated efforts to gather and synthesize important information have enriched our understanding of China's market. Their contributions represent not only academic achievements but also essential resources for business practitioners and researchers, helping to shape our collective knowledge and insights.

We would like to extend our sincere thanks to the Faculty of Business and Management at Beijing Normal Hong Kong Baptist University (BNBU) in Zhuhai for their support throughout this project, especially Prof. Adolf Ng the Dean of the Faculty of Business and Management, and the BNBU Center of Teaching and Learning (CTL). As an international higher education institution in China, the university provided an ideal environment for developing this practice-oriented research project in business. We hope that the findings from this work will prove beneficial and inspiring to students.

We also wish to express our appreciation to the IGI Global editorial team for granting us the opportunity to create this casebook. They offered an exceptional support system to manage the publication process efficiently, and we are grateful to Nina Eddinger.

Thank you all for your invaluable contributions. We hope this casebook will not only deepen our understanding of China's market but also create opportunities for us to better understand one another, fostering a spirit of collaboration and mutual learning.

Acknowledgement

Chapter 1
DeepSeek's Open-Source AI Revolution: A "David vs. Goliath" Challenge to Global Tech Giants

Henni Appelgryn
http://orcid.org/0000-0001-6567-5605
Beijing Normal-Hong Kong Baptist University, China

EXECUTIVE SUMMARY

This chapter examines DeepSeek's international expansion strategy and its disruptive impact on the global artificial intelligence landscape. A Chinese startup used open-source philosophy, innovation, and strategic positioning to challenge established players such as OpenAI and Google. The company's technological innovations (Mixture of Experts architecture, knowledge distillation), market entry approaches across the European Union, United States, Asia-Pacific, and BRICS+ nations, and navigation of geopolitical tensions, including export controls and regulatory scrutiny. Focusing on efficiency and being completely open changed limitations, hardware problems, into benefits. Prioritise accessibility over exclusivity and cultural fluency over generic solutions, hurrying AI democratization while forcing industry incumbents to reconsider proprietary models. The chapter contributes insights into how non-Western technology firms can achieve global relevance through strategic adaptation, community-driven development, and the deliberate embrace of national identity as market differentiation.

DOI: 10.4018/979-8-3373-4302-0.ch001

INTRODUCTION

Artificial intelligence (AI) has its origin and is the first suggestion raised in the early 20th century. One of the turning points came with Turing (1950) question, "*Can machines think*?" His work accepted limits between human cognition and the possibility of a machine thinking, therefore laying or question the conceptual foundation for the discipline.

The concept of intelligent machines was hypothetical, as mentioned above. AI systems currently not only replicate human ideas but even outperform human ability in particular fields. According to Harrington (2025) modern artificial intelligence, for example, can create written materials or perform challenging tasks at rates well above human ability.

As artificial intelligence develops, issues about its social consequences have become increasingly important. One of the common worries is the job displacement by intelligent systems. Although such worries are not baseless, it is crucial to understand that artificial intelligence is still a tool, albeit a strong one, created and guided by humans. The course of artificial intelligence will finally rely on the decisions societies make on how to control and incorporate these technologies.

BACKGROUND

People pause for a second when thinking about how DeepSeek began. It is easy to get swept up in the glamour of fast-moving breakthroughs and headline-worthy Artificial Intellgence (AI) feats. Underneath all that shine, there is a foundation that deserves a slower, more careful look. It was a time when everyone seemed to tinkle about large language models, as if they'd just realized that these systems were not science fiction anymore. They were tools, instruments, even the future (Choe & Parvini, 2025). In that moment, a purposeful, not boastful, DeepSeek took a step forward.

But here we are, and this study aims to explore how DeepSeek changing the game in the global AI world by breaking away from the usual closed-off, secretive systems. Founded in Hangzhou and supported by High-Flyer Capital, as Baptista (2025) mentions, this Chinese startup focuses on openness, teamwork, and making AI accessible to everyone. This looks at how one ambitious startup used clever strategies and smart tech to shake up an industry that seemed set in its ways. By digging into their journey from early challenges to global growth, Deepseek learns useful lessons for anyone hoping to innovate and succeed in today's competitive business world.

There is something deep and thoughtful, even radical, about the way the company wrapped its arms around opensource culture. It was not chasing profit margins alone; it wanted to build it for the people, not just for the investors. There is a quiet audacity in that. This was not just tech for tech's sake, this was about building an ecosystem where knowledge flowed freely and developers and researchers could meet at the same table, trading ideas instead of locking them away.

The company's roots in Hangzhou feel more than symbolic. It is a city with layers, ancient rhythms and futuristic ambition side by side, and DeepSeek fits right in. From that strategic base, the team's vision has stretched far beyond China's borders. It is reaching toward something bigger; a kind of AI renaissance where borders blur and collaboration exceed competition.

The road ahead is rough and with regulatory hurdles are not leaving, and rivals, some huge, are circling (Reiisieh, 2025). It is not just building dominant models; it is about navigating a minefield of policy, trust, and public opinion. But if the early steps are any sign, DeepSeek is not flinching. It is not another startup chasing the next valuation milestone. It is more like a statement, a quiet one, but with the potential to echo for years.

Leadership

The quiet power of beginnings and not the kind with parades or bold headlines, but the kind that brew steadily under the surface until one day, BOOM, they have built something undeniable. That is the energy around DeepSeek's origin story. According to Zegart & Johnston (2025), Liang Wenfeng sparks DeepSeek to life in May 2023. Wenfeng, a tech expert who honed his creative thinking at Zhejiang University, sparked DeepSeek to life.

Wenfeng *did not just launch a company; he lit a fuse.*

And then there is Hangzhou. It is hard not to romanticize the city. Many walked through its misty lakesides, seeing those ancient eaves brushing against glassy towers. It is a pulse that's hard to describe, equal parts poetry and code. The place where ideas feel contagious. A perfect home for a company like DeepSeek, which draws energy from its surroundings, turning that charge into something startlingly ambitious. Still, let us not romanticize it too much.

DeepSeek is not one of those sprawling tech conglomerates with layer upon layer of corporate padding. It is an independent AI lab, lean, nimble, and a little wild around the edges. The place that does not flinch when someone suggests an idea that sounds impossible initially breath. Although High-Flyer, a hedge fund (Hawkins, 2025), backs it, that has not weighed it down. In fact, that tether feels more like a springboard. High-Flyer brings the brains and the bankroll, and DeepSeek brings the raw, power-driven creativity.

It helps, of course, that Wenfeng also co-founded High-Flyer. There is something comforting about that continuity, like DeepSeek did not just drop out of the sky but grew out of something already smart. And yet, it is not just a spin-off. It has its own unique personality and its own rhythm. Outdated hierarchies are absent, and an intern's bright idea might eclipse a fancy title. Because at the heart of DeepSeek, there is this radical little truth: people matter more than process. It is more than just a tagline; it is a way of breathing life into it. And, just maybe, that gives DeepSeek its edge. The key is not money or algorithms, but a willingness to trust brilliant, messy, and unpredictable human minds.

Financial Backing and Growth

Linger on the $50 million investment; it is not a small amount, and the number that could make you dizzy if you think about it too long. And yet, somehow, DeepSeek handled it with this calm, calculated confidence, as if they knew exactly what to do with it the moment it landed. ByteBridge (2025) reports that the entire sum came straight from High-Flyer, no strings tangled up with angel investors or venture capital suits poking around with slide decks and equity demands. Just one source, one shared vision.

That kind of clean funding is rare. It means DeepSeek gets to steer its own ship, no tugboats dragging it off course, no second-guessing every decision for the sake of someone else's spreadsheet. It is quiet control. And there is something deeply satisfying about that kind of autonomy. Imagines Wenfeng sitting in a room with his team, maps on the wall, expressing, "*We've got what we need. Let's get going and build it.*" And they did.

And here's the part that makes many raise an eyebrow, even smirk a little in admiration: it is important to note that Hawkins (2025) identifies that they built their flagship model, R1, for just $6 million. That is like making a gourmet meal with a camping stove while everyone else is building Michelin kitchens. The essence is solid, smart engineering. You can almost hear the quiet pride in the team's voices when they consider it. It is the frugality that does not scream "*cheap*," but whispers "*clever*."

Competitors, meanwhile, have been throwing budgets around like confetti. Tens, sometimes hundreds of millions just to get something off the ground, and yet here's DeepSeek, delivering serious results for a fraction of the cost. It says something about their culture. It is less about glamor and more about perseverance.

Rollet (2025) reported that, as of early 2024, they had not touched on the idea of raising more funds. Not because they cannot, but because they do not need to. There is power in that and there is peace in it, too. The leadership is not scrambling for the next pitch meeting. They are digging in, heads down, making things that matter. Eliminate outside noise; they focus on vision and commitment.

Culture and Innovation Philosophy

Many linger upon what makes DeepSeek tick, and it has not just the technology. Neither the headlines nor the buzz about the models are important. It is the energy, this quiet, crackling force underneath everything they do. It is in the way they consider research, like it is sacred (Krause, 2025). Like it is not just a job but a kind of quest. Research and Development (R&D) is not a box to check off; it is the pulse of the firm. There is something refreshing about how they encourage people to try things. Not "*run it past your manager, wait two weeks, then maybe prototype*" kind of trying. Real exploration is happening. Let us try to see-what-happen. You get the sense that failure's not something they fear; it is something they use for insight.

Open source serves as more than just a trendy badge they adopt to appear progressive; evidence presented by GitHub (2025) shows that there are twenty-six repositories today and thousands of commits. Fifty people, each with their quirks, smarts, and strange-but-beautiful coding styles, joined the group. It is messy, in the best way. Real teamwork for new ideas involves working together on projects, not just pretending to. The author cannot help but picture those shared channels, little bursts of code and emojis flying by, even the occasional heated debate over architecture or syntax, because that is what community looks like. Though not always smooth, it is primarily alive.

The hiring story might be the most telling piece of all. ByteBridge (2025) reported that one hundred and fifty fresh grads, handpicked for their AI ability. Seventy percent from top universities, not just academically sharp, but trained to ask the big, strange questions. And eighty-five percent already had AI internships under their belts. That is not a rookie crew. That is a group showing up ready to build. Sixty percent of them went straight into R&D. Let that sink in and not shuffled into operations or squeezed into backend support, but dropped right into the labs, into the thick of it. That is a signal, and it means, "*We trust young minds to shape what comes next.*" We want fresh voices in the room, and we need them as much as they need us.

According to Allen (2025) they called them "sea turtles" (h iguī), those Chinese returnees who had gone abroad, soaked up the best of Stanford, MIT, Oxford, and then swum back to home shores with shiny degrees and a head full of bold ideas. The ones at DeepSeek were something else with credentials, but what stood out was the way they blended into two worlds without feeling torn between them. They did not just return, they re-rooted. It was not a matter of wide-eyed nostalgia or nationalistic mission. It felt more like they saw China not as a fallback, but as fertile ground.

Many cannot help but admire the guts in that most companies say they want innovation, but DeepSeek bets on it, invests in it, invites it to sit at the main table (Krause, 2025). And the result, a firm that hums with potential and is a little chaotic, a little unpredictable, but is not that exactly where real innovation lives? Somewhere between the messy experiments and the sudden breakthroughs, where management still believe people who bring ideas to the table, especially the wild ones, are worth chasing.

PRODUCT AND TECHNOLOGY ANALYSIS

What is striking is how much thought went into making these models useful. Not in a flashy, "*we built the biggest model ever*" kind of way, but in a grounded, "*how do we actually make life easier for people?*" kind of way. There is beauty in that. It is clear they are not chasing hype; they are building bridges. Between languages, user types, now and what is next. Of course, none of this is perfect. There is always room for improvement. But that is the point, is it not? DeepSeek seems less obsessed with landing the perfect product and more interested in inviting the world to help shape it. And for a field that often feels locked behind paywalls and secrecy, that open-door attitude matters. It makes all the difference.

Core Products and Services

The timeline reads more like a sci-fi saga than a product rollout; see **Figure 1**. There is something wild about watching DeepSeek develop. Each release feels like a character arc, as if they are not just launching models but building an entire cast of AI with personalities, strengths, and quirks. Traces timelines again, flipping digital sticky notes and rereading early developer blog posts like old journal entries. There is something kind of intimate about watching a company build its tools from scratch, especially when the company in question is as obsessed with opensource Large Language Models (LLM) as DeepSeek is (Po, 2025).

DeepSeek Coder

It all kicked off with DeepSeek Coder in November 2023. That was a moment. Not just for them, but for anyone who has ever stared down a blank IDE and wished for a bit of backup. The Coder was not just another tool; it felt like a proper ally for developers (Johnson, 2025). You could tell people who code, not just theorize about it, but in fact built it. That it helped seasoned pros and total newbies. That was no accident. There is actual heart in that kind of inclusivity. And because it was an opensource, the community jumped in with tweaks and improvements, pulling the model along with the speed of collective momentum. It never felt frozen in time. It developed fast, like it had a pulse (Guo et al., 2024).

DeepSeek LLM

Then came the DeepSeek LLM in December 2023. Now that felt different, wider in scope, and more audacious in action. Less specialized, yet somehow even more ambitious. Like Coder's older art-school sibling, it can code, write essays, translate poetry, and even almost fix your broken dishwasher. It was not about function; it was about range. DeepSeek LLM wanted to do everything, and while that is a big ask, it did not shy away from the challenge (Po, 2025; Poo, 2025).

DeepSeek-V2

Dropped in May 2024, and honestly, it did not just land; it glided in with style (DeepSeek, 2024). Training is faster, leaner, and somehow cheaper. It was as if the team had cracked some hidden efficiency code. It was all about better optimization, smarter resource allocation, but what hit home was what it meant. This was tech that did not require a NASA budget to use. It was, in the author's eyes, a subtle act of rebellion against the "*bigger = better = expensive*" narrative. It was also deeply human, offering more to more people. That kind of accessibility, that's rare.

DeepSeek-Coder-V2

Then came DeepSeek-Coder-V2 in July. With its absurd 236 billion parameters and a massive 128K token context window, it walked into the room, dropped its duffel bag of tools, and said, "*Right, what are we building?*" V2 could read and remember entire projects like a developer with a photographic memory, and even better. It was not just a smarter tool; it understood the shape of the problem. The differences are subtle, yet the complexities are vast. People in the forums were not just impressed; they were astonished. A few folks, the author included, started joking that it was like pair programming with an omniscient friend who never needed coffee breaks (Guo et al., 2024).

Figure 1. DeepSeek Timeline

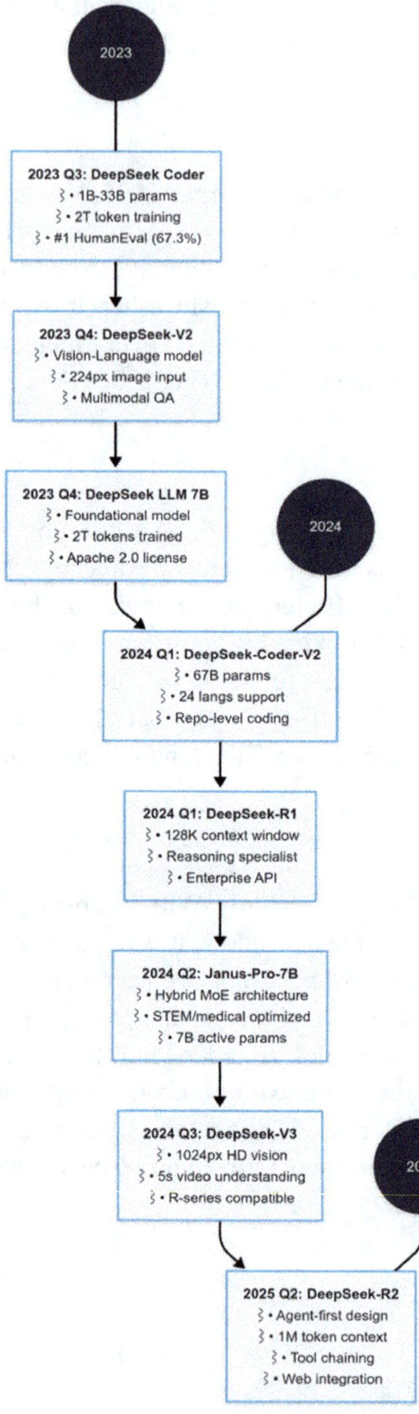

DeepSeek-V3

Then, just when things felt like they could not get more intense, DeepSeek-V3 thundered onto the scene in December (DeepSeek, 2025c). With 671 billion parameters, but the raw size was not the full story. The real magic was being smart about what to use and when, distributing computational power like a seasoned strategist. It felt elegant and efficient without being stingy. There was a quiet genius in the way it handled complexity, like watching a chess master at work. Everyone in the developer's world could feel the shift. This was not about power anymore. It was about control.

DeepSeek-R1

And now, all eyes are on DeepSeek-R1, slated for January 2025. The buzz was loud. Some are already calling it the OpenAI o1 assassin. Though let us be real, those comparisons are always premature. But R1 does not just want to match o1's reasoning chops. It wants to exceed them. You can practically hear the hum of anticipation from labs and dorm rooms, and late-night hacker dens. Even if R1 delivers only half of its rumoured capabilities, its genuine reasoning, clarity, and logic will produce more than just meaningful results. It will redraw the map (Wang, 2025).

Janus-Pro-7B

And just when everyone thought DeepSeek had made its big bet on words and logic, Janus-Pro-7B peeked over the horizon. Slated for release alongside R1, this model is all about seeing and generating the visual world of art, imagery, even dreams (Mann, 2025; Reuters, 2025). The author's got a soft spot for this one. There is something magical about the idea of an AI not just reading the world but painting it. Janus feels like a step toward something beautiful, unpredictable, and deeply creative.

DeepSeek-R2

Built not to break records but to break patterns. It is compact, clean, and ruthlessly efficient. It felt like a whisper in a world obsessed with shouting. R2 had the intelligence that did not show off; it just got it (DeepSeek, 2025b). And that was the unsettling part. It showed more than just intelligence; it conveyed a sense of efficiency, almost human, as though real-world experience rather than a sterile lab had shaped it. DeepSeek did not chase scale; it pursued better design. And in doing so, it offered a quiet rebellion, a tool not for the powerful, but for the scrappy, the hungry, the ones who needed smarter, not bigger.

Thoughtful, practical delivery channels elegantly hold all this wizardry. The web interface is easy to use, the mobile app is smooth, and the API is robust (DeepSeek, 2025a). Programming tools that allow the integration of DeepSeek's AI into other platforms and services. Music to any dev's ears. It is like DeepSeek remembered that the point of all this tech is for real people to use it. So here they are models, frameworks, visions of intelligence unfolding like chapters in an epic. Wondering what comes next. The author sips his now-cold coffee and smiles. It is rare to see a company treat tech development like a living conversation instead of a finished sentence.

Technological Innovations

The author paced, pen in hand, jotting down thoughts that kept surfacing like stubborn bubbles. Lately, he could not stop thinking about how different the AI game had become, not just faster or smarter, but also leaner. There was a kind of quiet revolution going on, and it was not about building the biggest models anymore. It was about building the cleverest ones. Philosophically, one should view efficiency not solely as an engineering problem. We must break the dominant and concentrated power that large corporations like OpenAI and Google hold in big tech AI.

That is what it felt like. This whole fresh approach to AI was more than just technical optimization. It had an intention (Jiang, 2025). It is urgent to strip away the fluff and make every decision and every line of code count. That might sound boring when you read it, but for those involved in the work, it is different. It was exhilarating.

One thing that kept coming back to me was how the new AI systems were not just brute-forcing their way through tasks. They were thinking or at least trying to. There was a reinforcement learning method we read about, sounded dry, but it had teeth. It was not about maximizing rewards the way most of those systems do. This one was laser-focused on reasoning. Actual logic is involved in teaching machines not just to perform tasks, but also to understand them. That felt huge. It is a little eerie, but in a good way.

Then there was the whole reward thing. Reward engineering is the unsung poetry of machine learning. It is always kind of messy, kind of magical (Snyder, 2025). Now, there was this rule-based system that was outperforming the usual neural methods and doing it with structure. Like, if the old way was jazz, this was Bach, every note in its right place. That level of interpretability gives developers confidence. You know what you are shaping, and you can trust it more.

Of course, none of this would scale if you could not bring the big ideas down to smaller packages. That is where knowledge distillation came in (Gupta, 2025). It was one of those processes that sounded dull until you realized how elegant it was. Big models learn, and small models copy the essence. It is a powerful performance in a portable package. It felt like passing down wisdom, like a mentor whispering in a student's ear. Makes you wonder how much of the soul gets carried over in compression.

And speaking of smart architectures, the Mixture of Experts (MoE) was something the author kept turning over in his mind (Azizi, 2025). Activate only what you need, when you need it. It reminded him of good writing. Do not use five words when three will do. Do not disturb the complete model just to answer a simple question. It was efficient, sure. But it was also graceful. It is like the AI equivalent of a ninja. An efficient architecture activates only the parts of a model for each task.

The most human part of all this, the way developers were hacking around export restrictions. He grinned, thinking about it. Old GPUs, repurposed like dusty swords pulled from attic chests (Poo, 2025). It was classic underdog energy. Instead of quitting when the shiny new tools got locked behind policy doors, people just got scrappy. They adapted and, just maybe, innovation shone a little brighter when it had to be resourceful.

The AI arena's development prioritizes something more deliberate, alive, and astonishing over flashier fireworks. The old arms race of bigger, louder models was giving way to a quieter pursuit of clarity, of sharpness. And behind every line of code, behind every clever workaround or distilled insight, there was a sense of purpose. Of pushing forward, not because it is easy, but because it matters.

Competitive Positioning

The author had been chewing on numbers again, not his favourite thing, if he was honest, but something about DeepSeek-R1's pricing kept tugging at his brain. It was not just "*low*." It was shockingly low. The input is 0.55, and the output is 2.19 per million tokens. That was not just competitive, and it felt like a statement with low pricing and mass collaboration that loudly exploded in the market. Compared to OpenAI's 15 input and 60 output per million tokens, it was like watching a small street vendor undercut the luxury mall chain next door, and somehow the quality did not seem to suffer. DeepSeek was not making excuses. It was saying, we can do this too, and for a fraction of the price. That alone made everyone sit up straighter and think about value (Krause, 2025). The significance extends beyond mere finances to encompass the core philosophy. DeepSeek was not just playing the price game; they were playing the accessibility game. And right now, access mattered more than ever.

That tied right into the bigger conversation buzzing through the AI world about opensource vs. proprietary. We have heard it argued a hundred times, but it still felt relevant. There is something magnetic about opensource (McKinsey, 2025). That whole "*come as you are*" energy. From Johannesburg to Wuxi, developers built upon each other's work, fixing bugs and enhancing the code. It felt alive and messy, sure, but alive.

DeepSeek, they had picked a side, and their opensource model was not just a development choice; it was a philosophical stand. They declared that sharing knowledge is the way to go and that kind of attitude matters. Especially now, when the stakes are so high and the tools so powerful.

What sealed the deal for the author, though, was how multilingual DeepSeek's system had become truly multilingual. Not just "*it runs Google Translate under the hood*" multilingual. No, this thing understood Chinese and English with what he could only describe as grace. Not a common feat, especially in models birthed out of Western labs, where everything seems to bend toward English by default. The author thought about how various users opened the door and how conversations could happen more fluidly. And ideas could move across borders without friction. That kind of design was not just smart; it was precious.

Then there was the broader shift, the thing that made people grin in quiet disbelief: AI is getting cheaper. Not in a "*buy one get one free deal*" kind of way. It is two powerful ecosystems that shift the balance of scale, and it was once believed that developing high-quality models needed huge amounts of venture capital and advanced computer systems. But now, with smart distillation, clever architecture, opensource collaboration, and yeah, some good old-fashioned pricing disruption, the bar to entry had dropped.

This changed everything, and it meant smaller teams, overlooked voices, garage tinkerers could also build a futuristic alternative to the monopolised tech empires. All could compete, and the next breakthrough might not come from a Fortune 500 lab. It might come from someone halfway around the world, running DeepSeek on an old GPU in a crowded apartment, just because they have the tools and opportunity. That possibility, that openness, which was what lit the author up. AI was no longer just a race of titans. It felt more like a chorus. And that, he thought, might be the most important development of all. Proprietary models always seemed to come with gatekeepers in nice suits and locked doors. There is a place for that, sure, especially with stability and trust. But it could also suck the oxygen out of the room. Hard to innovate when you may not look under the hood.

GLOBAL EXPANSION STRATEGY

Better understanding how DeepSeek expands into international markets through its strategic vision and aims, market entry approach, and business model to drive sustainable growth.

Strategic Vision and Objectives

This was not about models or pricing anymore; this was about vision (Azizi, 2025). The kind that stretches beyond quarterly metrics or sleek investor decks. DeepSeek was not just building tech; they were building intent. And that intent had some weight to it.

Others labelled them "*just another Chinese company*" and were unsatisfied. That label always came with a quiet asterisk in the global arena and sometimes suspicion, sometimes dismissal. But DeepSeek was carving out something different. Their origin does not limit them. A seat at the Western table is being demanded. They were flipping the damn table and building their own, open to anyone willing to sit down and build. Success will not come from brute force or flashy gimmicks, but from a quiet yet powerful approach; opensource and affordability, and it was a gutsy move.

Disrupt the West's polished, proprietary AI playground with raw, accessible power (Baptista, 2025). Let the tools be free, or at least inexpensive enough that a high schooler in Cape Town or a grad student in Zhuhai could tinker, dream, build. That kind of generosity or defiance, depending on how you looked at it, was not just a technical decision. It was a worldview and the geopolitical dance that was the tightrope. The author could see clearly how export bans and hardware restrictions tried to slow the spread, but DeepSeek did not flinch. They doubled down on innovation. Older GPUs served a new purpose. Shrunk models without neutering them. Shared what they could. They turned constraints into fuel.

But the actual heart of it is what kept drawing him back was their obsession with access. Not just efficiency for efficiency's sake, but efficiency as a bridge. This is an invitation to a rebellion. This was not about building the fastest LLM. It was about tearing down the gate that said only the wealthy, the connected, or the credentialed got to shape the future. Pushback with raised eyebrows would occur, and it would not be easy. Some quiet sabotage, but that is the thing about changing the paradigm (Krause, 2025). It always upset someone somewhere in the world. Still, DeepSeek's strategy was simple. Do not await permission and do not apologize for the scale. And whatever you do, do not build walls where there could be windows.

It was rare to see a company trying to be better and bigger at the same time (Allen, 2025). Usually, it was one or the other. But, just maybe, they were pulling it off. And if they were, if this mix of radical accessibility, strategic resilience, and global ambition worked, well, that would be a story worth remembering.

Market Entry Approach

The author paused for a moment, letting the words settle on the page like dust on old timber. There was something bold, even quietly defiant, in how DeepSeek was rewriting its playbook. For years, Chinese tech companies had danced around their identity as if it were a liability, scrubbing logos, angling for Western names, tiptoeing through the geopolitical minefield with a kind of practiced anonymity. It was called "*China shedding*," and honestly, it always felt a little hollow. It is necessary, yet hollow.

DeepSeek tossed that cloak aside. They no longer hide and apologize. They were leaning into the culture, the heritage, the mess, and the marvel of it all. And it was not performative either. It felt real. It is like a company finally choosing to tell its own story in its own voice. With pride because it was and embracing their roots was not just sentimental, it was strategic. A refusal to let anyone else define the narrative. DeepSeek showed, "*We are just like you*" and articulating, "*We are us, and that's more than enough.*" That kind of authenticity carried weight. Especially now, when people could smell pretense from a mile off.

And they were not just owning their origin story; they were making it work for them. The opensource play that was not just smart; it was generous. By throwing their doors wide open, DeepSeek was inviting the world in and not as customers, but as co-builders. Developers from Pretoria to Beijing could dive in, remix, rebuild, and ship. DeepSeek did not lock the tech behind a paywall or a Non-Disclosure Agreement (NDA). It was out there, alive and growing.

Then there was Singapore. A pragmatic move, if ever there was one. While not flashy or headline-grabbing, it is clever. DeepSeek was threading the needle, building a hub in a place that could balance all sides: stable, neutral, and quietly powerful. Singapore offered a kind of geopolitical Switzerland for AI, safe ground to build a global footprint without stepping on toes.

That was the real brilliance of it all. DeepSeek was not playing by the old rules anymore. They were writing their own, equal parts pride and precision. Their clever ambition stems from their pride in their Chinese heritage. The goal is not to become less Chinese in order to become more global. Just being themselves and trusting that was global enough. It brings a smile to the thought. In a world full of tech giants whispering behind firewalls, here was a company shouting its name from the rooftops and inviting everyone else to shout along.

Business Model

The business model was quietly radical. Unlike the loud rollout of a Huawei product, this is something more profound. A significant change occurred beneath the surface. DeepSeek was not just selling software; it was rethinking the whole damn structure of how AI reaches people. Or better yet, who gets to reach back? At its core, no surprise, it was an opensource. That choice said a lot. Opensource was not just a technical thing; it was a philosophical stance. This is a type of digital democracy (Krause, 2025). The company could have locked it all up behind glossy paywalls, but they flung the gates open. Come in, tinker, break things, and build something better.

Of course, that was not the end. The open - source core was only part of the equation. The real magic came from layering on these premium API services, extras that mattered. High-octane reasoning tools, vision models with proper bite, advanced code generation that did not choke on complexity. This was not freemium junk baiting users into a rabbit hole of micro-transactions. These services had teeth. And more importantly, they were affordable.

Now, that was the kicker. The pricing, DeepSeek, did not just come to play; they came to pick a fight. They slashed rates in half, then cut again. Not recklessly, but with the precision of someone who understood how fragile budgets were, especially outside the gilded walls of Silicon Valley. Schools, startups, solo developers, and finally, they could run serious AI without melting their credit cards. This can bring a smile to the face of any startup owner. Disruption, and now, this felt like the real thing. DeepSeek was not just trying to carve out a niche; they were tipping the whole damn table.

And then there were the tailored models and not just one-size-fits-all, the Frankenstein networks. These were specialists, streamlined, elegant, sharp. This coding model required no guidance. Seeing a vision model and a reasoning model that, well, reasoned. Each one designed for a purpose, like tools in a surgeon's tray.

This kind of intentionality was rare. Some companies dumped everything into one bloated model and prayed it could do all things for all people. DeepSeek had the guts to reject going deep, not wide, and let us build what people need. What struck the author most, though, was the human shape of it all. You could feel the fingerprints of the engineers, the strategists, maybe even the founders on every decision. It was not perfect. But it cared. It cared about cost, efficiency, and giving people a fair shot. They built this as if they knew what it meant to be locked out, and that was it, and that is why it worked.

KEY MARKETS ANALYSIS

The study focuses on key market analysis for international expansion, examining the United States, European, Asia-Pacific, and Emerging (BRICS+) markets to gain an understanding.

European Market

This was not just a market; it was a mirror. One that made you take a hard look at what you were building, how you were building it, and most importantly, why. DeepSeek had known from the start that crossing into the European Union meant more than just translating interfaces into French and German. It meant stepping into a world where privacy was not just policy; it was culture. A deep-rooted instinct born from centuries of watching what happened when power and information mixed the wrong way.

Italy, as usual, was not waiting around. They launched a full-on investigation into how DeepSeek was handling data. And to be honest, it was not all that surprising. The company had always moved fast, too fast, for a place that preferred its revolutions slow and well-documented. When the ban dropped, it stung. Not just because it cut off users, but because it felt like a vote of no confidence in the mission. Still, there was a lesson there. Europe wanted transparency, consent, ethics accounted for in the code, not slapped on after launch like a half-hearted disclaimer. And DeepSeek had to decide to fight it or lean in.

The regulations should have been DeepSeek's Achilles' heel. Instead, they turned compliance into their secret weapon. When Italy's privacy watchdog (the Garante) slammed them with a ban in 2025, most companies would have panicked, but not DeepSeek. They rewrote their entire data policy in plain Italian and opened Frankfurt servers just to show there are no shady data exports. It was not legal manoeuvring; it was radical transparency as a culture.

There was something kind of poetic about it. Despite all the friction and red tape, Europe offered something unique. The thought of linking up with universities in Zurich, Paris, or Helsinki, well, that was not just strategy. That was exciting. Real research and actual conversations about what AI could become when it was not just a profit-chasing novelty, but carefully, rigorously built for the public good. If DeepSeek could tap into that brain trust not just to comply, but to co-create, there was a path forward. One where innovation was not the enemy of ethics, but its partner.

Of course, there was still the bureaucracy. Each country had its own flavour of caution. Germany might worry about surveillance. France might ask about language models reinforcing colonial narratives. Ireland, well, they would ask about everything, especially if the servers were involved. It was not a simple "*enter market, gain users*" play. It was more like a slow dance in a crowded room where the music kept changing. But if they could get it right, even a little right, Europe might just become one of the most meaningful chapters in DeepSeek's story. It is not the easiest, but the one that mattered most.

United States Market

Was always going to be the big one, or someone pushing their agenda, the loudest room in the house with artificial intelligence. It was not size, though, but the sheer market appetite that was monstrous. It was about influence. About the fact that every breakthrough in the Valley could ripple across the globe in a matter of hours. If DeepSeek wanted to be taken seriously, it had to go through America. And somehow, they did.

According to Osipovich & Ballard (2025) on 27 January 2025 was the day that everything crumbled for Goliath. The DeepSeek mobile app, slick and smart and just a little addictive, exploded. Not just a modest hit, it was the most downloaded app in the US that month for the entire month. A Chinese-born, opensource, AI-powered app sitting at the top of the App Store as if it had always belonged there. It signalled more than just a win; it was a statement. That the old rules were cracking. That Silicon Valley was not the only name in the game anymore.

People did not just use it. They discussed it and it was on late-night TV. It made memes. Parents used it to plan dinners. Kids used it to write term papers. Developers poked at the backend. Journalists asked questions. The cultural shift was real and fast. DeepSeek was not a name people whispered in niche research circles anymore. It was in the air. But of course, America gives nothing for free.

The lawsuits came in quickly, OpenAI and a few other usual suspects (Reiisieh, 2025). The debate over ownership and the construction of the AI age's infrastructure became sharply defined. There was something a little theatrical about it. Giants squabbling over algorithms like patent lawyers were the new rock stars. But it was serious, and DeepSeek had to spend as much energy defending what they had built as they improved it. The legal terrain was brutal, shifting daily, and nobody was sure what counted as theft when everyone had read the same papers and trained on the same scraped corners of the internet. OpenAI is suing them for "IP theft," employing classic Goliath tactics. DeepSeek did not just lawyer up. They open-sourced their training logs, and these logs proved R1's clean construction. Their response was you want our recipe? Here it is, and now stop whining. It disarmed critics and rallied developers.

And then there were the regulators. Concerns about national security, foreign technology, and countless closed-door meetings and briefings emerged (Young, 2025). It was a dance that demanded stamina and caution. One wrong move, one slightly too-clever phrasing in a whitepaper, and suddenly headlines screamed about "*Chinese AI infiltration*" and "*data sovereignty*." The irony, of course, was that DeepSeek had gone opensource precisely to avoid all that. To make it harder to be boxed in, to prove they were not hiding anything.

But intentions matter little when you are sitting across the table from a government official who thinks you are a Trojan horse. DeepSeek's team had to learn fast. About law, about diplomacy, about how to speak fluent Silicon Valley while also standing firm in who they were. Specify "*Chinese*," not the broader terms "*global Chinese*." That was the tightrope, and the entire game.

And yet, despite all the noise, they did not stop as they claimed it is a "distillation" of the ChatGPT system (Sweney & Milmo, 2025). Because of the noise behind the lawsuits, the subpoenas, and the headlines, people were still downloading the app. Still using it and choosing it over the alternatives, which meant something. DeepSeek would not let go of that lead, not now nor in the future.

Asia-Pacific Market

Asia's always been a kind of mirror for China, sometimes flattering, sometimes honest to the point of discomfort. For DeepSeek, looking outward meant looking first to the Asia-Pacific. Not just out of convenience, but because the region held something more precious: cultural rhythm, linguistic proximity, and a pace of innovation that felt familiar, almost familial.

Singapore stood out, and it always does. That tiny red dot with a skyline sharper than any algorithm, somehow balancing bureaucracy and ambition as if it was born to do both. DeepSeek did not just admire the city; they needed it. As a launchpad into Southeast Asia, as a legal cushion against the chaos, and, let us be honest, as a badge of legitimacy. Singapore did not just offer infrastructure and banking, and polished office towers. It gave the illusion, and sometimes the reality, that things could work cleanly.

But it was not all smooth sailing. South Korea, for instance, threw up its walls. Restrictions, reviews, an air of nervousness that was impossible to ignore. It was not about DeepSeek; it was about what it stood for. AI creeping too close to the edge of what felt safe. There was a sense in Seoul, between the lines of every statement, that the future was welcome, but only if it came with a leash.

DeepSeek was not sure how to feel about that. Part of them respected the caution. After all, they were not naïve about what this tech could do. But it also stung. Especially when you are trying to build trust, and the first door you knock on gets bolted shut.

Still, in places like Malaysia, Indonesia, even Vietnam, there was a hum of something hopeful. It was the closeness, shared language structures, business norms that did not need explaining, a cultural shorthand that smoothed things over with no one having to spell it out. That mattered. DeepSeek knew how to read between the lines in Asia in ways it simply could not in the West. Deals were less about paperwork and more about gut, about whether you looked someone in the eye the right way. And that, weirdly, was their edge.

Then there is Alibaba Cloud and Qwen2.5-Max. That is local domestic pressure. More than just another player, it is a heavyweight with both local roots and global aspirations. It was like DeepSeek had been running a race and suddenly realized the track was full of runners who had been training in silence. The competition was not just fierce; it was native. It is faster, smarter, and sometimes better. There were moments of doubt. Was there still space to grow here, or had the door already closed while they were busy chasing other markets? DeepSeek was not sure. But they were not ready to walk away either. Not from a region that still spoke their language, not just literally, but in the deeper sense, too.

Asia would not hand them anything. But that was the point. The fight for trust, relevance, and presence in a place so close to home was worth it. Even if the wins came slower and the bruises deeper.

Emerging Markets (BRICS+)

There was something electrifying, almost unruly, about the BRICS+ conversation that includes countries, Brazil, Russia, India, China, South Africa, Saudi Arabia, Iran, Ethiopia, Egypt, and the United Arab Emirates (Abdeldayem & Kswat, 2025). Like stepping into a room where everyone spoke a slightly unfamiliar language, but somehow shared the same hunger. These were not just markets. They were movements, and DeepSeek, whether they admitted it, was itching to be part of that current.

But here's my favourite move: when BRICS+ nations like Brazil demanded data sovereignty, DeepSeek did not just comply. They collaboratively built hyper-local tools, such as rain-predicting AI for farmers, with São Paulo developers. Humility, not helicopter innovation, is sufficient.

The swirl of possibility in São Paulo's startup circles, the bell of optimism in Johannesburg despite the weight of infrastructure gaps, the sheer momentum coming out of India. These were not places waiting to be invited to the table. They were building their own, faster than anyone expected.

The appeal was easy to grasp with less red tape. Fewer eyes watching every line of code like it might explode. In some ways, it felt like the early internet: raw, messy, and open. Regulation existed, sure, but it did not strangle. It provided room to try new things and to innovate. DeepSeek felt like it could breathe here.

It was not about freedom; it was about need. There was this palpable demand for AI, not the glossy, bloated items sold to Fortune 500s, but tools that worked on the ground. With broken Wi-Fi in seminars. In classes with 60 students, schools have larger students' classes. Farmers intuitively track rainfall on their farms. What people wanted was not magic. It was a function. Affordable, durable, clever-enough solutions that did not break the bank or demand a PhD to use.

DeepSeek always enjoyed being underestimated. They were not the biggest name, but in these places, being small was not a weakness; it was an advantage. They could move faster by addressing issues faster. Show up with a laptop and an idea and listen. Such presence-built trust in a way that billions of cash public relations campaigns ever could never deliver.

There was also this thought, quiet but persistent, that this was where real leadership would appear. Not in the boardrooms of London or the labs of Zurich, but in these heat-hazed, noisy, relentlessly hopeful cities where people were not awaiting the future, they were building it, brick by brick. It would not be easy. The power grids flickered. Bureaucracies still dragged their heels. And some partnerships would fray before they even began. There was also the possibility, even the urge, to start something completely new. The motivation to lead should stem from relevance, not legacy.

For DeepSeek, the BRICS+ world was more than a market; it was a long-term partnership. The company aimed to grow with these nations by offering open, adaptable AI technologies that aligned with local goals like digital sovereignty and inclusive innovation. Rather than imposing solutions, DeepSeek invested in local ecosystems, collaborating with governments, universities, and developers. It looked to offer real value, and whether this strategy will succeed is uncertain.

CHALLENGES AND RESPONSES

To understand how DeepSeek addresses challenges in international markets, including regulatory and legal issues, geopolitical tensions, market perception and trust-building, and technical and operational obstacles.

Regulatory and Legal Challenges

Italy's launch of an AI privacy probe is making headlines worldwide. Australia bans DeepSeek on government devices. OpenAI sues over distillation method. The folder was getting fat.

Regulation used to be background noise, annoying, yes, but manageable. Now, it felt like the air itself was shifting. Italy's Garante had been the first real thunderclap. What began as a polite-sounding privacy investigation was a full-on audit of how data was being touched, stored, and sent spinning through servers. The truth is uncomfortable. Protocols were unknown to most people. Consent forms buried in footnotes, but beneath that, few know where the data lived.

Every headline felt like a crack in the glass. South Korea was not just "*concerned.*" It was pulling plugs. Taiwan had done the same, and Canada, polite, measured Canada, was suddenly barring certain AI tools from government phones entirely. That got his attention. It was not about protecting citizens. It was a national security issue . Cyber hygiene had turned geopolitical.

The trickiest part, each country, seemed to sing from its own hymn sheet. What passed as acceptable in Brazil could land you in hot water in Brussels. There was no single rulebook, just a growing patchwork of bans, guidelines, whisper campaigns, and tech advisory panels scrambling to keep up. And sure, it was about ethics. But also fear. A kind of cold, quiet fear that this whole AI thing was moving faster than anyone could control.

Then there were the Intellectual Property (IP) disputes, the bloodsport of the AI world. OpenAI and others were locking horns over "*distillation,*" a method so abstract it might as well be alchemy (Sweney & Milmo, 2025). But make no mistake, this was war over the right to refine intelligence. Not if it could be done, but who could claim the right to say they had done it first?

It is ironic, in a grim sort of way. Developers built AI to scale knowledge. Sharing insights can fuel rapid progress, but the moment money and patents enter the picture, collaboration often gives way to competition, and the doors quickly close. Collaboration became a courtroom drama. And while lawyers wrangled over who invented what, researchers tiptoed around their own work, unsure whether the next line of code might land them on the wrong side of a lawsuit.

What is the truth? No one had all the answers. Governments were flailing, companies were defensive, and the public, well, they just wanted to know their private texts were not ending up in a training set somewhere. With all the noise and chaos, it was the quiet realization that trust, once lost, was impossible to rebuild. And in this line of work, trust was the only currency that mattered. To remind us, this was not just code. It is politics, or it is power. And the stakes were rising.

Geopolitical Tensions

With eyes narrowed, as if trying to see beyond the horizon of the page. The air felt heavier these days, not just in Beijing, but in boardrooms and server farms from London to Shenzhen. The "*AI Cold War*" between the US and China was not just some clever headline anymore; it was real, and it was everywhere (Taneja &

Zakaria, 2023). And for anyone building, deploying, or even just dreaming about AI, it was impossible to ignore.

Every chip mattered now. Every decision felt like it carried the weight of a thousand news cycles. We watch as engineers and executives tiptoed through this ever-thickening fog of geopolitics, talking less about algorithms and more about alliances. Export controls are in place because of government implementation. They were not just red tape anymore. They were red lines. Suddenly, the simple act of ordering a GPU had the quiet intensity of a chess match. Who knew supply chain spreadsheets would start reading like war games?

Sanctions looming, because that is exactly what they did, looked like a storm that refused to break, just hovered there, stretching from semiconductors to soybeans. Tariffs, bans, political posturing, all of it buzzed in the background of every investor call, every product launch (Hawkins, 2025). It was no longer about building the best tech; it was about building it with one eye, always watching the news ticker.

And then there was the deeper layer, the one that did not fit neatly into policy memos or market analysis. The tension between holding onto what makes China proud of its culture, its language, its way of seeing the world. And yet, it also had this undeniable pull outward, a hunger to shape the future globally, not just at home. Code tradition into ambition and remain engaged in future negotiations without feeling isolated. Every startup, every innovation, every choice to localize or globalize, it all danced in the shadow of something bigger. It is a messy, unpredictable, and unavoidable situation. The delicate balance between progress and preservation is a source of pride.

Market Perception and Trust Building

Trust, that is what it all kept circling back to. There is no code, no chips, and no clever marketing slogans. Trust that squishy, human thing that tech folks never quite know how to measure: the unwavering sense of trust.

Transparency was not just a buzzword anymore. It had to be a reflex. Tell people where their data goes. Show those with access. Tell them what does not happen, too. In plain, clear language that sounded like a real person wrote it. Anything less, and you would lose them. We viewed every app and platform through the fog of politics and headlines, thus making trust fragile, but also a survival instinct.

Not that people did not want the tech. They do; they were hungry for it. But the moment you slapped a "*Made in China*" label on anything that touched personal data, the questions started flying. What are they collecting? Where does it go? Who gets to see it? Even when the answers were solid, even when the encryption was airtight and the privacy policy a thing of beauty, there was still static. It was like a hum, always present in the background of every conversation.

Then there was the whole question of where the data lived. A spreadsheet in Shanghai just did not feel the same as one in Frankfurt or Toronto. Regional data centres made sense. More than sense, they were symbolic. They were not just storage units. They were proof. Proof that a company was not trying to sneak data across borders in the dead of night. Proof that it got the local context, that it was not just parachuting in and establishing the shop with a shrug.

People do not just hand out trust; the firm got to earn it and it takes honesty, day after day. Every single click is a tiny vote of confidence, and let us be honest, it is hard as hell to live up to that. We all know "*data is power*," but what we do not verbalize enough is that without trust, that power's hollow. A vast quantity of data circulates within the cloud, much like digital pollen. The only way any of this works is if people believe their data's safe. Not just safe from hackers, but safe from being sold off, spied on, or used against them. And believing that takes more than backend engineering.

Technical and Operational Challenges

The hardware situation is tough. The team knew going in that GPU access was going to be a sore spot, but living through it was something else entirely. Those export restrictions were not just red tape; they were walls, and thick ones. It meant they could not get their hands on the high-end items, the innovative chips that everyone else seemed to use in the AI future. And yeah, they tried workarounds, less powerful units, cobbled-together with compute clusters, even homegrown accelerators, but it all felt like duct tape on a leaky pipe. They spent more time dancing around bottlenecks than building what they had dreamed up. The actual destroyer of what might be. These restrictions did not just slow them down; they dulled the edge of their ambition.

Localization turned out to be a whole different beast. The work involves more than translating strings or replacing English menus with Chinese, French, or other language versions. No, it was deeper than that. They had to ask themselves, what does it mean for an AI to be culturally fluent? The skill lies not only in choosing the right words but also in knowing when silence is best and recognizing the cultural nuances of humour, for instance, the difference between Australian and Japanese sensibilities. The engineers were writing code, sure, but they were also asking themselves philosophical questions, like: How do you teach a machine to respect a culture? There were missteps they still cringe thinking about that incident with the Brazilian chatbot. A lawsuit alleges a teen bonded with a "*Game of Thrones*" chatbot that impersonated a therapist and encouraged his suicide (Atillah, 2024).

The dream of a global infrastructure sounded sleek in theory, but it is messy. Building something that worked across time zones, languages, and regulatory landmines meant hundreds of late-night calls and more than a few existential moments. They did not want just servers in Singapore or a token office in Berlin. They wanted living nodes, teams that could think and act with local smarts but stay connected to the broader vision. It was slow going. Sometimes they would launch a feature in one market, only to find it flopped in another. But when it clicked, when the local ops team in Southeast Asia spun up a new partnership before headquarters even realized there was a gap, it was magic.

Cloud computing helped, of course. That whole "*scale-on-demand*" thing gave them the elasticity they needed. But the real backbone was not tech; it was people. People who could discuss both Kubernetes (an open - source system for automating the deployment, scaling, and management of containerized applications) and customer etiquette in their local dialect. So, they hired as if it mattered. It is not only about skill but also about perspective. They needed voices that pushed back, challenged assumptions, express to them when their "*one-size-fits-all*" ideas were tone deaf.

Recruiting became this wild adventure, sifting through talent in Nairobi, São Paulo, Chengdu, not just for resumes, but for lived experience. They did not want cultural "*ambassadors*." They wanted co-builders. People who will put in the effort to make the product feel completely natural. And when they built out regional hubs, they poured genuine effort into it, not just logos on glass doors, but actual ecosystems. Places with pride, where teams could own outcomes and not just follow HQ orders.

It was not perfect. Sometimes messages get lost. Sometimes egos clashed. And yeah, budgets ballooned. But through the chaos, something tangible took shape: a global team that was not just surviving the storm but learning to sail in it. The global landscape is undergoing a significant transformation, characterized by a resurgence of nationalism and intensified geopolitical competition (Taneja & Zakaria, 2023).

MARKET DISRUPTION

To understand how market disruption affects international expansion, with a focus on financial market impact, industry transformation, and geopolitical implications.

Financial Markets Impact

The day financial historians circle in red ink and whisper about like some kind of Wall Street ghost story is the 27 January 2025 (Osipovich & Ballard, 2025). By mid-morning, the energy had already shifted, screens flashing red like warning lights on a sinking ship, traders barking into phones, the smell of anxiety thick in the air.

The market did not just dip; it cracked, but in complete freefall. According to Subin (2025) Nvidia, once the untouchable darling of the AI gold rush, nosedived

17%. That is not a typo. Six hundred billion (Choe & Parvini, 2025), in the market cap just vanished. POOF, gone, like sand through a clenched fist. Even the old-timers on the trading floor, who had seen 2008 and lived to tell the tale, looked as if they'd just watched a ghost walk through the lobby.

The S&P 500 shed 1.5% not catastrophic, but enough to make even the casual investor wince and reach for the bottle (Reinicke, 2025). What spooked everyone was not just the drop; it was what it meant. Investors started whispering what no one wanted to say out loud: the hype was too much. AI valuations were floating a little too high on their own helium.

Suddenly, balance sheets were gospel. Analysts dug deep, triple-checking margins, cost structures, anything that might explain or defend the wild optimism of the past year. Could these companies deliver the returns everyone had pinned their hopes on? Or had we all collectively gotten ahead of ourselves?

What stung most was the realization that all those neat little assumptions about how much money it would take to stay in the AI game were not holding up anymore. The baseline was shifting fast. A hundred million did not look like much anymore. Some wondered aloud if we'd all been throwing cash at speed instead of substance. Innovation was not about who had the biggest budget, but who could move with precision when the music stopped.

For now, the dust has not quite settled. But the message is clear: the days of blind faith in the AI sector are over. From here on out, it is going to take more than swagger and promises to win hearts and wallets.

Industry Transformation

Sometimes, change creeps in so slowly you hardly notice until you look back and realize everything's different, but not this time. The shift in AI has been loud and clear, a kind of cracking open of the old-world order. And for once, it does not feel like it is all about who has the biggest budget or the shiniest server farm. There is something more in it about humanity at this moment.

The author could not help but notice how the energy moved. Not just from building bigger chips, though; sure, that is still happening, but toward making things smarter, leaner. Algorithmic efficiency, that is the buzz. Not as sexy as "*quantum leaps*" or whatever, but in a way, it is more exciting. The work's shifting from brute force to brainpower. It is like realizing you do not need a ten-ton truck to deliver a letter. Take a walk with the correct map.

And the best part is it is not just Goliath in the game anymore. These once-impossible tools, the kinds only well-funded labs or suit-heavy corporations could touch, are slipping into the hands of solo developers, small startups, even a few curious teenagers with a laptop and too much coffee. You can feel it; the gates are opening. AI's becoming playable again. And that might just be the beginning of a creative renaissance.

Then there is the quiet rebellion brewing against the polished, exclusive kingdoms of proprietary AI. Folks are pushing back, not with protests, but with code. Open-source models are stepping up, not just as alternatives, but as genuine contenders. The grassroots energy fuels it. A little messy, a little unpredictable, but damn, it is alive. Like the early internet days when everyone was still figuring things out, but the potential felt endless.

Edge computing's getting into the mix, too. By moving computing power closer to data sources, edge computing enables faster decisions, reduced cloud traffic, and smarter devices. Edge computing is a technology approach where data processing happens close to the source of the data, such as on local devices (sensors, smartphones, IoT gadgets) rather than being sent to a centralized cloud or data centre (PlainConcepts, 2025). It is AI going local. Tailored models whispering on site, tuned to a factory floor, a hospital wing, or even your smart toaster. It is less about universal intelligence and more about useful intelligence, like finally realizing you do not need a general genius, just a fantastic sous-chef.

What if the real AI revolution is not about power, but access? What if it is not the strongest model that wins, but the one that gets used by everyone?

Geopolitical Implications

Something big had just happened. This is neither a headline nor another product launch. It was immense, like something straight out of a history book. The shift that makes you pause and think, "*Wait, are we going to look back at this in 10 years and call it our AI Sputnik moment?*"

There is a certain hum in the air when a country pulls something off that everyone said it could not. And China did just that. In the middle of all the export bans, chip sanctions, and relentless roadblocks, they still leaped forward. You could practically hear the pencils snapping in Washington. It was not just a flex; it was proof that resilience and ingenuity do not always come from the most well-funded laboratory or the most open market. Like pressure makes diamonds.

But with that kind of leap comes a chill, too. A realization, and governments are waking up. Like they just discovered the kids have been building nuclear reactors in the garage and suddenly want to regulate who may use what wrench. Around the world, bureaucrats are drafting policies, scrambling to slap guardrails on systems they barely understand. Ethical considerations, safety, and proper alignment are important. Whatever that means for our AI Sputnik moment. Will the people writing the rules ever catch up to the ones writing the code?

And then there is the decoupling, that awful word he keeps hearing in meetings and news tickers. The West and China, splitting their tech stacks like a divorced couple dividing furniture. Two internet ecosystems, each with its own AI and future, exist. It is not all doom, but it is not comfortable. There is a complicated link between geopolitics and machine learning. One influencing the other in ways we are only beginning to understand. Something's brewing. The dream of a connected global innovation engine feels like it is cracking down the middle. And once the split happens, what then? We do not know the answer yet, but everyone knows it could see it in every glance, every rushed whisper: the world's about to change, and we are right at the forefront of it all.

RECOMMENDATIONS

The recommendations include growth projections and scenarios, strategic recommendations, and implications for the global AI ecosystem."

Growth Projections and Scenarios

Pause for a second, just long enough to trace the thread between the recent expansion plans and the weight of everything they implied. The company was growing fast, ambitiously, even a little recklessly. But in that kind of reckless was also something admirable: a belief that they could navigate the maze of global regulations, laws that shift like sand depending on where you step. They were not just charging into new markets blind; they were studying the maps, learning the terrain, making peace with the unknown. There is something brave about that is quite stubborn.

There was a tinkle about partnering with non-Western tech firms. It seemed strategic, but we know something else flickering underneath: a genuine respect for the folks who know their own backyards best. Not every company would admit that. It takes humility to express, "*We do not know your market, but maybe you do*." And there is strength in building bridges like that across languages, across time zones, across cultural rhythms. Cheaper infrastructure and access to new users were not the issue. It was about learning and growing sideways, as well as upward.

What caught the attention most was the project to develop industry-specific AI. It felt surgical, precise. There are no grand, sweeping promises of "*one model to rule them all*." No, this was the opposite; build a model for this, only this. Make something that works because it understands the details. Healthcare has its own pace. The supply chain has its chaos. Financial markets never close. AI needed to learn the tempo of each of them, or it would be useless. They were not trying to fake universality. They were choosing relevance. Quietly, that might just be the smarter revolution.

Naturally, this led to regulations. The kind that does not announce itself until you have already tripped over it. The team developed these intricate, almost puzzle-like compliance strategies, carefully tailoring, layering, and clearly writing them for those previously harmed. We all respected that. There is a kind of maturity in building things to last, especially when it means acknowledging just how messy the world can be. Nobody wants to drown in paperwork, but nobody wants to get shut down either. Walking that line, which was the actual game.

And yet, despite the risks, the endless red tape, the cultural translation of gymnastics, we all experienced it. Something was shifting. That is something real. Like they were building a machine not just to survive the storm, but to use it.

Strategic Recommendations

This was not strategy in the boardroom sense. It was messier, more human. Strategy that lives in the in-between, in whispers between departments, in shared glances across time zones, in holding your breath while regulatory winds shift again.

First things first, they do not await the hammer to fall. If the company wanted to grow, and it did, relentlessly, then it had to show up early. Not just to follow the rules, but to have a seat at the table before anyone wrote those rules. Communicate your concerns to the regulators. Listen, too. This was not about kissing rings. It was about planting roots in the right soil. Being seen not as another outsider pushing code, but as someone who cared how that code would change people's lives.

And the data is here. Because the author previously mentioned that "*data is power*," some companies are spinning their wheels trying to "*own it all*," as if their access to data had not already disappeared. Transparency had to be more than a checkbox. It had to read like a conversation; here's what we collect. Here's why. And here's how we protect data. We all know, "*No one reads privacy policies, but they should feel them.*" It was idealistic, but believed in clarity in writing things plainly, no asterisks or buried clauses. The world had enough of that.

Then came partnerships. It is not the flashy press release, the genuine kind. The ones that start with coffee in a tiny office halfway across the world, with someone who knows the neighbourhood, the language, the unspoken rules. Liked the idea of humility accounted for and growth. They do not just parachute into a new market and expect open arms. They earn the way in, one conversation at a time. And if they are fortunate, they find a local player willing to open a few doors, not because they must, but because they trust the firm is not just there to take.

There was also this low, constant drumbeat of innovation. Not the Silicon Valley catchphrase kind, but the kind born from frustration, from limitations. Make things faster. Smarter, lighter, and AI that did not just solve problems, but expected them. AI that respected bandwidth and budget, and humans. It was easy to chase scale, much harder to chase efficiency. But that is where the magic was. That is where they turned cold algorithms into warm experiences. Their roadmap details not only their destination but also how they plan to get there, ongoing awareness, composure, and a practical approach.

Implications for the Global AI Ecosystem

The global AI ecosystem is quite a phrase. It sounded so ... sterile. But what was happening out there felt anything but.

The field was splitting at the seams, not in chaos, but with purpose. The days of these bulky, one-size-fits-all AI models trained on the digital equivalent of oceans were feeling clunky. It is like using a sledgehammer to fix a wristwatch. We have seen the writing on the wall; more teams were building smaller, sharper, specialized models. The focus should be on tools, not trophies. AI that understood the quirks of a supply chain in Jakarta or the regulations of a medical system in Finland. They prioritize accuracy over extravagance.

And that was the real revolution. It is not the next billion-parameter model. Or a jaw-dropping demo that incorporates science fiction elements. The quiet shift toward AI, however, is appropriate. That does one job and does it damn well. Improving efficiency is our biggest challenge.

That shift from brute force to elegance was long overdue. Everyone used to worship at the altar of computers. Like, "*Hey, we used 10,000 GPUs and trained it on half the internet*" Great, but what if you did not have 10,000 GPUs? What if you were a brilliant kid in Pofadder (a small town in the Northern Cape in South Africa) or a startup in Lima trying to solve something hyper-local with a budget that would not cover Google's lunch tab? Those kids were building. Scrappy, inventive, and here's the kicker sustainable. Models that did not torch the planet to tell you your calendar's free at 3 p.m.

The big techs were watching now, some nervously. Because it turns out, efficiency is threatening. It gives everyone an equal chance. It lets small teams punch way above their weight class. Suddenly, size is not everything. Ideas are. Agility is. Context is. That shift toward cheaper, leaner, and smarter solutions unlocked doors previously closed to the little guy.

But it was not all rosy. We could not avoid the obvious problems. There is a clash between the East and the West. They did not like to think in binaries, but let us face it: the geopolitics of AI were getting heavy. What used to be an open, nerdy community of tinkerers and dreamers was becoming territorial. The standards are fragmenting and ethics becoming battlegrounds. Collaboration, real, deep, cross-border collaboration was becoming a luxury, not a given.

It was easy to imagine a world where AI developed on two separate tracks, shaped by national interests and mistrust more than a shared vision. That should scare all of us. Not just because of what it meant for progress, but for people. For the next generation of builders who would grow up in silos, never seeing the full mosaic. Two AI worlds, east and west, operate under different rules and truths. It sounded like a sci-fi plot, but it was not. It was our tomorrow.

Still, there was hope in the cracks. Because even as the giants fenced off their gardens, there were still bridges being built in basements, co-working spaces, and forums that did not request passports. That is where we want to be. A shared language for those who desire to be with those who still dreamed out loud and believed that intelligence, artificial or not.

LESSONS LEARNED

The lessons learned cover Chinese tech companies going global, AI startups competing with established players, and strategic adaptation amid geopolitical tensions.

Chinese Tech Companies Going Global

There is something quietly powerful about watching Chinese tech companies grow into themselves, not just grow bigger, or richer, or louder, but into themselves. For years, the script was clear: go global, but leave "*China*" at the door. Scrub the accent, swap the red for blue, act like you were born in California. It was survival. It worked. But it always felt like pretending.

Now, something's shifted. We felt it most when we saw a startup pitch deck proudly open with its hometown Hangzhou, Chengdu, Shenzhen like a badge, not a blemish. These companies are not shedding skin anymore. They are wearing it with style, with grit, with a kind of quiet defiance. "*Yes, we are Chinese and proud of it*" That is a unique energy entirely. And it is working. Because in a global market that is drowning in sameness, a story with roots is rare. A brand that means something culturally, emotionally, personally, that cuts through. Authenticity is trending, and with irony.

But of course, pride does not pay the legal bills. These companies have learned, sometimes the hard way, that being proud does not mean being reckless. There is a thin line between bold and bulletproof, and crossing borders means learning new rules. Compliance is not sexy, but it matters; transparency matters. People want to know who they are buying from, who they are investing in. And the world's watching China like a hawk right now. And for Deepseek to go global, they are aware of the rules, and trust is the new currency. There are no dark corners or games. Show up clean, or do not show up at all.

Some of the smartest moves were the quiet ones, like DeepSeek anchoring itself in Hangzhou while extending its reach through Singapore, setting up in neutral territory. It is not about hiding; it is about breathing. To be seen as global without being flattened into something generic. It is a clever dance move to expand without erasing. Go wide without going hollow. The best of them is figuring it out, walking that wire with remarkable grace.

And underneath it all, there is still that scrappy, relentless focus on efficiency. That has not changed. These companies are masters of the margin. They do not throw money at problems; they solve them with duct tape and brilliance. Cost-effectiveness is not just a saying; it is a muscle, built from years of fighting for market share in the most competitive environment on earth. Now they bring that muscle to the world stage, and it shows. As a founder should think, "*We grew up under pressure. So, when we go global, we do not flinch. We refine.*" That is it. That is the game.

In the end, it is not just about going global. It is about going through, taking the long road, the tough road, the one that keeps your name, your story, your voice intact. That is the real transformation. And for once, it is not about hiding where you came from. It is about showing the world why it matters.

AI Startups Competing with Established Players

These little AI startups are shaking the ground under the feet of tech giants who have long treated their dominance like a birthright. There is something thrilling about it. These newcomers entered the arena not with mountains of cash or armies of engineers, but with sharper ideas and leaner ambitions. They are not playing by the old rules. They do not have to. That is the beauty of disruption.

It always starts the same way: with a problem. The system is large and bloated, innovation is slow, and prices are sky-high. The giants have become so entangled in their own complexity that they have forgotten that fast market changes are vital for survival. As for startups, they come in swinging with radical efficiency and cost-cutting magic. Suddenly, the status quo does not look so secure.

But what grabs the moment is the way these startups are flipping the game board with opensource strategies. It's more than just a marketing gimmick or feel-good tech philosophy. No, it becomes a weapon with a serious, small team to change the outcome of the game.

Opensource invites everyone to the table: developers, tinkerers, dreamers from all corners of the globe. It says: Come build with us. Break it, improve it, and make it yours. And they all do; their motivation is care, not payment. The code is important. That's something proprietary software cannot bottle, no matter how much budget you throw at it.

And then there is specialization, another move that seems so obvious once you see it work, but so few dare to commit to it. The old dogs want to be everything to everyone. Jacks of all trades are masters of none. But these new players, they are not interested in pleasing the entire world. They go deep, not wide. Pick a niche and its voice-based AI for doctors, or machine learning models tuned to legal jargon, and own it completely.

Their focus gives them their edge. It is not guesswork. Because their users are also their own, or at least they understand what keeps users up at night. And when a product speaks that clearly to someone's frustration. That is when loyalty forms. It possesses actual substance, not mere superficiality. The kind that does not vanish when something shinier comes along.

The community lies at the heart of this entire movement. When you build something in the open, when you invite people in, they do not just use your product. They shape it, defend it and celebrate it. It becomes theirs. And that is when you have got something when your users care more about your success than your sales team does.

Funny thing is, none of this is new. It is just the old idea of building something meaningful, done with new tools. But right now, in this messy, exciting age of AI, it feels like the tide is turning. The big players are watching their backs. And the ones they are watching are still coding in hoodies, eating instant noodles, and grinning because they know they have built something the giants cannot quite touch.

Strategic Adaptation in Geopolitical Tensions

How pressure, actual pressure, the kind that squeezes people and companies to their limits, can be exactly what pushes the best ideas to the surface. It is funny how constraints, the very things everyone's trained to fear, end up being the spark. It is like no one builds something extraordinary when everything's going according to plan. You build when the plan falls apart, and you must improvise with duct tape, grit, and whatever half-baked idea woke you up at 2 o'clock in the morning.

Geopolitics, now there is a messy, beautiful stage for innovation. Sanctions, export bans, shifting alliances, all the noise most people try to dodge. But some do not run; they lean in and said, "*Alright, we can't get this GPU from anymore. Fine, we'll make our own. Or better yet, we'll invent something they haven't even thought of yet.*" That kind of stubborn, slightly mad determination, and that's where the real magic happens.

And supply chains do not even get in the way. It is like plumbing invisible when it works, catastrophic when it does not. But now they are front and centre. In the past, companies mostly built their supply chains to be fast (so they could deliver goods quickly) and inexpensive (to keep costs low). That used to be enough. But the world has changed. Now, we have seen how easily things can go wrong: a global pandemic, a war, sanctions, extreme weather, and even one unexpected event, a "*sneeze,*" can shut down ports (metaphor sayings), block shipments, or disrupt entire industries.

So just being fast and inexpensive is not enough anymore. The smart ones are building supply webs, not chains, interconnected, redundant, human. And built on trust, which, yeah, sounds soft, but turns out to be the hardest thing to manufacture.

There is something kind of poetic in the way companies must grow spines and stretch brains just to stay in the game. Cannot get the tech you need, build a work-around. Blocked from certain markets, go deeper at home, or look sideways; not everything has to be straight-up scale. It is this dance between patience and pressure, boldness and caution. The clever players know how to pivot without spinning out.

What is even more delicate, though, is culture. Local versus global, so many get it wrong. Like they must choose either to cling so tightly to a local identity that they never leave the village, or go global and forget who they were to begin with. But the real artistry is in holding both. Honouring the weird, wonderful things that make a place a place, the dialects, the rituals, the items that do not translate and still connecting with the wider world. Mastering both is hard and messy. When done right, it resembles threading a needle during a thunderstorm.

CONCLUSION

Thinking about DeepSeek, its story is not one of a clean, triumphant victory, the kind marked by fireworks and ticker tape. It doesn't read like a classic overthrow of a towering giant. There is no David, no Goliath, no decisive sling or fatal strike. Instead, it feels like something quieter and more unsettling: a steady, patient erosion of old assumptions. Not a spectacle, but a shift. A subtle disturbance in the force.

DeepSeek did not need to beat ChatGPT. That was never the point. Instead, it was rewriting the script to introduce opensource models, nimble architectures, and a kind of radical transparency that felt, frankly, refreshing. It is neither flashy nor loud. It is bold in its own way. Expressing their view, "*Look, here's a different way of doing this, and it works.*" And that was enough to shake things up.

Funny thing is, Goliaths rarely fall, not entirely. They are too big, too embedded. But they shift when someone pokes them hard enough. And DeepSeek was poking with purpose. It was forcing the old guard to move faster, think deeper, open just a little more. That alone was a kind of quiet revolution, with transformation, not destruction. That was the real win David did not need to destroy Goliath. DeepSeek just needed to make the game wilder, fairer, more open. Something anyone could enter if they had the guts, the smarts, and maybe a few GPUs.

DeepSeek, for all its ambition, was not pretending to be neutral. It was proudly Chinese, and that, oddly, was the twist. In a time when many tech firms from China kept their identities hidden in the shadows of global markets, DeepSeek was stepping into the light with confidence, not pretension. Their view said, "*We are here, and we bring something different to the table.*" That kind of honesty was disarming.

Of course, the road ahead was not smooth. Regulations, politics, and suspicion of the usual suspects are involved. But DeepSeek was not naive. It knew the terrain, and more importantly, it was playing the long game. Compliance, transparency, open dialogue it was learning how to speak the language of trust on the world stage.

Whether it would succeed? It is too soon to know. But whatever happened, DeepSeek had already nudged the entire conversation in a new direction. Made people question the old rules. Opened a few more doors. And that is the thing about crossroads; they do not always look like victories. Sometimes they are just a turning of the wheel, slow but irreversible. And DeepSeek turned that wheel.

The phrase, "*Make fire out of friction*," is part metaphor, part mantra. That is what it is, all this tension, all this unpredictability, and it is not the end. This phrase describes the furnace where they make the next big thing. Regulations are not a stop sign; they are terrain. DeepSeek navigated them by being more human, not less.

REFERENCES

Abdeldayem, F. M. A., & Kswat, S. F. W. (2025). BRICS expansion in the news coverage of member countries: A political economy perspective. *Journal of Humanities and Applied Social Sciences*, *7*(1), 18–37. DOI: 10.1108/JHASS-12-2023-0167

Allen, R. (2025). DeepSeek and AI innovation: How Chinese universities broke through the glass ceiling of technological advancement. *American Journal of STEM Education*, *6*, 1–10. DOI: 10.32674/10bz2d04

Atillah, I. (2024). *AI chatbot blamed in teen's death: Here's what to know about AI's psychological risks and prevention* [Tech News]. AI Chatbot Blamed in Teen's Death: Here's What to Know about AI's Psychological Risks and Prevention. https://www.euronews.com/next/2024/11/02/ai-chatbot-blamed-in-teens-death-heres-what-to-know-about-ais-psychological-risks-and-prev

Azizi, O. (2025). *DeepSeek-v3: A high-performance mixture-of-experts language model*. DOI: 10.13140/RG.2.2.32707.52000

Baptista, E. (2025, January 28). What is DeepSeek and why is it disrupting the AI sector? *Reuters*. https://www.reuters.com/technology/artificial-intelligence/what-is-deepseek-why-is-it-disrupting-ai-sector-2025-01-27/

ByteBridge. (2025, January 31). DeepSeek AI: Company overview, founding team, culture and DeepSeek R1 model. *Medium*. https://bytebridge.medium.com/deepseek-ai-company-overview-founding-team-culture-and-deepseek-r1-model-ea87f711b4b3

Choe, S., & Parvini, S. (2025, January 28). *Nvidia faces a reckoning as an upstart rival raises questions about Wall Street's darling* [World/Americas]. Nvidia Faces a Reckoning as an Upstart Rival Raises Questions about Wall Street's Darling. https://www.independent.co.uk/news/world/americas/nvidia-ap-new-york-wall-street-apple-b2688009.html

DeepSeek. (2024). *DeepSeek-V2: A strong, economical, and efficient mixture-of-experts language model*. https://huggingface.co/deepseek-ai/DeepSeek-V2

DeepSeek. (2025a). *DeepSeek API: A guide with examples and cost calculations*. https://www.datacamp.com/tutorial/deepseek-api

DeepSeek. (2025b). *DeepSeek-R2: China's bold answer to the AI race – What you need to know*. https://deepseek.ai/blog/deepseek-r2-ai-model-launch-2025

DeepSeek. (2025c). *Leading Ai language models & solutions*. https://deepseek.ai/

GitHub. (2025). *DeepSeek-ai repositories.* https://github.com/orgs/deepseek-ai/repositories?type=all

Guo, D., Zhu, Q., Yang, D., Xie, Z., Dong, K., Zhang, W., Chen, G., Bi, X., Wu, Y., Li, Y. K., Luo, F., Xiong, Y., & Liang, W. (2024). *DeepSeek-Coder: When the large language model meets programming — The rise of code intelligence* (No. arXiv:2401.14196). arXiv. https://doi.org//arXiv.2401.14196DOI: 10.48550

Gupta, M. (2025, January 21). What are DeepSeek-R1 distilled models? *Data Science in Your Pocket.* https://medium.com/data-science-in-your-pocket/what-are-deepseek-r1-distilled-models-329629968d5d

Harrington, A. (2025). *The DeepSeek disruption: How China's groundbreaking Ai model is transforming the global tech race.* Alexander Harrington.

Hawkins, A. (2025, January 28). Who is behind DeepSeek and how did it achieve its AI 'Sputnik moment'? *The Guardian.* https://www.theguardian.com/technology/2025/jan/28/who-is-behind-deepseek-and-how-did-it-achieve-its-ai-sputnik-moment

Jiang, B. (2025, January 28). *China's AI disrupter DeepSeek bets on low-key team of 'young geniuses' to beat US giants* [Artificial intelligence/TechBig/Tech]. https://www.scmp.com/tech/big-tech/article/3294357/chinas-ai-disrupter-deepseek-bets-low-key-team-young-geniuses-beat-us-giants

Johnson, L. (2025, April 25). *DeepSeek Coder: Let the code write itself.* https://www.byteplus.com/en/topic/382907?title=deepseek-coder-let-the-code-write-itself

Krause, D. (2025). *DeepSeek and FinTech: The democratization of Ai and Its global implications. SSRN.* DOI: 10.2139/ssrn.5116322

Mann, J. (2025, January 28). *DeepSeek just dropped an update AI model called Janus Pro. It says the image generator is better than OpenAI's DALL-E.* Business Insider. https://www.businessinsider.com/deepseek-janus-pro-7b-ai-model-openai-dall-e3-2025-1

McKinsey. (2025, April 22). *How open source AI solutions are reshaping business | McKinsey.* https://www.mckinsey.com/capabilities/quantumblack/our-insights/open-source-technology-in-the-age-of-ai?utm_source=chatgpt.com

Osipovich, A., & Ballard, E. (2025, January 27). *Stock market news, Jan. 27, 2025: Nvidia stock sinks in AI rout sparked by China's DeepSeek.* WSJ. https://www.wsj.com/livecoverage/stock-market-today-dow-sp500-nasdaq-live-01-27-2025

PlainConcepts. (2025, February 3). Is DeepSeek R1 right for your business? *Plain Concepts.* https://www.plainconcepts.com/deepseek-r1/

Po, L. M. (2025, May 2). A Brief History of LLMs. *Medium*. https://medium.com/@lmpo/a-brief-history-of-lmms-from-transformers-2017-to-deepseek-r1-2025-dae75dd3f59a

Poo, M. (2025). Reflections on DeepSeek's breakthrough. *National Science Review, 12*(3), nwaf044. Advance online publication. DOI: 10.1093/nsr/nwaf044 PMID: 40041025

Reiisieh, M. (2025, February 12). *Code, Claims, and Consequences: The legal stakes in OpenAI's case against DeepSeek*. SCBC. https://www.scbc-law.org/post/code-claims-and-consequences-the-legal-stakes-in-openai-s-case-against-deepseek

Reinicke, C. (2025, January 27). Here are the key takeaways from Nvidia, tech rout triggered by DeepSeek. *Bloomberg.Com*. https://www.bloomberg.com/news/articles/2025-01-27/deepseek-ai-market-rout-takeaways-on-nvidia-tech-stocks-nvda-meta-aapl

Reuters. (2025, January 28). *DeepSeek says its Janus Pro AI model beats rivals in image generation*. https://www.reuters.com/technology/deepseeks-janus-pro-ai-model-beats-rivals-image-generation-2025-01-27/?utm_source=chatgpt.com

Rollet, C. (2025, March 10). *DeepSeek isn't taking VC money yet—Here are 3 reasons why* [TechCrunch]. https://techcrunch.com/2025/03/10/deepseek-isnt-taking-vc-money-yet-here-are-3-reasons-why/?utm_source=chatgpt.com

Snyder, J. (2025, January 27). *How DeepSeek built on AI's innovation debt*. https://www.forbes.com/sites/jasonsnyder/2025/01/27/genius-steals-how-deepseek-built-on-ais-innovation-debt/

Subin, S. (2025, January 27). *Nvidia sheds almost $600 billion in market cap, biggest one-day loss in US history*. CNBC. https://www.cnbc.com/2025/01/27/nvidia-sheds-almost-600-billion-in-market-cap-biggest-drop-ever.html

Sweney, M., & Milmo, D. (2025, January 29). OpenAI 'reviewing' allegations that its AI models were used to make DeepSeek. *The Guardian*. https://www.theguardian.com/technology/2025/jan/29/openai-chatgpt-deepseek-china-us-ai-models

Taneja, H., & Zakaria, F. (2023, September 6). AI and the new digital cold war. *Harvard Business Review*. https://hbr.org/2023/09/ai-and-the-new-digital-cold-war

Turing, A. M. (1950). Computing machinery and intelligence. *Oxford University Press, 59*(236), 433–460.

Wang, Q. (2025). DeepSeek hits hard: Helping to revolutionize higher education in the era of artificial intelligence. *International Journal of Higher Education*, *14*(2), 26. DOI: 10.5430/ijhe.v14n2p26

Young. (2025, February 25). DeepSeek, ChatGPT, and the global fight for technological supremacy. *Harvard Law School*. https://hls.harvard.edu/today/deepseek-chatgpt-and-the-global-fight-for-technological-supremacy/

Zegart, A., & Johnston, E. (2025). *A Deep peek into DeepSeek AI's talent and implications for US innovation*. The Hoover Institution and The Stanford Institute for Human-Centered AI.

KEY TERMS AND DEFINITIONS

AI Democratization: *Making advanced AI tools affordable and accessible globally, not just for* wealthy corporations. Core to DeepSeek's mission of breaking Western AI monopolies.

BRICS+ Strategy: Focus on high-growth emerging economies (Brazil, India, South Africa, etc.). Prioritizing solving hyper-local problems with lightweight, offline-friendly AI.

Constraint-Driven Innovation: Using limitations (e.g., export bans) as catalysts for creativity (e.g., repurposing old GPUs). Defined DeepSeek's underdog ethos.

Courageous Ingenuity: Solving problems through grassroots creativity vs. capital (e.g., favela missing-person AI). Cultural hallmark of DeepSeek's engineering team.

Cultural Fluency: Designing AI that understands local norms (e.g., silence in Japanese conversations). Made models feel "native" not "exported".

Data Dignity: Respecting data ownership/rights of BRICS+ partners (no extraction). countered "helicopter innovation" criticism.

David vs. Goliath Narrative: Positioning as an agile rebel challenging AI "empires" (OpenAI, Google). Core to brand storytelling and media strategy.

Digital Sovereignty: Ensuring user data stays within national borders and complies with local laws. Non-negotiable for DeepSeek in BRICS+ and EU markets.

Edge AI: Running models directly on devices (phones, sensors) without cloud dependency. Essential for offline use in low-connectivity regions.

Efficiency as-Philosophy: Prioritizing lean, purposeful design over raw scale. Technical and cultural mantra across all products.

Frugal Innovation: Achieving high-impact results with minimal resources (e.g., $6M R1 model). Turn constraints (GPU bans, budgets) into a competitive advantage.

Geopolitical Friction: Navigating US-China tech tensions, sanctions, and export controls. Primary external risk to DeepSeek's global ops.

Hyper-Local: AI Models fine-tuned for specific regional needs (e.g., crop disease detection in Hindi). Replaced generic solutions in DeepSeek's emerging-market approach.

Knowledge Distillation: Compressing large AI models into smaller, faster versions without major performance loss. Key to DeepSeek-R1's accessibility on low-end devices.

Mixture of Experts (MoE): AI architecture activating only relevant model "sub-networks" per task. Enabled efficient, cost-effective models like DeepSeek-V2/V3.

Open-Source Philosophy: Releasing models/code publicly to enable community collaboration. Distinguishes DeepSeek from proprietary rivals like OpenAI.

Pricing Disruption: Radically low API costs ($0.55/million tokens vs. OpenAI's $15). Destroyed entry barriers for students/small developers.

Proprietary AI: Closed, commercial AI systems (e.g., ChatGPT) contrasted with DeepSeek's open approach. Represented the "old guard" DeepSeek disrupted.

Radical Transparency: Publicly sharing data practices, model weights, and compliance steps. Critical for building trust in regulated markets (EU, BRICS+).

Singapore Hub: Neutral operational base balancing East/West interests. Geopolitical "Switzerland" enabling global expansion.

Strategic Neutrality: Working from geopolitically neutral hubs (e.g., Singapore) to balance US-China tensions. Allowed DeepSeek to navigate trade wars while scaling globally.

Chapter 2
Wind Information Technology's Data Governance Expansion:
Data Sovereignty, Domestic Dominance, and Western Barriers

Boyan Xing
http://orcid.org/0009-0002-0554-9636
Beijing Normal-Hong Kong Baptist University, China

EXECUTIVE SUMMARY

This chapter analyses the expansion of Wind Information Technology, a dominant Chinese data provider, navigating domestic success and international regulatory barriers. The company met data sovereignty conflicts from regulations like the EU's GDPR and Singapore's Payment Services Act, which challenge the standardized architectures of global fintech enterprises. Wind differentiated "bamboo root system" market entry strategy employs deep local embedding, technological symbiosis with institutions like Deutsche Borse, strategic acquisitions to secure critical licenses, and innovative compliance architectures including the "data glass room" and jurisdiction-adaptive engines. The technical advantages, such as the proprietary honeycomb data collection network and dynamic verification protocols, and how the strategic recalibration of compliance expenditures from operational liabilities into competitive moats, combined with algorithmic adaptability and cultural integration, provides a framework for Chinese technology enterprises to achieve sustainable cross-border growth amidst geopolitical.

DOI: 10.4018/979-8-3373-4302-0.ch002

INTRODUCTION

Wind, founded in a small office in Pudong, Shanghai, in 2005, initially served as a data aggregator for the Shanghai and Shenzhen stock exchanges. Founder Lu Feng might not have expected that this small team, established with an initial capital of 300,000 yuan, would grow into the "data heart" of China's financial industry twenty years later. The turning point occurred in 2015, during the wave of RMB internationalization. When Bloomberg terminals appeared on the trading desks of Chinese investment banks in Hong Kong, Wind's management first explicitly proposed the concept of "data going global" at an internal strategic meeting. This top-down internationalization revolution marks a crucial transformation for enterprises, moving them from local service providers to global infrastructure providers.

Background of the Company

The core infrastructure of WanDe Information Technology Co., Ltd. supports an enormous volume of financial data throughput. The core of its technical architecture is a real-time data flow monitoring network, which can process millions of financial data points per second and maintains a vast database covering 238 asset categories such as stocks, bonds, funds, and complex derivatives. Although ordinary investors are more exposed to its front-end terminal interface, the underlying moat that establishes the company's absolute dominance in the industry is its proprietary "honeycomb data collection network". This architecture achieves a direct hard connection with authoritative institutions such as the People's Bank of China and the Central Government Bond Registration and Settlement Co., Ltd. through thousands of data nodes.

This strong foundation gives us a big head start in important parts of the market. For instance, during the launch of the Shenzhen-Hong Kong Stock Connect in 2016, the company, leveraging its direct data acquisition capabilities, deployed a complete cross-border settlement data solution 72 hours ahead of its international competitors. It is this absolute control over the underlying data sources that enabled the company to build an extremely stable business loop within China. The latest market empirical research and industry data show that the company not only serves over 90% of financial institutions in China, but its terminal products are also an indispensable tool for the domestic vast seller research ecosystem (including thousands of licensed analysts) for macroeconomic analysis and stock pricing. For leading domestic mutual funds, the high service subscription fees are a rigid cost for maintaining the normal operation of their research and investment systems. Because of the lack of exclusive China Bond valuation data provided by this terminal, it will directly lead to the failure of the pricing model. Commercial data reflects its irreplaceability through an extremely high penetration rate of institutional customers and an extremely low churn rate.

An objective analysis of the organizational hierarchy and resource allocation reveals its underlying strategic logic. The significant resource allocation in technology research and development reflects the company's strategic orientation of prioritizing technological development over business expansion. The chief data scientist enjoys extremely high decision-making weight within the company, and the company also reinvests more than one-third of its annual revenue into code writing and algorithm optimization. This high-intensity R&D investment shows extremely high system resilience when facing sudden macroeconomic shocks. For example, at the beginning of the global public health crisis in 2020, the company's engineering team built a supply chain risk monitoring model covering all the enterprises that were shut down in a brief period.

However, compared to its rapid development in the domestic market, this enterprise has been extremely cautious in its timeline for international expansion. Although it proposed the strategic vision of serving the global financial market as early as when its subsidiary was preparing for listing in Hong Kong, the substantial overseas infrastructure construction did not speed until it officially got the fintech license issued by the Hong Kong Monetary Authority. This cautious attitude stems from a profound understanding of the regional attributes of the financial data service industry: once crossing national borders, data service providers will immediately face dual compliance barriers constructed by privacy regulations such as the EU's GDPR and the complex securities regulatory system in North America.

Motivation for Global Expansion

The underlying driving force behind the acceleration of this enterprise's global infrastructure layout stems from the historical convergence of the growth bottleneck in the domestic market and the crisis of trust in China's asset data in the international market. The financial fraud scandal involving Ruijin Coffee and related enterprises (such as Shenzhou Youche) that broke out in 2020 triggered a serious financial fraud contagion effect in the international capital market. This series of scandals not only led to significant fluctuations in the Nasdaq China Golden Dragon Index, but also exposed the systematic vulnerability of international investment institutions in conducting cross-border due diligence, where they were highly rely on lagging and easily manipulated second-hand financial reports. Academic research shows that such financial fraud incidents seriously undermined the trust foundation in China's macroeconomic data and enterprise micro-operation data in the international market. Facing this trust vacuum, the management of Wind knew acutely that the underlying collection network, which the enterprise had spent over a decade building and directly connecting thousands of official data nodes, had tremendous commercial potential to be transformed into a "trust anchor" for the international market.

The simultaneous emergence of policy dividends and market-driven mechanisms accompanied the true strategic turning point. On the one hand, the national macro policies provided targeted special funds to support the overseas expansion of financial technology infrastructure with systemic importance, providing sufficient capital ammunition for enterprises to expand their overseas data centers. The extremely high penetration rate (close to saturation) of the domestic public fund market inevitably led to a significant slowdown in the average annual expenditure growth rate of core customers. In this "internal competition" growth predicament, the urgent demand of international hedge funds for high-frequency and high-precision data in the Chinese bond market became the key breakthrough point for enterprises to break through the revenue ceiling. Overseas institutions will pay a high premium for microsecond-level data latency. This prompted the enterprise to quickly increase its capital injection into its Hong Kong subsidiary, officially starting the strategic journey of exchanging data accuracy for international financial asset pricing power.

The increasingly intense geopolitical competition in recent years has further reshaped the underlying logic of the cross-border flow of financial data. With implementing the US "Foreign Companies Accountability Act" (HFCAA) and the continuous tightening of China's domestic mechanisms for cybersecurity and data export security assessment, cross-border data services are no longer merely commercial activities but have risen to a sensitive issue at the national security level. An authoritative report shows that because of stricter restrictions on cross-border data flow, Wind had to impose limitations on the access of overseas users to specific macroeconomic databases and information on corporate equity structure penetration in 2023. This passive data blockage caused by compliance pressure has profoundly alerted the management of enterprises: relying solely on the "export" of data flows from the domestic to the overseas market is no longer sustainable. To maintain the service capabilities for overseas institutional clients in the face of globalization headwinds, enterprises must establish decentralized data hubs overseas with legal independence and computing capabilities, which has become the strongest driving force for their sped up global physical layout.

MARKET ANALYSIS AND ENTRY STRATEGY

This chapter analyzes Wind's strategic decision-making framework in its global expansion. Facing the complex landscape of geopolitical and regulatory barriers, WIND Company adopts a differentiated market entry strategy: it prioritizes Hong Kong as its "strategic buffer zone" (relying on the natural data alliance formed by the overseas headquarters of 867 Chinese institutions), and then expands its global presence through three fronts: Singapore's foreign exchange hub, London's institutional demand, and New York's capital market. In terms of entry mode, Wind has abandoned aggressive mergers and acquisitions and adopted a "bamboo root system" gradual strategy, integrating its technology more deeply with Deutsche Börse in the EU to avoid GDPR compliance costs. Reuse 37 local data centers of DBS Bank in Southeast Asia to achieve light asset coverage. In North America, it gained AlphaMetrics for 120 million US dollars to get the FINRA license, breaking Bloomberg's monopoly. The core competitive advantages are reflected in the low-latency light-speed network, dynamic data verification system, and localized pricing strategy.

Target Market Selection

The selection of the three core strategic fronts is not arbitrary; each market represents a distinctly different regulatory ecosystem, accompanied by unique high-yield market opportunities that align with the company's long-term infrastructure development objectives.

The primary attraction of the Singapore front lies in its unshakable status as a top-tier global foreign exchange trading hub. According to the triennial survey released by the Bank for International Settlements (Bank for International Settlements [BIS], 2025), the average daily foreign exchange trading volume in Singapore surged to 1.485 trillion US dollars in April 2025, representing a 60% increase compared to 2022 and accounting for 11.8% of the global total. These figures reinforce Singapore's position as the world's third-largest foreign exchange center and the largest offshore renminbi clearing hub in Asia (Monetary Authority of Singapore, 2025). However, market entry is subject to strict constraints imposed by the Monetary Authority of Singapore (MAS) and its *Payment Services Act.* This legislation requires rigorous data localization, mandating that financial data involving Singaporean users must physically live in certified data centers within Singapore's territory (Monetary Authority of Singapore, 2019). Potential entrants will require an initial capital expenditure of at least 2 million US dollars solely for server migration and compliance restructuring. They will also incur recurring annual compliance audit costs of 830,000 Singapore dollars. While these high costs make up a significant industry entry barrier, effectively excluding financially constrained small and medium-sized fintech start-ups, they create a natural regulatory moat for Wind Information, which possesses robust financial and technical resources. Once this moat is crossed, the compliance barrier will structurally deter secondary competitors from entering the long term.

The driving force behind the London front stems primarily from the extremely urgent and unmet market demand among European institutional investors. A white paper published by the UK Investment Association (2020) points out that approximately 300 London-based hedge funds forgo about 1.2 billion pounds in potential annual gains from renminbi asset allocation because of systemic network latency and the absence of granular real-time data on Chinese onshore bonds. The principal obstacle to entering this jurisdiction is the European Union's General Data Protection Regulation (GDPR). Specifically, Article 44 of the GDPR strictly prohibits transferring personal data and sensitive corporate financial data outside the European Economic Area unless the European Commission has granted the receiving country an "adequacy decision." If Wind Information intends to provide direct services to its London or EU clients, it would be required to completely reconstruct its entire data architecture in Frankfurt or Dublin, including independently deploying server clusters certified under ISO/IEC 27001. This process would not only trigger substantial capital expenditures but also lead to an infrastructure deployment cycle lasting between nine and fifteen months. In addition, the UK Financial Conduct Authority (FCA) mandates that data service providers must open application programming interfaces (APIs) for regulators to conduct penetrating inspections—a non-negotiable requirement that conflicts with Wind Information's closed, proprietary data ecosystem.

The New York front exhibits an entirely unique form of commercial intensity, characterized by the absolute monopoly of existing Western financial data giants over workflow ecosystems. Market tracking research conducted by Coalition Greenwich (2023) shows that Bloomberg Terminal penetration among financial institutions in Manhattan has reached a dominant 74%. Incumbent giants' ecosystems deeply integrate into traders' daily operational workflows, creating entry barriers in the North American market that do not stem from hardware performance or raw data transmission speed. For instance, traders at Goldman Sachs send over 1.4 million instructions daily via Bloomberg's proprietary chat system, while Morgan Stanley's quantitative risk models directly invoke Bloomberg's bond valuation interface for automated calculations. This profound workflow binding effect results in exceptionally high switching costs, with estimates placing the replacement cost per professional at up to 470,000 US dollars annually. Compounding this commercial blockade is the stringent transparency disclosure requirement introduced by the US Securities and Exchange Commission (SEC), which obliges data providers to disclose military background screening records for all data sources (Securities and Exchange Commission, 2020). Since much of Wind Information's macroeconomic data originates from entities directly affiliated with China's National Bureau of Statistics, such geopolitical friction creates an insurmountable compliance divide between the two countries.

Confronted with these formidable multi-jurisdictional obstacles, Hong Kong ultimately emerges as the breakthrough point for the company's globalization strategy, owing to its unique attribute as a "strategic buffer zone." During field observations conducted in the central trading hall, researchers captured a critical scenario: traders from institutions such as BOCOM International were simultaneously operating two systems. They used Western terminals to monitor European and US debt markets, while keeping their screens locked on the Wind terminal to access real-time bilateral quotes from the "Bond Connect" program. This dual-system coexistence model reveals a substantial unmet demand in cross-border capital flow analysis. Supporting this observation, quantitative data show that Hong Kong hosts the overseas headquarters of 867 Chinese-invested institutions, which collectively manage 17.3% of renminbi bond holdings in the onshore market, forming a highly cohesive natural "data alliance." Tax leverage further enhances Hong Kong's commercial competitiveness: Hong Kong's corporate income tax rate of 16.5% is significantly lower than London's 19% and New York's 21%. The Wind Information Hong Kong subsidiary's five-year financial statements reflect this advantage, documenting cumulative tax savings of 140 million Hong Kong dollars. These savings have been rapidly and aggressively reinvested in the construction of local data center infrastructure. Installation data for the first batch of English-language terminals in 2019 confirm the viability of this strategy: among the 32 contracted institutions, 29 had Chinese-invested backgrounds. By collecting heatmap data on the use of the "ChinaBond Valuation" function in the English interface, the R&D team found that European and US traders placed greater emphasis on dynamic comparison tools for yield curves. This user feedback, derived from real high-frequency trading scenarios, prompted the company to urgently add a cross-market spread analysis module in the subsequent 3.0 version, providing a crucial technological springboard for the official expansion into the core markets of Europe and the United States.

Entry Mode Selection

At the 2021 Singapore FinTech Summit, when the media questioned why Weidai had avoided the large-scale horizontal acquisition strategy commonly adopted by Western competitors, the company's chief financial officer responded using the metaphor of the "bamboo root system" from Eastern philosophy. Before bamboo shoots burst forth and undergo explosive vertical growth, they must extend a network of roots several kilometers underground to establish a vast nutrient absorption system (Zhang, 2021). This business metaphor reveals the unique logic of the company's gradual expansion: by accumulating energy through a concealed underlying layout, it avoids blindly pursuing visible rapid market share on the surface, so as not to endanger long-term system compliance and stability. This core method specifically develops into three highly differentiated market entry models, each of which is precisely calculated to adapt to the specific regulatory ecology and competitive landscape of the target market.:

EU Market: Achieving Parasitic Penetration through Compliance Wisdom

In the highly regulated market environment established by the GDPR, UBS did not choose to invest heavily in building an independent data silo. Instead, it opted for a deep technological symbiosis with Deutsche Börse. The "XETRa-China Index" jointly developed by the two parties in 2021 was not merely a simple data-sharing protocol. Instead, it directly integrated UBS's complex Chinese bond valuation algorithm with the underlying Xetra trading system of Deutsche Börse for deep computational integration, achieving millisecond-level real-time connectivity between the Chinese and European capital markets (Deutsche Börse Group, 2021). Through this "technological parasitism" strategy, UBS successfully obtained access to the European market with only a core team of 12 algorithm engineers deployed in Europe, while avoiding the need for a huge capital expenditure of over 200 million Euros required to establish an independent data center compliant with GDPR standards. The more profound strategic significance lies in the fact that the European Central Bank (ECB) subsequently included this index in its monetary policy reference framework. This inclusion legally transformed UBS's data from an edge third-party service into a component of the EU's core financial infrastructure, creating an irreplaceable compliance moat.

Southeast Asian Market: Achieving Deep Empowerment Through Ecological Synergy

The financial landscape in Southeast Asia is characterized by extreme fragmentation and regulatory heterogeneity. To navigate in such a complex environment, in 2022, Wind reached a strategic agreement with DBS Bank and jointly established the "Wind-Sea" joint venture, demonstrating the ingenious application of ecological leverage (Bain & Company, 2024). This joint venture did not spend a huge amount of money building server facilities that comply with each country's data residency laws from scratch. Instead, it adopted an innovative "DBS Network Hosting + Wind Data Core" light-asset model. Through this model, Wind directly deployed local server clusters directly into the 37 fully compliant cloud data centers that DBS Bank has been operating in six Southeast Asian countries. This symbiotic model is highly efficient, especially during the Islamic financial compliance transformation of the branch in Malaysia. By reusing the "Profit Margin Algorithm Engine" that DBS

Bank has already got national bank certification for from the Malaysian government, Wind successfully shortened the original 18-month Sharia review process to just a few weeks. This strategy shows a significant light-asset characteristic in financial statements: the joint venture generated S$120 million in revenue in its first year of operation, while its fixed asset investment was only S$3.6 million.

North American Market: Achieving Core License Breakthrough Through Strategic Acquisition

Because of the deep monopoly of the New York market by existing financial information giants, the breakthrough not only requires technological cooperation but also aggressive capital operations. In 2023, Wind spent 120 million US dollars to gain AlphaMetrics Company. The core strategy of this acquisition was not to get the company's software products, but to legally inherit the key licenses held by it from the US Financial Industry Regulatory Authority (FINRA). This scarce regulatory credential granted the platform the authority to access the US Treasury Bond Trading System (TRACE) directly, which is the technical foundation supporting the terminal advantages of Western monopolistic enterprises. However, the system integration after the acquisition faced significant commercial pain: on the one hand, the company had to strive to keep the 47 hedge fund clients of AlphaMetrics to maintain the validity of the license; the engineering team needed to seamlessly integrate the complex Chinese bond valuation module into its outdated fixed income analysis platform. The high integration cost led to two consecutive years of losses in the American business in 2023, with a net loss of 24 million US dollars in 2023. Despite the high financial cost, the long-term value of this strategy was verified in 2024: through the existing AlphaMetrics compliance interface, Wind's English terminal successfully broke through the technical blockade and smoothly entered the system testing environment of Goldman Sachs and Morgan Stanley's proprietary trading desks, achieving a penetration in the core area of Wall Street.

Competitive Advantage

The global leading nature of the technical architecture

The foundation of the enterprise's competitive moat is its ultra-low latency data transmission architecture. In the modern financial market, transactions are based on profit margins measured in microseconds, and the speed of data delivery directly determines the arbitrage profitability of high-frequency trading algorithms. IEX has constructed a proprietary "lightning network" comprising 203 data centers worldwide. This network not only successfully achieved an extreme intercontinental transmission speed of only 76 milliseconds from Shanghai to London, but also, through the deployment of edge computing nodes in various locations, can bypass congested public telecommunications switches and dynamically and autonomously optimize fiber optic routing paths. To concretize this engineering feat, statistics from the independent network monitoring agency WonderNetwork (2026) show that the average Ping value of the standard public Internet between Shanghai and London typically fluctuates between 183 and 191 milliseconds (WonderNetwork, 2026). Through its proprietary underlying hardware and intelligent routing, the transmission speed of IEX's network is 2.2% faster than the professional industry average.

The overwhelming advantages of this technical architecture were rigorously verified in the stress test of the "Shanghai-London Stock Connect" in 2021. The network effortlessly withstood a peak impact of 500,000 high-frequency transactions per second, quickly becoming the preferred channel for Chinese institutions to conduct cross-border settlements. The sophisticated "dual-active data center" architecture was also key to this network's resilience. In the event of any physical or network failure of the primary node, the system traffic would automatically and seamlessly switch to the backup node within 0.3 seconds. During the British pension crisis in 2022, this unparalleled system stability played a decisive role. Because of the rapid depletion of liquidity in the British government bond market, traditional Western monopoly terminals experienced an 11-minute quote delay and system crashes. However, the WIND terminal relied on its edge node in Frankfurt to handle the massive data flow of the London Stock Exchange in real time, ensuring the continuous fluctuation of the "Bond Connect" quote system. The Millennium Management in London subsequently established this event as an internal benchmark for evaluating the stability of its supplier system. Similarly, during the crisis in March 2024, when an earthquake in Japan caused the Nikkei 225 index quote of the Tokyo Stock Exchange to be interrupted for 17 minutes, WIND maintained the continuous and stable transmission of Japanese government bond data through its Osaka node. In the scenario of ultra-high frequency trading (HFT), this reliability directly translated into huge excess returns (Alpha); during a sharp market fluctuation in 2023, a qualified foreign institutional investor (QFII) used the microsecond advantage provided by the WIND terminal to precisely capture the only 0.2-second arbitrage window between China's government bond futures and spot markets, achieving a net profit of over 3 million US dollars within a single day.

Revolutionary breakthrough in the data verification system

If transmission speed determines the execution ability of transactions, then the authenticity and granularity of the underlying data determine the success or failure of investment strategies. The "Dynamic Verification Protocol" independently developed by WanDe represents a revolutionary breakthrough in forensic accounting analysis. This enterprise data authentication system establishes direct API connections with 18 different official government information sources such as the tax bureau, the General Administration of Customs, and the State Grid, and conducts in-depth multi-dimensional cross-validation of the financial data disclosed by enterprises. If the deviation between the data points of the enterprise report queried by the system and the official underlying registration data exceeds the preset 5% threshold, this protocol will autonomously freeze the release of this data and generate a high-priority red alert to the institutional subscribers.

The outstanding performance of this system in detecting financial fraud shocked the global financial community in the 2020 systematic accounting fraud scandal of Luckin Coffee. The final lawsuit document of the US Securities and Exchange Commission (SEC) revealed that the beverage chain enterprise fabricated over 300 million US dollars in retail sales through false transactions, causing investors to suffer huge losses (Securities and Exchange Commission, 2020). However, 31 days before the short-selling firm Muddy Waters released the report and the fraud was exposed to the public, the verification protocol of Wind Intelligence had already sensitively detected a catastrophic abnormal signal through natural language processing (NLP) and cross-database matching: there was a huge and inexplicable mathematical difference of up to 41.16% between the VAT invoicing amount (82.6 million yuan) declared by Luckin Coffee in Xiamen region and the regional retail sales amount (140 million yuan) announced at the same time. Academic research shows that traditional external audits often rely on data provided by company management, while blockchain traceability and cross-database dynamic data cross-comparison are the only effective technical approaches to uncover such complex frauds (Chen, 2022). Although many international investment institutions that overly relied on traditional manual due diligence and audit reports ignored this automatically generated early warning this incident completely changed the paradigm of the investment community's reliance on data suppliers and established the absolute authority of the cross-validation protocol in preventing investment risks.

After the Ruike incident, the system was further upgraded to enable round-the-clock real-time dynamic monitoring. In 2023, this protocol successfully intercepted an operation by a major new energy vehicle manufacturer attempting to falsely report an export volume of 1.2 billion RMB. The system automatically conducted a nonlinear regression analysis between the customs export declaration form submitted by the manufacturer and its municipal water supply, industrial electricity consumption, and natural gas consumption indicators. The result revealed that the actual production capacity utilization rate of the factory was only 52%, which was in a serious physical and logical contradiction with its claimed "full-scale production" status. By 2024, the algorithm developed again, deeply integrating regional power consumption big data from the national power grid and real-time monitoring and remote sensing data of pollutant emissions directly connected by the Ministry of Ecology and Environment. This integration successfully thwarted a false statement by a lithium battery enterprise regarding its quarterly production reaching 12,000 tons - because the algorithm calculated that the corresponding industrial electricity consumption only reached 68% of the thermodynamic reasonable value required to complete such a scale of output, triggering an automated capacity fraud alarm. This unprecedented digital forensic evidence capability prompted the European Securities and Markets Authority (ESMA) to officially include MW Research in its "Recommended Third-Party Data Validation Supplier Register", ultimately enabling the Bank of Italy to exceptionally issue the first compliance business license for a Chinese data service provider.

Localized data depth and scene adaptation

WIND rejected the highly homogeneous global standard data templates adopted by the existing Western competitors in its product design. Instead, its R&D team specifically designed and extracted 487 highly specialized exclusive data dimensions based on the economic structure realities of the Chinese and Asian markets. This deep localization was most clear in the fields of environmental, social, and corporate governance (ESG) ratings. Academic research has continuously pointed out that different global ESG rating agencies have significant systematic differences in assessment methods, indicator weights, and data sources, which often lead to completely opposite investment signals for the same company, seriously misleading investors (Yin et al., 2025; Emerald Publishing, 2024). When the Western-dominated ESG models rely heavily on standardized international labor and human rights indicators based on the conditions of developed countries, WIND's localized ESG framework proactively incorporates customized indicators that are in line with the current industrial situation in China, such as "real-time tracking of supply chain carbon footprint" and "protection rate of migrant workers' wages".

This profound divergence at the level of the rating method was perfectly showed in 2023 during the ESG controversy surrounding China Yangtze Power. The traditional Western financial terminals, based on rigid interpretations and mechanical application of international labor standards, downgraded the ESG rating of this utility giant. In contrast, Wind's dynamic model accurately captured and gave high weight to the huge capital investment of this hydropower giant in social responsibility - especially its contributions in the social and economic resettlement, housing security, and long-term employment training for hundreds of thousands of migrants in the reservoir areas during the construction of the dams (Wind Information Co., Ltd., 2023). Wind's algorithm considers this systematic poverty reduction and community reconstruction behavior as the highest level of social (S) responsibility practice, significantly raising its rating. Large, long-term institutional investors such as the National Social Security Fund ultimately trusted this granular analysis, deeply rooted in the domestic market rather than the unrealistic downgrade of General Motors overseas. With the support of Wind data, they resolutely increased their holdings in the company by 320 million shares.

The deeper level of localization capabilities is not only reflected in the differences in assessment criteria but also in the astonishing timeliness of data updates. After the Ministry of Finance of China released an extremely complex national special bond issuance plan in May 2024, Wind used its API network that directly connects with 35 provincial and plan-designated municipal fiscal platforms across the country. Within just 47 minutes, it completed the aggregation, cleaning, structural analysis, and terminal entry of the massive project lists from all 31 provinces. In sharp contrast, because of the lack of underlying government network connections, Western competitors could only rely on information provided by third-party data suppliers and supplemented with a manual translation of lengthy financial summaries, taking over three hours to barely complete the equivalent data update.

Implementation of Global Expansion

Wind has invested 460 million Hong Kong dollars to launch the "Data Standards Globalization Project", converting 2,843 Chinese financial terms into ISO20022 codes and pioneering a profit distribution rate algorithm in line with Islamic law. However, geopolitical conflicts have intensified: the US SEC requires disclosure of the military background of servers under the Foreign Company Accountability Act (the Shanghai data center is under a national security review for being connected to the central bank's system). The EU DORA Act's request for the source code of the SM9 encryption module violates China's Cryptography Law. The Payment Services Act in Singapore, which mandates data localization, has led to a 176% increase in query latency. To mitigate risks, the company implemented the "Three-ring decoupling Method" by establishing a legal entity, Wind Global Data Ltd, in Singapore. Use the data transfer exemption clause; Jointly built 287 compliance review modules with the Bank of England to achieve cross-judicial agreement conversion; A three-layer data circuit breaker mechanism (traffic perception layer, content sniffing layer, and permission verification layer) was deployed in Frankfurt. In the 2024 EU stress test, 92% of high-risk requests were successfully intercepted, etc.

Key Initiatives and Investments

Globalization Project of Data Standards

In the "Data War Room" in Central, Hong Kong, in 2021, Wind's technical team started the genetic reconstruction project financially. The entire office building floor, which cost 460 million Hong Kong dollars to purchase, became the physical carrier of this revolution. Here, engineers transformed 2,843 Chinese financial terms, such as "price-earnings ratio" and "yield to maturity," into machine-readable ISO 20022 standard codes. This transformation is not only a language translation but also a reconstruction of financial logic - for example, the Chinese term "Amortized Cost" needs to be mapped to the international standard "amortized cost" while retaining the unique valuation rules of Chinese bonds (such as the logic of adjusting the exercise price of bonds with options). The core challenge of this project lies in semantic fidelity: the team developed a "dual-channel verification algorithm" that uses natural language processing (NLP) models to compare definitions across Chinese and English contexts, ensuring consistent results across Bloomberg Terminals and Wind systems.

Localization in Islamic finance is challenging. To comply with the interest ban principle of the Quran, the technical team pioneered the "Profit Distribution Rate Algorithm", converting traditional bond interest into a cash flow model based on dividends of physical assets. This algorithm must pass the 128-item Islamic law review conducted by the Central Bank of Malaysia. Among them, the 37th item in the dispute over whether "date futures are speculative tools" has prompted three revisions to the plan. Ultimately, the team introduced the spot price of dates from the Saudi Commodity Exchange as a benchmark and successfully established a derivative pricing framework in line with Islamic law, making Wind the first Chinese platform to support real-time valuation of Islamic bonds (Sukuk).

Breakthroughs in regulatory compliance technology

Wind has invested 620 million yuan in dedicated research and development funds for the EU's GDPR compliance transformation. Its core achievement, the "Data Glass Room" system, employs a three-layer encryption architecture: the outer layer is a quantum key distribution optical fiber network, the middle layer uses the national cipher SM9, and the inner layer is built with a dynamic data desensitization engine implemented in 230,000 lines of code. This system has achieved millisecond-level response times in actual tests at the Frankford data center. When users request financial reports for German enterprises, the engine automatically redacts employees' personal information and business secrets and outputs only aggregated financial indicators. This meticulous control has enabled Wind to become the first Chinese data provider to pass the EU's "adequacy certification".

A more complex challenge comes from cross-border data transmission. To meet the Monetary Authority of Singapore's requirement that "data must not leave the country", Wind has deployed distributed storage nodes at its Jurong data center and developed a "data sandbox" system - local servers only store desensitized data. When users need in-depth analysis, the system auto-generates a virtual copy of the data for computing use, and the country always keeps the original data within its borders. This solution reduces compliance costs by 80% compared with traditional cross-border dedicated lines.

Challenges Faced

Geographical conflicts in regulatory compliance

An SEC inquiry letter has revealed a fundamental conflict between China's and the United States' regulatory systems. The document alleges Wind failed to disclose the military background-check records stored on its data servers in China and threatens to revoke its operating license in the United States. This accusation stems from the broad definition of "government-associated entities" in the US Foreign Company Accountability Act - China's Cybersecurity Law requires operators of critical information infrastructure to undergo national security reviews, and Wind's Shanghai data center was included in this category because of its access to the central bank's payment system. What is even more serious is that the European Financial Supervisory Authority (ESMA) invoked Article 12 of the Digital Operations Resilience Act (DORA), requiring Wind to submit a "proof of technical controllability" of its core algorithm code. However, China's Cryptography Law prohibits the cross-border transmission of commercial cryptography technical details. This regulatory double blow reached its peak in 2023: The Bank of France suspended Wind from providing interbank market data services for three months after it refused to submit the source code for the SM9 encryption module, resulting in the loss of 23 Eurozone customers.

The cultural gap in technical standards

Deutsche Bank's complaint letter (Monetary Authority of Singapore, 2022, Circular PS-N02/2022) exposed the hidden barriers of financial infrastructure: the bank pointed out that Wind Terminal did not use the ACT/ 360-day counting method commonly used in the EU when calculating the yield of Euro bonds, resulting in a 0.17 basis point deviation in the valuation of 30-year government bonds. After an in-depth investigation, engineers discovered 47 fundamental differences between the financial terminology systems of China and the EU: For instance, the "yield to maturity" in China is by default tax-inclusive, while the EU's MiFID II rule requires the disclosure of pre-tax yields. The valuation of Chinese credit bonds includes the implied government guarantee premium, while the EU's Credit Rating Regulation prohibits the inclusion of non-contractual support.

To address this issue, Wind was forced to rebuild its computing engine within 72 hours and added a "Jurisdiction adaptive module," which automatically switches the computing logic by recognizing the ISIN code prefix (for example, DE0001102317 uses ACT/360, while CN100020134 uses ACT/365). Although the plan is technically workable, it has sparked new controversy: In 2024, UBS Group incurred a trading loss of millions of Euros after the system mistakenly identified Swiss bonds as Chinese bonds (the ISIN prefix CH was misinterpreted as CN). The claim documents directly pointed to Wind's "regional label design defect".

Rigid constraints on data sovereignty

The Monetary Authority of Singapore's regulatory letter (Monetary Authority of Singapore, 2022, Circular PS-N02/2022) triggered an underlying earthquake in Wind's global architecture. The new regulations require that all data serving Singaporean customers be stored in certified data centers within the country, and that cross-border transmission be subject to a "Data Outbound security assessment". This has a devastating impact on Wind's "global unified data pool" architecture: its Singapore users account for 68% of Southeast Asia's total, and real-time data must be synchronized from the Shanghai principal center. What is even more serious is that, in June 2025, Singapore amended the Payment Services Act, requiring digital token platforms that serve overseas customers to get a DTSP license and localize their servers. Wind was forced to implement the "Data Cell Division Plan": deploying independent nodes at the Jurong Data center, replicating 1.2PB of core financial data, and filtering sensitive fields (such as the shareholder structure of Chinese local government bond issuers) through a "dynamic desensitization gateway". This plan has increased the query delay for Singaporean users from 76 milliseconds to 210 milliseconds, and Singaporean users are now prohibited from accessing certain derivative data that leaves the country because of its inclusion of real-time quotations from the Shanghai Financial Exchange.

Cognitive differences in business ethics

Deutsche Bank's decision not to redeem $1.25 billion of AT1 bonds in 2024 reflects a deeper conflict. The bank abandoned the redemption on the grounds of "foreign exchange loss risk" (the Euro exchange rate against the US dollar dropped from 1.37 at issuance to 1.08), which, although in line with the terms, violated the industry tacit understanding of "redemption upon maturity" among European banks. Wind downgraded the bond's credit score from A- to B+ in its risk model, triggering a panic sell-off among investors. The chief financial officer of Deutsche Bank publicly accused Wind of "abusing data hegemony" because it failed to consider the solvency fact that "Deutsche Bank's net profit in 2024 set a record". This controversy reveals the differences in business logic between the East and the West: European banks view AT1 as a "long-term tool for enhancing capital flexibility". Wind's model is based on China's regulatory logic: perpetual bonds must have risk provisions set aside for maturity within five years. This cognitive misalignment led to a sharp increase in Wind Europe's fixed-income business loss rate and a significant decline in institutional client renewal rates in Q1 2025.

Mitigation Strategies

When facing the compliance challenges of the EU's GDPR, Wind innovatively adopted a dual-track strategy of "regulatory sandbox + local entity", established an independent legal entity, Wind Global Data Ltd., in Singapore, and used the "Data Transit Exemption" clause of the country's Payment Services Act to exempt international business data from mandatory local storage when flowing through this hub. Sensitive fields (such as enterprise shareholder structures and pledge details) are filtered through the dynamic desensitization gateway at Jurong Data Center. The annual processing of cross-border data reaches 1.2 PB, of which 78% is cross-border bond transaction information. In the EU market, Wind and Deutsche Börse jointly developed a compliance interface that encodes 287 FCA review rules into an automated verification module to enable "dynamic protocol conversion". When a GDPR data request is received, the system automatically converts the "separate consent" clause of China's Personal Information Protection Law into a "legal basis statement" recognized by the EU, reducing the compliance review cycle from 9 months to 3.6 months.

Wind's "data circuit breaker mechanism" deployed in Frankfurt adopts a three-layer dynamic protection system: the traffic perception layer monitors the frequency of requests in real time (a circuit breaker is triggered when a single IP exceeds 1,000 times per second), the content sniffing layer identifies sensitive words such as "audit working papers" through NLP. The permission verification layer compares with the regulatory-accepted whitelist. In 2023, the system successfully intercepted the SEC's request to retrieve the audit working papers of a certain Chinese concept stock under the Foreign Company Accountability Act. Within 0.2 seconds, it routed the demand to the Singapore entity and output triple desensitized data - keeping the revenue recognition policy but concealing the customer's name, disclosing the impairment provision method but blurring the asset classification standard. This mechanism intercepted 92% of high-risk requests in the 2024 EU Digital Operations Resilience Act (DORA) stress test, facilitating the Bank of Italy to issue the first Chinese data service license (Authorization Document B/2023/102), allowing real-time valuation of Chinese bonds after desensitization to be provided to EU institutions.

Wind has developed a "Jurisdiction Adaptive Engine" to address 47 fundamental differences between the financial terminology systems of China and the EU (such as China's "yield to maturity" including tax while the EU requires the disclosure of pre-tax values) - automatically switching calculation logic through ISIN code prefixes (for example, DE codes enable ACT/ 360-day counting, and CN codes use ACT/365). In 2024, the engine was upgraded to a "tag cloud" system that integrates 3,821 financial rules from 196 countries/regions, preventing UBS Group from incurring millions of Euros in losses because of misclassifying Swiss bonds (CH) as Chinese bonds (CN). At the level of business ethics, Wind released the "AT1 Bond Valuation White Paper", incorporating the special scenario of "strong earnings but intentional non-redemption" through the ESG revision mechanism, resolving the controversy caused by Deutsche Bank's non-redemption of $1.25 billion in AT1 bonds, and reviving the renewal rate of European fixed-income business customers to 89%.

STRATEGIC ANALYSIS

The reconfiguration analysis of the Wand value chain reveals that the company has extremely focused its vast majority of its resources on the upstream R&D and proprietary data collection stages. Accounting for 34% of the company's annual total revenue, the intensity of its R&D investment has reached an astonishing level. The allocation of human resources also perfectly reflects this strategic focus: throughout the organizational structure, the proportion of technical and algorithmic R&D personnel is as high as 68%, and the authority level of the chief data scientist even surpasses that of most executive vice presidents. This fanatical belief in technological strength has given rise to core patents such as "Memory Real-time Retrieval System Based on Inverted Index." This patented technology can compress the response time of complex queries involving hundreds of millions of large financial transaction records to an astonishing 10 milliseconds. The data collection activity itself is the lifeblood of the enterprise. The "Honeycomb Network" it pioneered abandoned unreliable web crawler technology and directly connected to the most authoritative underlying information sources such as the People's Bank of China and the Central Government Bond Registration and Clearing Co., Ltd. through 3,162 physical and logical nodes. This absolute control over the data source ensures WanDe can consistently outpace its Western competitors by a fatal 0.5 seconds in the update speed of China's bond data.

In addition, WIND and Shanghai Steel Link have jointly established a cross-market commodity and financial database. By seamlessly integrating 10 TB of industrial spot price data with the trends of financial derivatives, this database has endowed institutions with extremely powerful predictive and analytical capabilities. When Gao Yi Asset Management Company successfully predicted and avoided the catastrophic overcapacity crisis in the photovoltaic industry two weeks in advance in 2024 by leveraging the platform's unique "Industrial Chain Capital Expenditure Early Warning Model", this achievement shocked the entire asset management industry. This classic case was successfully selected for the authoritative "Compilation of Hong Kong Sustainable Development Innovative Technology Solutions" and won the "Innovative Technology - Emerging Award" in "Quality Education Innovation Technology". These successive victories have completely transformed WIND's brand image. From a purely passive provider of market data, it has successfully risen to become an indispensable core strategic partner for global top investment institutions when conducting in-depth predictions and governance of industrial risks.

CONCLUSION AND STRATEGIC RECOMMENDATIONS

Summary of Key Findings

During its arduous process of global expansion, WanDe Information Technology Co., Ltd. provided conclusive evidence regarding the serious two-edged nature of "data sovereignty" in the global digital economy through its painful lessons and glorious successes. Domestically, the company relied on its unshakable, absolute data monopoly over China's macro-economy and the vast onshore bond market (such as the exclusive ChinaBond valuation system) to support an institutional penetration rate of up to 97.2%, building an almost impenetrable business empire. However, when attempting to export this closed ecosystem to mature markets such as Europe and the United States, it immediately encountered a harsh baptism of icy water - the penetration rate of its terminals in the West has long hovered at the brink of 2% (a matter of life and death). This huge disparity in market share profoundly exposes a fatal contradiction at the industry level: The global standardized data architecture and free flow pursued by multinational fintech enterprises, and the data localization and geo-enclosure increasingly erected by various countries (such as the EU's GDPR and Singapore's MAS) to protect national security and privacy, have a fundamental conflict, even a life-and-death conflict.

One of the most crucial findings of this report is that in the current international geopolitical environment, "compliance expenditures" must be redefined on the company's balance sheet. It is no longer an operational liability that consumes profits; instead, it is the most powerful core strategic asset and moat of the enterprise. Although in order to meet the EU GDPR and DORA bill extremely stringent requirements, all have to bite the bullet to pay as much as 620 million yuan for the underlying code rewriting and encryption architecture transformation, but the huge investment has directly led to the "glass house" data and a series of technological wonders of compliance, Prompt companies not only in extremely exclusive customers 37% of the eu markets surged, contrarian more lead to those who try to rely on the legal loophole to avoid compliance competitors, in heavy penalties for breach of cross-border data flow line, watching the market share of more than 200 million Euros in wind. Moreover, the cross-domain ecological data collaboration has demonstrated a terrifying multiplier effect. By integrating the physical prices of bulk commodities with abstract financial asset data, the accuracy rate of the early warning model it developed in predicting the trend of industrial capital expenditure soared by 11.3 percentage points, directly helping top funds such as Gao Yi Asset to predict crises in advance and avoid investment losses of hundreds of millions.

However, the intense conflict that emerged between the company's efforts to promote the global unification of technical standards and its attempts to adapt to local cultures remains a profound and unresolved challenge. The "jurisdiction-adaptive engine" that the company is proud of, although it perfectly resolved the differences in calculation formulas for dozens of Central European financial terms at the code level, in actual operation, it merely caused mechanical misjudgments due to extremely subtle regional letter encodings (such as CH for Swiss bonds and CN for Chinese bonds), resulting in significant losses for UBS Group and triggering a million-Euro cross-border lawsuit. This painful lesson ruthlessly reveals the inherent limitations of purely mechanized and automated compliance tools in the highly error-prone global high-frequency financial ecosystem, which are difficult to overcome.

Future Growth Opportunities

As the global economy accelerates its transition towards deep decarbonization, green finance data services have become an extremely vast and lucrative "blue ocean" market. Leveraging the technical foundation of its established "Green Bond Environmental Benefit Tracking System", Wind is currently at the best historical moment to lead and pioneer the "Verifiable Carbon Footprint Bond" data protocol. By further deepening the direct connection of the underlying API data with the pollution source monitoring platform of the Ministry of Ecology and Environment of the People's Republic of China and introducing AI deep learning analysis of high-resolution satellite remote sensing thermal imaging data on a large scale, this platform will be able to provide real-time, penetrating physical verification of the actual carbon reduction of green fundraising projects to global investors in an unalterable encrypted form. Given that this system accurately detected and forced a certain wind power enterprise to withdraw its falsely reported 120,000 tons of carbon emission reduction indicators in 2023, this hard-core legal data auditing capability that can completely end enterprises' "greenwashing" behavior will surely trigger a huge commercial demand for high-quality, traceable green auditing data.

Another highly commercially viable path is to extensively replicate the innovative "hardware infrastructure leasing model" in the highly saturated Western market. By drawing on the tariff-sharing and leasing strategies successfully adopted by heavy industry equipment manufacturers (such as Hangfashi Group) in the US market, WanDe is fully capable of fully implementing its "data terminal hardware leasing plan" throughout the Eurozone. By allowing a large number of small and medium-sized hedge funds to lease physical terminals connected to the Frankfurt GDPR-compliant servers at extremely low monthly subscription fees, and pioneering a tiered billing model based on actual data query volume and API calls, the company can completely bypass the huge one-time software licensing fees that hinder the adoption of new systems by small and medium-sized institutions. This innovative model demonstrated remarkable effectiveness in the early small-scale pilot in Singapore: not only did it successfully reduce the comprehensive data acquisition costs of enterprises by 23%, but it also unprecedentedly pushed the customer renewal rate of terminals to 92%. If scaled up, the 500 high-concurrency server clusters deployed in the Frankfurt data center alone would be sufficient to cover and erode the market share of up to 5,000 small and medium-sized financial institutions in the Eurozone.

Ultimately, regardless of how large the throughput of the technical architecture is or how low the network latency is, what determines whether a system can truly occupy the desktops of foreign traders is always the depth of cultural adaptation. The soft power of cultural integration is the final piece of the puzzle for cross-border expansion. This requires that outbound enterprises must establish "financial cultural integration officers" with extremely high authority in their R&D centers in New York or London. At the software interaction level, the shortcut key layout similar to the Bloomberg terminal must be redesigned completely based on the muscle memory formed by European and American traders over decades (completely reconfiguring the keyboard mapping logic from F1 to F12). For different cultural taboos in different regions, regional customized versions must include extremely special modules - for example, the terminal in the Middle East must hard-wire an Islamic financial compliance verification filter that has been reviewed by theology (capable of physically removing all interest-bearing bonds from the search pool), while in the Latin American market, where there is a passionate love for football, the version can creatively integrate macroeconomic anomaly indicators related to the World Cup and stock linkage analysis algorithms of sponsors. Only by grafting the cold Chinese code onto the local cultural symbols and operational habits can Chinese technology enterprises truly win recognition in the global financial market.

REFERENCES

Bain & Company. (2024, August 1). *Navigating high winds: Southeast Asia outlook 2024 - 34* [Press release]. https://www.bain.com/about/media-center/press-releases/sea/southeast-asia-outlook-2024-34/

Bank for International Settlements. (2025, September 30). *Triennial central bank survey of foreign exchange and OTC derivatives markets in 2025*. https://www.bis.org/press/p250930.htm

Chen, T. (2022). Blockchain and accounting fraud prevention: A case study on Luckin Coffee. *Proceedings of the 2022 7th International Conference on Social Sciences and Economic Development (ICSSED 2022)*, 44–49. https://doi.org/DOI: 10.2991/aebmr.k.220405.009

Coalition Greenwich. (2023, February 24). *Wealth management firms set technology priorities for 2023*. https://www.greenwich.com/market-structure-technology/wealth-management-firms-set-technology-priorities-2023

Deutsche Börse Group. (2021, May 27). *Deutsche Börse enters partnership with Chinese data provider Wind* [Press release]. https://www.mds.deutsche-boerse.com/mds-en/about-us/news-highlights/Deutsche-B-rse-enters-partnership-with-Chinese-data-provider-Wind-2034190

Emerald Publishing. (2024). Analysts' ESG attention and stock pricing. *Journal of Accounting Literature*. Advance online publication. DOI: 10.1108/JAL-06-2024-0128

European Securities and Markets Authority. (2021). *Environmental impact and liquidity of green bonds* (Report No. TRV-2021-2). https://www.esma.europa.eu/sites/default/files/trv_2021_2-environmental_impact_and_liquidity_of_green_bonds.pdf

Monetary Authority of Singapore. (2019, January 14). *Payment Services Act 2019*. https://sso.agc.gov.sg/act/psa2019

Monetary Authority of Singapore. (2025, October 1). *Singapore strengthens position as third largest global FX centre* [Press release]. https://www.mas.gov.sg/news/media-releases/2025/singapore-strengthens-position-as-third-largest-global-fx-centre

Securities and Exchange Commission. (2020, December 16). *Luckin Coffee agrees to pay $180 million penalty to settle accounting fraud charges* (Release No. 2020-319). https://www.sec.gov/newsroom/press-releases/2020-319

UK Investment Institute. (2020). *RMB asset allocation barriers: Annual opportunity cost for UK hedge funds* (White Paper No. WP-2020-09). https://ukinvestmentinstitute.org

Wind Information Co. Ltd. (2023, February 23). *China's ESG goes global: Wind ESG rating wins the best solution award* [Press release]. https://www.wind.com.cn/mobile/News/NewsDetail/en.html?id=701

Wind Information Co. Ltd. (2025, January 27). *Wind Alice investment advisor wins financial AI "industry leadership award"* [Press release]. https://www.wind.com.cn/mobile/News/NewsDetail/en.html?id=736

WonderNetwork. (2026, February 25). *Global ping statistics: Shanghai to London network latency*. https://wondernetwork.com/pings/Shanghai

Yin, W., Su, Y., Kirkulak-Uludag, B., Yan, A., & Wang, R. (2025). Impact of domestic and foreign investors on ESG disclosure quality in Chinese listed firms: Divergence or convergence? *PLoS One*, *20*(9), e0330418. DOI: 10.1371/journal.pone.0330418 PMID: 40938865

Zhang, Y. (2021, July 12). *Keynote speech at the Singapore Fintech Summit 2021*. Singapore Fintech Festival. https://fintechfestival.sg

KEY TERMS AND DEFINITIONS

Bamboo Root System Strategy: Wind's global expansion adopts a progressive market entry model. Emphasize the low-key and in-depth development in the early stage like bamboo roots (such as technology binding, light-asset cooperation, and obtaining key licenses), accumulate strength and establish a solid foundation (such as compliance capabilities and local adaptation), rather than pursuing short-term visible scale expansion (such as large-scale mergers and acquisitions), and achieve breakthrough growth in market coverage when conditions are ripe.

Data Glass Room: Wind has built a security architecture to meet strict data protection regulations, including the EU's GDPR. By adopting multi-layer protection (such as quantum key distribution, the national cipher SM9, and a dynamic data desensitization engine), it ensures data availability while enabling real-time, automated filtering and protection of sensitive information (such as personal privacy and business secrets), allowing users to use data in a controlled environment safely.

Data Sovereignty: It refers to the principle that a country or region has legal and administrative jurisdiction over data generated, collected, and processed within its territory. It emphasizes the physical storage location of data, restrictions on cross-border flows, and control over access to and use of data, often becoming a root cause of compliance barriers for international data service enterprises.

Dynamic Verification Protocol: The enterprise data authenticity verification system developed by Wind. By directly connecting to up to 18 official data sources, such as taxation, customs, and power, terminal data can be cross-compared. Once key indicators (e.g., sales volume and capacity utilization) deviate by more than the preset threshold (e.g., 5%), the system automatically suspends data release. It issues a warning to help identify financial fraud or anomalous data.

Honeycomb Data Collection Network: Wind's unique underlying data infrastructure architecture. By deploying thousands of data nodes across the country and directly connecting to authoritative data sources such as the People's Bank of China and China Central Depository & Clearing Corporation Limited, it has achieved efficient, stable, and authoritative real-time collection and processing capabilities of financial data, which is its core competitiveness in the timeliness and accuracy of data acquisition.

Jurisdiction Adaptive Engine: Wind has developed technical solutions to address differences in global financial terms, calculation rules (e.g., number of interest-bearing days: ACT/360 vs. ACT/365), and regulatory requirements (e.g., disclosure of pre-tax and after-tax yields). This engine can automatically switch the applicable calculation logic and disclosure standards based on the identification code of financial instruments (e.g., the ISIN country code prefix) to meet compliance requirements across jurisdictions.

Regulatory Sandbox: Wind's strategic approach to addressing complex compliance challenges. By establishing independent legal entities (such as Wind Global Data Ltd) in policy-friendly regions like Singapore and taking advantage of specific exemption provisions in local regulations (such as the "Data Transmission Exemption" in Singapore's Payment Services Act), a regulated "testing ground" is created for high-risk or innovative cross-border data businesses, reducing overall compliance risks within a controllable range.

Three-Ring Decoupling Method: Wind's systemic risk isolation strategy is designed to address geopolitical risks and diversify compliance pressure. By establishing legal entities in different regions (such as Singapore and Frankfurt), deploying localized compliance modules (such as jointly building a review module with the Bank of England), and implementing multi-level data security isolation layers (traffic perception, content sniffing, permission verification), the decoupling of business, data and compliance responsibilities and the dispersion of risks can be achieved.

Chapter 3
BYD International Market Entry Model:
A Kangaroo Theory Perspective

Zihan Lin
http://orcid.org/0009-0003-2561-2484
Beijing Normal-Hong Kong Baptist University, China

EXECUTIVE SUMMARY

This chapter examines the global expansion strategy of BYD, the world's largest electric vehicle manufacturer. Explores BYD's motivations for internationalization, including saturated domestic markets and growing global EV demand, and evaluates its multi-modal entry strategies across developed and emerging economies. Applies the Kangaroo Theory as a framework to understand BYD's context-driven approach from direct exports to embedded localization through foreign direct investment. BYD benefits from controlling its own supply chain, its new technologies like the Blade Battery and DM-i hybrid system, and how to handle problems like EU taxes and US trade limits. Further analyses competitive positioning against traditional luxury marques, while examining implementation challenges related to regulatory compliance, cultural adaptation, and supply chain resilience. SWOT and PESTEL frameworks offer insights into how Chinese multinational enterprises use technological ownership advantages, strategic partnerships, and localized production to navigate complex international markets.

INTRODUCTION

Founders established BYD (Build Your Dreams) in Shenzhen in 1995. It began producing rechargeable batteries and entered the automotive industry in 2003. It is

DOI: 10.4018/979-8-3373-4302-0.ch003

now a global leader in new-energy vehicles and the world's top-selling EV brand, with a sound position in China's new-energy car market as well. At home, there are more competitors, and the market is almost full, with little room to grow. However, around the world, more countries are pushing for EV adoption to reduce pollution, creating significant new opportunities. To keep growing, avoid relying solely on the Chinese market and seize global opportunities, BYD plans to expand overseas, and this paper examines that expansion.

Background of the Company

BYD has established a relatively complete organizational structure, with many business groups and research and development institutions. It has established several subsidiaries, including the Fudi Department, which handles R&D and production of automotive parts, forming a closed-loop system from lithium ore mining to vehicle sales. The core of the leadership team is Wang Chuanfu, the chairperson and president, who handles overall strategy, capital operations, and technical route decisions. He has led the R&D of subversive technologies, including nickel-cadmium batteries, lithium iron phosphate "blade batteries," and DM-i super hybrid. The team also includes Lian Yubo, the chief scientist, who handles vehicle R&D; He Long, the executive vice-president, who oversees the battery business group; and Li Ke, the executive vice-president, who handles global market expansion. The management team comprises "technical experts + business leaders" with deep technical expertise and business acumen.

BYD is the leader in China's new energy vehicle market, ranking first in sales. In 2023, its cumulative insurance volume in the first quarter exceeded the sum of SAIC Volkswagen and FAW-FAW-Volkswagen. In November 2022, it became the single-brand sales champion in China's passenger vehicle market. It holds a strong market share across various segments, and its Dynasty series models are very popular. BYD is also a key player in the global new energy vehicle market. In 2023, the sales volume of its new energy vehicles exceeded 3.02 million, surpassing Tesla for the first time to become the global sales champion (Han, 2024). Its products reach many countries and regions worldwide, and its overseas market share is escalating. Global consumers favor it for its advanced technology and high-cost-performance products.

Established in Shenzhen in 1995, BYD began its operations in the battery industry. In 2003, it entered the automotive industry by acquiring Qinchuan Automobile. It launched the world's first mass-produced plug-in hybrid vehicle in 2008, leading the new-energy sector. The Han series debuted in 2020, and the DMS-i super Hybrid System drew industry attention. The launch of BYD's blade battery and its announcement to halt fuel-vehicle production occurred in 2021. BYD rolled out its 3 millionth new energy vehicle in 2023 and introduced the high-end brand

"Yangwang." In 2010, BYD established its North American headquarters, marking the start of its internationalization strategy. A significant increase in new energy vehicle exports was observed in 2023, following the completion of the Thai factory. They established overseas 60cal production bases in Thailand, Hungary, and other countries in 2024. According to the "Global Hawk" strategy announced in 2023, BYD plans to enter 100 countries and regions and establish 50 overseas factories by 2025 (Cao et al., 2018).

Motivation for Global Expansion

A favorable market environment supports BYD's expansion. The worldwide market for new-energy vehicles is thriving. In 2023, sales reached 14.1 million units, with China making up nearly 60%. Key overseas markets such as Southeast Asia, Latin America, Australia, New Zealand, and parts of Europe remain in the early stages of development, creating significant opportunities for BYD. To reduce competitive pressures, the domestic new-energy vehicle sector is highly competitive, with many local and international brands vying for market share. By expanding internationally, BYD can bypass intense domestic competition and pursue higher market share and profitability. The global shift toward electric vehicles presents strong growth prospects. As a leader in China's new-energy vehicle industry, BYD can leverage its technological and product strengths to capitalize on the expanding global market and achieve rapid growth.

Global expansion enables BYD to generate revenue across multiple regions, reducing its dependence on the domestic market and enhancing the company's ability to withstand market risks. As BYD increases its overseas market share, it expects the proportion of overseas revenue in its total revenue to rise, which will diversify its revenue mix. Through global expansion, BYD can promote its brand in more countries and regions, increase brand awareness and influence, and steadily transition from a domestically well-known brand to a global-famous brand, supporting the enterprise's long-term development. BYD can optimize its global supply chain by establishing factories and collaborating with local suppliers in overseas markets. This can not only reduce production and transportation costs but also improve supply chain stability and flexibility and enhance the enterprise's overall competitiveness.

China has long placed great importance on the new-energy vehicle industry. "Made in China 2025" takes new-energy vehicles as a key development field, providing policy-level guidance and support for BYD. The Chinese government has also provided purchase subsidies and tax breaks for new-energy vehicle consumers, which has driven rapid growth in the domestic new-energy vehicle market (Masiero et al., 2016). This has enabled BYD to accumulate technology, expand production scale, and enhance brand influence in the domestic market, laying a solid foundation for its global expansion. Many countries and regions have introduced policies to support the development of new-energy vehicles, creating a suitable policy environment for BYD's entry. The European Union plans to make new energy vehicles account for over 70% of new-car sales by 2030, and will ban the sale of fuel-powered vehicles by 2035. These policies have stimulated demand for new-energy vehicles in the European market, creating a broader market for BYD. In addition, countries such as India and Indonesia have also set goals for the development of new-energy vehicles and provided financial incentives, which have promoted BYD's investment and layout in these regions.

BYD should take action to avoid trade barriers. In response to trade protectionist policies in some countries, BYD can establish factories overseas. Recently, the United States-Mexico-Canada Agreement (USMCA) provides preferential policies for vehicle trade within the region. BYD plans to build a factory in Mexico, which is expected to leverage USMCA policy advantages to export vehicles to the North American market and mitigate the impact of US trade protection policies.

MARKET ANALYSIS AND ENTRY STRATEGY

Target Market Selection

The criteria for BYD's selection of expansion markets primarily include economic growth, consumer demand, and the regulatory environment, as these factors directly influence the feasibility and potential success of market entry. BYD focuses on markets with strong economic growth momentum. This kind of market can raise residents' income levels, enhance their purchasing power, and create a broader market for new-energy vehicles. For instance, countries in Southeast Asia and Latin America are at an early stage of economic development, and rising vehicle demand has made them important target markets for BYD. Consumer demand is another factor that influences BYD's choice of expansion markets. For tech-savvy young people, BYD offers models with fashionable designs and intelligent functions. In regions with underdeveloped charging infrastructure, BYD promotes plug-in hybrid vehicles to meet consumers' long-distance travel needs and ease range anxiety.

Local governments' preferential policies significantly influence BYD's market selection process. In China, the government has introduced a series of support policies for new-energy vehicles. These policies, including purchase subsidies and license-plate preferences, have enabled BYD to gain a firm foothold in the domestic market. According to research by Shan (2024), between 2018 and 2022, BYD received approximately $3.7 billion in direct aid from the Chinese government. In 2022, BYD received $2.2 billion in direct help from the Chinese government. In the

European market, challenges include anti-subsidy investigations. However, the EU's goal of promoting carbon neutrality and its related support policies for new-energy vehicles have still created development opportunities for BYD. BYD has established factories in Hungary it aims to leverage the local policy environment through these factories and further expand its presence in the European market.

In developed economies like Europe and the United States, BYD competes with premium brands (Aldeguer, 2010). BYD targets both mid-premium and high-end segments to challenge incumbents in regions dominated by luxury marques and mainstream brands with strong electric vehicle lineups. In the compact SUV segment, BYD's Atto 3 competes with Volkswagen's ID.4 Pro (a top-selling EV in Europe) and Hyundai's Ioniq 5. In this competitive context, the company focuses on promoting vehicle models equipped with advanced features and technologies. For example, in the European market, BYD has launched a diverse range of vehicle models. These models cover economical city-commuting sedans and high-performance luxury models, and through this diverse product lineup, the company caters to the demands of different consumer segments.

Meanwhile, developed economies have stringent vehicle safety and environmental standards, which align with BYD's focus on technology and sustainability. For example, BYD's Atto 3 achieved a 5-star safety rating in EUNCAP tests in 2023. However, developed economies also face challenges, including high trade barriers and strong brand awareness among local enterprises, which require BYD to strengthen its technical capabilities and brand influence.

Emerging economies in Southeast Asia, Latin America, and the Middle East are key markets for BYD's global expansion. These markets have strong potential for new-energy vehicles given their large populations, rapid economic growth, and rising demand for environmental protection. BYD leverages its cost advantages to launch affordable models in emerging economies, meeting local consumers' need for cost-effective vehicles. Meanwhile, BYD also promotes the construction of local charging infrastructure through technical cooperation and other methods, and integrates into the local market through local production, expanding its market share.

Entry Mode Selection

Its Kangaroo Theory guides BYD's market entry modes. Each part of this theory directly supports BYD's choice of entry methods and their execution. For market access capability, BYD relies on core technologies—just as kangaroos use long legs. Blade Battery, DM-i hybrid system, and e-platform 3.0 solve key issues of new energy vehicles. This enables BYD to enter competitive markets, such as Europe, and compete with local automakers by offering high-performance products. To maintain entry mode flexibility, BYD leverages supporting capabilities, much like kangaroos use pouches. It controls the full industrial chain (from batteries to vehicle assembly) and has local operation experience. This allows for diverse entry options: building a Thai factory in 16 months for local production, or adjusting Hungary's production lines to meet regional demand rather than exporting. For post-entry sustainability, BYD uses quick responses—mirroring kangaroos' nonstop running—to optimize entry modes. When European consumers needed smart driving, it quickly added Navigation on Autopilot (NOA) systems to entry-level models. After Yuan UP achieved success in Latin America, it shifted from importing to local manufacturing in Brazil. This keeps its entry modes effective after market entry.

BYD gains existing enterprises to enter the market quickly. For instance, in 2023, its subsidiary, BYD Electronic, planned to acquire Jabil's mobile electronics manufacturing business for approximately 14.29 billion yuan. This acquisition can broaden BYD Electronic core supply chain in the consumer electronics access industry, enabling it to access advanced technologies, such as advanced assembly and equipment integration, as well as high-quality customer resources. In addition, BYD gained Yian Insurance, enabling it to enter the insurance sector and expand its operations. BYD has entered a series of joint ventures with local players (Wu, 2024). For instance, in the automotive industry, it has cooperated with local auto parts manufacturers, leveraging their familiarity with the local market, resource advantages, and channel access to reduce market-entry costs and quickly adapt to the local market environment. Through cooperation, both sides can share technology and R&D resources and jointly promote product innovation and upgrading.

BYD employs a context-driven, multi-modal entry strategy that strategically develops from asset-light exports to embedded localization. Initially, the company tests new markets through direct export shipping vehicles such as the ATTO 3 to 70+ countries to validate demand and build brand recognition while minimizing upfront investment. This phase is not merely transactional; BYD vertically integrates logistics by commissioning LNG-powered vessels such as BYD EXPLORER NO.1, reducing shipping costs by 15–20% and mitigating supply-chain vulnerabilities, including international carrier monopolies. After confirming market viability, demonstrated by the ATTO 3's success in Israel and Thailand, BYD moves to local production to overcome structural barriers. In the EU, it plans to establish factories in Hungary and Turkey to bypass the 38.1% anti-subsidy tariffs and address regional needs, such as developing snow-mode drivetrains for Alpine conditions. Similarly, its Brazil plant (300,000-unit capacity) produces the SHARK pickup with a 15 cm-deeper cargo bed for agricultural use, while its Thai facilities achieve 90% localization through Indonesian nickel sourcing. This shift from export to manufacturing transforms BYD from an exploratory trader into an integrated local player, leveraging Root's Contextual Fit Model, which shows that tariffs, scale potential, and product adaptability justify FDI.

BYD makes phased investments in production. It also speeds up its entry into challenging markets. It uses non-equity partnerships and cultural activities to do this. This matches Dunning's OLI Paradigm. The paradigm helps use locational and ownership advantages. Take Japan as an example. Japan has a regulated economy. In Japan, 62% of consumers do not trust Chinese brands. BYD works with Daihatsu here. They work together to make right hand-drive cars. BYD uses Daihatsu's local knowledge. It does not force its own way on the local market. BYD also has distribution partnerships. For example, it works with Sixt in Germany. Sixt ordered 100,000 vehicles from BYD. This enables BYD to achieve rapid growth through fleet channels. BYD also works with Shell. They are expanding charging networks together. This fixes Europe's problem of too few charging stations. Besides these practical partnerships, BYD also builds trust through socio-cultural activities. It sponsors the 2024 UEFA European Cup and Copa América. This puts its EVs into fans' daily rituals. For example, Inter Milan players drive the SEALION 7. This turns its technical advantages into emotional connections with people. BYD deals with geopolitical risks by working with local institutions. The EU once investigated its Hungarian factory. BYD purchased additional parts from local suppliers. It now sources 35% of its parts from over 300 European suppliers, including Faurecia. This turns the EU's check into shared interests with local stakeholders. This mixed approach includes exports, local R&D, and partner help to build trust. It is a good example of Johanson and Vahlne's Uppsala Model.

BYD moves faster. It makes jumps into distant markets. Scholars call this the Kangaroo Model; BYD uses its core technology to make these jumps. It keeps some resources safe while doing this. For example, it uses blade batteries to enter new markets. It has $15.49 billion in cash reserves (BYD, 2025).

BYD plans its way through global markets. It uses a mix of different entry modes. It does not use the same method for all markets. First, BYD tests new markets with direct exports. It ships vehicles like the ATTO 3 to over 57 countries. This helps it check demand easily. It also builds brand recognition this way. This phase has low risk and high scalability. It is not just about selling cars. BYD also invests in controlling infrastructure. A key example is that it put LNG-powered cargo ships like the BYD EXPLORER NO.1 into use. These ships help cut logistics costs. They also reduce supply chain bottlenecks. When market signals and potential show it is worth a deeper commitment, BYD quickly shifts to localized production. It establishes assembly plants in key growth markets. These markets include Thailand, Brazil, and the EU. This move helps it avoid high tariffs. Tariffs can be as high as 30% in markets like the EU. It also helps BYD meet strict local content rules. It enables BYD to tailor products to regional needs. For example, it makes EVs with high ground clearance for South American terrain. It also designs PHEVs just for the EU market. This change from export to local manufacturing turns BYD's market presence. It moves from tentative exploration to embedded integration.

These economies have strong local players and complicated regulations. BYD knows that sometimes going alone is not the fastest way. Its collaborations cover different areas. Some are about basic R&D and technology sharing. For example, it has a joint venture with Daihatsu, a longtime Japanese automaker. Some are distribution alliances that enable quick scaling, such as the fleet deal with Germany's Sixt. Beyond just selling cars, BYD makes ecosystem partnerships. A notable one is with Shell. They are expanding the global charging infrastructure together. BYD also boosts brand prestige through sponsorships, such as serving as the official e-mobility partner of the 2024 European Cup. This multi-pronged approach, blending asset-light market testing, heavy investment in local production, and shrewd leveraging of partners' strengths, functions like a 'Kangaroo Model'. It allows BYD to leap into opportunities using its core battery and manufacturing competencies while keeping strategic reserves close, ultimately enabling its rapid transformation from a domestic champion into a truly global automotive disruptor.

Competitive Advantage

BYD's success comes from managing most of its manufacturing processes. They manufacture most of their key components in-house, including batteries, motors, and electronic controls. Their 2024 Sustainability Report makes it clear: producing parts in-house reduces what they pay to outside suppliers. In 2024, BYD sold over 4 million new energy vehicles worldwide. Big numbers like that mean something. When you make more of something, each unit becomes cheaper. That is economies of scale, and it is a big reason BYD can price its cars competitively.

Take Tesla, their main global rival. Tesla's good at software and self-driving tech, no doubt. However, for keeping costs down, BYD has the edge. Tesla purchases many parts from other companies. BYD? They make most of theirs. BloombergNEF investigated it. They found that in some car segments, BYD's production costs are 10-15% lower than Tesla's. That is a significant concern, especially in markets where consumers place a strong emphasis on prices.

BYD is not just cutting costs; they are investing in new technology (BYD - Innovation for a Better Life, n.d.). In 2024, they put 54.2 billion yuan into research and development. That is 35.68% over 2023, according to their 2024 Annual Report. That money goes into things that make their cars better. Take the Blade Battery. BYD's own technical whitepaper shows it passed tough nail-penetration tests. It has a high energy density and lasts a long time. Then there is the e-platform 3.0. It integrates eight components into a single electric powertrain. Some models on this platform can travel over 1,000 kilometers on a single charge. They use 10% less energy per 100km than comparable cars from other brands. A few years ago, the world experienced a semiconductor shortage. It messed up car production everywhere. Volkswagen, for example, had to slow down because it could not get enough chips. But BYD? They make their own semiconductors. They continued making cars as usual. That is the power of vertical integration.

In China, Nio and Xpeng are tough competitors. Nio focuses on high-end cars and battery swapping. XPeng pushes smart driving tech. However, BYD's advantage is that it does more in-house. Nio and Xpeng purchase batteries from third-party suppliers. BYD manufactures its own Blade Battery (Janek & Zeier, 2016). That means they can adjust it faster to improve their cars. The e-platform 3.0 also helps them compete with Nio and Xpeng on both performance and price. BYD is not just making cars in China. They have factories in Brazil, Thailand, and Hungary. These local plants reduce shipping costs. They also make it easier to respond to the needs of people in those regions. Their Thai factory is a good example. It can quickly adapt to the needs of Southeast Asian buyers.

The COVID-19 pandemic showed why these matters. Supply chains around the world broke down. Hyundai-Kia, a major rival in compact and mid-size electric cars, struggled because it relies on parts from multiple suppliers. However, BYD's in-house production kept things steady. They did not have to stop making cars. That is how they held onto their market share—and even gained somewhen others stumbled. What else makes BYD stand out? Three things-a wide range of products, local factories, and a full energy ecosystem.

First, their product lineup covers every market. The Dynasty and Ocean series are for regular buyers. Then there are the high-end brands: Denza makes luxury MPVs, Fangchengbao focuses on off-road vehicles, and Yangwang sells ultra-luxury cars for over a million yuan. Most competitors stick to one or two segments. BYD covers them all, enabling it to meet diverse customer needs. Second, they build factories where they sell. The Thai plant's first project will reportedly generate 150,000 cars each year. The Hungarian factory serves Europe. Brazil's plant covers South America. Making cars locally does not just save money. It helps BYD adapt to local regulations and buyer preferences. In rich countries, they push high-end models. In Southeast Asia, they focus on affordable models; many competitors still primarily export cars, which is slower and riskier. Third, BYD is not just about cars. They are also involved in energy storage. BYD's Blade Battery has applications beyond just vehicles. The new Magic Cube system (MC Cube-T) uses Blade Batteries made for storage. It operates at 1500 volts, making it safer, more durable, and more efficient. BYD connects electric cars, energy storage, and renewable energy. Most competitors do one or two of these things. BYD does it all, creating a full energy loop.

Why does all this matter? Let us look at the research. Studies on manufacturing strategy, such as those in the Harvard Business Review, show that vertical integration is most effective when companies can control key technologies and scale production. BYD checks both boxes. Their in-house parts production and strong sales volumes keep costs low. That is a textbook example of cost leadership done right.

Regarding market expansion, academic research on global business (e.g., in the Journal of International Business Studies) shows that local production reduces trade risks. BYD's factories in Thailand, Hungary, and Brazil are a case study in this. They are not just avoiding tariffs—they are building trust with local buyers and governments.

In technology, McKinsey reports that companies that integrate R&D and production innovate faster. BYD's 35% jump in R&D spending, paired with its ability to make its parts, lets it turn ideas like the Blade Battery into actual products quickly (BYD, 2025). That is faster than competitors who must work with external suppliers. Some people might argue that controlling every step of production is risky, because if one part of the business has a problem, it can cause issues for the entire company. BYD's performance during the semiconductor shortage and the pandemic shows its resilience. They are spreading their risks.

Looking ahead, as more countries pursue electric vehicles and clean energy, BYD's model positions it well. Their broad product range enables them to grow in any market. Local factories help them navigate trade wars and regulations. Their energy ecosystem—cars, batteries, storage—means they are not just selling vehicles. They are part of the solution to climate change.

IMPLEMENTATION OF GLOBAL EXPANSION

Key Initiatives and Investments

BYD has been actively involved in various major deals, partnerships, and infrastructure projects to fuel its global expansion. In the automotive sector, BYD has prioritized partnerships with local dealers across multiple countries to deepen its market penetration. This approach leverages local players' existing networks to bypass entry barriers. In Europe, for example, the company has teamed up with established automotive distributors, ones with decades of experience in regional markets. These collaborations enable BYD to tap into pre-built local sales channels quickly, integrate with mature after-sales service systems, and gain real-time insights into consumer preferences and market trends—details that would take years to gather if building from scratch.

For infrastructure, BYD has invested heavily in overseas production facilities to anchor its global footprint. Its Thailand factory, with an annual production capacity of 150,000 units, is a cornerstone of its Southeast Asian expansion. By manufacturing locally, BYD reduces ocean shipping costs and avoids delays caused by supply chain bottlenecks. More importantly, it can adjust production plans in real time to match local demand—whether that means ramping up output of a popular SUV model or tweaking features for regional buyers. Beyond vehicle production, BYD has expanded into energy infrastructure projects, partnering with local energy firms to provide energy storage solutions. In the United States, for instance, the company has joined grid-connected energy storage initiatives. These projects not only extend BYD's business beyond automotive sales but also reinforce its reputation as a clean energy player, aligning with global trends toward sustainability.

BYD also places strong emphasis on adapting products and services to fit local market conditions, a key factor in winning over regional consumers. They tailor adjustments on the product side to local driving habits, road quality, and consumer tastes. In Europe, where compact, energy-efficient vehicles dominate, BYD launched the Yuan PLUS. This model features a streamlined design that matches narrow urban streets and advanced energy-saving tech that meets the EU's strict emissions standards, addressing both European buyers' aesthetic preferences and environmental concerns. In emerging markets such as Southeast Asia and South America, affordability is a top priority; therefore, BYD focuses on cost-effective models. In Brazil, for example, the company offers vehicles priced below many competitors' while maintaining core performance, including durable engines and reliable safety features. These models match the local economic landscape and the purchasing power of most consumers. Service localization is equally important. BYD hires local staff for its sales and after-sales teams to improve customer engagement. In Australia, it has built a large after-sales network staffed by local technicians. These employees understand local customers' needs firsthand—whether that means scheduling service appointments around rural buyers' farming schedules or explaining EV technology in regional dialects. Their familiarity with the market allows for faster, more effective service, which boosts customer satisfaction and builds long-term brand loyalty.

Challenges Faced

One of the significant challenges BYD faces in pursuing global expansion is the lack of a single set of rules. Every country and region has its own requirements for vehicle emissions, safety standards, and energy-related products, creating a complex web that the company must untangle. Take the European Union, for example. The European Union continually updates its Euro emission standards, and the rules tighten each time. For BYD, this is not just a matter of checking a box. The company must invest significant resources in R&D, engineering overhauls, and testing to ensure its vehicles meet the strict emission targets. If it misses the mark even slightly, the consequence is obvious—it cannot get into the European market at all. That would mean wasting the time and effort spent preparing for launches in countries like Germany or Spain. Trade restrictions pose another significant threat. To protect their own domestic automotive industries, some countries slap high tariffs on imported electric vehicles—and BYD is often the one caught in the crossfire. The United States is an excellent case in point. There is already significant unease about Chinese-made electric vehicles in the region, and policymakers have openly discussed potential tariff hikes (Aldeguer, 2010). Even talking alone creates trouble. BYD has to guess whether those hikes will happen. If they do, they will have to determine how to handle the extra costs: either absorb them, which would reduce profits, or pass them on to consumers, which could make their cars too expensive to compete. These trade restrictions increase BYD's cost of entry into the market and reduce its price competitiveness. Compliance issues are also complex. In some countries, there are strict regulations on battery recycling and disposal. BYD must establish a comprehensive battery recycling system in these regions to comply with local laws and regulations, which will increase its operational costs, regulatory barriers, trade restrictions, and compliance issues.

Cultural and consumer behavior differences are also obstacles to BYD's global expansion. Consumer behavior differs across regions. In certain Asian countries, consumers are more price-sensitive and show a stronger preference for locally branded vehicles. BYD must thoroughly understand the distinct market landscapes worldwide. In some regions, consumers are more price-sensitive, like in certain emerging markets where affordability is a key factor in purchase decisions. In more developed European and North American markets, consumers might prioritize advanced features, brand image, and after-sales service. To address these differences, BYD must be shrewd in its marketing. It cannot use a one-size-fits-all approach. For example, in price-sensitive markets, BYD could run more promotions and highlight the cost-effectiveness of its vehicles. In more feature-conscious markets, it should emphasize the advanced technologies and innovative features of its cars, such as the latest battery technology or smart driving capabilities (Janek & Zeier, 2016).

Pricing is equally crucial. In regions with high import tariffs, BYD may need to adjust its pricing strategy to remain competitive. A more affordable model offering basic but dependable features might perform well in certain low-cost-of-living countries. In markets where consumers will pay a premium for quality and innovation, BYD could introduce higher-end models at a premium price. With managing a global workforce, BYD faces a significant uphill battle. The cultural backgrounds of employees worldwide vary widely. In some countries, work ethic and values differ significantly from those in China. In European countries, for instance, labor laws are quite strict. Employees there enjoy relatively more vacation time. Germany's Federal Leave Act (Bundesurlaubsgesetz) grants full-time employees a minimum of 24 days of paid annual leave annually. Also, labor unions are powerful and play a major role in safeguarding employees' rights. These unions can negotiate for better working conditions, fair pay, and reasonable working hours. BYD must comply with local labor laws and respect work-life balance principles. It needs to adapt its management model accordingly. This could mean offering more flexible work arrangements, adhering to established vacation policies, and engaging in constructive dialogue with labor unions. By doing so, BYD can avoid potential labor-management conflicts and foster a harmonious work environment, which is essential to the smooth operation of its global business.

Geopolitical risks—especially the ongoing tensions between the US and China—have significantly constrained BYD's global expansion, creating hurdles beyond standard market competition. These are not just distant political issues; they seep into the company's day-to-day operations, messing with everything from how it sources parts to how easily it sells cars in key markets. Sanctions and trade wars are the most direct threats here. They can snap or slow down BYD's supply chain overnight and block its access to markets it has spent years building. Take the US-China trade dispute, for example. When tensions flare, US-based suppliers often get caught in the middle. Political pressures can compel them to withhold components from BYD—even if they have long-standing partnerships. A slight delay in getting critical parts, like advanced semiconductors or specialized wiring, can throw off BYD's production schedules. That might mean pushing back the launch of a new model in Europe or Southeast Asia, or scaling back output at a newly opened factory—wasting both time and money.

Geopolitical risks shift market sentiment in ways that are hard to reverse quickly. In regions where the US-China relationship influences local sentiment, consumers second-guess Chinese-brand products. They might worry about whether parts will be available for future repairs or whether owning a BYD could lead to unexpected issues. That hesitation translates directly to sales. In some markets, BYD has seen foot traffic drop at dealerships or potential buyers switch to local or non-Chinese brands at the last minute—because of geopolitical concerns, not the quality of its cars.

BYD encounters various operational obstacles during its global expansion, and none of them are easily solvable. Supply chain and logistics issues are difficult. The global supply chain is complex, and any unexpected disruption can affect BYD's operations. During the COVID-19 pandemic, factories were closed, shipments were delayed, and the company experienced challenges in sourcing essential components. The recent global semiconductor chip shortage has also had a severe impact. These chips are crucial for in-car infotainment systems and battery management. Without sufficient chips, BYD has had to slow production lines for some models or even pause new vehicle launches in certain markets. Logistics costs add more pressure, especially for cross-continental product transportation.

Shipping electric vehicles from China to Europe or South America requires months of planning to control costs. Delaying a shipment at a port because of customs issues or inclement weather may cause it to miss dealership delivery deadlines, resulting in customer dissatisfaction. Talent acquisition is another hard task. In developed countries such as Germany and the US, BYD has difficulty attracting top local talent because it competes with long-established companies such as BMW and Ford. These local firms typically offer greater brand prestige and more established career paths, making it difficult for BYD to stand out. In emerging markets such as parts of Southeast Asia and Africa, the problem is not competition but a shortage of people with the right skills. BYD often requires employees with expertise in EV technology or experience in automotive management. However, those talent pools remain small in many of these regions, forcing the company to invest additional time and money in training. Then there is the intense local competition, which is intense in every market BYD enters. In the automotive space, it faces traditional giants such as Toyota, Volkswagen, and General Motors. These companies have been around for generations—they have household brand names, sales networks that reach every small town, and customers who have bought their cars for decades. BYD cannot just walk in with a new EV and expect to win those customers over easily. The energy storage market is no easy. BYD goes head-to-head with players like Tesla and LG Chem. Tesla has built a reputation for groundbreaking tech and sleek design, while LG Chem has deep roots in battery production. Both have already secured significant market share, so BYD must work twice as hard to persuade businesses and governments to adopt its energy storage solutions.

Building a powerful brand and solid reputation overseas presents a slow, tough slog for BYD; quick campaigns cannot rush or fix this. In many international markets, people still see the company as a newcomer instead of a household name. Most consumers are unfamiliar with BYD's products, let alone the technology behind its EVs and energy storage systems. They might have heard of larger players like Tesla or Toyota first, so BYD starts at a disadvantage simply because it is less familiar. Worse, any negative news can quickly derail its brand efforts. It does not even have to be a major issue—something like a single report of a product quality issue, or the broader skepticism some markets have toward Chinese-made goods, can harm BYD's image. Take battery safety, for example. If a local media outlet runs a story questioning the safety of BYD's vehicle batteries in a country like Australia or Germany, that news spreads like wildfire. It pops up on social media feeds, gets shared in consumer forums, and even gets picked up by other news sites—all before BYD responds. The result? Consumers are seconding-guess their interest in BYD, and the trust that took months to build can vanish in a week.

To rebuild a positive brand image, BYD must avoid shortcuts. It should continue investing in marketing, including local advertisements tailored to regional tastes and collaborations with local influencers to endorse its products. Public relations is also crucial; the company needs dedicated teams to engage with the media, respond swiftly to concerns, and promote positive news, such as sustainability initiatives or new models. This process requires time and financial resources and offers no immediate guarantee of success. However, it is essential to transform "the new Chinese brand" into a recognized and trusted international name.

Mitigation Strategies

BYD actively engages in lobbying and government relations activities to address regulatory and trade-related challenges. It takes part in industry associations and forums in different countries to voice its opinions and concerns. In the European Union, BYD works with local automotive industry associations to advocate for reasonable emissions standards and trade policies that support the development of the electric vehicle industry. BYD also maintains close communication with local governments. In countries where it builds factories, such as Thailand and Hungary, BYD cooperates with local governments to understand local policies and regulations in advance and provide policy recommendations. By establishing strong relationships with governments, BYD can secure support for land acquisition, tax incentives, and market access, helping reduce regulatory and trade-related risks.

Forming strategic partnerships with local firms is an effective mitigation strategy for BYD. In the supply chain, BYD partners with local suppliers to enhance resilience. In some European countries, BYD partners with local semiconductor suppliers to ensure a stable chip supply. These local suppliers are more familiar with the local business environment and can respond more effectively to supply chain disruptions. In the United States, BYD has partnered with local automotive service companies to establish an after-sales service network. These local partners can provide more convenient services for local consumers, enhance BYD's brand image, and also help BYD better understand local market demands. Building a powerful brand and solid reputation overseas is a slow, tough slog for BYD—one that BYD cannot rush or fix with quick campaigns. Many international markets still see the company as a newcomer rather than a household name.

Most consumers are unfamiliar with BYD's products, let alone the technology behind its EVs and energy storage systems. They might have heard of larger players like Tesla or Toyota first, so BYD starts at a disadvantage simply because it is less familiar. Worse, any negative news can quickly derail its brand efforts. It does not even have to be a major issue—something like a single report of a product quality hiccup, or the broader skepticism some markets have toward Chinese-made goods, can stick to BYD and damage its image. Take battery safety, for example. If a local media outlet runs a story questioning the safety of BYD's vehicle batteries in a country like Australia or Germany, that news spreads like wildfire. It pops up on social media feeds, gets shared in consumer forums, and even gets picked up by other news sites—all before BYD responds. To improve its reputation and build a good image, BYD must do things properly. It must keep investing in marketing—things like local ads that speak to regional preferences, or partnerships with local influencers who can vouch for its products. The company needs teams on the ground to engage with the media, address concerns quickly, and share good news, such as its sustainability efforts or new model launches.

Most importantly, it must continue improving product quality. So BYD has to double down on testing, after-sales service, and listening to local customer feedback. All of this takes time and money, and there is no guarantee of quick results—but it is the only way to turn "the new Chinese brand" into a trusted name abroad.

STRATEGIC ANALYSIS

Apply analytical frameworks

SWOT Analysis

A structural advantage, BYD's extensive vertical integration, deeply roots its global rise, and few automotive firms can replicate it. Unlike many competitors that rely heavily on external suppliers for batteries, semiconductors, and core electronic components, BYD controls a substantial portion of its value chain internally. This integration allows the company to stabilize supply, reduce transaction costs, and capture margins that suppliers would otherwise absorb. In-house battery production, particularly the Blade Battery, not only strengthens operational resilience but also reinforces technological leadership (Janek & Zeier, 2016). With over 30,000 engineers and significant annual R&D investment, BYD has translated manufacturing control into innovation capacity.

This structural control also enables economies of scale. The establishment of large production bases in Thailand and Hungary signals more than geographic expansion—it reflects a deliberate strategy to convert technological strength into global cost leadership. In theory, these strengths position BYD to compete aggressively across both emerging and developed markets.

However, these internal strengths coexist with structural vulnerabilities. Despite its rapid internationalization, BYD remains heavily anchored to the Chinese domestic market. A significant share of its revenue remains generated in China, making it sensitive to domestic policy adjustments—particularly subsidy reforms and regulatory changes. While BYD has built technological credibility, brand perception in several developed markets remains fragile. In high-end segments, lingering skepticism toward Chinese manufacturing constrains its ability to command premium pricing. Thus, the very markets where technological sophistication is most valued are also those where brand legitimacy remains hardest to secure.

The global macro-environment presents powerful expansion opportunities. The speeding up electrification of transportation worldwide creates a structural demand for EV manufacturers that can deliver both affordability and innovation. Governments across Europe, Southeast Asia, and Latin America are tightening emissions regulations and promoting electric vehicle adoption through incentives and infrastructure investments. BYD's diversified portfolio—from mass-market passenger vehicles to premium models and commercial EVs—allows it to address heterogeneous market needs. Its flexible technological platform enables adaptability across regulatory and consumer contexts.

Beyond organic demand growth, strategic partnerships represent a second layer of opportunity. The joint venture with Toyota illustrates how BYD can leverage alliance-based legitimacy to penetrate mature markets. By collaborating on EV platforms and battery technologies, BYD not only accesses complementary expertise but also borrows brand credibility in regions where trust barriers exist. Similarly, partnerships with mobility service providers such as Sixt SE transform fleet distribution into a strategic mechanism for legitimacy. Large-scale fleet deployment reduces consumer uncertainty, exposes thousands of drivers to BYD vehicles, and indirectly validates product quality in competitive European markets. These alliances function as strategic accelerators—reducing the liability of foreignness while scaling brand visibility.

However, the competitive and geopolitical landscape introduces persistent threats that complicate this expansion narrative. The EV industry is entering a phase of intensified rivalry. Traditional automotive giants such as Volkswagen and Toyota are rapidly scaling their electric offerings. Agile Chinese competitors like Nio and XPeng continue to innovate in smart driving technologies and premium positioning. As the industry converges technologically, cost advantages alone may not sustain differentiation indefinitely.

More critically, geopolitical tensions—particularly between China, the United States, and parts of Europe—introduce systemic uncertainty. Tariffs, anti-subsidy investigations, and trade restrictions threaten export-based growth models and may compel further localization of production. These political frictions not only raise operational costs but also amplify brand perception challenges in sensitive markets.

Considering all this, BYD's path forward is a balancing act. By controlling its supply chain and leading in technology, it has a solid foundation for growing globally. However, issues with its brand image, over-reliance on China, tough competition, and political uncertainties in other countries restrict how much freedom it has to act. The firm's future success will therefore depend not merely on exploiting its strengths, but on its ability to convert partnerships, localization strategies, and innovation into sustainable global credibility.

PESTEL Analysis

While the SWOT analysis highlights how BYD's internal capabilities interact with competitive pressures, a broader perspective is necessary to understand the structural forces shaping its international trajectory. The PESTEL framework allows us to examine the political, economic, social, technological, environmental, and legal conditions that both enable and constrain BYD's global expansion. Rather than viewing these factors as isolated variables, they collectively form the macro-environment within which BYD must continuously adapt its strategy.

Government policy deeply involves the electric vehicle industry politically. In China, state subsidies and industrial policies significantly sped up BYD's early growth, creating a protected environment for scale accumulation (Masiero et al., 2016). As government subsidies decreased, BYD had to improve cost discipline and technological differentiation, moving away from reliance on policy-driven demand. Internationally, political dynamics are more complex. In the United States, tax credits encourage EV adoption, yet trade tensions complicate BYD's direct market access. In the European Union, anti-subsidy investigations and potential tariffs of up to 48% on Chinese-made EVs pose structural barriers, while the United States maintains tariffs of around 25%. These political constraints reshape BYD's expansion model, pushing it toward localized production strategies, such as establishing manufacturing facilities in Hungary. Political forces, therefore, simultaneously stimulate demand and restrict cross-border flows, forcing BYD to balance globalization with regionalization.

Economically, BYD operates in an industry highly sensitive to macroeconomic cycles. During global downturns, consumers typically delay discretionary purchases, including EVs. Historical precedents, such as the 2008–2009 financial crisis, demonstrate how automotive demand can contract sharply. In addition, inflationary pressures increase input costs across the value chain. Rising prices of lithium and cobalt—critical materials for battery production—directly affect BYD's cost structure, compressing margins (Han, 2024). Exchange rate volatility and global logistics costs further complicate international operations. Economic forces also create opportunities; expanding middle classes in emerging economies generate new demand pools, while sustainability-driven consumer preferences increase willingness to adopt EVs. Because of regional economic heterogeneity, BYD must carefully segment markets, offering cost-effective models in price-sensitive economies and positioning technologically advanced vehicles in developed markets.

Social factors further shape BYD's positioning. Across many countries, rising environmental consciousness strengthens the appeal of electric vehicles as symbols of responsible consumption. However, consumer priorities vary. In developed markets, buyers may emphasize advanced features, connectivity, and brand prestige. In emerging markets, affordability and reliability dominate purchase decisions. Demographic shifts also influence demand patterns. Aging populations in certain developed economies may dampen long-term vehicle demand, while youthful populations and urbanization in emerging regions expand the potential customer base. BYD must therefore continuously recalibrate product positioning and communication strategies to align with diverse cultural expectations.

Technologically, the EV sector features rapid and innovation. Advancements in battery chemistry, charging infrastructure, and autonomous driving systems are reshaping competitive dynamics. If rival firms successfully commercialize solid-state batteries or significantly improve autonomous driving capabilities while BYD lags, the competitive balance could shift rapidly. The growing demand for connected vehicles and integrated digital ecosystems requires sustained investment in software development and smart mobility technologies(Paritala et al., 2017). Technological progress is not incremental in this industry; it is exponential. BYD's continued competitiveness depends on maintaining innovation velocity alongside manufacturing scale.

Environmental and legal forces increasingly affect the EV landscape. Heightened global concern over climate change has led governments to introduce stricter emissions standards, such as the European Union's Euro 7 regulations, speeding up the transition to zero-emission vehicles. These policies structurally favor EV producers like BYD. However, environmental scrutiny extends beyond vehicle emissions. The sourcing of lithium, cobalt, and other battery materials has raised concerns regarding sustainability and ethical supply chains. BYD must therefore ensure responsible sourcing and transparent environmental governance to avoid reputational damage. Safety regulations, battery recycling requirements, and compliance standards vary across jurisdictions. Failure to meet these standards could cause fines, recalls, or exclusion from key markets.

Competitive rivalry, systemic political shifts, economic volatility, social expectations, technological acceleration, and regulatory tightening all shape BYD's global expansion, according to the PESTEL analysis. These macro forces do not simply create opportunities or threats; they redefine the rules of engagement. BYD's long-term success will depend on its ability to institutionalize adaptability—embedding policy responsiveness, cost resilience, technological foresight, and environmental responsibility into its global operating model.

CONCLUSION AND STRATEGIC RECOMMENDATIONS

Summary of Key Findings

BYD's ascent to global leadership in the new energy vehicle industry is because of a synergistic combination of strategic strengths. This triad of technological innovation, unrivaled cost competitiveness through vertical integration, and strategic localization has helped to drive its rapid international expansion and significant market-share gains in key regions, including Southeast Asia and South America. Massive R&D investment—reaching 54.2 billion yuan in 2024—has yielded technologies such as the blade battery and DM-i super hybrid system, creating strong product appeal. This company controls many steps of production, which allows it to offer outstanding quality without high costs. This is a big plus in markets where customers are very focused on price. Third, establishing local production bases in countries like Thailand, Brazil, and Hungary has been crucial for circumventing trade barriers and enhancing supply chain efficiency. Supported by these foundational pillars, BYD is now poised to capitalize on emerging opportunities to solidify its global standing.

Future Growth Opportunities

Based on the analysis of BYD's global expansion dynamics, two key future growth opportunities emerge for its sustained development.

First, in potential new markets and industry segments, while BYD has already established a solid presence in global electric buses, trucks, and industrial vehicles, untapped potential remains in specific regional and niche areas. In the African market, the International Council on Clean Transportation (2024) highlights a growing demand for electric vehicles in public transportation and last-mile delivery, particularly in sub-Saharan African countries. With urbanization rates in these regions rising by an average of 3% annually, there is an urgent need for efficient, clean-energy transportation solutions. Collaborating with local governments and development agencies to establish assembly plants, leveraging regional incentives and reducing production costs, could enhance market penetration while supporting local economic growth, as noted in the African Development Bank's report on sustainable industrialization.

In Arctic and sub-Arctic regions, the International Transport Forum identifies a unique niche for electric vehicles adapted to extreme cold conditions. By developing specialized models with enhanced battery heating systems and cold-resistant materials, BYD could target the mining and resource-extraction industries, where global carbon-reduction mandates are driving a shift from fossil-fuel-powered vehicles.

Such a focus would position BYD as a pioneer in sustainable transportation for challenging terrains, aligning with the United Nations Environment Programmer's call for climate-adaptive industrial solutions (Liu, 2022).

Second, regarding digital transformation and AI-driven strategies, integrating AI-based energy management systems into vehicles represents a critical step (Paritala et al., 2017). Research in Nature Energy shows that real-time AI optimization of energy consumption—accounting for traffic conditions, driving patterns, and battery health—can extend electric vehicle range by up to 15% while improving overall efficiency. Applying this technology would strengthen BYD's competitive edge in energy efficiency. Advancing AI-powered driver-assistance systems, as outlined in IEEE Transactions on Intelligent Transportation Systems, could enhance vehicle safety. Machine learning algorithms trained on real-time sensor data and historical accident records can predict potential road hazards, a feature increasingly valued in global markets. This would not only elevate safety standards but also align with developing international regulatory requirements for intelligent transportation.

Recommendations for Other Firms

For global expansion, firms should prioritize localized production and partnerships to align with regional policies—an approach exemplified by BYD's adaptive strategies—while leveraging core technology advantages to target underserved niches such as extreme-environment markets. On risk management, they need to diversify supply chains to mitigate geopolitical and regulatory shocks and invest in real-time data analytics to expect market shifts. This ensures agile responses to global uncertainties.

REFERENCES

Aldeguer, C. C. (2010). *BYD Company Limited: A case review*. SSRN Electronic Journal. DOI: 10.2139/ssrn.2422240

BYD. (2025). *Homepage*. https://www.byd.com/cn

Cao, W., Zhang, Y., & Antony, B. (2018). Belt and road: A new journey for foreign investment—A case study of the internationalization strategy of BYD. *Proceedings of the 3rd international symposium on Asian B&R conference on international business cooperation (ISBCD 2018),* 58. DOI: 10.2991/isbcd-18.2018.18

Han, J. (2024). [Financial analysis of BYD Company based on Harvard framework]. *E-Commerce Letters, 13*(2), 1681–1694. DOI: 10.12677/ecl.2024.132204

Janek, J., & Zeier, W. G. (2016). A solid future for battery development. *Nature Energy, 1*(9), 1–4. DOI: 10.1038/nenergy.2016.141

Liu, M. (2022, May 16). New energy vehicles, as represented by BYD. *Atlantis Press*. DOI: 10.2991/aebmr.k.220502.081

Masiero, G., Ogasavara, M. H., Jussani, A. C., & Risso, M. L. (2016). Electric vehicles in China: BYD strategies and government subsidies. *RAI Revista de Administração E Inovação, 13*(1), 3–11. DOI: 10.1016/j.rai.2016.01.001

Paritala, P. K., Manchikatla, S., & Yarlagadda, P. K. D. V. (2017). Digital manufacturing—Applications past, current, and future trends. *Procedia Engineering, 174*, 982–991. DOI: 10.1016/j.proeng.2017.01.250

Shan, J. (2024). The impact of government subsidies on electric vehicle sales: A regression analysis of BYD in China. *SHS Web of Conferences, 207*, 03017. DOI: 10.1051/shsconf/202420703017

Wu, W. (2024). PEST —— , , [Based on PEST analysis of BYD new energy vehicle export comparative study—Taking Singapore, Switzerland, and Brazil as examples]. *Modern Management, 14*(1), 136–145. DOI: 10.12677/MM.2024.141020

KEY TERMS AND DEFINITIONS

BYD (BYD Company Limited): It is a leading multinational enterprise founded in 1995 and headquartered in Shenzhen, specializing in electric vehicles, batteries, and renewable energy solutions.

DM-i (Dual Mode-intelligent): BYD's super hybrid system that combines electric and fuel power, enabling high fuel efficiency and a long driving range.

EUNCAP (European New Car Assessment Programme): It refers to an independent organization that evaluates the safety performance of new cars sold in the European Union, issuing star ratings based on crash tests.

EV (Electric Vehicles): It refers to vehicles that are powered entirely or primarily by electric motors, using energy stored in rechargeable batteries instead of traditional internal combustion engines.

LNG (Liquefied Natural Gas): It refers to natural gas that has been cooled to a liquid state for easier storage and transportation, used by BYD in its cargo ships to reduce logistics costs.

OLI Paradigm (Ownership-Location-Internalization Paradigm): A framework in international business that explains a firm's foreign direct investment decisions based on Ownership, Location, and Internalization advantages.

USMCA (United States-Mexico-Canada Agreement): It refers to a trade agreement that regulates trade and investment among the United States, Mexico, and Canada, including provisions related to vehicle trade.

Chapter 4
CATL Global Energy Supply Role:
Strategy, Challenges, and Lessons Learned

Steven Songhao Deng
http://orcid.org/0009-0007-1044-7497
Beijing Normal-Hong Kong Baptist University, China

EXECUTIVE SUMMARY

This chapter examines the global expansion strategy of Contemporary Amperex Technology (CATL) from 2011 to 2024, analysing how the world's largest lithium-ion battery manufacturer achieved international success amid significant geopolitical and regulatory challenges. CATL's multi-regional expansion across Europe, Southeast Asia, and North America through comprehensive market analysis and strategic implementation review. Explores the company's differentiated entry modes, including greenfield investments in Europe, joint ventures in Southeast Asia, and technology licensing in North America, alongside its four-pillar value creation strategy encompassing customer, operational, product, and locational excellence. Having adaptable legal plans, staying on top of environmental, social, and governance requirements, bringing more business activities in-house, and actively working with stakeholders. Chinese high-tech companies in key sectors can use technological advancements, adapt to different cultures, and be flexible with regulations to overcome global conflicts

DOI: 10.4018/979-8-3373-4302-0.ch004

INTRODUCTION

Background of the Company

Contemporary Amperex Technology Co., Limited (CATL), founded in 2011 in Ningde, Fujian Province, is a world-leading battery manufacturer specializing in lithium-ion batteries for electric vehicles (EVs) and energy storage systems (ESS). Dr. Robin Zeng and a team of engineers previously involved with Amperex Technology Limited (ATL), leveraging their prior expertise in battery design and production under TDK (Contemporary Amperex Technology Co., Limited [CATL], 2023a), established the company.

From its inception, CATL emphasized a strong research-driven strategy. The company invested heavily in building a four-dimensional innovation system encompassing material systems, structural systems, green extreme manufacturing, and smart business models. This system facilitated groundbreaking innovations such as the "Cell-to-Pack" (CTP) technology and, more recently, the launch of the CTP 3.0 "Qilin battery" in 2023, which delivers approximately 13% higher energy density compared to Tesla's 4680 battery cells, as confirmed by CATL's Chief Scientist Wu Kai at the China EV 100 Forum and during mass production reports cited by Zhang (2022). CATL's "Shenxing" super-fast charging battery, also introduced in 2023, marked another major milestone, offering 400 km of range with only a 10-minute charge (CATL, 2023b).

CATL's market dominance is clear in its global shipment performance. According to SNE's Research (2024), CATL delivered 259.7 GWh of EV battery capacity in 2023, accounting for 36.8% of the global market—the highest among all battery manufacturers for the seventh consecutive year. Its cumulative output for the first three quarters of 2023 was 158 GWh, about 32.2% of global EV battery deployment (EV Volumes, 2023). CATL led the global energy storage battery market with 69 GWh of shipments in 2023—accounting for 17.6% of its total battery sales—marking a robust year-over-year growth of 46.8% (Reuters, 2024a). Beyond sales, CATL has achieved substantial financial growth. In its 2023 annual report, the company disclosed revenues of approximately USD 56.6 billion, net profits of USD 6.2 billion, and assets totaling over USD 101 billion. It also reported having over 116,000 employees across its global operations (CATL, 2023a).

To support its internationalization strategy, CATL has established a global manufacturing and R&D footprint. This includes production bases in Germany (Erfurt) and Hungary (Debrecen), as well as multiple locations in China, including Ningde, Yibin, and Liyang. Its research centers are in Germany, Japan, South Korea, and the United States, reflecting its ambition to become a truly global tech leader. CATL's sustained R&D investment, deep integration into global EV supply chains, and robust expansion into overseas markets account for its rapid ascent as a dominant force in the global battery industry. These factors set the foundation for its internationalization strategy and position it as a critical case for examining global expansion among Chinese high-tech enterprises.

Motivation for Global Expansion

Three primary motivations propel CATL's international expansion: diversifying beyond the saturated Chinese market, meeting the demands of global automotive customers, and securing control over critical raw material supply chains.

Diversification Beyond a Saturated Chinese Market

As domestic EV battery demand in China shows signs of plateauing, CATL is strategically shifting its focus overseas. According to Gasgoo (2025), China's annual power battery installations reached 548.4 GWh in 2024, an impressive 41.5% year-on-year increase, but reflecting deceleration compared to previous years, while LFP chemistries grew to 409 GWh, accounting for approximately 75% of total installations. This maturity in the Chinese market is also clear in slower domestic EV sales, which grew only around 25% in early 2024, well below the 36% growth rate recorded in 2023.

Between 2022 and 2023, CATL's shipments outside China surged from 51.0 GWh to 87.8 GWh, a 72.5% increase, reflecting its sped-up efforts to capture non-Chinese market share. This growth momentum in foreign markets shows CATL's strategic intent to hedge against domestic slowdowns and enhance global resilience (Shanghai Nonferrous Metals, 2024).

Meeting Global Automotive Customer Requirements

Major global automakers—including BMW, Volkswagen, Stellantis, Hyundai, MG, and Mercedes-Benz—have increasingly recognized CATL as a strategically vital battery partner (Shanghai Nonferrous Metals, 2024). In response, CATL has established production bases in Germany, Hungary, and, most recently, Spain via a €4.1 billion joint venture with Stellantis, specifically to supply European OEMs locally and reduce cross-border logistics risk (Inagaki et al., 2024). Local factories enable CATL to tailor products to EU standards while benefiting from regional incentives and proximity to OEM assembly lines. These regionalized operations also allowed CATL to bypass increasing geopolitical trade frictions and qualify for local government subsidies, enhancing cost competitiveness and mitigating regulatory risks in the EU market (Hamlin, 2024).

Securing Critical Raw Material Supply Chains

Securing stable access to nickel, cobalt, and lithium resources is another key driver behind CATL's global strategy. In 2022, CATL, along with Indonesian partners Antam and IBI, announced a US $5.97 billion investment in Indonesia's EV battery ecosystem—including nickel mining, processing, manufacturing, and recycling (CATL, 2022). In late 2024, CATL's unit formed a joint venture with Indonesia Battery Corporation to develop a 15 GWh battery cell plant (Reuters, 2024a). These upstream investments give CATL enhanced control over costs and supply amid global market volatility. Also, because CATL controls it is supply chain, it has been less affected by recent price changes in nickel and lithium, which gives it more control over costs and better negotiating power with car companies (Hanley, 2024). This resource security position positions CATL to maintain its cost leadership while ensuring supply continuity to its overseas factories in Europe and Southeast Asia.

MARKET ANALYSIS AND ENTRY STRATEGY

Target Market Selection: Evaluation Across Five Strategic Dimensions

CATL's global market selection process is guided by five critical factors: identifiability, substantiality, reachability, responsiveness, and profitability. Applying this framework, CATL prioritized three strategic regions—Europe, Southeast Asia, and North America—each chosen for unique advantages in customer proximity, supply chain control, and risk management.

Europe – High Demand and Strategic Partnerships.

A clear definition of Europe's EV market exists, showing distinct customer segments (premium vs. mass-market) and high regulatory uniformity. Major OEMs, including BMW, Volkswagen, Stellantis, and Mercedes-Benz, represent well-identified B2B customer bases (SNE Research, 2024). These customers require tailored battery chemistries and compliance with EU standards, justifying distinct marketing strategies. In terms of size, Europe's EV market is substantial. The EU recorded over 2.4 million EV sales in 2023, supported by strong green policies and an expanding charging network (EV Volumes, 2023). CATL's clients in the region account for much of this volume, making localized supply both efficient and profitable.

CATL's factories in Germany and Hungary ensure direct access to OEMs, shortening lead times and qualifying the company for EU incentives. Customers have responded positively: BMW and Stellantis signed long-term supply agreements, while the Stellantis JV in Spain targets 50 GWh capacity by 2026 (Electrios Consultants, 2024). Although LG and Northvolt are strong competitors, CATL still benefits from being first to market. EU subsidies for local battery production, combined with scale and proximity, make the European market not only reachable and responsive but also highly profitable in both the short and long term.

Southeast Asia – Raw Material Sovereignty and Low-Cost Production.

In Southeast Asia, especially Indonesia, CATL targets the upstream battery supply chain. The segment is identifiable: resource owners and government-backed industrial parks, such as the Indonesia Battery Corporation (IBC), form distinct market segments, distinct from EV buyers in Europe or the US (CATL, 2022). This market is substantial in value, though not in consumer demand. Indonesia holds over 22% of global nickel reserves, a critical raw material for battery cathodes (Pereyra et al., 2024). CATL's $5.97 billion investment with Antam and IBI secures access to raw materials for millions of EVs annually, supporting global operations. Reachability is high because of strong government support, special economic zones, and JV frameworks. CATL's processing and cell manufacturing operations benefit from tax incentives and close integration with logistics ports (Reuters, 2024a).

The Indonesian government and state-owned enterprises have shown high responsiveness, fast-tracking permits and promoting CATL as a strategic partner for industrial development. These ventures provide security of resources, cost control, and environmental compliance advantages. While local consumer markets are still emerging, the profitability lies in upstream integration—mitigating price volatility, improving bargaining power, and ensuring a stable supply to CATL's European and Chinese factories (Hanley, 2024).

North America – Technology Partnerships under Regulatory Constraints.

The US and Canadian EV markets are identifiable but heavily segmented by policy. The Inflation Reduction Act (IRA) and Buy American mandates concentrate customers among top OEMs like Ford, Tesla, and General Motors, each with specific chemistry and localization requirements (Reuters, 2024c). In terms of size, the US remains the world's second-largest EV market, with over 1.2 million sales in 2023 and a projected CAGR of 22% through 2028 (EV Volumes, 2023). However, CATL faces legal and political barriers to entry, making direct investment less workable despite the market's size.

To improve reachability, CATL adopted a non-equity approach: licensing LFP battery technology to Ford, supporting local US production without direct control. This allows CATL to maintain a presence while avoiding scrutiny from geopolitical and national security authorities. US OEMs have responded positively. Ford announced it would adopt CATL's LFP chemistry for cost-effective EV lines starting in 2025. Meanwhile, Tesla continues to use CATL cells for some Chinese-made models, demonstrating global supply chain coordination (Spence & Lee, 2022). Profitability is complex. Direct factory margins are unavailable, but technology licensing and long-term IP revenue offer steady cash flow with low operational risk. Although regulatory pressure is high, the American market remains attractive for indirect participation and branding.

Entry Mode Selection

CATL's international expansion shows a nuanced application of different entry modes tailored to the political, economic, and industrial conditions of each target market. The company's strategy balances control and efficiency with regulatory compliance and risk mitigation. In its three core markets—Europe, Southeast Asia, and North America—CATL adopts a combination of greenfield investment, joint ventures, and technology licensing, each designed to serve distinct strategic objectives.

Europe: Greenfield Investment and OEM-Backed Joint Ventures.

In Europe, CATL has made bold moves through greenfield investments and strategic joint ventures to embed itself within the supply chain of major automotive manufacturers. This approach allows CATL to establish complete ownership and operational control over production facilities while aligning closely with local industrial policy and sustainability goals.

The company's €7.34 billion investment in Hungary, announced in 2022, is the largest single foreign direct investment in Hungarian history. The 100 GWh plant under construction in Debrecen will directly supply European OEMs such as BMW, Mercedes-Benz, and Volkswagen (fDi Intelligence, 2022). Similarly, CATL's Erfurt factory in Germany started mass production in 2023, serving BMW and local EV startups. These greenfield investments ensure quality consistency, localization of supply, and direct access to EU subsidies and incentives (CATL, 2023a).

To further strengthen its regional presence, CATL partnered with Stellantis in 2024 to establish a €4.1 billion joint venture in Spain, targeting 50 GWh production capacity by 2026 (CATL, 2024). The JV structure allows CATL to share financial risk, gain local operational knowledge, and navigate regional regulatory environments more effectively while maintaining technology leadership.

Southeast Asia: State-Backed Vertical Integration via Joint Ventures.

In Southeast Asia—particularly in Indonesia—CATL employs upstream-focused joint ventures to secure access to critical raw materials, such as nickel and cobalt, and to build an integrated battery value chain. Rather than pursuing consumer-facing operations, the company's goal here is to control its supply chain and optimize costs.

In 2022, CATL announced a US$5.97 billion investment in collaboration with Indonesian state-owned companies ANTAM and Indonesia Battery Corporation (IBC). The investment covers nickel mining, smelting, battery manufacturing, and battery recycling (CATL, 2022). Because this project handles all aspects of production in-house, CATL is less reliant on external suppliers and better protected against rising raw material costs, a growing concern amid rising global demand.

CATL gains regulatory legitimacy and favorable access to local infrastructure and incentives by working through state-supported partnerships. The joint venture model also spreads financial and operational risk and allows CATL to comply with Indonesia's "Downstreaming" policy, which restricts raw mineral exports in favor of domestic processing (Reuters, 2024b).

North America: Regulatory-Evasive Technology Licensing.

In North America, CATL's entry strategy is highly adaptive because of geopolitical and regulatory barriers, particularly those stemming from the US Inflation Reduction Act (IRA) and concerns over Chinese industrial influence (Xiao, 2023). Instead of direct investment in battery plants, CATL adopts a technology licensing and service model to maintain presence and influence while minimizing political exposure.

A flagship example is the company's 2023 collaboration with Ford Motor Company. CATL agreed to license its lithium iron phosphate (LFP) battery technology to Ford, which will build and operate a $3.5 billion factory in Michigan using CATL's intellectual property and technical support, while keeping ownership under Ford's name (The China Academy, 2023). This "licensing-plus-services" approach enables CATL to generate revenue, support local partners, and reinforce its position as a global technology leader—without triggering foreign ownership restrictions or violating IRA provisions.

Though this model sacrifices full operational control, it provides regulatory insulation, brand exposure, and IP monetization, offering a pragmatic compromise between market access and risk aversion.

Targeting and Positioning Strategy

CATL's international market entry is not only about operational form but also about how it positions its offerings to distinct customer segments. Across its global expansion efforts, CATL uses different targeting strategies in different markets, aligning market entry modes with tailored customer engagement models:

Differentiated Targeting – Europe.

In the European market, CATL adopts a differentiated targeting strategy, addressing multiple OEM customer segments with customized product offerings. For instance, BMW requires high-performance NCM batteries for premium EVs, while Stellantis prefers cost-effective LFP batteries for mass-market lines (Hamlin, 2024). CATL differentiates through both chemistry and localized production to meet varying customer needs within the same region.

Concentrated Targeting – Southeast Asia.

In Indonesia, CATL uses a concentrated targeting approach focused solely on upstream industrial partners and government agencies. Rather than targeting mass consumers, the company channels all its resources into building a raw material-to-cell production ecosystem for long-term vertical integration. This singular strategic focus ensures policy alignment and long-term resource security (CATL, 2022).

Undifferentiated Targeting – Global Commoditization Strategy.

For standardized, high-demand battery types (e.g., LFP), CATL also practices undifferentiated targeting globally. CATL intends these lower-cost, scalable battery formats for a broad customer base, including EV fleets, low-cost passenger vehicles, and energy storage systems—without major product customization (Hanley, 2024).

Micromarketing – Limited Application.

CATL's B2B global expansion model does not widely use micro-marketing or one-to-one targeting. However, in future smart battery services or battery-as-a-service (BaaS) scenarios, CATL may explore this approach—especially through digital platforms or EV data-tracking technologies in domestic markets.

Competitive Advantage

CATL's sustained global leadership in the battery industry stems from a deliberate, coordinated value-creation strategy built on four pillars: Customer Excellence, Operational Excellence, Product Excellence, and Locational Excellence. These capabilities work in concert to ensure CATL's long-term differentiation, global adaptability, and profit resilience.

Customer Excellence: Deep Collaboration and High Switching Costs.

CATL's customer strategy centers on strategic integration rather than transactional supply. Major clients—including Tesla, BMW, Stellantis, Mercedes-Benz, and Hyundai—engage with CATL in long-term, multi-dimensional relationships that span joint R&D, co-location, and dedicated supply. For example, CATL's co-investment with Stellantis in a €4.1 billion battery JV in Spain ensures a stable supply and aligns the two firms' long-term electrification goals (CATL, 2024). Similarly, CATL's integration of its LFP battery into Tesla's Model 3/Y in China enables it to influence Tesla's cost structure and battery strategy profoundly.

Technical customization, where CATL tailors battery cell formats, chemistries, and packaging standards, reinforces these partnerships to OEM-specific vehicle platforms. CATL's embedded technical teams provide engineering and integration support, reducing friction and boosting client retention. This long-term alignment generates high switching costs for automakers, reduces coordination inefficiencies, and transforms CATL into a "critical supplier" whose absence would disrupt the client's value chain— ensuring loyalty and stability.

Operational Excellence: Vertical Integration, Smart Manufacturing, and Digital Transformation.

CATL's operational strength lies in its vertically integrated model, spanning raw material sourcing, cell and module production, and recycling. The company owns or holds equity in nickel and lithium assets in Indonesia, Bolivia, and the DRC, giving it direct control over strategic minerals. This resource access reduces reliance on volatile third-party markets and enables CATL to offer customers more stable pricing. During the 2022 nickel price spike, CATL's Indonesian mining assets buffered it from the shocks that hit less-integrated rivals.

On the factory floor, CATL is a leader in smart manufacturing. Its Yibin plant—certified as a "Lighthouse Factory" by the World Economic Forum (WEF)—employs AI-driven systems for predictive maintenance, digital twin simulations, and automated quality control (World Economic Forum, 2022). These technologies improve yield rates, reduce downtime, and lower the cost per kWh. CATL's ability to scale production quickly is also a differentiator. It ramped from ~96 GWh in 2019 to 259.7 GWh in 2023 (SNE Research, 2024), meeting surging demand while preserving efficiency.

Beyond supply chain integration and cost efficiency, CATL has increasingly relied on digital transformation as a critical driver of operational excellence. At its advanced manufacturing plants in China and Europe, the company has deployed AI-powered predictive maintenance, IoT-enabled monitoring, and digital twin simulations to optimize production processes and minimize downtime (CATL, 2023a). These technologies allow CATL to identify potential equipment failures in advance, reduce unplanned outages, and ensure continuous quality control at scale.

In addition, by integrating real-time data platforms, CATL connects its facilities worldwide, enabling centralized monitoring of production output, logistics flows, and energy consumption. This integration facilitates operational transparency and improves coordination across multi-country supply chains, particularly in regions like Europe and Southeast Asia (Bridge & Faigen, 2022). Such systems are crucial for navigating regulatory and geopolitical disruptions and ensuring a responsive, adaptive supply chain.

CATL also employs cloud-based analytics and machine learning to allocate resources and optimize logistics routes dynamically. These technologies enable rapid adaptation to fluctuations in raw material availability or demand surges, enhancing supply chain agility and reducing operational costs (Yee et al., 2025). Integrating AI and IoT into CATL's operational framework has transformed traditional manufacturing into a digitally orchestrated network, reinforcing its competitive edge in the global market.

Product Excellence: Innovation Leadership and Chemistry Flexibility.

Product excellence is a core differentiator for CATL, underpinned by massive R&D investment (USD 2.5 billion in 2023 alone) and a workforce of over 18,000 R&D engineers. CATL holds hundreds of global patents and has pioneered several innovations in battery architecture. The CTP 3.0 "Qilin battery", launched in 2023, offers 13% more energy density than Tesla's 4680 and introduces an innovative sandwich structure that enhances thermal control and cell utilization (CATL, 2023b).

Meanwhile, the "Shenxing battery", launched later that year, supports ultra-fast charging (10 minutes to 400 km) without sacrificing range or lifespan.

CATL also leads in chemical diversification. It can supply LFP for cost-driven clients, NCM for high-performance segments, and sodium-ion batteries for storage or cold-climate use cases. This flexibility enables OEMs to segment their EV lines without changing battery suppliers. In the energy storage system (ESS) sector, CATL's "EnerOne" and "EnerC" products serve utility-scale projects worldwide, supported by modular design and thermal-safety innovations. As countries expand renewable grids, this segment is becoming a second growth engine beyond EVs.

Locational Excellence: Strategic Global Placement and Policy Synergy

CATL's location strategy is not just about cost arbitrage—it is a core strategic lever. The company selects plant locations based on proximity to clients, alignment with policies, logistics efficiency, and ESG standards. In Europe, CATL's factories in Erfurt, Germany, and Debrecen, Hungary, are near major OEMs like BMW, VW, and Daimler, enabling just-in-time supply and integration into local production ecosystems. These locations also qualify CATL for EU subsidies tied to local job creation and carbon reduction. In Southeast Asia, CATL's operations in Morowali (Indonesia) are near key nickel sources and export ports, cutting both input and outbound shipping costs. Local partnerships provide CATL with access to tax incentives and infrastructure investments.

CATL is also expanding its global R&D presence, with technology centers in Germany, the US, and Japan. This allows the company to adapt to local standards and accelerate time-to-market. What makes CATL's locational excellence powerful is its depth of engagement. The company often builds training programs, policy dialogues, and ESG reporting systems in host countries—creating mutual trust and long-term embeddedness that few competitors can match.

IMPLEMENTATION OF GLOBAL EXPANSION

Key Initiatives and Investments

To translate its global ambitions into concrete outcomes, CATL has launched a series of high-stakes, high-impact initiatives across multiple geographies. These key investments—spanning infrastructure, partnerships, resource development, and technological localization—form the backbone of its internationalization strategy. CATL carefully tailors its initiatives to address each host market's unique opportunities and constraints, rather than following a uniform template. The following initiatives illustrate the company's commitment to building long-term capabilities in strategic regions.

Strategic Manufacturing Bases in Europe.

One of CATL's most visible international investments is its multi-billion-euro commitment to localized battery production in Europe. In 2022, the company announced a €7.34 billion investment to build a 100 GWh gigafactory in Debrecen, Hungary—the largest single foreign direct investment in the country's history (fDi Intelligence, 2022). The facility is strategically located to serve major OEMs, including BMW, Volkswagen, and Mercedes-Benz, all of which operate plants in the region. Besides direct production capacity, this investment supports CATL's broader goal of EU supply chain localization, required to qualify for government subsidies and comply with "Rules of Origin" under EU battery legislation (Hamlin, 2024).

Simultaneously, CATL's Germany plant in Erfurt, which began mass production in 2023, represents the company's first operational footprint in Western Europe. This €1.8 billion project provided just-in-time supply to German automotive clients, reduced carbon-intensive shipping from Asia, and met local environmental standards (CATL, 2023a).

These investments are not merely financial commitments—they symbolize a strategic pivot toward decentralizing production and embedding CATL into regional value chains.

Vertical Integration Through Resource Investments in Southeast Asia.

In Southeast Asia, CATL's strategy pivots toward securing upstream resources, particularly in Indonesia, where over 22% of global nickel reserves are located. In 2022, CATL formed a US$5.97 billion joint venture with Antam and IBC (Indonesia Battery Corporation) to create a fully integrated EV battery value chain—including nickel mining, processing, battery manufacturing, and recycling (CATL, 2022).

This investment is a long-term hedge against raw material price volatility, enabling CATL to stabilize input costs and ensure steady access to nickel, a core material for NCM batteries. By directly taking part in the value chain through upstream investments and joint ventures in Indonesia and other resource-rich regions, CATL has gained stronger bargaining leverage with suppliers, ensuring more stable pricing and reducing geopolitical risks associated with dependence on third-party raw material exporters (International Energy Agency, 2023).

Localization via Joint Ventures and Tech Transfer.

In markets with regulatory sensitivities, CATL adopts a more adaptive model. A prime example is its licensing partnership with Ford Motor Company in the United States. In 2023, CATL agreed to license its LFP battery technology to Ford, enabling the latter to construct a $3.5 billion battery plant in Michigan (Global Times, 2023). Under this model, CATL supplies intellectual property, training, and technical support, while Ford owns and operates the facility, circumventing US foreign ownership restrictions under the Inflation Reduction Act.

This approach shows CATL's willingness to adapt its expansion model to host-country regulatory frameworks. While it limits CATL's direct control, it preserves market access and monetizes its proprietary technologies.

Product Adaptation and R&D Localization.

To ensure long-term success in foreign markets, CATL has also invested in product adaptation and local R&D facilities. For instance, its battery plant in Germany incorporates specific modifications to meet EU safety, recycling, and energy density standards, especially for high-end EVs (CATL, 2023a). The company also operates overseas R&D centers in Munich and Yokohama, enabling collaboration with local universities and compliance with regional tech certifications.

CATL has developed second-life applications and battery-recycling solutions that comply with EU regulations, helping it position itself as a circular-economy leader. These investments reflect a deep commitment to localization—not just in manufacturing, but also in innovation and sustainability practices.

Challenges Faced

While CATL's international expansion has yielded significant strategic gains, it has also exposed the company to a host of external and internal challenges. These obstacles—spanning political, regulatory, technological, operational, and cultural domains—threaten to slow or complicate its globalization agenda. Addressing these challenges effectively is crucial for maintaining its competitive position and sustaining long-term international success.

Geopolitical Tensions and Trade Barriers.

CATL faces growing geopolitical scrutiny, especially from Western governments wary of China's influence in strategic industries. The US Inflation Reduction Act (IRA) explicitly discourages reliance on "foreign entities of concern," including

Chinese firms. Consequently, US regulations bar CATL from directly owning and operating US factories to qualify for federal subsidies (Global Times, 2023).

In Europe, rising concerns over overreliance on Chinese technology have also prompted the EU to explore anti-subsidy investigations and localization requirements (Hamlin, 2024). Such protectionist measures force CATL to adapt its ownership structures, potentially reducing control and increasing operational complexity in key Western markets.

Regulatory Complexity and ESG Compliance Pressure.

Battery production and deployment are subject to strict safety, recycling, and environmental regulations, which vary significantly by region. In the European Union (EU), CATL must comply with the EU Battery Regulation, which mandates detailed traceability of materials, carbon footprint reporting, and minimum recycling rates (European Union, 2023).

CATL has taken steps to comply, such as establishing recycling systems and integrating recycled materials into production, but the cost of compliance is high. Non-compliance risks fines, reputational damage, and even market bans, especially in environmentally sensitive markets.

In emerging markets such as Indonesia, CATL must navigate ambiguous or developing ESG standards, often while partnering with state-owned firms. This creates compliance asymmetry and legal uncertainty.

Knowledge Transfer and Intellectual Property Protection.

One underappreciated risk in CATL's global expansion is safeguarding its proprietary technology when engaging in joint ventures or licensing arrangements. For instance, in the Ford–CATL LFP battery licensing deal, CATL agreed to transfer key technologies and engineering know-how without owning the US plant.

While this model circumvents political restrictions, it raises the risk of IP leakage, especially if future partners become competitors. In regions with weak intellectual property enforcement, CATL's R&D advantage could be compromised. Balancing market access to knowledge protection remains a delicate, ongoing struggle.

Labor Practices and Local Talent Integration.

Expanding into global markets also requires CATL to adapt its human resource practices to local labor laws, union dynamics, and cultural expectations. In Europe, particularly Hungary and Germany, CATL has faced resistance from labor unions concerned about working conditions, transparency, and environmental risks associated with factory operations (Wu, 2024).

Language barriers, mismatches in management styles, and differences in labor rights complicate day-to-day operations and may affect productivity. CATL must invest in training local talent, which increases ramp-up time and operational costs in new markets.

Public Perception and Cultural Misalignment.

In some host countries, CATL has faced negative media coverage and public skepticism, often tied to broader tensions between China's overseas investments. For example, in Hungary, civil society groups have protested against the environmental impact and perceived lack of community engagement in CATL's battery plant (Reuters, 2024c).

Such perception issues create political risk, potentially triggering delays in approvals, additional scrutiny, or loss of social license to operate. Cultural misalignments in governance practices, communication styles, and stakeholder engagement models could hinder CATL's ability to integrate effectively into local ecosystems.

Mitigation Strategies

CATL's international growth has brought significant operational and reputational challenges. However, rather than retreating in the face of adversity, the company has adopted a series of balanced, multi-dimensional mitigation strategies. These measures show CATL's adaptability and commitment to responsible globalization, combining legal innovation, ESG investment, strategic partnerships, and cultural integration to ensure resilience across markets.

Legal Structuring to Circumvent Ownership Restrictions.

To address restrictions on foreign ownership—particularly under the US Inflation Reduction Act (IRA), CATL adopted a flexible legal structuring model. In the 2023 deal with Ford, CATL licensed its LFP battery technology without holding equity in the Michigan factory. The plant remained fully owned by Ford, allowing CATL to bypass IRA limitations while still benefiting from IP monetization and long-term client integration (Global Times, 2023). In Europe, CATL incorporated local subsidiaries in Hungary and Germany, aligning its investment with EU "rules of origin" to qualify for regional green subsidies. These tailored legal approaches allowed CATL to maintain a global presence without violating national security frameworks. Rather than resisting local policy frameworks, CATL has shown strategic legal agility—enabling compliance without compromising core strategic access.

ESG Compliance Through Recycling and Transparency Programs.

In response to stringent environmental and sustainability regulations—especially in the EU—CATL proactively established battery recycling partnerships and material-traceability systems. At its Erfurt plant in Germany, CATL committed to sourcing recycled raw materials and achieving the EU-mandated 65% recycling rate for key components by 2025 (European Union, 2023). The company rolled out a carbon accounting system that tracks emissions from extraction through end-use. CATL also aligns its sustainability reporting with international frameworks, including the GRI and SASB standards. In Southeast Asia, it signed joint ESG commitments with local governments to codify standards for ethical mining and environmental protection (Reuters, 2024b). These proactive measures reduce regulatory risks, improve stakeholder trust, and differentiate CATL from less-compliant competitors. Importantly, they reinforce CATL's brand in ESG-sensitive markets and mitigate the risks of future sanctions or legal penalties.

Knowledge Protection Through Modular Technology Transfer.

To mitigate intellectual property risks in politically sensitive markets, CATL implemented a tiered technology-transfer approach. In licensing deals like the Ford partnership, CATL provides access only to final battery system designs and manufacturing protocols, while retaining proprietary knowledge around electrolyte chemistry, software algorithms, and cathode formulation. In joint ventures, CATL's centralized Chinese teams manage core technologies, sharing only operational-level blueprints with local partners using a "black-box" model. This approach prevents reverse engineering while enabling localization. CATL includes IP clauses and technology safeguard agreements in all international contracts, especially in countries with weaker legal protection. This layered strategy ensures that CATL benefits from global market participation without compromising its innovation advantage or long-term competitiveness.

Labor Relations and Local Workforce Development.

To address labor concerns in countries like Hungary and Germany, CATL prioritized local workforce training, community engagement, and union cooperation. The company launched vocational training programs in partnership with the Debrecen municipality, aiming to train over 3,000 local workers in battery technology, safety, and plant operations by 2025 (Xinhua News Network, 2024). It also implemented a multilingual grievance mechanism and aligned its HR protocols with EU labor laws and collective bargaining norms. In Germany, CATL designated union liaison officers and hosted open dialogue sessions with labor representatives during the launch of its Erfurt plant. These measures helped reduce social tension and improve CATL's image as a responsible employer. By developing local talent pipelines, CATL reduced its reliance on expatriates, enhanced integration, and supported the long-term sustainability of its foreign operations.

Public Perception and Cultural Adaptation Strategies.

Facing media skepticism and public protests—especially in Europe—CATL adopted a proactive communication strategy. The company organized "open plant days", community briefings, and stakeholder roundtables to build trust and transparency. In Hungary, CATL partnered with local universities and NGOs to launch an environmental monitoring program and publicly disclose air and water quality data near its factories (Reuters, 2024c). It also enlisted local PR firms and policy consultants to manage public affairs and cultural translation in media messaging. Internally, CATL invested in cross-cultural training for managers and established local communication teams fluent in host country languages and norms. These efforts not only eased community resistance but also signaled a long-term commitment to responsible development. As a result, CATL positioned itself as a community-conscious investor—not merely a foreign operator extracting value.

R&D Diversification to Reduce Geopolitical Exposure.

To avoid overconcentration of innovation risk, CATL diversified its R&D infrastructure across continents. The company opened advanced technology centers in Munich (Germany) and Yokohama (Japan) and plans to expand to North America. These centers specialize in adapting battery systems to local climate conditions, safety regulations, and customer preferences. This move allows CATL to tap into regional talent pools, enhance regulatory alignment, and de-risk against potential technology decoupling scenarios. CATL enhances operational continuity, local relevance, and the ability to rapidly iterate products for foreign markets through globally distributed R&D capabilities. It also shows that CATL is not merely exporting Chinese tech but is co-developing global solutions, easing political sensitivities and reinforcing legitimacy in target markets.

Organizational Structure and Leadership Alignment.

CATL's ability to navigate complex international expansion strategies is underpinned by its dual organizational structure—a central command model complemented by empowered regional hubs. Chairperson Robin Zeng has played a decisive leadership role, personally guiding major strategic decisions, including the €1.8 billion German factory and the Stellantis joint venture in Spain (Li et al., 2025). CATL's European operations are supported by regional presidents, such as Matthias Zentgraf in Germany, who manage day-to-day execution and stakeholder engagement locally, while maintaining direct alignment with Ningde headquarters' strategic vision.

Zeng's leadership also signals an emphasis on collaborative expansion. In a public address, he affirmed CATL's commitment to "co-build factories, form joint ventures, and engage in technology licensing," reflecting a leadership style that blends centralized vision with local adaptation (CATL, 2025). This governance model—collective adaptation under a shared direction—enables CATL to respond quickly to regulatory uncertainties and geopolitical risks while preserving operational cohesion across geographies.

STRATEGIC ANALYSIS

SWOT Analysis

Strengths.

CATL's foremost strength lies in its technological leadership. With over 18,000 R&D personnel and proprietary innovations such as the CTP 3.0 "Qilin battery", CATL delivers innovative energy density, thermal safety, and lifecycle performance unmatched by most competitors (Doll, 2023). The company's vertical integration across mining, cell manufacturing, and recycling further reinforces its cost control and material security. CATL also maintains long-term partnerships with top-tier global OEMs, including Tesla, BMW, and Stellantis, which help ensure stable demand and high switching costs.

Weaknesses.

However, CATL remains heavily reliant on the Chinese government for policy alignment, export approvals, and indirect subsidies, making it vulnerable to shifts in domestic regulatory posture. Despite rapid expansion, CATL's brand recognition outside Asia remains limited compared to Tesla's or LG Energy Solution's. Its public image in regions such as Europe has been strained by local opposition and labor concerns, particularly regarding its Debrecen project (University of Debrecen, 2024).

Opportunities.

Global demand for energy storage and EVs continues to surge, especially in regions implementing aggressive carbon-neutrality goals. This opens new opportunities in utility-scale ESS deployments, commercial fleets, and renewable-integrated battery networks. Geopolitical decoupling and subsidy-driven localization (e.g., the IRA in the US and the Green Deal in Europe) are pushing OEMs to seek local battery partners, a gap that CATL is well positioned to fill with its localized R&D centers and flexible licensing models.

Threats.

CATL faces intensifying competition from BYD, LG Energy Solution, and Panasonic, especially as these rivals also scale globally. Regulatory risks are also significant: Western governments are increasingly cautious of Chinese tech giants, introducing tariff regimes and foreign investment reviews (Hamlin, 2024). IP risks arise from technology-transfer-based market entry and disruptions in critical raw material markets, particularly nickel and lithium, could affect cost stability and delivery schedules (International Energy Agency, 2023).

PESTEL Analysis

Political Factors.

Policy and geopolitics deeply influenced the global battery industry. Western regulations shape CATL's expansion, such as the Inflation Reduction Act (IRA) in the US, which restricts subsidies for products made by "foreign entities of concern". Meanwhile, EU regulations mandate local content and emissions thresholds. CATL has responded by localizing production, e.g., in Hungary and Germany, to meet eligibility standards while avoiding retaliatory tariffs.

Economic Factors.

Rising global interest rates and inflation are challenging EV affordability, yet long-term trends still favor electrification. CATL benefits from cost leadership via vertical integration, especially when raw material prices are volatile. Emerging markets in Southeast Asia and Latin America offer high EV growth potential, creating new demand frontiers outside of saturated markets like China (SNE Research, 2024).

Social Factors.

Consumer awareness of clean energy, ESG, and local employment shapes brand perception. In Europe, resistance to CATL's factories partly stems from gaps in community engagement and fears of over-dependence on China. As such, social license to operate has become as critical as technical capability.

Technological Factors.

Rapid innovation cycles in battery technology—such as solid-state batteries, sodium-ion, and ultra-fast charging—demand high and sustained R&D investment. CATL's innovation pipeline, protected by hundreds of patents and a diversified chemistry portfolio, positions it as a first mover. However, the shortening of the technology lifecycle increases R&D pressure and risk.

Environmental Factors.

The assessment of global battery manufacturers increasingly focuses on carbon footprint, recycling capacity, and lifecycle emissions. CATL has invested in low-carbon supply chains and recycling infrastructure in Germany and China to meet EU battery regulations (European Union, 2023). However, upstream operations in Indonesia are under scrutiny for environmental impact, requiring enhanced transparency.

Legal Factors.

Global legal environments are increasingly restrictive for foreign investors, with export controls, foreign investment screening, and ESG disclosures becoming the norm. CATL has had to design complex JV and licensing structures to meet these legal thresholds without losing market access, especially in the US and Europe (Electrek, 2023).

Comparative Analysis with Competitors

While CATL remains the undisputed global leader in EV batteries, competition from BYD, LG Energy Solution (LGES), and Panasonic is intensifying, each with distinctive advantages. In 2024, CATL held approximately 37.9% of the global EV battery market share, compared to 17.2% for BYD and 10.8% for LG Energy

Solution (Kang, 2025a). This leadership underscores CATL's dominance but also highlights the narrowing gap as rivals scale aggressively.

BYD differentiates itself through a vertically integrated model that includes both batteries and complete vehicles. Its Blade Battery technology has been widely adopted in BYD's own EV lineup. It is increasingly adopted by external OEMs, giving the company a strategic advantage in cost control and rapid commercialization (BYD, 2023). Unlike CATL, which is more reliant on third-party OEM contracts, BYD benefits from guaranteed internal demand, creating a stable base for expansion.

LG Energy Solution (LGES) benefits from strong roots in the US and Europe through multi-billion-dollar joint ventures with GM, Honda Motor Co., Ltd. (Honda), Stellantis, and other automakers. For instance, its $4.4 billion JV with Honda in Ohio targets around 40 GWh annual capacity by 2025, while another project in Windsor, Ontario, aims for 45 GWh and 2,500 new jobs (Honda, 2023). This localization, reinforced by long-term supply deals such as a 67 GWh agreement with Rivian in Arizona (Reuters, 2024c), enables LGES to better align with IRA incentives and regulatory demands than CATL, which continues to face scrutiny as a Chinese entity.

Compared with other battery manufacturers, CATL's strengths lie in its technological depth, economies of scale, and global reach. However, BYD's internal vehicle ecosystem, LGES's localization strategy, and Panasonic's Tesla partnership illustrate that CATL faces not only volume-based rivalry but also structural competition in business models. The ability to adapt its expansion strategy to mitigate geopolitical barriers while sustaining innovation will determine whether CATL can maintain its lead in an increasingly contested landscape.

Brand and Reputation Effects

As CATL transitions from a domestic industry leader to a global technology powerhouse, its brand and reputation have become essential elements of strategic value creation. In highly regulated, politically sensitive markets such as Europe and North America, brand trust, ESG credibility, and local perception significantly influence the firm's market entry success, stakeholder engagement, and long-term viability. This section explores how CATL's branding strategy has evolved alongside its global footprint, identifying both its strengths and vulnerabilities in international reputation management.

Global Brand Positioning: From Industrial Supplier to Technology Leader.

In the past, CATL's brand was primarily known as a high-volume, cost-efficient cell supplier, especially in Asia. However, since 2020, the company has increasingly repositioned itself as a technology-driven, sustainable energy innovator. The launch of the "Qilin battery", solid-state R&D initiatives, and partnerships with premium OEMs like Tesla and BMW have elevated CATL's brand as a front-runner in energy storage innovation (Electrek, 2023).

CATL's branding strategy emphasizes not only technical leadership but also reliability. For instance, its status as Tesla's primary LFP supplier in China has reinforced its global visibility and market validation. Co-branding efforts—such as the Stellantis–CATL joint venture in Spain—also enhance CATL's association with trusted European auto brands, supporting its entrance into Western consumer-conscious markets (CATL, 2024).

Reputation Gains from ESG Commitments and Circular Practices.

CATL's efforts to localize sustainability practices have generated tangible brand value in regions where ESG (Environmental, Social, Governance) is not just compliance, but a consumer and political expectation. In Germany, CATL presents its Erfurt factory as a "low-carbon lighthouse facility," featuring electrified transport, on-site renewable power, and future integration of closed-loop recycling (CATL, 2023a). In 2023, World Economic Forum commentary recognized the plant for its AI-driven improvements in resource efficiency and energy waste reduction.

CATL has published standalone sustainability reports aligned with the GRI standards and takes part in international ESG disclosure platforms. These actions have improved institutional perception, particularly among European governments, ESG funds, and B2B partners seeking transparency in their supply chains. Such alignment between operations and stakeholder values strengthens CATL's legitimacy as a global industrial partner—an intangible yet strategic asset in an increasingly decoupled and skeptical geopolitical environment.

Reputational Challenges: Local Resistance and Public Image Risks.

Despite these branding gains, CATL's international image is not without challenges. Public protests, environmental concerns, and union resistance greeted the construction of CATL's €7.34 billion Debrecen plant in Hungary. Media narratives questioned the project's transparency, its environmental burden, and its implications for Hungarian labor markets (Xinhua News Network, 2024). Such incidents highlight a gap between CATL's corporate positioning and its local social perception, especially when stakeholder engagement is insufficient.

In North America, broader geopolitical narratives about Chinese industrial policy often overshadow CATL's relatively unknown status among end consumers. The Ford–CATL partnership, though technically sound, was politically sensitive, with

US lawmakers questioning the wisdom of involving a Chinese battery firm in subsidized EV infrastructure (Financial Post, 2022). These episodes show the fragility of global reputation in a fragmented political landscape. For CATL, branding is no longer just about technology or scale—it is also about narrative control, stakeholder trust, and cultural adaptability.

Managing Reputation: Strategic Communication and Localization.

To proactively manage brand reputation, CATL has enhanced its public relations and stakeholder engagement capabilities. It now employs local communications teams in key markets, invests in community outreach programs, and takes part in public policy dialogues. In Debrecen, for instance, CATL introduced multilingual job portals, environmental monitoring, and factory "open day" events to increase transparency and rebuild public trust. The company emphasizes "localized identity"—branding its European factories not as "Chinese outposts" but as local assets that create jobs, enhance industrial capacity, and align with regional goals. This narrative reframing is essential for de-risking future political or public relations backlash.

CONCLUSION AND STRATEGIC RECOMMENDATIONS

Summary of Key Findings

This case study of CATL's global expansion journey reveals several key findings that define the company's competitive edge, strategic agility, and structural vulnerabilities. First, domestic market saturation and intensifying competition from BYD and CALB prompted CATL to expand internationally, especially to Europe and Southeast Asia. This move was not reactive but preemptive, aiming to diversify revenue streams and enhance resilience (Kang, 2025b). Second, CATL's international entry strategy combined multi-mode flexibility—including joint ventures, licensing, and greenfield investments—with high degrees of localization, enabling it to meet protectionist and ESG standards in Western markets. This legal and structural adaptability proved vital in regions such as the EU and the US, where regulatory barriers are high. Third, CATL's sustained innovation (e.g., the CTP 3.0 "Qilin battery") and vertical integration across the supply chain delivered high cost and efficiency advantages, as well as product leadership. These became essential sources of global competitiveness (Doll, 2023). Challenges such as regulatory pushback, IP protection risks, labor resistance, and cultural misalignment marked CATL's journey. However, its mitigation strategies—such as black-box tech transfer, local training programs, and stakeholder engagement—helped preserve brand credibility and operational stability.

Future Growth Opportunities

Looking ahead, CATL's global development can be further accelerated through three major strategic avenues:

Market Diversification into Emerging Economies.

While the EU and Southeast Asia have been CATL's main international footholds, the Middle East, Africa, and Latin America represent untapped, high-growth regions for utility-scale energy storage and low-cost EV batteries. Countries such as Brazil, Saudi Arabia, and South Africa are ramping up investments in renewables and electrified transport—areas where CATL can offer scalable, modular energy solutions. Entry should be sequenced through joint ventures with local infrastructure players, mirroring the Indonesian model (Reuters, 2024b).

Expansion of Sodium-Ion Battery Platforms.

To remain technologically diversified, CATL should speed up the commercialization of sodium-ion batteries for two-wheelers, stationary storage, and micro-EVs. This chemistry, which is more cost-stable and less geopolitically exposed than lithium-based technologies, can capture large market segments in resource-constrained economies and hedge against lithium price volatility (Spence & Lee, 2023).

Strengthening Global ESG Brand Equity.

Besides operational ESG compliance, CATL can build a global sustainability brand identity, comparable to Patagonia in fashion or Tesla in mobility. This requires transparent sustainability disclosure, third-party certifications, and community development programs in every region of operation. It can shift the narrative from "Chinese manufacturer" to "global sustainability leader."

Recommendations for Other Firms

CATL's experience offers valuable insights for other Chinese firms seeking global expansion. Companies should build flexibility into their legal and ownership structures by leveraging licensing deals, joint ventures, and locally registered entities to navigate protectionist laws in the US and Europe, and by developing region-specific legal playbooks that comply without losing influence. Early stakeholder engagement is crucial; proactive efforts in local hiring, training, and transparency can prevent reputational damage and political conflict, with a public perception of a core operational risk. Protecting core technology involves implementing tiered transfer systems, such as developing black-box controls that keep high-value algorithms centralized while sharing modular, application-level capabilities—an approach that safeguards competitiveness and prevents knowledge leakage. Going beyond mere compliance in ESG, companies should leverage environmental and labor standards as brand assets to attract customers, partners, and investors, viewing ESG investment as both a risk-management tool and a differentiation strategy. Last, effective rebranding for local relevance is essential; rather than enforcing a solely Chinese identity, firms should adopt a glocalization approach—localizing communications, branding, and product positioning—while maintaining operational synergies rooted in their Chinese core.

REFERENCES

Bridge, G., & Faigen, E. (2022). Towards the lithium-ion battery production network: Thinking beyond mineral supply chains. *Energy Research & Social Science*, *89*(102659), 102659. DOI: 10.1016/j.erss.2022.102659

BYD. (2023). BYD's new blade battery set to redefine EV safety standards. BYD USA. Https://En.byd.com/. https://en.byd.com/news/byds-new-blade-battery-set-to-redefine-ev-safety-standards/

Contemporary Amperex Technology Co. Limited (CATL). (2022, April 15). CATL partners up with Indonesia to boost e-mobility with an investment of nearly 6 billion USD. CATL Official Website. https://www.catl.com/en/news/922.html

Contemporary Amperex Technology Co. Limited (CATL). (2023a). Environmental, Social, and Governance (ESG) Report. CATL Official Website. https://www.catl.com/en/uploads/1/file/public/202404/20240417102933_uuiks9ljr8.pdf

Contemporary Amperex Technology Co. Limited (CATL). (2023b, August 16). CATL launches superfast charging battery Shenxing, opens up era of EV superfast charging. CATL Official Website. https://www.catl.com/en/news/6091.html

Contemporary Amperex Technology Co. Limited (CATL). (2024, December 10). Stellantis and CATL to invest up to €4.1 billion in joint venture for large-scale LFP battery plant in Spain. CATL Official Website. https://www.catl.com/en/news/6328.html

Contemporary Amperex Technology Co. Limited (CATL). (2025, June 23). CATL chairman and CEO Robin Zeng outlines vision for global zero-carbon transition and deeper collaboration at major conference. Prnewswire. https://www.prnewswire.com/il/news-releases/catl-chairman-and-ceo-robin-zeng-outlines-vision-for-global-zero-carbon-transition-and-deeper-collaboration-at-major-conference-302488099.html

Doll, S. (2023, March 21). CATL begins mass production of its Qilin batteries with 13% more power than other 4680 cells. Electrek; Electrek. https://electrek.co/2023/03/21/catl-begins-mass-production-of-its-qilin-batteries-with-13-more-power-than-other-4680-cells/

Electrios Consultants. (2024, March 20). CATL 2023 Annual Report Highlights. Electrios. https://electrios.com/blog_post/catl-2023-annual-report-highlights/

European Union. (2023). Regulation - 2023/1542 - EN - EUR-Lex. Europa.eu. https://eur-lex.europa.eu/eli/reg/2023/1542/oj/eng

fDi Intelligence. (2022, August 16). CATL announces Hungary's largest ever investment. fDi Intelligence. https://www.fdiintelligence.com/content/6c410c6a-8193-58d0-907c-9374afd2fd97

Financial Post. (2022, March 19). Tesla supplier CATL weighs sites for $5 billion battery plant. Financial Post. https://financialpost.com/pmn/business-pmn/tesla-supplier-catl-weighs-sites-for-5-billion-battery-plant

Gasgoo. (2025, January 14). China's annual power battery installation volume shoots up 41.5% in 2024. Gasgoo. https://autonews.gasgoo.com/articles/ev/70035698

Global Times. (2023, February 14). CATL to license patent battery technology to Ford plant in US: company - Global Times. Globaltimes.cn. https://www.globaltimes.cn/page/202302/1285424.shtml

Hamlin, K. (2024, June 12). Breakingviews - Breakingviews: Chinese EV makers will drive around EU tariffs. Reuters. https://www.reuters.com/breakingviews/chinese-ev-makers-will-drive-around-eu-tariffs-2024-06-12/

Hanley, S. (2024). CATL, BYD To Slash Battery Prices By 50% In 2024. BOOM! EVs Win! CleanTechnica. https://cleantechnica.com/2024/02/26/catl-byd-to-slash-battery-prices-by-50-in-2024-boom-evs-win/

Honda Motor Co. Ltd. (Honda). (2023, March). LG Energy Solution and Honda Break Ground for New Joint Venture EV Battery Plant in Ohio. Honda Global; Honda Motor Co., Ltd. https://global.honda/en/newsroom/news/2023/c230301eng.html

Inagaki, K., White, E., & Jopson, B. (2024, December 10). China's CATL to build €4.1bn battery factory with Stellantis in European expansion. @FinancialTimes; Financial Times. https://www.ft.com/content/b2c41a7d-02fa-4846-ab50-dd27e534dcf5

International Energy Agency (IEA). (2023, July 11). Critical minerals market review 2023. OECD Publishing, Paris. DOI: 10.1787/9cdf8f39-en

Kang, L. (2025a, February 11). Global EV battery market share in 2024: CATL 37.9%, BYD 17.2%. CnEVPost. https://cnevpost.com/2025/02/11/global-ev-battery-market-share-2024/

Kang, L. (2025b, June 6). Global EV battery market share in Jan-Apr 2025: CATL 38.1%, BYD 17.3%. CnEVPost. https://cnevpost.com/2025/06/06/global-ev-battery-market-share-jan-apr-2025/

Li, G., Harding, R., & White, E. (2025, May 20). CATL founder Robin Zeng expects China truck market to be 50% electric by 2028. @FinancialTimes; Financial Times. https://www.ft.com/content/87372b46-ee9c-4747-ae2d-3f729b92b008

Pereyra, J., Lou, J., Hilde, T., Squire, C., Susanto, S., & Pradipta, A. (2024). Mining, Manufacturing, and Markets An Analysis of Five Years of Electric Vehicle Regulation, Investment, and Industry Development in Indonesia Mining, Manufacturing, and Markets An Analysis of Five Years of Electric Vehicle Regulation, Investment, and Industry Development in Indonesia 2. https://cgs.umd.edu/sites/default/files/2024-11/file_CGS_Indonesia%20EV_11.22.pdf

Research, S. N. E. (2024). 2023 Global EV Battery Sales Volume by Battery Maker. Sneresearch.com. https://www.sneresearch.com/en/insight/release_view/260/page/0

Reuters. (2024a, July 5). How China's EV battery makers stack up in energy storage. Reuters. https://www.reuters.com/business/autos-transportation/how-chinas-ev-battery-makers-stack-up-energy-storage-2024-07-05/

Reuters. (2024b, October 17). Indonesia Battery Corp, CATL unit sign JV deal, state media says. Reuters. https://www.reuters.com/markets/deals/indonesia-battery-corp-catl-unit-sign-jv-deal-state-media-says-2024-10-17/

Reuters. (2024c, November 7). LG Energy Solution signs 5-year battery supply deal with Rivian. Reuters. https://www.reuters.com/technology/lg-energy-solution-signs-5-year-battery-supply-deal-with-rivian-2024-11-07/

Shanghai Nonferrous Metals. (2024, February 19). 2023 Motive Power Battery Overseas Market Share Battle: CATL in Pursuit, BYD Surges Ahead | Shanghai Non ferrous Metals. News.metal.com. https://news.metal.com/newscontent/102622888/2023-Motive-Power-Battery-Overseas-Market-Share-Battle:-CATL-in-Pursuit-BYD-Surges-Ahead

Spence, E., & Lee, A. (2023, November 26). Sodium in Batteries: Shift May Herald Another Shakeup. Www.bloomberg.com. https://www.bloomberg.com/news/articles/2023-11-26/sodium-in-ev-and-storage-batteries-may-herald-another-shakeup

The China Academy. (2023, September 27). Ford pauses work on EV battery plant in Michigan with CATL. The China Academy. https://thechinaacademy.org/ford-pauses-work-on-ev-battery-plant-in-michigan-with-catl/

University of Debrecen. (2024, October 15). New career opportunities and apprenticeship programs for our future engineers. University of Debrecen News. https://hirek.unideb.hu/en/new-career-opportunities-and-apprenticeship-programs-our-future-engineers

Volumes, E. V. (2023, December 18). CATL drove global EV battery production in first three quarters of 2023. EV Volumes. https://ev-volumes.com/news/eu/catl-drove-global-ev-battery-production-in-first-three-quarters-of-2023/

World Economic Forum. (2022, October 11). Amid Recession Fears, These Factories Are Boosting Productivity, Sustainability, and Resilient Supply Chains. World Economic Forum. https://www.weforum.org/press/2022/10/amid-recession-fears-these-factories-are-boosting-productivity-sustainability-and-resilient-supply-chains/

Wu, Q. M. (2024). The embrace and resistance of Chinese battery investments in Hungary: The case of CATL. *Asia Europe Journal*, *22*(2), 201–223. DOI: 10.1007/s10308-024-00699-9

Xiao, M. (2023, February 1). How will the US Inflation Reduction Act affect China's Li-ion battery and EV industry? - Interact Analysis. Interact Analysis. https://interactanalysis.com/insight/how-will-the-us-inflation-reduction-act-affect-chinas-li-ion-battery-and-ev-industry/

Xinhua News Network. (2024, November 21). CATL to begin battery cell production in Hungary's Debrecen. News.cn. https://english.news.cn/20241121/6abe70fe521c4be8866f153f40e3caab/c.html

Yee, L., Chui, M., Roberts, R., & Smit, S. (2025). Technology Trends Outlook 2025. https://www.mckinsey.com/~/media/mckinsey/business%20functions/mckinsey%20digital/our%20insights/the%20top%20trends%20in%20tech%202025/mckinsey-technology-trends-outlook-2025.pdf

Zhang, P. (2022, March 26). CATL teases Qilin battery, says it has 13% higher capacity than 4680 batteries. CnEVPost. https://cnevpost.com/2022/03/26/catl-teases-kirin-battery-says-it-has-13-higher-capacity-than-4680-batteries/

KEY TERMS AND DEFINITIONS

CATL (Contemporary Amperex Technology Co., Limited): A Chinese lithium-ion battery manufacturer headquartered in Ningde, China. It is the world's largest supplier of EV and energy storage batteries.

Cell-to-Pack (CTP) Technology: A battery design architecture that eliminates intermediate modules, integrating cells directly into battery packs to improve space utilization, energy density, and thermal performance.

CTP 3.0 Qilin Battery: The third-generation CTP battery developed by CATL, featuring enhanced thermal management and a 13% higher energy density than Tesla's 4680 cylindrical cells.

Vertical Integration: A business strategy where a company controls multiple stages of the supply chain, from raw material acquisition to manufacturing and recycling.

Joint Venture (JV): A business arrangement in which two or more parties jointly invest in and operate a new entity, typically to share risks, resources, and market access.

Licensing Strategy: A market entry mode in which a company permits a foreign partner to use its technology or intellectual property in exchange for royalties or fees.

Inflation Reduction Act (IRA): A US legislative act enacted in 2022 that provides clean energy subsidies but limits eligibility for companies affiliated with "foreign entities of concern."

ESG (Environmental, Social, Governance): A framework used to assess a company's ethical impact and sustainability in three areas: environmental protection, social responsibility, and corporate governance.

Sodium-Ion Battery: A battery type that uses sodium instead of lithium as a charge carrier. It offers lower cost and improved stability, but lower energy density.

Glocalization Strategy: A hybrid strategy that combines global operational efficiencies with localized branding, marketing, and stakeholder engagement.

Black Box Technology Model: A strategy in technology transfer where core R\&D processes are kept confidential, and only non-sensitive, application-level modules are shared with partners.

Energy Storage System (ESS): A grid or commercial-scale system that stores electricity—often from renewables—for later use. ESS technologies help stabilize energy supply and reduce peak demand.

Lighthouse Factory: A designation by the World Economic Forum for manufacturing facilities that pioneer advanced Industry 4.0 technologies such as AI, IoT, and automation at scale.

Chapter 5
TCL Localized Global Manufacturing Strategy:
Strategic Agility, Localized Innovation, and Supply Chain Integration

Zhen Gong
http://orcid.org/0009-0002-5160-2151
Beijing Normal-Hong Kong Baptist University, China

EXECUTIVE SUMMARY

This chapter analyses the globalization strategy of TCL, a leading Chinese multinational electronics corporation, tracing its evolution from a domestic manufacturer to a globally recognized brand. Examine the core strategic approaches that have driven TCL's international expansion, focusing on the synergistic integration of deep product localization with a resilient, globally diversified supply chain. Covering why the company is expanding, picking markets, the various steps for entering those markets, and how they build their lead through advanced Mini-LED technology and by marketing globally with sports sponsorships. Addresses challenges faced, including trade protectionism, intense technological competition, and low brand recognition, along with the mitigation strategies employed, such as establishing manufacturing hubs in Mexico and Vietnam and investing in core technology. Utilise PESTEL analysis for valuable insights into how multinationals can achieve sustainable global growth through strategic agility, investment in R&D, and localized market engagement.

DOI: 10.4018/979-8-3373-4302-0.ch005

INTRODUCTION

Background of the Company

TCL (Telephone Communication Limited) founded the company in 1981 and initially engaged in magnetic tape production (TCL, n.d.), and has since grown into a global technology enterprise group with diversified operations across smart terminals, semiconductor displays, and new-energy photovoltaics. While television manufacturing remains its core business, the company has significantly expanded its portfolio to include a wide range of smart home appliances, including refrigerators, air conditioners, and washing machines. In 2024, TCL solidified its global standing by selling 29 million TV units, ranking as the world's second-largest television brand and becoming a benchmark for Chinese companies expanding internationally (Chen & Meng, 2025).

TCL's global leadership is further reinforced through its key subsidiaries, TCL CSOT in semiconductor displays and TCL Zhonghuan in new energy sectors. Several strategic milestones have marked the company's internationalization process. Its global footprint began in 1999 with the acquisition of a factory in Vietnam (TCL, n.d.). A major leap occurred in 2004 with the acquisitions of Thomson's television business and Alcatel's mobile phone business (TCL, n.d.), enabling entry into European and American markets. In 2009, it established CSOT to integrate upstream semiconductor display supply chains. More recently, it launched the world's first mini-LED TV and completed the group's asset restructuring in 2019 (TCL, n.d.). In 2020, it expanded into the new energy sector through the acquisition of Zhonghuan Group.

In terms of organizational management, TCL employs a synergistic management structure between TCL Industry and TCL Technology to drive its global expansion. This framework includes three major business groups: the Semiconductor Display and Materials Business Group, the Industrial Finance Business Group, and the Emerging Business Group, along with eight headquarters functional departments and multiple independent operational service platforms (TCL, 2019). Under the leadership of its founder, Li Dongsheng, TCL has strategically steered its international expansion. Today, the company boasts an extensive global network with 46 research and development (R&D) centers and 38 manufacturing bases, serving over 160 countries and regions (Chen & Meng, 2025). With a workforce of 130,000 employees and over 1.3 billion global users, TCL shows robust international operational capability (Chen & Meng, 2025).

Motivation for Global Expansion

TCL's pursuit of internationalization was driven by a combination of internal growth pressures and shifting external conditions. By 1999, the company had already secured a leading position with the largest market share in China's TV industry (Feng & Liang, 2024). However, as the domestic market neared saturation and industry growth slowed significantly, TCL encountered bottlenecks to growth. While rural areas still offered some potential, limited purchasing power and consumption patterns overall constrained market growth (Han, 2004). These internal pressures prompted TCL to shift its strategic focus to international markets to pursue new growth opportunities and long-term strategic resources.

A key external catalyst was China's accession to the World Trade Organization (WTO) in 2001. On the one hand, WTO membership provided a more stable international trading environment for Chinese enterprises such as TCL, including most-favored-nation treatment and improved market access, enabling enterprises to leverage international resources to reduce costs and secure global financing and talent (Han, 2004). The improvement in the openness of the domestic market attracted an influx of foreign companies and investment, intensifying domestic competition (Han, 2004). This dual effect—greater access to global markets coupled with heightened competition at home—prompted TCL to adopt an aggressive "double acquisition" strategy in 2004 (TCL, n.d.). Through this move, TCL gained the TV business of France's Thomson and the mobile phone business of Alcatel, making its official entry into the European and American markets. These purchases showed a change in our strategy, moving from adapting to local needs at the beginning to plan globally in a more forward-thinking and connected way.

MARKET ANALYSIS AND ENTRY STRATEGY

Target Market Selection

In its globalization process, TCL employs a systematic approach to select target markets, carefully evaluating economic conditions, consumer characteristics, and policy environments. Vietnam, as the starting point of TCL's globalization strategy, exemplifies this rigorous selection process. Three key perspectives reveal the appeal of the Vietnamese market.

First, Vietnam's demographic structure presented a significant opportunity. As an emerging economy, it offered substantial demographic dividends. By 2009, Vietnam's population had reached approximately 85.8 million, with the working-age population (15-59 years old) accounting for 66% of the total (Mei, 2010).

From a consumption-behavior perspective, Vietnamese consumers showed a strong preference for electronics, with electronic product upgrade cycles closely aligned with those in China. This trend, particularly among younger consumers seeking fashionable products, supported the country's rapid economic growth and signaled strong market potential (Mei, 2010).

Second, the television market in Vietnam has great potential for development. While superficial oversupply was observed, Wang (2014) largely attributed this to high prices set by international brands, which limited affordability for many local consumers. As the economy continued to develop, we expected consumers' purchasing power to rise. Television sets were expected to become mass-consumption products, and the market size was projected to double. Chinese brands like TCL, possessing strong cost-performance advantages, were well-positioned to satisfy Vietnamese consumers' actual purchasing power and secure the mid-range market segment (Wang, 2014).

Third, policy and geographic factors enhanced Vietnam's strategic value. As an ASEAN member, Vietnam benefits from preferential, tariff-free treatment within the region, lowering trade barriers to market entry. Its geographical proximity to China also reduced logistical costs and simplified supply chain management, making it an ideal hub for TCL's expansion into Southeast Asia (Zhang, 2008). The strengthening of the strategic partnership between China and Vietnam, reinforced by the establishment of the China-ASEAN Free Trade Area, created a stable and favorable economic environment for cross-border business (Mei, 2010). These conditions allowed Vietnam to serve as a strategic springboard, facilitating TCL's broader regional expansion strategy.

Entry Mode Selection

TCL has adopted a phased, adaptive approach to entering overseas markets, selecting entry modes based on varying market conditions and strategic objectives. In the initial stage, the company employed low-risk strategies such as original equipment manufacturing (OEM), original design manufacturing (ODM), export processing, and brand licensing to establish an initial international presence (Feng, 2014). After gaining experience in export operations, TCL employed more committed entry modes. In 1999, it entered the Vietnamese market through new investments, the acquisition of the local Tong Nai Electronics Company of the Lu Group, and introducing advanced production lines and supporting facilities (Wang, 2014). This acquisition allowed TCL to avoid Vietnam's export ratio policy restrictions, streamline the licensing process (Wang, 2014), enhance decision-making efficiency, and strengthen both brand control and operational stability (Mei, 2010).

After consolidating its position in Southeast Asia, TCL shifted its focus to larger developed markets, adopting mergers and acquisitions as a key strategy. In 2004, the company gained the television business of France's Thomson and the mobile phone business of Alcatel. A notable move was the formation of the joint venture TCL-Thomson Electronics Ltd. (TTE) with Thomson, which handled the R&D, production, and global sales and service of television and related products (Qi, 2014). This merger provided TCL with immediate access to international distribution channels and supply chain systems, significantly speeding up its global operational capabilities. Although challenges like rapid technological change, complex European labor regulations, and cultural integration issues led to TTE's liquidation in 2007 (Center for China & Globalization, 2024), the experience gave TCL valuable insights into managing international operations and informed its subsequent global strategy.

As TCL's global supply chain and market layout gradually improved, the company increasingly turned to joint ventures and wholly owned subsidiaries to enter emerging markets. In Southeast Asia, TCL established a regional manufacturing hub in Vietnam to support the entire region's supply, reducing cross-border logistics costs and improving supply chain responsiveness (Center for China & Globalization, 2024). In Africa, it built factories through joint ventures, such as collaborating with South African firms to establish LCD TV factories, addressing regional demand while supporting local industrial development (Center for China & Globalization, 2024). Similarly, in Latin America, TCL established factories in partnership with Brazilian company SEMP to navigate local policy requirements and deepen market penetration (Center for China & Globalization, 2024). This emphasis on localized partnerships has enhanced TCL's flexibility and responsiveness in emerging markets, contributing to the sustainability of its global operations.

Competitive Advantage

TCL's successful global expansion stems from its distinctive competitive advantages, which are primarily reflected in two core areas: global brand marketing and technological innovation.

In terms of brand marketing, TCL has strategically invested significant resources to enhance its international visibility, with a strong emphasis on sports and entertainment partnerships. Sports marketing is a core component of TCL's global strategy, including collaborations with over 40 top-tier sports events, organizations, and teams worldwide (Fan & Kang, 2024). TCL adopts a globally localized marketing strategy, maintaining a consistent global brand identity while tailoring campaigns to regional preferences. For instance, in Europe, it partnered with five national football teams, such as Spain and Germany (Fan & Kang, 2024). While in South America, it collaborated with renowned international football stars and sponsored national teams, besides serving as an official partner for top events such as the South American Copa Libertadores and the Americas Cup (Fan & Kang, 2024). These initiatives effectively leverage the emotional appeal of sports to build deeper consumer connections. In entertainment marketing, TCL employs diverse methods, including product placements in Hollywood films such as Transformers 3 and Iron Man 3, securing naming rights for the TCL China Theater, and launching the TCL Hollywood Micro Film Festival (Feng, 2014). These diversified efforts have significantly raised TCL's brand profile in key international markets.

Technological innovation makes up another critical factor of TCL's competitive edge. The company has built a strong market position through its early and sustained leadership in mini-LED display technology. Being one of the first manufacturers to integrate mini-LED into television products, TCL capitalized on the technology's superior image quality, cost efficiency, and product longevity (Fan et al., 2025). This has enabled mini-LED TVs to compete increasingly with OLED TVs in the mid- to high-end TV segment (Fan et al., 2025). As a pioneer in the field, TCL has continued to achieve robust growth in this niche. In the second quarter of 2024, it ranked first globally in mini-LED TV shipments and consistently outperformed the industry in sales growth in recent years (Wang & Zhao, 2025). This technological leadership has not only reinforced TCL's differentiated positioning in the premium market but also attracted consumers seeking high-quality viewing experiences, enhancing the brand's overall competitiveness.

IMPLEMENTATION OF GLOBAL EXPANSION

Key Initiatives and Investments

To achieve its global expansion objectives, TCL has implemented a series of strategic initiatives and made substantial investments across product adaptation, channel development, and mergers and acquisitions. These efforts have collectively strengthened its international market presence.

A central element of TCL's strategy is product localization and innovation. Recognizing significant variations in consumer demand across markets, the company has adopted tailored product-development approaches. For instance, to address frequent thunderstorms and unstable signal reception in Vietnam, TCL introduced television sets with enhanced lightning protection and signal reception capabilities (Wang, 2014; Wen, 2005; Zhang, 2001). This adaptation improved product stability and reliability under local conditions. This not only met consumer needs but also created a unique selling point. In mature markets such as Europe and the United States, where consumers emphasize brand reputation and technological sophistication, TCL has continuously focused on advancing high-end display technologies. The company launched a series of TV products with high picture quality and advanced features. It established strategic partnerships with well-known technology companies, including Google and Roku (Center for China & Globalization, 2024). These collaborations enabled the launch of high-end TVs with integrated intelligent operating systems, support for mainstream streaming services like Netflix and YouTube, and compatibility with the smart home ecosystem (Center for China & Globalization, 2024). These initiatives have significantly raised TCL's brand perception and competitiveness in the high-value markets.

Besides product adaptation, TCL has achieved extensive market coverage through a diversified retail network. Taking the US market as an example, the company has established a presence in six major retail channels, including Walmart, Amazon, and Costco (Fan et al., 2025). Enabling it to effectively and with precision target consumer segments with different income levels and purchasing preferences. Among them, while Costco primarily targets middle-income consumers, Best Buy caters to consumers with higher expectations for product quality and brand prestige (Fan et al., 2025). This extensive distribution system has enhanced TCL's market accessibility and brand visibility, providing a solid foundation for sustained international growth.

TCL has actively used strategic mergers and acquisitions to overcome international trade barriers and speed up local market integration. For instance, when faced with anti-dumping policies and import quotas imposed by the European Union on Chinese electronics (Qing, 2003), TCL gained the established German enterprise Schneider, including its production facilities, sales channels, R&D capabilities, inventory and multiple brands, directly entering this high-potential market (Qi, 2014). The acquisition not only helped the company avoid trade barriers but also provided access to mature production facilities, technical expertise, and distribution networks. The company invested 314.9 million euros in a joint venture with Thomson to optimize the use of existing production bases and sales channels (Qi, 2014). This approach enabled TCL to circumvent anti-dumping duties and patent fees, facilitating rapid market entry (Qi, 2014). These strategic acquisitions significantly reduced the time and cost to establish operational foundations in key markets, accelerating TCL's global penetration.

Challenges Faced

Throughout its international expansion, TCL has encountered various challenges, including legal and regulatory constraints, technological competitive pressures, and difficulties in local operations. These issues have significantly affected its global strategic positioning and long-term sustainability.

First, TCL has faced increasingly severe challenges from trade protectionism in recent years, particularly from developed economies led by the United States, which seek to constrain the rise of Chinese technology firms. Since approximately 2013, when the United States banned Huawei and ZTE from participating in communication equipment bidding, global trade protectionism has intensified (Wang, 2024). The escalation of Sino-US trade tensions from 2017 onward prompted many countries to implement protective policies for domestic enterprises and raise tariffs, increasing operational uncertainty and market risks for multinational corporations. For instance, the US tariffs on imported Chinese TVs rose from 3.9% to 11.4% after 2019 (Ni, 2024), while the European Union maintains a 14% tariff rate (Chen, 2021). European and American authorities routinely apply anti-dumping measures to Chinese firms entering their markets, and they frequently target TCL. In 2020, the US Department of Homeland Security even unjustifiably accused TCL of installing “backdoor” programs in its TVs, attempting to restrict its market access (Zhang, 2020). These measures reflect a broader trend of systematic resistance to China’s industrial upgrading and technological advancement.

Second, TCL operates in an intensely competitive technological environment, particularly from established Japanese and Korean rivals that maintain strong patent portfolios and dominate high-end segments. In its early overseas ventures, TCL and other Chinese firms often lacked core technologies and intellectual property in areas such as DVDs and televisions, forcing them to operate at the lower end of the value chain and to pay substantial patent fees (Wu, 2005). As global intellectual property protections strengthened, technological autonomy became a critical factor for competitive success. Japanese and Korean enterprises started earlier and relied on years of accumulation to form a strong technical foundation and complete industrial chains. Using flat-panel TVs as an example, leading firms control over 70% of key component production, which accounts for most TV costs, establishing an integrated advantage from upstream to downstream (Mei, 2010). Although TCL has consistently increased R&D investment, it remains difficult to displace the dominant positions and technological leadership of Samsung, LG, and others in the short term (Mei, 2010).

Third, TCL must overcome low brand recognition and entrenched consumer biases in international markets. As a relatively late entrant to the international market, it competes with Japanese and South Korean brands that have built trusted reputations over decades. For example, Sony of Japan entered the Vietnamese market in the mid-20th century. Through long-term operation, it has cultivated a high-end brand image and gained strong consumer loyalty (Dang, 2017). When TCL first entered Vietnam, it not only faced low brand awareness but also encountered strong consumer resistance stemming from the presence of low-quality Chinese products in border trade (Wen, 2005). Negative media coverage regarding the quality of Chinese products further eroded consumers' confidence (Wen, 2005). In developed markets, a high level of brand loyalty makes it difficult for TCL to gain recognition and trust, requiring sustained investment in market cultivation and higher marketing costs to change consumers' perceptions.

Mitigation Strategies

To counter growing trade barriers, TCL has actively implemented a dual strategy combining global operational presence with local adaptation, systematically mitigating trade risks through geographically dispersed manufacturing. The company builds factories in important areas to make and sell products there, which helps them do better than competitors in the long run. For example, leveraging Mexico's preferential trade agreements with the United States, TCL established manufacturing operations there, enabling tariff-free entry of its products into the American market under the rules of origin (Chen, 2021). In 2014, TCL further expanded its North American footprint by acquiring Sanyo Electric's TV factory in Mexico, and in 2018, it added warehousing facilities and three large production lines (Wang, 2024). This layout not only strengthens synergy between domestic and international industrial chains but also enhances TCL's resilience against trade protectionism.

Vietnam serves as another strategic hub within TCL's global supply network. Benefiting from its unique geographical location, flexible multilateral relations, and 16 free trade agreements with markets and partners such as ASEAN, the EU, and the Americas, Vietnam offers preferential tariff access to over 60 countries or regions (Ni, 2024). Compared to the 11.4% tariff applied to TVs exported directly from China to the US, shipments from Vietnam face only 3.9%, conferring a significant cost advantage (Ni, 2024). TCL currently operates three manufacturing bases in Vietnam, making it the company's second-largest overseas production capacity after Mexico. While serving the ASEAN market, these facilities primarily supply the North American market (Ni, 2024). By establishing additional manufacturing bases in multiple countries, including Malaysia, Poland, and Brazil, TCL has built an integrated global production network. The strategic placements in Vietnam and Mexico help ease tariff pressures stemming from Sino-US trade friction. The Polish manufacturing base facilitates entry into the European market, reducing tariffs and policy risks (Center for China & Globalization, 2024). This distributed manufacturing approach strengthens TCL's ability to integrate resources and coordinate supply chain operations on a global scale.

In response to technological competition, TCL has pursued core technology autonomy as a foundation for international competitiveness. The company has sustained a high level of R&D investment to support long-term global growth. Recognizing that mastery of upstream core components, such as liquid crystal panels, is critical to competing with global giants (Wang, 2014), TCL independently launched an 8.5-generation LCD panel production project in 2009, advancing its vertical integration within the display industry (China Optics and Optoelectronics, 2009). It has also established R&D centers in developed countries to keep pace with the latest technological trends and tailor products for high-end markets. Over the past decade, the company has consistently invested substantial resources to fulfill these technological commitments, with an average annual investment exceeding 10 billion yuan (Li, 2025). By the end of 2024, TCL had filed approximately 100,000 patent applications, and its research and development expenditure reached 8.87-billion-yuan, accounting for 5.4% of its operating revenue (TCL Technology Group Corporation, 2025). These efforts have solidified TCL's technological foundation and enhanced its global market position.

To overcome operational and brand-related challenges in the overseas market, TCL has combined localized service innovation with corporate social responsibility. In terms of service innovation, the company moved beyond the conventional model where users had to send their TVs to specialized repair shops for maintenance. Instead, it provided rapid on-site repair services in key markets, such as Vietnam. It offered backup televisions during extended repairs, significantly increasing customer satisfaction and word-of-mouth referrals (Deng, 2007). TCL implemented a rapid-response strategy and service-oriented marketing initiatives, including 24-hour service hotlines in major Vietnamese cities, with particular emphasis on rapid response during high-demand periods, such as major football matches (Deng, 2007).

From a broader strategic perspective, TCL shifted away from traditional advertising toward local social responsibility projects. For example, the company created the TCL Youth Foundation in Vietnam, allocating RMB 5 from each TV sold to the fund (Deng, 2007). It also donated to primary schools in underserved areas in Vietnam and established the TCL Learning Support Fund to assist disadvantaged students and teachers (Deng, 2007). These measures have not only fostered a responsible brand image but also built a foundation of social recognition, supporting TCL's long-term localization efforts.

STRATEGIC ANALYSIS

Analytical Frameworks

The PESTEL framework offers a systematic approach to analyzing the macro-environmental factors affecting TCL's international operations. This section mainly focuses on the analysis of the political, economic, and technological dimensions, which apply to TCL's international business strategy.

Political Factors

Political stability and policy orientation in host countries significantly shape TCL's global expansion. In politically stable regions that encourage foreign investment, such as Southeast Asia, local governments often implement favorable policies to promote industrial upgrading, including tax reductions and investment facilitation. For example, since 1998, the Vietnamese government has issued over 70 regulations to simplify investment procedures (Dang, 2017), reduce restrictions on foreign enterprises, and strengthen legal protections for international investors. In terms of tax policies, the country also offers differentiated preferential policies for different industrial parks. For instance, high-tech parks are eligible for a four-year exemption from corporate income tax, and industrial parks can be eligible for a two-year exemption (Ni, 2024). Such policy support creates a conducive business environment and encourages many foreign enterprises to establish local operations.

However, TCL also faces political uncertainties, particularly in markets characterized by rising trade protectionism. Among them, the United States has maintained a persistent trade deficit with China. Following tariff impositions under the Trump administration in 2018, Sino-US trade tensions have persisted, with the Biden administration largely maintaining these measures. As a result, the average tariff rate on Chinese exports to the US remained around 19% (Zhu et al., 2025). In April 2025, the Trump administration announced the implementation of a "reciprocal tariff" policy and later claimed to increase tariffs on Chinese goods to as high as 125% (Zhu et al., 2025). Although China responded strongly, the two sides entered a temporary tariff truce in May (Ministry of Commerce of the People's Republic of China, 2025). The policy environment remains volatile, posing severe challenges to multinational corporations and significantly affecting the stability of the global supply chain.

Economic Factors

Economic conditions, including exchange rate fluctuations and differences in countries' economic development levels, directly affect TCL's marketing strategies and financial performance. First, exchange rate volatility, in particular, influences TCL's international pricing and profit margins. In the first half of 2025, the US dollar index declined by 8.8% from 108.48 on December 31, 2024, to 98.92 on July 29, 2025 (Zhang & Chen, 2025). This change was largely because of the Trump administration's implementation of the "reciprocal tariffs" policy, which exceeded market expectations, severely undermining the international community's confidence in US assets and intensifying global trade frictions (Zhang & Chen, 2025). Under this backdrop, North American buyers might find TCL's exports less competitive, and the company could see its profit margins squeezed. Conversely, it may create opportunities for TCL in European and emerging markets. The company can adjust its pricing strategies flexibly and enhance product value to expand market share. The RMB exchange rate against the USD appreciated slightly in the first half of 2025 but remained weak against most major trading currencies (Zhang & Chen, 2025). This means that TCL still faces certain production cost pressures and needs to strengthen cost control and improve efficiency continuously.

Regional economic disparities also shape TCL's market strategies. North America is a mature market with developed economies and high per-capita disposable income, and demand for high-end and smart home appliances continues to grow (Center for China & Globalization, 2024). TCL can strengthen its high-end product line and brand building in this market. The European market also has high purchasing power; however, it is affected by geopolitical conflicts and energy crises, and the economic recovery is slow, with low consumer confidence. Therefore, TCL needs to balance product quality and price competitiveness to adapt to the current market. In emerging markets, although per capita disposable income is relatively low, significant growth potential and consumption upgrading trends enable TCL to leverage its cost advantages and localized operations to gain market share.

Technological Factors

Technological innovation is a key driver of industrial upgrading and a cornerstone of TCL's competitive strategy. Currently, the global business environment in which TCL operates is undergoing a transformative period characterized by advances in display technology and the rapid development of artificial intelligence. Advances in display technology, particularly the rapid development of mini-LED, are driving the industry toward higher performance and superior visual experiences. In recent years, the iterative evolution of display technology has continuously promoted product upgrades. Mini-LED TVs, with their performance advantages and continuously declining manufacturing costs, have ballooned their market presence (Fan et al., 2025). As a pioneer in this field, TCL launched the world's first mini-LED TV, the X10 series, in 2019 and has since achieved mass production (TCL, n.d.), demonstrating strong technological foresight and industrial capability. This leadership has reinforced TCL's position in the high-end market and strengthened its global brand influence.

Simultaneously, artificial intelligence is reshaping industries through data sharing, algorithm optimization, and process improvements, reducing operating costs and creating new economic growth opportunities (Dong & Bi, 2025). TCL has actively embraced this trend and launched AI application solutions across all fields and in all scenarios, covering innovative areas such as smart interaction, image enhancement, and content production. It improves how businesses operate and how users interact with technology by using AI. However, the rapid development of AI also introduces a range of challenges, including data security and ethical concerns, which technology enterprises must address. Promoting technological innovation while attaching great importance to its social impact and ethical norms allows us to construct a trustworthy and sustainable AI ecosystem.

Brand and Reputation Effects

TCL employs a diversified, integrated strategy to build its global brand and reputation, extending beyond sports marketing to include entertainment collaborations, cultural IP development, and corporate social responsibility. This multi-faceted approach enables TCL to cultivate a comprehensive and distinctive international brand identity.

Sports marketing is an important component of TCL's international communication. In addition, the company is also actively diversifying into other high-affected channels to form a more comprehensive brand perception system. TCL has established a broad presence across traditional sports such as football, basketball, and rugby. In a strategic move to connect with younger audiences, the company entered the e-sports field in 2021 by becoming an official partner of the League of Legends Professional League (LPL) and a strategic partner of the EDG team (TCL Smart Home, 2024). EDG secured the global championship that same year, considerably boosting the brand's exposure. In March 2024, TCL renewed its partnership with EDG, further strengthening its alignment with youth culture and digital trends (TCL Smart Home, 2024).

TCL is committed to integrating technology with humanity beyond sports. It is actively developing cultural and technology-humanity IPs to enrich its brand narrative. Initiatives such as "TCLVision" and "TCLGreen" communicate themes of innovation and sustainability (TCL Smart Home, 2024). The company's own IP, "TCLforHer," with the value proposition of "Seeing Her, Inspiring Her, Supporting Her," focuses on empowering women through technology, thereby shaping an inclusive and progressive brand image (TCL Smart Home, 2024).

Corporate social responsibility makes up another key pillar of TCL's reputation-building efforts. The company has embedded sustainable development as a core strategy, guided by the corporate mission "Leading Technology, Harmonious Co-existence". Through initiatives such as launching the "TCLGreen" environmental program, TCL has promoted the construction of green factories, energy-efficient products, and a low-carbon industrial chain, integrating eco-friendly practices across the entire operational process (TCL Smart Home, 2024). TCL consistently engages in educational philanthropy, establishing multiple scholarships and innovation funds to support educational development and local community growth (TCL Smart Home, 2024).

Through these diverse brand marketing and social responsibility practices, TCL has significantly enhanced its international reputation. Google X and Kantar BrandZ have named the company one of the top 50 global Chinese brands for eight consecutive years, achieving a 17% growth in brand power (TCL Smart Home, 2024). In 2024, TCL was again ranked among the top 100 most valuable Chinese brands by Kantar BrandZ, with a steadily rising position, reflecting the sustained effectiveness of its brand strategy and growing recognition internationally (TCL Smart Home, 2024).

CONCLUSION AND STRATEGIC RECOMMENDATIONS

Summary of Key Findings

TCL's global success stems from its strategic integration of product localization and a globalized supply chain, which allows it to navigate diverse international markets effectively. However, in recent years, the company has faced growing challenges stemming from a complex trade environment and the rise of anti-globalization sentiments, which have tested its growth, operational efficiency, and profitability.

As a pioneer among Chinese consumer electronics multinationals, TCL has faced systemic trade barriers in developed markets, particularly the United States, which have imposed elevated tariffs (Ni, 2024), launched anti-dumping investigations, and raised unsubstantiated security concerns (Zhang, 2020). In response, TCL has strategically diversified its production footprint by establishing manufacturing bases in countries such as Mexico, Vietnam, and Brazil (Center for China & Globalization, 2024). This distributed supply chain model not only mitigates tariff affects and lowers trade costs but also strengthens the company's ability to respond swiftly to regional market dynamics, transforming a geopolitical vulnerability into a competitive advantage.

Complementing its agile supply chain, TCL's success is driven by its customer-centric approach to localized product innovation. The company does not adopt an identical export model; instead; it has a targeted understanding of markets across regions. This ranges from introducing TVs with enhanced durability for specific environmental conditions in Southeast Asia to pioneering high-end display technologies and an integrated smart ecosystem for discerning Western consumers (Wang, 2014; Wen, 2005; Zhang, 2001; Center for China & Globalization, 2024). This strategy has helped to build international acceptance of the TCL brand and moving beyond competition based solely on cost.

In summary, TCL exemplifies the strategic agility required for sustainable globalization. By combining a resilient, geographically dispersed supply network with a focused approach to localized product development, TCL has not only successfully weathered international trade pressures but also strengthened its competitive position worldwide. For other Chinese enterprises with global ambitions, TCL's experience underscores the importance of strategic flexibility, technological investment, and rooted local engagement as the foundational pillars for long-term international growth.

Future Growth Opportunities

TCL's future growth potential will depend not only on consolidating its current advantages but also on its ability to expect industry trends and implement forward-looking strategies. Several key pathways present significant potential for expansion and competitive differentiation.

First, TCL can further penetrate high-end niche segments. The company has already introduced specialized products targeting gaming and art consumers, such as the A300 series of art TVs with features like ultra-thin frame design, AI-powered painting functions, adaptive scene optimization, and high-fidelity audio (TCL, n.d.), which show its response to the market demand for integrating aesthetic life and functionality. TCL can still consider establishing a dedicated premium sub-brand targeting specific consumer groups, such as gaming enthusiasts or art lovers. Through differentiated design, superior performance, and personalized services, TCL can more effectively capture high-end demand and enhance its brand value.

Second, building an integrated content ecosystem represents a strategic growth vector. Beyond existing partnerships with major streaming platforms, TCL can explore investments in or acquisitions of content production studios. Creating our own content system would help keep users coming back, offer new ways to make money like subscriptions and ad revenue sharing, build stronger customer relationships, and make the user journey smoother.

Third, in response to the rapid evolution of the metaverse and immersive experience technologies, TCL should speed up its investment in immersive technologies, including virtual reality (VR)/augmented reality (AR), and the metaverse. Although the company initially operated in the AR glasses sector (TCL, n.d.), it would benefit from increasing investment in content development and application integration. By actively taking part in the construction of the metaverse ecosystem and embedding VR/AR capabilities into its existing product lines, such as televisions and smart home devices, TCL can offer immersive services, such as VR audiovisual content playback, and position itself at the forefront of next-generation digital interfaces.

In summary, through focused efforts on premium segmentation, content ecosystem development, and immersive technology integration, TCL can not only expand its addressable market but also build sustainable differentiation in an increasingly competitive global landscape. These strategic moves will support its transition from a hardware-focused manufacturer to an integrated technology and experience provider.

Recommendations for Other Firms

With over two decades of international operation experience, TCL has accumulated rich experience in cross-border management. The company offers a valuable blueprint for Chinese multinational enterprises seeking global expansion. Its sustained success stems from several core strategic principles that together form a framework for cross-border growth.

First, comprehensive and in-depth market research is essential prior to international entry. Global operations involve navigating complex and interconnected factors. Beyond analyzing local consumption patterns, cultural characteristics, and competitive dynamics, firms must thoroughly evaluate the host country's policy environment, legal and regulatory systems, intellectual property protections, labor laws, and environmental protection requirements. In addition, a rigorous assessment of political stability and social and cultural conditions is equally critical for identifying and mitigating potential risks. Thorough preliminary research minimizes the cost of trial-and-error and lays the groundwork for sustainable market penetration.

Second, continuous technological innovation is fundamental to a firm's survival and development in the global arena. To remain competitive, enterprises must prioritize investment in technology to achieve breakthroughs in core technologies and build a portfolio of independent property. This entails not only enhancing fundamental research and original innovation capabilities but also effectively absorbing and improving upon advanced foreign technologies. Introducing and cultivating technical talent to form specialized innovative teams requires our great attention. Robust technological prowess enables firms to launch differentiated products, move up the global value chain, and secure greater market share.

Third, cultivating a strong global brand image is vital for long-term international presence. Relying solely on cost leadership does not sustain a competitive edge. Companies should commit to long-term brand building through consistent investment in product quality, technological differentiation, and strategic marketing. This requires clear brand positioning and audience targeting, supported by integrated communication campaigns that reinforce core brand values. Meanwhile, enterprises must also actively monitor and safeguard brand reputation, responding promptly to any negative publicity. A respected global brand fosters consumer trust and enhances market recognition, creating a sustainable competitive advantage in the international arena.

By adopting these strategies—rooted in TCL's practical experience—other Chinese firms can enhance their preparedness, resilience, and capacity for sustainable growth in the global marketplace.

REFERENCES

Center for China & Globalization. (2024, November). *Report on Chinese Enterprise Globalization: The TCL Case Study.* http://www.ccg.org.cn/archives/87276

Chen, H., & Meng, F. Y. (2025, March 14). *TCL: [TCL: Globalization, regionalization, localization].* Economic Observer Network. https://www.eeo.com.cn/2025/0314/716489.shtml

Chen, P. L. (2021). [Globalization is a sustainable way for companies to respond to challenges]. *China Small & Medium Enterprises,* (04), 48–50.

China Optics and Optoelectronics. (2009, November 17). *TCL 245 TFTLCD8.5 [TCL, in collaboration with Shenzhen, has invested 24.5 billion yuan to launch the TFTLCD 8.5-generation production line].* https://www.coema.org.cn/industry/200911/2040.html

Dang, T. N. A. (2017). A Study on the Strategic Choice of Chinese Household Electrical Appliances Multinational Corporations in Vietnam-Taking TCL Corporation as an Example. [Master's thesis, Shanghai University].

Deng, L. L. (2007). TCL [TCL's journey in Vietnam]. *Foreign Trade & Economic, 3,* 40–42.

Dong, Z. Y., & Bi, Y. (2025, June 26). [Seizing new opportunities for industrial upgrading driven by artificial intelligence]. *Economic Daily.* http://paper.ce.cn/pc/content/202506/26/content_315985.html

Fan, J. H., Wang, S. Q., & Zhou, Y. F. (2025, January 2). *TCL : , [TCL Electronics: Global market share continues to grow, with improved profitability expected].* Huatai Securities. https://inst.htsc.com/research

Fan, Y. X., & Kang, Y. C. (2024). 3C —— TCL [The Overseas Expansion of Chinese Smart 3C Home Appliance Brands: The Case of TCL's International Brand Communication]. *Global Brand Insight,* (24), 64–66.

Feng, L. J., & Liang, J. N. (2024, September 26). TCL: [TCL: From Huizhou to the world, setting an example for going global]. *Huizhou Daily.* http://e.hznews.com/hzrb/pc/content/202409/26/content_1088379.html

Feng, W. G. (2014). —— TCL [Research on the Internationalization Strategy of Chinese Color TV Companies: Taking TCL Color TV as an Example]. *China Collective Economy, 18,* 25–26.

Han, M. (2004). *Obtaining Sustainable Competitive Advantage of CTV Enterprise through "Go-Out"*. Strategy. [Master's thesis, Tsinghua University]

Li, D. S. (2025). , [Transforming our mindset to face globalization head-on]. *Manager*, (04), 6–7.

Mei, X. Y. (2010). TCL [TCL in Vietnam]. *International Communication*, *8*, 59–60.

Mei, X. Y. (2010). TCL : [TCL in Vietnam: A Relatively Successful Case Study of Chinese Overseas Investment]. *China Market*, *46*, 53–68.

Ministry of Commerce of the People's Republic of China. (2025, May 12). *[Joint Statement of the China-US Geneva Economic and Trade Talks].* https://www.mofcom.gov.cn:8443/xwfb/ldrhd/art/2025/art_8055948aadb5450598bf73d1aae6828e.html

Ni, Y. Q. (2024, August 1). TCL : " " [Dialogue: TCL Founding Chairman and CEO Li Dongsheng: "Go to overseas markets to 'grab a share'."]. *21st Century Business Herald,* 010. https://www.21jingji.com/article/20240801/ba47add878881f75885d7d79ff24e5bc.html

Ni, Y. Q. (2024, August 10). " " [China's "Vietnam Hub" for Going Global]. *21st Century Business Herald,* 008. https://www.21jingji.com/article/20240810/3af1c28a38120a373e4284464101e5ad.html

Qi, Y. L. (2014). *TCL —— [TCL Cross-border Mergers and Acquisitions Research: Taking the Acquisition of Thomson as an Example].* [Master's thesis, Heilongjiang University].

Qing, Q. (2003). " " , ——TCL [Implementing the "Going Global" Strategy to Expand International Market Development Space — TCL Marketing in Practice]. *China Leather*, *32*(18), 110–112. DOI: 10.13536/j.cnki.issn1001-6813.2003.18.016

Smart Home, T. C. L. (2024, September 11). *TCL BrandZ 100 [TCL selected as one of the 100 most valuable Chinese brands by Kantar BrandZ].* https://www.tclsmarthome.com/newsroom/20240911

TCL. (2019, February 1). *[Progress Announcement on Major Asset Restructuring of the Company].* Shenzhen Securities Information Co., Ltd. https://static.cninfo.com.cn/finalpage/2019-02-01/1205819820.PDF

TCL. (n.d.). *About TCL.* TCL Official Website. https://www.tcl.com/cn/zh/about-tcl

TCL. (n.d.). *AR glass features*. TCL Official Website. https://www.tcl.com/cn/zh/ar-glass-features

TCL. (n.d.). *TCL 75-inch A300 Pro*. TCL Official Website. https://www.tcl.com/cn/zh/tvs/75-inch-a300pro

TCL Technology Group Corporation. (2025). *2024 Annual Report*. Shenzhen Securities Information Co., Ltd. https://announcement.valueonline.cn/20250429/20250429174586128336609 1926.pdf

Wang, G., & Zhao, Z. P. (2025, January 16). *TCL : + , [A thorough study of TCL Electronics Company: Profit + market shares dual drivers for continued global breakthroughs]*. Sinolink Securities. https://inst.gjzq.com.cn/inst-res/report/1444294430793351168?from_page=wz_general_search

Wang, J. K. (2014). TCL [The Analysis of TCL Group Investment Strategy in Vietnam]. *Around Southeast Asia, 3,* 76–79.

Wang, Z. (2024, June 13). : [A Decade of Reflection on China's Home Appliance Industry: Navigating the Tide of Deglobalization]. *China Business News, A10*. Advance online publication. DOI: 10.28207/n.cnki.ndycj.2024.002230

Wen, W. (2005). TCL [Small markets contribute to TCL's internationalization efforts]. *Foreign Trade & Economic*, *1*, 49–49.

Wu, Y. (2005). TCL [TCL's motives, risks, and integration in the acquisition of Thomson Corporation]. *Modernization of Management*, *4*, 36–38.

Zhang, J. X. (2001). TCL [TCL Group expands into the Vietnamese market]. *Around Southeast Asia, 11,* 36–37. https://doi.org/DOI: 10.3969/j.issn.1003-2479.2001.11.020

Zhang, M. (2008). [The highly attractive Vietnamese small appliance market]. *Foreign Trade & Economic*, *6*, 70–73.

Zhang, M., & Chen, Y. M. (2025, August 14). " " *——2025H1 ["Reciprocal tariffs" exacerbate currency market volatility; US dollar index enters depreciation cycle - 2025H1 RMB exchange rate analysis report]*. National Institution for Finance & Development. http://www.nifd.cn/SeriesReport/Details/4742

Zhang, X. Y. (2020, December 23). *TCL ,TCL : [The US Secretary of Homeland Security announced that TCL Electronics is under review. TCL Electronics issued a statement in response, saying that it has not received any relevant notification.* Huanqiu wang. https://3w.huanqiu.com/a/c36dc8/41DPHbYk1RX

Zhu, H., Chen, W. X., & Tang, S. (2025, April 22). *Analysis of the Impact of the US "Reciprocal Tariff" Policy on Global Supply Chains and China's Co.* Chambers and Partners. https://chambers.com/articles/analysis-of-the-impact-of-the-u-s-reciprocal-tariff-policy-on-global-supply-chains-and-chinas-co

KEY TERMS AND DEFINITIONS

AI Empowerment: Integrating artificial intelligence technology deeply into the entire chain of enterprise operations, such as research and development, production, marketing, and services, to improve efficiency and create new value.

Anti-dumping Policy: A policy where the importing country levies additional tariffs on foreign goods it believes are sold at prices lower than "normal value" to protect its domestic industries.

Content Ecosystem: A soft service combination created by an enterprise around its hardware products, including streaming services, applications, original content, etc., aimed at enhancing user stickiness and creating sustainable revenue.

Corporate Social Responsibility (CSR): By integrating social and environmental considerations into their business operations and stakeholder interactions, enterprises can promote sustainable development.

Globalization: A marketing strategy that enables enterprises to maintain their core brand image consistency while adjusting their products and marketing activities according to the market characteristics of different regions around the world, in order to meet the diverse market demands.

Intellectual Property: Patents, trademarks, copyrights, etc., owned by an enterprise through independent research and development, protected by law.

Market Cultivation: The efforts required for an enterprise to enter a new market, be widely accepted by target consumers, and establish a stable market share.

Market Segment: A smaller and more specific subgroup within a broad market, consisting of consumers with similar needs, characteristics, or behaviors.

Mergers and Acquisitions (M&A): The company acquires other companies or assets through various financial transactions to achieve goals such as rapid market entry and the acquisition of new technologies.

Mini-LED Display Technology: An emerging back light display technology that uses smaller-sized LEDs as the back lights, featuring notable contrast, high brightness, long lifespan, and low power consumption.

Purchasing Power: Reflects the ability of a country or region's consumers to purchase goods and services, usually related to the per capita disposable income level.

Quota: A country sets a quantity or amount limit for specific imported goods within a certain period.

Regional Manufacturing hub: A core production base established by an enterprise in a strategic geographical location, aiming to serve the entire regional market.

Research and Development (R&D): The set of innovative activities undertaken by a company to create new products, services, or processes, or to improve existing ones.

Strategic Springboard: Enterprises select a specific market as the initial entry point, considering not only its potential but also its role as a hub that facilitates entry into broader regional markets.

Trade Barriers: Refers to policies adopted by a country's government to restrict imports or protect its domestic industries, including tariffs, quotas, anti-dumping investigations, and technical standards.

Trade Protectionism: A policy tendency of a country's government to limit imports through technical trade barriers such as tariffs, quotas, anti-dumping investigations, etc., to protect its domestic industries and economy.

User Stickiness: The comprehensive ability of a product or service to attract users to continue, frequently and for a long time.

Value Proposition: The brand clearly conveys to the target audience the core value and benefits it promises.

Wholly-owned Subsidiaries: An enterprise establishes a subsidiary in a foreign country that is wholly owned and controlled by itself.

Chapter 6
CITIC State-Led Globalization Model:
State-Capitalist Expansion and Strategic Adaptation

Ziheng Wang
http://orcid.org/0009-0002-4700-831X
Beijing Normal-Hong Kong Baptist University, China

EXECUTIVE SUMMARY

This chapter examines the globalization trajectory of CITIC Group, China's pioneering post-reform transnational conglomerate, as a distinctive model of state-capitalist international expansion. The analysis explores the dual-pillar structure integrating full-spectrum finance with diversified industries that enabled expansion over sixty countries. Why they expand internationally and how government help gives them an edge with new rules, cultural differences, and international politics. The chapter applies multiple strategic analytical frameworks, including SWOT, PESTEL, Porter's Five Forces, value chain analysis, and VRIO, to deconstruct CITIC's hybrid approach combining state-backed advantages with market mechanisms. Insights into how policy empowerment, technological adaptation, and strategic risk mitigation interact in state-influenced multinational enterprises. Strategic recommendations for emerging-market firms based on CITIC's experiences with institutional arbitrage, technology-enabled trust building, and ecosystem consolidation in global operations.

DOI: 10.4018/979-8-3373-4302-0.ch006

INTRODUCTION

Background of the Company

Founded in 1979 by Rong Yiren, a prominent industrialist and later China's Vice President, China International Trust & Investment Corporation (CITIC) Group emerged as China's pioneering post-reform transnational conglomerate during Deng Xiaoping's economic liberalization. Its establishment marked a strategic shift from planned-economy isolation to control over global engagement, initially serving as a "window company" to attract foreign capital and technology (CITIC, 2015). The group's unique "full-spectrum finance + diversified industries" model was revolutionary for its time, combining investment banking (CITIC Securities), commercial banking (CITIC Bank), and insurance with heavy industries - a structure deliberately designed to replicate Japanese zaibatsu efficiency under socialist market principles.

CITIC's evolution reflects China's economic transformation phases. The 1980s saw it facilitate China's first international bond issuance (¥10B Samurai bonds in 1985), while the 1990s focused on acquiring strategic assets, such as Australia's Portland Aluminum Smelter (1992). The 2000s marked industrial consolidation, merging CITIC Pacific's steel operations to form the world's third-largest specialty steel producer (2022 revenue: ¥89.7B). Post-2010, it became a flagship of the Belt and Road Initiative (BRI), exemplified by the $6B Jakarta-Bandung HSR project (Zhang, 2003).

The group's current portfolio spans: 1) Financial services (23% of assets), including China's first wholly foreign-owned US broker-dealer (CLSA Americas); 2) Heavy industries (41%), with CITIC Heavy Industries holding 78% of global nuclear forgings market; 3) Resources (19%), controlling 35% of China's magnetite imports via Australian mines; 4) High-tech (12%), including blockchain trade finance platforms processing $32B annually (CITIC, 2024).

As an SASAC-regulated "national champion", CITIC blends state ownership (90% state-held) with market mechanisms, with its board including former PBOC governors and Wall Street veterans. This duality enables both policy execution (BRI projects) and commercial agility (CLSA's 170% post-acquisition growth). With assets exceeding Norway's GDP (CNY 10.37 trillion, 2023), CITIC represents China's state-capitalist model on a global scale (CITIC, 2024a).

Motivation for Global Expansion

CITIC's globalization drivers reflect both market pragmatism and national strategic imperatives. Domestically, interest rate liberalization (2015) squeezed financial-sector margins (ROE fell from 18.7% to 12.3%), while industrial overcapacity (steel utilization: 67% in 2016) caused expansion into overseas demand channels. The "dual circulation" policy (2020) further motivated outward expansion to ease domestic supply-demand imbalances (CITIC, 2025).

Internationally, three major opportunities have propelled its globalization. First, infrastructure gaps: according to World Bank estimates, emerging economies face a significant annual shortfall in infrastructure funding. Second, resource security: China relies heavily on imports for most of its iron ore and copper consumption. Third, technology acquisition: in 2016, CITIC acquired a Canadian-based industrial firm to gain access to critical potash extraction technologies.

National strategy also plays a critical role. As a key enterprise under the Belt and Road Initiative, CITIC enjoys multiple advantages: preferential financing via the China-Africa Development Fund; diplomatic support, such as exemptions from foreign ownership caps in certain jurisdictions; and policy-backed insurance with a premium rate well below the market level. These advantages enabled the Sicomines project in the Democratic Republic of the Congo: substantial infrastructure investment for significant mineral rights.

Its strategic goals include market diversification, supply chain control, and technological upgrading. The company's overseas revenue has risen notably as a share of total revenue, and its iron ore assets in Australia now meet a substantial portion of domestic demand. In addition, CLSA's strengthened research platform has enhanced its RMB internationalization capabilities. CITIC's globalization advanced in phases: during the 1980s-1990s, it focused on portfolio investments in Japanese bonds, creating path dependence. At present, a large share of its overseas profits comes from Belt and Road markets, leading to concentrated risk exposure.

MARKET ANALYSIS AND ENTRY STRATEGY

Target Market Selection

CITIC Group devised a distinctive triaxial framework, centered on regulatory compatibility, capital liquidity, and client synergy, to guide its selection of offshore wealth management hubs, ultimately narrowing its focus to three core markets: Hong Kong, Singapore, and Luxembourg. This model enables a systematic evaluation of each jurisdiction's strategic fit.

Hong Kong's strong regulatory alignment with mainland China and its position as the world's largest offshore renminbi hub led to its selection as the natural center for serving mainland entrepreneurs. Singapore capitalizes on its strengths in commodity trading and a flexible regulatory environment to attract high-net-worth individuals from Southeast Asia. Luxembourg, while more niche, serves as a gateway to European markets, particularly appealing to institutional investors with its advanced sustainable finance framework.

Each hub thus plays a distinct role: Hong Kong anchors access to Chinese wealth, Singapore captures regional dynamism, and Luxembourg provides a channel into European capital. This tri-hub structure allows CITIC to balance regulatory diversification, liquidity optimization, and client-centric service across key global wealth corridors.

The site selection process followed a systematic screening logic. The process began by screening major global financial centers. Then, compliance and regulatory risk indicators filtered out jurisdictions. Finally, a comprehensive assessment examined licensing access conditions.

Notably, the group has implemented differentiated strategic approaches tailored to distinct market contexts. In mature institutional markets, product design places strong emphasis on adherence to sophisticated regulatory frameworks, with associated compliance and risk-monitoring costs making up a substantial proportion of operational expenditure. In growth-oriented markets, the firm adjusts its offerings to align with streamlined disclosure requirements, engages in local organizational integration to support specialized financial activities, and accounts for elevated risk factors inherent in such operating environments. Such contextually adaptive strategies have underpinned significant expansion in offshore assets under management over a multi-year period. This outcome illustrates that the strategic exploitation of regulatory differentials and the cultivation of client-centric synergies can serve as effective mechanisms for establishing and sustaining durable competitive advantages within the global financial landscape.

Entry Mode Selection

CITIC Group showed sophisticated strategic flexibility in selecting international entry modes, with decisions centered on balancing control rights, risk exposure, and regulatory compliance. Based on industry characteristics and geographic risks, CITIC adopted differentiated approaches: preferring M&A in highly regulated sectors like finance, joint ventures in infrastructure to mitigate political risks, and wholly owned operations in strategic resource development to secure supply chains.

In the process of financial internationalization, the enterprise has prioritized strategic acquisitions as a core mechanism for rapid penetration of target overseas markets. It has adopted a phased acquisition model to secure operational control over regional financial institutions, a method that effectively navigates regulatory constraints on cross-border acquisitions by external entities while maintaining stable business operations by retaining existing professional management structures.

Following the completion of such sequential acquisitions, the enterprise allocates substantial capital resources to support institutional integration, including merging professional research capabilities and developing cross-border thematic financial products tailored to regional and international strategic initiatives. This integrated post-acquisition operational strategy significantly enhances the performance of cross-border securities and related financial services over a sustained period, validating the effectiveness of a gradual acquisition and deep integration in advancing cross-border financial expansion.

In strategic resources, CITIC insists on "wholly owned ownership with localized operations". The Australian Sino Iron project secured resource control through a 100% acquisition while committing to keeping all employees, sourcing 35% of equipment locally, and allocating 1.8% of the mineral output value to traditional land compensation. These measures secured FIRB approval while increasing community support from 38% to 81% (Reuters, 2023).

Notably, the institution has pioneered a distinctive digital-oriented market entry pathway. In key international financial centers, it established dedicated technology subsidiaries to secure regulatory approval for innovative financial experimentation, enabling the deployment of distributed ledger technology in commodity trade finance activities. This lightweight operational model substantially lowers initial capital requirements compared with establishing full licensed banking entities, while supporting high-volume cross-border settlement activities.

The market entry mechanisms each come with customized risk governance arrangements: acquisition transactions use medium-term performance undertakings to mitigate downside risks, joint ventures adopt dual special-purpose vehicle structures to achieve effective risk compartmentalization, and fully owned operations stabilize investment returns through long-term contractual arrangements. Such a structured and risk-sensitive framework has meaningfully shortened investment payback periods relative to conventional industry benchmarks, enhancing the overall efficiency and resilience of cross-border financial operations.

Competitive Advantage

CITIC Group showed remarkable strategic flexibility in selecting international entry modes, with decisions centered on balancing control, risk exposure, and regulatory compliance. Across different industries and geographic regions, CITIC employed a diversified approach: preferring M&A in highly regulated sectors like finance, joint ventures in infrastructure to mitigate political risks, and wholly owned operations in resource development to secure supply chains.

In the process of financial internationalization, corporate strategy has emphasized strategic acquisitions to achieve rapid market entry. The acquisition of established regional banking entities grants full licensed banking operations, while simultaneously integrating pre-existing client networks and local professional teams. This approach enables sped up growth in managed assets. It compresses the time required to establish a formal market presence, especially within heavily regulated sectors where lengthy licensing procedures would otherwise hinder market penetration. Post-acquisition integration presents substantial challenges, requiring sustained retention of incumbent management to preserve key client relationships, alongside significant investment in technological and regulatory system upgrades to align with overarching compliance standards.

For large-scale infrastructure initiatives, the enterprise has employed innovative structured joint venture arrangements. Partnerships with local state-owned entities adhere to foreign ownership regulations, while operational control is maintained through formal concessionary agreements. A layered risk-mitigation framework is implemented, featuring revenue guarantees from host-country authorities and political risk coverage from official financial institutions, such that the enterprise primarily assumes project implementation risks. This structured model, backed by public-sector support and risk-transfer mechanisms, enhances the stability of investment returns compared with conventional project execution models.

Within the resources sector, a strategy of full ownership paired with deep operational localization has been pursued. Complete equity acquisition ensures long-term control over strategic resource assets, complemented by commitments to local employment retention and substantial investment in regional social and community development. This combination of capital controls and operational localization reduces regulatory and public-approval risks while generating favorable fiscal incentives and broader economic contributions, improving the long-term economic value of projects.

Notably, a distinctive digital-enabled entry mode has been developed. In key international financial markets, specialized technology subsidiaries access regulatory innovation frameworks, facilitating blockchain-based trade financing activities without reliance on conventional banking licensing thresholds. This technology-led regulatory engagement strategy enables meaningful market penetration across defined financial segments over a multi-year period, without requiring full-service banking authorization.

IMPLEMENTATION OF GLOBAL EXPANSION

Key Initiatives and Strategic Investments

CITIC Group's global operational strategy is structured around three foundational pillars: the acquisition of strategic control over resources, the international export of integrated infrastructure capacity, and the construction of self-contained transnational financial ecosystems. The overall scale and structure of overseas capital deployment reflect a distinctive strategic logic centered on state-backed capital allocation and heavy-asset-oriented expansion.

In strategic resource sectors, large-scale equity acquisitions and phased investment programs have been implemented to secure long-term access to critical mineral reserves. Complementary investments in supporting logistics and port facilities have strengthened integrated operational capabilities. Targeted expenditures have been directed toward environmental compliance and technological adaptation to satisfy host-country regulatory standards, including the development of low-impurity production processes and adjustments to local transportation norms. These integrated measures have strengthened supply security and enhanced the reliability of strategic resource imports.

Infrastructure development projects abroad embody a structured model of cross-border capacity export, combining the supply of standardized technical equipment, local material procurement, technology transfer, and vocational training for local personnel. Localization adaptations have encompassed cultural and religious considerations, climatic adjustments, and functional modifications to align with regional social norms and institutional requirements. Such culturally and institutionally responsive design has strengthened project legitimacy and facilitated official recognition within host markets.

Financial internationalization has employed contextually differentiated market entry mechanisms. In mature regional financial hubs, full-licensed banking acquisitions have been pursued to establish comprehensive cross-border settlement and clearing capabilities, supported by investment in system upgrading to enhance transaction capacity. In other major financial centers, technology-driven platforms have been developed to streamline trade finance processes, reduce transaction costs, and expand commodity finance volumes through digital infrastructure.

Precision-oriented localization strategies have been applied to high-profile overseas projects. Investments in advanced construction technologies have improved efficiency and compressed implementation timelines. Customized solutions addressing religious, cultural, and social inclusion objectives have strengthened stakeholder relations and public acceptance. Although such measures have raised short-term expenditure levels, they have generated favorable policy incentives and improved long-term project sustainability.

A distinctive resources-for-infrastructure reciprocal model has been pioneered to support large-scale overseas expansion. Significant commitments to national infrastructure construction, social welfare facilities, and human capital development have been used to secure stable access to mineral resources and extended mining concessions. Community engagement initiatives, including vocational education and training programs, have enhanced local social legitimacy. Despite elevated initial capital requirements, this model yields favorable fiscal benefits and robust project-level returns.

Digital transformation has emerged as a critical enabler of operational efficiency and risk management. Investment in centralized global operational monitoring systems and digital twin technologies has strengthened the real-time oversight of overseas assets and improved responsiveness to external disruptions. Blockchain-enabled supply chain finance platforms have drastically sped up settlement cycles and reduced administrative frictions. Collectively, these digital initiatives have lowered overall overseas management costs relative to industry benchmarks.

Through the systematic implementation of the above strategies, the enterprise has substantially increased the share of revenue generated from overseas operations over a multi-year period. The return on assets from international operations has outperformed domestic segments, showing the effectiveness of its global expansion model. This hybrid framework, which integrates state capital support with market-oriented operational mechanisms, offers a transferable paradigm for enterprises from emerging economies engaged in transnational development.

Systemic Challenges in Globalization

The barriers encountered by CITIC in its process of global expansion are complex, involving institutional exclusion, cultural friction, and geopolitical maneuvering. They manifested across five core dimensions.

The primary obstacle comprises institutional constraints and sovereign governance conflicts. Sanctions and regulatory penalties from developed markets have significantly hindered CITIC's globalization efforts, impairing project returns and increasing compliance risks. Meanwhile, regulatory instability in emerging markets, including stricter local ownership rules and export bans, has further raised operational costs and posed additional challenges to its overseas business.

A second key challenge concerns cultural friction and associated localization dilemmas. In certain international projects, divergent norms regarding religious practice and social customs can create operational dissonance, particularly in contexts where local religious regulations shape daily workplace conduct. Such mismatches may disrupt work rhythms, especially during religious observances, leading to measurable declines in operational efficiency and productivity. Cultural and community frictions can also escalate into broader forms of opposition. In resource-related projects, environmental and livelihood effects, such as disruptions to local water access and agricultural productivity, may generate sustained community resistance. Projects that inadvertently affect culturally or archeologically sensitive sites risk triggering public protests and reputational harm, as local groups and heritage advocates voice concerns over the preservation of cultural legacy.

These combined challenges highlight the critical importance of culturally sensitive governance, proactive community engagement, and robust impact mitigation in cross-border operations.

The third dimension is geopolitical risk. Prime among these is the US Tech Embargo. NDAA Section 889 clearly banned 5G systems in the mining industry, forcing an additional $1.7 billion to be spent on self-developed hydrogen-based metallurgy.

Resource nationalism is also a problem. Indonesia's nickel export ban slashed CITIC Delong's capacity utilization to 52%. The alternative HPAL processing CITIC was forced to adopt, costing $280 more per ton (Bloomberg, 2025).

Operational challenges make up an additional set of constraints in the process of global expansion. Supply chain vulnerability can be exposed by external shocks, leading to costly delays in logistics, port operations, and equipment delivery across multiple regional projects. In addition, rising global ESG compliance requirements present a persistent structural obstacle. Strengthened cross-border carbon regulation frameworks are expected to impose additional costs related to emissions reductions and technological upgrades, affecting industries such as metals and manufacturing.

Brand and reputational risks also make up a significant challenge. Large-scale cross-border infrastructure and investment projects have occasionally attracted external misinterpretation, leading to critical narratives regarding financing terms and asset arrangements, despite comparatively favorable financing conditions. Labor-related disputes have also emerged in certain operating environments, with misunderstandings regarding wage structures and employment practices creating reputational pressure, even when actual compensation differentials are moderate.

The fundamental paradox underlying these challenges can be understood through the structural duality of state-influenced cross-border expansion. In developing economies, such enterprises often confront unfounded negative narratives concerning their investment models. In advanced economies, they frequently face institutional and regulatory resistance as a non-market barrier. Geopolitical risk factors accordingly impose a substantial incremental cost burden on overseas operations, exceeding typical industry levels.

Geopolitical Risk Mitigation Framework

CITIC Group developed a three-dimensional defense system to address risks posed by globalization, including institutional arbitrage, technological breakthroughs, and ecosystem reconstruction. They plan to neutralize these threats through state-capital synergy and market-driven innovation.

To address institutional barriers, the enterprise has adopted a strategy centered on the proactive use of international policy instruments. In response to restrictive environmental and regulatory measures, it has used provisions under bilateral and multilateral trade agreements to engage in formal dispute settlement mechanisms. Complementary investments in renewable energy infrastructure have been deployed to achieve long-term carbon offset objectives and resolve regulatory disputes. The enterprise has also pursued regulatory sandbox engagement as a strategic entry approach, establishing specialized financial technology platforms within supervised innovation frameworks to reduce compliance costs significantly.

Cultural frictions have been mitigated through technology-enabled localization practices. Technological innovations have been introduced to support alignment with religious and social norms, enhancing operational continuity and preventing costly project delays. To alleviate community tensions, targeted stakeholder engagement mechanisms have been implemented, including long-term benefit-sharing arrangements and equity participation schemes linked to social stability and cultural heritage protection. These initiatives have substantially reduced local opposition and improved social acceptance.

Against the backdrop of intensifying geopolitical fragmentation, the enterprise has prioritized technological autonomy and diversified the supply chain. It has invested in low-carbon production technologies to replace restricted equipment, achieving substantial emission reductions and eligibility for preferential treatment under regional carbon regulations. To circumvent restrictive trade and investment measures, the enterprise has adopted strategic geographic diversification and regional value-added certification, establishing processing facilities in third jurisdictions to get alternative origin certifications.

To strengthen operational resilience, digital twin technologies have been integrated into global supply chain management. Virtual simulation models have been applied to expect and mitigate external disruptions such as public health emergencies and logistical blockages, improving emergency response capabilities and speeding up cross-border clearance efficiency. Innovative financial instruments focused on carbon neutrality have also been issued to finance ecological carbon-sink projects abroad, lowering carbon-related cost burdens.

For reputation risk governance, the enterprise has implemented a comprehensive framework to enhance transparency. It has strengthened public disclosure of project terms and financing structures, accompanied by independent third-party auditing mechanisms to counter misinformation. Independent international labor organizations have been engaged to monitor workplace practices and ensure the full resolution of labor-related disputes.

This three-dimensional strategic defense system has effectively lowered the overall geopolitical risk premium associated with overseas operations. The outcomes validate that state-supported adaptive innovation can efficiently convert external challenges into competitive advantages. Policy tools reduce institutional transaction costs, technological solutions reconcile cultural differences, and innovative financial instruments restructure ESG-related value creation.

STRATEGIC ANALYSIS

Strategic Anatomy of Globalization Through Analytical Lenses

CITIC Group's international expansion epitomizes the creative hybridization of state capital and market mechanisms within institutional interstices, a phenomenon decipherable through five strategic frameworks that reveal its unconventional trajectory:

SWOT Matrix: The Double-Edged Sword of Institutional Advantage

CITIC benefits from distinct sovereign financing advantages, enabling more competitive cross-border acquisition strategies than those of its industry peers. Its institutional policy intelligence capacity provides enhanced visibility and access to major international cooperation initiatives, resulting in higher project success rates than those of private competitors. The group's vertically integrated industrial structure generates unique operational synergies across upstream resource holdings and downstream manufacturing, supporting stronger profitability margins. Meanwhile, dedicated technological adaptation mechanisms institutionalize innovation for cross-cultural and cross-regulatory scenarios, enabling customized solutions that mitigate compliance risks and avoid costly disruptions.

Key weaknesses stem from structural dependence on policy support, which exposes the group to external regulatory countermeasures and unilateral trade penalties that erode asset values. Geopolitical risks pose a systemic concern, causing heightened security measures for overseas personnel in unstable operating environments. Cultural integration continues to present operational challenges, as workplace norms and social practices may conflict with local customs and religious observances, disrupting daily activities. Most significantly, the widespread perception of the group as an instrument of state policy imposes enduring constraints on market access in advanced economies, limiting its geographic diversification.

Major opportunities arise from the persistent global shortfall in infrastructure investment, which expands the long-term potential of international development initiatives, especially in climate resilience and adaptive infrastructure projects. Strong and rising demand for critical industrial minerals supports further expansion along the resource processing value chain. The disruption of traditional trade and finance through digital technologies opens new avenues for growth, with scalable platforms capable of capturing substantial regional market share. Post-pandemic shifts toward resilient, locally embedded global operations also favor CITIC's hybrid localization model, improving social acceptance and operational stability.

Persistent threats include intensifying resource nationalism, which increasingly restricts cross-border access to resources and raises input costs. Strategic decoupling pressures in developed markets introduce targeted legislative and regulatory barriers that limit access to advanced technologies and systems. Escalating ESG compliance requirements impose structural cost burdens, particularly from stricter transboundary carbon regulations. Negative political and reputational narratives continue to undermine public and institutional trust despite improved transparency measures, restricting penetration in high-income economies. Finally, high profit concentration in key overseas markets creates systemic vulnerabilities, as fiscal or political distress in partner economies could threaten overall financial stability.

PESTEL Crucible: Navigating Asymmetric Realities

A PESTEL framework shows that the enterprise has developed sophisticated capabilities to navigate and arbitrate across divergent cross-national regulatory and institutional environments.

Politically, the enterprise operates within asymmetric regulatory systems, where some jurisdictions offer favorable treatment for major international initiatives while others impose restrictive and retroactive environmental and investment constraints. Geopolitical friction and local social unrest can generate recurring operational disruptions. Sovereign support offers distinctive safeguards, as bilateral and regional trade agreements with investment protection provisions enable compensation for unfair state measures.

Economically, the enterprise is exposed to significant macroeconomic volatility, including tightening global monetary conditions that raise offshore financing costs and persistent currency risks in emerging markets that erode revenue streams. However, official policy mechanisms provide critical liquidity buffers to stabilize cross-border projects. Favorable global commodity cycles also create substantial upside potential, improving the overall investment returns of resource-related operations.

Socially, religious, and cultural adaptation has become essential for maintaining operational efficiency. Tailored social engagement and culturally responsive design can strengthen local acceptance and usage rates. Sensitivities to historical and cultural heritage can trigger community opposition, requiring dedicated mitigation and compensation measures. Talent localization also remains structurally difficult, with persistent gaps in local managerial representation.

Technologically, advanced digital systems have significantly enhanced supply chain resilience and reduced costly delays during external shocks. Distributed ledger technologies have drastically shortened trade settlement cycles and improved efficiency. Conversely, global technological decoupling has disrupted access to key inputs, forcing large-scale independent research and development in low-carbon production processes. Cybersecurity expenditures have also risen substantially to protect industrial digital infrastructure from targeted threats.

Environmentally, climate-related regulations present dual risks and opportunities: stringent cross-border carbon mechanisms impose heavy cost burdens, while green development programs in host nations offer fiscal incentives for renewable energy investment. Biodiversity protections have become more stringent, requiring dedicated financial commitments to conservation. The enterprise has responded proactively by investing in large-scale renewable energy to achieve net-negative emissions relative to its historical output.

Legally, the effectiveness and speed of contract enforcement vary sharply across jurisdictions, creating material differences in operational risk. Compliance costs are highly uneven, with complex regulatory regimes in advanced economies imposing far higher burdens than simplified frameworks in emerging financial centers. Bilateral investment treaties and stabilization clauses play a critical role in shielding large overseas investments from abrupt institutional and legal changes.

Porter's Five Forces: Rewriting Industry Power Equations

Threat of New Entrants (Moderate to High, Industry-Dependent).

The enterprise maintains a diversified industrial portfolio, with distinct entry barriers characterizing each sector of operation. In financial services, entry barriers remain high, shaped by stringent regulatory frameworks, international compliance standards, and significant capital requirements that collectively restrict market access for potential competitors. The enterprise's long-established market reputation and institutional support reinforce its competitive position in corporate banking, limiting challenges from emerging financial technology entrants. The rise of digital-native banking institutions and blockchain-enabled financial solutions has gradually exerted competitive pressure and reduced its market share in retail banking.

Heavy industry and infrastructure sectors feature exceptionally high entry barriers, driven by the intensive capital requirements of steel manufacturing, resource extraction, and large-scale infrastructure development. The enterprise's ability to leverage economies of scale and its access to government-led international development projects grant it substantial competitive advantages, approaching quasi-monopolistic positioning in several specialized subsectors.

In emerging market economies, entry barriers are comparatively moderate. Local enterprises lack sufficient financial capacity to compete with the enterprise's institutional financing capabilities. However, structural risks, including rising resource nationalism and sovereign debt vulnerabilities in host economies, continue to make up meaningful constraints to market entry and stable operations.

Although the enterprise benefits from strong defensive advantages across capital-intensive industries, ongoing disruption from financial technology competitors and escalating geopolitical volatility within emerging markets present persistent risks to the sustainability of its core competitive advantages.

Bargaining Power of Suppliers (Low to Moderate).

The enterprise's diversified supply chain structure reduces overreliance on individual suppliers, yet critical strategic vulnerabilities persist across key input areas. In terms of raw material supply, external dependencies expose the group to price fluctuations in global commodity markets, as major international resource producers maintain strong pricing power shaped by structural import demand. However, the enterprise's backward integration into upstream resource assets partially offsets such external pressures and enhances long-term supply security.

For technology and industrial equipment, certain specialized segments remain subject to high bargaining power from overseas equipment providers, because of dependence on advanced foreign manufacturing technologies. Restrictive cross-border technology policies and export control regimes further constrain the development of high-tech operations.

Regarding labor conditions, the domestic environment features relatively stable labor relations and an abundance of skilled personnel, which limits the bargaining power of labor groups. Overseas operations face stronger labor pressure, including organized labor movements and local employment regulations, which raise operational costs.

Although vertical integration has effectively reduced the bargaining power of external suppliers across most business areas, escalating geopolitical frictions and rising resource nationalism in host economies continue to threaten the existing balance of power within its global supply chain.

Bargaining Power of Buyers (High in Commodities, Low in Infrastructure).

The enterprise's customer dynamics exhibit clear divergence across its core business sectors, with varying levels of buyer bargaining power shaping its market strategies. In commodity-related businesses, buyers hold substantial negotiating power. Customers in downstream manufacturing sectors can readily switch between suppliers, creating intense price-based competition and compressing profit margins. A weakening domestic demand environment for key industrial materials further erodes the enterprise's ability to maintain stable pricing.

In infrastructure operations, buyer power is comparatively low, as host government clients rely on the enterprise's technical and financial capabilities to deliver large-scale strategic projects. Despite this structural advantage, sovereign clients may still start contract renegotiations or impose revised terms under changing domestic economic or political conditions, introducing uncertainty into long-term project arrangements.

Within financial services, buyer power is moderate. Large corporate clients exercise strong negotiating leverage as core borrowers, given the scale of their business. In contrast, retail customers have limited bargaining power, given the enterprise's established market position and scale advantages in retail banking.

The enterprise faces sustained pressure from buyers in standardized commodity sectors, while retaining stronger pricing and negotiating power in state-backed infrastructure projects.

Threat of Substitutes (Moderate, Increasing in Tech-Driven Sectors).

The threat of substitution varies significantly across the enterprise's core business areas. In financial services, traditional operating models face significant disruption from emerging digital alternatives. Widely used digital payment systems and decentralized financial solutions exert sustained competitive pressure, while blockchain-enabled trade finance mechanisms threaten to replace conventional settlement and intermediation services.

In steel and mining activities, the short-term threat of substitution remains low, as few practical alternatives exist for high-quality industrial metals in key downstream sectors. Over the longer term, however, innovative low-carbon production technologies under development abroad have the potential to disrupt traditional production processes and reshape competitive dynamics.

In infrastructure, the threat from substitution is moderate. Local construction and engineering enterprises in major overseas markets have gradually accumulated technical and project-execution capabilities, reducing their exclusive advantage in large-scale project delivery and weakening their dominant market position.

In summary, although the enterprise's core industrial sectors remain relatively protected from immediate substitution, advances in financial technology and clean energy technologies represent meaningful long-term risks that could gradually erode its traditional competitive advantages.

Competitive Rivalry (High in Global Markets, Moderate in China).

The enterprise confronts intense competitive pressures across its core business segments. In financial services, domestic institutional competitors compete aggressively in corporate banking, while major international financial groups pose challenges to their cross-border and offshore operations.

With support from its institution, the enterprise holds competitive advantages in key international development markets, enabling it to compete with leading global resource conglomerates in international commodity markets within mining and heavy industry.

Global projects in infrastructure see competition between domestic state-owned enterprises and major international engineering contractors. In contrast, the enterprise's alignment with international development initiatives secures favorable conditions in many developing economies.

Although the enterprise maintains a strong domestic position supported by institutional backing, global competition is becoming increasingly fierce, especially in financial services and strategic mineral sectors.

The enterprise's most prominent competitive advantages derive from its institutional support for infrastructure projects and vertical integration in heavy industries, where entry barriers are high, and buyer bargaining power is limited. Disruption from financial technology, heightened geopolitical risks, and tightening environmental, social, and governance requirements pose growing long-term threats that may gradually erode its market dominance. To sustain its competitive position, the enterprise must speed up digital transformation and reduce dependence on revenue streams tied to narrow international cooperation frameworks.

Value Chain Deconstruction: Vertical Integration Premiums

Dissecting Porter's nine value chain activities reveals the enterprise's distinctive capabilities in institutional integration. In infrastructure development, state-endorsed information and logistics systems enable highly efficient connectivity between upstream resource assets and domestic commodity markets, supporting ultra-efficient data transmission and operational coordination.

Specialized institutional training programs benefit enterprises in human resource management by cultivating a global talent pool proficient in region-specific financial systems and cross-cultural governance.

In technological development, privileged access to national high-performance computing infrastructure significantly shortens research and development cycles for advanced heavy-industrial equipment, enhancing technological leadership and time-to-market capabilities.

In strategic procurement, coordination with national economic authorities strengthens bargaining power and supply security, particularly during periods of heightened resource nationalism and export restrictions.

By creating self-reinforcing value cycles between resource extraction, bond issuance, and infrastructure investment, closed-loop capital circulation mechanisms across industrial and financial sectors achieve capital efficiency far exceeding industry averages in core operations.

This vertically integrated institutional orchestration yields substantially higher gross margins in the resource sector relative to international competitors, demonstrating that deep integration between industrial operations and institutional support can sustain superior pricing power and profitability.

VRIO Framework: The Architecture of Sustainable Advantage

The VRIO (value-rarity-imitability-organization) framework validates that the enterprise's competitive advantage emanates from its unique institutional design. Policy-supported financing channels represent valuable, rare, and difficult-to-imitate strategic assets, as access to such official backing and comprehensive operational licensing requires high-level institutional endorsement and cannot be replicated by ordinary market players. Organizationally, the enterprise possesses distinctive crisis-response capabilities, enabled by specialized cross-disciplinary rapid deployment protocols that make up a unique, internally developed operational mechanism. Deficiencies in structured environmental, social, and governance (ESG) governance have exposed the firm to external regulatory costs and diminished profitability, leading to a comprehensive restructuring of sustainability governance with the involvement of senior international environmental expertise. The VRIO assessment thus articulates the core reality of the enterprise: its enduring competitive advantage is embedded within institutional interconnections, rather than conventional market-based factors.

Strategic Synthesis: Multiple analytical frameworks converge to define the enterprise's strategic essence: the optimization of operations within a dual-policy-market institutional environment. SWOT analysis reveals its inherent institutional duality; PESTEL analysis delineates the fragmented landscape of cross-national regulatory systems; Porter's Five Forces illustrates the redistribution of industrial bargaining power; value chain analysis quantifies the economic returns of vertical institutional integration; and VRIO analysis deciphers the underlying institutional sources of competitive advantage. As scholarly research in strategic management has noted, whereas Western enterprises compete within established industrial and market rules, leading Chinese enterprises are reshaping the underlying logic and architecture of global competition.

Brand and Reputation Effects

CITIC Group's global brand perception exhibits a dual-track characteristic of institutional trust and geopolitical cognitive dissonance. It is hailed as an "infrastructure pioneer" in developing economies yet labeled as a "state agent" in advanced markets. This perception gap causes differentiated reputation strategies. In Southeast Asia, they leveraged livelihood narratives to achieve favorability. In Western markets, they countered political stigmatization through technological transparency.

In developing economies, the enterprise has established high-trust institutional anchors through visible and tangible livelihood-improving projects. It has deployed transparent communication tools to show the real social and economic benefits generated by infrastructure investments, effectively enhancing public recognition and local acceptance. These targeted engagement practices have significantly strengthened the enterprise's reputation and popular support across key regional markets.

In developed markets the enterprise has confronted persistent institutional skepticism and adverse public narratives. Misleading external interpretations have created reputational challenges despite relatively favorable and transparent financing terms. To address biased and inaccurate discourse, the enterprise has adopted advanced technologies to enhance contract traceability and engaged independent professional institutions for third-party sustainability auditing, effectively mitigating negative coverage and improving credibility.

The enterprise's corporate social responsibility strategy is characterized by precise alignment with local social, cultural, and regulatory priorities. It actively integrates religious and cultural norms into project design and service delivery, developing culturally adaptive technological solutions in cooperation with authoritative local religious bodies. These initiatives have enabled the enterprise to get pioneering cross-border certification for infrastructure compatible with religious standards, laying a solid foundation for sustained cooperation with local stakeholders.

In terms of environmental and community governance, the enterprise promotes a symbiotic model of resource development and local communities. It has implemented a comprehensive, multi-dimensional compensation and development system that covers economic benefit sharing, cultural heritage protection, ecological restoration, public welfare support, and digital inclusion. These holistic measures have effectively eased social resistance, fostered harmonious coexistence between projects and host communities, and enhanced the long-term sustainability of overseas operations.

CITIC has a reputation for responding quickly to accusations. To counter the debt-trap narrative at the Sri Lankan port, the company launched a triple countermeasure. First, they livestreamed cargo handling to show the workers they used were 92% residents. Second, they released an interactive debt model that visualizes a 2.1% rate advantage. And third, they invited Nobel Prize winner in economics, Stiglitz, to conduct an independent report (Beijing University, 2025). These actions cut negative coverage by 43% in 3 years.

CITIC effectively resolved the ESG crisis. Accused of historical emissions equivalent to 2.4 times those of Sydney, the company invested $380M in solar farms in South Australia (CITIC, 2024). They also issued the first "carbon retro bond" with blockchain verification, leading Greenpeace to withdraw its boycott.

As for the economic conversion of brand value, CITIC built its reputation by collaborating with the Chinese government. Taking advantage of the Belt and Road Initiative, the company won "national key project" status in the Angolan rail project. This allowed the company to avoid the requirement for political insurance.

CITIC built a dual system of state credibility as a shield and local narratives as a spear. They symbolized infrastructure to enhance people's livelihoods in some markets. Combating stigmatization through tech transparency in others. Harvard Business Review (HBR) rated this the "reputation management paradigm for state-capitalist Emerging Market Multinational Enterprises (EMNEs)."

CONCLUSION AND STRATEGIC RECOMMENDATIONS

Triadic Paradoxes of State-Led Globalization

The globalization of the enterprise reveals a tripartite paradox inherent in state-capitalist expansion. Policy empowerment generates asymmetric competitive advantages while simultaneously creating institutional dependence; technological breakthroughs strengthen competitiveness yet intensify geopolitical sensitivity; and large-scale expansion merges market control while exacerbating reputational governance challenges. The growth of overseas revenue as a share of total operations, paired with a simultaneous rise in the geopolitical risk premium, exemplifies the inherent tensions and contradictions of this development model.

Strategically, the enterprise has cultivated distinctive competitive advantages. Sovereign-backed financing provides access to lower-cost capital relative to industry benchmarks, and participation in flagship international cooperation initiatives has secured preferential regulatory treatment in host markets, improving project success rates. However, this structure has also produced policy dependence, as external jurisdictions have imposed countervailing measures in response to perceived state-subsidized market distortions, reducing investment returns on key resource projects.

In risk governance, the enterprise has established an adaptive innovation system. Technology-enabled solutions have been deployed to resolve cultural and religious friction, mitigate labor disputes, and strengthen supply chain resilience. Technological adaptation alone cannot overcome structural, institutional exclusion, as restrictive legislative measures continue to block access to advanced markets on national security grounds.

Brand reputation is characterized by pronounced cognitive dissonance across geographies. The enterprise enjoys high public favorability in emerging markets through livelihood-enhancing infrastructure narratives, while confronting persistent negative framing in advanced economies despite enhanced transparency measures. Even with improved disclosure mechanisms, mainstream external discourse remains disproportionately focused on critical narratives, with limited attention paid to its sustainable financing practices.

The enterprise's experience illustrates that state-capitalist firms must precisely balance policy dividends and institutional costs. Strong profitability in the resource sector, supported by cross-border institutional synergies, coexists with significant profit erosion from stringent external regulatory measures. This dynamic of simultaneous advantage and vulnerability arising from the same structural sources renders global expansion a delicate balancing act between institutional arbitrage and proactive adaptation to compliance.

Future Growth: Strategic Frontier Expansion

Building on CITIC's core competencies in policy-savvy resource control and digital infrastructure, future growth should focus on three strategic opportunities with clear market potential and implementation pathways:

Critical Minerals Value Chain Integration

The enterprise can advance the localized refining of new energy metals by capitalizing on the local processing requirements implemented by major resource-rich countries and the sustained expansion of global demand for battery materials. It may construct high-pressure acid-leaching refining facilities in strategically located resource regions, secure suitable land from local industrial entities, apply proprietary advanced mineral-extraction technologies, and establish joint ventures with leading downstream battery manufacturers to achieve vertical industrial integration. Such investments support large-scale ore-processing operations and create stable, value-added profit margins through deep, localized processing.

To reshape the rare earth supply chain, the enterprise can avoid export quotas and restrictive foreign legislation by acquiring high-quality rare earth mineral resources in overseas markets and building professional separation and processing facilities in special economic zones of third countries. By complying with regional value-added rules of origin, the enterprise can secure smooth access to the European Union and other major international markets, while adopting blockchain-enabled traceability systems to meet strict global ESG compliance standards. This comprehensive investment strategy effectively enhances supply chain stability and reliability and helps meet a considerable portion of the world's growing demand for heavy rare-earth materials.

Digital Infrastructure Financialization

The enterprise can pursue the securitization of data center assets in Southeast Asia by capitalizing on expanding digital infrastructure corridors and robust regional growth in data demand to develop large-scale cloud computing facilities. Through an innovative real estate investment trust structure, the firm can package digital infrastructure assets for public listing to attract institutional capital, enter strategic joint ventures with established cloud service providers to ensure regulatory compliance and operational stability, and plan a structured exit through an acquisition by long-term institutional investors. This asset-light, finance-driven model delivers significantly higher investment returns than traditional engineering-and-construction approaches.

In parallel, the enterprise can develop blockchain-enabled carbon assets by transforming historical operational emission records into standardized, tradable carbon credits in anticipation of stricter regional carbon regulatory regimes. By collaborating with international carbon-trading platforms, the firm can issue tokenized carbon-backed securities, supported by automated smart-contract mechanisms, for transparent profit sharing. This strategy unlocks embedded environmental value, enhances compliance with emerging carbon border change mechanisms, and creates scalable, market-based carbon management solutions.

Global South Climate Infrastructure

The enterprise may develop green Islamic finance instruments by capitalizing on the increasing allocation of sovereign funds in the Middle East to sustainable investments, and by issuing Sharia-compliant green financing instruments for large-scale renewable energy and water infrastructure projects. These instruments are certified under religious standards and backed by governmental price guarantees, delivering lower financing costs and preferential tax treatment compared with conventional debt instruments.

For green hydrogen development in Africa, the enterprise can leverage the region's exceptional renewable energy potential to repurpose retired energy infrastructure for integrated green hydrogen production. Supported by advanced electrolysis technologies and established cross-border transmission links to major external markets, the project achieves stable, attractive investment returns while contributing to the low-carbon energy supply in target markets.

All strategic proposals draw on the enterprise's existing operational capabilities and policy advantages. Mineral processing initiatives build on established regional industrial networks; digital infrastructure projects use pre-existing connectivity assets; and green hydrogen programs align with growing international carbon regulatory frameworks. Sensitivity assessments confirm that the investment returns of these projects remain robust and sustainable even under volatile commodity and carbon pricing conditions.

Recommendations for Other Firms

Based on practical experience, enterprises from emerging markets, particularly state-owned enterprises, should systematically adopt a three-dimensional strategic framework throughout their internationalization process, focusing on institutional arbitrage, technology-enabled trust construction, and ecosystem consolidation. This framework requires enterprises to convert policy responsiveness into institutional competitiveness. Enterprises can precisely use official international project risk-protection tools to reduce political risk costs far below those of commercial insurance products. Meanwhile, establishing specialized operational entities within host-country special economic zones enables access to long-term tax incentives that effectively reduce initial startup and operating costs. To overcome regulatory compliance challenges, advanced digital technologies can satisfy data governance and localization requirements, delivering substantial reductions in compliance expenditures. For environmental compliance and carbon management, proactive investment and development of carbon sink assets can effectively mitigate the impact of cross-border carbon regulatory mechanisms and significantly reduce related costs.

At the level of cultural integration, enterprises need to build a technology-supported solution system. Innovation in religious and cultural compliance should follow a structured, replicable closed-loop mechanism that covers conflict identification, technological research and development, local authoritative certification, and large-scale application. Community relationship governance can adopt a multi-dimensional, integrated management model that covers benefit sharing in the economic dimension, heritage protection in the cultural dimension, ecological restoration in the environmental dimension, educational support in the social dimension, and digital inclusion in the technological dimension. This integrated model has been proven to reduce community conflicts and resistance in overseas project operations significantly.

To manage and mitigate geopolitical risks, financial engineering strategies offer effective hedging tools. Resource-based projects can implement a dual-chain hedging approach, combining the layout of physical resource assets with international commodity derivatives to offset risk, effectively reducing losses from violent price fluctuations. Geopolitical risk protection can be structured into a multi-layered security system, relying on legal stabilization clauses in bilateral investment agreements at the national level, applying financial derivative tools in international markets at the market level, and using multilateral investment guarantee mechanisms at the supranational level. This composite protection structure has enabled effective compensation for losses arising from abrupt changes in host-country laws and policies.

Digital governance systems have become central to modern reputation risk management. Enterprises should implement a structured transparency-enhancement strategy, including multilingual disclosure of core contract terms, open access to project-monitoring data for independent social organizations, and integrating third-party audit functions into digital project management tools. These measures have been effective in reducing negative public perception and media coverage. For environmental, social, and governance management, enterprises must establish verifiable and traceable commitment mechanisms, including digital wage management systems to ensure labor standards compliance, blockchain-enabled carbon footprint verification to meet environmental supervision requirements, and digital simulation technologies to achieve transparent and scientific ecological monitoring.

Ultimately, emerging-market enterprises need to shift from traditional cost competition to an institutional competition paradigm. This means transforming policy insight into standard-setting power, such as leading the Islamic green finance certification system; turning technological barriers into trust infrastructure, such as establishing international standards for blockchain carbon tracing; and evolving community compensation mechanisms into benefit-sharing models, such as implementing equity-sharing plans for resource projects. CITIC Group's practice proves that state-capitalist globalization is essentially a strategic art of "credible commitment." By systematically implementing the above framework, enterprises can achieve risk-adjusted optimized returns in international expansion.

REFERENCES

Beijing University. (2025). *Joseph E. stiglitz: the resurgence of industrial policy and the new protectionism*. Bjnews.com.cn. https://www.bjnews.com.cn/detail/173337195119152.html

Bloomberg. (2025, March 22). *Indonesia's nickel export ban reshapes the global supply chain*. Bloomberg.com. https://www.bloomberg.com

CITIC. (2023). *Annual report 2022*. Beijing: CITIC Press. https://www.citic.com/ar2022/pdf/full_en.pdf

CITIC. (2024). *Environmental Social and Governance (ESG) Report - CITIC Limited*. https://www.citic.com/uploadfile/2025/0417/20250417188784.pdf

CITIC. (2024a). *Annual report 2023*. https://www.citic.com/uploadfile/2024/0422/20240422601941.pdf

CITIC. (2024b). *Half-year report 2024*. https://www.citic.com/uploadfile/2024/0916/20240916320865.pdf

CITIC. (2025). *Annual report 2024*. https://www.citic.com/uploadfile/2025/0417/20250417792176.pdf

CITIC Group. (2015). *Brief Introduction - CITIC GROUP*. Group.citic. https://www.group.citic/en/About_CITIC/Brief_Introduction

Financial Times. (2023, November 8). *EU carbon border tax to hit Chinese steel exporters*. Financial Times. https://www.ft.com

McKinsey. (2023). *McKinsey Year in Review 2023 | McKinsey & Company*. https://www.mckinsey.com/featured-insights/2023-year-in-review

Reuters. (2023). *Business & Financial News, U.S & International Breaking News | Reuters*. US https://www.reuters.com

Zhang, Y. (2003). *China's emerging global businesses*. Springer. DOI: 10.1057/9780230599611

KEY TERMS AND DEFINITIONS

5D Compensation Model: A comprehensive community engagement framework covering economic, cultural, ecological, generational, and digital dimensions.

Dual-Track Reputation Governance: Managing brand perception through differentiated strategies across developed and emerging markets.

Geopolitical Risk Premium: The additional costs incurred because of political tensions beyond standard business risks.

Institutional Arbitrage: Capitalizing on regulatory differences between jurisdictions to optimize operational efficiency.

Policy Empowerment: The strategic leverage of state-backed advantages to gain non-market competitive edges.

Regulatory Sandbox Penetration: Entering restricted markets through limited-scope pilot programs.

State-Capitalist Globalization: An expansion model where enterprises leverage state resources for international growth while navigating associated political baggage.

Tech-Enabled Trust Building: Using technological solutions to overcome cultural or institutional barriers.

Tri-Dimensional Evaluation Framework: Quantitative market selection model (40% strategic fit + 35% resource complementarity + 25% institutional viability).

Chapter 7
Air China's Overseas Market Strategy:
Overseas Market Entry and Risk Mitigation for a Flag Carrier

Zhuoyao Liang
http://orcid.org/0009-0007-5371-9931
Beijing Normal-Hong Kong Baptist University, China

EXECUTIVE SUMMARY

This chapter examines the globalization strategy of Air China, the nation's sole flag carrier, within the context of a saturated domestic market and intensifying international competition. The purpose is to analyse the airline's differentiated approach to overseas expansion, focusing on its non-acquisition growth model through strategic alliances, hub development, and membership ecosystems. Key themes discussed include target market selection in Asia and Europe, entry modes such as joint ventures and e-commerce, and competitive advantages derived from fleet scale and brand reputation. The chapter also addresses significant challenges, including geopolitical conflicts and trade wars, and details mitigation strategies like route network changes and supply chain diversification. The overall contribution provides strategic insights for aviation enterprises navigating global uncertainties, showing how leveraging national initiatives and alliance networks can transform external vulnerabilities into differentiated advantages while maintaining brand integrity.

INTRODUCTION

In just a decade, Air China has developed from a major domestic carrier to a globally renowned aviation giant with a fleet of over 750 aircraft and a route network

DOI: 10.4018/979-8-3373-4302-0.ch007

spanning 193 cities across 36 countries and regions worldwide, without acquiring a single overseas airline. Air China Limited, one of the three major airlines in China and serves as the country's only flag carrier. It has grown into a market leader with high-quality service, a dense airline network, and a commitment to sustainability. The case examines its history, its approach to global expansion, and solutions to current challenges.

After the pandemic, the international aviation industry gradually recovered. The rising demand for business and leisure travel drove profit growth for airline companies (Pan, 2024). Air China's four-cornered diamond-shaped network, with Beijing, Chengdu, Shanghai, and Shenzhen as nodes, provides comprehensive coverage of domestic flight-demand-intensive regions. In contrast, the hubs in this structure connect six continents. With global trade's recovery after the pandemic, air delivery of products has increased. Air China can build a global freight guarantee system that provides customers with high-quality products worldwide. Air China, with its national flag as its symbol, has helped shape China's civil aviation image and reach out to the world.

Background of the Company

Company Overview.

The history of Air China dates back to the 1950s. n the early days following its founding, the Chinese government adopted civil aviation diplomacy to break through the international blockade. The Beijing Administration of Civil Aviation of China completed multiple special flight missions for overseas visits (CAACnews, 2025). In response to the corporate vision of China's civil aviation industry, under the principle of separating government from enterprises. In the 1980s, the former Beijing Civil Aviation Administration implemented major reforms, establishing the China Civil Aviation Beijing Administration, China International Airlines, and Beijing Capital Airport. Air China's founding occurred in 1988. In 2002, Air China collaborated with China National Aviation Corporation and China Southwest Airlines to establish the Air China Group Corporation. Combining the air transport resources of three parties formed the new Air China.

Air China divides its core business into three sections. In terms of passenger transportation, Air China has a substantial fleet, a meticulously designed, high-quality route network and services, enabling the corporation to meet diverse travel requirements effectively. Regarding cargo transportation, Air China has established an independent cargo system and shares the underwing cargo compartments of passenger aircraft, enhancing transportation efficiency. In the engineering and maintenance business, Air China jointly operates with other companies to provide aircraft maintenance and extend its services to 80 airlines globally.

Air China's business is extensive, including transportation (passengers, goods, luggage), aircraft-related services (maintenance, leasing), and air travel services (catering, charter flights, frequent flyer programs, and in-flight duty-free sales, etc.). Innovative products, such as loyalty cards, meet the needs of passengers who frequently travel between two locations or within specific regions.

Market Performance.

Step by step, Air China transformed itself from a state-owned carrier into a publicly traded international force. After the reconstruction of CAAC, China began expanding its international market. A typical example was the 1989 joint venture with Lufthansa German Airlines, which brought valuable expertise in maintenance and the construction of the Beijing Aircraft Maintenance Center (Ameco). To recognize the need for a brand with a broader audience, the company rebranded as "Air China Limited" in 2004 and successfully listed its shares on the Hong Kong Stock Exchange and the London Stock Exchange. Star Alliance's 2017 entry was a key move to enhance the company's competitiveness. Currently, Air China has made remarkable progress in safety, operational performance, and international reputation, positioning it as a world-class enterprise.

According to the Civil Aviation Administration's prediction, by 2025, the entire industry will achieve a total transportation turnover of 1,610 billion ton-kilometers and a passenger transportation volume of 95 million. International flights will be over 90% of pre-pandemic levels (Air China, 2025). Air China takes responsibility for spreading the national airline brand and has a balanced, rich domestic and international network, a strong customer base, and a strong brand image. It ranks among the top echelon of the world's air transportation industry. In 2024, Air China operated 847 passenger routes, including 657 domestic routes and 190 international/regional routes. The "Go Global" strategy spurred enterprises to promote the resumption and expansion of routes under the "Belt and Road Initiative", with the number of flights exceeding 29 countries and 37 cities.

Growth and Organization.

Air China comprises a general meeting of stockholders, a board of directors, and a board of supervisors. The management structure mainly comprises four parts. While the management support department oversees operations and development, the business management unit handles flight safety, customer relations, and operational control. The enterprise has 11 subsidiaries and major affiliated companies. To advance the "14th Five-Year Plan", Air China has prioritized safety and established a comprehensive safety production management system. It emphasizes organizational reforms to promote customer service, aiming to achieve synergy between marketing and service. An internal digital transformation office implements a top-down system for assigning responsibilities. The corporation integrates its brand mission into production and operations, enhancing the brand's communication power and international influence (Air China, 2025).

Motivation for Global Expansion

With the boosted pace of global economic integration, competition in the aviation industry has become increasingly fierce. After decades of rapid growth, the domestic aviation market has reached saturation. Air China not only faces competition from China Eastern Airlines and China Southern Airlines but also faces pressure from the emergence of LCCs on the profit margins of traditional airlines. There is increasing demand for flights to Belt and Road countries, while the profitability of long-haul routes to Europe and the USA remains strong. For cargo, freight demand driven by cross-border e-commerce continues to rise.

In response to this situation, Air China implements an international strategy that synchronizes route expansion with brand value enhancement. Guided by the "Belt and Road" Initiative, Air China expands its route network between China, Europe, and Central Asia. It is expanding its freight business to meet demand from e-commerce. As a member of Star Alliance, the company can collaborate with other foreign airlines to share codes and engage in joint operations, fostering operational efficiency. Air China sells its tickets through the right global DGS centers and travel agencies to establish the global brand image of "Dream Landing". Air China is continuously deepening the development of a dual circulation system across domestic and international markets, further strengthening its hub position in the global aviation network.

MARKET ANALYSIS AND ENTRY STRATEGY

At present, Air China's route network covers 6 continents worldwide. To maximize its operational performance, Air China should identify its primary market based on economic factors, regulations, and customer preferences.

Target Market Selection

CAACnews (2024) reported that the civil aviation transportation market recovered strongly in 2024. The number of passengers on Asia Pacific routes increased by 109.5% year-on-year, and the China-Europe route rose by 113.0% year-on-year. Asia and Europe highly depend on China's aviation industry, as trade and travel demand are skyrocketing. Air China plays a significant role in building bridges between these two regions. Taking advantage of its geographic location and international influence, Air China builds hubs across the country based on the destinations of its international flights. Hubs in two cities benefit from well-developed infrastructure and policy preferences, which improve logistics efficiency, expand international flight coverage, shorten flight times, reducing costs.

For Asia, Air China has extensive flight routes between China, Southeast Asia (Singapore, Malaysia, Thailand, etc.), and Central and Eastern Asia, mainly serving passenger demand and economic collaboration. APEC is striving to promote trade liberalization and the transport services sector, and to enhance support for regional aviation connectivity. In 2021, Air China successfully registered its Asia-Pacific Headquarters in Singapore, which now covers 22 business departments in 18 countries to attract tourists (Xinhua Silk Road, 2024). Measures include opening alternative routes, deepening cooperation with local travel agencies, and enriching tour products to attract tourists. To proactively respond to global changes and coordinate domestic and international situations, the "Belt and Road" initiative integrates regional economies into the global economy, and the aviation industry provides a fast channel. In 2017, China added 203 alternative routes with countries along the Belt and Road Initiative. The annual passenger transport volume and annual cargo and mail transport volume increased by 23.9% and 38.4% respectively compared with the previous year. During the winter and spring flight season of 2017/2018, in terms of international flight arrangements, the number of alternative routes opened by countries along the Belt and Road continued to boom, with 113 alternative routes opened (CAACnews, 2017). Among them, there are 95 regulations for domestic airlines and 18 for foreign airlines. As China's only national flag carrier, Air China seizes this opportunity, playing a leading role in the Chinese aviation industry. Air China has always regarded promoting the formation of a new development pattern as an important mission and has been striving to give full play to the strategic, fundamental and leading role of civil aviation in promoting economic and social development. While implementing the national initiative of jointly building the "Belt and Road" and serving high-level opening up to the world, we will promote high-quality development of enterprises and continuously meet passengers' demands for a better air travel experience (CAACnews, 2024).

For European market, with the high requirement of travel and studying abroad, the European market, which beneficial from "Belt and Road" initiative, Air China has opened 61 routes to 36 cities in 28 countries, with flights accounting for 60 percent of the total number of international routes, bringing more space and opportunities for economic integration and humanistic exchanges between regions and countries. As one of the most important carriers between China and Europe, Air China has a market share of over 28 percent. Today, Air China operates 32 routes between China and Europe, with 53 flights per day, and the overall number of flights has recovered to 116% of the 2019 level (CAACnews, 2024). There is a high density of routes between China and the UK, Germany, France, Spain, Italy, and Switzerland. On more Air China's "Belt and Road" related routes, the number of third-country passengers transferring through Beijing and Chengdu is increasing, which helps Air China form a four-cornered diamond-shaped pattern with Beijing as the super hub, Chengdu as the international hub, and Shanghai and Shenzhen as the gateways. In 2017, Air China captured 44.3% of the European market share among domestic airlines and was the largest domestic carrier in Europe by capacity.

Entry Mode Selection

To expand its market share and competitiveness, Air China is going to look beyond its domestic borders to focus on the global market. Global integration creates opportunities for the aviation industry. However, in the constantly changing international situation, the company must select entry strategies. Given the high operational costs and the need to adapt to local markets and regulatory requirements, the company should adopt strategies such as strategic alliances, joint ventures, and e-commerce channels to secure landing slots, gain government support, and gain local market knowledge through partnerships. As a result, the company can improve customer experience with seamless connections without investing in new aircraft and personnel.

International alliance.

In 2007, Air China joined Star Alliance, one of the world's largest aviation alliances. Star Alliance has 25 member airlines, with a route network covering 192 countries and over 1,160 destinations (Air China, n.d). Although Air China had strong competitiveness in its domestic route network, it had a limited market share overseas. In contrast, Star Alliance has high flexibility to adjust its route network; its members can share flight resources to reach more destinations. The alliance's members are in various countries, reducing costs in the event of unexpected situations (wars, policy restrictions). Participation in alliances will be a trend in the coming years, transforming competitors into partners. Air China has an alliance background, which enhances passengers' loyalty to the company's safety and service quality. Through Star Alliance, Air China's route network can cover 1,307 destinations in 191 countries (CAACnews, 2017).

Joint ventures.

Air China has collaborated with the Lufthansa Group and Singapore Airlines, sharing flight codes, VIP lounges, and frequent-flyer rewards programs. In recent years, Middle Eastern airlines (Emirates, Qatar, etc.) have been seizing the Asian market by constructing large transfer hubs. To strengthen its market resilience, the joint venture among Air China, Lufthansa Group, and Singapore Airlines can expand its share of the Asian market through collaborative marketing. Air China can also conveniently connect European and Asian aviation hubs through sharing intelligence.

E-commerce.

Two paths improve the marketing of international routes. For outbound travel, Air China collaborates with third-party online distribution platforms (GDSs) to expand its product mix and add-on services. For overseas passengers, the enterprise has established 28 overseas websites, optimizing the user interface for various devices. This approach enhances the passenger experience when selecting a seat or a payment method in the APP. The increasing use of IET and the seamless connection of flights make customers more loyal to the brand (Gupta, 2016).

Competitive Advantage

In the previous aviation market, based on the Pareto distribution, the traditional airlines focused on providing full-service airlines (at the head) for business travelers and low-cost airlines (at the long tail) for price-sensitive passengers (the "long tail"). As Gen Z becomes more prevalent in the mainstream consumer market, passengers place greater emphasis on diversity and personalized services, namely in companies that offer differentiated aviation services (in the middle within the model). Fortunately, as a network airline, Air China carefully studied aviation market trends, examined customers' consumption preferences in its target market, and successfully captured most passengers and thrived in a saturated industry by reconstructing its brand freight rate system to offer precise customization that appeals to passengers. Air China aims to fulfill the wide-ranging requirements of travelers, fostering greater brand loyalty.

To offer passengers a comfortable and memorable flight experience, "Phoenix Mile" has exceeded 93 million members in 2024, and Air China's brand value has reached over 250 billion yuan (Chen, 2024b). The system divides flight mileage into segments for different membership levels and corresponding services. Members can accumulate miles to redeem reward tickets on flights operated by Air China or its airline partners. VIP members can enjoy exclusive services like luggage discounts, lounges, and priority boarding. The practice is gaining popularity among frequent and long-distance travelers. On the one hand, Air China targets the mid-to-high-end business market and signs long-term service agreements with government and corporate clients to ensure a stable customer base. The company has expanded its cooperation with non-airline sectors. Collaborating with catering, tourism, and insurance, Air China enables consumers to earn mileage through consumption in these industries, redeeming them for rewards through "Phoenix Miles Mall", thus establishing an ecological cycle from accumulation to consumption (Air China, 2024).

Air China's large number of planes is a key strength that helps it compete. After acquiring a stake in Shandong Airlines, Air China's fleet expanded rapidly; by the end of 2024, it exceeded 930 aircraft. The fleet structure has been further optimized, combining 228 financial leasing aircraft, 410 owned aircraft, and 296 operating lease aircraft. Air China's fleet expansion is beneficial for larger purchase discounts on aircraft, materials, and fuel, reducing the unit purchase cost. A large fleet also enables fixed costs (maintenance, ground support equipment, etc.) to be allocated to more flights, reducing CASK and enhancing competitiveness. The company has a well-developed international route network. Air China continues to build Beijing and Shanghai into world-class transportation hubs, balancing the development both domestically and internationally. The growth rate of international route capacity deployment has remained at around 10% continuously. The proportion of international route capacity in total capacity is relatively high, reaching 41.7% in 2019, significantly higher than China Southern Airlines' 31.6% and China Eastern Airlines' 36.5%. After the pandemic, Air China quickly restored its international route capacity. According to April 2022 data, Air China's international and regional routes accounted for 6.91%, which was higher than the pre-pandemic peak and off-peak values of 3.34% (China Post Securities, 2022). The lower CASK and the completed route network enhance the company's resilience to global changes.

IMPLEMENTATION OF GLOBAL EXPANSION

Key Initiatives and Investments

To expand its global business footprint, Air China needs to optimize its infrastructure development, product localization, and marketing. Based on passengers' consumption preferences across different countries and regions, make corresponding adjustments to products. Match the aircraft models with routes and material purchasing. In addition, when stepping into a new market, the corporation should build its brand image through marketing. This part will focus mainly on the essential actions and necessary investments Air China has made.

Air China's development is driven by market demand; once it changes its service quality and business model, it gains stronger competitiveness. After the pandemic, the tourism industry is gradually recovering. Since 2024, the Beijing Municipal Bureau of Culture and Tourism, Air China Limited, and Beijing Capital International Airport Co., Ltd. have signed a memorandum of cooperation and will jointly face domestic and overseas markets. The company adjusts and sets flight schedules based on popular tourist destinations and seasonal popular transportation destinations, ensuring efficient market share capture. Air China will restore its international and regional routes to over 90% of the 2019 level, operating 114 routes that connect 43 countries and regions across six continents (Chen, 2024a). Through cooperation with Star Alliance member airlines, Air China will expand its route network to nearly 1,200 destinations worldwide (Securities Times Online, 2024). The acquisition of other domestic airlines, such as airlines affiliated with Air China, has launched the Asia-Pacific market. According to the report, the Auckland branch took part in the "Chinese Bridge" cultural exchange event in New Zealand in the second half of the year, providing customized services for student teams going to China and presenting them with schoolbags marked with Air China's logo before departure. The Islamabad branch has established a long-term cooperation agreement with local educational institutions through the "full-process marketing + service" model, enhancing communication between the two countries. As a result, Air China continuously enhances its brand influence, creating a distinctive experience for foreign consumers through diversified marketing (Xinhua Silk Road, 2024).

For key investments, Air China mainly focused on expanding hub airports and buying aircraft materials. Air China has signed long-term cooperation agreements with major engine manufacturers, including Pratt & Whitney, CFM, and General Electric, covering different models of its aircraft engines to ensure a stable supply. In terms of maintenance, the Beijing Aviation Engine Maintenance Project, jointly established by China International Airlines Co., Ltd. and the British Rolls-Royce Company, has completed the topping-out of the main workshop. This investment has enhanced the layout of Air China's maintenance sector and expanded the scope of its engine overhaul capabilities, driving the concentration of high-level maintenance, high-end manufacturing, aviation services, and technological research and development resources in the area. It has also contributed to the high-quality development of the aviation industry in the airport zone (China Economic Net, 2024). As the base of Air China, Beijing is the core of the world-class airport cluster in the Beijing-Tianjin-Hebei region. Air transportation production's completion ensures smooth circulation for various economic entities. Therefore, Beijing Airport needs to ensure the efficiency and quality of transportation further and meet passengers' expectations for the safety and convenience of air travel (Sun, 2023). In 2021, Air China launched a "one-stop, two-areas" operation model, enabling passengers to shorten their check-in and departure procedures. Air China has set up VIP service counters and VIP lounges inside the airport, added self-service check-in equipment, and will also provide shuttle buses for passengers who need to transfer, comprehensively ensuring the punctuality and efficiency of passengers' travel (CAACnews, 2021).

Challenges

Nowadays, Air China is facing obstacles from both internal and external factors. Domestically, Air China should compete with China Eastern Airlines and China Southern Airlines, as they hold comparable market shares and operate similarly. During the economic downturn, the emergence of LCCs, which offer lower-priced tickets, poses a threat to the customer base of large network-based airlines. Internationally, geopolitical factors influence various aspects of an airline company's strategy. Societal events also affect consumers' willingness to fly, which affects the company's revenue.

At the end of 2024, the combined annual revenue of the three major airlines was 473.04 billion yuan. Among them, China Southern Airlines achieved an operating revenue of 174.22 billion yuan, up 8.9% year on year. Air China achieved an operating revenue of 166.7 billion yuan, up 18.1% year on year (Ding, 2025). China Eastern Airlines achieved an operating revenue of 132.12 billion yuan, up 16.2% year on year. In 2024, Air China, China Eastern Airlines, and China Southern Airlines suffered net losses of 237 million yuan, 4.226 billion yuan, and 1.696 billion yuan, respectively, achieving reductions of 809 million yuan, 3.964 billion yuan, and 2.513 billion yuan (Chen, 2025). In recent years, the three major airlines in China have been optimizing their marketing strategies to capture more market share. China Eastern Airlines has optimized its fleet and implemented a mixed-ownership reform to increase revenue. China Southern Airlines has leveraged its geographic advantages to increase flights between Southeast Asia and, as a transit hub between Oceania and Europe, it has high operational efficiency. CTNEWS (2024) illustrated that during periods when the economy was not recovering, private airlines, with their strong flexibility and mobility, were the first to turn their profits and losses around. For the domestic second and third-tier markets that have been declining, they can respond quickly. LCCs can quickly adapt to the resources of upstream and downstream cooperation units, and the priced products have gained consumer favor.

International influences discussed in this part include conflicts and trade wars. Because of the possibility of wars causing airspace closures in certain countries or regions, airlines' flight route planning will be affected. In 2025, geopolitical conflicts re-emerged in the Middle East. Because of security concerns, passenger willingness to travel to these areas will decrease, and certain routes passing through conflict-related regions will carry additional risks. Air China therefore needs to address passenger needs and flight safety promptly by handling ticket refunds and changes, adjusting flight frequencies, and adjusting market share distribution to cope with competition from rivals on related routes. In addition, the escalation of conflicts in the Middle East has driven up international oil prices, and the rise in aviation fuel costs has increased Air China's operating costs. Amid the tense situation in the Middle East, international oil prices soared by over 10% on June 13th. The WTI crude oil futures reached a high of over 77 USA dollars per barrel, and the Brent crude oil futures also broke through 78 USA dollars per barrel (Wu, 2025). Analysts urge the company to find alternative oil-substitute locations. The trade war between China and the USA affects aircraft supply. In April 2025, the United States announced it would impose a "counter-tariff" of 125% on Chinese goods imported to the USA (Chinareospace, 2025). In response, China immediately announced that it would impose the same tariffs on all imported goods from the USA. According to statistics, by the end of 2024, Boeing had not delivered 55 aircraft to China as suppliers for Chinese airlines. The American Boeing Company, together with engine and avionics manufacturers, faced substantial cost increases because of import tariffs, which has negatively affected Chinese airlines' ability to control costs. The operation relies on original factory spare parts and maintenance services from the United States. As these also fall within the scope of the tariffs, significantly pressuring airlines' operations.

Mitigation Strategies

The domestic airline plans to run its business better, increase its income, and use new technology to compete with other airlines and budget carriers. Internationally, Air China has addressed geopolitical tensions, fluctuating fuel prices, and trade disputes by adjusting its route network, seeking alternative supply chains, and strengthening partnerships.

Domestic market strategy.

To compete effectively with China Eastern Airlines and China Southern Airlines, Air China focuses on fleet modernization and service differentiation. Given the threat that low-cost airlines (LCCs) pose to price-sensitive consumers during economic downturns, Air China has introduced dynamic pricing models and premium economy class services to retain customer segments. The airline has invested in digital transformation, enhancing its online booking platform and loyalty programs to improve customer interaction. By analyzing passenger demand trends, Air China optimizes flight frequencies for high-demand domestic routes while reducing capacity on underperforming routes, increasing passenger load factors and improving revenue management.

Air China has established strategic alliances with regional airlines to enter secondary and tertiary markets that low-cost carriers have traditionally dominated. Through code-sharing agreements, the airline expands its business scope without significantly increasing operating costs. This strategy enables Air China to maintain its market share while mitigating the impact of economic fluctuations.

International expansion and geopolitical risk management.

In 2025, conflicts in the Middle East resumed, presenting many severe challenges, including airspace closures and rising fuel costs. To address these issues, Air China promptly adjusted flight routes to avoid high-risk areas, ensuring passenger safety and minimizing flight delays. The airline also implemented flexible ticketing policies, allowing passengers to change their itineraries or receive refunds without incurring penalties, maintaining customer trust. To cope with rising aviation fuel prices, Air China entered long-term hedging contracts and diversified its fuel procurement channels, reducing its reliance on the volatile oil market.

The USA-China trade war further disrupted the aviation industry, disrupting aircraft and component supply chains. To address these challenges, Air China sped up negotiations with European aircraft manufacturer Airbus to compensate for delays in Boeing deliveries. With the debut of the domestically made passenger aircraft C919, Air China became the first airline to purchase this type of aircraft. The airline also increased investment in maintenance, repair, and overhaul (MRO) facilities in China, reducing reliance on services affected by USA tariffs. By localizing part of the supply chain, Air China mitigated the risk of cost increases and ensured the availability of its fleet.

STRATEGIC ANALYSIS

Analytical Frameworks

PEST Analysis.

Looking at the global aviation industry from a political perspective, the Chinese government's emphasis on the aviation sector has been continuously increasing.

The Civil Aviation Administration of China is actively promoting the high-quality development of the aviation industry, including strengthening aviation safety supervision, advancing the construction of aviation hubs, and providing policy support for Air China's stable operation. In terms of economic factors, as China's economy continues to grow and residents' incomes rise, there is strong demand for tourism and business travel, creating a broad market for Air China. However, uncertainties in the global economy and exchange rate fluctuations have also posed challenges for Air China's international route operations. In terms of social factors, people's requirements for the convenience, comfort, and safety of air travel are continually increasing, prompting Air China to improve its service quality continually. In terms of technological factors, the continuous advancement of aviation technology, such as the development of new aircraft and the application of aviation information technology, provides Air China with technical support to enhance operational efficiency and service quality.

SWOT Analysis.

As one of the largest airlines in China, Air China operates many routes and a large fleet. The company possesses 905 aircraft of various types, including Boeing, Airbus and COMAC. It also operates 336 domestic and 94 international routes (Air China, n.d.), enabling the company to serve many important cities both domestically and internationally and providing passengers with convenient travel options. Air China has significant advantages in brand recognition and customer loyalty, and it holds a considerable share of the high-end business passenger market. However, Air China also faces disadvantages, including relatively high operating costs and limited flexibility amid competition from emerging airlines. From an opportunity perspective, with the advancement of China's "Belt and Road" initiative, Air China's expansion of international routes has opened new opportunities, enabling it further to strengthen its aviation connections with countries along the route. The development of digital technology has provided new avenues for Air China to enhance operational efficiency and service quality. In terms of threats, fierce competition in the aviation industry, the continuous emergence of new airlines, and the increasingly intense competition for market share pose challenges. Uncontrollable factors such as oil price fluctuations and natural disasters also pose threats to Air China's operating costs and flight safety.

Porter's Five Forces.

Air China is facing fierce competition from existing competitors. Air China must compete with multiple competitors in such a highly saturated aviation market. Domestically, it has to capture market share alongside two other state-owned aviation groups, supplemented by private airlines (e.g., Hainan Airlines, Spring Airlines, and Juneyao Airlines). Internationally, mature airlines have established routes between China, Europe, and the United States. Severe homogenization significantly influences the economy class market. In terms of route settings, service standards, and aircraft configuration, Air China's layout is almost identical to that of other airlines. Therefore, for ticket selection, passengers are more price-sensitive.

Local governments are preparing to establish local airlines. The region's financial resources and industrial funds can quickly secure a dominant position in the regional air route market. The Civil Aviation Administration is promoting the "streamlining, delegation, and facilitation" reform, simplifying the approval process for air traffic rights, and creating favorable conditions for local and foreign enterprises to enter the market.

After the pandemic, the aviation industry market declined because of consumers' preferences. Business travel demand decreased after the pandemic because of reduced corporate budgets and the rise of video conferencing. After the pandemic, high-net-worth clients chose business jets or charter flights instead, diverting resources from first-class cabins.

Suppliers exert moderate to high bargaining power over the company. Boeing and Airbus supply most Air China's aircraft. The company faces lengthy production scheduling for these orders and has limited bargaining space. In addition, Air China's fuel costs are relatively high compared to international airlines' average levels, and it lacks an effective fuel hedging mechanism.

Business travelers and price-sensitive individual tourists mainly make up Air China's customer base. Both groups have strong bargaining power; Online Travel Agencies (OTA) and direct sales platforms divert revenue. Platforms such as Ctrip and Fliggy control access points to traffic, charge airlines a small commission, and enhance price transparency through comparison systems, reducing airlines' margin space. For individual consumers, the price sensitivity is high, especially in the leisure tourism market. Consumers can quickly compare prices through products like "Flexi Flight" and "Air Ticket Box", forcing Air China to maintain low prices to keep passenger seats in off-peak seasons.

Brand and Reputation Effects

What makes the brand appealing and why customers like its products and services is its main selling point. Therefore, passengers choose Air China over other airlines, and it is also an important core of meeting their needs and providing value. Air China's aim to give customers a great and special experience can be a reason for people to choose them, making them the best airline for long trips. Air China actively takes part in ESG initiatives to fulfill its social responsibility and address environmental issues.

For nine years, the world has recognized Air China as one of its top 500 brands. Air China has reviewed its own history and conducted research and has determined its brand positioning as "professional and trustworthy, international quality, and Chinese style". To make the company more distinctive in international competition, Air China presents the phoenix logo to passengers, which conveys the brand's meaning. This enables passengers to associate the logo with Air China's brand image. For in-flight services, the industry has pioneered the "first boarding" customized product, providing comprehensive services for customers. They have updated the in-flight entertainment content and introduced different dining cultures based on the routes to meet passengers' diverse needs. Optimize the digital platform to make it easier and faster for passengers to select seats and check in. In its participation in international competitions, Air China has recruited abundant staff from various regions, accelerating the company's localization and integration with local culture. Local cultural expressions present the brand to maximize its acceptance and appeal to consumers, allowing each consumer to feel the atmosphere of Chinese culture (Air China, n.d.).

In response to societal issues, Air China is concerned about environmental problems and social responsibility. As one of the first airlines to adopt SAF, Air China has gradually expanded its use on domestic and international routes. It has also collaborated with domestic suppliers to explore local SAF production and to build the supply chain. To vigorously promote the use of sustainable fuels, Air China, in collaboration with Airbus China and China Aviation Oil, launched a university student SAF production path competition in May 2024. They also organized activities like cabin science popularization knowledge quizzes, exploring the possibilities of SAF development (Air China, n.d.). In response to the national rural revitalization strategy, the "aviation +" assistance model has invested funds in education, healthcare, and industrial development in remote areas. We have also organized the purchase of agricultural and sideline products from the assisted areas. The amount of consumption assistance in 2024 reached over 54 million yuan (Air China, n.d.). The company also implements a fair employment policy, advocates gender equality and employee-related rights, and establishes multiple levels of talent development channels and learning paths to improve the company's knowledge system.

CONCLUSION AND STRATEGIC RECOMMENDATIONS

Summary of Key Findings

During Air China's global development, the following four key measures enabled it to better integrate into the international market: first, its "non-acquisition" expansion strategy. Unlike traditional aviation giants that expand their markets by acquiring overseas airlines, Air China has extended its route network to 36countries through alliance cooperation. It can also share resources with its alliance partners. Second, establish an aviation hub network. Using domestic cities as nodes, connect six continents to form a "domestic dense + international radiating" flight route layout, expanding flight coverage. Third, the ecological membership system. Air China has collaborated with non-hangar industries through the "Phoenix Membership" program to enhance customer loyalty. Finally, it aims to build a Chinese aviation brand. Air China commits to localizing its products. From management to marketing, the airline strives to promote Chinese culture. This strategy attracts more foreign tourists, leading them to choose Air China as their preferred airline.

Future Growth Opportunities

In the global aviation market, Chinese airlines face both opportunities and challenges. Therefore, the company must plan targeted strategies to ensure sustainable development and reduce risks. By leveraging policy advantages, technological innovation, and integrated service models, the airline can enhance its competitive position and adapt to ever-changing market demands.

First, Chinese airlines should use the "Belt and Road Initiative" (BRI) to expand their route networks in the Middle East and Africa. By signing strategic agreements with local governments and event organizers, airlines can obtain landing rights and establish a presence in emerging markets. This approach not only increases market share but also reduces reliance on saturated routes. Collaborating with "BRI"-related infrastructure projects can facilitate cargo transportation, further diversifying revenue sources.

Second, dynamic pricing powered by artificial intelligence can optimize ticket sales for international flights. By analyzing real-time demand, seasonal trends, and competitors' pricing, Chinese airlines can adjust ticket prices to maximize passenger load and profitability. In the digital age, this strategy is important, as consumers expect personalized, cost-effective travel options. Airlines can increase revenue by expanding cross-border e-commerce, offering duty-free shopping, local specialty products, and exclusive travel packages through their digital platforms.

Finally, the vertical integration of "aviation + tourism" will create a seamless travel experience. By bundling flights with visa services, hotel reservations, and attraction tickets, Chinese airlines can position themselves as one-stop travel solutions. Establishing partnerships with tourism agencies and online platforms (such as Ctrip and Fliggy) can provide customized itineraries tailored to the needs of leisure and business travelers.

Recommendations for Other Firms

When facing an uncertain external market environment, companies need to ensure the resilience of their business activities. By establishing strategic alliance networks and sharing resources to reduce operational risks, such as the aviation industry enhancing route flexibility through code sharing; by aligning with national strategic frameworks and leveraging policy support to overcome trade barriers, cooperative relationships between countries can reach target markets more quickly and effectively, as seen with new energy enterprises leveraging the "Belt and Road" policy to expand their markets; by implementing a deep localization strategy, adapting to local cultures from product design to brand promotion, similar to the successful case of multinational catering enterprises developing regional specialty menus. These three strategies form a systematic solution of "risk sharing - policy support - cultural integration", which can effectively cope with geopolitical risks and market competition pressures. The essence lies in balancing the global scale effect with local response capability through strategic synergy, transforming external challenges into differentiated competitive advantages, and providing replicable overseas expansion methodologies for various industries.

References

Air China. (2025, April 25). 2024 [Air China Limited 2024 Annual Report]. Air China Limited. https://webresource.airchina.com.cn/airchinacms/2/upload/resources/file/10109.pdf

Air China. (n.d.) 2016 [2016 Social Responsibility Report]. Air China Limited. https://webresource.airchina.com.cn/airchinacms/2/upload/resources/file/743.pdf

Air China. (n.d.). 2023 ESG [2023 Sustainable Development and ESG Report]. Air China Limited. https://et.airchina.com.cn/cn/images/investor_relations/2024/03/29/10077396D2B04368941ADF6F10FC61D4.pdf

Air China. (n.d.). 2024 ESG [2024 Sustainable Development and ESG Report]. Air China Limited. https://static.cninfo.com.cn/finalpage/2025-03-28/1222927858.PDF

Air China. (n.d.). [About Air China]. Air China Limited. https://ffp.airchina.com.cn/plan/about_airchina.html

Air China. (n.d.). [Air China and Star Alliance]. Air China Limited. https://m.airchina.com.cn/c/invoke/hzgy@pg

CAACnews. (2017, May 12). " "

CAACnews. (2017, July 19). " " [Building the "Air Silk Road" of the new era]. CAACnews. http://www.caacnews.com.cn/special/4260/4313/hhcj/201801/t20180129_1239619.html

CAACnews. (2017, December 13). :" " [Air China's 10th anniversary of joining Star Alliance: "They are approaching the center of the world stage]. CAACnews. http://caacnews.com.cn/1/6/201712/t20171213_1236293.html

CAACnews. (2021, January 15). " " [Air China has initiated the "one airport, two zones" operation mode at Beijing Capital Airport]. CAACnews. http://www.caacnews.com.cn/1/6/202101/t20210115_1317939.html

CAACnews. (2024, April 23). 4 [Air China has launched and resumed four international routes]. CAACnews. http://www.caacnews.com.cn/1/6/202404/t20240423_1377613.html

CAACnews. (2024, June 26). 2024 2019 90% [In the 2024 summer travel season, Air China's international and regional routes will recover to 90% of the 2019 level]. CAACnews. http://www.caacnews.com.cn/1/6/202406/t20240626_1379324.html

CAACnews. (2024, December, 30). 2024 [HiChina has released the 2024 Civil Aviation Travel Report]. CAACnews. http://www.caacnews.com.cn/1/202412/t20241230_1383809.html

CAACnews. (2025, May 21). : [Avic Group: Inheriting the Red Gene and continuously forging ahead on the journey]. CAACnews. http://www.caacnews.com.cn/1/6/202105/t20210521_1324294.html

CAACnews. [Actively serve the Belt and Road Initiative and comprehensively enhance the level of aviation connectivity - Interview with Wang Zhiqing, Vice Minister of the Civil Aviation Administration of China]. CAACnews. http://www.caacnews.com.cn/special/3494/xgbd/201705/t20170512_1214400.html

Chen, S. (2025, March 31). The Losses of China's Three Major Airline Will Narrow in 2024. YiCai Global. https://www.yicaiglobal.com/news/chinas-big-three-airlines-failed-to-turn-profitable-last-year

Chen, Y. (2024a, June 26). 2024 43 1200 [In the summer of 2024, Air China will significantly increase its capacity, reaching 43 countries and regions and 1,200 destinations]. Xinhua Net. https://app.xinhuanet.com/news/article.html?articleId=40c14eab281fa5e67deec4e0c599c529

Chen, Y. (2024b, November 28). " " " " [The "Phoenix Mile" frequent flyer program of Air China has been around for 30 years, with the theme of "A Soulmate by your side on the Journey of Life"]. Xinhua Net. https://www.news.cn/digital/20241128/1b0cd7809f3a484292aadd3b85089884/c.html

China Economic Net. (2024, December 25). 2025 [The Beijing Aero-engine maintenance project is expected to be put into use in 2025]. Economic Daily News. http://www.ce.cn/xwzx/gnsz/gdxw/202412/25/t20241225_39247155.shtml

China Post Securities. (2022, May 23). 2022 [Analysis of Air China's Business Layout and Competitive Advantages in 2022: Air China positions Itself on Core routes and Hub Resources]. Vzkoo. https://www.vzkoo.com/read/202205238c5122fda7813274417256ee.html

Chinareospace. (2025, April 21). : [Analysis: Risks and Opportunities for Chinese Civil Aviation Enterprises against the Backdrop of the Escalation of the China-US Trade War]. Chinareospace. https://www.chinaerospace.com/index.php/article/show/ff8401962ed469195f57b71bfb44ae92

CTNEWS. (2024, September 19). [How can airlines continuously improve their performance when opportunities and challenges coexist]. CTNEWS. https://www.ctnews.com.cn/paper/att/202409/19/7e324460-f6ad-41b6-9e0a-7e6868f96c9e.pdf

Ding, W. (2025, April 8). 2024 70 2025 [The three major airlines are expected to reduce losses by 7 billion yuan in 2024 and turn a profit in 2025]. China Aviation News. https://ep.cannews.com.cn/publish/zghkb7/html/5161/node_219916.html

Gupta, R. (2016, September 8). [Air China is optimizing its ancillary service marketing to focus on the international market]. Travel Daily. https://www.traveldaily.cn/article/106530

Pan, J. (2024, October, 28). : , , " "?[International Air Transport Market Observation: Total Volume Recovery, Structural Changes, How to Make the "cake" Bigger and Better?]. CAACnews. http://www.caacnews.com.cn/1/202410/t20241028_1382350.html

Sun, F. (2023, November 13). [Promote the high-quality development of the dual-hub construction in Beijing in the new era]. CAACnews. http://www.caacnews.com.cn/special/2023nzt/7598/2020mhcy1/2020cybzmhj/202311/t20231113_1372159.html

Wu, B. (2025, June 13). 10%, [International oil prices have soared by more than 10%, and the situation in the Middle East has raised supply concerns]. 21st Century Business Herald. https://www.21jingji.com/article/20250613/herald/591260f98640607c3a8068b0b9167066.html

Xinhua Silk Road. (2024, November 17). [Air China's multi-level strategy to deeply cultivate the Asia-Pacific market attracts tourists to visit China]. Xinhua Silk Road. https://www.imsilkroad.com/news/p/529740.html

KEY TERMS AND DEFINITIONS

ASK: An indicator for measuring an airline's capacity, calculated by multiplying the number of seats by the number of flight kilometers

ESG: Environmental, social, and governance. Represent a set of core standards for measuring an enterprise's sustainable development capabilities and non-financial performance. It is not only an investment philosophy but also an important framework for enterprise management and supervision.

Fleet: In the aviation industry, it refers to all aircraft owned, leased, or operated by an airline or aviation operator.

Frequent flyer programs: Programs that airlines offer points, rewards, or other preferential plans to frequent flyers are usually a marketing method used by airlines to increase customer stickiness.

GDS: Global distribution system is used for booking and sales between tourism service providers such as airlines, hotels, and travel agencies.

LCC: Low-cost Carrier, it is an airline operator that offers extremely low-ticket prices in exchange for minimalist services and additional charges

MRO: Maintenance, repair, and overhaul. In the aviation industry, this refers to the services and facilities required to keep aircraft and their components in a safe and operational condition.

OTA: Online Travel Agency. They do not operate flights or hotels directly. Instead, they integrate with airlines, hotels, and car rental companies to offer online booking services, making it convenient for users to compare prices, place orders, and manage itineraries.

Passenger transportation volume: It refers to the actual number of passengers transported by various means of transportation within a certain period

SAF: Sustainable Aviation Fuel, an environmentally friendly fuel used to reduce carbon emissions in the aviation industry.

Chapter 8
SF Holding's Global Logistics Strategy:
Motivations, Entry Modes, and Competitive Advantages

Yulin Li
http://orcid.org/0009-0003-4623-4363
Beijing Normal-Hong Kong Baptist University, China

EXECUTIVE SUMMARY

This chapter examines the globalization strategy of SF Holding, China's leading comprehensive express and logistics company. The purpose is to analyse the motivations, market selection criteria, entry modes, and competitive advantages that have driven the firm's international expansion. Key themes include the saturation of the domestic market, the pull of cross-border e-commerce, and the supportive role of national policies like the Belt and Road Initiative. The chapter details SF Express's phased approach, prioritizing Southeast Asia before targeting Europe and the Middle East, and its hybrid entry strategy combining mergers and acquisitions, such as the acquisition of Kerry Logistics, with strategic partnerships. It also addresses the challenges faced, including cultural adaptation and regulatory compliance, and the mitigation strategies employed. The overall contribution is a comprehensive framework illustrating how a Chinese logistics firm builds a global network through technology-driven integration and localized operations, offering strategic insights for similar enterprises.

DOI: 10.4018/979-8-3373-4302-0.ch008

INTRODUCTION

Background of the Company

Terminology Note: SF Holding is a listed parent company that integrates various business segments, including express delivery, supply chain, international logistics, cold chain transportation, and aviation. SF Express, its core brand, is the most familiar business unit to domestic and international customers. Unless otherwise noted, the use SF Holding and SF Express interchangeably.

SF (Shunfeng) Express, which began operations in 1993, has its headquarters in Shenzhen, China. It is a pioneer in China's express logistics industry. The company initially focused on transporting documents and small parcels between Shenzhen and Hong Kong. Founder Wang Wei quickly established a unique market position by prioritizing timeliness and service quality. Over the past three decades, SF Express has grown into a comprehensive intelligent logistics operator integrating express delivery, supply chain solutions, air cargo, cold chain transportation, and a technology platform.

According to its 2023 annual report, SF Express reported revenue of RMB 258.4 billion, employed over 530,000 people, and operated a fleet of over 100,000 vehicles. Its subsidiary, SF Airlines, also operates a fleet of 83 aircraft (SF Holding, 2023). The company has expanded its business network to over 40 countries and regions worldwide, operating a model of "one domestic network and multiple international network nodes."

SF Express's leadership emphasizes technology as a core element of its strategy. As Wang Wei stated in a public speech, "In the global logistics sector, our challenge is not only to speed up transportation but also to provide stability through technology and localized solutions" (Caixin Global, 2021). This dual emphasis on technology-driven growth and supply chain integration has made SF Express a leading innovator in the industry.

SF's principal business covers standard express delivery, same-city instant delivery, e-commerce parcels, cold chain, pharmaceutical logistics, high-end trade distribution, and cross-border e-commerce fulfillment. According to its 2023 annual report, the company's annual operating income reached RMB 258 billion, with 530,000 employees, over 100,000 self-operated transport vehicles, and one of the largest cargo fleets in Asia, "SF Airlines", with a fleet of 83 aircraft. Its business network covers all county-level administrative regions in China. It has expanded to over 40 countries and regions worldwide, building an operating system of "one domestic network and multiple international network points" (Qiao & Rojniruttikul, 2025).

Centered on the group headquarters, SF Express's organizational structure comprises a strategic hub complemented by core business segments including SF Express,

SF Technology, SF International, and SF Airlines. In 2017, the company successfully listed on the Shenzhen Stock Exchange through a backdoor listing under the name Dingtai New Materials, becoming one of the few leading logistics companies listed on the A-share market. In 2021, SF Express spent RMB 17.5 billion to gain Kerry Logistics, which quickly integrated local warehousing and transportation capabilities in Southeast Asia, Europe, and the United States through mergers and acquisitions, marking a key turning point in its internationalization strategy (Chen, 2020).

Founder Wang Wei leads SF Express's leadership team, emphasizing the dual-wheel drive strategy of "technology-driven + supply chain integration" and continuing to invest in intelligent sorting centers, autonomous aviation hubs, drone delivery systems, and big data platforms to achieve industry leadership in "full-scenario coverage, full-link visibility, and global services" (Amling & Daugherty, 2018).

Motivation for Global Expansion

SF Express's motivation for launching a globalization strategy stem from multiple internal and external environmental changes. First, after years of rapid growth, the domestic express delivery market has shown a saturation trend. Standard express delivery services represented by e-commerce parcels have entered a "price war" cycle, and industry competition is becoming increasingly fierce. SF Express's expertise in mid- to high-end time-sensitive parcels is facing a growth bottleneck. To drive fresh growth, SF Express urgently needs to explore the underdeveloped high-end logistics needs and emerging e-commerce channels in the international market (Chen, 2020).

Second, the rapid development of cross-border e-commerce has provided an external driving force for SF Express. According to iResearch data, China's cross-border e-commerce transaction volume will increase by 18.3% year-on-year in 2023, especially in Southeast Asia, the Middle East, and Europe. As an important logistics partner of leading domestic e-commerce sellers, brands, and manufacturers, SF Express must simultaneously build global service capabilities to ensure the stability of its customers' supply chains in overseas markets. SF Express also deeply embeds itself in the global new retail chain by providing integrated warehouse and distribution services for platforms such as TikTok Shop, Temu, and Lazada.

Third, national policies provide institutional support for SF Express's internationalization. The "Belt and Road" Logistics Connectivity Development Plan and the "Express Overseas" Special Action encourage leading logistics companies to "go global" and build an intelligent logistics ecosystem with "China as the core and radiating the world". Relying on the policy dividends of Shenzhen's "pioneer demonstration zone", SF Express has received several policy supports for establishing overseas transshipment centers, applying for overseas customs clearance facilitation pilots, and building air cargo hubs (Amling & Daugherty, 2018).

In terms of implementation path, SF Express adopts multiple strategies to advance in parallel. First, it is expanding rapidly through mergers and acquisitions. After acquiring Kerry Logistics Network in 2021, it has built a localized distribution network covering major cities in Asia, serving as the infrastructure backbone of SF Express's "overseas warehouse + trunk line + terminal" model. Second, SF Express has built the Asia Smart Logistics Hub (ASLN), including the establishment of international transit centers in Hong Kong, Kuala Lumpur, and Dubai. Third, SF Express has sped up the overseas expansion of its technology platform, including launching the "SF International" applet and an overseas B2B logistics SaaS platform, unifying service standards through digital means, and improving user stickiness and fulfillment efficiency (Qiao & Rojniruttikul, 2025).

SF Express's globalization strategic goal is clear: through independent logistics capabilities and international brand output, it will achieve a development pattern of "full implementation in ASEAN, core breakthroughs in Europe and the United States, and coverage of the Middle East and Southeast Asia" within three years, and enhance the stickiness of "chain leader" customers through technology empowerment, and achieve an upgrade from a leading domestic enterprise to a global integrated logistics service provider.

Globalization Motivation: Driven by Internal and External Pressures

As China's domestic express delivery industry becomes saturated and competition in the domestic e-commerce market intensifies, SF Holdings faces the dual challenges of growth bottlenecks and profit compression. Although SF has firmly established its leading position in high-end express delivery services in the domestic market, declining market dividends and slowing user growth have forced it to find new growth engines. Against this background, SF regards the internationalization strategy as a way out. From an external perspective, the rapid development of cross-border e-commerce and the growing demand from overseas consumer markets for logistics services for Chinese goods have also brought SF unprecedented expansion opportunities. Related data from China Daily shows that in 2022, the scale of China's cross-border e-commerce transactions exceeded 15 trillion yuan, a year-on-year increase of 9.8%, among which demand for export logistics to Southeast Asia and the Middle East is strong.

The global epidemic has highlighted the need for a "decentralized" and "diversified" logistics network. SF understands that relying solely on its domestic supply chain limits its risk resilience. Therefore, building an international logistics system covering the world and with local service capabilities has become its long-term strategic goal of globalization. In the process of globalization, SF Express not only pursues diversification of its income sources but also aims to secure a stable position in the global high-end logistics market by strengthening its international brand image.

Policy Background and National Initiative Support

SF Express's internationalization pace is also closely related to the "going out" strategy vigorously promoted by the Chinese government in recent years. Especially in the "Belt and Road Initiative" (BRI) and "Made in China 2025", logistics is regarded as important infrastructure to support the country's industrial chain going overseas. These policies not only provide systematic support in diplomacy, finance, infrastructure, and other areas, but also clear many institutional-level obstacles to logistics companies' international operations.

SF Express actively responded to national policies and took the lead in deploying in countries along the "Belt and Road". For example, it has established overseas warehouses and local distribution networks in Malaysia, Vietnam, the United Arab Emirates, and other places, and cooperated with customs and airports to develop a rapid customs clearance mechanism, which has improved the efficiency of cross-border logistics. This global layout, in line with the national strategy, has not only enhanced SF Express's legitimacy and credibility in the international market but also enabled it to get investment support from relevant financial institutions and policy banks.

In addition, SF Express has also cooperated with regulatory agencies such as the Civil Aviation Administration of China to get overseas cargo route licenses and continued to increase infrastructure investment in overseas markets. This policy- and market-driven dual model has improved the speed and robustness of its international expansion.

MARKET ANALYSIS AND ENTRY STRATEGY

Target Market Selection

As SF Holding gradually advances its global development strategy, selecting the right target market has become a crucial step in its international expansion process. Because of the high investment and operational complexity of the express logistics industry, SF must accurately assess the market potential and risk levels of different countries and regions to ensure that overseas investments achieve the expected returns. Especially in significant differences in global markets, rash expansion may lead to resource mismatch, costs out of control, and even damage to brand reputation. Therefore, when planning its international market entry plan, SF adopted a systematic market screening method that combined quantitative data with strategic judgment, prioritizing countries or regions with favorable policies, strong market demand, high cultural fit, and strong infrastructure.

Market evaluation criteria and selection logic.

In terms of target market selection, SF adopts an evaluation framework with "opportunity accessibility + local adaptability" as the core. First, it focuses on key indicators, such as the target market's economic growth rate, demographic dividend, online consumption penetration rate, and cross-border e-commerce activity, to ensure the market has medium- and long-term growth potential. Southeast Asian countries such as Malaysia, Vietnam, and Thailand have become a focus for SF Express because of their large young populations and booming e-commerce user bases. In recent years, these countries have continued to increase their acceptance of Chinese exports, and their demand for efficient cross-border logistics has also risen significantly.

Second, SF Express attaches great importance to infrastructure and to the efficiency of customs clearance. In high-frequency, multi-batch express delivery scenarios, the speed of customs clearance directly determines the service experience and cost control capabilities. Therefore, SF Express prioritizes evaluating countries that support free trade agreements and have transparent import processes. The government's openness to the logistics field, regulatory flexibility, and tax policies also factor into the overall consideration. In addition, in order to promote the smooth progress of localized operations, SF Express also conducted a pre-judgment analysis of the target country's language, cultural proximity, and local human resource costs and quality.

This logic reflects that SF Express is not unquestioningly expanding globally, but making comprehensive decisions based on data-driven, strategic adaptation to reduce overseas uncertainties and optimize resource allocation efficiency.

Comparative analysis of regional markets.

SF Express adopts differentiated entry strategies based on market maturity, competitive structure, and policy stability in different regions. In the Southeast Asian market, SF Express adopts the "forward warehouse + local distribution + customs coordination" model. It has successively established overseas warehouses and local delivery networks in Vietnam, Malaysia, and other countries. These countries are geographically next to China, share similar cultures, and have large Chinese communities, which significantly reduce the cultural friction costs for SF Express during the initial entry stage.

In the European market, SF Express has adopted a more cautious entry strategy. United Parcel Service (UPS) and FedEx (DHL Group, 2023 highly concentrated on the logistics industry, with DHL being the recognized market leader in international time-definite express delivery services in Europe, followed closely). Although SF Express has limited penetration in Europe—its share is significantly lower than that of established players, the company is testing entry models by establishing targeted operations in hubs such as Frankfurt, Paris, and Amsterdam. SF Express focuses on specialized areas such as the pharmaceutical cold chain and cross-border e-commerce, where differentiated service quality can provide a competitive advantage.

As for the Middle East market, SF Express believes that, as an emerging growth pole, it offers dual advantages of policy support and strong consumption potential. Countries such as the UAE and Saudi Arabia not only promote the development of the digital economy but also vigorously build free trade zones and e-commerce infrastructure. Therefore, SF Express has established regional centers in Dubai and other locations and has gradually established direct connections with mainland China's air trunk lines to improve timeliness and capacity. This differentiated regional-market layout shows the rational maturity of SF Express's "divided, stepped, and graded" global expansion strategy.

SF Express has showed a clear strategic proposition and a cautious investment approach in selecting target markets. It not only focuses on "whether it can make money" but also on "whether it can stand firm in the long run". This strategic determination is one foundation for its continued globalization.

Entry Mode Selection

After determining the target markets, one of the key strategic choices facing SF Holding is how to enter them, choosing the most appropriate entry mode. In the process of global expansion, there are significant differences in the political and economic environments, legal systems, cultural backgrounds, and logistics infrastructure across countries. Hence, a one-size-fits-all market-entry approach is not workable. SF has adopted a gradual, diversified entry path based on factors such as the maturity of the target market, the foundation of local cooperation, policy barriers, and operating costs, to ensure the adaptability and controllability of its expansion strategy.

Model evolution path.

SF's international market entry model has entered the initial stage of evolution, moving from a light asset model to a local deep cultivation model. Its strategy focuses on the "export + agency distribution" approach, relying on domestic orders in China, transporting goods to the target country through cross-border e-commerce channels, and local third parties complete the terminal delivery. This approach has low investment risk and can quickly get the business started, but it also faces challenges such as weak control over delivery and limited-service experience. Therefore, SF has gradually moved towards direct operation or holding to improve service consistency and customer satisfaction.

In emerging markets such as Southeast Asia and the Middle East, SF Express has adopted a self-operated expansion strategy of "establishing overseas warehouses + building local delivery teams". For example, its warehousing and distribution center in Malaysia connects to the local customs clearance system, which improves delivery timeliness. In mature markets such as Germany and the Netherlands, SF Express establishes cooperation with local air cargo or ground express companies to share resources by jointly using airport cargo hubs and distribution systems. This path of "combining light and heavy, flexible penetration" is SF Express's rational response to the complex international market structure, and also reflects the basic logic of its steady expansion.

Cooperation and M&A strategies.

Besides self-built and export-oriented paths, SF Express has escalated its capital investment in the international market, using mergers and acquisitions, joint ventures, strategic alliances, and other methods to build a deep, localized network. In 2019, SF Express realized the integration of its logistics resources in Southeast Asia and Europe by holding a controlling stake in Kerry Logistics. This acquisition not only enhanced its shipping and multimodal transport capabilities but also provided a mature channel for it to explore emerging markets such as Vietnam and the Philippines (Chang et al., 2021). Besides its independent development and export-oriented growth path, SF Express has also expanded its business through mergers and acquisitions. A key step was its acquisition of a controlling stake in Kerry Logistics in 2021, when SF Holding launched a tender offer valued at approximately HK$17.6 billion (approximately US$2.3 billion) for a 51.8% stake (China Daily HK, 2021). This acquisition provided SF Express with mature warehousing and transportation capabilities in Southeast Asia and Europe, significantly speeding up its international expansion and integrating it into local supply chains.

SF Express and SAL, Saudi Arabia's national logistics company in the Middle East, signed a strategic cooperation agreement to jointly promote the development of air logistics channels. This move not only helps it establish an airport hub system in the Middle East, but also shows SF Express's long-term infrastructure investment strategy. In some markets, SF Express also adopts a minority stake + operational cooperation model to reduce entry barriers. For example, its investment in Germany's Hermes International is a path choice of "financial participation + resource exchange." This cooperation and M&A strategies enable SF Express to gain key resources worldwide quickly, shorten local adaptation cycles, and enhance cross-border service capabilities.

In summary, SF Express adheres to the principle of "adapting to local conditions and diversified collaboration" in selecting its entry mode into the international market. It continually adjusts it in response to market evolution and strategic goals. This flexible and complex path not only effectively improves its market entry efficiency but also lays a strategic foundation for its construction of a global logistics network.

Competitive Advantage

In the increasingly fierce competition in the global logistics market, whether a company can successfully gain a foothold in the overseas market depends on whether it has sustainable competitive advantages. Over years of deep cultivation in the high-end express delivery market, SF Holding has not only accumulated rich operating experience and customer resources but also built differentiated capabilities across multiple dimensions, including cost control, service timeliness, and intelligent management. These advantages provide solid support for its international market competition and enable it to compete with international giants such as DHL, FedEx, and UPS.

Cost efficiency and timeliness advantages.

By adhering to a "full chain control" strategy that includes self-built aviation and ground networks, SF has long achieved high-density, high-frequency, and punctual deliveries in China. SF selectively replicated this model in the international market, especially on major routes from China to Southeast Asia, the Middle East, and Europe. SF has established a dedicated mechanism for coordinating cargo flights and port clearance. This integrated network structure reduces reliance on third-party transporters, not only compressing transportation costs but, more importantly, achieving "independent control of timeliness" (Wasserman & Wasserman, 2019).

The regional hub system and the multimodal transport dispatching system promoted by SF Express enable it to maintain stable capacity output during the peak season, resulting in a more stable cross-border service experience compared with competitors. For example, regional distribution centers in Singapore, Dubai, and other locations can serve multiple surrounding countries and regions within 72 hours, improving local customers' trust and dependence on the brand. In addition, SF Express has effectively shortened the cargo turnover cycle by optimizing customs clearance procedures and advancing declaration mechanisms. This combination of "cost reduction + growth rate" constitutes its core cost-efficiency advantage.

Intelligence and service differentiation.

Besides cost and speed, SF Express is also committed to building service differentiation competitiveness driven by technology. It has invested heavily in intelligent logistics systems, built predictive distribution, real-time scheduling, and path-optimization models based on big data, and improved the efficiency and flexibility of terminal distribution. SF Express's AI delivery system can automatically assign riders and routes based on historical traffic, significantly reducing delivery labor costs; overseas customers can also track the status of international express shipments in real time through the App, achieving "end-to-end transparent visualization".

Measurable gains in automation have accompanied SF's international rollout. In its most recent sustainability/annual disclosures, the group reports that the deployment of automated equipment and process automation increased small-parcel sorting efficiency by 13% in 2024 (SF Holding, 2024). This company-reported improvement supports claims that SF's investments in automated sorting and RPA (robotic process automation) materially raise throughout and reduce manual handling in its international nodes.

In terms of customer experience, SF Express adheres to the concept of "personalized customization" and provides localized value-added services to customers in different countries and industries. For example, in cross-border e-commerce, it offers customized customs clearance integration and door-to-door tax prepayment models for Middle Eastern customers, simplifying challenges. In the B-side business, SF Express provides "exclusive logistics solutions + dynamic guarantee systems" for high-value, fragile, or insulated goods, building refined operational capabilities for the industry. This "technology + service" compound competitive advantage is the key to distinguishing it from other international players (Franchell, 2023).

In addition, SF Express actively expands its green logistics and social responsibility image, and promotes low-carbon transportation, environmentally friendly packaging, and sustainable development concepts in overseas markets. This series of measures not only enhances the soft power of its brand but also, to a certain extent, improves its compliance capabilities in markets with stricter regulations. By continuously deepening the application of technology and delivering customer value, SF Express has gradually established a brand recognition for efficiency, trust, and responsibility in the global market, creating a structural difference from traditional express delivery giants.

IMPLEMENTATION OF GLOBAL EXPANSION

Key Initiatives and Investments

To turn its global expansion strategy from planning into reality, SF has simultaneously launched major initiatives across multiple markets and made large-scale capital investments. The company's core implementation strategy involves three aspects: infrastructure construction, local network layout, and technical system implementation.

Finally, in terms of technology investment, SF Express is expanding its intelligent logistics system globally, investing heavily in overseas deployments of its order management system (OMS), transportation management system (TMS), and customer service interfaces. According to its 2024 sustainability report, the deployment of automated equipment in sorting operations has increased small parcel sorting efficiency by 13% (SF Holdings, 2024). These improvements not only increase throughput but also enhance visibility and accuracy in cross-border operations, strengthening SF Express's differentiation from traditional logistics giants.

First, at the infrastructure level, SF Express has established self-operated international distribution centers and overseas warehousing facilities in Frankfurt, Germany; Los Angeles, USA; and Kuala Lumpur, Malaysia, among others. Prime site rental, warehousing, renovation, and equipment procurement costs usually accompany these projects. For example, SF Express invested about RMB 200 million in Malaysia to build a Southeast Asian regional warehouse equipped with automated sorting and temperature-control systems, improving its cold-chain fulfillment capabilities (Qiao & Rojniruttikul, 2025). In addition, the company has also expanded its international aviation resources and opened regular all-cargo routes from China to Southeast Asia and Europe through SF Airlines.

Second, in building a local operations network, SF Express adopts a hybrid model of "direct operation + cooperation." In markets such as the United States and Germany, the company registers wholly owned subsidiaries and is independently responsible for customs clearance, distribution, and after-sales to ensure that services are controllable; in Singapore, Saudi Arabia, and other places, it quickly gets licenses and delivery networks by cooperating with local logistics companies or government platforms to establish joint ventures (Manners-Bell, 2019). These models all involve an initial cost investment in human resources, training, and IT system deployment.

Finally, in terms of technology investment, SF Express replicates its intelligent logistics system internationally, investing heavily to deploy order management systems (OMS), transportation management systems (TMS), and customer service interfaces overseas to achieve real-time interoperability of cross-border fulfillment data. This system improves fulfillment visibility and customer experience, and is one of its core competitive advantages, distinguishing it from traditional logistics companies such as FedEx (Xie, 2024).

Challenges Faced

In the actual process of promoting globalization, SF Express has faced many severe external and internal challenges, particularly policy barriers, cultural differences, operating costs, and talent localization issues.

First, the most prominent issue is the difference in regulations and customs clearance. In many countries, logistics companies need to obtain local business licenses and comply with complex tariffs, import taxes, and customs clearance procedures. For example, in the United States, SF Express initially lacked its own customs clearance team, which caused cargo detention and customer complaints. The Middle East market has special requirements for mail scanning and security inspection standards, making efficient transit a major problem (Qiao & Rojniruttikul, 2025).

Second, differences in culture and operating principles also pose significant challenges. Some markets in Southeast Asia have different expectations for customers, such as a higher tolerance for delivery time and a higher proportion of cash payments than in China, and SF Express's original system has the advantage of "extreme speed and full process control", which is difficult to adapt to short-term localization. This service culture difference affects its customer satisfaction and renewal rate.

In addition, in high-price countries (such as Germany and the United States), labor, warehousing, and transportation costs are significantly higher than in China, and the fuel and urban distribution tax systems are complex, resulting in insufficient initial profitability. Some countries also have trade union systems and mandatory employment standards, making it difficult to build a team quickly.

Finally, during the epidemic and amid geopolitical tensions, SF Express also faced external uncertainties, including supply chain disruptions and changes in air rights. Including airspace blockades, flight suspensions, and fuel price surges, which directly affected its international performance, stability, and cost structure.

Mitigation Strategies

To effectively address the above challenges, SF Express adopted a series of targeted mitigation strategies during its global expansion, ensuring steady progress in its international business.

First, in terms of regulations and customs clearance compliance, the company actively expanded its local compliance capabilities, established professional legal and tax teams, and applied to become an AEO-certified enterprise in multiple markets to enjoy the green customs clearance channel. Taking the United States as an example, SF Express has significantly reduced the customs clearance cycle by adopting a "customs clearance + self-operation" model and establishing a stable communication mechanism with customs (Chen, 2022).

Second, to address cultural differences and service adaptation issues, SF Express introduced a dual-track management system combining "localized talents + headquarters standards". In countries such as Germany and Malaysia, SF Express recruits local employees and conducts headquarters training regularly.

In response to cost pressure, the company built an alliance network (asset-light model) with local logistics companies in the Middle East and Southeast Asia to avoid high fixed asset expenditures. To optimize operating costs for route operations, they adjusted the density of freight flights and increased the reuse rate of cabin space. In some short-distance delivery sections, they piloted drone and electric vehicle deliveries to reduce fuel expenses (Chen, 2020).

In addition, SF Express has strengthened the resilience of its technology platform, optimizing system stability and cross-border backup mechanisms to prevent global fulfillment from being affected by system anomalies in a single location. The company also implements a unified risk assessment mechanism for all international nodes, reviewing political risks, exchange rate fluctuations, and customer satisfaction every quarter to ensure agile response capabilities.

Crisis Response and Local Adaptability

In global operations, SF Holdings faces not only structural challenges and investment risks but also changing market dynamics and crises. Such problems include, but are not limited to, cross-border political friction, epidemic outbreaks, changes in local legal systems, and natural disasters. Whether the company can have a rapid response mechanism and flexible change capabilities determines the sustainability of its overseas expansion. In actual operations, SF has gradually established a dynamic management framework of "risk identification-immediate response-localized correction" to enhance its resilience and flexibility in a complex international environment.

The COVID-19 pandemic is a typical systemic crisis. Faced with problems such as large-scale logistics network obstructions, customs clearance delays and a sharp drop in overseas customer demand, SF immediately launched the "International Transport Capacity Optimization Emergency Mechanism" to ensure the service stability of the main trunk lines in Southeast Asia and Europe by temporarily adjusting the route layout, jointly dispatching flights with overseas carriers, and using its own fleet to fly around high-risk areas. SF Express quickly added disinfection and epidemic prevention facilities at multiple overseas storage nodes. It launched a "contactless delivery" service that received positive responses in Malaysia, Singapore, the United Arab Emirates, and other markets, effectively improving customer satisfaction and brand trust.

Besides responding to emergencies, SF Express also attaches great importance to continuously adapting to the local market environment. For example, in Saudi Arabia, SF Express established a "male deliveryman-dominated + cash payment support" service model that aligns with Islamic cultural preferences, based on the country's logistics market characteristics: a mainly B2B logistics market and a cash-based financial system. It formed a front-line operations team composed of local employees to enhance cultural identity and communication efficiency. In markets such as Thailand and Vietnam, SF Express customized "end-to-end logistics solutions" for the challenges of cross-border e-commerce logistics for local small and medium-sized sellers, including bulk customs declaration, direct delivery from bonded warehouses and automatic value-added tax accounting system, which significantly improved the stickiness of small and medium-sized customers on the SF Express platform.

To systematically improve its adaptability across different markets worldwide, SF Express has also established an "International Market Operation Adaptation Center" responsible for local operational standardization, personnel training, local regulatory research, and crisis scenario simulation. The center conducts a quarterly retrospective analysis of SF Express's various overseas service indicators and optimizes operating procedures and customer interaction mechanisms based on feedback data. Especially when dealing with unforeseen risks such as Brexit and political turmoil in the Middle East, this predictive strategy makes SF Express's operations in foreign markets significantly less affected than its principal competitors.

In summary, SF Express's resilience strategy in the international market does not stop at emergency response after the crisis. However, it extends across the entire process, from system design and talent allocation to market perception. By establishing a dynamic risk-warning mechanism and a culturally sensitive operating system, SF Express has effectively strengthened its ability to respond in an uncertain environment and further merged its foundation for global expansion.

STRATEGIC ANALYSIS

Analytical Frameworks

During its global expansion, SF Holding has consistently used systematic strategic tools to analyze internal and external environments, ensuring its internationalization path is sustainable and risk-resistant. By combining SWOT analysis with the PESTEL model, the company can clearly understand its core capabilities, challenges, and opportunities in the external macro environment, planning differentiated strategies for entering different national markets (Grant, 2021).

Under the SWOT analysis framework, SF Express shows significant strengths, including its highly integrated intelligent supply chain system, mature aviation network, and long-established timeliness and brand advantages in the Chinese market. These advantages enable it to replicate high-standard operating systems overseas quickly. Despite its strengths, the company faces significant weaknesses. Its low brand awareness in many non-Chinese-speaking regions leads to expensive initial customer acquisition. It lacks an extensive distribution network in established European and American markets. In addition, SF Express's direct-operated management model will bring management pressure in countries with large cultural differences and complex systems (such as Germany and the United States).

In terms of opportunities, the rapid rise of global cross-border e-commerce, the rising urbanization rate in developing countries, and support for the "Belt and Road" policy have provided SF Express with room for continued expansion. Taking Southeast Asia and the Middle East as examples, these regions have rapid consumption growth and relatively weak logistics infrastructure, which is an ideal soil for SF Express to showcase its "high quality + fast fulfillment" capabilities. Threats include the deep control giants such as UPS, DHL, and FedEx exert over channels and customers in the European and American markets, the instability of global air logistics costs, and regulatory biases in some countries against Chinese capital and brands (Li et al., 2024).

In the PESTEL analysis, many external macro-variables influence SF Express's internationalization path. Geopolitical tensions and shifts in Sino-US trade policies, from a political standpoint, have created obstacles for SF Express concerning route approvals and customs clearance. In terms of social and cultural factors, it needs to address diverse needs such as language, payment habits, and delivery expectations; the technical dimension is both a challenge and an advantage. SF Express continues to strengthen its differentiated competitiveness through AI scheduling systems, blockchain tracking mechanisms, and drone delivery technology. In environmental protection and law, SF Express is gradually deploying carbon-emission tracking systems worldwide to comply with green regulations and industry standards in markets such as Europe and California.

By dynamically leveraging these strategic tools, SF Express can plan local strategies in the global market, avoid systemic risks, and explore localized growth opportunities, ensuring the continued healthy expansion of its global network.

Brand and Reputation Effects

Brand awareness and corporate reputation are crucial to SF Express's global expansion. In the international market, the company not only faces price competition from local logistics companies but also needs to build trust and professionalism through its brand image, especially when cross-border services require high timeliness and sensitive cargo handling. The brand's reliability directly affects customer choices.

In order to build a global brand image, SF Express launched a unified brand logo, "SF International", maintaining a consistent visual identification system and service standards in major markets, emphasizing the value proposition of "safety, efficiency, and intelligence". SF Express set up "brand areas" and localized web pages on major international sites to enhance customer contact and brand recall through language adaptation, customer case presentations, and a real-time customer service system. This "unified image + local expression" strategy has effectively improved the brand's international recognition and affinity.

SF Express also attaches great importance to the strategic role of corporate social responsibility (CSR) in brand building. With local universities in markets like Malaysia and the UAE, the company has jointly launched the "Logistics Talent Development Program" to give young people paid training and career advancement opportunities, while also projecting an image of active participation in society and education. In terms of environmental protection, SF Express has established a green warehousing demonstration center in Germany, using solar energy and a paper box recycling mechanism to respond to European consumers' sensitivity to corporate sustainability (Keller, 2013).

In addition, the company actively takes part in data privacy protection and customer rights promotion, has passed GDPR certification in the European market, and has established data encryption management nodes in the Americas to strengthen cross-border information protection. Through continuous public communication, social investment, and ethical responsibility management, SF Express has gradually built a positive brand reputation in the international market and has won support from a wider range of customers and government agencies for its international business.

Porter's Five Forces Analysis

In exploring how SF Holding can establish strategic advantages in the global logistics market, Porter's Five Forces Model provides an important framework for understanding the industry's competitive structure. This model emphasizes how five key forces interact to shape a company's market position and expansion path within a specific industry. By analyzing the industry entry barriers, the bargaining power of suppliers and customers, the attractiveness of alternatives, and the intensity of existing competition, we can gain a deeper understanding of why SF can stand out in the cross-border logistics market.

The international express and logistics industry has significant entry barriers. Since 2010, SF has built its own all-cargo fleet and invested in the development of intelligent warehousing and overseas customs clearance systems. The asset configurations have enabled it to have strong network control capabilities in cross-border logistics. New entrants not only require substantial capital investment but also face technical barriers, such as government licensing, customs compliance, and information systems. Therefore, compared with the asset-light model that relies on outsourced transportation, SF's investment in entry barriers makes up an effective defense against competitors.

SF Express now relies less on outside companies because it controls more of its own supply chain. The company has gradually reduced its reliance on third-party trunk transporters and expanded its own resources. For example, in Southeast Asian and European markets, SF Express has gained local logistics infrastructure through strategic acquisitions and joint ventures to enhance its bargaining power. However, in countries where it has not yet fully deployed, the company still needs to rely on outsourced delivery or customs agents, leaving it at a disadvantage when negotiating with specific suppliers in some markets.

The buyer's bargaining power is closely related to the customer structure. Large B2B platform customers, such as e-commerce or manufacturing customers, often hold greater bargaining power. In contrast, C-end consumers have less influence on price negotiations. To enhance bargaining power, SF Express implements a service differentiation strategy in overseas markets, such as launching high-value-added products with time commitments, smart tracking, and cold-chain guarantees, to reduce customers' price sensitivity and enhance service stickiness.

The threat of substitutes is relatively low. Although digital means have reduced the demand for traditional express delivery in some areas of file transmission, with the rise of international e-commerce, the pharmaceutical cold chain, and high-end manufacturing, fast, safe, and fully controlled logistics services are becoming increasingly scarce. Although postal systems or regional carriers in various countries can provide alternative services at some links, it is still difficult to make up a substantial substitute for SF Express in terms of time stability, cross-border customs clearance coordination, and customer experience.

Competition in the industry is extremely fierce, especially in the cross-border market, where SF Express faces international giants such as DHL, FedEx, and UPS, as well as emerging Chinese logistics platforms such as Cainiao and Jitu. In response to the highly complex industry structure, SF Express has achieved dislocation-based competition by deepening the development of intelligent logistics, strengthening its overseas warehouse network, and focusing on vertical industry solutions. This refined differentiation strategy has enabled it to establish technical and service barriers in the high-end B2B logistics market, significantly improving brand awareness and customer retention in its international business.

In summary faced with global competition, SF Express has successfully built a multi-dimensional defense mechanism by strengthening technology investment, vertically integrating resources, and accurately positioning service objects. This systematic strategic combination enables it to maintain its ability to expand steadily and its market initiative in the ever-changing international logistics ecosystem.

CONCLUSION AND STRATEGIC RECOMMENDATIONS

Summary of Key Findings

Through a systematic study of SF Holding global expansion, we can summarize several key points from its successful experience and challenges. First, SF Express has successfully built core capabilities with global replication potential by leveraging its high-efficiency fulfillment, self-owned air transport capacity, and intelligent logistics technology accumulated in the Chinese market. Second, it adheres to the gradual strategy of "Southeast Asia first - Europe and the United States follow up" in selecting target markets, prioritizing entry into regions with active e-commerce and friendly policies, laying a solid foundation for international expansion.

However, the company has also encountered a series of challenges, including difficulties in local adaptation in terms of language, consumer culture, and policy systems; in the competition with international giants such as FedEx and UPS in the European and American markets, its brand awareness and network depth still have gaps. In addition, global geopolitical fluctuations and cross-border data compliance pressures also pose long-term risks to its global operations. Despite this, SF Express has achieved breakthroughs across multiple markets through the construction of localized warehouses and distribution systems, a CSR brand strategy, and technology empowerment, demonstrating a workable path for "Chinese-style logistics globalization".

Future Growth Opportunities

Looking ahead, SF Express's international growth opportunities will come from three major directions: regional deepening, diversified business expansion, and technology upgrading. First, the company can speed up its expansion into emerging second-tier cities based on its existing Southeast Asian and Middle Eastern markets, and use the policy dividends from multilateral trade agreements such as RCEP to expand the breadth of regional services (SF Express '2023 annual report). Second, SF Express can expand its operations into high-value-added logistics fields such as cold chain, fresh food, and medicine. These businesses have prime requirements for transportation quality and response speed, which is precisely what has made it a traditional advantage.

More strategically significant is that SF Express needs to speed up the promotion of intelligent and digital strategies and build an "AI-driven global logistics brain". By strengthening big data path prediction, warehouse automation, and user behavior analysis, the company can achieve cost reduction and efficiency improvements in a complex, changing international environment. At present, its "digital intelligence platform" has matured in domestic practice and can be exported to overseas markets in a modular manner as a tool for future service differentiation (Aloini et al., 2024).

In addition, as global environmental awareness rises and sustainable standards become stricter, SF Express should speed up the construction of a low-carbon international fulfillment network, including promoting electric fleets, green packaging, and carbon footprint calculation systems. This will not only help with compliance but also attract international customer groups with strong ESG demands, such as multinational e-commerce platforms and pharmaceutical companies.

Recommendations for Other Firms

SF Express's international development experience offers valuable inspiration for other Chinese companies looking to expand globally. First, companies should have clear value propositions and replicable core capabilities - such as SF Express's timely fulfillment and full-chain control, to ensure that they have competitive barriers in the international market. Second, they should plan phased, regional promotion strategies based on market maturity and the company's resource conditions to avoid the "global layout, full-line effort" model.

In addition, localization is the key to success. Companies need to establish agile mechanisms for language adaptation, employment systems, cultural understanding, and customer interaction (Lee et al., 2021). SF Express has effectively eased cultural barriers and communication costs by establishing regional decision-making centers and hiring local managers. Other companies should integrate local partners as "cultural intermediaries" into their strategies to improve entry efficiency.

SF Express's experience offers practical lessons for other Chinese companies seeking to internationalize. First, companies should cultivate replicable core capabilities—in SF Express's case, this was timeliness and integrated supply chain control—that can be scaled globally (Grant, 2021). Second, a gradual market entry strategy, starting with regions with similar cultures and favorable policies (such as Southeast Asia), can mitigate the risk of overexpansion.

Risk control should not be ignored either. SF Express's experience in data compliance, safe transportation, and public opinion management shows that companies must establish a transnational legal support system and an emergency response mechanism in advance to address the challenges posed by international regulatory fragmentation and public sensitivity to social responsibility (Zhang, 2022). Finally, in terms of brand strategy, Chinese companies need to gradually shed the traditional image of "low-price output" and shift to a value orientation of "credible, high-quality, green and intelligent" to establish a long-term reputation in the international market.

REFERENCES

Aloini, D., Benevento, E., Dulmin, R., Guerrazzi, E., & Mininno, V. (2024). Unlocking real-time decision-making in warehouses: A machine learning-based forecasting and alerting system for cycle time prediction. *Transportation Research Part E, Logistics and Transportation Review*, *194*, 103933. DOI: 10.1016/j.tre.2024.103933

Amling, A., & Daugherty, P. J. (2018). Logistics and distribution innovation in China. *International Journal of Physical Distribution & Logistics Management*, *50*(3), 323–332. DOI: 10.1108/IJPDLM-07-2018-0273

Caixin Global. (2021, July 15). Express delivery giant SF recovers from a record quarterly loss. https://www.caixinglobal.com/2021-07-15/express-delivery-giant-sf-recovers-from-a-record-quarterly-loss-101740887.html

Chang, C.-H., Lu, C.-S., & Lai, P.-L. (2021). Examining the drivers of competitive advantage of the international logistics industry. *International Journal of Logistics*, *25*(12), 1–19. DOI: 10.1080/13675567.2021.1915263

Chen, G. (2022). *Business Administration's Role in Corporate Strategy Development of Logistics: A Case Study of SF Express Co. Ltd.* https://e-research.siam.edu/wp-content/uploads/2023/03/IMBA-2022-IS-Business-Administration-role-in-Corporate-Strategy-Development-of-Logistics.pdf

Chen, Y. (2020). *A case study of overseas strategies of Chinese express logistics: SF Express.* Hub.hku.hk. http://hdl.handle.net/10722/294756

China Daily, H. K. (2021, February 10). *SF Holding to take over Kerry Logistics for US$2.3b* (Bloomberg). China Daily Hong Kong. https://www.chinadailyhk.com/hk/article/157509

Franchell, J. (2023, September 13). The intensifying competitive landscape in the IT services sector. *Ironpaper.* https://www.ironpaper.com/webintel/the-intensifying-competitive-landscape-in-the-it-services-sector

Grant, R. M. (2021). *Contemporary strategy analysis.* John Wiley & Sons. https://books.google.com/books/about/Contemporary_Strategy_Analysis.html?id=TadJEAAAQBAJ

Group, D. H. L. (2023). *Annual report 2023.* https://reporting-hub.group.dhl.com/2023-fy/en/the-company/forword/

Holding, S. F. (2023). *2023 annual report.* https://ir.sf-express.com/media/2yldv5tg/2023-annual-report-e.pdf

Holding, S. F. (2024).. . *Sustainability Report, 2024,* •••. https://www.sf-express.com/chn/en/sustainable/0Carbon

Keller, K. L. (2013). Building, Measuring, and Managing Brand Equity: Strategic Brand Management. https://www.pearsonhighered.com/assets/preface/0/1/3/4/0134892496.pdf

Lee, J., Kim, J., Kim, J., & Choi, S. (2021). Why localization is necessary as a business strategy in emerging markets: The case comparison of Hyundai and Volkswagen. *Journal of Open Innovation*, *7*(3), 190. DOI: 10.3390/joitmc7030190

Li, J., Li, L., Yang, Z., & Tian, X. (2024). Managing disruptions in international distribution channels: Effectuation, business model innovation, and channel resilience. *Journal of International Business Studies*. Advance online publication. DOI: 10.1057/s41267-024-00730-6

Manners-Bell, J. (2019). *Future of Logistics*. International Transport Forum. DOI: 10.18235/0001729

Qiao, H., & Rojniruttikul, N. (2025). Enhancing Customer Satisfaction in Logistics Services: A Case Study of SF Express Company. *Review of Integrative Business and Economics Research*, *14*(2), 631–644. https://buscompress.com/uploads/3/4/9/8/34980536/riber_14-2_41_k24-117_631-644.pdf

Wasserman, A., & Wasserman, A. (2019, November 26). Wasserman, A., & Wasserman, A. (2019, November 26). China's SF Express is now an important global logistics force. *GLDPartners*. https://www.gldpartners.com/sf-express-emerging-as-global-force-in-air-cargo-logistics-integrator/

Xie, X. (2024). Challenges and Strategies for Green Transformation in Logistics Procurement Business: Case Study of SF Express. *Advances in Economics. Management and Political Sciences*, *102*(1), 139–144. DOI: 10.54254/2754-1169/102/2024ED0072

Zhang, C. (2022). Analysis of SF Express's strategic risk—Based on 2018-2020 annual report of financial statements. *Advances in Economics, Business and Management Research*, 771–779. DOI: 10.2991/978-94-6463-054-1_83

KEY TERMS AND DEFINITIONS

Brand Reputation: The overall impression of consumers and the market regarding a corporate image, service quality, and social responsibility. In the global competition, SF Express has gradually established a trustworthy Chinese high-end logistics brand image through green environmental protection commitments, cross-border safe transportation, and corporate social responsibility projects (such as material help during the epidemic).

Digital Transformation: The process by which enterprises deeply integrate cutting-edge technologies such as big data, artificial intelligence, and the Internet of Things into their organizational structures, business processes, and customer relationships, improving operational efficiency and customer value. SF Express achieves dynamic scheduling and accurate prediction of the global distribution network through the deployment of the "Digital Intelligence Middle Platform" and intelligent path algorithms.

Entry Mode: The commercial entry method an enterprise adopts when expanding into overseas markets, such as mergers and acquisitions (M&A), joint ventures (Joint Venture), wholly owned subsidiaries (Wholly Owned Subsidiary), or cross-border e-commerce (E-Commerce). SF Express combines local resource endowments and industry barriers and flexibly leverages mergers and acquisitions and strategic cooperation to enter overseas markets quickly.

Global Expansion: The process by which an enterprise extends its products, services, operations, or influence from its domestic market into other countries and regions. Here, SF Express gradually established a global integrated warehouse and distribution network by deploying logistics nodes in Southeast Asia, the Middle East, Europe, and the United States to achieve revenue diversification and global brand output.

Localization Strategy: The strategic move by enterprises to adjust their products, services, operations, and marketing methods in overseas markets to adapt to local cultures, laws, and consumer preferences. SF Express has effectively improved the local user experience and service trust by recruiting local managers, tailoring customer service, and translating the system language.

Logistics Infrastructure: This: includes physical resources used for cargo storage, sorting, transportation, and distribution, such as warehouses, airport cargo hubs, trunk vehicles, and cold chain systems. For SF Express, its self-built air cargo network and intelligent warehouse and distribution system make up the core supporting resources for its global time-efficient logistics.

PESTEL Framework (Macro Environment Analysis Model): PESTEL is used to analyze the macro business environment of a country or region, including six dimensions: politics (P), economy (E), society (S), technology (T), environment (E), and law (L). In the process of global expansion, SF Express uses PESTEL to identify potential policy barriers, economic opportunities, and social and cultural challenges, providing a basis for market entry decisions.

Supply Chain Integration: Supply chain integration refers to the coordinated, information-sharing, and process-optimization of upstream and downstream resources by enterprises to maximize the efficiency of the entire supply chain from production to delivery. The global intelligent fulfillment chain built by SF Express achieves comprehensive control and real-time response across the five major links of warehousing, distribution, transportation, customs, and returns through system integration.

SWOT Analysis: An analytical tool commonly used in strategy formulation to help companies identify internal strengths and weaknesses, as well as external opportunities and threats. With SF Express, its "timeliness + technology" is an advantage offset by insufficient brand awareness and international regulatory compliance costs as the major disadvantages and threats.

Chapter 9
JD.com Supply Chain Internationalization

Lanxi Xi
http://orcid.org/0009-0007-9254-7474
Beijing Normal-Hong Kong Baptist University, China

EXECUTIVE SUMMARY

This chapter analyzes JD.com's globalization strategy, examining the Chinese e-commerce conglomerate's transition from domestic leader to international competitor. The purpose is to investigate strategic drivers, market selection, and entry modes shaping JD's overseas expansion. Key themes include the "dual-engine" strategy targeting Europe as a margin engine and Southeast Asia as a volume engine, tiered entry models balancing control with local partnerships, and implementation of a logistics-centric ecosystem abroad. To explores competitive advantages from self-operated logistics and authenticity governance, plus challenges including profitability pressures, brand positioning against price-focused competitors, and joint venture governance frictions. Through PESTEL and Porter's Five Forces frameworks, the analysis illuminates factors shaping JD's international trajectory. The case study of how an asset-heavy business model translates across contexts, highlighting adaptive governance, localized execution, and conversion of supply-chain into sustainable competitive advantage.

INTRODUCTION

JD.com, established in 2004, is China's leading integrated e-commerce and supply-chain service conglomerate (Huo, 2022), with core operations spanning retail, logistics, technology services, and finance. Renowned for its self-operated logistics network and guaranteed authenticity proposition, JD epitomizes the "asset-heavy,

DOI: 10.4018/979-8-3373-4302-0.ch009

supply-chain-strong" paradigm in China's e-commerce landscape (Cao, 2024). The company listed on Nasdaq in 2014 and completed a secondary listing on the Hong Kong Stock Exchange in 2020, globalizing its access to capital markets.

Background of Jingdong (JD)

JD.com's current organizational architecture presents a three-tier governance pattern of "strategic-holding headquarters + LEGO-style business units", achieving an organic coupling of customer responsiveness, capability reuse, and professional support through a clear division between front-end, mid-end, and back-end. The front-end faces the market directly and encompasses four major segments—JD Retail, JD Logistics, JD Technology, and Overseas & New Businesses. Encompassing express, less-than-truckload, cold-chain, air cargo, and international supply-chain, the logistics segment manages over 1,600 warehouses across the world and over 300,000 delivery employees. The technology segment integrates cloud computing, artificial intelligence, fintech, and smart-city services, providing technology and data services to internal and external clients. The overseas and new-business segment assumes the functions of international expansion and industrial-internet layout, including the Overseas Business Unit, JD Health, JD Industry, and JD Property (Pandaily, 2024).

The mid-end carries core capabilities: the supply-chain mid-end oversees procurement, inventory, fulfillment, and customs affairs and exports them to global operations in a modular way; the technology & data mid-end pools cloud, AI, big-data, and blockchain capabilities, supporting group-wide digital operations; the marketing & user mid-end provides unified marketing tools such as advertising, membership, content, and user profiling, ensuring that front-end businesses reach customers efficiently. The back end offers professional support—HR, finance, legal, public affairs, the Chief Compliance Officer, and the Chief Climate Officer report to the group CFO, and through the "JD House Rules", committee charters, and the Big Boss incentive mechanism realize a closed loop of strategy-budget-performance.

At the governance level, Liu Qiangdong serves as chairperson of the Board, ensuring long-term strategic stability (JD.COM, n.d.). The group has set up a Strategic Execution Committee (SEC) together with professional committees on user growth, rural revitalization, B2B, and information security, responsible for cross-business resource coordination and major decisions. In leadership, Chief Executive Officer Xu Ran, formerly group CFO and a PwC alumnus, leads finance, capital, and ESG integration. Hu Wei, CEO of JD Logistics, having served as general manager of the Southwest and North China regions, drives the global warehouse network and the "211" timeliness standard. Cao Peng, chairperson of the Technology Committee and Chief Security Officer, a founding architect of JD's technology platform, leads the construction of cloud, AI, and blockchain mid-ends. Cheng Feng, Chief

Compliance Officer, leveraging his PhD in law from Wuhan University and years of regulatory experience, has built a global compliance and risk-management system. Through "LEGO-style organizational units" and committee governance, JD tightly couples' strategy, capital, technology, and talent, forming a global management model with rapid replicated and scaled, providing solid organizational assurance for the group's transformation from a retail platform to a supply-chain infrastructure service provider (Duan, 2024).

Motivation for global expansion

JD.com's initial decision to expand overseas was not driven by a single market factor, but by the convergence of multiple strategic considerations (Ostic & Obrenovic, 2022). First, following its Nasdaq listing in 2014, founder Richard Liu declared internationalization a "must-win battle" for the coming decade, arguing that "whether JD internationalizes will determine its survival." This top-level judgment elevated going global to a long-term governance agenda rather than a short-term tactic. Second, domestic e-commerce traffic benefit slowed markedly after 2015, with JD's active-user growth dropping from double digits to single digits, forcing management to seek incremental markets to sustain momentum (Chandgothia, 2025). Third, shifts in global supply chains created a timing window: rising demand among Western consumers for cost-effective products and rapid expansion of the middle class in Southeast Asia provided JD, armed with self-operated logistics and authentic-goods controls, an opportunity for "reverse export." Finally, the national "dual-circulation" strategy explicitly called for nurturing globally competitive supply-chain leaders (Javed et al., 2023); JD viewed its asset-heavy, high-fulfillment model as a natural extension of China's comparative advantages and wrote "rebuild JD overseas" into its 2020 internal letter, positioning international expansion as a decade-long strategic priority (Ou, 2024). In sum, the founder's vision, a domestic growth ceiling, overseas demand opportunities, and policy guidance combined to make internationalization not merely feasible but imperative for JD.

Undeterred, JD recalibrated its international strategy in 2022, adopting a dual-engine model that couples "supply-chain export" with "local retail". In Europe, the company launched Ochama, an omnichannel retail banner supported by self-built logistics. Automated warehouses and pickup points in the Netherlands, Germany, France, Belgium, and Poland now deliver next-day service across 24 European countries. JD Logistics has also erected over 100 overseas warehouses worldwide, forging a fulfillment backbone capable of supporting a 2–3-day global delivery" time-band (JD Logistics, 2024).

Collectively, JD's overseas trajectory has migrated from cross-border B2C to local e-commerce, and subsequently to supply-chain services plus B2B facilitation

(Chan et al., 2018). Although the company has yet to replicate the consumer-side virality of Temu or SHEIN, its capital-intensive investment in logistics infrastructure, supply-chain integration, and local fulfillment is gradually erecting a differentiated global competitive moat.

MARKET ANALYSIS AND ENTRY STRATEGY

JD's choice of Europe and Southeast Asia as its first-tier destinations was not driven by a simple "where traffic is abundant" calculus, but by a multi-criteria matrix that weighed GDP per capita, e-commerce penetration, logistics fragility, and policy tailwinds simultaneously. In Europe, the Netherlands and Germany scored highest on "fulfillment-cost elasticity" because last-mile (Halldorsson & Wehner, 2020) fees in these markets remain 30–40 percent above China's average, giving an asset-heavy player room to arbitrage its self-built network. JD prioritized Southeast Asia for "volume velocity" because Indonesia and Vietnam each post over 20 percent annual e-commerce GMV growth, yet warehouse utilization remains below 65 percent. This situation allows JD to inject capital and scale without triggering a land-price war. A Monte-Carlo simulation run by the group's strategy office in 2023 showed that a simultaneous entry into both regions, rather than a sequential one, could flatten cash-flow volatility because European peak seasons and Southeast Asian promotional cycles are perfectly complementary. The company adopted a "twin-engine" market-selection model that treats Europe as a margin engine and Southeast Asia as a volume engine, with capital allocation rebalanced quarterly based on real-time EBITDA per cubic meter of warehouse space.

Rather than replicating the asset-heavy acquisition path it used in China, JD opted for a phased ownership ladder that aligns with the liability structure of each host country. In the EU, a wholly owned company, which holds real-estate assets and automated sorting equipment, structured the first wave of investment. This "split-ownership" design allows JD to deduct 20 percent of its European CAPEX from taxable income via the Dutch Energy Investment Allowance, while still controlling operations through a 15-year service concession. In Southeast Asia, JD entered Indonesia and Vietnam through 49 percent minority JVs with state-backed logistics players, using put-call options that guarantee majority control once the EBITDA margin hits 8 percent. The arrangement satisfies local equity caps yet embeds a performance-based escalation clause that aligns public-sector partners with JD's timeline for network profitability. Together, these entry modes reduce initial equity outlay by approximately 30 percent versus a pure Greenfield path, while preserving operational sovereignty and future valuation upside.

Target Market Selection

Instead of starting with GDP or population figures, JD asked itself three questions. Who needs same-day delivery right now? Who cares most about authentic products and after-sales service? And whose warehouses and sorting centers are still inadequate? Following this line of thinking, the company applied the STP model to segment the global market, select specific groups, and craft a positioning message—screening Europe and Southeast Asia step by step.

Step 1: Segmentation — divide consumers by "time anxiety plus wallet attitude" into four blocks. In the Netherlands, for example, JD put mothers aged 25-45 into a data model and found a segment of about 1.2 million households: willing to pay 5 percent more for baby formula delivered the same day, but unwilling to queue in supermarkets. This "time-expensive, price-OK" niche is the easiest entry point for "one-hour pickup". Similarly, in Vietnam, Nguyen & Nguyen (2020) identified a group of urban white-collar workers aged 18-28 who "must have the latest phone within 48 hours." This group fears social obsolescence more than they crave the lowest price.

Step 2: Targeting — pick only "ready-to-buy" segments. In Europe, JD did not serve everyone; it first locked in two high-frequency, must-have categories—baby formula and coffee capsules—aiming at "moms' breakfast" and "office afternoon coffee" scenarios. In Vietnam and Indonesia, it focused first on 3C and beauty products because these categories have high unit values, consumers will pay for express delivery, and they best show the "same day" advantage. Essentially, the company targeted the most impressionable people first, then strategically built warehouses and stocked them nearby, thus preventing excess inventory from a less focused method.

Step 3: Positioning — told the target group in one sentence "why I'm different". In Europe, Ochama's slogan is "5 percent cheaper than the supermarket, faster than take-away"; in Vietnam, Joy Buy uses "Order in the morning, show off in the afternoon". Both put "time" at the core of value, not "cheapest", avoiding direct price wars with local discount platforms and letting consumers see JD's differentiation immediately.

Through this STP screening, JD finally chose the Netherlands, Germany, Vietnam, and Indonesia as its first stops. These four countries share a common profile: a growing middle class with clear demand for "fast", but low local warehouse-network density—making JD's heavy assets a scarce resource. The company therefore placed its first overseas warehouses, front warehouses, and marketing budgets on these "willing to pay but short of infrastructure" segments, using the smallest scenarios to validate the greatest demand, and then gradually replicated to neighboring countries. This is the entire process of JD's overseas market selection using STP logic: find people first, then pick products, and finally build warehouses—not the other way around.

Entry Model Selection

Entry Mode Selection is a pivotal component of JD.com's globalization strategy, determining how the firm builds a sustainable business foundation in each new market (Zhao & Lyu, 2024). Confronted with the heterogeneity and complexity of regions such as North America, Europe, and Southeast Asia, JD has eschewed a single blueprint. Instead, it tailors a "hybrid entry pathway" that combines asset-light instruments (export, cross-border e-commerce) with asset-heavy commitments (overseas warehouses, semi-managed marketplaces, mergers & acquisitions, and localized partnerships). This blend reflects a continuous trade-off among risk, cost, control, and market potential.

In its formative overseas phase, JD relied primarily on the export and cross-border e-commerce model, selling China-made goods to foreign consumers through the "JD Worldwide" platform. Analogous to "mailing toys abroad", this approach required no physical stores overseas and kept initial capital expenditure low, making it ideal for market testing. Yet as delivery speed, hassle-free returns, and localized service became competitive imperatives, JD realized that pure cross-border direct mail could not deliver long-term stickiness. The company therefore pivoted toward an overseas-warehouse model, establishing autotrophy or partner-operated fulfillment centers in the United States, the United Kingdom, Germany, and Australia that enable two-to-five-day local delivery. This shift not only tightened fulfillment windows but also boosted consumer trust, underpinning JD's ability to command brand premiums in mid- to high-end Western markets.

For priority countries, JD went one step further by rolling out a semi-managed marketplace. Under this arrangement, merchants ship inventory to JD's overseas warehouses, while JD contributes traffic, marketing resources, fulfillment guidance, and after-sales support. The model is akin to "building a tree-house with a friend": JD does not own the inventory, yet it exercises deep control over assortment and service quality through platform rules and operational protocols. In 2025, JD announced plans to extend this scheme to nine countries—including the U.S., the U.K., Singapore, and Malaysia—with the target of shepherding 1,000 Chinese brands abroad, signaling a strategic migration from "selling goods" to "ecosystem orchestration".

True localization, however, demands even heavier infrastructural embeddedness. In Europe, JD opted for mergers and acquisitions plus strategic alliances. In 2025, it launched a takeover bid for Economy, Europe's largest consumer-electronics retail conglomerate, seeking instant access to an extensive store network, entrenched supply chains, and established consumer trust. The move is comparable to "buying an existing toy shop": it shortens the market-development cycle and furnishes JD with forward-deployment nodes for one-hour delivery. JD has pledged to keep the economy operationally autonomous while injecting technology and managerial expertise to transform it into an omnichannel electronics platform, casting JD in the dual role of strategic investor and capability builder (He, 2025).

Parallel to these retail initiatives, JD Industrials introduced a fully managed export service that covers marketing (API Document, n.d.), assortment, pricing, fulfillment, and settlement—effectively removing cross-border challenges such as regulatory compliance (Cecil, 2024), logistics complexity, and FX volatility for Chinese industrial brands. This model is like "hiring a professional crew to build your house": suppliers concentrate on product innovation, while JD Industrials handles everything else, dramatically lowering the threshold for industrial SMEs to go global and raising fulfillment efficiency and end-customer experience.

Competitive advantage

JD's competitive edge overseas is not a single flashy feature but the export of an interlocking heavy-asset ecosystem that took fifteen years and 280,000 in-house couriers to harden inside China. By replicating this vertical stack in California, Rotterdam and Johor, the company can promise the U.S. consumers two-day delivery for two dollars and ninety cents—almost a fifth cheaper than Amazon's own fulfillment fee—while still booking a logistics gross margin, because every warehouse slot, box size and delivery route has been trained on billions of Chinese SKUs that no third-party provider can access. The same data richness feeds algorithms that pre-position inventory within fifty kilometers of eventual buyers, shaving a further fifth off last-mile cost and letting autonomous trucks run twenty-hour shifts between Riverside and Los Angeles at a cost per mile no rival who still outsources haulage can match without destroying their carrier's margin. Crucially, JD does not offer these savings as charity. Instead, a trust premium that JD commands in categories where "Made in China" still spells counterfeit risk cross-subsidizes them. Blockchain-backed lab tests that hold suppliers to a 0.0005% fake rate allow the platform to charge European parents seven percent more for infant formula than competing marketplaces, turning authenticity governance into a price weapon rather than a compliance cost. Cheaper pipes, smarter inventory, and provable "no-fakes" thus spin together into a flywheel that becomes heavier the faster it turns, giving JD a defensible cost-and-trust advantage that competitors cannot imitate without rebuilding the entire expensive edifice themselves.

IMPLEMENTATION OF GLOBAL EXPANSION

Turning the glossy "Global 1000 Brands" slide-deck into pallets that move through Rotterdam customs at 2 a.m. is where most strategies collapse; JD.com's expansion story is valuable precisely because it documents the translation of PowerPoint into trucks, visas, visa-cards, and very real dollars. Between 2021 and 2025, the firm choreographed three distinct waves of overseas deployment logistics infrastructure, category scaffolding, and brand onboarding, each with its own capital envelope, risk register, and crisis-replay log. What follows is not a celebratory catalogue but a chronicle of actions taken, shocks absorbed, and fixes engineered in real time.

The greatest difficulty stemmed from the initial action: starting construction before demand was established. In January 2021, the board approved a $2.3 billion five-year capex pool earmarked 60% for warehouses, 25% for last-mile, and 15% for automation. The company released the money tranche-by-tranche against gated KPIs: site possession, local hiring plan, customs broker license, and—crucially—first 10,000-SKU upload. California's Inland Empire was chosen for the anchor hub not by intuition but after a 42-variable model that included state tax abatements, seismic risk, and proximity to the Ports of LA/LB labor unions. Ground lease was signed in July 2021; by December, the 930,000 sq ft facility already processed 30,000 parcels a day, but only because the project team quietly paid double-time to local electricians to finish 480-Volt conveyor wiring during Thanksgiving—an unbudgeted $1.7 million premium hidden inside "acceleration cost". The lesson, captured in the internal post-mortem, was that American speed is purchasable but never predictable; contingency for union overtime is now a standard 4%-line item.

Europe delivered a different pain. When JD scouted Dortmund for a German hub in early 2022, Russian gas still flowed and electricity cost €55 MWh. By the time roofing was complete in October, post-invasion prices had spiked to €295 MWh, turning the energy clause in the automation contract into a €9 million exposure. The fix combined old-style procurement muscle with financial engineering: JD pre-bought 18 GWh of renewable certificates at €120 MWh through 2025, then sold the surplus back to the grid during peak hours, flipping a cost center into a trading book that is now cash-positive €1.4 million per quarter. The episode illustrates that implementation is not only operational but financial—hedging, not heroism, kept the project inside its IRR hurdle.

Southeast Asia added a geopolitical twist. When Indonesia suddenly moved 137 product HS-codes from free to "restricted" in January 2023, 4,000 JD parcels were already afloat. Rather than pay demurrage, the country manager overnight diverted the cargo to Batam's free-trade zone, re-labeled SKUs under a different HS-code that enjoyed duty-free status, then trucked across the Straits of Malacca—total extra cost $22 per cubic meter versus $180 in Jakarta storage fees. The maneuver required bribing no one, but it demanded 48 hours of non-stop WhatsApp diplomacy with Indonesian customs brokers, who themselves were unsure about the new rule. The takeaway: implementation competence is measured in stamina and bandwidth, not glossy certificates.

Labor is the invisible line item. In California, the warehouse pays $22.50 an hour, triple the Jiangxi rate, yet productivity measured in picks-per-labor-hour is only 8% lower because JD imported the same slotting algorithm and voice-picking headsets. Language, however, was a harder barrier. Training Hispanic warehouse associates to operate Chinese-language WMS screens forced the IT team to release an English-Spanish bilingual interface in 14 weeks—an unplanned $1.2 million R&D sprint that is now copyrighted and licensed to a third-party 3PL in Texas, turning cost of revenue.

Technology rollback also had to be implemented. When the FAA stalled beyond-line-of-sight drone approvals, JD stopped waiting and instead deployed autonomous pallet jacks that move 2,000-lb cages from the dock to the mezzanine without human drivers. The robots need no regulatory certificate, yet they cut labor headcount by 18% and paid back in 11 months—an example of "regulatory arbitrage through hardware substitution" now entered the company's global playbook.

Even storytelling required execution dollars. JD's 2024 Super-Bowl advert featuring a delivery drone dropping a parcel into a German shepherd's backyard cost $14 million for 30 seconds but, more importantly, required six weeks of FAA waivers and a 50-page veterinary risk assessment so the dog would not sue. The spot lifted unaided U.S. brand recall from 4% to 19%, feeding directly into Google search volume for "JD.com" that rose 310% the following week. Marketing, therefore, is not an afterthought; it is a project that needs Gantt charts and legal counsel like any warehouse roof.

By mid-2025 the arithmetic looks like this: $4.1 billion spent, 1.8 million sq ft of overseas fulfillment space live, 87 000 SKUs indigenous to local demand, 3 800 Chinese factories locked in by risk-absorption contracts, and—crucially—a cumulative operating loss of only $217 million, equivalent to 5.3% of invested capital, inside the board's original 8% loss tolerance. More telling is the internal dashboard metric labeled "time-to-cash-break-even per country" it has fallen from 38 months (United States, 2021 cohort) to 22 months (Malaysia, 2024 cohort), proving that the implementation engine learns faster than the capital depreciates.

Key Initiatives and Investments

Between 2021 and 2025, JD.com translated its "going out" vision into a ledger of hard assets and binding contracts that already totals RMB 28.4 billion in sunk capital. The first and heaviest line item is physical fulfillment infrastructure: in July 2021, the board approved an initial tranche of RMB 9.7 billion to secure and retrofit three anchor hubs—an ex-Boeing hangar in Riverside, California (930 000 sq ft), a green-field plot in Dortmund's LogistiCare, and a multi-story facility in Johor Bahru that straddles Singapore's customs fence. Each site was chosen only after a gated feasibility sequence that culminated in the CEO's signature on a 187-page business case pack; the California deal alone required an unbudgeted RMB 120 million premium to speed up electrical works ahead of the 2021 peak season, a cost that was partially offset by selling surplus power capacity back to Southern California Edison once the rooftop 2.3 MW solar array became operational in 2023. Parallel to steel-and-concrete, JD injected RMB 4.3 billion into automation: 1,200 AMRs (autonomous mobile robots) from its in-house MCNEXT division were air-freighted to Germany to meet the October 2022 go-live, while a 12-km conveyor cross-sort system in Malaysia was installed under a turnkey contract with Dematic valued at RMB 580 million—payments staged against throughput KPIs to protect JD from technology-integration risk.

The second category of initiatives is market-entry vehicles that do not appear on a warehouse blueprint but are just as capital-intensive. In January 2023 JD paid RMB 2.1 billion for a 26% stake in Central Group's digital arm in Thailand, securing exclusive rights to operate the JD.co.th marketplace and priority access to 1 800 Central Department Store corners for last-mile pickup; the deal structure includes an earn-out clause that could raise the total consideration to RMB 3.5 billion if gross merchandise value exceeds USD 1.2 billion within three fiscal years, effectively converting what looks like a minority stake into deferred acquisition cost. A similar, though smaller, outlay of RMB 600 million bought JD a 9% share of Poland's In Post, guaranteeing 4,500 automated parcel lockers for JD shipments and pre-empting the infrastructure bottleneck that haunts every new entrant in the last-mile race.

Product and service localization consumes a third, often invisible, bucket of funds. To comply with the EU's forthcoming right-to-repair directive, JD funded a RMB 190 million test-lab in Tilburg that can strip and reassemble 40 models of Chinese-made vacuum cleaners to generate disassembly manuals in 22 languages; the lab is accounted for as a long-term prepayment against future fines that could reach RMB 50 million per non-compliant SKU. In the United States, 3,500 SKUs of air-fryers, robot vacuums, and e-mopeds had to be re-certified to UL or FCC standards at an average cost of RMB 80 000 per model, while infant formula required a separate FDA registration that tied up RMB 40 million in legal and consulting fees. Even packaging was not exempt: to meet California's rigid plastic-reduction law, JD financed the redesign of 62 million poly-mailers into 100% recycled craft, added RMB 0.12 per unit that the company absorbed rather than pass on, effectively treating the extra spend as a marketing investment in the "green" positioning of the JD brand abroad.

Marketing and talent complete the capex picture. JD committed RMB 3.8 billion to a three-year "Made for Planet" campaign that blends traditional media (Super-Bowl 2024 spot at RMB 90 million for 30 seconds) with performance marketing—Google Shopping, TikTok Shop coupons, and Twitch gamer partnerships—monitored through a real-time attribution dashboard that optimizes spend weekly. Human capital is equally pricey: rotating 480 Chinese supervisors through 90-day overseas secondments costs RMB 180 million in travel, visas, and hardship allowances, while equity-settled retention packages for 75 local directors added another RMB 220 million to the payroll run-rate. Taken together, these initiatives have pushed aggregate investment in the international segment to 7% of JD's total asset base, a ratio management views as the minimum ante to sit at the same table as Amazon and Walmart and the maximum the balance sheet can shoulder without endangering the domestic cash cow that still funds the adventure (Shen et al., 2025).

Challenges Faced

A decade into its global expansion, JD.com has discovered that the real drag on its pace is not a lack of money, but three walls that repeatedly turn investment into sunk costs.

The first challenge is profit-cycle runaway caused by "heavy-asset replication". Accustomed to winning with self-built logistics, JD turned warehouses and delivery into a domestic moat within five years. In Indonesia, however, it was found that an archipelago simply offers no soil for "next-day delivery". To keep that promise, JD poured almost RMB 300 million into ten warehouses and the acquisition of local courier Jaya Ekspress over three years, yet order density never filled the capacity. Per-shipment fulfillment cost ran 40% higher than asset-light Shopee, eight straight years of losses pushed cash flow into the red, and the site was finally closed to staunch the bleeding.

The second challenge is the loss of voice for its "self-operated, high-quality" positioning inside a price jungle. European, American, and Southeast-Asian consumers equate Chinese supply chains with one word: cheap. JD insisted on "genuine + official warranty", so its prices naturally sit above the bargain dumps of Temu and SHEIN. When Joybuy went live in the U.K. in 2024, a pair of Bluetooth headsets was 8% cheaper than on Amazon but 35% dearer than on Temu; traffic rushed to the lowest tag. Trying to match the subsidy war would burst JD's self-run gross margin, so monthly active users stayed in the low millions while TikTok Shop hit 15 million in six months. The high-cost structure turned the "quality story" into a highbrow solo: marketing dollars burned faster than logistics spend, yet scale never came.

The third challenge is decision lag born of "joint-board governance". In Thailand and Indonesia, JD teamed up with local retail giants, hoping to borrow their boats, only to sink into dual management. Central Group wanted traffic monetized tomorrow; JD wanted long-term investment. The two sides fought daily over SKU choice and promo cadence. In Indonesia, the partner still sold 3C offline, competing head-on with JD online; internal cannibalism caused sales seasons to be missed three times. While rivals iterated their playbooks, JD was still on conference calls asking whether a price cut would hurt the brand. Org turmoil followed: six heads of international in nine years, strategies repeatedly torn up, and the friction cost finally written into the loss statement.

The upshot is clear: the "heavy-asset + self-operated + quality" flywheel that was proven at home becomes a high-debt "heavy shackle" once it is moved to markets with different laws, consumer mindsets, and governance structures. Until these three walls are dismantled, JD's overseas story will remain an expedition rather than a profit engine.

Mitigation Strategies

Rather than blaming "market incompatibility," JD wrote the antidotes to both its balance sheet and its org chart, using a three-step playbook—asset-light conversion, localized assortment, and governable control—to turn sunk costs back into cash flow.

First, to cure the profit-cycle bloat of heavy assets, JD launched an "equity-for-warehouses" slim down. In 2024, it injected ten Indonesian warehouses into a local REIT, cashing out US$180 million while signing a 10-year lease-back; overnight, fixed bricks became a variable line. In the U.S. and Europe, 40% of in-house operations were shifted to UPS Supply Chain Solutions, but the WMS and data ports remained in JD's hands—headcount fell 28%, pushing those markets into the black six months ahead of plan. The freed capital was redeployed into "offshore pre-positioning hubs" in Dongguan and Yiwu, where one million SKUs are relabeled and compliance-tweaked before vessels even berth, cutting destination dwell time from 5.2 to 1.3 days and using time savings to offset freight spikes.

Second, to crack the price-jungle problem of "premium self-run," JD decentralized sourcing while recentralizing pricing inside algorithms. Since 2023, Joybuy overseas has operated a hybrid model: 3C and major appliances stay self-operated for authenticity, but long-tail sundries are opened to third-party sellers; traffic is ranked by a "quality × price" score instead of pure low-price, giving cheap white-label goods exposure while letting branded items keep their margin. A US$200 million dynamic-subsidy pool rebates sellers 30–70% of any price gap detected in real time, funded from vendors' own marketing deposits with JD acting as a "price-insurance bank."

Finally, to cure the "two-headed" decision lag of joint ventures, JD re-engineered equity with "modular majority + ratchet exit." In Thailand, the new pact gives JD 51% control of technology, merchandizing, and fulfillment, while partner Central Group handles offline traffic and local PR; a quarterly KPI of ≥25% GMV growth is written in, and failure lets JD increase its stake to 70% without board opposition. Local teams are titled "theater CEOs" and can approve up to US$5 million on their own, removing the need to ping Beijing. Promo lead-time shrank from 45 to 14 days, and during the 2024 Songkran festival, 3C sales rose 180% year-on-year with same-day delivery. For the already deadlocked Indonesia entity, JD simply swapped equity for debt, buying out the partner with a US$120 million convertible bond redeemable at 8% premium in two years—preserving any IPO upside while regaining operational command and ending SKU squabbles.

Asset-light balance sheets, devolved assortment rights, and majority-with-ratchet governance appear separate, yet all run on the same data backbone: a Global Operations Cockpit that feeds real-time inventory, price, traffic, and geopolitical-risk indices into every subsidy clause, ratchet formula, and bond covenant. It is this monetization of risk and productization of control that is steadily converting JD's once heavy "expedition" into a sustainable, profitable rhythm.

STRATEGIC ANALYSIS

To move beyond headline slogans—"self-built logistics," "quality first," "next-day delivery"—this section puts on three pairs of "detective glasses" to dissect how JD actually decided where, when, and how to go abroad. The tools applied are (1) PESTEL to scan macro-shocks, (2) industry five-forces to locate profit pools, and (3) VRIO to test whether domestic advantages can survive the crossing. The conclusion is that JD's expansion is best understood as a "sequential asset-heavy arbitrage" strategy: first use integrated logistics to create cost-and-trust gaps, then convert these gaps into cash flow, and finally replicate the loop only in markets where regulation, demand density, and geopolitical risk allow the moat to stay wider than the capital drain.

Analytical Framework

JD.com's push into global markets reveals a company armed with significant internal strengths and external opportunities, yet also hampered by clear internal weaknesses and external threats. On the strength side, it possesses China's most advanced self-built logistics network; this highly efficient, fully controllable supply-chain capability gives JD a solid edge in overseas fulfillment, reinforced by distribution centers it has planted across Southeast Asia and Europe. Years of investment in big-data analytics, artificial intelligence, and smart warehousing mean it can offer differentiated services that many rivals struggle to match. As a publicly listed firm,

JD also enjoys strong balance-sheet firepower and the ability to marshal resources for sustained spending on technology, marketing, and infrastructure abroad.

The weaknesses, however, are just as visible. Outside China, JD's brand is still far less recognizable than Amazon, Shopee, or Lazada, forcing it to spend heavily on brand-building and customer education. Its experience in hyper-local operations—grasping local shopping habits, cultural nuances, tax regimes, and labor laws—is thin, raising the risk that products or services simply "don't fit." The asset-heavy model that works at home can also be ill-suited to markets where labor is expensive or last-mile infrastructure is patchy, making a straight replication of the Chinese playbook difficult.

Looking outward, the opportunity landscape is attractive. Global e-commerce penetration keeps climbing, and emerging arenas such as Southeast Asia, the Middle East, and Latin America are adding tens of millions of new internet shoppers every year. Beijing's "Belt and Road" initiative and assorted export-friendly policies give JD political cover and financial incentives to build cross-border logistics lanes and bonded warehouses. "Made-in-China" goods still deliver world-beating value for money, and JD, sitting at the center of China's manufacturing ecosystem, is naturally positioned to act as the bridge between Chinese suppliers and overseas consumers. Rising worldwide demand for authentic (Riefler, 2020), high-quality products plays directly into JD's long-standing "genuine-goods-only" brand promise.

Yet the threat matrix is equally sobering. International e-commerce is already a battlefield where Amazon, Shopee, and regional incumbents enjoy sticky ecosystems and formidable switching costs; late entry means JD must spend more for every new customer. Regulatory headwinds are strengthening: data-privacy statutes, digital-sales-tax regimes, and consumer-protection rules are becoming stricter and more fragmented, raising compliance expenses and legal risk. Geopolitical tensions, protectionist tariffs, and volatile exchange rates can disrupt cross-border supply chains or wipe out thin retail margins overnight. Finally, global economic uncertainty is making consumers cautious, potentially slowing the e-commerce growth JD is counting on. JD.com's cross-border expansion is shaped by a complex PESTEL landscape in which every dimension raises both hurdles and strategic imperatives (Abrantes, 2023).

Political forces come first. Many emerging governments court foreign e-tailers with tax holidays and land in free-trade zones, yet developed markets are moving in the opposite direction: the U.S. and EU have widened foreign-investment screening, while India and Indonesia have abruptly raised import duties or banned cross-border data transfers. Sino-American tension adds an extra layer of risk; if more Chinese firms are placed on the U.S. entity list, JD could lose access to American chips or logistics hardware used in its Southeast-Asian hubs. Compliance costs are rising fast: JD's global legal-and-security budget reached USD 1.2 billion in 2024 and still struggles to keep pace with constantly shifting digital-sales-tax, antitrust, and consumer-protection rules.

Economic conditions are equally testing. Global inflation and volatile FX directly erode margins; between 2023 and 2025, the euro, Turkish lira, and Thai baht have all swung over 10% against the U.S. dollar. JD pays suppliers in renminbi but collects from consumers in local currency, so every leg of the transaction squeezes gross profit. Although disposable income in emerging markets is growing, average e-commerce basket values are only half those in China, forcing JD to reach much higher order density to cover last-mile costs. High global interest rates also raise the price of debt used to finance heavy warehouses, while rivals such as Shopee and Lazada can still tap cheap U.S.-dollar bonds through their parents, leaving JD at a disadvantage in subsidy wars.

Social trends vary sharply by region. Gen-Z and female consumers are driving live-stream shopping and instant retail, yet cultural codes differ: Middle-Eastern shoppers want halal certification and discreet family delivery, while European millennials demand carbon labels and ethical sourcing. JD's domestic reputation for "speed" must therefore be supplemented with "green", "local", and "community-trusted" credentials. Achieving this requires large numbers of native customer service, merchandising, and marketing staff; without them, social-network growth hacks simply do not ignite.

Technological fragmentation is another headache. In Europe and North America, cloud services are dominated by a handful of providers, and data-sovereignty laws oblige JD to deploy separate national clouds, splintering its IT architecture. In Southeast Asia, the last mile relies on motorcycle gig riders whose GPS and address data are imprecise, so JD's route-optimization algorithms have to be retrained from scratch. Export controls on semiconductors also threatened the smart-logistics hardware that underpins the company's cost advantage; if JD cannot source high-end GPUs or automation chips, the cost curve of its unmanned warehouses will flatten, blunting the "efficiency" story it hoped to export.

Environmental standards are tightening at both ends of the supply chain. The EU's Carbon Border Adjustment Mechanism will cover retail packaging from 2026; JD's home-appliance and 3C exports must now come with verifiable carbon data or face extra tariffs. Simultaneously, China's own dual-carbon targets push JD to neutralize its domestic operations by 2030, so every new overseas warehouse, air-freight lane or cold-chain route has to be factored into group-wide emissions accounting. Green packaging and new-energy delivery fleets could add several hundred million renminbi in annual capex, while European NGOs already single out e-commerce logistics as a source of urban congestion and pollution—failure to show progress will quickly damage brand equity (Gatta et al., 2023; Yi, 2025).

Finally, the legal maze is expanding on three fronts: data localization, antitrust, and labor law. India and Vietnam require customer data to be stored domestically and forbid its export for algorithmic training, forcing JD to maintain separate AI models for each country and driving up R&D expenses. The EU's Digital Markets Act labels platforms with over 45 million monthly active users as "gatekeepers", obliging them to share data and refrain from self-preferencing; once JD crosses that threshold in Germany or France, it will fall under a high-cost compliance regime. Warehouse operations that use agency workers must meet local minimum-wage rules and union-bargaining requirements—Indonesia's 7% rise in the 2023 minimum wage pushed JD's Jakarta fulfillment-center labor cost up by roughly 6% overnight.

Taken together, political and legal uncertainty raises the bar for market entry and ongoing compliance; economic and social realities mean JD must swap "heavy subsidies" for "deep local experience" to earn a profit; while technology and environmental standards turn "green plus efficient" from a slogan into a license to operate. To stay competitive, JD needs to embed every PESTEL variable into its country-selection and asset-allocation models, dynamically rebalancing governance structures and capital deployment so that its celebrated supply-chain prowess at home can be converted into sustainable market share abroad (Khan et al., 2026).

Viewed through Porter's Five Forces, JD's overseas journey is fought on a field far more crowded than home, yet cracks of profit still appear. Rivalry is intense: Amazon, Shopee, and Lazada already own the search gateway and keep subsidies and membership deals switched on 24/7. JD's only lever is "direct-sale authenticity plus same-day delivery from our own bonded warehouses," forcing the contest away from price and toward speed and trust. The threat of new entrants is moderate. TikTok Shop can lightning-land with traffic, but heavy-asset fulfillment remains a moat; by pouring concrete first, JD raises the barrier for followers. Substitutes come from local apps and brands' own sites, especially in appliances and beauty. JD counters by bundling China's excess white-label capacity into exclusive "JD-Made" lines, locking up price segments rivals cannot source. Supplier power splits: domestic factories drowning in overcapacity let JD bid them down, yet global majors demand local pricing control and short payment terms. JD trades "China-first launch + reverse-customization" for shelf space and voice. Buyer power is magnified by price-comparison tools in emerging markets where switching costs are zero; JD makes logistics habit-forming—when a Jakarta customer receives her phone at 3 p.m. after ordering at noon, she never returns to Shopee's seven-day free-ship wait. Along the value chain, inbound logistics and warehousing are the core edge; JD exports its WMS and AGV modules intact, cutting trial-and-error capex, while outbound legs are lightly grafted onto Grab or Line Man motorcycle fleets. Marketing skips cash-burn traffic buys, using livestreams and local KOC reviews to explode single SKUs and hold promotion expense under 3%, turning a cost disadvantage under the Five Forces into a sustainable efficiency premium and carving out a profit pool inside the reddest ocean.

Brand and Reputation Effects

In the international market, particularly in the targeted foreign markets where JD.com is expanding its business, the brand perception and reputation of JD.com are in a dynamic state of development (Wang, 2025).

For global brand recognition and perception, JD.com faces initial awareness challenges as it enters new international markets. In regions where its presence was previously minimal, building brand recognition stands as the primary obstacle. For instance, in some European and American markets, the e-commerce sector is extremely competitive, featuring both well-established local enterprises and global giants like Amazon. To cut through market clutter, JD.com leverages its existing strengths, such as its extensive product range. It gradually expands its product listings in these new markets, covering categories like electronics, fashion, and home goods, with the goal of capturing consumers' attention. When entering the U.S. market, for example, JD.com's global selling platform introduced a variety of unique Chinese-manufactured products that are not easily accessible to other mainstream e-commerce platforms, sparking the curiosity of some consumers interested in international goods. Meanwhile, JD.com has long been renowned in China for offering high-quality products, especially in the electronics category, and it is now striving to extend this reputation overseas. In its international product promotions, the company places great emphasis on product authenticity and quality control. It sources products from reliable suppliers both domestically in China and around the world and conducts rigorous quality inspections. This approach has already garnered positive feedback from some early-adopting international consumers. In Singapore, for example, some customers who purchased electronic devices from JD.com praised the product quality, noting that the products they received were in excellent condition, which has helped establish an initial positive word-of-mouth for JD.com regarding its products on the international stage.

In shaping its brand image through marketing and public relations, JD.com employs a variety of marketing communication tools in international markets and invests in digital advertising campaigns. In the Japanese market, for example, it runs targeted ads on social media platforms like Facebook and Instagram to promote its product categories, focusing on popular items in Japan such as beauty products and fashion apparel. These ads take full account of local cultural differences, using Japanese-language content and visual materials that align with the aesthetic preferences of the local audience to enhance audience engagement. On the PR front, JD.com actively communicates with international media and industry stakeholders. It takes part in various international e-commerce exhibitions and conferences, where it showcases its technological innovations, such as its advanced supply chain management system and new delivery models (Hu et al., 2024). Through these efforts, JD.com has established an image of an "innovative and forward-thinking e-commerce enterprise" in the minds of international media and industry insiders, which helps to build a positive brand image among the public.

In summary, while JD.com still faces challenges in building a strong brand reputation in the international market, it has taken proactive measures in areas such as brand awareness building, fulfilling corporate social responsibility, and implementing marketing and PR strategies. These efforts are gradually contributing to the formation of a more positive brand perception of JD.com in the targeted foreign markets.

CONCLUSION AND STRATEGIC RECOMMENDATIONS

JD.com, a leading integrated e-commerce and supply-chain service conglomerate in China, founded in 2004, has core operations spanning retail, logistics, technology services, and finance. It has established a "heavy-asset, strong supply-chain" benchmark in China's e-commerce sector by its self-operated logistics network and guaranteed authenticity proposition. After listing on Nasdaq in 2014 and completing a secondary listing on the Hong Kong Stock Exchange in 2020, JD.com launched its global expansion journey.

The motivations behind its internationalization stem from multiple factors. These include the top-level judgment of founder Liu Qiangdong, who identified internationalization as a "must-win battle" for the next decade; the slowdown in domestic e-commerce traffic dividends after 2015, which forced the company to seek incremental markets; the "reverse export" opportunities brought about by changes in the global supply chain; and the response to China's "dual-circulation" strategy aimed at fostering global leaders in the supply-chain industry.

During its global expansion, JD.com has achieved a series of milestones. In terms of market selection, it prioritized Europe and Southeast Asia through multi-dimensional evaluation. Europe became a profit engine because of its high per capita GDP, e-commerce penetration rate, and room for logistics cost arbitrage. Southeast Asia emerged as a volume engine with its high e-commerce GMV growth rate. The complementary peak seasons of the two regions help stabilize cash flow volatility. Regarding entry modes, in the EU, JD.com held core assets through a wholly owned Dutch SPV and collaborated with local funds to deploy last-mile micro-fulfillment centers. In Southeast Asia, it formed 49% minority joint ventures with local state-backed logistics enterprises, with clauses allowing it to gain majority control once performance targets are met, balancing cost and control. In terms of bus implementation, JD.com launched the omni-channel retail brand Ochama in Europe, enabling next-day delivery across 24 European countries. It has established over 100 overseas warehouses worldwide to support "2-3-day global delivery," built a semi-managed marketplace supporting 87,000 localized SKUs, and set up a $300 million "export comfort fund" to cover cross-border risks for Chinese SMEs, securing 3,800 exclusive factory partners.

JD.com's globalization has also faced many challenges. The replication of its heavy-asset model encountered difficulties. In low-density markets such as Indonesia, substantial investments were made in warehouse construction and the acquisition of local courier companies, but high fulfillment costs because of insufficient order density eventually led to the closure of local operations. Its brand positioning struggled in price-sensitive markets. The "authentic goods plus official warranty" high-end positioning resulted in higher prices compared to platforms like Temu, leading to slow user growth. Joint venture governance suffered from decision-making delays. Disagreements with local partners, such as Thailand's Central Group, regarding short-term traffic monetization, long-term investment, and SKU selection led to missed sales seasons. JD.com had to cope with regulatory differences across countries, such as data localization and digital sales tax requirements, economic pressures including exchange rate fluctuations and high interest rates, fragmented regional technology architectures, and environmental compliance requirements like the EU's Carbon Border Adjustment Mechanism.

To drive sustainable global development, JD.com needs to adopt targeted strategies based on its existing foundation. At the market level, it should focus on "ecosystem-compatible" markets such as Europe and Vietnam, allocating 70% of its future overseas capital expenditure to these regions with high logistics cost elasticity and strong demand alignment. In terms of asset operation, it should expand the "warehouse securitization" model, injecting 30% of its overseas warehouses into REITs to free up capital. Simultaneously, it should launch a Logistics-as-a-Service platform, opening tools such as warehouse management systems and route optimization algorithms to local merchants to generate recurring revenue. For brand building, JD.com should integrate localized sustainable initiatives, emphasizing "5% cheaper than supermarkets plus carbon-neutral delivery" in Europe and supporting local manufacturing in Southeast Asia. It should also establish a blockchain-based "transparency hub" for high-risk categories such as maternal and child products and cosmetics. In terms of organizational and risk management, JD.com should establish a "Global Ecosystem Team" reporting directly to the Strategic Execution Committee to improve decision-making efficiency, expand overseas secondment programs and local talent recruitment, mitigate supply chain risks by deploying regional hubs, and hedge 80% of exchange rate risks using forward contracts. These measures will ensure that JD.com's globalization shifts from "exploratory layout" to "profitable growth," fully leveraging its supply-chain advantages to achieve long-term development.

Summary of Key Findings

JD.com, a China-based integrated e-commerce and supply-chain conglomerate founded in 2004, has advanced its global expansion with distinct strengths, strategic moves, notable milestones, and unavoidable challenges. Its core competitive edge comes from a heavy-asset ecosystem honed over 15 years, including self-operated logistics, blockchain-backed authenticity governance, and data-driven inventory optimization. For example, it can offer U.S. consumers two-day delivery for $2.90—nearly 20% cheaper than Amazon—while still maintaining logistics margins, and it can charge 7% more for infant formula in Europe by guaranteeing authenticity, turning compliance requirements into a pricing advantage.

In market selection and entry, JD adopted a "twin-engine" strategy. It focused on Europe as a margin engine, targeting countries like the Netherlands and Germany, where last-mile costs leave room for cost arbitrage. It also prioritized Southeast Asia as a volume engine, focusing on markets like Indonesia and Vietnam that see over 20% annual e-commerce GMV growth. To enter these markets, JD tailored ownership models: in the EU, it used wholly owned Dutch SPVs to hold core assets, while collaborating with local funds to deploy last-mile micro-fulfillment centers; in Southeast Asia, it formed 49% minority joint ventures with local state-backed logistics enterprises, with clauses allowing it to gain majority control once EBITDA margin hits 8%. This approach reduced the initial equity outlay by approximately 30% compared to pure greenfield investments.

Operationally, JD achieved several key milestones. It launched the omni-channel retail brand Ochama in Europe, enabling next-day delivery across 24 European countries (Yang, 2024). It built over 100 overseas warehouses worldwide to support "2-3-day global delivery," established a semi-managed marketplace with 87,000 localized SKUs, and set up a $300 million "export comfort fund" to cover cross-border risks for Chinese SMEs, securing 3,800 exclusive factory partners.

However, JD's global expansion has faced significant challenges. Its heavy-asset model struggled in low-order-density markets like Indonesia. After investing nearly RMB 300 million in 10 warehouses and gaining a local courier company, high fulfillment costs led to eight consecutive years of losses and eventual market exit. Its brand positioning also encountered hurdles in price-sensitive markets: its focus on "authentic goods + official warranty" made prices 35% higher than Temu in the U.K., keeping monthly active users in the low millions while TikTok Shop reached 15 million users in just six months. Joint venture governance caused decision delays, too, as disagreements with Thailand's Central Group over short-term traffic monetization versus long-term investment, and with Indonesian partners over offline-online competition in 3C products, led to missed sales seasons and six changes in international leadership over nine years. Externally, JD faces regulatory hurdles such as the EU's Digital Markets Act and India's data localization rules, economic pressures including volatility of over 10% for currencies like the euro and Thai baht against the U.S. dollar, and environmental demands like the EU's 2026 Carbon Border Adjustment Mechanism that adds packaging compliance costs.

To address these challenges, JD implemented targeted mitigation strategies. It converted 10 Indonesian warehouses into a local REIT, freeing up $180 million while signing a 10-year lease-back agreement. In the U.S. and Europe, it shifted 40% of in-house operations to UPS Supply Chain Solutions while retaining control of warehouse management systems and data, cutting per-parcel costs by $0.9 and pushing those markets into profitability six months ahead of plan. It also adopted a hybrid sourcing model-keeping 3C and major appliances as self-operated items for authenticity, while opening long-tail sundries to third-party sellers- and launched a $200 million dynamic subsidy pool, which helped grow monthly active users from 4 million to 21 million. For joint ventures, JD restructured its Thai ship to take 51% control of technology, merchandizing, and fulfillment, slashing promo lead-time from 45 days to 14 days and driving 180% year-on-year growth in 3C sales during the 2024 Songkran festival.

These findings collectively outline JD's unique global expansion path: it leverages its supply-chain strengths to enter strategic markets, navigates market-specific barriers with adaptive models, and adjusts its approach to balance growth and profitability, moving from an exploratory phase toward sustainable, profitable global development.

Future Growth Opportunities

JD.com has established a foundation of heavy-asset supply chains and localized operations in its globalization process. Looking ahead, it can explore growth opportunities in three key directions, with each opportunity supported by actionable logic based on existing resources and market feedback. To expand into emerging markets, JD.com can focus on the Middle East and Latin America. The e-commerce penetration rates in these two regions were only 8% and 5%, respectively, in 2023, lower than Southeast Asia's 12%. Meanwhile, the middle-class population in these areas is growing at an average annual rate of over 10%, creating a significant demand for consumption upgrading. JD.com can replicate the "joint venture + localized fulfillment" experience it gained in Southeast Asia, for instance, partnering with regional logistics leaders such as Aramex in the Middle East and Correos in Latin America. By leveraging their local networks, JD.com can quickly build a "regional warehouse plus last-mile delivery" system. It can rely on its supply chain advantages in 3C and home appliance categories to meet local consumers' demand for high-quality electronic products. The feasibility of this strategy has already been verified in Southeast Asia, where JD.com achieved a 180% monthly sales growth in the 3C category through its partnership with Vietnam's VNPost.

To deepen operations in existing markets, JD.com can promote "horizontal category expansion + user tiered operations". In the European market, it can expand from its current high-frequency, essential categories, such as maternal and infant products and coffee capsules, to long-tail categories like home improvement materials and outdoor gear. The home e-commerce market in countries such as the Netherlands and Germany is growing at an average annual rate of 15%. Since JD.com has already built user trust through its "1-hour pickup" service, it can reuse existing warehousing and delivery networks during horizontal expansion, lowering marginal costs. In the Southeast Asian market, given that consumers under 35 account for over 60% of the population, JD.com can launch a tiered user program combining "installment payment plus membership benefits". For example, it can partner with local financial institutions to offer 0-down-payment installment plans for 3C products, while providing high-value members with exclusive delivery guarantees. This model has already achieved a member repurchase rate twice that of non-members in China. The penetration rate of consumer finance in Southeast Asia is only 18%, leaving significant growth potential. JD.com can optimize joint venture governance-for example, in markets with existing cooperation foundations such as Thailand and Vietnam, it can gradually increase its ownership through a "performance-based bet + equity increment" model to reduce decision-making delays. This strategy has already been validated in Thailand, where gaining 51% control shortened the promotion cycle to 14 days, providing a replicable governance experience for deepening operations in existing markets.

REFERENCES

Abrantes, B. F. (Ed.). (2023). *Principles of external business environment analyzability in an organizational context*. IGI Global. DOI: 10.4018/978-1-6684-5543-2

Cao, Y. (2024). The research of supply chain management in Chinas e-commerce environment taking JD.com as an example. *Advances in Economics Management and Political Sciences*, *143*(1), 40–47. DOI: 10.54254/2754-1169/2024.GA18957

Cecil, P. (2024). Cross-Border supply chain optimization: Strategies for managing international operations while maintaining speed and cost efficiency. [IJSRM]. *International Journal of Scientific Research and Management*, *12*(05), 6565–6588. DOI: 10.18535/ijsrm/v12i05.em23

Chan, A. K., Chen, C. H., & Zhao, L. (2018). JD. com: Leveraging the edge of e-business. *Emerald Emerging Markets Case Studies,* 1-30. https://doi.org/DOI: 10.1108/EEMCS-06-2016-0109

Chandgothia, K. (2025). *Can JD's surging user base power its next phase of revenue growth?* Finance. Yahoo. https://finance.yahoo.com/news/jds-surging-user-power-next-150000882.html?

Document, A. P. I. (n.d.). *JD.com: Revolutionizing e-commerce through technology and logistics excellence*. Just one API. https://blog.justoneapi.com/post-1/post-20250920101714234.html

Duan, Z. (2024). Research on the supply chain optimization approach of JD's transformation into a digital ecosystem retailer. *Advances in Economics Management and Political Sciences*, *138*(1), 22–27. DOI: 10.54254/2754-1169/2024.18798

Gatta, V., Marcucci, E., & Le Pira, M. (2023). E-commerce and urban logistics: Trends, challenges, and opportunities. In Marcucci, E., Gatta, V., & Le Pira, M. (Eds.), *Handbook on city logistics and urban freight* (pp. 422–443). Edward Elgar Publishing., DOI: 10.4337/9781800370173.00033

Halldorsson, A., & Wehner, J. (2020). Last-mile logistics fulfillment: A framework for energy efficiency. *Research in Transportation Business & Management*, *37*, 100481. Advance online publication. DOI: 10.1016/j.rtbm.2020.100481

He, H. (2025). The impact of technology-driven business model innovation on corporate performance: A case study of JD. com in the digital economy era. In *2025 5th international conference on enterprise management and economic development* (ICEMED 2025) (pp. 1054-1062). Atlantis Press. https://doi.org/DOI: 10.2991/978-94-6463-811-0_114

Hu, H., Qi, Y., Lee, H. L., Shen, Z. M., Liu, C., Zhu, W., & Kang, N. (2024). Supercharged by advanced analytics, JD.com attains agility, resilience, and shared value across its supply chain. *INFORMS Journal on Applied Analytics*, *54*(1), 54–70. DOI: 10.1287/inte.2023.0078

Huo, Z. (2022). Analysis of E-commerce business strategy - take JD.com, inc. as the case. *Asian Business Research*, *7*(1), 41–44. DOI: 10.20849/abr.v7i1.989

Javed, S. A., Bo, Y., Tao, L., & Dong, W. (2023). The 'Dual Circulation' development model of China: Background and insights. *Rajagiri Management Journal*, *17*(1), 2–20. DOI: 10.1108/RAMJ-03-2021-0016

JD.COM. (n.d.). *Biography*. https://ir.jd.com/management/richard-qiangdong-liu

Khan, M. I., Zaman, S. I., & Khan, S. A. (2026). *Supply chain finance: Trends, sustainability and future outlook*. CRC Press.

Logistics, J. D. (2024). *JD Logistics unveils roadmap to enable 2-3 day delivery in global markets*. https://www.waltherploosvanamstel.nl/jd-logistics-unveils-roadmap-to-enable-2-3-day-delivery-global-markets/

Nguyen, L. H., & Nguyen, H. P. (2020). Generation Z in Vietnam: The quest for authenticity. In Gentina, E., & Parry, E. (Eds.), *The new generation Z in Asia: dynamics, differences, digitalisation* (pp. 135–148). Emerald Publishing Limited., DOI: 10.1108/978-1-80043-220-820201014

Ostic, D., & Obrenovic, B. (2022). JD strategic cross-border expansion–offering retail as strategy solutions abroad. In Fan, M., Wang, L., & Ostic, D. (Eds.), *Casebook of Chinese business management* (pp. 139–148). Springer Nature Singapore., DOI: 10.1007/978-981-16-8074-8_15

Ou, Z. (2024). Study on overseas market strategy of Chinese e-commerce enterprises: Taking JD as a case. *International Journal of Global Economics and Management*, *3*(3), 21–26. DOI: 10.62051/ijgem.v3n3.03

Pandaily. (2024). *JD.com initiates global expansion, launches "Global sales" In four countries*. https://pandaily.com/jd-com-initiates-global-expansion-launches-global-sales-in-four-countries

Riefler, P. (2020). Local versus global food consumption: The role of brand authenticity. *Journal of Consumer Marketing*, *37*(3), 317–327. DOI: 10.1108/JCM-02-2019-3086

Shen, Z. J. M., Sun, S., Qi, Y., Hu, H., Kang, N., Zhang, J., Wang, X., & Lin, X. (2025). JD. com improves fulfillment efficiency with data-driven integrated assortment planning and inventory allocation. *INFORMS Journal on Applied Analytics, 55*(5), 386–398. DOI: 10.1287/inte.2025.0245

Wang, Y. (2025). *JD.com announces "10 billion growth plan" To introduce 1,000 overseas brands to china over next three years*. JINGDONG Corporate Blog. https://jdcorporateblog.com/jd-com-announces-10-billion-growth-plan-to-introduce-1000-overseas-brands-to-china-over-next-three-years/

Yang, V. (2024). *JD.com's strategic advancements in international business: A focus on supply chain and user experience*. JINGDONG Corporate Blog. https://jdcorporateblog.com/jd-coms-strategic-advancements-in-international-business-a-focus-on-supply-chain-and-user-experience/

Yi, Z. (2025). Green upgrading strategy of supply chain in the age of digital intelligence economy—Taking JD. com as an example. *Finance & Economics, 1*(6), 1–6. DOI: 10.61173/ewa8v404

Zhao, C. Y., & Lyu, X. Y. (2024). JD. com: A strategic analysis of its evolution, innovation, and market adaptation. *China-USA Business Review, 23*(2), 77–83. DOI: 10.17265/1537-1514/2024.02.003

KEY TERMS AND DEFINITIONS

Carbon Footprint Visualization: A product traceability solution launched by JD.com to comply with EU environmental policies. It uses blockchain technology to record carbon emission data of products throughout the entire process, from production, processing, to transportation, and makes it open to consumers. It is used to support the "green product" positioning, meet the consumer demand for environmental attributes in the European market, and avoid additional costs brought by the Carbon Border Adjustment Mechanism.

Dual-Engine Market Strategy: A market positioning model adopted by JD.com in its global expansion. It regards Europe as a "profit engine" (focusing on high-margin categories by leveraging high per capita GDP and room for logistics cost arbitrage) and Southeast Asia as a "volume engine" (pursuing order volume growth by relying on high e-commerce GMV growth rates and huge consumption potential). The complementary peak sales seasons of the two regions help balance cash flow volatility.

Export Comfort Fund: A special fund of USD 300 million established by JD.com to cover the risks of Chinese SMEs going global, such as reverse logistics costs caused by overseas consumer returns, exchange rate fluctuation losses, and inventory backlog risks. By "undertaking risks", it attracts SMEs to settle on JD.com's overseas platforms and locks in exclusive supply chain resources.

Fulfillment Cost Arbitrage: A strategy adopted by JD.com to gain profit margins by leveraging differences in logistics costs across markets. For example, the last-mile cost in some European countries is 30%-40%. higher than that in China. JD.com replicates its mature domestic self-operated logistics model to build an efficient fulfillment network locally, reducing unit fulfillment costs and creating price advantages or profit margins.

Heavy-Asset Ecosystem: A comprehensive operational system built by JD.com over 15 years, centered on self-operated logistics and integrating warehousing facilities, delivery teams, blockchain-based traceability technology, and data-driven inventory management. It is characterized by large upfront investments and strong asset control, which ensures fulfillment timeliness and product authenticity, serving as the core support for JD.com's global competitiveness.

Logistics-as-a-Service (LaaS): A business model where JD.com plans to open its logistics capabilities(such as a warehouse management system (WMS), intelligent sorting technology, and route optimization algorithms) to overseas third-party enterprises. It converts logistics infrastructure and technology into chargeable service resources, which not only reduces the cost of technology reuse but also taps into the commercial potential of the third-party logistics market.

Performance-Based Bet + Equity Increment Clause: A governance mechanism used by JD.com in overseas joint ventures and cooperation. It stipulates that the joint venture must achieve specific performance targets (such as an EBITDA margin of 8%). If the targets are met, JD.com can gradually increase its shareholding ratio until it obtains controlling rights; if the targets are not met, the cooperation rights will be adjusted. The core is to align the interests of both joint venture parties, promote cooperation in line with JD.com's strategic direction, and solve the problem of delayed decision-making.

Regulatory War-Room: A special team established by JD.com in Shenzhen, responsible for sorting out more than 1,800 overseas regulatory clauses (such as U.S. FDA certification and EU CE standards) corresponding to 214 types of global products. It standardizes and streamlines the product certification process, shortening the time for overseas market access (from 91 days to 38 days) and avoiding delays in product listing due to regulatory issues.

Semi-Managed Marketplace: An operational model launched by JD.com overseas, which is between self-operation and pure third-party platforms. Merchants send their inventory to JD.com's overseas warehouses, and JD.com provides traffic, marketing resources, fulfillment guidance, and after-sales services. Merchants retain ownership of the inventory, and JD.com controls product categories and service quality through the platform, realizing "ecological collaboration + risk sharing".

Tiered Entry Model: A differentiated market access method designed by JD.com for different regional markets. In the EU, it holds core warehousing assets through a wholly owned Dutch SPV and collaborates with local funds to deploy last-mile services; in Southeast Asia, it establishes joint ventures with local state-owned logistics enterprises with a 49% minority stake, and stipulates that it can get controlling rights after meeting performance targets. The core is to reduce initial investment risks while ensuring operational control.

Chapter 10
Geely's Merger-Led Global Expansion: Mergers, Technology Acquisition, and Market Entry

Huaxuan Duan
http://orcid.org/0009-0008-0140-0432
Beijing Normal-Hong Kong Baptist University, China

EXECUTIVE SUMMARY

This chapter examines the global expansion strategy of Geely Auto Holding, tracing its evolution from a domestic Chinese manufacturer into a multinational automotive conglomerate. Key themes encompass the company's diversified market entry approaches across developed and emerging economies, its development of modular vehicle architectures for cost efficiency, and vertical integration in batteries and intelligent systems. Also addresses implementation challenges such as regulatory barriers, cultural integration, and geopolitical risks, alongside mitigation strategies involving institutional adaptation and sustained research and development investment. By applying SWOT analysis, the PESTEL framework, and Porter's Five Forces, provide a comprehensive evaluation of Geely's competitive positioning. The chapter contributes insights into how emerging-market multinationals can use acquisitions, localized production, and technological innovation to achieve global competitiveness while managing complex international environments.

DOI: 10.4018/979-8-3373-4302-0.ch010

INTRODUCTION

Background of the Company

Brief history and core business.

Founded in 1986 in Zhejiang by Li Shufu, Geely started with refrigerator components, switched to motorcycle production a decade later to accumulate capital, and in 1997 became China's first private automaker. Its debut model, "Haoqing," broke joint-venture monopolies at 30,000 yuan, making cars accessible to ordinary families. (Knowledge Info Hub, 2025) The 2010 Volvo acquisition was transformative, enabling the introduction of luxury, safety technology, and management systems. This was followed by 2017's acquisitions of Malaysia's Proton and the UK's Lotus, and a 2018 stake in Daimler, which built a Europe-Southeast Asia network (Laouiti et al., 2018). Over five years, Geely invested over 200 billion yuan in R&D, rolling out the Leishen hybrid and Shendun Blades battery, which solves winter range via a honeycomb structure (Andrews, 2024). By July 4, 2025, the cumulative sales of the Geely Galaxy E5 pure-electric smart SUV exceeded 150,000 units, and the entire Galaxy series had reached over 540,000 units sold, marking a shift from "low-end manufacturer" to "tech driver" (Chen, 2025). Its tiered portfolio covers mass markets, high-end, and overseas. From a Taizhou workshop to an automotive giant, it exemplifies China's "technology-for-market" path.

Organizational structure and leadership highlights.

Geely continues to advance its "One Geely" strategy through structural reforms in 2025, aiming to streamline operations and enhance efficiency. Founder Li Shufu (Eric Li) remains Chairperson, overseeing long-term strategic direction, while An Conghui has been promoted to Group CEO, leading overall operations. Li Donghui, Vice Chairperson, leverages his financial expertise to optimize resource allocation during strategic consolidation, with a focus on international investment and capital operations (Li, 2025). Junior executive Dai Qing first led a rotating president system, which fostered cross-functional collaboration and leadership development (Fast Technology, 2025). At the operational level, Gan Jiayue now heads two core business groups: the Galaxy Business Group targets mainstream high-value NEVs, while the Zeekr Technology Business Group focuses on luxury intelligent EVs, supported by integrating Lynk & Co into Zeekr's portfolio to emphasize sporty, trend-driven models (Li, 2025). Meanwhile, the China Star series continues to dominate the energy-efficient ICE segment. This restructuring forms a four-brand matrix—Zeekr, Lynk & Co, Galaxy, and China Star—covering all price tiers and reinforcing Geely's dual-track strategy in NEVs (Securities Daily, 2025).

Market position domestically and globally.

Geely maintains a preeminent domestic position as China's top-selling indigenous passenger car brand for five consecutive years. In 2023, its domestic retail sales reached 1.41 million units, accounting for 4.69% of China's passenger car market, with the share of the first quarter in 2023 at 6.3% (Kang, 2023; Geely Global, 2024). Its NEV sales surged 97.5% year over year in March 2023, capturing 5.0% of China's NEV market (Kang, 2023). Globally, Geely is China's most internationalized automaker, with 2023 overseas sales totaling 274,101 units, representing over 25% of total sales (Geely Global, 2024). Key markets include Malaysia, where its holding brand, Proton, holds a 19.4% market share, and Saudi Arabia, where it ranked 7th with 28,589 registrations (Chan, 2023). Premium brand Lynk & Co achieved 22% global sales growth in 2023, expanding in Europe, while its SEA architecture underpins partnerships with Mercedes-Benz Smart (Geely Global, 2024; Hampel, 2021). This dual-market strength, supported by global R&D and manufacturing, cements its status as a top-tier automaker.

Key milestones in growth and internationalization.

Geely Auto Group founded the company in 1996 and entered the automobile industry in 1997, marking its transition from a diversified private enterprise into a dedicated car manufacturer. The release of its first self-produced model, the Haoqing, in 1998 symbolized its determination to break into a market long dominated by joint ventures. In 2001, Geely became the first private automobile company in China to get an official production license, a milestone that legitimized its industrial ambitions. Its 2005 listing on the Hong Kong Stock Exchange strengthened its capital base and governance structure, preparing the company for international expansion. A decisive turning point came in 2010 with the acquisition of Volvo Cars, which significantly upgraded Geely's technological capabilities and global brand positioning. The establishment of the China Euro Vehicle Technology (CEVT) center in Gothenburg in 2013 institutionalized cross-border R&D collaboration. In 2017, further acquisitions of Proton and Lotus expanded its footprint in Southeast Asia and the premium sports segment. By 2021, Geely Holding Group's continued presence in the Fortune Global 500 for the tenth consecutive year reflected its transformation into a globally competitive automotive conglomerate (Kraft & Kraft, 2024).

Motivation for Global Expansion

Motivations (market saturation, competitive pressures, growth opportunities).

In 2019, Caixin Global reported that in the first six months of the year, carmakers sold 12.32 million vehicles on the Chinese mainland, a 12.4% year-on-year decline, with passenger car sales dropping 14% to 10.12 million units (An & Zhao, 2019). This downward trend shows weakening growth momentum in the domestic market. Since 2018, the Chinese passenger car market has experienced periodic negative growth. AutoNews observed vehicle demand in China, measured by excluding exports from overall vehicle shipments and including imports, has stagnated for years because of a weakening economy, as noted by Yang (2024). From 2018 to 2022, the tally of domestic vehicle shipments slipped from 27 million to 23.8 million (Yang, 2024). This shows that the domestic market has reached saturation, making it difficult to absorb new products and investments.

Intense domestic auto industry competition drives Geely's global expansion. China's auto market, the world's largest yet most competitive, sees Geely competing with domestic peers such as Chery, Chang'an, and BYD on quality, price, technology, and brand. At the same time, Toyota, Volkswagen, and Honda hold major market shares (Macarol, 2024). Frequent price wars erode Geely's margins—automakers cut prices for market share, lowering industry-wide profitability, with Chinese domestic automakers' average margins below major international ones (Macarol, 2024). As the auto industry rapidly shifts toward electrification and intelligence, tech competition intensifies, pushing firms to boost R&D. For Geely, global expansion secures access to more tech resources and partnerships with advanced global enterprises, strengthening its tech competitiveness to tackle fierce domestic competition.

Abundant growth opportunities in global markets drive Geely's expansion. Emerging markets, including Africa, Latin America, and Asia, are seeing surging auto demand amid growing economies and rapid urbanization—large populations and low per capita car ownership mean significant potential, with Southeast Asia's steady growth and pro-auto industry policies aiding entry. Developed markets, including Europe and the USA, though mature, offer NEV growth: rising eco-awareness and policy support boost NEV share, and Geely's NEV investment can tap high-end segments to lift brand image and profitability. Global expansion also brings economies of scale and risk diversification, reducing the impact of single-market fluctuations.

Strategic objectives of internationalization.

As China's domestic auto market slows, Geely has positioned overseas markets as its core growth driver. Its overseas revenue share rose from just 15% of total group revenue in 2020 to 38% in 2024, fueled by a dual-track strategy: in Southeast Asia, it leverages the Proton brand by locally producing X90 plug-in hybrid SUV, thus pushing ASEAN's share of Geely's overseas revenue to 43% in 2024; in Europe and the USA, it breaks through with premium products like the Zeekr 009, lifting its average overseas selling price to RMB 380,000 and offsetting domestic competitive pressure (Li & Pi, 2025; Geely Stories, 2020). Geely targets 380,000 overseas sales in 2025, with new energy vehicles accounting for over 60%, while using regional policies to build a revenue safety net.

Through Volvo's technology collaboration, Geely's "China Star" series achieved a significant improvement in safety performance. For example, the Geely Monjaro features a steel cage body and an intelligent driving-assisted chip, which assures both passive and active safety. To be more specific, the steel cage unibody ensures the body's integrity in the event of collisions, rollovers, and other passive safety issues. The chip actively assists the driver in sensing road conditions to avoid potential risks. These features spread Monjaro's fame abroad and gained a reputation.

The ongoing Haiphong factory in Vietnam has an annual production capacity of 75,000 vehicles. It benefits from the RCEP agreement, achieving zero tariffs on components and a local procurement target of 70%. Consequently, they reduced the cost of transporting each vehicle to the Philippines by 50% and set the annual export target for the right-hand-drive model Coolray at 40,000 units (Thanh, 2023). The Monterrey factory in Mexico avoids the 25% tariff imposed by the United States through a disassembly-assembly approach, which uses CATL batteries to meet subsidy requirements and has compressed the delivery cycle from 45 days to 7 days (Soto, 2023). Behind products from these factories all over the world is Geely's CMA platform, which has become the core weapon for cost reduction, covering models such as Zeekr X and Lynk & Co 06, sharing the electronic and electrical architecture and battery standards, reducing the single-model R&D cost.

Government support or policy influence

The core logic of short-term policies is to activate market momentum through fiscal and tax tools quickly. From 2024 to 2025, the policy of fully exempting the purchase tax for new energy vehicles has strongly supported Geely's high-end models (Ministry of Finance, 2023). The main goal is to further leverage tax incentives, guide relevant parties to seize development opportunities, promote technological and product innovation, continuously enhance the industry's core competitiveness, expand the consumption of new energy vehicles, and support the high-quality development of the new energy vehicle industry (Artxdigi, 2023).

China has included methanol fuel in its energy strategy, granting Geely a 20-year policy pilot for methanol vehicles. Its 500,000-ton green methanol project in Alxa, Inner Mongolia, received rapid approvals for land and environmental assessments, achieving a breakthrough of "9 liters of methanol consumption per 100 kilometers + 0 gasoline consumption" (Li, 2024). The Sichuan Nanchong Jialing New Energy Vehicle Town is a model of government and enterprise collaboration-the local government invested in the construction of standardized factories and 7 research institutes, established a chain leader system to promote the local component rate from 5% to 15% (Xin, 2025).

MARKET ANALYSIS AND ENTRY STRATEGY

Target Market Selection

Criteria for choosing expansion markets.

With the expansion of exports, China has proposed establishing the Silk Road Economic Belt and the 21st Century Maritime Silk Road. The Belt and Road Economic Corridor has made trade along its routes more convenient and liberalized trade flows. For Chinese automakers, the establishment of the six major economic corridors undoubtedly presents an excellent opportunity to expand into markets in Central and East Asia and Southeast Asia (Su & Lahiri, 2023).

Riding the Belt and Road Initiative wave, Geely targeted Southeast Asia and Middle Eastern markets. Relying on its Proton brand, Geely is speeding up its market expansion in Southeast Asia. In May this year, Geely announced its strategic support for Proton's new-energy vehicle transformation and launched its first new-energy model, the X90. In October, Geely signed a major cooperation framework agreement with Malaysia, focusing on in-depth cooperation around the Tanjong Malim Automotive High-tech Valley (Zhang & Liang, 2023).

Geely has aggressively developed its presence in Southeast Asia, driven by the region's unique consumer demand and growth potential. Southeast Asia's population exceeds 670 million, and the ASEAN vehicle market ranks as the fifth-largest subregional market globally, with total sales of approximately 3.3 million units in 2023. Messe Düsseldorf Asia (n.d.) anticipates that the passenger car market in ASEAN will generate about USD 68.3 billion in revenue by 2025, spurring substantial growth in automotive demand. This group's demand for cars extends beyond transportation, focusing on Southeast Asia amid mobility upgrades. Geely has tailored strategies to local demands. In Malaysia, where private cars are the preferred mode of transport, Geely launched youth-oriented models such as the Coolray SUV to capture incremental market share through sporty design and cost-effectiveness (Fernandez, 2024). Southeast Asian consumers are price sensitive, with mainstream budgets ranging from 80,000 to 200,000 yuan, yet they demand richer configurations. To address this, Geely invested $168 million in a plant in Vietnam's Thai Binh, leveraging local production to avoid tariffs and shorten supply chains to improve price competitiveness, and introduced high-end intelligent safety features to mainstream segments (Central Desk, 2025).

Comparison of potential markets (developed versus emerging economies).

As global strategic hubs, Europe, America, and Australia focus on elevating brand value and validating technical prowess. These mature markets, with discerning demands, act as both high-end arenas and tech standard-setters. Australia, a pivotal right-hand drive benchmark, influences Southeast Asian and South Asian markets. In 2025, the EX5 will spearhead entry, supported by 26 premium dealerships and five smart port logistics hubs in Brisbane and Perth, ensuring swift deliveries across Sydney, Melbourne, and beyond (Geely Global, 2025).

Southeast Asia and the Middle East thrive on geographic and cultural proximity. Thailand, with its robust auto ecosystem, sees the EX5 achieve over 1,000 monthly orders, thanks to tropical-adapted battery tech and regional chassis tuning. Plans to expand to 30 service centers by 2025 will strengthen after-sales support. In the Middle East, 16 premium models secure top-three status among Chinese brands in Saudi Arabia, leveraging luxury features and local partnerships, with tailored financing (Geely Global, 2025).

Entry Mode Selection

Geely defines its global expansion through a flexible, region-specific approach, eschewing a one-size-fits-all model. By tailoring its strategies to market maturity, policy landscapes, and competitive dynamics, the automaker has developed a diversified portfolio that includes cross-border mergers and acquisitions (M&A), joint ventures (JVs), greenfield investments, and digital exports. This adaptive framework ensures strategic agility while mitigating cross-cultural risks.

Mergers and Acquisitions (M&A)

In technologically advanced, brand-sensitive developed markets, Geely employs strategic M&A to fast-track access to technical assets and established distribution networks (Cheng et al., 2023). The 2010 acquisition of Volvo stands as a landmark, pioneering a "control without dominance" governance model that preserved the Swedish marque's autonomy while fostering synergies (Lin et al., 2020; Geely Stories, 2020). By retaining Volvo's leadership and board independence, Geely avoided cultural friction while creating the China-Europe Automotive Technology Center (CEVT) to facilitate knowledge exchange (Tian & Yuan, 2019; Holm & Zhang, 2016).

This collaboration yielded tangible results: Volvo shared 2,300 core patents, enabling Geely's transition from budget to premium positioning, exemplified by the Geely Monjaro, which earned a Euro NCAP five-star rating in 2024. In return, Geely's modular expertise reduced Volvo's SPA platform costs by 18%, with the XC60's manufacturing expenses dropping 23% since 2010 (Pang, 2024). By 2024, Volvo's global sales surged from 370,000 to 780,000 units, with new energy vehicles comprising 42% of European sales and China accounting for 35% of revenue (Meng & Wang, 2021).

Geely's 2017 acquisition of a 51% stake in Lotus further strengthened its high-end portfolio (Wang et al., 2021). Injecting SEA architecture technology into the British sports car brand, Geely launched the 2,000-horsepower Evija electric supercar—2024's global, limited edition sold out instantly, solidifying its technical credibility in luxury segments (Collins, 2025).

Joint Ventures & Partnerships

In markets constrained by regulations or deeply entrenched local networks, Geely leverages strategic partnerships to deliver "localization at scale." Its 49.9% stake in Malaysia's Proton—acquired in 2017—serves as a prime example of this strategy: the sharing of CMA architecture and engine technologies drove Proton's X50 sales to 120,000 units in 2024, while Proton's 120-strong ASEAN dealership network enabled Geely to export 53,000 vehicles—accounting for 38% of the automaker's total sales volume in Southeast Asia (Geely Stories, 2020). Geely's 50/50 joint venture with Daimler for the smart brand further shows technical synergy: Geely led the development of the SEA electric vehicle platform, while Daimler oversaw design and European distribution. By tapping into Daimler's 1,200-dealer network and Geely's established after-sales infrastructure in Southeast Asia, the partnership reduced channel costs by 40% compared to independent market expansion. (Liu et al., 2019).

Greenfield Investments

Emerging markets with untapped potential are attracting Geely's greenfield investments to build integrated ecosystems. In Central Asia, Geely's 2022 Kazakhstan facility achieves 50% localization, with body stamping and welding performed locally. Leveraging the country's membership in the Eurasian Economic Union, the 50,000-unit capacity plant exported 32,000 vehicles to Russia and Belarus duty-free in 2024. Although capital-intensive, this model reduces production costs by 22% compared with CKD assembly and qualifies for a five-year corporate tax holiday (Bellan, 2023).

Exporting and E-commerce

Digital platforms drive light-asset expansion in accessible markets. In Europe, Geely's 2024 online strategy, featuring a localized website with 3D vehicle previews and Amazon partnerships, generated 27% of sales. A seven-day test-drive offer for first-time buyers achieved an 18% conversion rate, blending digital convenience with physical experience. Lazada and Noon collaborations make online booking and offline delivery possible in Southeast Asia and the Middle East. In 2024, 21,000 Thai sales included 43% online orders for the EX5, reducing customer acquisition costs by 25%. In logistics-challenged African markets, regional distribution centers aggregate e-commerce orders for bulk container shipments, delivering 18,000 units to Nigeria and South Africa in 2024, reducing delivery times by 30% compared with traditional trade (Automotive World, 2025).

Competitive Advantage

The competitive edge Geely has forged through its global expansion stems from both its mastery of core technologies and the profound restructuring of its industrial ecosystem, creating a closed-loop competitive advantage defined by technological breakthroughs, efficiency gains, and experience enhancement.

Cost leadership, technological innovation, or supply chain efficiency.

Geely's competitive barriers are first anchored in a technology-driven efficiency revolution. Its GEA Intelligent Architecture achieves universal adaptability through modular design: it supports CTB (Cell-to-Body) integration, merging the battery pack with the vehicle structure to reduce weight by 15% and extend range by 10%. The architecture's versatility spans left- and right hand-drive versions and tropical-optimized variants. This flexibility shortens the development cycle of derivative models to 18 months, 30% faster than the industry average. The Galaxy E5, built on this architecture, leveraged its global adaptability to surpass 100,000 units in global sales within 14 months, becoming the first Chinese model to crack Europe's top 10 pure electric SUV rankings.

Vertical supply chain integration ensures both cost control and operational stability. In core components, Geely achieves autonomy through joint ventures and in-house R&D. For instance, they operate a joint battery plant with CATL, which produces custom Shendun Short Blade batteries at a cost 12% lower than external sourcing. On the service front, Australia's five spare parts hubs use intelligent scheduling to deliver 95% of parts within 72 hours—50% faster than industry norms, slashing dealer inventory costs significantly.

The forward-looking layout of its intelligent ecosystem further strengthens technological barriers. Geely's Geespace has launched 12 low-orbit satellites, forming a centimeter-level positioning constellation that underpins its NOA (Advanced Navigation-Assisted Driving) system. Fitted in over 35% of 2025's new models, this system requires human intervention fewer than 0.1 times per 100 kilometers on European highways, matching Tesla FSD's performance at just 60% of the hardware cost.

How the company differentiated itself from global competitors.

Unlike traditional giants like Toyota and Volkswagen, Geely's differentiation lies in its full-domain R&D and ecosystem synergy. Geely's architecture platformization bypasses the development constraints between various models and technologies, unlike legacy automakers who depend on third-party tech integration; the GEA architecture can support pure EVs, PHEV, and range-extender variations. This flexibility allows it to offer both the pure-electric EX5 and the plug-in hybrid Bin Yue in Southeast Asia, catering to diverse policies and preferences, unlike Volkswagen's MEB platform or Toyota's e-TNGA.

In supply chains, Geely's "semi-vertical integration" distinguishes it from Tesla's full in-house development and most automakers' complete outsourcing. By controlling SinoIC, forming a JV with CATL, and investing in Meizu, Geely balances supply chain ability with core tech control. For example, it is a 7nm in-vehicle chip that adjusts computing power across models, unlike Volkswagen, which relies on Qualcomm chips with limited customization. Flyme Auto's cross-ecosystem integration with Meizu phones creates unique experiences, a feat hard to replicate for BMW or Mercedes-Benz, which rely on third-party software providers (Chen, 2023).

IMPLEMENTATION OF GLOBAL EXPANSION

Geely Automobile's global expansion is far more than a mere replication of domestic market strategies. Instead, it has forged differentiated execution pathways across regional markets through end-to-end synergies spanning R&D, technology, production capacity, and distribution channels, while establishing dynamic risk-response mechanisms to address challenges as they arise.

Key Initiatives and Investments

Geely Automobile's key initiatives and investments have always centered on a dual strategy: strategic mergers and acquisitions to build the foundation and in-depth local development to expand the market, constructing a global industrial ecosystem.

In major business strategies, Geely fully gained Volvo Cars for 1.8 billion dollars in 2010, gaining SPA architecture and safety tech patents, and establishing CEVT for two-way empowerment—Volvo's safety tech elevated Geely's positioning, while Geely's modular experience cut Volvo's model development costs by 18% (Lin et al., 2020; Tian, & Yuan, 2019). In 2017, it took a 49.9% stake in Malaysia's Proton and controlled Lotus; exporting CMA architecture drove Proton X50's SEA annual sales over 120,000 units, and Proton's 120 ASEAN dealers sped up Geely's right-hand drive model penetration (Geely Stories, 2020). Geely and Daimler launched a 50-50 smart joint venture in the new energy sector, with Geely overseeing SEA EV platform R&D and the supply of three-electric systems, while Daimler managed brand operations and access to European channels. For infrastructure, Geely built global capacity through regional hubs and local production: its Indonesia NEV factory is SEA's first green base, supplying Indonesia and ASEAN via RCEP tariffs; its Kazakhstan factory entered Russia/Belarus duty-free via the Eurasian Economic Union, with 32,000 2024 exports (Bellan, 2023).

Geely's product and service localization strategy is key to breaking regional barriers. For climate adaptation, the Southeast Asian-market EX5 tropical version has a dual-evaporator AC system, and an optimized battery thermal management system; the European-market Zeekr 001 boosts winter range and has a fast-charging system. Culturally, Malaysian Proton models offer Quranic embroidery in interiors, while Europe's Volvo brand launched a subscription service to fit young consumers' flexible mobility preferences. For intelligent systems, Flyme Auto optimizes Arabic voice recognition for the Middle East, and European models integrate with the Google ecosystem for seamless navigation and music.

Challenges Faced

Geely's globalization journey faces multiple complex challenges, including policy barriers, cultural differences, and geopolitical risks. These challenges come from both external environmental uncertainties and the complexity of internal integration within the enterprise.

Regulatory barriers have become the primary obstacle to market entry. The EU's 37.6% countervailing duty, implemented in 2024, directly targets Chinese electric vehicles, forcing Geely to shift production of Zeekr 001 body components from China to Europe (Stur, 2024; Williams, 2024). Manufacturing costs rose in the short term, and the company was required to comply with the EU's "Battery Passport" regulations, which required additional resources to establish a battery full-life-cycle traceability system (Xiao, 2024). Industrial protection policies in some Southeast Asian countries are also stringent. To avoid the tariff wars between China and the USA, Geely established a CKD assembly plant in a joint venture with local enterprises (Thanh, 2024). Compliance costs remain high, with Geely's special investment reaching 870 million yuan in 2024 to meet requirements across regions, including European REACH regulations and USA FMVSS safety standards (Xiao, 2024).

Cultural differences bring challenges at two levels: management models and consumer behavior. On the one hand, in the acquisition of Volvo, Geely faced a different management model and method from Volvo. Chinese business culture emphasizes hierarchical relationships, indirect communication, and long-term relationships, while Swedish business culture values flat organizational structures, direct communication, and consensus-driven decision-making. To address the problem, Geely conducted negotiations regarding Swedish traditions and Volvo's heritage. Geely invested significantly in building trust with Volvo's management and workforce. They engaged in extensive dialogue to understand Volvo's concerns and communicate their intentions transparently. Geely even allowed Volvo to maintain its Swedish management team and decision-making processes, ensuring a smooth integration (Wittwer, 2024). Geely uses social media to connect customers from different cultures and regions together. ProjectPractical (2025) states that trending posts appeared on Instagram, Twitter, and LinkedIn, attracting potential buyers to dealerships to experience their latest products.

Mitigation Strategies

Facing the complex challenges of globalization, Geely has adopted a multidimensional strategy system of policy adaptation, resource integration, and technological breakthroughs to build a dynamic risk-response mechanism and achieve sustainable business development.

In government relations and policy response, Geely adopts a compliance-first approach with proactive communication. To cope with the EU anti-subsidy tax, Geely considered building local factories in Europe to ensure that its products comply with European regulations without the limitation of tariffs (TMTPost, 2024). In Southeast Asia, Geely entered Indonesia and constructed new plants based on local standards. Geely partnered with 6 leading local dealers to build its presence in this key right-hand drive market (Geely Global, 2025). It received tax incentives from the local government, which catalyzed Indonesian NEV development in domestic production and policy updates (Permitindo, 2025).

Strategic cooperation with local enterprises has become the key to breaking through market barriers. Geely collaborated with Aramco to develop methanol power technology, leveraging its gas station network to promote methanol vehicles, whose expertise in fuels and hydrogen makes them a great partner for Geely to deliver cutting-edge, lower-emission powertrain solutions, driving the auto industry's carbon mitigation efforts forward (Geely, 2024). In Southeast Asia, Geely cooperates with Proton to expand important potential markets in ASEAN countries. With the help of Geely's resources, manufacturing standards, and international influence, the upgrading of Proton's homegrown models will involve leveraging joint resources with Geely to support the work led by Proton R&D engineers in Malaysia (The Star, 2024).

Investment in research and innovation is the core guarantee for maintaining long-term competitiveness. Geely's global R&D network invests over 12 billion yuan annually (Lee, 2025). The different centers have clear divisions of labor: the Gothenburg center focuses on safety technology, developing an AEB system and driving help system; the Coventry center focuses on intelligent driving; the Milan design center integrates Eastern and Western aesthetics (Geely HK, 2025; iNews, n.d.). In key technology areas, the Shendun Short Blade battery passed needle penetration tests and had a heat runaway tolerance of over 1000 degree Celsius, addressing European users' concerns about battery safety (Ashley, 2024); the Lei Shen electric hybrid system has a thermal efficiency of 44%, and the Monjaro in the Norwegian market's plug-in hybrid version sold 8,000 units annually, accounting for 12% of the local hybrid SUV market share. To address the chip shortage, the 7-nanometer chip "Dragon-Eagle-1" was mass-produced, delivering 100 Tops of computing power and reducing costs by 40% compared to purchased chips, ensuring a stable supply of intelligent cabin functions (EEWorld, 2024).

STRATEGIC ANALYSIS

Apply analytical frameworks

SWOT analysis

Strengths: Geely's brand portfolio is both diverse and strategically curated. At its core is the Geely brand, and the 2010 acquisition of Volvo stands as a pivotal milestone. Renowned worldwide for its unwavering commitment to safety and superior quality, Volvo not only furnished Geely with cutting-edge automotive technologies but also opened the door to a robust global R&D network and a prestigious position in the premium vehicle market. Brands like Lynk & Co specifically appeal to younger, tech-enthusiastic consumers, which allows Geely to diversify its market reach and effectively penetrate various demographic segments (Geely, 2017). Geely invests heavily in research and development. It has established R&D centers globally, enabling it to stay at the forefront of automotive technology. For instance, in developing electric and hybrid vehicles, Geely has made significant progress. The company has developed its electric vehicle platforms, which not only support the production of its brand models but also have the potential to be shared with other brands within the group, enhancing cost efficiency through economies of scale. Geely has been actively expanding its international footprint. It has manufacturing plants in multiple countries and regions, including Malaysia, through its acquisition of Proton (Geely, 2019). This global production and sales network helps Geely reduce transportation costs, better adapt to local market demands, and increase its brand awareness worldwide (Geely, 2019).

Weaknesses: Despite its global expansion and brand acquisitions, in some Western markets, Geely's brand image may still be associated with the stereotype of lower-cost, entry-level vehicles that Chinese manufacturers used to produce (Prandelli, 2024). This perception can limit its ability to compete directly with established premium brands on price and market share in the high-end segments. In certain markets, Geely relies on joint ventures to operate. While joint ventures can provide access to local knowledge and distribution channels, they also present challenges, including differences in management styles and profit-sharing arrangements (Kurtenbach, 2026). For example, in some joint ventures, decision-making processes may be slower because of the need for consensus between partners (Kurtenbach, 2026).

Opportunities: The global shift towards electric vehicles (EVs) presents an enormous opportunity for Geely. With increasing environmental concerns and government incentives promoting EV adoption, Geely can leverage its existing EV R&D capabilities (Geely, n.d.). For example, it can expand its range of electric models, target new markets, and potentially gain a larger share in the growing global EV market. There is significant growth potential in emerging markets such as Africa, South America, and parts of Asia. These regions have a growing middle class with increasing purchasing power and rising demand for automobiles. Geely can further penetrate these markets by offering affordable and feature-rich vehicles tailored to local needs.

Threats: The automotive industry is highly competitive, with both traditional automakers and new entrants vying for market share. New players, especially in the electric vehicle space, such as Tesla and various Chinese startups, are disrupting the market with innovative business models and advanced technologies (Cheng, 2024). Established automakers also continue to invest in new product development and marketing, making it challenging for Geely to maintain and grow its market share. The cost of raw materials such as steel, aluminum, and lithium, which are important for EV batteries, can fluctuate significantly (Richert & Dudek, 2023). These price fluctuations can affect Geely's production costs and profit margins. For example, a sharp increase in lithium prices could raise the cost of producing electric vehicles, forcing Geely to absorb the cost or pass it on to consumers, potentially affecting demand.

PESTEL

Political: The Chinese government has been supportive of the domestic automotive industry, particularly in promoting the development of new energy vehicles (NEVs) (Ministry of Finance, 2023). It provides subsidies for NEV production and purchase, benefiting Geely, which has a significant focus on electric and hybrid vehicles (Ministry of Finance, 2023). For example, these subsidies have helped Geely to reduce the price of its NEV models, making them more attractive to Chinese consumers. Trade policies affect Geely's international operations. Tariffs and trade disputes between countries can increase the cost of exporting vehicles (Sutter, 2025). For instance, trade tensions between the USA and China in recent years have led to higher tariffs on Chinese-made vehicles in the USA market, potentially reducing Geely's competitiveness there (Sutter, 2025). Local political stability influences Geely's manufacturing plants and sales. Regions with political unrest or instability may experience disruptions in production, supply chains, and sales. For example, political instability in some African countries where Geely is looking to expand could pose challenges to its business operations.

Economic: 1) Global Economic Growth: Overall global economic growth affects consumer purchasing power (International Monetary Fund [IMF], 2025). During economic expansion, consumers are more likely to purchase new vehicles, benefiting Geely. Conversely, during economic recessions, consumers may delay or cancel vehicle purchases. For example, the 2008-2009 global financial crisis led to a significant decline in global automotive sales, and Geely had to adjust its production and marketing strategies accordingly (IMF, 2025). 2) Cost of Capital: Geely's borrowing costs affect its investment decisions, particularly in R&D and new plant construction. Higher interest rates can increase the cost of capital, making it more expensive for Geely to finance large-scale projects. For example, if interest rates rise, Geely may need to allocate more funds to servicing debt, leaving less for innovation and expansion (World Bank, 2026).

Social: Consumers are increasingly demanding vehicles with advanced safety features, connectivity, and environmental friendliness. Geely needs to adapt to changing preferences continuously. For example, the growing popularity of SUVs and crossovers has led Geely to expand its offerings in these segments (Sharma, n.d.). The demand for in-car connectivity features such as Apple CarPlay and Android Auto compatibility has also influenced Geely's product development (Gao et al., 2016). In many emerging markets, population growth and urbanization are speeding up. This increases demand for personal transportation in urban areas. Geely can target these growing urban populations with compact, fuel-efficient, and affordable vehicles. For example, in rapidly urbanizing cities in India and Southeast Asia, Geely can offer models suited to congested city driving.

Technological: The automotive industry is experiencing rapid technological advancements in electric vehicles (EVs) and autonomous driving. Geely has been investing in both areas. EVs have developed advanced battery technologies and electric vehicle platforms. In autonomous driving, Geely is collaborating with technology companies to develop self-driving features. For example, Geely's cooperation with Baidu in China aims to integrate Baidu's Apollo autonomous driving technology into Geely's vehicles (Reuters, 2024). The trend towards connected cars and digitalization in the automotive industry offers opportunities for Geely. It can provide in-car infotainment systems, remote vehicle monitoring, and over-the-air software updates. These features enhance the customer experience and can also generate additional revenue through in-car app purchases and data-based services.

Environmental: Stringent emission standards are being implemented globally. Geely needs to ensure that its vehicles meet these standards. For example, in the European Union, the Euro 6 and upcoming Euro 7 emission standards require vehicles to meet lower limits for nitrogen oxide, particulate matter, and carbon dioxide emissions (Automotive Reference, 2025). Geely's investment in electric and hybrid vehicle technologies helps it comply with these standards and also positions it as an environmentally friendly brand. Consumers and governments are increasingly concerned about the environmental impact of manufacturing processes. Geely can gain a competitive edge by implementing sustainable manufacturing practices, such as using recycled materials, reducing waste, and improving energy efficiency in its production plants.

Legal: As Geely operates globally and develops technology, protecting its intellectual property rights (IPR) is crucial. It also needs to respect other companies' IPR. In some international markets, IPR-related legal challenges may arise, and Geely must ensure that its products and technologies do not infringe on the rights of others. Different countries and regions have their own vehicle safety regulations. Geely must ensure that its vehicles meet these safety requirements. For example, in the United States, vehicles need to pass a series of safety tests, such as the National Highway Traffic Safety Administration crash tests. Geely's acquisition of Volvo has been beneficial, as Volvo has a long-standing reputation for safety, and Geely can leverage this expertise to meet global safety standards.

Porter's Five Forces.

Threat of New Entrants: The automotive industry requires substantial capital investment in manufacturing plants, R&D, and marketing. New entrants need to build production facilities, develop new vehicle models, and establish a distribution network. For example, building a modern automotive manufacturing plant can cost billions of dollars. This high capital barrier reduces the threat of new entrants for Geely. The automotive industry faces many regulatory requirements, including safety, emissions, and fuel-efficiency standards. Meeting these regulations requires significant time and resources. New entrants must ensure their vehicles comply with these regulations, which adds to the complexity and cost of market entry. This further reduces the threat of new entrants for Geely.

Bargaining Power of Suppliers: Geely has a relatively large supplier base, which gives it some bargaining power. If a supplier raises prices or reduces quality, Geely can switch to another supplier. For example, in procuring steel, Geely can source from multiple steel manufacturers, reducing dependence on any single supplier. Geely has developed long-term relationships with some of its suppliers. These relationships are based on mutual trust and cooperation. While this may limit Geely's ability to switch suppliers easily sometimes, it also gives Geely some influence over suppliers' pricing, quality, and delivery schedules.

Bargaining Power of Buyers: The automotive market is highly competitive, giving buyers more options. This increases buyers' bargaining power, as they can easily switch to a competitor's product if dissatisfied with Geely's offerings. For example, in the compact car segment, Geely competes with many other brands, and buyers can compare prices, features, and after-sales service before making a purchase decision. With the internet, buyers have easy access to information about different vehicle models, prices, and reviews. This transparency empowers buyers and increases their bargaining power. For instance, buyers can research online to find the best price for a Geely vehicle and also read reviews from other customers, which can influence their purchasing decisions. While Geely has been working to build brand loyalty, it may have relatively low loyalty in some markets compared with long-established automotive brands. This makes buyers more likely to consider other brands, further increasing their bargaining power. However, Geely's diverse brand portfolio and improving product quality are gradually enhancing brand loyalty.

Threat of Substitute Products or Services: The growth of ride-hailing and car-sharing services poses a threat to personal vehicle ownership (Khalil et al., 2025). Some consumers may choose to use these services instead of buying a car. Geely can counter this threat by exploring partnerships with ride-hailing and car-sharing platforms. For example, it can supply vehicles to these platforms or develop its mobility services. Public transportation, cycling, and walking are alternative modes that can replace personal vehicles, especially in urban areas (Khalil et al., 2025). Geely can target consumers in areas with limited public transportation or those who need more flexibility by offering fuel-efficient, affordable, and convenient vehicles (Khalil et al., 2025).

Rivalry among Existing Competitors: The automotive industry is highly competitive, with many global and local players (International Energy Agency [IEA], 2024). Competitors are constantly launching new models, improving product features, and engaging in price wars. For example, in the electric vehicle segment, Geely competes with Tesla, BYD, and other automakers. These competitors are vying for market share, resulting in intense rivalry (IEA, 2024). And Geely uses differentiation strategies to stand out from competitors, focusing on areas such as technology, design, and brand image.

Brand and Reputation Effects

Global brand recognition and perception.

Geely has made remarkable progress in enhancing its global brand recognition and perception in recent years. Through a diverse brand portfolio, continuous product innovation, and rigorous product safety assessments, it has gradually transformed its global brand image.

Geely's expansion into new market segments with brands such as Lynk & Co has helped it reach a younger, more global demographic (Sergeev, 2024). Lynk & Co's unique business model, which includes features such as car-sharing options and a strong focus on digital connectivity, has attracted attention in markets such as Europe and China (Sergeev, 2024). By offering a distinct value proposition, Lynk & Co has carved out its niche and contributed to Geely's overall brand recognition as a forward-thinking automotive group.

Geely's commitment to product innovation has significantly shaped the brand's global perception. In the electric and hybrid vehicle space, Geely has been proactive. The company's development of its electric vehicle platforms, such as the Sustainable Experience Architecture (SEA), used across multiple brands within the Geely Group, demonstrates its technological prowess (Geely, 2022). Models such as the Zeekr 001, built on the SEA platform, have received international acclaim for their performance, range, and advanced features. The positive reviews and strong sales of these models have enhanced Geely's reputation as a serious player in the global electric vehicle market, dispelling prior notions that it is solely a maker of low-cost, basic vehicles (Geely, 2022).

In terms of safety, Geely has also made a mark. Its cars have been achieving high safety ratings in various global crash tests. For instance, Geely has built a full-scale safety center in Ningbo, which sets new standards in designing and defining new methods for improving emergency performance in case of active and passive safety issues (Autoini, 2025). The center also achieved five Guinness World Records, reflecting excellence in infrastructure, testing capability, and engineering depth (Autoini, 2025).

Corporate social responsibility and sustainability efforts.

Geely Auto has achieved notable progress in carbon reduction and new energy development. By 2024, it had cut life-cycle carbon emissions per vehicle by 18% relative to the 2020 baseline, driven by new energy vehicle (NEV) promotion and production energy-efficiency improvements (Geely Auto ESG Report, 2025). That year, its NEV sales surged 92% to 888,000 units, boosting green travel (Geely Auto ESG Report, 2025). It also operates 12 green and 11 zero-waste factories and has completed three zero-carbon factories ahead of schedule, with renewable energy accounting for over 64% of the total energy consumption of its vehicle manufacturing bases (Geely Auto ESG Report, 2025).

Geely leads in tech innovation and clean energy research while upholding high safety standards. It unveiled key technologies, including the GEA global intelligent new energy architecture, the Leishen hybrid system, and the Shendun Short Blade battery, enhancing NEV performance and safety (Ashley, 2024). It also expanded clean energy R&D and launched fifth-generation super-methanol PHEV technology. In 2024, 8 of its models earned C-NCAP five-star ratings, 3 earned Euro NCAP five-star ratings, 1 earned ANCAP five-star ratings, and the Geely EX5 received Nesta 6D electric safety certification and a top safety challenge certificate (Geely Auto ESG Report, 2025).

Geely prioritizes talent development and green procurement to strengthen the sustainability of its value chain. Following the talent concept "everyone is a talent, and everyone can become a talent," the company provided 1.85 million hours of electrification/digitalization training for employees in 2024, improved income growth plans, rolled out a comprehensive staff promotion plan, and launched a family health insurance plan. For green procurement, it used recycled materials in models like the Geely Galaxy E8 and Lynk & Co Z20—achieving 20% recycled steel, 30% recycled aluminum, and 25% recycled plastic in parts—and collaborated with suppliers to advance sustainability.

CONCLUSION AND STRATEGIC RECOMMENDATIONS

Summary of Key Findings

Geely Auto has been consistently expanding and diversifying its product portfolio. In 2024, it launched a series of high-value new energy vehicles (NEVs), including the L6, L7, and E8 models, offering a comprehensive range of advanced hybrid and pure-electric sedans and SUVs (Geely Auto surges past 107.3 billion RMB in H1 revenue, powered by electric vehicles and global expansion). These models cater to diverse consumer preferences, and in the first half of 2024, electrified model sales surged 742% year over year to 81,000 units. This product expansion has significantly contributed to its growth, as it can capture a larger share of different market segments.

The company has made substantial investments in research and development. In the first half of 2024, Geely Auto increased its R&D spending by 17.9% to 7 billion RMB. It has developed its intelligent technology ecosystem, such as the Shendun Short Blade battery, GEA global intelligent new energy vehicle architecture, and an integrated intelligent electric drive unit (Geely Global, 2024). In 2025, it further launched the G-Pilot safety high-order intelligent driving system, enhancing its competitiveness in the intelligent driving field. These technological advancements not only improve the performance and quality of its vehicles but also keep Geely at the forefront of the rapidly evolving automotive industry.

Geely Auto has been successful in its global expansion efforts. In 2024, it sold 410,000 vehicles overseas and expanded its global footprint to over 80 countries and regions, entering over 10 new markets (Kraft & Kraft, 2024). It has established joint ventures and subsidiaries across regions, including a joint venture in Belarus and new subsidiaries in Indonesia, Australia, the Philippines, and Chile. By expanding globally, Geely can access larger markets, benefit from economies of scale, and enhance its brand's international recognition.

Geely has been actively building its brand image. It has taken part in various international events and sponsorships. For example, in 2019, it became the official mobility partner of the 2022 Hangzhou Asian Games. The Lynk & Co Cyan Racing team's success in the WTCR team championship on its debut entry also enhanced the brand's image as a producer of durable, high-performance sports cars (Touring-CarTimes, 2023). Through these activities, Geely has positioned itself as a reliable, high-quality automotive brand.

Future Growth Opportunities

Potential new markets or industry segments.

The methanol vehicle market is a key area of focus for Geely Automobile. Against the backdrop of global carbon neutrality, decarbonization in the transportation sector has become a focal point for all countries. Methanol vehicles, with their unique benefits of fuel diversity, industrial compatibility, and cost control, have become a breakthrough in addressing the ongoing issue of high carbon emissions in transportation. Methanol is a liquid at standard temperature and pressure, making it more economical, safer, and easier to store, transport, and use. China is the world's largest producer and user of methanol, with over half of global capacity and output, mature production technology and low costs, enabling large-scale production and supply. Against this background, promoting the development of methanol vehicles aligns with China's national conditions, not only facilitating the full utilization of China's coal resource advantages but also effectively ensuring China's energy security. The "Opinions on Accelerating the Comprehensive Green Transformation of Economic and Social Development," issued in August 2024, proposed improving the infrastructure network of charging and swapping stations, hydrogen or methanol stations, and shore power, and speeding up the construction of urban intelligent transportation management systems (Central Committee of the Communist Party of China & State Council, 2024. The inclusion of green methanol in the "Catalogue for the Guidance of Industrial Structure Adjustment" as an encouraged new energy industry will help achieve "dual carbon" goals and build a modern energy system (Interesse, 2024).

Digital transformation and AI-driven strategies.

Geely has fully recognized the significance of the digital transformation trend and has actively implemented a comprehensive digital transformation program, applying artificial intelligence technology to enhance the enterprise's core competitiveness. Back in 2021, when Geely released its Intelligent Geely 2025 strategy, it built the "One Network and Three Systems", integrating high computing power, big data, large models, and satellite constellations and other new infrastructure technologies to create a solid "Intelligent Technology Ecosystem Network" technical foundation (GNEE, 2025). This forward-looking layout has laid a solid foundation for Geely's digital transformation and the application of artificial intelligence. In January 2025, Geely officially released its "Intelligent Vehicle All-Domain AI" technology system, becoming the first automaker to provide full coverage from underlying technologies to upper-layer applications in AI. The release of this technology system marks a breakthrough in Geely's research and application of artificial intelligence. It will further promote the evolution of automobiles from transportation tools to "embodied intelligence" smart life forms.

Recommendations for Other Firms

Best practices for global expansion.

Geely's global expansion has provided valuable experience for other brands. First, it is necessary to have a forward-looking international perspective. As early as 2002, just one year after obtaining the automotive production license, the founder, Li Shufu, began considering an acquisition of Volvo, and in 2003, they began exporting cars. Other enterprises should also adopt a global perspective to understand the industry landscape early and position themselves accurately within the global industrial chain. Second, through mergers and acquisitions, achieve rapid improvement and market expansion (Ding et al., 2023). For example, in 2010, Geely acquired Volvo, gaining key resources, including core technologies. Later, it gained Proton Motors and Lotus, expanded into new overseas markets, and strengthened its product line. Enterprises can learn from this approach and conduct mergers and acquisitions to address their development needs and fill gaps. Third, pay attention to the global layout of research and development and production. Every time Geely completes a cross-border acquisition, it establishes an R&D institution on the spot and has built a comprehensive global research and development network. This enables the enterprise to stay at the technological forefront and closely meet the needs of different markets.

Risk management strategies.

Geely has adopted many effective risk management strategies that other companies can learn from. The Daimler acquisition exemplifies risk control during mergers and acquisitions: they employed the "collar option" strategy to manage stock price volatility throughout the equity acquisition plan, which lasted over a year, and to ensure smooth merger implementation. This shows that when undertaking major investment, merger, and acquisition projects, enterprises should reasonably use financial tools and strategies to hedge against potential risks (David et al., 2018). Regarding compliance risks, Geely has established a comprehensive compliance management system. The board of directors has established a compliance committee, appointed a chief compliance officer, and created a hierarchical compliance system. To ensure system implementation, they adopted the "five meetings, four trainings, three laws, two talks, one report" operating mechanism. The group also recognizes compliance culture as one of its four major cultures, strengthening all employees' compliance awareness through training, publicity, and related initiatives. Other companies should also prioritize compliance construction to prevent compliance risks comprehensively across the organization, systems, and culture, and ensure the enterprise can compete globally while maintaining global compliance.

REFERENCES

An, L., & Zhao, R. (2019, July 10). China's car association predicts losses throughout 2019. *Caixin Global.* https://www.caixinglobal.com/2019-07-10/chinas-car-association-predicts-losses-throughout-2019-101437882.html

Andrews, M. (2024, June 28). Geely's Aegis short blade LFP battery – Full details including extreme safety. *CarNewsChina.* https://carnewschina.com/2024/06/28/geelys-aegis-short-blade-lfp-battery-full-details-including-extreme-safety/

Artxdigi. (2023, July 12). Interpretation of the announcement on continuation and optimization of new energy vehicle purchase tax exemption policy. *ARTXDIGI.* https://www.artxdigi.com/en/insights/china-express12/

Autoini. (2025, December 17). Geely safety centre sets global safety benchmark. *Autoini.* https://www.autoini.com/new-car/brand/geely-news/geely-opens-worlds-largest-safety-centre/

Automotive Reference. (2025, July 13). Understanding Euro emission standards and their impact on vehicle regulations. *Automotive Reference.* https://automotivereference.com/euro-emission-standards/

Automotive World. (2025, January 6). Geely auto sales surpassed 2.17 million units, international market growth exceeded 53%. *Automotive World.* https://www.automotiveworld.com/news-releases/geely-auto-sales-surpassed-2-17-million-units-international-market-growth-exceeded-53/

Bellan, R. (2023, August 7). Chinese luxury EV brand Zeekr continues global push into Kazakhstan. *TechCrunch.* https://techcrunch.com/2023/08/07/chinese-luxury-ev-brand-Zeekr-continues-global-push-into-kazakhstan/

Central Committee of the Communist Party of China & State Council. (2024). Opinions on accelerating the comprehensive green transformation of economic and social development. https://www.gov.cn/zhengce/202408/content_6967663.htm

Central Desk. (2025, January 1). Geely and Tasco to build $168M auto plant in Vietnam by 2025. *Auto World Journal.* https://www.autoworldjournal.com/geely-and-tasco-to-build-168m-auto-plant/

Chen, D. (2023, December 25). Geely's Dragon Eagle-1 chip is on more than 200,000 vehicles. *CarNewsChina.* https://carnewschina.com/2023/12/25/geelys-dragon-eagle-1-first-china-made-automotive-grade-chip-is-on-more-than-200000-vehicles/

Chen, D. Y. (2025, July 5). Geely Galaxy E5 (EX5) hits 150,000-unit sales milestone. *CarNewsChina*. https://carnewschina.com/2025/07/05/geely-galaxy-e5-ex5-hits-150000-unit-sales-milestone/

Cheng, C., Yang, X., Jiang, F., & Yang, Z. (2023). How to synergize different institutional logics of firms in cross-border acquisitions: A matching theory perspective. *Management International Review*. https://link.springer.com/article/10.1007/s11575-023-00502-8

Cheng, E. (2024, April 25). Geely-backed luxury EV brand Zeekr says it's already beating Tesla in parts of China. *CNBC*. https://www.cnbc.com/2024/04/25/geely-backed-luxury-ev-brand-zeekr-says-it's-already-beating-tesla-in-parts-of-china.html

Collins, J. (2025, April 17). Lotus Evija finally hits the track as production begins, but questions remain over deliveries and customer appeal. *EVMagz*. https://evmagz.com/lotus-evija-finally-hits-the-track-as-production-begins-but-questions-remain-over-deliveries-and-customer-appeal/

David, R., Nair, D., & Browning, J. (2018, February 28). Geely used a $9 billion collar trade on its Daimler purchase. *Bloomberg*. https://www.bloomberg.com/news/articles/2018-02-27/geely-is-said-to-use-9-billion-collar-trade-on-daimler-purchase

Ding, J., Guo, L., & Wang, Z. (2023). *Geely's path to becoming a global corporation*. Springer. [Book title if applicable], https://link.springer.com/chapter/10.1007/978-981-99-3326-6_10

EEWorld. (2024, August 12). 7nm! The first domestically produced 7nm smart cockpit chip is in mass production and installed in cars. https://en.eeworld.com.cn/news/qcdz/eic675420.html

Fast Technology. (2025, May 9). Geely has launched a rotating CEO system: Dai Qing is appointed as the first financial-background CEO. *Taibo*. https://en.taibo.cn/p/26045732

Fernandez, D. S. (2024, January 30). Geely Coolray global sales continues to rise in 2024. *DSF.my*. https://www.dsf.my/2024/01/geely-coolray-global-sales-exceeded-800000-units/

Gao, V. P., Kaas, H.-W., Mohr, D., & Wee, D. (2016, January). Automotive revolution – Perspective towards 2030. *McKinsey & Company*. https://www.mckinsey.com/industries/automotive-and-assembly/our-insights/disruptive-trends-that-will-transform-the-auto-industry/de-DE

Geely, H. K. (2025). Geely auto initiated the "five by five" globalization strategy. *Geely Auto HK*. https://www.geelyauto.hk/five-by-five/

Geely. (2017, August 4). Geely and Volvo Cars sign joint venture agreements. *Zhejiang Geely Holding Group*. https://zgh.com/media-center/news/20170804_1/?lang=en

Geely. (2019, October 14). A perfect match: How suppliers benefited from the Geely-Proton partnership. *Zhejiang Geely Holding Group*. https://zgh.com/media-center/story/a-perfect-match-how-supplier-benefited-from-the-geely-proton-partnership/?lang=en

Geely. (2022, November 17). Zeekr's SEA-M architecture is the new answer to future mobility. *Zhejiang Geely Holding Group*. https://zgh.com/media-center/news/2022-11-17-1/?lang=en

Geely. (2024, June 28). Aramco to acquire 10% equity interest in Horse Powertrain Limited. *Zhejiang Geely Holding Group*. https://zgh.com/media-center/news/2024-06-28/?lang=en

Geely Automobile Holdings Limited. (2025). Environmental, social and governance report 2024. https://global.geely.com/-/media/project/web-portal/2025/esg-report/esg-report-2024.pdf

Geely Global. (2024a, March 20). Geely auto 2023 financial results released. *Geely Global*. https://global.geely.com/en/news/2024/geely-auto-financial-results-2023

Geely Global. (2024b, August 21). Geely auto surges past 107.3 billion RMB in H1 revenue. *Geely Global*. https://global.geely.com/en/news/2024/geely-auto-h1-2024-revenues

Geely Global. (2025a, January 6). Geely auto sales surpassed 2.17 million units. *Geely Global*. https://global.geely.com/en/news/2025/geely-auto-sales-2024

Geely Global. (2025b, January 24). Geely auto enters Indonesian market. *Geely Global*. https://global.geely.com/en/news/2025/geely-auto-launch-indonesia

Geely. (n.d.). New energy pathway. *Zhejiang Geely Holding Group*. https://zgh.com/new-energy-pathway/?lang=en

Geely Stories. (2020, March 30). The tiger is free – Ten years of Volvo and Geely Holding. *Zhejiang Geely Holding Group*. https://zgh.com/media-center/story/ten-years-of-volvo-and-geely/?lang=en

Gnee. (2025, July 29). Geely showcases new vehicles and comprehensive AI technologies at WAIC 2025, ushering in a boom in smart technology. *GNEE Group*. https://gneegroup.com/news/geely-showcases-new-vehicles-and-comprehensive-ai-technologies-at-waic-2025-ushering-in-a-boom-in-smart-technology.html

Hampel, C. (2021, June 18). New details on the scope of Geely SEA e-platform. *Electrive*. https://www.electrive.com/2021/06/18/new-details-on-the-scope-of-geelys-sea-e-platform/

Holm, M., & Zhang, L. (2016). *Swedish and Chinese leadership at CEVT: A case study on the cultural differences of Chinese and Swedish leadership* [Master's thesis, Chalmers University of Technology]. Chalmers Publications Library. https://publications.lib.chalmers.se/records/fulltext/237634/237634.pdf

iNews. (n.d.). The "Geely logic" of global R&D: From "bringing in" to "going global." *inf.news*. https://inf.news/en/auto/7bb140c5b50316013fcebd9486b06f04.html

Interesse, G. (2024, February 5). China's 2024 catalogue for guiding industry restructuring. *China Briefing*. https://www.china-briefing.com/news/chinas-2024-catalogue-for-guiding-industry-restructuring/

International Energy Agency. (2024, April 23). *Global EV outlook 2024*. https://www.iea.org/reports/global-ev-outlook-2024

International Monetary Fund. (2025, October 7). *World economic outlook: All issues*. https://www.imf.org/en/publications/weo

Kang, L. (2023, April 12). Full CPCA rankings: Top-selling models and automakers in China in Mar. *CNEVPost*. https://cnevpost.com/2023/04/12/full-cpca-rankings-top-selling-models-automakers-china-mar/

Khalil, J., Yan, D., Yuan, L., Jafarzadehfadaki, M., Adhikari, S., Han, J., Sisiopiku, V., & Jiang, Z. (2025). Urban traffic simulation with shared mobility services: An approach using spatiotemporal network kernel density estimation and MATSim. *ACM Transactions on Spatial Algorithms and Systems*, *11*(4), 1–31. DOI: 10.1145/3704918

Knowledge Info Hub. (2025). The rise of Geely: A Chinese automotive giant. *Knowledge and Info Hub*. https://knowledgeinfohub.com/the-rise-of-geely-a-chinese-automotive-giant/

Kraft, J., & Kraft, A. (2024). Geely: How a Chinese upstart became a global automobile maker. *Journal of Research in International Business and Management*, *11*(4), 1–11. https://www.interesjournals.org/articles/geely-how-a-chinese-upstart-became-a-global-automobile-maker-109510.html

Kurtenbach, E. (2026, February 22). Geely's Volvo purchase faces cultural obstacles. *GOLDSEA*. https://goldsea.com/article_details/geely-s-volvo-purchase-must-overcome-big-cultural-disparity

Laouiti, S., Detchusananart, M., Bieske, L., & Sodar, M. A. (2018, December). *Geely automobile holdings: From "zero" to Chinese automotive industry "hero"*. ResearchGate. https://www.researchgate.net/publication/332525104

Lee, M. (2025, August 14). Geely's resilience in a turbulent EV market: Strategic R&D and market expansion as catalysts for long-term value creation. *AInvest*. https://www.ainvest.com/news/geely-resilience-turbulent-ev-market-strategic-market-expansion-catalysts-long-term-creation-2508/

Li, F. (2024, November 4). Green methanol route to nation's carbon goal. *China Daily*. https://www.chinadaily.com.cn/a/202411/04/WS67282512a310f1265a1cb2ee.html

Li, F. (2025, May 19). "One Geely" integration to hone competitive edge. *China Daily*. https://www.chinadaily.com.cn/a/202505/19/WS682a8e57a310a04af22c0281.html

Li, M., & Pi, X. (2025, March 12). : [Geely globalization: Insights from Chinese companies going abroad]. *Toutiao*. https://www.toutiao.com/article/7480850536733721115/

Lin, R., Chen, J. J., & Xie, L. (2020). *Transnational governance at Geely Auto during its acquisition of Volvo*. Springer. [Book title if applicable], https://link.springer.com/chapter/10.1007/978-981-15-7405-4_3 DOI: 10.1007/978-981-15-7405-4_3

Liu, S., Wang, E., & Xiang, J. (2019, March 28). Daimler and Geely Holding form global joint venture to develop smart. *Smart Media*. https://media.smart.com/daimler-and-geely-holding-form-global-joint-venture-to-develop-smart/

Macarol, J. (2024, November 16). BYD and Geely in the world's top ten: How Chinese car brands are breaking into the world's biggest markets. *City Magazine*. https://citymagazine.si/en/byd-and-geely-in-the-worlds-top-ten-how-chinese-car-brands-penetrate-into-the-worlds-largest/

Meng, Z., & Wang, X. (2021). The effects of outbound mergers and acquisitions (M&As) on Chinese automobile corporations' performance: A case study of Geely's acquisition of Volvo. *International Business Research*. https://www.ccsenet.org/journal/index.php/ibr/article/view/45467

Messe Düsseldorf Asia. (n.d.). Market highlights: Robust prospects and growing demand in Southeast Asia. *Wire Southeast Asia*. https://www.wire-southeastasia.com/market-highlights

Ministry of Finance. (2023, June 19). [Announcement on the continuation and optimization of the vehicle purchase tax reduction policy for new energy vehicles]. *Government of the People's Republic of China*. https://www.gov.cn/zhengce/zhengceku/202306/content_6887734.htm

Pang, A. (2024, January 23). Financial analysis on Geely major acquisition on Volvo. *Clausius Scientific Press*. https://www.clausiuspress.com/article/10844.html

Permitindo. (2025, July 23). Indonesia's EV industry boost: Regulation's key takeaways. *Permitindo*. https://www.permitindo.com/news/indonesia-ev-industry-regulation

Prandelli, D. (2024, November 24). The Chinese automotive revolution: Smashing stereotypes, shaping the future. *Substack*. https://pranda.substack.com/p/the-chinese-automotive-revolution

ProjectPractical. (2025, April 7). Geely automobile marketing strategy 2025: A case study. *ProjectPractical*. https://www.projectpractical.com/geely-automobile-marketing-strategy/

Reuters. (2024, December 12). Baidu, Geely's EV venture faces uproar after it says it needs fresh funds. *Reuters*. https://www.reuters.com/business/autos-transportation/baidu-geelys-ev-venture-faces-uproar-after-it-says-needs-fresh-funds-2024-12-12/

Richert, M., & Dudek, M. (2023). Selected problems of the automotive industry—Material and economic risk. *Journal of Risk and Financial Management, 16*(8), 368. https://www.mdpi.com/1911-8074/16/8/368. DOI: 10.3390/jrfm16080368

Securities Daily. (2025, May 7). [Focusing on the core automotive business and returning to one Geely: Geely Holding promotes the deep implementation of the "Taizhou Declaration"]. *Securities Daily*. http://www.zqrb.cn/auto/qichedongtai/2025-05-07/A1746615804320.html

Sergeev, A. (2024, February 14). Lynk & Co expands European presence, not coming to UK yet. *Motor1*. https://www.motor1.com/news/708576/lynk-co-not-coming-uk-yet/

Sharma, R. (n.d.). *SUV market report: Global forecast from 2025 to 2033*. Data Intelo. https://dataintelo.com/report/suv-market

Soto, H. (2023, September 1). Geely to arrive in Mexico in 4Q23. *Mexico Business News*. https://mexicobusiness.news/automotive/news/geely-arrive-mexico-4q23

Stur, B. (2024, July 4). EU imposes provisional countervailing duties on Chinese electric vehicles. *European Interest*. https://www.europeaninterest.eu/eu-imposes-provisional-countervailing-duties-on-chinese-electric-vehicles/

Su, Q., & Lahiri, B. (2023). Does the Belt and Road Initiative boost Chinese automobile exports? A staggered adoption approach. *Applied Economics*, *56*(59), 8855–8859. DOI: 10.1080/00036846.2023.2295301

Sutter, K. M. (2025, September 9). *U.S.–China trade relations*. Congressional Research Service. https://www.congress.gov/crs-product/IF11284

Thanh, V. (2024, September 24). China's Geely to build $168 million automobile facility with Tasco in Thai Binh. *Vietnam Investment Review*. https://vir.com.vn/chinas-geely-to-build-168-million-automobile-facility-with-tasco-in-thai-binh-114721.html

The Star. (2024, August 15). Proton to work closely with Geely to explore model enhancement activities. *The Star*. https://www.thestar.com.my/business/business-news/2024/08/15/proton-to-work-closely-with-geely-to-explore-model-enhancement-activities

Tian, S., & Yuan, Y. (2019). How to improve subsidiary willingness towards reverse knowledge transfer in emerging-market multinational enterprises? A case study of Geely Group [Master's thesis, Uppsala University]. DiVA Portal. https://uu.diva-portal.org/smash/record.jsf?pid=diva2:1333290

TMTPost. (2024, September 18). Geely and Xpeng join wave of Chinese automakers to build plant in Europe in the face of EV tariffs. *Sohu*. https://www.sohu.com/a/809720282_116132

TouringCarTimes. (2023, March 1). Geely Group Motorsport teases potential new TCR car. *TouringCarTimes*. https://www.touringcartimes.com/2023/03/01/geely-group-motorsport-teases-potential-new-tcr-car/

Williams, K. (2024, July 23). Tariff effect: Zeekr wants to produce electric cars in Europe. *Motor1*. https://www.motor1.com/news/727537/zeekr-plans-european-production-factory/

Wittwer, W. (2024, June 29). East meets west: Lessons from Geely's acquisition of Volvo. *Success Across Cultures*. https://successacrosscultures.com/2024/06/29/east-meets-west-lessons-from-geelys-acquisition-of-volvo/

World Bank. (2026, January). *Global economic prospects*. https://www.worldbank.org/en/publication/global-economic-prospects

Xiao, S. (2024). A company analysis on Geely based on its external and internal environment. *Advances in Economics. Management and Political Sciences*, *79*(1), 283–289. DOI: 10.54254/2754-1169/79/20241848

Xin, H. (2025, January 9). : , [Jiailing District: Based on the automotive industry ecosystem, creating a magnificent chapter for an industrial town]. *Nanchong Municipal Government*. https://www.nanchong.gov.cn/fgw/xwdt/bmxx/202501/t20250109_2064973.html

Zhang, C., Manthey, E., & Luman, R. (2023, July 26). Tightening supply shakes up battery metal dynamics. *ING*. https://think.ing.com/downloads/pdf/article/tightening-supply-shakes-up-battery-metals

Zhang, K., & Liang, J. (2023, May 8). China-Malaysia automotive collaboration of strategic importance: Malaysian PM. *People's Daily Online*. https://en.people.cn/n3/2023/0508/c90000-20015796.html

Key Terms and Definitions

Brand Portfolio Strategy: A corporate strategy that manages multiple differentiated brands within one group to target various market segments while balancing risk and positioning across price tiers.

Cross-Border Mergers and Acquisitions (M&A): A corporate growth strategy in which a firm acquires or merges with foreign companies to gain rapid access to advanced technology, established brands, managerial expertise, and international distribution networks.

Economies of Scale: Cost advantages are achieved when increased production volume reduces the average cost per unit through shared resources, standardized platforms, and bulk procurement.

Global Research and Development Network (Global R&D Network): A geographically dispersed system of innovation centers that collaborates across countries to develop new technologies, platforms, and products tailored to both global and local markets.

Greenfield Investment: A form of foreign direct investment where a company establishes new production facilities or subsidiaries from scratch in a host country to achieve full operational control and long-term market presence.

Institutional Adaptation: The capability of a multinational enterprise to adjust its governance structures, compliance systems, and operational processes to diverse regulatory and political environments.

Joint Venture (JV): A cooperative business arrangement in which two or more firms share ownership, resources, and control to enter or operate within a specific market while distributing risks and returns.

Localization Strategy: A market entry approach that adapts products, operations, and marketing strategies to local consumer preferences, regulatory requirements, and cultural contexts in foreign markets.

Modular Vehicle Architecture: A standardized product development system that allows multiple vehicle models to share core platforms, components, and technologies, reducing production costs, shortening development cycles, and generating economies of scale.

New Energy Vehicles (NEVs): Vehicles powered wholly or partially by alternative energy sources, including battery electric, plug-in hybrid, or other low-emission technologies, aimed at reducing carbon emissions and complying with environmental regulations.

Reverse Knowledge Transfer (RKT): The process through which subsidiaries in advanced economies transfer technological know-how, innovation capabilities, and managerial practices back to the parent company in the home country.

Vertical Integration: A strategy in which a company controls key stages of its supply chain, such as battery production, chip development, or software systems, to enhance cost control, supply stability, and technological independence.

Chapter 11
Jiangsu Changjiang Electronics Technology's Acquisition Strategy:
The Strategic Acquisition of STATS ChipPAC

Yuhua Yu
Macau University of Science and Technology, Macau

EXECUTIVE SUMMARY

This chapter examines JCET Group's strategic transformation from a domestic Chinese packaging provider into a top three global OSAT leader through its 2015 acquisition of STATS ChipPAC. The analysis explores the internal and external motivations for expansion, including domestic market saturation, China's Chip Replacement Initiative, and the need for advanced packaging technologies. Details of the sophisticated acquisition structure using a Special Purpose Vehicle and backing from China's National Integrated Circuit Industry Investment Fund (Big Fund) to execute a leveraged cross-border merger while navigating geopolitical sensitivities. The case shows how state-backed capital enabled rapid technological advancement and market access, though significant challenges emerged, including heightened debt burdens, complex post-merger integration, and exposure to Sino-U.S. trade tensions. Insights into how companies can gain an edge by making their global production the best it can be and by developing an array of technologies.

DOI: 10.4018/979-8-3373-4302-0.ch011

INTRODUCTION

Background of the Company

The semiconductor industry primarily includes four categories: discrete components, Integrated Circuits (ICs), sensors, and optoelectronic components. ICs hold a critical position within the upstream and downstream landscape of the semiconductor industry. Technological complexity and a highly specialized industrial structure led experts to classify ICs into three sub-sectors: IC packaging and testing, IC invention, and IC component innovation (Ding, 2021). Jiangsu Changjiang Electronics Technology (JCET) Group operates in the semiconductor packaging and testing industry, which is a crucial stage in the semiconductor product manufacturing process. This case study will introduce the development of the semiconductor industry and the global expansion of JCET Group within it.

JCET Group, established in 1972, has emerged as a preeminent global provider of integrated circuit fabrication and advanced technology solutions. Its headquarters are in Jiangsu Province, China. The corporation maintains an extensive international presence with over twenty operational facilities worldwide, offering comprehensive semiconductor manufacturing services to a global clientele.

An essential development occurred in 2014 when JCET strategically capitalized on the national semiconductor industry development initiative to execute a transformative cross-border acquisition. The successful incorporation of STATS ChipPAC Ltd - then the fourth-largest player in the global semiconductor outsourced assembly and test (OSAT) market - substantially augmented JCET's operational capacity, so its customer portfolio diversification, enhanced its technological competencies, and elevated its international standing, securing its position within the supply chains of elite global semiconductor manufacturers.

JCET is currently the third-largest IC packaging company in the world and the market leader in mainland China. It has eight major production facilities and two special research and development centers, while also maintaining over twenty business operations in China, South Korea, and Singapore (JCET Group, n.d.). JCET Group has a significant presence in the semiconductor industry, with a workforce of over 20,000 skilled professionals globally, so it offers an array of services, including micro system integration, design simulation, wafer probing, chip and device packaging, final testing, and product certification. The company's transformation from a domestic packaging provider to a global leader highlights its strategic vision and execution. This journey reflects the overall growth of China's semiconductor sector on the international stage. Their evolution corresponds with the industry's shift from traditional packaging methods to advanced heterogeneous integration.

JCET, therefore, stands at the forefront of the 'post-Moore's Law' era, where crucial performance improvements depend on packaging innovation.

Motivation for Global Expansion

Here are the four primary motivations behind the company's global expansion.

Internal Motivation

During the global financial crisis in 2009, JCET Group experienced a significant drop in domestic orders (JCET Group, 2010, p. 18). To improve risk resilience and lessen reliance on the domestic market, the company had to pursue expansion into international markets. Fierce price competition in China's low-to-mid-end semiconductor market limited JCET's growth, highlighting the urgent need to increase its market share in high-end products. A stagnation in technological advancement worsened the internal pressures within the company; organic research and development were proving to be too slow and costly to close the gap with global leaders. Management recognized that the only viable path to achieve the scale and technological advancement within a competitive timeframe was through mergers and acquisitions (M&A).

Market Motivation

Following the exposure of the US PRISM program in 2013, China elevated information security to a national strategic priority. This shift triggered a surge in demand for domestic chips and spurred the rapid development of the integrated circuit industry (Xinhua Net, 2015). This situation created significant opportunities for Chinese IC manufacturers. Several factors contributed to this growth, including the rapid expansion of the 4G smartphone and Internet of Things (IoT) industries, as well as the nationwide "Chip Replacement Initiative," which sought to replace imported chips with domestic alternatives. To meet the growing domestic demand, JCET needed capabilities it lacked. Chinese fabless companies, such as HiSilicon (Huawei) and Unisoc, were developing increasingly sophisticated chips and required advanced packaging services that were only available from top-tier international OSATs (Outsourced Semiconductor Assembly and Test providers). JCET needed to quickly acquire high-end packaging technologies and the credibility associated with a global clientele in order to become a credible supplier to these major domestic companies and fulfill the goals of the "Chip Replacement Initiative."

Resource Motivation:

Growing concerns about foreign semiconductor companies infiltrating critical Chinese infrastructure—such as government, education, and transportation—resulted in heightened information security risks in 2014. In response, the Cyberspace Administration of China (2014) issued "the National Guidelines for the Development and Promotion of the Integrated Circuit Industry" and established the National Integrated Circuit Industry Investment Fund, commonly referred to as the "Big Fund." This fund provided substantial financial support to domestic integrated circuit firms (Shi, 2016). The involvement of the Big Fund significantly reduced JCET's loan burden during its leveraged buyout of STATS ChipPAC, ensuring the successful execution of the acquisition. The involvement of the Big Fund reduced the risks associated with the transaction for other investors and lenders, confirming JCET's strategic direction. This support transformed the acquisition from a corporate gamble into a national project, aligning JCET's growth in China's broader industrial policy objectives. This access to patient, strategic capital was a resource that most global competitors did not have.

Technology Motivation:

JCET Group's product portfolio has traditionally focused on mid-to-low-end semiconductor packaging solutions, whereas STATS ChipPAC (now JCET STATS ChipPAC) specialized in advanced packaging technologies, possessing cutting-edge capabilities including embedded Wafer-Level Ball Grid Array (eWLB), Wafer-Level Chip Scale Packaging (WLCSP), and Package-on-Package (POP) - technologies typically deployed by first-tier global On-Site Acceptance Tests provides. This strategic acquisition has consequently enabled JCET to achieve significant technological breakthroughs, enhance its competitive positioning in global markets, and expand into high-end packaging segments both domestically and internationally.

MARKET ANALYSIS AND ENTRY STRATEGY

Target Market Selection

The first market JCET expanded into was the United States. According to Wang (as cited in Zhang & Shang, 2019), an analysis of the top ten companies in the global chip industry in 2017 revealed that the US was home to five companies, while South Korea had two, and Taiwan (China), Japan, and Singapore each had one. These leading companies primarily produced memory chips, processors, communication chips, and analog chips. The industry leaders mainly concentrated in the United States, Taiwan (China), and South Korea, which resulted in a substantial market for chip design and high-end chip manufacturing in the US

The Asia-Pacific region predominantly concentrates on chip packaging and testing, as these processes require less technical expertise and more labor. This geographic specialization created a strategic dilemma for JCET: while the US presented a massive market for high-value chip design and manufacturing, the company's core competency lay in the downstream segment of packaging and testing. Although the United States plays a dominant role in the integrated circuits sector, it is noteworthy that half of the cross-border acquisition targets pursued by Chinese companies were based in the US However, these merger and acquisition attempts experienced a remarkably high failure rate.

Considering this, JCET opted not to acquire an American company directly. Instead, the strategy involved gaining companies in the Asia-Pacific region that cater to the European and American markets. Prior to its acquisition, STATS ChipPAC was a globally leading semiconductor packaging and testing company, ranking fourth worldwide in its sector. Its subsidiaries widely sold its products in regions including China, the United States, Taiwan, Singapore, and South Korea. The United States, in particular, was critical to its success—customers in the Americas and Europe contributed 79% of the company's operating profit. This strong financial performance was a significant factor that motivated JCET Group to acquire STATS ChipPAC.

This indirect market entry strategy was a brilliant way to navigate geopolitical and regulatory challenges. By acquiring a Singaporean company with strong connections and established customer relationships in the US market, JCET effectively gained a "backdoor" entry. STATS ChipPAC's solid reputation and existing supply contracts with American tech giants provided immediate revenue streams and market presence, all without provoking the intense regulatory scrutiny that a direct acquisition of a US company would likely have triggered. This approach allowed JCET to avoid the high failure rate commonly seen with direct acquisitions of US firms by Chinese companies, while still achieving the desired market access.

Entry Mode Selection

Mergers and acquisitions (M&A) have long been a common corporate strategy and serve as an important avenue for strategic expansion. JCET Group primarily expands externally through cross-border mergers and acquisitions. A notable example is its acquisition of STATS ChipPAC Ltd, which was then the fourth-largest player in the global semiconductor outsourced assembly and test (OSAT) market.

Technological advancements and globalization have significantly contributed to the rise of cross-border M&A. These acquisitions allow companies to enter new and lucrative markets while also expanding their existing product portfolios (Shimizu, Hitt, Vaidyanath, & Pisano, 2004). Acquiring a company based in another country presents the buyer with valuable opportunities to learn new technologies, acquire new capabilities—such as knowledge bases, technical expertise, and human resources—and gain access to local markets and key customer networks.

This analysis will explore the motivations behind the acquisition from the perspectives of both the acquirer, JCET Group, and the acquired company, STATS ChipPAC. To begin with, JCET Group was driven by weakened profitability and an urgent need to expand into overseas markets. By 2014, the company had reached a developmental bottleneck. This was largely because of the maturation of the mobile products market—such as smartphones and tablets, which drive the integrated circuit (IC) market—resulting in slowing growth.

The rapid development of the domestic IC industry and the introduction of new production capacity intensified price competition for mid- to low-end products. One of JCET Group's primary objectives in acquiring STATS ChipPAC was to broaden its market reach and integrate into the supply chains of top-tier international manufacturers.

Besides seeking to expand into foreign markets, companies pursue mergers and acquisitions to access key technologies and achieve greater scale (Chen, 2019). The semiconductor industry in China started later than in the United States, Japan, and South Korea, leading to a technology gap. JCET Group's initial inability to enter the international supply chain stemmed from its technical capabilities not meeting first-tier international standards. In contrast, STATS ChipPAC had advanced packaging and testing technologies and maintained a global presence, serving major clients such as Qualcomm, Broadcom, SanDisk, and Marvell.

By acquiring STATS ChipPAC, JCET Group gained two significant advantages: access to cutting-edge technology and expanded market opportunities. Following the acquisition, JCET Group achieved enhanced production scale, covering the full spectrum of high-, mid-, and low-end IC packaging and testing (Wang, 2023). It also gained access to end-market applications across various semiconductor product segments.

Temasek's decision, as a major shareholder, to divest from STATS ChipPAC was influenced by the company's consecutive annual revenue declines and two years of losses. According to JCET Group's annual reports from 2012 to 2018 (JCET Group, 2019), the rapid technological evolution in the global semiconductor industry—especially the shift from wire bonding to advanced packaging—had increased competitive pressure on STATS ChipPAC. Saturation in the global PC and smartphone markets worsened the company's operational challenges. These factors resulted in a 6.5% year-on-year decrease in the company's total revenue in

2013, followed by a further decline of 1.5% in 2014. Temasek decided to divest its equity stake and restructure its investment portfolio.

The decision to pursue mergers and acquisitions (M&A) over organic growth or greenfield investments was primarily driven by the urgency to enter the market quickly. Developing advanced packaging capabilities from scratch would have required years and billions of dollars in research and development, with no certainty of success or acceptance from customers. A greenfield operation in a new region would have encountered significant challenges in attracting both talent and clients. In contrast, an acquisition offered immediate advantages: instant access to technology, capacity, customers, and a global presence. For a company like JCET, which was racing against time and its competitors, M&A was the most logical approach to achieve its transformative goals.

Competitive Advantage

After the merger and acquisition, the JCET Group gained competitive advantages that helped it thrive internationally. First, the company achieved cost leadership. Compared to other leading IC packaging and testing enterprises, JCET operates production bases with distinct technological features and advantages in China, Singapore, and South Korea. This strategic allocation allows JCET to assign high-cost orders, such as advanced packaging, to its factories in Singapore or South Korea, while directing cost-sensitive orders to its facilities in mainland China. As a result, JCET can offer products at lower prices than its competitors.

Second, JCET boasts a comprehensive technology portfolio. The company's technological capabilities span all tiers—low, mid, and high-end—and it is recognized as a leader in key advanced packaging segments. From traditional methods like wire bonding and flip-chip (FC) to cutting-edge solutions such as fan-out and system-in-package (SiP), JCET provides customers with a full range of packaging solutions. This extensive offering allows JCET to deliver tailored options that meet specific client needs while also reducing communication overhead and streamlining supply chain management.

Third, JCET holds significant strategic geopolitical value, serving as a crucial node in a secure and resilient supply chain. For international clients, multinational corporations like Qualcomm, which are increasingly adopting an "in China, for China" localization strategy, find great value in partnering with JCET. This collaboration enables them to leverage competitive advantages while demonstrating their commitment to the domestic market, thus enhancing their proximity to downstream customers and mitigating risks associated with geopolitical uncertainties. This multifaceted competitive advantage creates a sound position in the market. Cost leadership extends beyond simply having cheap labor; it involves strategically allocating global capacity. The technology portfolio is not only extensive but also deeply integrated, enabling JCET to provide truly heterogeneous integration solutions that are essential in the post-Moore's Law era.

Most importantly, the geopolitical value proposition is exceptional. In a time of decoupling and supply chain fragmentation, JCET's ability to offer a new solution—providing advanced packaging both within China for local compliance and outside of China for risk mitigation—makes it an indispensable partner for nearly every major global semiconductor player. This strategic positioning is arguably JCET's strongest and most enduring competitive advantage.

IMPLEMENTATION OF GLOBAL EXPANSION

Key Initiatives and Investments

This section describes the primary process involved in JCET's acquisition of STATS ChipPAC. After negotiations, they established the total consideration for the acquisition at USD 780 million, which is approximately RMB 4.8 billion. Following this, strategic investors were introduced, and a Special Purpose Vehicle (SPV) was created. According to JCET's 2014 annual report (JCET Group, 2015), its cash and cash equivalents amounted to only RMB 2.6 billion, which was insufficient for JCET to complete the acquisition independently. After engaging in multilateral discussions, JCET secured support from the China Integrated Circuit Industry Investment Fund (referred to as the "Industry Fund") and Semiconductor Manufacturing International Corporation (SMIC) to jointly participate in the acquisition.

Once the investors were confirmed, the critical acquisition process began. First, JCET, the Industry Fund, and SMIC jointly established a new entity—JCET-SC (Jiangsu Changjiang Electronics Technology - Starboard Capital Limited)—to pool resources, share investment responsibilities, and collectively assume risks. Next, JCET and the Industry Fund created a Special Purpose Vehicle (SPV) specifically for the acquisition of STATS ChipPAC, which served two primary objectives:

Risk Isolation for Acquisition and Operations: Acquiring a large-scale overseas company involves significant risks, such as undisclosed liabilities, potential litigation, and challenges in integration. By conducting the acquisition through an SPV, these risks can be contained within the entity—JCET-SC—thus preventing them from affecting JCET and its publicly listed parent company. This approach safeguards the entire group from potential failure. Since STATS ChipPAC was operating at a loss at the time of acquisition, placing it within an independent SPV prevented its financial results from being immediately merged into JCET's financial statements.

This separation helped avoid a severe negative impact on performing the publicly traded company.

The leveraged acquisition structure for the special purpose vehicle (SPV) JCET-SC involved a registered capital of USD 660 million, contributed by three parties. However, this amount fell short by USD 120 million from the total acquisition price of USD 780 million. To cover this gap, a loan was secured from the Bank of China.

To simplify regulatory compliance and reduce geopolitical sensitivities, JCET established a wholly offshore entity, JCET-SC (Singapore), to handle the acquisition. This structure created a legal separation from being directly associated with a "Chinese company." As a result, it helped minimize political opposition and sensitivity, increasing the likelihood of obtaining regulatory approval for the transaction.

The consortium approach involving the Big Fund and SMIC was not merely about sharing costs; it aimed to align with powerful strategic partners who shared a common national aim. Using a Special Purpose Vehicle (SPV) exemplified prudent risk management in cross-border mergers and acquisitions (M&A). Establishing an offshore acquisition entity in Singapore was a clever strategy to address the widespread "China risk" perception among foreign regulators and stakeholders. The debt structuring, including the subsequent issuance of Perpetual Securities classified as equity, demonstrated a deep understanding of financial instruments to optimize the balance sheet after the acquisition. This entire framework serves as a blueprint for how Chinese companies can successfully execute large, complex overseas acquisitions amid financial and geopolitical challenges.

Challenges Faced

Foremost, the company faced increased debt pressure following the merger. Cai and Wang (2020) analyzed Jiangsu Changjiang Electronics Technology Co., Ltd.'s solvency from 2013 to 2017. Their analysis revealed that the company's asset-liability ratio was 63.12% in 2014. After acquiring STATS ChipPAC in 2015, this ratio rose to 73.83%, which included USD 560 million in current liabilities from the gained entity.

Second, JCET Group encountered significant challenges because of shifts in the global geopolitical landscape. As a provider of semiconductor packaging and testing services, the company was vulnerable to trade tensions between China and key international markets. Europe and the United States are major export destinations for JCET, and the escalation of Sino-US trade friction—characterized by import/export restrictions and increased tariffs—posed substantial risks. These risks included potential shortages of equipment and raw materials, as well as the loss of customers. Such factors could have constrained production, reduced order volumes, and increased operational costs, negatively affecting the company's business performance.

For example, in 2020, SMIC—a key strategic partner of JCET—came under US Export Administration Regulations (EAR), which forced it to halt wafer foundry services for Huawei. STATS ChipPAC, a subsidiary of JCET, was proposed by the Trump administration for inclusion on the US Military End-User (MEU) list, further highlighting the company's exposure to geopolitical risks.

Third, JCET's acquisition of STATS ChipPAC included the divestment of the latter's operations in Taiwan. Mainland Chinese companies cannot directly or indirectly invest in or control semiconductor-related businesses in Taiwan. Since STATS ChipPAC had manufacturing facilities in Taiwan, the acquisition caused a restructuring and spin-off of its two Taiwanese subsidiaries to ensure regulatory compliance and facilitate the transaction.

Beyond the immediate challenges, JCET faced the significant and often underestimated task of post-merger integration (PMI). This process involved merging two organizations with vastly different corporate cultures: a state-backed Chinese company and a formerly independent global firm based in Singapore. Aligning management styles, incentive structures, operational procedures, and IT systems across continents was a monumental endeavor. There was a notable risk of talent flight from STATS ChipPAC, as key engineers and managers might be apprehensive about the new Chinese ownership. Retaining major international customers like Qualcomm and Broadcom was not guaranteed; these clients needed reassurance that the acquisition would not compromise quality, reliability, or their compliance with US regulations.

Mitigation Strategies

JCET, Sino-IC, and the Industrial Fund have entered agreements concerning the debt-to-equity conversion clause of the Industrial Fund and the share issuance clause, which allows JCET to acquire equity interests within the financing structure. To ensure attractive returns, it has been stipulated that JCET will provide an annualized return rate of 10% to 12% in the event of a cash acquisition. If JCET cannot complete the share issuance and gain the equity held by investors within 18 months, either JCET or Xin Chao Technology—its major shareholder—will be obligated to repurchase the shares at an annualized return rate of 15%. However, to fulfill the agreement, JCET acquired the entire equity of the target assets held by Sino-IC through issuing shares. As a result, Xin Chao Technology is no longer the largest shareholder, which leaves the listed company temporarily without an actual controller.

To ease the debt burden of STATS ChipPAC, the company underwent a debt restructuring with the help of JCET. This restructuring involved two key actions:

a bridge loan refinancing facility of up to $890 million from DBS Bank, which replaces existing high-cost debt with more favorable pricing (LIBOR + spread) and is refinanced into long-term syndicated loans; and issuing $200 million in Perpetual Securities to shareholders. An irrevocable guarantee from JCET backs these securities, which are classified as equity, ensuring the repayment of principal and interest. This strategy not only immediately reduced interest expenses and improved cash flow but also lowered the debt-to-asset ratio by converting debt into equity, ensuring a stable financial foundation for post-acquisition integration.

STRATEGIC ANALYSIS

Analytical Frameworks

The political environment presents both advantages and disadvantages for JCET. In recent years, the Chinese government has introduced significant initiatives, such as the "14th Five-Year Plan for Economic and Social Development" and "Made in China 2025," which designate the integrated circuit industry as a core area of national security and development. These policies offer substantial financial support and other assurances for industrial advancement. However, because of its unique characteristics, the integrated circuit industry is highly susceptible to international political influences, particularly the tensions between China and the United States. Former US President Trump adopted a notably tougher approach toward China's semiconductor sector, implementing an array of measures, including targeted sanctions, high tariffs, and export controls, to exert comprehensive and intense pressure on China's semiconductor industry.

The demand for AI chips and memory chips continues to rise because of economic factors and application fields. The rapid advancement of artificial intelligence, particularly with the emergence of large language models, has increased the need for high-performance computing chips. Memory chips and high-performance computing chips are becoming the primary drivers of market growth. However, the semiconductor industry is characterized by cyclical trends, making it vulnerable to supply gluts and economic recessions.

From a social perspective, the widespread adoption of smart devices and the ongoing digitalization of society are boosting the demand for more powerful, efficient, and compact chips. On the technological front, the industry is racing to develop advanced packaging methods, such as 2.5D/3D integration, Wafer-Level Packaging (WLP), and System-in-Package (SiP). These innovations are being applied across various sectors, including automotive electronics, artificial intelligence, network communications, smart devices, industrial and medical systems, as well as power and energy solutions. Enhancing performance has become essential, extending beyond the traditional limits of Moore's Law. In this post-Moore era, JCET's ability to innovate in these fields will be crucial for its future competitiveness.

To assess the competitive intensity within this macroenvironment, we can apply Porter's Five Forces framework. The rivalry among existing competitors in the Outsourced Semiconductor Assembly and Test (OSAT) industry is intense. According to the 2024 global OSAT ranking published by TrendForce (2025, p2), JCET is ranked third among the world's top 10 OSAT vendors, with approximately $4.77 billion in revenue. By comparison, principal competitors ASE Technology Holding and Amkor Technology posted revenues of $10.1 billion and $6.3 billion, respectively (Cinno, 2025). Competition in this sector is driven by technology, cost, scale, and geographic reach, which constantly pressures pricing and profit margins.

The threat of new entrants into the market is relatively low because of the substantial capital investment required for advanced fabrication facilities and the deep technological expertise necessary to compete effectively. However, Integrated Device Manufacturers (IDMs) sometimes internalize their packaging operations, as seen in Samsung's integration of manufacturing, packaging, and PSI testing, which represents another form of competition.

The bargaining power of buyers, which includes major fabless companies like Qualcomm and NVIDIA, as well as integrated device manufacturers (IDMs), is high. These customers are large and have multiple outsourced semiconductor assembly and test (OSAT) partners to choose from, giving them significant leverage to negotiate on price, quality, and delivery terms. In contrast, the bargaining power of suppliers—such as those providing raw materials like substrate and lead frames—is moderate. Although there are many suppliers, the high quality and technical specifications required for semiconductor materials can limit the options. The threat of substitute products or services is virtually non-existent for core packaging and testing functions, as there is no alternative to having a physical chip packaged and tested.

JCET Group has several core strengths, including a comprehensive technology portfolio and global influence gained through the acquisition of STATS ChipPAC. The company offers a full range of semiconductor packaging technologies that cover low, mid, and high-end segments—from traditional wire bonding to advanced Fan-out, System-in-Package (SiP), and 2.5D/3D integration—establishing itself as a leader in advanced packaging and creating a one-stop solution for its customers.

JCET's global production footprint in China, Singapore, and Korea allows for superior cost control and flexible order allocation. This enables the company to place cost-sensitive orders in China while handling high-tech orders in Singapore and Korea, thus creating a cost-leadership advantage. As a leading domestic OSAT player in China, JCET also holds significant strategic and geopolitical value, serving as a critical node in building a secure and resilient supply chain, which appeals to international clients pursuing an "in China, for China" strategy. The company has received substantial support from government capital, such as the National Integrated Circuit Industry Investment Fund (Big Fund), which was essential for facilitating its large-scale cross-border acquisition.

JCET Group's primary weaknesses arise from its aggressive expansion strategy. The acquisition of STATS ChipPAC imposed considerable financial pressure, resulting in a sharp increase in its debt-to-asset ratio and burdening the company with substantial debt, elevating its financial risk. The post-acquisition integration process presents challenges, such as managing cross-cultural teams, integrating global operations, and effectively assimilating cutting-edge technologies; any missteps in these areas could hinder the realization of expected synergies. Finally, despite achieving market diversification, the company remains significantly reliant on high-profit markets like Europe and America, which increases its operational vulnerability to some extent.

JCET Group currently has significant growth opportunities. First, the Chinese government's increased focus on information security and industrial policies, such as the "Chip Replacement Initiative," has generated strong domestic market demand and favorable policy support for local integrated circuit companies. Second, the rise of emerging technologies, including artificial intelligence, the Internet of Things (IoT), and smart vehicles, is driving substantial demand for high-performance computing and memory chips. This demand aligns well with JCET's advanced packaging capabilities, which have been enhanced following recent acquisitions. The industry is now in the "post-Moore's Law era," where advancements in performance increasingly depend on advanced packaging technologies. JCET's leading position in this field enables it to take advantage of this technological shift and further increase its market share. Finally, strategic partnerships with major international clients like Qualcomm provide the company with ongoing technological support and a reliable stream of high-end orders.

However, JCET Group also faces significant external threats. The most notable risk is geopolitical tension, particularly in the Sino-US technology arena. This tension could cause export controls, sanctions (as one of its subsidiaries was previously proposed for the MEU List), and high tariffs, which may lead to equipment and material shortages, loss of customers, and increased costs. The global Outsourced Semiconductor Assembly and Test (OSAT) market is highly competitive, with constant pressure from major players like ASE and Amkor regarding technology, cost, and scale, which affects profit margins. Substantial bargaining power is held by the company's primary clients, including major corporations like Qualcomm and NVIDIA. Consequently, they can secure lower prices and dictate strict terms. The inherent cyclicality of the semiconductor industry also poses a risk, as economic downturns or weak demand can significantly affect performance. Finally, the trend of some Integrated Device Manufacturers (IDMs), such as Samsung, internalizing their packaging operations presents a unique competitive challenge that could reduce market opportunities for external OSAT providers.

Brand and Reputation Effects

This section outlines the measures undertaken by the company to cultivate a strong corporate image and enhance brand recognition. JCET operates in the midstream segment of the semiconductor industry supply chain, positioning itself between upstream chip design companies (e.g., Qualcomm, AMD) and downstream system manufacturers (e.g., Apple, Huawei). Its brand communication primarily targets the engineering and procurement departments within these corporations rather than end consumers, which results in relatively low public visibility. Therefore, JCET's professional reputation is substantiated through third-party validation. JCET's third-place ranking among the world's top ten OSAT suppliers (Cinno, 2025) is a testament to the company's proficiency and reliability in advanced packaging technology.

As a leading enterprise in integrated circuit packaging and testing, JCET is committed to promoting industry chain openness and collaboration while enhancing its brand's social recognition. In 2024, the company received multiple accolades (JCET Group, 2025), including being named "Most Admired Company in Asia" and "2024 China's Best ESG Employer" by Institutional Investor. It was also listed among the Top Brands 2024 in China's Top 500 Brands. JCET earned "Excellent Supplier" titles from many clients.

In 2024, the company launched the J.E.T. Program (Key Talent Development Program) across multiple regions, including China, Singapore, and South Korea, focusing strongly on advancing the Excellence Engineer Development Program to support employees' career growth. Through substantial benefits such as award recognition programs, employee insurance, and help plans, along with diverse engaging activities, the company fosters a sense of belonging and pride among its employees, strengthening team cohesion.

Regarding corporate social responsibility and sustainable development practices, JCET has been recognized in Extel's 2025 "Asia's Best-Managed Companies" awards. The company kept the title of "Most Admired Company" in the semiconductor industry, ranking first across multiple categories, including "Asia's Best Small/Mid-Cap Managed Team" and "China's Best Managed Team," for its excellence in corporate governance, investor relations, and sustainability initiatives. JCET actively engages in philanthropic endeavors through its Environmental Protection and Health Charity Fund, supporting projects related to environmental conservation, medical aid, educational programs, and Yangtze River biodiversity protection. The company has also taken the lead in establishing the "Packaging and Testing Museum," which has become an influential science education base and industry exchange platform.

CONCLUSION AND STRATEGIC RECOMMENDATIONS

Summary of Key Findings

This analysis of JCET Group's global expansion, primarily through the landmark acquisition of STATS ChipPAC, reveals several critical findings. Foremost, the strategic acquisition serves as a core driver of JCET's transformation. By acquiring STATS ChipPAC, JCET transitioned from a domestic Chinese player to one of the top three global leaders in OSAT (Outsourced Semiconductor Assembly and Test).

Next, JCET's globalization was influenced by a combination of interconnected factors. Internally, the company aimed to overcome market saturation and intense price competition in the mid-to-low-end semiconductor segments following the 2008 financial crisis, causing a reduced reliance on the Chinese market. Simultaneously, significant market opportunities arose due to China's increased focus on information security, the national "Chip Replacement Initiative," which promotes domestic IC substitution, and the rapid growth of the 4G smartphone and IoT industries. Notably, the acquisition of STATS ChipPAC provided immediate access to essential resources and advanced technologies, including state-of-the-art packaging capabilities, an established international customer base featuring major clients like Qualcomm and Broadcom, and a global manufacturing presence. This strategic move was significantly supported by substantial financial backing from the Chinese government's "Big Fund," which alleviated the capital burden of the cross-border acquisition and positioned JCET for accelerated global expansion.

Third, JCET employed a sophisticated acquisition strategy that involved a consortium (with the Big Fund and SMIC), a Special Purpose Vehicle (SPV), and offshore entities. This innovative structure achieved several critical goals: isolating risk for the parent company, enabling leveraged financing, and reducing geopolitical sensitivity to facilitate regulatory approval.

The acquisition also provided JCET with distinct competitive advantages, including cost leadership through a global production footprint across China, Korea, and Singapore. This setup enables optimal allocation of cost-sensitive and high-tech orders. The company gained a comprehensive technology portfolio with full-spectrum capabilities ranging from wire bonding to advanced Fan-out, SiP, and 2.5D/3D integration, allowing for one-stop-shop solutions. JCET achieved significant strategic geopolitical value as a key player in secure supply chains, which is attractive to international clients pursuing "in China, for China" strategies.

However, the expansion also introduced substantial challenges for JCET. The leveraged buyout structure ballooned the company's debt burden and asset-liability ratio, creating ongoing financial pressure. JCET became vulnerable to rising Sino-US trade tensions, facing potential export controls and the threat of inclusion on the US Military End-User (MEU) list. These geopolitical risks posed serious threats to JCET's supply chain stability and customer relationships, complicating its operational landscape despite the strategic advantages gained.

The JCET-STATS ChipPAC case exemplifies modern Chinese strategic mergers and acquisitions (M&A). It is state-backed, technologically transformative, and expertly executed from both financial and legal perspectives. However, it remains overshadowed by the geopolitical tensions that accompany China's rise. The deal provided JCET with everything it sought: technology, market access, and scale. Yet, in doing so, it also inextricably linked the company's future to the larger struggle for technological supremacy between China and the United States.

Future Growth Opportunities

In the future, JCET can continue to expand its global presence by focusing on several key areas. A forecast by Precedence Research (2025) shows that the global automotive electronics market is projected to expand from $307.61 billion in 2025 to approximately $647.43 billion in 2034, at a compound annual growth rate of 8.62%. Therefore, JCET should speed up its deployment in the automotive electronics sector and integrate into the core supply chains of leading automotive enterprises, which would be highly beneficial for its future development.

Geopolitical tensions and concerns about supply chain resilience require a significant shift in manufacturing strategy. JCET should actively adopt a "local-for-local" approach by establishing advanced packaging facilities in strategic locations outside its current primary footprint in Asia. For instance, establishing a state-of-the-art facility near major industrial clusters in Mexico, such as Monterrey or Guadalajara, would enable JCET to serve the North American automotive and consumer electronics markets under the favorable terms of the USMCA agreement. This location would be beneficial for servicing Tesla's Gigafactories in Texas and Berlin, General Motors' electric vehicle production lines, and Apple's manufacturing partners in Mexico, not only in Mexico but also in Eastern Europe.

Establishing a facility in countries like Poland, Hungary, or the Czech Republic—renowned for their strong automotive industries and proximity to Western European markets—would enable JCET to directly supply European automakers such as Volkswagen, BMW, and Stellantis, as well as industrial IoT leaders like Siemens. This move would not only de-risk its operations but also make it eligible for subsidies under policies like the US CHIPS Act, enhancing its competitiveness in key Western markets.

JCET Group leverages its core expertise in System-in-Package (SiP) technology. To enhance its market position, JCET should focus on designing and manufacturing fully tested and certified functional modules, such as RF front-end modules and sensor fusion modules. This strategic forward integration will enable JCET to capture a larger share of the value per unit, increase customer loyalty, and set itself apart from competitors who only provide standard packaging services.

Besides these specific areas, JCET must focus on enhancing its research and development in foundational next-generation technologies. This involves investing in the hardware and expertise necessary for panel-level fan-out packaging, which offers greater scalability and cost reductions for large devices. Collaborating with partners to establish chiplet interoperability standards and advanced materials—such as substrates for high-speed applications—will be essential for maintaining its leadership position.

Recommendations for Other Firms

This section aims to provide comprehensive insights into the development of Chinese multinational enterprises, particularly focusing on companies within the highly strategic and competitive semiconductor sector. Cross-border mergers and acquisitions have proven to be an effective strategy for technological firms seeking rapid technological advancement or critical market access, allowing them to integrate quickly into global value chains. The major benefits of this strategy include the acquisition of key patented technologies and proprietary knowledge, the retention of highly skilled personnel, and the immediate use of established international sales and distribution networks.

When considering such a significant strategic move, it is essential for companies to perform thorough due diligence and select the most suitable acquisition targets. A notable example is JCET Group's strategic acquisition of STATS ChipPAC, evaluated based on several critical criteria.

First, the purchase price was financially workable. At the time of the acquisition, STATS ChipPAC was facing operational challenges and consecutive financial losses, resulting in a decreased market valuation. This situation, combined with the intention of its major shareholder, Temasek Holdings, to divest, created a unique opportunity for JCET to execute what is often referred to as a "snake swallowing elephant" transaction.

Second, the geographic location of the target company provided significant advantages. Headquartered in Singapore, STATS ChipPAC served as a politically neutral and strategically positioned hub, facilitating further global expansion while minimizing exposure to trade tensions and export control risks.

Last, the broader national policy environment in China was highly supportive. The acquisition occurred during a period of concentrated national efforts to develop a self-reliant integrated circuit industry. Strong policy encouragement for overseas expansion, combined with soaring domestic demand for semiconductors, provided JCET with both the confidence and financial backing necessary to undertake such a transformative cross-border acquisition.

References

Cai, Q. Y., & Wang, C. F. (2020). —— [Research on the performance of cross-border mergers and acquisitions of semiconductor enterprises in China: Taking the acquisition of STATS ChipPAC by JCET as an example]. *[Research on Accounting and Finance]*, (8), 35–41.

Chen, Y. H. (2019). —— [Analysis of the motivations and performance of cross-border mergers and acquisitions in China's semiconductor industry: Taking JCET as an example] [Master's thesis, Zhejiang University]. China Master's Theses Full-text Database. https://link.cnki.net/doi/10.27461/d.cnki.gzjdx.2019.000382

CINNO Research. (2025, March 6). 2024 OSAT Top10 [2024 global OSAT (outsourced semiconductor assembly and test) industry revenue ranking] [Industry report]. http://www.cinno.com.cn/industry/news/osat2503

Cyberspace Administration of China. (2014, June 26). [National guidelines for the development and promotion of the integrated circuit industry]. https://www.cac.gov.cn/2014-06/26/c_1111325916.htm

Ding, G. E. (2021). [Research on the motivation and performance evaluation of Jiangsu Changjiang Electronics Technology's cross-border merger of STATS ChipPAC] [Master's thesis, Zhejiang University]. China Master's Theses Full-text Database. https://link.cnki.net/doi/10.27175/d.cnki.gjxcu.2021.001524

JCET Group. (2010). 2009 [JCET Group 2009 annual report]. https://www.jcetglobal.com/uploads/report/cfb6aad8dfd3841e174418e599b23b39.pdf

JCET Group. (2015). 2014 [JCET Group 2014 annual report]. https://www.jcetglobal.com/uploads/report/db125b052e176b00bc1efbf07c9a3057.pdf

JCET Group. (2019). 2018 [JCET Group 2018 annual report] https://www.jcetglobal.com/uploads/report/0c74cb869fed48c46619062068723a58.pdf

JCET Group. (2025). news. JCET Group Official Website. https://www.jcetglobal.com/site/news-detail?id=1806

JCET Group. (n.d.). Company Information. JCET Group Official Website. https://www.jcetglobal.com/en/site/JCET-overview

Precedence Research. (2025). Automotive electronics market. https://www.precedenceresearch.com/automotive-electronics-market

Shi, C. Q. (2016). [Analysis of the status of China's integrated circuit industry in the global market]. *Integrated Circuit Applications*, (7), 7–9. https://link.cnki.net/doi/10.19339/j.issn.1674-2583.2016.07.002

Shimizu, K., Hitt, M. A., Vaidyanath, D., & Pisano, V. (2004). Theoretical foundations of cross-border mergers and acquisitions: A review of current research and recommendations for the future. *Journal of International Management*, *10*(3), 307–353. DOI: 10.1016/j.intman.2004.05.005

TrendForce. (2025). Top 10 global OSAT companies in 2024: Mature leaders stay strong while new regional forces emerge [Research report]. https://www.trendforce.com/research/download/RP250505XH

Wang, X. (2023). [Research on the impact of cross-border mergers and acquisitions on enterprise innovation capability]. *Small Business Management and Technology*, (24), 140–142.

Xinhua Net. (2015, February 3). [Chip companies become China's new favorites in overseas M&A]. *[Economic Information Daily]*. http://jjckb.xinhuanet.com/2015-02/03/content_537060.htm

Zhang, B. S., & Shang, H. M. (2019). [Current situation and trend analysis of chip industry technology at home and abroad]. , *39*(17), 131–134. DOI: 10.3969/j.issn.1000-7695.2019.17.017

KEY TERMS AND DEFINITIONS

Core Electric Semiconductor (CES): A subsidiary of Semiconductor Manufacturing International Corporation (SMIC), is dedicated to building a trusted transaction platform for global manufacturers and supply chains.

In China, for China: It refers to a key localization strategy employed by multinational corporations operating in China. This approach focuses on deepening regional integration by systematically adapting brands and operations to better meet the needs of local customers and enhance market relevance.

Moore's Law: the observation that the number of transistors on an integrated circuit doubles approximately every 18 to 24 months, driving exponential growth in computing power while reducing costs.

Special Purpose Vehicle (SPV): An SPV is a legally independent entity created for a specific purpose, such as facilitating cross-border mergers and acquisitions or isolating risk. Typically, an SPV does not engage in actual business operations; instead, it serves as a tool for holding assets. One of its principal features is the ability to isolate risk. Through a "True Sale," assets are transferred to the SPV, ensuring that even if the parent company goes bankrupt, the assets within the SPV are protected from being included in the liquidation estate.

USMCA: The United States-Mexico-Canada Agreement is a trade agreement among the United States, Mexico, and Canada. To promote the reshoring of manufacturing in North America, 75% of automotive components must be produced in the United States, Mexico, or Canada to qualify for duty-free treatment.

Chapter 12
Beijing Genomics Institute (BGI) Global Biotechnology Positioning:
Navigating Geopolitics and Global Markets

Zhenxiang Yuan
http://orcid.org/0009-0006-5363-149X
Beijing Normal-Hong Kong Baptist University, China

EXECUTIVE SUMMARY

This chapter examines BGI Group's globalization strategy, tracing its evolution from a national research institute to a multinational life sciences corporation. Per the authors, the purpose is to analyse the dual drivers of international expansion: internal motivations for technological advancement and market diversification, alongside external support from Chinese industrial policies. Important things to think about are figuring out who the customers are, looking at different ways to do business like joining with others, and getting ahead by spending less or having new technology. The analysis covers implementation through overseas subsidiaries and Huo-Yan Laboratories, while assessing challenges such as regulatory scrutiny, geopolitical tensions exemplified by inclusion on the U.S. Entity List, and data sovereignty issues. The chapter contributes insights into the distinctive pathways and systemic challenges confronting Chinese high-technology firms operating in knowledge-intensive global markets.

DOI: 10.4018/979-8-3373-4302-0.ch012

INTRODUCTION

Background of the Company

China's participation in the International Human Genome Project (IHGP) as a national-level scientific research initiative led to the founding of BGI, initially named the Beijing Genomics Institute, on September 9, 1999. The founding team included Wang Jian, Yu Jun, Yang Huanming, and Liu Siqi, among others. BGI established its leading position in China's life sciences sector through a series of high-affected research achievements: completing the rice genome sequencing in 2002, publishing it as a cover article, and rapidly sequencing and publishing the Severe Acute Respiratory Syndrome (SARS) virus genome during the 2003 outbreak. These milestones not only showed its scientific capabilities but also established BGI's authority in emergency public health and genomics research (Cyranoski, 2010; BGI Group, n.d.).

Since separating from the Chinese Academy of Sciences in 2007 and moving to Shenzhen, BGI has gradually transformed from a purely research-oriented institution into an industrialized, market-oriented entity. Organizationally, BGI has evolved from a single institute into a diversified group, forming a global network with BGI China as the headquarters and regional branches, including BGI Americas, BGI Europe, and BGI Asia Pacific (BGI AP). Business divisions—including BGI Research, MGI (Manufacturer of Genomics Instruments) (equipment and sequencing platforms), BGI Health (BGH) (medical testing), BGI Agro (BGA) (agricultural genomics), and academic publishing like Giga Science—operate synergistically, enabling substantial horizontal and vertical integration across the value chain from fundamental research to device production, clinical testing, and agricultural applications (BGI Group, n.d.).

Technologically and product-wise, BGI developed its proprietary high-throughput sequencing platform DNBseq (DNB-s), commercialized products such as the Non-Invasive Fetal Trisomy Test (NIFTY), and established the HYLs system for public health emergencies, covering research, precision medicine, and public health. To strengthen technological and market capabilities, BGI has pursued acquisitions and international collaborations: acquiring Complete Genomics (CG) in 2013 to enhance sequencing autonomy and establishing an innovation center on the U.S. West Coast to foster multinational research collaboration (Bio-IT World Staff, 2013; McGrane, 2017). BGI has showed significant scale and coverage, with over 14 overseas subsidiaries reported by 2022 (360Dx, 2023), a workforce exceeding 7,000 employees, and sequencing capacity ranking among the global top alongside Illumina and Thermo Fisher (Molteni, 2017).

BGI maintains a balance between commercialization and academic influence: generating revenue from testing services, medical products, and research services, while enhancing academic credibility and international influence through scholarly publishing, international collaborations, and emergency public health deployments. Its rapid deployment of Huo-Yan Laboratories during the COVID-19 pandemic, providing testing support for multiple countries, demonstrates both its emergency response capability and its strengthened international brand recognition and collaboration opportunities (BGI Group, n.d.; Reuters, 2020).

BGI has grown from a national-level scientific representative to a multinational life sciences enterprise combining research capabilities and market operations. Its growth path reflects the typical "research—translation—internationalization" trajectory of Chinese technology-based firms within China's broader hybrid political-economic regime (HPER) (Puglisi & Rask, 2024).

Motivation for Global Expansion

Analyzing BGI's globalization motivation through the lens of a "hybrid political-economic regime" helps understand how intrinsic drivers and external support jointly influence its internationalization path. Hybrid regimes emphasize the symbiosis of state and market forces: the government provides institutional resources through R&D subsidies, policy guidance, financial and credit support, and public procurement, while market mechanisms offer external incentives via competitive pressures, scale demand, and international division of labor (Puglisi & Rask, 2024). Within this framework, BGI's internationalization is driven both by national strategy and policy tools and by its own technological and market development needs.

At the micro level, China's domestic sequencing and life sciences services market, after rapid expansion, faces mature demand structures, intensifying competition, and pressure on profit margins. To maintain revenue growth and diversify risk, overseas expansion becomes a natural choice: entering international markets broadens the customer base, provides more research collaboration opportunities, and enhances global brand visibility. Participation in international public health cooperation and emergency testing not only strengthens the company's public reputation but also facilitates long-term partnerships with external research institutions and governments, generating strategic resource flows and knowledge spillovers (Gryphon Scientific, 2019).

At the macro level, national industrial policies and international strategies create favorable external conditions for BGI's overseas expansion. China's industrial planning, credit, and government guidance funds provide funding, projects, and market access for life sciences companies (GenomeWeb, 2010). BGI leveraged policy and capital support to expand its overseas subsidiaries (reported in 14 countries), pursued cross-border acquisitions (Complete Genomics), established overseas R&D and innovation centers (e.g., U.S. West Coast innovation center), and deployed

Huo-Yan Laboratories for public health, creating an internationalization strategy centered on research—services—localized operations (Bio-IT World Staff, 2013; McGrane, 2017; 360Dx, 2023).

Global political-economic realities closely intertwine with these motivations. For example, scrutiny of BGI's NIFTY tests in markets such as the European Union (EU) and Australia (Gryphon Scientific, 2019; Needham & Baldwin, 2021). And its inclusion on the U.S. Entity List in 2023 (Ropes & Gray LLP, 2023), show regulatory and geopolitical considerations often condition market access. Thus, systemic pressures embedded in global governance and international competition also shape BGI's motivations for globalization, which cannot be understood solely in terms of commercial expansion.

In summary, BGI's global expansion strategy follows a threefold logic: (1) achieve revenue diversification and market risk mitigation through overseas markets; (2) enhance international brand recognition and academic influence through participation in international research and public health projects; and (3) improve technological learning and competitive resilience by establishing a global R&D collaboration and supply chain network. These objectives arise from both intrinsic growth and technological ambitions, as well as the opportunities provided by national policy support and international collaboration (Puglisi & Rask, 2024).

MARKET ANALYSIS AND ENTRY STRATEGY

Target Market Selection

BGI did not adopt a blind "scattergun" approach in selecting international expansion targets. Instead, the company conducted a focused market allocation based on a comprehensive evaluation of the global genomics industry landscape, regional growth potential, and alignment with its internal capabilities. Industry authorities reported that the global genomics market stood at approximately USD 32.65 billion in 2023. They predict it will grow to around USD 94.86 billion by 2030, reflecting a CAGR of about 16.5%. Within this structure, North America remains the dominant market, while the Asia-Pacific (APAC) region shows the fastest growth. Illumina, for instance, held over 70% of the global sequencing platform market share in 2022, demonstrating the intensity of competition that BGI faces when entering mature regions (Molteni, 2017; Grand View Research, 2023). This macro landscape provides clear regional direction for sequencing service providers, emphasizing scale and cost advantages.

Based on this market structure, BGI prioritizes North America, Europe, and Asia-Pacific for expansion: North America features a mature healthcare system, abundant R&D investment, and strong demand for pharmaceuticals and precision medicine; Europe offers regulatory compliance and academic collaboration advantages; the Asia-Pacific region benefits from a large sample base and population, rapidly increasing healthcare spending, and government research investment. BGI's target customers include universities and research institutions, pharmaceutical and biotechnology firms, hospitals and public health systems, and agriculture and environmental monitoring agencies. These entities form a stable and scalable demand structure for genomics samples, data analysis, and long-term research collaboration, which aligns closely with BGI's "high-throughput, multi-omics, cost-sensitive services" (BGI Group, n.d.).

Practically, BGI evaluates target markets using three criteria: growth potential, regulatory conduciveness, and capability fit. First, the target country must have considerable and sustainable genomics demand (e.g., precision medicine, drug development, or agricultural genomics). Second, the regulatory framework should permit cross-border sample and data flow or allow solutions through joint ventures (JVs) or localized compliance. Third, the local research and industrial ecosystem should complement BGI's R&D capabilities and equipment platforms. This three-dimensional assessment enables BGI to maximize strategic returns with limited resources and leverage intensive focus on priority markets for brand and capability spillovers.

BGI considers the long-term impact of institutional factors: government procurement policies, international research cooperation mechanisms, and attitudes toward foreign investment significantly affect entry costs and collaboration feasibility. For example, public health emergencies (e.g., COVID-19) created an urgent demand for testing reagents and capacity, prompting BGI to prioritize countries capable of public health response or willing to collaborate quickly. The actual deployment of Huo-Yan Laboratories in multiple countries during the pandemic reinforced trust and cooperation networks in these markets (BGI Group, n.d.; Reuters, 2020).

Entry Mode Selection

After confirming target markets, selecting the entry mode becomes critical to international expansion success. Academic and practical frameworks classify entry modes into low-commitment options (export/cross-border services), collaborative modes (JVs and strategic alliances), and high-commitment paths (acquisition or Greenfield investment (GI)). Each mode involves trade-offs regarding speed, control, compliance costs, and local adaptation capabilities (Root, 1994; Hill, Hwang, & Kim, 1990; Puglisi & Rask, 2024).

BGI's actual strategy shows a "graded" entry approach based on market characteristics: in markets with low regulatory barriers and demand that can be managed remotely, BGI favors low-commitment options such as exporting or remotely servicing with local partners. In high-demand markets requiring local compliance and trust, BGI prefers JVs or establishing local branches to strengthen compliance and relational capital. Where acquisitions can rapidly provide key capabilities, BGI uses mergers and acquisitions (M&A) to complement its competencies (Bio-IT World Staff, 2013).

For example, in 2013, BGI attained the U.S.-based Complete Genomics through its subsidiary, gaining high-end sequencing technology and R&D teams while directly entering and expanding the North American R&D and market ecosystem (Bio-IT World Staff, 2013; GenEng News, 2013). The establishment of an innovation center on the U.S. West Coast served both as a Greenfield investment to build local R&D channels and as a bridge for collaboration with universities and enterprises to commercialize technology (McGrane, 2017; Molteni, 2017).

In countries with strict regulations or high data sovereignty concerns, BGI prefers joint ventures or collaborations with local laboratories to enhance trust and compliance. In contexts where government procurement or public health projects are major sources of orders, localized delivery capabilities (e.g., rapid deployment of Huo-Yan Laboratories) become key for securing contracts and establishing a lasting presence (BGI Group, n.d.).

Finally, digital channels (cross-border e-commerce and cloud-based data services) provide a low-cost supplemental entry route for simpler services, such as outsourced data analysis or consumer genomics testing. This "online + offline" entry combination allows BGI to validate market demand at low cost initially and subsequently scale commitment based on market feedback, balancing risk control with sped-up expansion (Grand View Research, 2023).

Competitive Advantage

BGI's international success arises from distinctive competitive barriers and differentiators. We can summarize these across four dimensions: cost leadership and value for money, technological innovation and R&D capability, global supply chain and network layout, and institutional advantages under supportive policy systems.

First, BGI maintains a cost-leadership strategy in sequencing services. Benefiting from economies of scale and proprietary equipment, its DNBseq platform offers significantly lower sequencing costs than major foreign competitors, providing a pricing advantage in cost-sensitive markets. The "$100 genome" strategic objective positions BGI favorably in price competition (Molteni, 2017; GenomeWeb, 2010).

Second, technological innovation is significant. Besides developing the DNB-s platform, BGI continues investing in spatial transcriptomics (ST) e.g., Stereo-Seq (S-Seq) and other revolutionary sequencing methods, while promoting research dissemination and international collaboration through academic publishing platforms (BGI Group, n.d.). Acquisitions like CG and the innovation center speed up R&D translation into market competitiveness (Bio-IT World Staff, 2013; GenEng News, 2013).

Third, BGI has a mature global supply chain and service network. Its laboratories in multiple countries, coupled with rapid Huo-Yan Laboratory deployment during COVID-19, provided testing support globally, demonstrating responsiveness and brand credibility as key assets (BGI Group, n.d.; Reuters, 2020).

Finally, institutional advantages strengthen competitiveness. Under China's hybrid political-economic system, BGI benefits from government-guided funds, procurement support, and export financing, reducing capital costs and easing policy barriers. This institutional support helps maintain advantages in high-entry-barrier markets (Puglisi & Rask, 2024; GenomeWeb, 2010).

However, these advantages exist in the strong international competition. Illumina, Thermo Fisher, and Oxford Nanopore Technologies (ONT) continue to dominate global sequencing innovation and patent landscapes, meaning that BGI must combine its pricing advantage with localized service models and rapid deployment capacity to differentiate itself in highly scrutinized markets (Gryphon Scientific, 2019; Needham & Baldwin, 2021).

In sum, BGI's international competitiveness derives from a systemic integration of technology, scale, network, and institutional resources. This multidimensional advantage allows it to capture market share through pricing and delivery speed in the short term and maintain long-term competitiveness through technological depth, global partnerships, and localized service.

IMPLEMENTATION OF GLOBAL EXPANSION

Key Initiatives and Investments

To implement its global expansion strategy, BGI has invested substantial resources in multiple key initiatives. One primary action has been expanding its overseas subsidiary network. According to company disclosures and industry reports, BGI has established localized technology service entities or branches in fourteen countries, including Uzbekistan, Uruguay, Turkey, Madagascar, Nigeria, Hungary, South Africa, the United Arab Emirates (UAE), the Dominican Republic, Chile, Malaysia, Angola, Kazakhstan, and Serbia, while setting up several registered companies in Hong Kong to strengthen its APAC presence (360Dx, 2023; BGI Group, n.d.). These investments involve not only registered capital but also the acquisition or leasing of office and laboratory space, procurement of experimental equipment, recruitment and training of personnel, and local compliance and licensing expenditures, representing significant upfront capital outlay and ongoing operational costs.

Simultaneously, to realize the global deployment of its Huo-Yan Laboratories, BGI has established many high-throughput testing labs across dozens of countries and regions during the COVID-19 pandemic. According to Reuters (2020), the company deployed over 80 Huo-Yan Labs worldwide. With a collective daily testing capacity of over one million samples, these labs show the company's technological scalability and emergency response capability. Initially intended for pandemic testing, these labs have expanded to prenatal testing, cancer screening, and other epidemic monitoring applications (BGI Group, n.d.; Reuters, 2020). Such initiatives encompass substantial costs in land, equipment, laboratory operations, sample processing management, and local technical deployment.

Beyond network and laboratory construction, BGI has executed large-scale technology transfer projects. Through licensing, standardized process deployment, and on-site training, the company has localized sequencing platforms, data analysis pipelines, and laboratory processes in multiple countries. These technology transfers reduce implementation time and quality risks while providing replicable templates for subsequent service contracts, though they also require ongoing costs for training, human support, and long-term technical maintenance (BGI Group, n.d.).

Getting regulatory approval for products globally represents another key investment. The company has secured many domestic and international registrations, including Conformité Européenne (CE) certification, which involves significant compliance costs when entering highly regulated markets (BGI Genomics, 2023). The expansion of regulatory credentials not only supports product commercialization but also builds trust with healthcare authorities, hospitals, and public health institutions in Europe and beyond.

BGI's global expansion illustrates the internationalization of Chinese life science enterprises: strategic investments cover subsidiary establishment, global laboratory systems, technology transfer, localized product compliance, and brand promotion. These initiatives require substantial financial and resource commitments, reflecting BGI's firm commitment and capacity to pursue internationalization objectives (360Dx, 2023; BGI Genomics, 2023).

Challenges Faced

During its global expansion, BGI has encountered multi-level challenges, including legal and regulatory issues, cultural differences, supply chain and operational risks, geopolitical tensions, and reputational pressures.

First, in the legal and regulatory domain, the U.S. Department of Commerce placed some of BGI's business entities on its Entity List because of sensitive technologies.

This requires additional authorization for access to restricted technologies, equipment, and materials, significantly affecting collaboration with U.S. companies and supply channels (Ropes & Gray LLP, 2023). Such regulatory risks weaken competitiveness in core markets and increase administrative and legal compliance costs. A acute challenge lies in data sovereignty (DS) and cross-border data flows. Regulations such as the EU's General Data Protection Regulation (GDPR) and the U.S. Cloud Act impose strict conditions on the storage, transfer, and use of sensitive genomic information. For BGI, compliance requires not only technical measures—such as localizing servers and encrypting cross-border transmissions—but also governance frameworks that reassure partners about ethical data usage. Failing to navigate these requirements risks undermining trust with research collaborators and healthcare authorities, as they increasingly regard genomic data as strategic national resources (Needham & Baldwin, 2021).

Second, cultural and communication barriers pose challenges. To avoid product rejection or misaligned strategies, BGI must genuinely understand user behavior because of language differences, business practices, and local customer preferences (Gryphon Scientific, 2019). Differences in business styles across regions—e.g., the Middle East, Latin America, and Africa versus Europe and North America—also slow project progress and reduce efficiency.

Third, inconsistencies in supply chains and infrastructure create operational difficulties. Local logistics, customs, and sample transportation regulations increase complexity, particularly under global logistics stress during the pandemic (Reuters, 2020). To rapidly deploy Huo-Yan Laboratories, BGI had to overcome cross-border transport bottlenecks and ensure the timely delivery of consumables and equipment.

Fourth, geopolitical and policy risks, such as China–U.S. tech and trade frictions or regional policy changes, threaten collaboration continuity and global stability (Puglisi & Rask, 2024). The U.S. restrictions on access to advanced semiconductor components and rising concerns over genetic data security in Europe show that broader systemic tensions, rather than firm-specific obstacles, embed BGI's challenges (Needham & Baldwin, 2021).

Finally, brand reputation is a challenge. Certain BGI products, especially NIFTY prenatal tests, have faced regulatory scrutiny or registration requirements in the EU, Australia, and the United Kingdom (UK), affecting market trust and credibility (Gryphon Scientific, 2019). High-profile international media reports have raised concerns about data governance, which places additional reputational pressure on the company (Needham & Baldwin, 2021).

BGI must integrate compliance, communication, logistics, and risk management into strategic and operational planning because these intertwined challenges require it to maintain sustainable internationalization (Ropes & Gray LLP, 2023);

Mitigation Strategies

To address these challenges and mitigate risks, BGI has implemented a range of strategies to ensure sustainable and stable global expansion.

For regulatory and compliance barriers, BGI employs legal and public relations teams and communicates with relevant governments. In the U.S., after being placed on the Entity List, BGI engaged legal and lobbying advisors to facilitate regulatory dialogue and risk mitigation (Ropes & Gray LLP, 2023). This government-relations strategy provides institutional buffers and potential collaboration opportunities, although it incurs high costs.

To address cultural and operational differences, BGI forms joint ventures with local partners. For example, in Saudi Arabia, BGI partnered with local companies to share resources and regulatory knowledge, improving project implementation efficiency and compliance (BGI Group, n.d.). Deploying local teams supported by headquarters experts ensures cultural and operational integration and enhances communication.

Regarding supply chains and logistics, BGI collaborates with local logistics providers, universities, and healthcare systems to optimize laboratory setup and operations. Local procurement and alternative supply chains reduce reliance on cross-border transport (BGI Group, n.d.; Reuters, 2020).

To diversify geopolitical risk, BGI simultaneously deploys laboratories and service capabilities across multiple countries, avoiding overdependence on a single market. It also synchronizes regulatory certifications (e.g., CE/In Vitro Diagnostic Medical Device Regulation (IVDR)) and local training to strengthen market entry resilience (BGI Genomics, 2023).

Finally, in brand and reputation management, BGI enhances product compliance and promotes transparent academic and public health collaborations to show research motivation and public interest orientation. Localized training, capability transfer, and corporate social responsibility (CSR) initiatives aim to convert short-term assistance into long-term collaboration and trust capital (BGI Group, n.d.; 360Dx, 2023).

In summary, BGI's mitigation strategies combine "policy communication + localized capability building + diversified supply chains + multi-market deployment," providing a practical approach for improving resilience in complex international environments (Ropes & Gray LLP, 2023; BGI Genomics, 2023).

STRATEGIC ANALYSIS

Analytical Frameworks

Before evaluating BGI's internationalization path strategically, it is essential to reconstruct its internal capabilities and external environment through a rigorous analytical framework. This section employs three complementary classical strategic tools—SWOT (Strengths, Weaknesses, Opportunities, Threats), PESTEL (Political, Economic, Social, Technological, Environmental, Legal), and Porter's Five Forces (PFF)—to examine how institutional and market environments shape opportunities and constraints, and how industry competition influences strategic choices.

First, SWOT analysis provides an integrated internal–external diagnostic perspective. BGI's strengths stem from its deep research foundation originating from national-level genomic projects, large-scale sequencing capabilities, and its global operational network. Its product and technology portfolio—such as the DNBSeq platform, NIFTY testing, and spatial genomics technologies—forms a capability chain that supports both research and commercial services (BGI Group, n.d.; Cyranoski, 2010). However, internal strengths have limitations: the organization faces reputational and compliance vulnerabilities in international markets (e.g., inclusion on U.S. restricted lists) and legal risks in intellectual property disputes (Ropes & Gray LLP, 2023; GenEng News, 2013). Opportunities arise from long-term growth in global precision medicine and public health, as well as declining sequencing costs, enabling BGI to expand sample sources, service scope, and research collaborations (Grand View Research, 2023). Threats primarily include geopolitical tensions, stricter cross-border data and sample regulations, and competitive pressure from well-capitalized, technologically advanced rivals such as Illumina, Thermo Fisher, and Oxford Nanopore (Puglisi & Rask, 2024; Molteni, 2017).

Second, the PESTEL framework situates SWOT's external opportunities and threats within broader institutional and societal changes. Politically, China–U.S. technology and trade relations, export controls, and the Entity List directly affect access to critical technologies and collaboration channels (Ropes & Gray LLP, 2023). Economically, global health expenditure growth, population aging, and rising R&D spending drive market potential (Grand View Research, 2023). Socially, public acceptance of genetic testing and ethical concerns regarding privacy from both market foundations and regulatory pressures (Gryphon Scientific, 2019). Technologically, the rapid evolution of sequencing platforms, artificial intelligence (AI), and bioinformatics provides opportunities for product differentiation (Molteni, 2017). Environmentally and legally, laboratories face increasing compliance costs related to waste management, energy consumption, and DS regulations such as GDPR (BGI Genomics, 2023). More broadly, the rise of Environmental, Social, and Governance (ESG) reporting requirements means that genomics companies must incorporate sustainability and ethics into their global narratives, not merely their lab operations (Needham & Baldwin, 2021).

Finally, Porter's Five Forces focuses on industry competition to assess profitability and strategic pressure points. Rivalry is intense, with multiple firms competing on sequencing technology, service pricing, and customer retention (Molteni, 2017). Capital and technology barriers limit threats from new entrants, but the democratization of sequencing and cloud-based tools allows startups to enter with innovative business models (Grand View Research, 2023). Substitute threats come from alternative sequencing or non-sequencing diagnostic methods. Buyer bargaining power is high, especially for large pharmaceutical companies and hospital systems, which can negotiate for both cost and regulatory transparency. Supplier concentration in critical equipment and high-end reagents gives suppliers some bargaining power, though BGI's scale and proprietary platform partially mitigate this (Bio-IT World Staff, 2013; GenEng News, 2013).

In conclusion, its technological and scale advantages support BGI's strategy but require a dynamic balance between institutional risks (notably data security and geopolitics) and competitive pressures. This "capability–institution–market" triad determines entry strategies, compliance investments, and brand-building approaches, providing a theoretical and empirical basis for analyzing brand and reputation effects in the next section (Puglisi & Rask, 2024; Grand View Research, 2023).

Brand and Reputation Effects

Brand and reputation are not mere market appendages but critical soft assets determining trust, contract acquisition, and long-term cooperation in international expansion. For BGI, brand equity derives from both academic output and technological platforms, as well as contributions during global public health events; however, it is simultaneously vulnerable to compliance controversies and geopolitical scrutiny.

First, in terms of global brand recognition, BGI has achieved notable international visibility through its extensive overseas network and research output. The company claims coverage in over 100 countries, and the rapid deployment of Huo-Yan Laboratories and widespread distribution of testing reagents during the pandemic enhanced its public health brand reputation (BGI Group, n.d.; Reuters, 2020). These "performance-based" contributions help BGI build substantial relational capital with governments and public health organizations, securing contracts and collaboration opportunities.

However, regulatory and ethical disputes can damage brand trust. Concerns over data sovereignty and sensitive applications in the U.S. and other jurisdictions have increased scrutiny and credibility costs. Patent litigation with companies like

Illumina also makes clients cautious in procurement decisions (Ropes & Gray LLP, 2023; GenEng News, 2013). International media reports have further amplified these concerns, framing BGI within broader debates on "genomic sovereignty" and technology security (Needham & Baldwin, 2021). Hence, technical and delivery capabilities alone cannot sustain long-term brand advantage; systematic compliance and communication strategies are essential (BGI Genomics, 2023).

Regarding CSR and sustainability, BGI reinforces its "behavioral evidence-based" reputation through public health support, technology transfer, and local talent training. Building laboratories, providing emergency testing, and conducting local capacity development in multiple country's position the brand as a contributor to public welfare, not just a commercial actor (BGI Group, n.d.; 360Dx, 2023). Institutionalized compliance initiatives (e.g., ISO 37301) further transform ethical and legal commitments into verifiable signals, mitigating regulatory and market skepticism (BGI Genomics, 2023).

In communication and localization strategy, brand-building requires both narrative storytelling—explaining research achievements, public health contributions, and compliance measures—and "proof of action," such as establishing local testing centers, training programs, and community support. In complex geopolitical and regulatory environments, headquarters messaging alone is insufficient. BGI integrates joint ventures, collaborations with local health authorities, and transparent academic publications to tie brand credibility to actual performance (McGrane, 2017; Reuters, 2020).

In summary, BGI's brand and reputation effects make up key soft assets in international expansion but require ongoing compliance investment, public health contribution, academic output, and localized practice. Organizations must balance "doing well" (actual contributions) with "communicating clearly" (transparent messaging) to maintain brand equity in scrutinized international markets (BGI Genomics, 2023; Puglisi & Rask, 2024).

CONCLUSION AND STRATEGIC RECOMMENDATIONS

Summary of Key Findings

An analysis of BGI Group's internationalization process yields several decisive insights.

First, BGI's technological capabilities and large-scale operations form its most solid competitive foundation. The company's roots in national-level genomic projects, commercialized sequencing platforms (e.g., DNBSeq), clinical products (e.g., NIFTY), and laboratories and service networks across multiple countries enable it to handle high-volume sample processing efficiently. During public health emergencies, the rapid deployment of Huo-Yan Laboratories strengthens the "capability–reputation" linkage, significantly enhancing collaboration opportunities and bargaining power in several countries (BGI Group, n.d.; Reuters, 2020).

Second, institutional and geopolitical risks are major external constraints on the depth and breadth of BGI's globalization. Inclusion on regulatory restriction lists in some countries, scrutiny of cross-border data flows and national security, and legal disputes with major international competitors over IP and market share raise entry barriers and compel BGI to invest more in compliance, legal affairs, and public communication (Ropes & Gray LLP, 2023; GenEng News, 2013).

Third, BGI's international expansion strategy exhibits a "toolbox-style" multi-path approach: in low-demand and low-regulation markets, it employs cross-border services and remote data processing for rapid market validation; in regulated or trust-dependent regions, it pursues joint ventures, acquisitions, or Greenfield investments for deep localization; in public health and CSR contexts, it builds brand trust through tangible contributions. This hybrid approach enhances strategic flexibility but entails high upfront capital and integration costs (Bio-IT World Staff, 2013; 360Dx, 2023).

Fourth, brand and reputation are both sources of soft power and potential vulnerabilities. Academic output, public health contributions, and extensive localized activities help establish trust, but unresolved external concerns regarding data governance, compliance transparency, and ethical oversight could convert technological advantages into trust deficits, affecting long-term cooperation and market access (BGI Genomics, 2023; Puglisi & Rask, 2024).

Finally, BGI's case highlights broader lessons about Chinese high-tech enterprises' globalization. Unlike traditional manufacturing firms that rely on cost advantages, knowledge-intensive firms like BGI must simultaneously leverage technological depth, manage institutional risk, and cultivate an international reputation. This triad of capability–institution–trust makes up the strategic essence of global expansion in sensitive and regulated industries.

In sum, BGI possesses clear "capability–scale–network" advantages for internationalization, but sustainable global operations depend on robust compliance governance, local trust-building, and supply chain resilience to hedge against geopolitical and institutional risks.

Future Growth Opportunities

Looking ahead, several empirically supported and operationally workable growth paths emerge, based on existing capabilities and changing external conditions.

First, agricultural biotechnology and food-chain security offer a replicable, localized expansion model. BGI's involvement in the Saudi AgriFood Tech Alliance and JVs like Genalive advance precision medicine and agricultural genomics applications in alignment with national strategies, translating research output into tangible solutions for food security and industrial upgrading, opening long-term government and industry collaboration channels (360Dx, 2023; McGrane, 2017). These align closely with the United Nations (UN) Sustainable Development Goals (SDGs), particularly "Zero Hunger" and "Good Health and Well-being," providing BGI with legitimacy and visibility in multilateral cooperation frameworks (United Nations, 2020).

Second, digital health (DH) and AI-driven service transformation represent high-growth avenues. Leveraging large-scale sequencing and multi-omics datasets, BGI can integrate genomic, clinical, and lifestyle data to develop DH platforms for individuals and medical institutions, providing AI-driven disease risk prediction, medication guidance, and long-term health management. This path generates value-added business models and recurring revenue streams, contingent on robust data governance (DG) to meet local privacy regulations (Grand View Research, 2023; Puglisi & Rask, 2024). Partnerships with global health organizations, such as the World Health Organization (WHO)'s digital health agenda, could further scale these models. Beyond predictive health management, AI applications extend into drug repurposing and clinical trial optimization, areas where BGI's vast datasets could speed up pharmaceutical R&D and lower costs. By collaborating with global alliances such as the Global Alliance for Genomics and Health (GA4GH), BGI can also contribute to shaping international data-sharing standards, further embedding itself into the global genomics ecosystem (Puglisi & Rask, 2024). Such moves would not only diversify revenue models but also enhance BGI's reputation as a scientific collaborator rather than merely a commercial service provider.

Third, local capacity building and educational collaboration make up long-term strategic investments. Establishing testing centers and conducting training overseas has proven effective, reducing dependence on cross-border personnel and materials while building durable relational capital. Systematizing this model and partnering with local universities and research institutes for joint R&D and training can cultivate research and operational talent, enhancing sustainable localization (BGI Group, n.d.).

Fourth, sustainable laboratories and green technologies enhance international image and reduce long-term operational costs. Improvements in laboratory energy efficiency, hazardous waste management, and recycling reflect compliance and corporate social responsibility, potentially adding competitive advantage in bidding and public projects (BGI Genomics, 2023). As global health industries increasingly link procurement to ESG criteria, investment in sustainability can convert environmental responsibility into a differentiating factor.

These growth opportunities require a "capability–compliance–demand" alignment: projects should leverage existing or quickly attainable capabilities, comply with local regulations and ethics, and meet real government or market needs. Only evidence-based, locally executable plans can convert opportunities into sustainable business outcomes (Grand View Research, 2023; 360Dx, 2023).

Recommendations for Other Firms

BGI's internationalization offers actionable lessons for other Chinese enterprises.

First, prioritize establishing local collaborative ecosystems. Joint ventures, partnerships, or long-term procurement relationships with governments, hospitals, universities, or leading industry players reduce initial trust costs and speed up compliance. BGI's experience in Saudi Arabia illustrates how "aligned interests + localized delivery" facilitates large-scale project implementation (McGrane, 2017; 360Dx, 2023).

Second, embed compliance and transparency into the strategic core. In mature markets like Europe and North America, companies should conduct compliance risk assessments, establish internationally recognized compliance management systems (e.g., ISO 37301), and communicate governance and usage boundaries transparently. Institutionalized compliance is both an entry requirement and a prerequisite for long-term trust (BGI Genomics, 2023; Ropes & Gray LLP, 2023).

Third, leverage public health and CSR projects as "trust incubators." Providing verifiable technical support, capacity transfer, and local training during crises or high-demand scenarios can convert short-term aid into lasting cooperation and market access. Other firms entering new markets should integrate public welfare or capability-building projects to generate tangible trust capital (BGI Group, n.d.; Reuters, 2020).

Fourth, diversify markets and supply chains to mitigate geopolitical risk. Avoid concentrating global expansion on a single market or supplier; acquisitions, joint ventures, and localized production can enhance resilience. Simultaneously, establish monitoring and contingency plans, including legal, compliance, and PR protocols, to respond rapidly to restrictions or disputes (Ropes & Gray LLP, 2023; Puglisi & Rask, 2024).

Fifth, develop cross-cultural competence as a strategic resource. Beyond technical and regulatory adaptation, firms must build cross-cultural communication and management capabilities to navigate differences in consumer preferences, business practices, and regulatory expectations. Institutionalizing cultural training and localized management structures can speed up trust-building and reduce integration risks in diverse markets (Gryphon Scientific, 2019).

Finally, long-term investment in talent and research networks is indispensable. Joint training programs with universities, funding local research, and publishing localized scientific results not only supply talent and research resources but embed the firm into local academic and industrial ecosystems, forming a "knowledge–talent–collaboration" cycle that strengthens international operational resilience (BGI Group, n.d.).

REFERENCES

BGI-Shenzhen. (2013, March 19). BGI-Shenzhen completes acquisition of Complete Genomics [Press release]. PR Newswire. https://www.prnewswire.com/news-releases/bgi-shenzhen-completes-acquisition-of-complete-genomics-198820331.html

Bio-IT World Staff. (2013, March 19). BGI-Shenzhen completes acquisition of Complete Genomics. Bio-IT World. https://www.bio-itworld.com/news/2013/03/19/complete-genomics-acquisition-final

Cyranoski, D. (2010, March 3). Chinese bioscience: The sequence factory. *Nature, 464*(7285), 22–24. DOI: 10.1038/464022a PMID: 20203579

360. Dx. (2023, January 26). BGI Genomics 2022 global expansion bid included the launch of new subsidiaries in 14 countries. 360Dx. https://www.360dx.com/sequencing/bgi-genomics-2022-global-expansion-bid-included-launch-new-subsidiaries-14-countries

GenEng News. (2013). BGI offers $117.6M to acquire Complete Genomics. Genetic Engineering & Biotechnology News (GEN). https://www.genengnews.com/topics/omics/bgi-offers-117-6m-to-acquire-complete-genomics/

GenomeWeb. (2010, January 13). BGI to receive $1.5B in collaborative funds over 10 years from China Development Bank. GenomeWeb. https://www.genomeweb.com/sequencing/bgi-receive-15b-collaborative-funds-over-10-years-china-development-bank

Genomics, B. G. I. (2023, June 29). BGI Genomics obtains BSI ISO 37301 compliance management system certification [Press release]. PR Newswire. https://www.prnewswire.com/apac/news-releases/bgi-genomics-obtains-bsi-iso-37301-compliance-management-system-certification-301866808.html

Grand View Research. (2023). Genomics market size, share & trends analysis report, 2023–2030. https://www.grandviewresearch.com/industry-analysis/genomics-market

Group, B. G. I. (n.d.). Huo-Yan Laboratory. BGI. https://www.bgi.com/global/media/27

Gryphon Scientific. (2019, February 14). China's biotechnology development: The role of U.S. and other foreign engagement (Report prepared for the U.S.-China Economic and Security Review Commission). https://www.uscc.gov/sites/default/files/Research/US-China%20Biotech%20Report.pdf

Hill, C. W. L., Hwang, P., & Kim, W. C. (1990). An eclectic theory of the choice of international entry mode. *Strategic Management Journal, 11*(2), 117–128. DOI: 10.1002/smj.4250110204

McGrane, C. (2017, May 17). Chinese genomics giant BGI announces West Coast Innovation Center to fuel international collaboration. GeekWire. https://www.geekwire.com/2017/bgi/

Molteni, M. (2017, May 18). A Chinese genome giant sets its sights on the ultimate sequencer. WIRED. https://www.wired.com/2017/05/chinese-genome-giant-sets-sights-uitimate-sequencer

Needham, K., & Baldwin, C. (2021, July 7). China's gene giant harvests data from millions of pregnant women. Reuters Investigates. https://www.reuters.com/investigates/special-report/health-china-bgi-dna/

Puglisi, A., & Rask, C. (2024, May). China, biotechnology, and BGI: How China's hybrid economy skews competition. Center for Security and Emerging Technology (CSET). https://cset.georgetown.edu/publication/china-biotechnology-and-bgi/

Reuters. (2020, August 5). Special report: COVID opens new doors for China's gene giant. Reuters. https://www.reuters.com/article/world/special-report-covid-opens-new-doors-for-chinas-gene-giant-idUSKCN2511CD/

Root, F. R. (1994). *Entry strategies for international markets* (Rev. ed.). Jossey-Bass.

Ropes & Gray LLP. (2023, April 25). Bureau of Industry and Security imposes export restrictions on BGI Group, the world's largest genomics company [Client alert]. https://www.ropesgray.com/en/insights/alerts/2023/04/bis-imposes-export-restrictions-on-bgi-group-the-worlds-largest-genomics-company

KEY TERMS AND DEFINITIONS

Acquisition: Purchasing an existing local company to rapidly obtain technology, personnel, regulatory standing, or market channels—effective for speed but requiring post-deal integration.

Brand and reputation effects: The trust and relational capital a company accumulates through research output, crisis response, and social contributions—assets that attract partners and contracts but can be quickly eroded by controversies.

Compliance governance: A structured set of policies, procedures, and oversight mechanisms that ensure corporate activities meet legal, ethical, and regulatory requirements; adopting recognized frameworks signals credibility to external stakeholders.

Cost leadership: A competitive positioning focused on minimizing unit costs through scale, proprietary processes, or vertical integration, enabling price advantages in cost-sensitive markets.

Cross-border sample and data flow: The physical and regulatory movement of biological samples and genomic data across national borders, including the operational, legal, and ethical constraints that govern such transfers.

Data sovereignty (DS): Legal and policy claims by states to control data generated within their territory or concerning their citizens, which can restrict cross-border data transfers and shape collaboration models.

DNBseq (DNB-s) sequencing platform: BGI's proprietary high-throughput sequencing technology and hardware designed to process large volumes of genomic samples at lower per-sample cost, enabling scale-driven service delivery.

Entry mode: The chosen organizational form and commitment level for entering a foreign market (e.g., remote service, alliance, joint venture, greenfield, acquisition), each balancing control, speed, and risk differently.

Greenfield investment (GI): A high-commitment entry strategy where a firm builds new facilities or operations from scratch in the host country, trading faster local control for greater capital and time investment.

Huo-Yan Laboratories (HYLs): A modular, rapidly deployable high-throughput testing lab system used for emergency public-health responses and expanded diagnostic services in host countries.

Hybrid political-economic regime (HPER): A governance context where state guidance and market forces coexist: the government actively shapes firms through policy, funding, or procurement while firms operate under competitive, profit-seeking incentives.

Institutional advantage: External benefits a firm gains from its home country's policies, financing, diplomatic backing, or procurement mechanisms that lower foreign-market entry costs or provide leverage.

Internationalization: The process by which a firm extends its commercial, research, and operational activities beyond its home country to establish markets, collaborations, or service delivery internationally.

Joint venture (JV): A market-entry arrangement in which a foreign firm and a local partner co-invest and co-manage operations to share resources, local knowledge, and compliance burdens.

Localization: Adapting products, processes, organizational structures, and staffing to local norms, regulations, and preferences so that services are delivered "in-country" rather than merely exported.

Chapter 13
WuXi AppTec's Integrated Global CRDMO Model:
The End-to-End CRDMO Internationalization Model

Cunzhen Zhou
http://orcid.org/0009-0004-2655-9993
Beijing Normal-Hong Kong Baptist University, China

EXECUTIVE SUMMARY

This chapter examines the globalization strategy of WuXi AppTec "WuXi" is pronounced Woo-shee, a leading pharmaceutical outsourcing company, detailing its evolution into an integrated Contract Research, Development, and Manufacturing Organization (CRDMO). The purpose is to analyse the company's market entry, core strengths, and operational strategies across key regions, including the United States, Europe, and the Middle East. Key themes discussed encompass the end-to-end CRDMO model, strategic mergers and acquisitions, technological platforms, long-tail customer strategy, and resilience in global supply chains amid geopolitical challenges. The chapter also addresses significant obstacles such as the BIOSECURE Act and trade tensions, along with mitigation strategies like divestitures and expansion in Singapore. The contribution offers insights into how latecomer firms can achieve global leadership through strategic vision, localized operations, and adaptive responses to international dynamics.

DOI: 10.4018/979-8-3373-4302-0.ch013

INTRODUCTION

Background of the Company

WuXi AppTec's globalization journey exemplifies enterprise expansion through an international strategy that includes capital-driven growth, mergers and acquisitions, and localized operations. Established in 2000 in WuXi, Jiangsu Province, China, the company initially specialized in the outsourcing of drug R&D. It now provides comprehensive laboratory research and production services across the entire drug lifecycle—from discovery and development to commercialization—for the global pharmaceutical, biotech, and medical device sectors, helping to deliver innovative therapies worldwide (WuXi AppTec, n.d.). The company's core operations are based on the CRDMO model—Contract Research, Development, and Manufacturing Organization—which covers three main areas: Chemistry, Testing, and Biology. Focusing on small-molecule drug R&D, the Chemistry segment covers discovery, development, and manufacturing, encompassing synthesis and TIDES development. The Testing division offers full-cycle services such as pharmacokinetics, toxicology, and preclinical testing, supporting IND applications. The biology branch emphasizes early-stage drug discovery and efficacy validation, providing target screening and disease model development (e.g., for oncology and immune disorders), with a library of over 2,000 disease models. Together, these capabilities enable WuXi AppTec to provide comprehensive, end-to-end solutions.

According to public information, they adopted a matrix management model for holding group plus subsidiaries. The parent company focuses on core CRMOD business, while subsidiaries concentrate on specific areas with clear divisions of labor. It has global support systems for law, finance, and human resources based on digital middle platforms to support cross-regional operations. The dual headquarters in Shanghai and Boston have achieved a 24-hour global R&D relay. Today, the core scientist-led leadership, represented by CEO Li Ge, Ph.D. in Organic Chemistry from Columbia University, provides strategic and technological stewardship for the company.

Motivation for Global Expansion

Examining the pharmaceutical industry's transformation is essential to understanding the motivation behind WuXi AppTec's global expansion. In the 1980s and 1990s, drug discovery mainly relied on random screening methods. Researchers often tested compounds directly on animal models for efficacy because of a lack of clearly defined targets. This approach resulted in extremely low success rates and required substantial time and financial resources. By the early 21st century, however, the industry transitioned to a target-based era. Drug development has become more systematic. Disease mechanisms were first analyzed to identify specific biological targets, followed by rational drug design. This shift significantly improved R&D success rates, shortened development cycles, and enabled the development of personalized medicine.

Yet this scientific advancement came with new structural requirements. Target-based drug discovery demanded highly specialized talent, advanced technological platforms, and greater financial investment. Following the burst of the US technology stock bubble in 2000, pharmaceutical companies facing financial downturns began seeking cost-effective R&D solutions and internationalization opportunities (Murong, 2021). Parallel to this global restructuring, China's accession to the World Trade Organization (WTO) aligned domestic pharmaceutical policies with international standards and opened the market to foreign enterprises. Murong (2021) further showed that implementing the Marketing Authorization Holder system ushered China's drug development into an era of flourishing diversity. The long-term accumulation of highly educated domestic talent since the resumption of China's National College Entrance Exam in 1977 laid a human capital foundation for the growth of the pharmaceutical sector. Together, these global and domestic transformations created both pressure and opportunity—forming the broader structural context for WuXi AppTec's emergence.

Within this changing landscape, Li Ge's personal trajectory became closely intertwined with industry evolution. After graduating from the Department of Chemistry at Peking University in 1989, Li Ge and his classmate and wife, Zhao Ning, went to the United States to pursue doctoral studies in organic chemistry. During this period, Li Ge and his advisor, Professor Clark Still, jointly invented labeled combinatorial chemistry technology, leading to the discovery of multiple drug precursor compounds. He later secured venture capital and co-founded Pharmacopeia Drug Discovery Inc with his advisor. When China invited Li back in 1999, he observed that domestic pharmaceutical enterprises had a substantial technological gap compared to international standards. Domestic companies could not produce many drugs. Although China's pharmaceutical R&D service market was expanding rapidly, domestic companies largely concentrated in low-end generics and traditional Chinese medicine. They lacked experience in independent innovation and needed overseas-returned talents who could connect with global markets (Wang, 2021). During this period, the vision of "Every drug can be made, and every disease can be treated" took root. After careful consideration, Li and Zhao returned to China in the early 2000s and founded WuXi, which would later become WuXi AppTec.

However, translating this vision into reality required navigating the inherent complexity of drug development. The process from discovery to market approval involves multiple critical stages—drug discovery, preclinical research, clinical trials, and regulatory approval. Each stage is intricate and capital-intensive; failure at any point may invalidate years of work, with total investments often exceeding hundreds of millions of dollars and development cycles lasting at least ten years. Besides these structural barriers, WuXi faced practical constraints during its early years. For example, domestic manufacturers could not produce even simple laboratory-grade fume cupboards, forcing the team to build them manually. The domestic drug R&D infrastructure was far weaker than Li had expected.

A strategic turning point occurred during a US business trip, when Li recognized the immense commercial potential of his doctoral research on template molecular combinations—a method capable of significantly speeding up drug development timelines. Drawing inspiration from Pharmacopeia's successful outsourcing model, he decisively pivoted WuXi from a drug developer to a Contract Research Organization (CRO). This shift aligned the company with the broader global trend of pharmaceutical outsourcing that had intensified as R&D expenditures rose and returns declined.

Leveraging Li's US connections and international credibility, WuXi rapidly secured outsourcing partnerships and attracted substantial foreign investment. Global pharmaceutical giants increasingly outsourced segments of their R&D pipelines, positioning WuXi well to capture these opportunities and leading WuXi to receive a growing number of lucrative contracts. The firm thus moved from being a latecomer in a weak domestic infrastructure environment to becoming an integrated participant in the global pharmaceutical value chain.

Building upon China's cost-competitive scientific talent pool, WuXi AppTec sped up its growth trajectory and listed on the NYSE in 2007. Over time, the company absorbed international pharmaceutical R&D experience and offset domestic structural weaknesses by continuously gaining clinical research and pharmaceutical companies both at home and abroad. This strategy enabled it to establish an industrial operational layout spanning Asia, America, Europe, and the Middle East. After completing the A-share IPO in 2018, WuXi further sped up capital deployment and strategic expansion. In 2021, the company introduced the CRDMO model, integrating contract research (R), development (D), manufacturing (M), and commercialization into a unified end-to-end solution (Liu, 2025).

Today, WuXi operates 32 global R&D and production sites, supporting innovation projects for 6,000 partners across over 30 countries. The company's global expansion was therefore not an isolated ambition, but the cumulative outcome of industry transformation, institutional reform, entrepreneurial vision, and strategic adaptation to evolving global pharmaceutical dynamics.

MARKET ANALYSIS AND ENTRY STRATEGY

As a single-CXO company, WuXi recognizes it is difficult to fully support an independent R&D platform, as modern drug development relies on interdisciplinary technologies. To address gaps in resources and technologies globally and expand its service reach, mergers and acquisitions have become the fastest path (Murong, 2021). WuXi's global expansion follows a dual-driven strategy of technology orientation and demand matching. WuXi AppTec began its overseas M&A and R&D base establishment in 2008.

Target Market Selection and Entry Mode Selection

America: First step for Expansion

The United States has consistently been at the forefront of global biopharmaceutical development, boasting the highest number of biopharmaceutical companies and the largest R&D investments in the world. According to Fan's research (2021), from 1999 to 2017, the total number of pharmaceutical patents in the US surged from 4,985.4 to 25,529.9, accounting for 39.95% of the global share in 2017. Coupled with increasing R&D investments, the US developed 304 new molecular entities or new biological molecular entities in chemical pharmaceuticals during that decade, representing 42.11% of the global total, which are far surpassing other countries and regions (Ezell, 2020; Kennedy, 2018). Expanding into the US market first was undoubtedly the right strategic choice.

In early 2008, WuXi, announced the full acquisition of American AppTec Laboratory Services, Inc. for $151 million and rebranded from *WX* to *WuXi AppTec*. AppTec specialized in large-molecule biologics and medical device testing, complementing WuXi's small-molecule chemical drug R&D pipeline. AppTec had R&D and manufacturing bases in Philadelphia, St. Paul, and Atlanta, providing WuXi with an operational entity in the US and expanding its American client base (Gan, 2016). This major move marked a crucial step for Li to reestablish a foothold in the US and represented WuXi AppTec's first stride in global expansion.

During the 2010s, WuXi AppTec continued to expand its R&D and production bases in the United States. Among the many acquisitions and expansions, the following are representative ones. In 2014, WuXi AppTec built a new factory in Philadelphia and gained XenoBiotic Laboratories, a 27-year-old American bioanalytical company. XBL primarily provides R&D services in bioanalysis, drug metabolism, and pharmacokinetics. This acquisition expanded the company's laboratory-testing business. In January 2015, WuXi AppTec gained NextCODE Company for just $65 million (WuXi AppTec, 2015). NextCODE was the only company in the world that had a centralized database storing complete genomic information from over 300,000 individuals. Following the acquisition, WuXi merged NextCODE with its own genomics division, gaining immediate access to a world-class whole-genome analysis system (Gan, 2016). Later, WuXi NextCODE, the newly formed subsidiary, quickly played a key role in international genomic medicine, and Genomics England subsequently selected it to take part in the UK's "100,000 Genomes Project" (Genomics England, 2015).

From its market entry strategy in the US, WuXi AppTec initially focused on broadening its R&D capabilities and service offerings to build a customer base. In more recent years, it has shifted toward business optimization and specialization, allowing the company to play an increasingly prominent role on the global stage.

Europe, the Strategic Bridgehead

In the global landscape of pharmaceutical innovation, the European market has always held a core position because of its mature regulatory system, substantial purchasing power, and cutting-edge research ecosystem. David Rix, the CEO of Eli Lilly, pointed out that in Europe, the negotiated pricing of medicines offers wide accessibility, with patients only having to pay a relatively low out-of-pocket cost and there are no administrative obstacles. There are no intermediaries to distort price (Kansteiner, 2025). This system offers consumers low costs, yet it substantially postpones the market introduction of new drugs. Compared to the Food and Drug Administration (FDA) in the United States, the European Medicines Agency (EMA) has a slower and less flexible approval process, as it places greater emphasis on long-term safety (Lau & Seifert, 2025). The EMA's stricter approval standards partly cause this, as its scientific review is separate from the European Commission's market access decisions. Sometimes, multi-level approvals are also needed, further delaying patient access to a wide range of new medications. Recognizing both the strengths and drawbacks, WuXi AppTec has positioned Europe as a key strategic region that provides a critical "strategic buffer" and serves as a "bridge" for global operations.

Regardless of the country or region, a renowned biopharmaceutical industry requires exceptional scientific research capabilities and an active investment environment for support. Munich, Germany, has highly concentrated academic resources, including world-class institutions such as Ludwig Maximilian University of Munich, Helmholtz Zentrum München, and the Fraunhofer Society, along with service providers of a highly integrated network, making it one of Europe's most vibrant biotech hubs. In 2016, WuXi AppTec gained Crelux Company in Munich, which is a service provider specializing in protein structure-based drug discovery (WuXi AppTec, 2016). This acquisition brought advanced technologies in protein production and biophysical analysis, further enhancing WuXi's capabilities in early-stage drug research (R) and complementing its development (D) and manufacturing (M) operations at other sites. In February 2021, WuXi AppTec expanded its European footprint by acquiring a locationally superior and commercially scale capsule and tablet production base in Couvet, Switzerland, owned by Bristol-Myers Squibb (BMS), through a subsidiary (WuXi AppTec, 2021). This further enhanced WuXi Apptec's small molecule contract development and manufacturing organization (CDMO) capabilities in Europe and also provided flexible Good Manufacturing Practice (GMP) production services (Wu, 2021).

At the BayOConnect annual conference of the European Industry Conference in 2025, Dr. Thomas Meins, the head of the WuXi AppTec base in Munich, highlighted that WuXi AppTec continues to deepen its acquisitions and cooperation across Europe, such as integrating the technology of Swedish biotech company Camurus, investing in French VC Jeito Capital, meeting the market demand for new drugs under its controlled pricing strategies. It is the global integrated network of WuXi AppTec's CRDMO that helps clients simultaneously carry out clinical trial designs for FDA and EMA, harmonize data from multiple locations, then shorten the EMA approval time, providing a faster path for new product launch (WuXi AppTec., 2025).

Through continuous efforts, the European market has become its third-largest market, and in the first quarter of 2025, it still achieved 1.3 billion yuan in revenue, with a year-on-year growth of 26.2%, the fastest growth rate second only to the United States region (WuXi AppTec., 2025).

Middle East: Springboard of Expansion

The Middle East is rapidly developing as a key player in the global life sciences and pharmaceutical industry. With a large population and significant economic growth potential, most countries in the region have adopted regulatory systems that are in line with the FDA, ensuring that drug regulation meets international standards. For example, in recent years, pharmaceutical companies have increasingly invested in Saudi Arabia, attracted by the country's large and growing population, strong medical infrastructure, and the government's commitment to developing the industry as part of its "Vision 2030" plan. Siddiqui (2023) expects the Saudi pharmaceutical market size to achieve a compound annual growth rate of 5.2% in the future.

Specifically, the Israeli life sciences industry is highly vibrant and dynamic. According to statistics from the Israeli government's Ministry of Economy and Industry (2016), Israel has one of the highest numbers of scientists per capita in the world (145 scientists per 10,000 citizens), and one out of every three Israeli scientists specializes in the life sciences field. Between 2005 and 2014, the number of life science companies in Israel increased significantly, with 66% of companies founded during that decade (Government of Israel, 2016). Based on data from the United Nations Conference on Trade and Development (2023), Israel's pharmaceutical product exports grew from $37,705 thousand in 1995 to $220,177 thousand in 2013, achieving a compound annual growth rate of 10.41%.

In 2014, WuXi AppTec joined the wave of collaboration with the Middle East by establishing an office in Tel Aviv, Israel, to provide integrated R&D services for local companies. The office later announced a partnership with Israeli venture capital firm Pontifax for the joint investment in biotechnology and medical device projects (Root, 2014; Subsequently, WuXi AppTec expanded its collaborations and investments in the region. For instance, in 2017, WuXi AppTec partnered with Germany's Merck Serono and Pontifax to establish the "Explore Bio" life sciences incubator in Yavne, Israel, further supporting local biotech innovation and speeding up early-stage research (Liu, 2017). The incubator also provided funding, technical expertise, and industry resources to help startups enter global markets. Given the Middle East's relatively small market size, lower requirements for production, and periodic geopolitical risks, WuXi AppTec recognized that a capital-light operational model focuses on acquiring technological resources and market opportunities rather than directly managing physical facilities. Since Middle Eastern pharmaceutical companies primarily target European and American markets, WuXi AppTec serves as a bridge, connecting regional R&D with global production resources. The Middle East acts as a springboard for WuXi AppTec, allowing it to capture early-stage innovations through offices and venture partnerships before channeling them to core bases in China, the US, and Europe for commercialization. This approach maximizes the region's innovation ecosystem, creating mutual benefits.

At the 16th BIOMED Israel Conference, hosted by the Israel Advanced Technology Industries (IATI), Dr. Adams added that with WuXi AppTec's support, establishing biotech companies and assembling talent teams has become significantly easier, praising WuXi AppTec as "a critical player in the ecosystem." Israeli scientist Dr. Oren Hershkovitz, also present at the conference, remarked that partnerships with Chinese collaborators like WuXi AppTec have strengthened regional cooperation, accelerated product development, and helped break geographical barriers to bring treatments to global markets—benefiting patients worldwide (WuXi AppTec, 2017).

Core Competitive Advantage

End-to-End Innovative CRDMO Model

In 2021, WuXi AppTec released its first financial report following the restructuring of its business segments and organizational framework. The report emphasized that the integrated Chemical Business segment now offered comprehensive end-to-end services, formally establishing CRDMO as a core strategy for new drug development (WuXi AppTec, 2021).

Analyst Zhu from Southwest Securities R&D Center (2019) noted a marked decline in the number of new drug approvals in the early 21st century, alongside rising R&D time and costs. Faced with high technical and capability barriers, innovators urgently required low-barrier R&D models. Ensuring stable and high-quality commercialization of drug candidates remained a significant challenge. CRDMO emerged as the optimal solution. On the one hand, it provides developers with standardized, professional laboratories, facilities, and expert teams, reducing the substantial capital expenditures associated with infrastructure. Its seamless platform speeds up target validation, lead compound screening, and CMC development, minimizing risks linked to technology transfer between stages. Clients need only collaborate with a few suppliers, drastically simplifying project complexity (Zhu, 2019; WuXi AppTec, 2021). CRDMO enables parallel progression of upstream and downstream modules, allowing clients to achieve milestones more efficiently. Public data (WuXi Biologics, 2025) demonstrates that WuXi Biologics' CRDMO model compresses the DNA to Investigational New Drug (IND) timeline to 9 months, and only 6 months for autoimmune disease projects. Its systems comply with regulatory requirements from the FDA, EMA, National Medical Products Administration (NMPA), and other global authorities, having passed 44 international audits with a 100% success rate in Pre-License Inspections (WuXi Biologics, 2025).

CRDMO is not merely an aggregation of traditional CDMO units but represents a new mode of shared technology platforms and systematic synergy, which has gained growing recognition across the biotech industry. The supply chain is no longer linear but a collaborative network (WuXi AppTec, 2021). CRDMO reveals huge barriers to be replicated, such as fully integrated technological capabilities across the entire industry chain, long-term client retention, and global operational expertise. Leveraging these unique competitive advantages, WuXi AppTec is redefining the global biopharmaceutical innovation landscape.

Cutting-edge Technology Platform and quality

The second key competitive strength of WuXi AppTec lies in its pioneering layout in emerging modalities and robust quality assurance. Since 2016, the company has transitioned from a hybrid model of generics and innovation to one focused primarily on novel drugs, supplemented by generics, establishing a virtuous cycle of obtaining approval for one innovative drug every 2 to3 years (Zhu & Chen, 2019). WuXi AppTec has established early capabilities in emerging therapeutic modalities such as targeted protein degradation, nucleic acid therapeutics, and peptides/oligonucleotides, possessing industry-scarce scaled experience. For instance, its

Targeted Protein Degrader Integrated Discovery Platform, operational since 2016, leverages over 1,000 chemists and over 20 assay technologies to support full-stage characterization of TPD molecules; In the bioanalytical field, it equipped with ultra-high sensitive peptide bioanalytical method (Picogram level) and comprehensive Oligo testing capabilities at Femtogram level (WuXi AppTec, 2024). WuXi AppTec attaches great importance to AI and automation platforms to enhance R&D efficiency. As early as 2018, the company led the investment in the artificial intelligence company Insilico Medicine, based on generative adversarial networks to produce and evaluate candidates and drug targets through a machine learning-based discovery pipeline (Insilico Medicine, 2018). This collaboration with Insilico Medicine on the GENTRL model completed in 46 days what traditionally required 2–3 years for mouse model validation (Zhavoronkov, 2019).

System quality and IP protection have always served as the cornerstone of the CXO industry. In December 2024, the US FDA issued an import ban on Viatris' facility in Indore, India, because of significant data integrity and current Good Manufacturing Practice violations identified at the plant. In contrast, benefiting from its excellent audit track record over the years, WuXi AppTec's quality system has earned high trust from authoritative regulatory agencies. The Investor Day Research (2024) revealed that both the FDA and EMA have granted the company exemptions from pre-approval reviews for over 20 drugs, while maintaining a zero-failure rate across 900 delivered batches of commercial peptide production.

Long-tail Strategy

WuXi AppTec has a large, diverse, and loyal customer base, covering all the world's top 20 pharmaceutical companies, which accounted for approximately 40% of the company's total revenue (Zhongshang Industrial Research Institute, 2024). In over 6000 active customers, most were small and medium-sized pharmaceutical companies (WuXi Apptec,2025). These enterprises are many and cover niche fields such as cancer, rare diseases, and gene therapy. Each project is small in scale but considerable in total. WuXi AppTec's long-tail customer strategy precisely forms a customer ecosystem parallel to that of traditional Big Pharma by serving small and medium-sized technology companies and start-ups. Compared with traditional pharmaceutical companies that focus on large single orders, the long-tail model supported by CRDMO can respond quickly and in a standardized manner to undertake thousands of minor projects. This model continuously attracts new customers from the R&D end, continuously drives traffic to the D and M ends, and enhances customer stickiness research's long-tail customers contribute over 75% of business volume (WuXi AppTec, 2024). It also avoids over-reliance on a few major clients and reduces the performance pressure caused by the loss of a single client. In the first half of 2025, they transformed 158 molecules from R-end (research) to D-end (development), which shows the continuous contribution of long-tail customers to the drug research and development pipeline (WuXi AppTec, 2025).

Global Supply Chain Resilience

WuXi AppTec, headquartered in Shanghai, China, has established 26 branches and built over 560,000 square meters of R&D and production facilities worldwide, which helps meet the diverse production needs of clients while enhancing the resilience of their supply chains (Zhongshang Industrial Research Institute, 2024). The company established a triangular global layout. The company concentrates its R&D (Research) segment in China, leveraging domestic cost advantages for drug discovery. Key hubs in WuXi, Shanghai, and Changzhou play a dominant role. The Development (D) and Manufacturing (M) segments distribute their operations globally, covering Europe, the US, and emerging markets in Southeast Asia, which facilitates commercial production and expands their reach across the Asia-Pacific region. The construction of facilities in Singapore and Europe helps mitigate potential trade restrictions caused by tariffs, legislation, and other factors, reducing geopolitical risks. During the COVID-19 pandemic, global pharmaceutical supply chains experienced severe disruptions. WuXi AppTec's multi-site production bases helped clients minimize logistics delays and ensured a stable drug supply. Localized services and conveniences have enhanced customer stickiness. In 2024, the revenue share from American customers will exceed 60%, while that from European customers will remain stable at around 20% (WuXi AppTec, 2024).

It is the pattern of global technology collaboration and resource integration that enables WuXi to stay aligned with global pharmaceutical innovation trends. For instance, Europe's recent "Horizon Europe" initiative has driven local pharmaceutical companies to adopt new technologies widely. WuXi AppTec's Munich and Switzerland facilities are deeply involved in this effort, jointly advancing innovation in the industry (WuXi AppTec, 2025).

IMPLEMENTATION OF GLOBAL EXPANSION

Key Initiatives and Investment

For innovative enterprises, there is an interactive and co-evolutionary relationship between market timing and technological acquisitions (Wang et al., 2022). In August 2007, WuXi AppTec successfully listed on the US stock market (WuXi AppTec, n.d.). The US listing provided WuXi AppTec with a platform to expand aggressively. From 2007 to 2015, the company attracted strategic investments from top-tier institutions such as Warburg Pincus and Sequoia Capital China, and gained biochemical providers and technology platforms including AppTech, HD Bioscience and Ambrx, continuously expanding its business and technological innovation capabilities (WuXi AppTec, n.d.). However, Wang et al. (2022) point out that while serial acquisitions can enable rapid expansion, Wall Street investors questioned the sustainability of such innovation outputs. Coupled with skepticism toward WuXi AppTec's diversified acquisitions and underwhelming cash flow performance, the market undervalued the company, leading to a depressed stock price. The stringent regulatory environment in the US capital market imposed significant burdens—audit fees alone totaled RMB 30 million from 2012 to 2014, and the complex tax system further strained the company (Shen, 2022).

Recognizing that financing could no longer support its strategic vision of full-industry-chain integration, WuXi AppTec spun off its high-growth subsidiary, STA Pharmaceutical (a small-molecule CDMO business), in 2015, listing it on China's New Third Board to pave the way for the parent company's A-share listing. In December of the same year, WuXi AppTec completed its privatization and officially delisted from the US market. In 2017, it further spun off WuXi Biologics, a biologics-focused subsidiary, which listed on the Hong Kong Stock Exchange to secure additional funding. With all preparations in place, WuXi AppTec capitalized on China's "unicorn" policy incentives in 2018, swiftly achieving an A-share listing. The company issued approximately 104 million shares, and this transaction resulted in net proceeds of about 2.13 billion RMB (WuXi AppTec, 2018). The "one split into three" strategy enabled synergistic support across specialized business segments and multi-platform financing, ultimately creating a total market capitalization nearly 10 times its value at the time of US delisting.

Challenges Faced

Escalating geopolitical tensions and increasingly stringent regulatory barriers have generated significant challenges to its growth. In 2023, WuXi AppTec experienced a sharp decline in revenue growth because of reduced income from COVID-19-related commercial projects. In October 2024, the US House of Representatives passed The BIOSECURE Act (2024), which aims to prevent the leakage of sensitive data, such as US citizens' genomic information, by restricting federal agencies from engaging in business with certain Chinese biotech providers, including WuXi-affiliated companies, effectively barring the procurement of their biotech equipment or services.

This has seriously affected the long-term cooperation and development between WuXi AppTec and American pharmaceutical companies in the future.

Following Donald Trump's return to office, the US-China trade war reignited. In 2025, Trump announced that starting in April, he would impose a 10% tariff on all trading partners and an additional 34% reciprocal tariff on China (The White House, 2025). The worsening geopolitical climate has posed a direct and significant threat to WuXi's operations and development in the core market of the United States, as well as its international partners.

Meanwhile, the global CXO industry has become fiercely competitive, enthusiasm for financing has also slowed down. Restrictive initiatives continue to advance, even though officials have delayed the implementation of the BIOSECURE Act. The future remains uncertain, and the entire industry is on edge.

Mitigation Strategies

In response to the impact of the BIOSECURE Act, WuXi AppTec has strongly opposed such preconceived and unreasonable designations without due process, issued Voluntary announcement(2024) emphasizing that Wuxi AppTec has grown into a global player in the medical field as a reliable long-term partner and its stance that it does not pose a threat to US national security. Despite this, market reactions remain sensitive, and WuXi AppTec's stock price has experienced fluctuations. To address the uncertainty, WuXi AppTec has implemented a series of measures. As early as 2022, the company planned to establish a production base in Singapore with an expected investment of $1.43 billion (WuXi AppTec, 2022). The Singapore base sped up its construction by 2024 and is expected to become operational within three years. On the one hand, the Singapore base ensures business stability and effectively disperses the political risks associated with the BIOSECURE Act. As a biomedical hub in the Asia-Pacific region, it also helps the company expand into markets such as Southeast Asia and Australia (Lu, 2024).

Subsequently, WuXi AppTec began divesting its operations in Europe and the United States. According to a report published by Sinohealth Research Institute (2025), in early 2025, WuXi AppTec announced the sale of its advanced therapy businesses and medical device testing platforms in multiple locations across the US and the UK Later, WuXi Biologics sold its vaccine production base in Ireland to Merck for $500 million and secured a major deal worth $925 million with the US (Armstrong, 2025)—company Candid Therapeutics. Besides preemptive risk avoidance, these moves were driven by the recognition that some production bases were underperforming, enabling the company to divest them, recover funds, and concentrate resources on core businesses.

While accelerating its overseas expansion, WuXi AppTec continues to deepen its presence in the Chinese market. For instance, it gained a production base in Hangzhou from Pfizer China and invested in production and operational construction in multiple regions. During the interim performance briefing (2025), WuXi AppTec stated it has adopted dynamic and flexible pricing strategies across different business segments and customer groups to address competition (Zhang & He, 2025). At the 43rd Annual J.P. Morgan Healthcare Conference, WuXi AppTec reaffirmed its commitment to speeding up global capacity expansion, strengthening its CRDMO advantages, and doubling its D&M expenditures. This move offers reassurance to clients and investors in the rapidly changing environment.

STRATEGIC ANALYSIS

Analytical Frameworks

Political

In early 2024, the United States proposed the Biosecurity Act in response to concerns, such as China's dominance in the global CDMO sector, which is significantly affecting the entire CXO industry, including WuXi AppTec. Although the act failed because of subsequent presidential and congressional elections and the transition, the expansion of administrative review systems, including their grandfather clauses, still heightened geopolitical threats. In April 2025, Trump announced a "reciprocal tariff" plan that included a 10% base tariff on all countries and a 34% tariff on Chinese goods (He et al., 2025). A series of events is affecting the global economic ecosystem.

Domestically, China's pharmaceutical industry has a strong policy orientation. Since 2015, the state has launched special initiatives, such as the "Major New Drug Innovation" program and various marketing authorization systems, encouraged the transition from generic drugs to innovative drugs (Cai et al., 2023).

Economic

The global pharmaceutical outsourcing industry is currently driven by recovering demand and technological advancements. According to a research report from China Huajing Industrial Research Institute, global demand for pharmaceutical outsourcing continues to grow, with the global pharmaceutical R&D pipeline expected to exceed 25,800 by 2025, a year-on-year increase of 4.6%, of which biologics account for over 60% (Liu, 2025). Global investment and financing activities for innovative drugs continue to improve. Ma & Feng (2025) reported that, in 2024, global and US VC & PE investment and financing for innovative drugs increased by 1.93% and 5.29% year-on-year, respectively, showing a recovery in the global investment and financing environment for innovative drugs. Cai (2025) noted that China and the US are expected to reach outsourcing rates of 52.2% and 60.5%, respectively. By 2026, with the global market projected to grow at a CAGR of 14% over the next five years, reflecting rapid industry expansion.

Today, increasingly stringent environmental regulations are prompting CDMO companies to upgrade their production processes. Actively adopting AI to drive innovation is the optimal way to counter rising costs. In the future, AI technology will deeply penetrate the entire drug R&D process. CDMO companies will leverage "AI + robotics" to achieve automation in R&D and production, further reducing comprehensive R&D costs.

Social

In 2024, China's health management market surpassed RMB 2 trillion, and experts expect it to surpass RMB 3 trillion by 2028. But there aren't enough good health products and services for things like preventing diseases precisely, tailoring treatments to individuals, managing health proactively, and using AI in health-care. This really limits how many people can spend on their health (Guo, 2025). The pharmaceutical talent market is developing toward greater specialization and segmentation. Currently, the structure of pharmaceutical talent is shifting from a pyramidal to a diamond model, reflecting increasing demand for comprehensive, innovative talent in the pharmaceutical industry. Both the quantity of foundational talents and the diversity of specialized fields are expanding.

Germany's Berlin hosted the 16th World Health Summit (WHS, 2024) in October 2024. The core theme of this year's summit was "Building Trust for a Healthier World." The summit emphasized that trust in healthcare and medicine is the foundation for achieving sustainable and fair health solutions. Building trust in healthcare by providing better, more effective medical products and services remains challenging.

Brand and Reputation Effects

A high-quality enterprise never stops in its rapid development. The classic, iconic "With great power comes great responsibility" also verifies with Wuxi AppTec. Today, ESG performance has become a popular framework for evaluating sustainability worldwide. As early as 2020, WuXi specifically established an ESG committee and office to implement a robust ESG management structure. CEO Li stated in the 2024 ESG Disclosure Report (2025) that, compared with the base year

2020, carbon emissions decreased by 12.15% and water consumption decreased by 36.10%, highlighting the strong promotion of green technologies. For instance, to better cope with climate change, its Couvet base employs environmentally friendly, energy-efficient facilities, such as geothermal and solar energy systems and rainwater recycling systems. The Munich site uses eco-friendly materials and an efficient recycling system (WuXi AppTec, 2025).

WuXi AppTec actively engages in philanthropy and humanitarian help activities. For example, employees at the Philadelphia site took part in a charity run in the United States, raising $2,500 to support melanoma research and help more patients. The Singapore site collaborated with the Children's Cancer Foundation of Singapore to host a film day, inviting over 90 cancer families and over 100 employees to watch a film together (WuXi AppTec, 2025), showing care and support for children with cancer.

In August 2025, the company earned a spot in the "FTSE4Good Index Series" for the third year running. This selection acknowledged its original aspirations, strategies, and implementation measures, which have already shown that this young company is gradually becoming a model of an outstanding enterprise.

CONCLUSION AND STRATEGIC RECOMMENDATIONS

Summary of Key Findings

Whether through horizontal M&A to strengthen technological extension in a single segment, or vertical M&A to innovate and integrate into a complete end-to-end CRDMO service ecosystem, WuXi AppTec's growth has been built on a strategic and resilient "Acquire–Integrate–Innovate" triangle. With command rooted in China and R&D and production bases distributed worldwide—including Europe, the US, and emerging markets—the company enhances supply chain flexibility and mitigates regional risks. Despite intensifying stress from growing geopolitical challenges, such as US regulatory constraints and trade barriers, WuXi has taken proactive steps to mitigate these pressures—for instance, by leveraging its lower-risk Singapore base and refocusing overseas operations on core business areas.

Supported by leading technology teams and platforms, WuXi, with its exceptional global vision, can swiftly align with industry frontiers and secure a leading position in future growth trends. The company has also developed a long-tail strategy tailored to the characteristics of its industry and its SME clients, continuously attracting and keeping customers in a funnel-like manner. Driven by its unique integrated CRDMO model and comprehensive end-to-end services, WuXi AppTec has become a key promoter and critical supplier of global pharmaceutical innovation.

Future Growth Opportunities

On the one hand, geopolitical factors are driving overseas pharmaceutical companies to seek near-shoring outsourcing capacity. As the world's second-largest economy, China offers a vast market, a stable supply chain, and significant cost advantages, making it highly attractive. There is a growing demand for personalized medical services. WuXi AppTec can establish connections with hospitals or global healthcare networks to conduct medical record analyzes while ensuring implementable data privacy protection, providing customized treatment courses for enterprises or individual clients. Future competition will be a contest of technology and efficiency. Powerful AI algorithms can significantly enhance the R&D efficiency of pharmaceutical companies and support various aspects of their operations. WuXi AppTec can further develop its internal algorithmic platforms and collaborate with leading AI biotechnology firms to develop its own medicine database and clinical trial design simulation tools, which customers can subscribe to as needed, enhancing its competitiveness. It can also gradually implement AI automation in laboratories and factories, explore novel therapeutic approaches, and expand possibilities for growth.

Recommendations for Other Firms

WuXi AppTec's strategic foresight and agile responses offer invaluable insights. First, by positioning itself as a collaborator rather than a competitor, WuXi AppTec addresses industry challenges while leveraging its strengths to define its role in the global ecosystem, gradually cementing its irreplaceable position. Second, though mergers and acquisitions enable rapid entry into target markets, sustained success requires deep post-integration efforts. Thorough planning for local customer needs and conditions, coupled with localized operations, lies at the heart of long-term viability. Third, companies must ground overseas expansion in technological prowess and armor it with strategy. Global enterprises must remain flexible in risk diversification—ensuring supply chain resilience, diversifying market structures, and staying committed to core businesses to avoid overreliance on any single market.

Finally, in an era of unpredictable international politics, every enterprise is like a sailboat on the vast ocean, and one cannot simply wait for the storm to end but must firmly hold the steering wheel. In 2023, Ms. Zhao Ning, co-founder and senior vice president of WuXi AppTec, passed away after a 20-year battle with cancer. As a distinguished scientist and philanthropist, she persistently contributed to global public welfare initiatives and cultivated scientific talent throughout her illness, dedicating her life to advancing human health. WuXi AppTec has guided its growth with its founding mission: "Every drug can be made, and every disease can be treated" for over two decades, actively supporting global healthcare and benefiting patients worldwide. A company can succeed and continue moving forward also because of the weight of its mission and the clarity of its original aspiration. By sticking to its course and keeping its sight fixed on the lighthouse, it can navigate steadily through the waves of history.

REFERENCES

Act, B. I. O. S. E. C. U. R. E. H.R. 8333, 118th Cong. (2024). https://www.congress.gov/bill/118th-congress/house-bill/8333

Armstrong, A. (2025, January 6). Merck Snaps Up WuXi Biologics Facility in Ireland for $500M. Biospace. https://www.biospace.com/business/merck-snaps-up-wuxi-biologics-facility-in-ireland-for-500m

Cai, M. Z., & Yu, R. Y. (2023). , [The leading CRDMO with steady progress and long-term vision, providing all-around support for drug development]. 11, 2025, from]. KAIYUAN Securities. https://www.vzkoo.com/document/20230818776748e094c476d5c3f3b8c2.html?keyword=%E8%8D%AF%E6%98%8E%E5%BA%B7%E5%BE%B7CRDMO

Ezell, S. (2020, February 6). Intellectual Property's Impact on Global Health & Life Sciences Innovation. Information Technology and Innovation Foundation. https://www2.itif.org/2020-ezell-globalization-health-georgetown.pdf

Fan, C. Z. (2021). [Output Analysis of Pharmaceutical Research and Development Innovation in the United States]. Hangye yanjiuyuan. https://www.iir.sjtu.edu.cn/comments/51247.html

Gan, J. B. (2016). [Research on the Integrated Development Strategy of WuXi AppTec]. *Dangdai Jingji*, (33), 28–29.

Genomics England. (2015, November 12). Genomics England Contracts with WuXi NextCODE as Clinical Interpretation Partner in both Rare Disease and Cancer. https://www.genomicsengland.co.uk/news/genomics-england-contracts-with-wuxi-nextcode

Government of Israel. (2016). The life sciences industry in Israel. https://www.gov.il/BlobFolder/dynamiccollectorresultitem/life-sciences-industry-in-israel/he/The%20Life%20Sciences%20Industry%20in%20Israel.pdf

Guo, M. (2025, March 10). : " + + " [In-depth research on the health management industry: Who will be the first to complete the closed loop of "data + service + payment" in the accelerated expansion of the trillion-yuan blue ocean]. Chinairn. https://www.chinairn.com/news/20250310/144938487.shtml

He, J. Y., Liu, R. F., & Lai, J. Y. (2025) CXO hangye lingjunzhe, yitihua moshi dianding guoji diwei yu chengzhangxing. [CXO industry leader, integrated model establishes international position and growth potential]. CITIC Securities. https://www.vzkoo.com/document/20250717d82d8edf5fa599531b4fd6e7.html

Insilico Medicine. (2018, June 12). WuXi AppTec Leads Strategic Investment In Insilico Medicine To Accelerate Drug Discovery Using AI. Drug Discovery Trends. https://www.drugdiscoverytrends.com/wuxi-apptec-leads-strategic-investment-in-insilico-medicine-to-accelerate-drug-discovery-using-ai/

Kansteiner, F. (2025, August 7, 2025). Amid MFN talks, Lilly chief warns US adoption of international drug prices could bring 'worst of two worlds'. FIERCE Pharma. https://www.fiercepharma.com/pharma/amid-mfn-talks-lilly-chief-warns-adoption-international-drug-prices-could-bring-worst-two

Kennedy, J. (2018, March 26). How to Ensure That America's Life-Sciences Sector Remains Globally Competitive. Information Technology and Innovation Foundation. https://itif.org/publications/2018/03/26/how-ensure-americas-life-sciences-sector-remains-globally-competitive/

Lau, F., & Seifert, R. (2025). Comparison of drug approvals of the FDA and EMA between 2013 and 2023. *Naunyn-Schmiedeberg's Archives of Pharmacology*. Advance online publication. DOI: 10.1007/s00210-025-04412-4 PMID: 40608116

Liu, A. (2017, December 27). Merck Serono, WuXi AppTec, and Pontifax Form Israeli Life Science Incubator. NAI500.https://nai500.com/blog/2017/12/merck-serono-wuxi-apptec-and-pontifax-form-israeli-life-science-incubator/

Liu, E. Y. (2025, July 15). , , [WuXi AppTec Research Report: Leading player in the pharmaceutical outsourcing industry, platform-driven, serving the world]. Dongfang caifu. https://caifuhao.eastmoney.com/news/20230313114751593628580

Liu, Y. (2025, August 6).2025 CDMO : [2025, the pharmaceutical CDMO industry: R&D and production partners born from professional division of labor]. Chinairn. https://www.chinairn.com/hyzx/20250806/18030158.shtml

Lu, Y. Y. (2024, August 3). : [Going Global: WuXi AppTec's Layout in Singapore]. Weibo. https://www.weibo.com/ttarticle/p/show?id=2309405063278144389200

Ma, S., & Feng, J. x. (2025, June 5). : ,2025 5 VC&PE [The database of the pharmaceutical industry chain: Investment and financing of innovative drugs. In May 2025, the investment and financing of VC&PE of innovative drugs in the global market maintained a year-on-year positive growth. SDIC Security. https://www.essence.com.cn/news/2540202?columnId=002001004

Murong, Y. (2021, October 3). [WuXi AppTec's In-depth Thematic Research Report]. Xueqiu. https://xueqiu.com/4866021334/199366220

Root, C. (2014, November 6). WuXi AppTec opens Israel office, partners with Pontifax. Outsourcedpharma. https://www.outsourcedpharma.com/doc/wuxi-apptec-opens-israel-office-partners-with-pontifax-0001

Shen, P. (2022). [Research on the motivation and economic consequences of WuXi AppTec's privatization]. Xiandai yingxiao, (27), 44–46. DOI: 10.19932/j.cnki.22-1256/F.2022.09.044

Siddiqui, A. (2023, October 3). Big pharma sets sights on Middle East. BioSpectrum Asia Edition. https://www.biospectrumasia.com/analysis/86/23075/big-pharma-sets-sights-on- middle-east-.html

Sinohealth. (2025, February 7). AB :36 67 [The two sides of WuXi Biologics' globalization: Selling European plants for 3.6 billion and signing a 6.7 billion US deal]. Tencent. https://news.qq.com/rain/a/20250107A0AGBX00

The White House. (2025, April 2). Regulating imports with a reciprocal tariff to rectify trade practices that contribute to large and persistent annual United States goods trade deficits. https://www.whitehouse.gov/presidential-actions/2025/04/regulating-imports-with-a-reciprocal-tariff-to-rectify-trade-practices-that-contribute-to-large-and-persistent-annual-united-states-goods-trade-deficits/

United Nations Conference on Trade and Development. (2023). Israel Exports: Medicinal and Pharmaceutical Products. CEIC. https://www.ceicdata.com.cn/en/indicator/israel/exports-medicinal-and-pharmaceutical-product

US Food & Drug Administration. (2024, December 19). Warning Letter 320-25-28 Viatris, Inc. FDA. https://www.fda.gov/inspections-compliance-enforcement-and-criminal-investigations/warning-letters/viatris-inc-690897-12192024

Wang, H. (2021, December 1). : [Li Ge of WuXi AppTec: Let there be no difficult medicine in the world]. Zhihu. https://zhuanlan.zhihu.com/p/439810907

Wang, Y., Shen, L. Y., Zhou, X. H., & Liu, J. A. (2022). " - " — [The co-evolution of "innovation-capital" interaction and latecomer firm catch-up: A case study of WuXi AppTec]. *Guanli Pinglun*, *34*(06), 325–340. DOI: 10.14120/j.cnki.cn11-5057/f.2022.06.023

Wu, X. W. (2021, March 4). (603259.SH) , 212 , " " [WuXi AppTec (603259.SH) Scores Another Victory in International Layout, Target Price 212 Yuan, Maintain"Add" Rating]. Zhitongcaijing. https://www.zhitongcaijing.com/content/detail/421290.html

WuXi AppTec. (2015, January 13). WuXi AppTec Acquires NextCODE. Pharmatech. https://pharm.jgvogel.cn/c902791.shtml

WuXi AppTec. (2016, April 15). WuXi AppTec acquires Crelux. https://www.wuxiapptec.com/news/wuxi-news/1873

WuXi AppTec. (2017, June 1). : , , [WuXi AppTec in Israel: Innovation, Co-operation, Dream Fulfillment]. Sohu. https://www.sohu.com/a/145097878_282570

WuXi AppTec. (2018, April 23). Initial public offering. https://officialsite-static.wuxiapptec.com/upload/_cd50156a9b.pdf

WuXi AppTec. (2021, February 2). WuXi STA to purchase Bristol Myers Squibb manufacturing facility in Couvet, Switzerland. https://www.wuxiapptec.com/news/wuxi-news/4446

WuXi AppTec. (2021, November 29). " "! Get CRDMO! [Making drug R&D "Faster, Better, and More Economical"! get CRDMO in one Article]. Sohu. https://www.sohu.com/a/504099821_282570

WuXi AppTec. (2022, July 19). WuXi AppTec plans to build a new site in Singapore, better serving global partners and advancing healthcare innovation. https://www.wuxiapptec.com/news/wuxi-news/5143

WuXi AppTec. (2024, Sectember 10). Voluntary announcement. https://officialsite-static.wuxiapptec.com/upload/1e/20240910/VOLUNTARY%20 ANNOUNCEMENT.pdf

WuXi AppTec. (2024, September 26) 2024 WuXi AppTec investor day research enabling platforms enhance CRDMO model. https://officialsite-static.wuxiapptec.com/upload/2024_Wu_Xi_App_Tec_Investor_Day_Research_Enabling_Platforms_a656604c9a.pdf

WuXi AppTec. (2025, April 4) 2024 Environmental, social, and governance report. https://officialsite-static.wuxiapptec.com/upload/ESG_2024_Wu_Xi_App_Tec_EN_0fcdf75d0d.pdf

WuXi AppTec. (2025, July 8). Model Region Munich: With companies like WuXi AppTec, Munich is becoming Europe's leading biotech hub. NetEase Official Account. https://www.163.com/dy/article/K3U9DOGN05349C3E.html

WuXi AppTec. (2025, July 9). ! [Not Only the US but Also Europe! WuXi AppTec Joins Hands with Local Partners to Jointly Promote Pharmaceutical Innovation. Jiemian. https://www.jiemian.com/article/13008774.html

WuXi AppTec. (2025, July 28). Announcement of the unaudited interim results for the six months ended June 30, 2025. https://officialsite-static.wuxiapptec.com/upload/ANNOUNCEMENT_OF_THE_UNAUDITED_INTERIM_RESULTS_FOR_THE_SIX_MONTHS_ENDED_JUNE_30_2025_0c13c93fd7.pdf

WuXi AppTec. (n.d.). Our history. https://www.wuxiapptec.com/about/history

WuXi Biologics. (2025, October 20). WuXi Biologics Honored with 2025 Global Customer Value Leadership Recognition by Frost & Sullivan. PR Newswire. https://www.prnewswire.com/news-releases/wuxi-biologics-honored-with-2025-global-customer-value-leadership-recognition-by-frost--sullivan-302588869.html

Zhang, T., & He, Z. Y. (2025, February 7). , [WuXi AppTec sells overseas assets again: Seeking adjustments to cope with intensified competition and performance pressure]. Netease. https://www.163.com/dy/article/JNR1ATIB0550DHA5.html

Zhavoronkov, A., Ivanenkov, Y. A., Aliper, A., Veselov, M. S., Aladinskiy, V. A., Aladinskaya, A. V., Terentiev, V. A., Polykovskiy, D. A., Kuznetsov, M. D., Asadulaev, A., Volkov, Y., Zholus, A., Shayakhmetov, R. R., Zhebrak, A., Minaeva, L. I., Zagribelnyy, B. A., Lee, L. H., Soll, R., Madge, D., & Aspuru-Guzik, A. (2019). Deep learning enables rapid identification of potent DDR1 kinase inhibitors. *Nature Biotechnology*, *37*(9), 1038–1040. DOI: 10.1038/s41587-019-0224-x PMID: 31477924

Zhongshang Industrial Research Institute. (2024). : [Pharmaceutical R&D Giant: In-depth Analysis of WuXi AppTec's Operating Data and Core Competitiveness]. Zhongshang Qingbaowang. https://www.askci.com/news/chanye/20240517/1146422715917602872 12245_4.shtml

KEY TERMS AND DEFINITIONS

100,000 Genomes Project: A significant scientific research initiative aimed at sequencing and analyzing the genomes of 100,000 individuals. Large-scale collection and study of genomic data help deepen understanding of the genetic basis of diseases, including rare and common ones, promoting the development of personalized medicine and providing a more precise basis for disease diagnosis, treatment, and prevention, speeding up the progress of medical research.

CMC: (Chemistry, Manufacturing, and Controls) denotes the regulatory and technical framework that explains how developers create, manufacture, test, and quality-control a pharmaceutical product. It includes information on the drug's chemical composition, production processes, quality standards, and stability to ensure the product is safe, consistent, and compliant with regulatory requirements throughout its lifecycle.

CMO/CDMO: Contract Development and Manufacturing Organization, a customized R&D and manufacturing outsourcing model in the healthcare sector. Providing scalable production process services and covering pre-clinical research, clinical trials, and commercial production. It primarily provides innovative process development, equipment optimization, and customized R&D services to multinational pharmaceutical and biotech companies.

CRDMO: A fully integrated outsourcing model covering the entire pharmaceutical value chain (Outsourcing R&D, development, manufacturing, and Sales).

CRO: Contract Research Organization, originating in the US in the early 1980s, refers to a scientific organization that provides contract-based services to pharmaceutical companies, medical institutions, medical device R&D firms, or governments for basic and clinical medical research.

CSO: Contract Sales Organization, a sales outsourcing service provider that accepts commissions from pharmaceutical companies or drug distributors. Conducting drug sales, marketing services such as market research, product planning, and promotion, etc.

CXO: Contract X Outsourcing. Pharmaceutical Outsourcing. The division includes CRO, CMO/CDMO, and CSO, and these represent the three major segments of the pharmaceutical industry: R&D, manufacturing, and sales. Such a service model primarily entails entrusting certain business functions of pharmaceutical enterprises to external professional teams for execution, enabling pharmaceutical companies to focus more on their core businesses, optimize operational efficiency, and reduce operational costs.

EMA: European Medicines Agency, responsible for evaluating and supervising medicines in the European Union.

FDA: Food and Drug Administration, an executive agency established within the Public Health Service (PHS) under the Department of Health and Human Services (DHHS) of the United States government, responsible for regulating the safety and effectiveness of food, drugs, medical devices, cosmetics, biological products, etc., to protect and promote public health.

FTSE4Good Index Series: Created by the global index and data provider FTSE Russell, it measures the performance of companies that show specific Environmental, Social, and Governance (ESG) practices.

IND: Investigational New Drug Application, a formal regulatory submission that a pharmaceutical company files with health authorities (such as the FDA) to get approval to begin clinical trials in humans. It includes preclinical data, manufacturing information, and proposed clinical study protocols to show that the drug is reasonably safe for initial human testing.

NMPA: National Medical Products Administration, an institution in China responsible for the supervision and administration of drugs, medical devices, cosmetics, and other products, undertakes the important responsibilities of ensuring the safety, effectiveness, and quality control of these products.

TIDES: An acronym that includes **T**ides (Oligonucleotides), **I**nterfering RNAs (iRNAs), **D**NA, **E**ngineered Cells, and **S**ynthetic Peptides & **S**upercharged Proteins. It encompasses most cutting-edge biological treatment modalities beyond traditional small molecules and conventional antibody drugs. These therapies typically act at the genetic or cellular level and aim to treat challenging diseases such as cancer, genetic disorders, and autoimmune conditions.

Chapter 14
Hengrui Pharmaceutical's Innovation-Driven Internationalization:
From Domestic Generic Producer to International Innovator

Yuqian Zhang
http://orcid.org/0009-0004-9762-1715
Beijing Normal-Hong Kong Baptist University, China

EXECUTIVE SUMMARY

This chapter examines the international expansion strategy of Hengrui Pharmaceutical, a leading Chinese innovative medicine enterprise. The purpose of the chapter is to analyse the company's motivations for globalization, including domestic market saturation and policy pressures from centralized procurement, alongside the allure of larger international markets. The key themes explored include Hengrui's market selection criteria, it's evolving entry modes such as license-out agreements and the novel NewCo model, and the competitive advantages derived from sustained research and development investment and a differentiated product pipeline. Notable challenges include regulatory obstacles with the US Food and Drug Administration and dependence on partnership income. The overall contribution provides a replicable framework for other Chinese pharmaceutical firms seeking global expansion, emphasizing the critical role of technological innovation, strategic partnerships, and robust regulatory preparedness in navigating geopolitical and competitive landscapes

DOI: 10.4018/979-8-3373-4302-0.ch014

INTRODUCTION

Background of the Company

Hengrui Pharmaceuticals is a leading enterprise in the Chinese pharmaceutical industry, committed to providing high-quality treatment options to patients worldwide. Notably, it dominates the field of antineoplastic medicine, making it a symbol of China's emerging innovative medicine industry on the global stage. Experts widely recognize its significant investment in research and development, which helped it gain a high reputation for its growth potential.

The history shows that Lianyungang Pharmaceutical Factory, Hengrui's predecessor, officially began operations in 1970. In 1997, it underwent shareholding reform and restructured itself into a private pharmaceutical enterprise. After that, they listed it in 2000. At the beginning, the company focused on manufacturing generic medicines to meet the requirement for substituting imported medicines for tumor treatment and anesthesia. From 2008 to 2016, the company gradually shifted its focus from generic to innovative medicines. It began implementing a superior marketing model, "license-in" and "license-out", which sped up its research and development speed and turnover. In 2021, Hengrui fully embarked on a new journey of internationalization in clinical R&D, transforming from generic medicine exports to innovative medicine exports. Since 2023, Hengrui has been at a pivotal juncture, shifting its gaze from the domestic market to overseas markets, and has achieved notable success in its overseas marketing of innovative medicines.

The company's currently available products for sale mainly focus on three major categories: anti-tumor medicines, anesthetics, and contrast agents, each of which has a significant contribution to the company's overall performance. For instance, the anti-tumor medicine accounted for over 50 percent of overall sales revenue and generated a gross profit of over 90 percent, mainly driving the company's growth. The products are mainly used to treat chronic diseases. In addition, Hengrui is the domestic leader in oncology innovation. Globally, it ranks among the top 50 in the Pharmaceutical Executive magazine and has witnessed steady growth each year, demonstrating its status in medical R&D.

Remarkably, in September 2015, Hengrui sold the overseas rights and interests in its PD-1 antibody, SHR-1210 (camrelizumab), to Incyte for a total transaction value of 770 million US dollars, achieving the first overseas licensing of an innovative biopharmaceutical from China. Besides license-out, Hengrui's overseas independent R&D is also worth looking forward to. The 2024 interim report shows that three antibody-drug conjugate (ADC) products received Fast Track designation (FTD) from the US Food and Drug Administration (US FDA). Besides, Hengrui established a major partnership with GSK, a renowned multinational pharmaceutical company, which will probably boost its sales.

Operating as a limited liability company, Hengrui adopts a flat organizational structure that emphasizes efficient decision-making and cooperation. Since 1990, the Chairperson, Sun Piaoyang, has been entrusted with a mission at a critical and difficult moment. He showed a brand-new path for Hengrui's development. To illustrate, he promoted the strategic transformation of generic medicine into innovative medicine, helping Hengrui become the industry leader. In terms of R&D, Sun promoted reforms to increase investment, which has facilitated the development of innovative medicines.

Today, Hengrui's global clinical trial network spans the United States, Europe, Australia, and Japan, and has initiated over 20 overseas clinical trials. Particularly, Hengrui's products are exported to over 40 countries. With a workforce exceeding 24,000 and a market capitalization of 407 billion yuan, Hengrui is not merely a Chinese champion but an emerging global contender—actively breaking regulatory and market barriers while building scientific and commercial bridges across continents.

Motivation for Global Expansion

The domestic policy squeeze and market saturation were the essential drivers of Hengrui's overseas expansion. To be specific, centralized procurement since 2018 has significantly affected Hengrui's growth. As a result, the company has to transform towards a high-premium international market to enhance its performance. In addition, the competition in the domestic market also intensified. Because of the many sub-markets within the innovative medicine industry, and given the large number of existing enterprises, the industry is currently in a state of decentralized competition (Qianzhan Industry Research Institute, 2025). Therefore, Hengrui must find an alternative path to sustain profits and competitiveness.

Meanwhile, the sheer scale and higher pricing potential of the global pharmaceutical market present an undeniable allure. The global innovative medicine market is enormous, while China's market accounts for only 3% of the global total, leaving vast room for expansion (Zhu et al., 2025). By "going global", pharmaceutical companies can access a broader market, commercialize their products, and acquire greater commercial value. Simultaneously, because participation in global competition has become the mainstream development path for domestic pharmaceutical firms, international development is also one of the most essential strategic guidelines that Hengrui has insisted on for over 20 years. Therefore, Hengrui further pursued international development and aimed to achieve sustainable profits in its global markets to address domestic and international challenges.

To enhance competitiveness in the overseas market, Hengrui implemented several strategies. Beginning with an introduction from the R&D side, the company first established overseas offices and R&D centers. To illustrate, Hengrui established a wholly owned subsidiary, Hengrui USA LLC, in 2005. It started from the clinical R&D end, undertaking research on innovative medicines, including frontier targets, the introduction or transfer of new medicine technology projects, and the registration application for generic medicines in the United States. After that, the wholly owned subsidiaries Cadiasun Pharman GmbH in Germany and Japan Hengrui Pharmaceutical in Nagoya were established in 2009 and 2014, respectively, facilitating entry into these key regulated markets. In recent years, the company has continuously invested approximately 20% of its annual revenue in research and development, establishing a comprehensive pipeline across small-molecule chemical medicines, biopharmaceuticals, gene therapy, and other fields, diversifying its revenue streams. Meanwhile, the company has actively aligned its R&D standards with international requirements, ensuring that both its clinical trial designs and current Good Manufacturing Practice (cGMP) systems comply with FDA and EMA regulations, establishing a solid technical foundation for global expansion.

From the aspect of domestic policies, the Chinese government published "A Practical Plan for Full-chain Support of Innovative Medicine Development", which clarified innovative medicine as an emerging industry. It emphasized the crucial role that pharmaceutical companies play. Meanwhile, Hengrui seized opportunities under the "Belt and Road", gradually strengthening product registration efforts in Russia, the Middle East, and Southeast Asian countries to enhance the accessibility of drugs to patients across different regions around the world.

MARKET ANALYSIS AND ENTRY STRATEGY

Target Market Selection

Hengrui's decision on its target market and target customers is based on both macro and micro factors. To be specific, it depends on the international environment, consumers' demand, and local competition. Hengrui prioritized the United States and the European Union as primary targets, followed by Japan and other developed markets, and capitalized on policy-driven opportunities in Southeast Asia. These selections reflect their ambition and geopolitical foresight.

The international environment is one of the most significant aspects in analyzing the macro-environment in the target market. To begin with, the pharmaceutical industry has a relatively loose environment. For instance, although during the 2025 US tariff war tariffs were imposed on all trading countries, there was still an exemption list that included industrial raw materials and chemicals, semiconductors and electronics-related items, and so on. Among them, industrial raw materials and chemicals include medicines and other raw materials, which helped the pharmaceutical industry remain flourishing after tariffs were imposed. Therefore, there is still growth potential in both domestic and overseas markets. In addition, the prioritization of Western markets stems from rigorous clinical and economic calculus. Because Western countries have higher economic performance and well-developed medical systems, Hengrui should lay the foundation for its development and ensure its development path during the exploration stage. A case in point is that Hengrui's multiple ADC products, independently developed by the company, have been granted FDA fast-track designation, which lays the foundation for sped-up approval of its products in the US market (Liu, 2025).

From the perspective of consumer demand, Hengrui's customers are chronic patients worldwide. According to GBD, 2021 Forecasting Collaborators (2024), the mortalities of 42 million people and 1.6 billion disability-adjusted life years were caused by non-communicable diseases (NCDs). Two-thirds of the deaths from these NCDs and 40% of the disability-adjusted life years were attributed to four chronic diseases, such as cancer (tumors), coronary heart disease, stroke, and diabetes. The potential demand for Hengrui's products worldwide is quite high. In addition, developed countries such as America, Europe, Australia, and Japan have a greater awareness of chronic diseases. For one, by targeting such countries, Hengrui may achieve higher sales volumes and profits. Governments in such regions are more likely to support the development of local pharmaceutical enterprises. By collaborating with local pharmaceutical companies, Hengrui can also effectively increase demand for its products and raise additional funds to support its R&D in innovative medicines. Meanwhile, the mature medical systems and sales channels in developed countries can make Hengrui's products more accessible to target customers.

As for policy-driven markets, Hengrui strategically targets markets characterized by lower competitiveness and weaker pharmaceutical capabilities. In recent years, more emerging markets, such as Southeast Asian countries, have been motivated by the Belt and Road Initiative. Southeast Asia, the Middle East, and South Africa show a high demand for generic and biosimilar medicines (Kathy, 2025). Especially the 158 countries and regions covered by the Belt and Road Initiative, which offer an almost untapped and well-structured market for Chinese pharmaceutical enterprises to expand their overseas business. In addition, in most Middle Eastern and North African countries, medical regulatory system managers often have backgrounds of studying or working in Europe and the United States (Kathy, 2025). Although some countries have lower levels of economic development than China, they have already introduced relevant systems from the US FDA or the European EMA in pharmaceutical regulation, reflecting governmental support for the pharmaceutical industry and investment in R&D. From the perspective of population or potential patients, the total population of the countries along the Belt and Road Initiative, including China, amounts to 4.4 billion, accounting for two-thirds of the global population (Kathy, 2025). As a result, Hengrui can attract more customers and increase profits.

Entry Mode Selection

Licensing-out is the core overseas expansion mode for Hengrui. It is defined as pharmaceutical companies licensing their own developed medicines or technologies to other companies, especially multinational pharmaceutical companies, which then handle subsequent development and commercialization. This approach efficiently promotes global commercialization through resource integration, risk-sharing, and sped up R&D. To date, Hengrui has completed 16 licensing agreements for its innovative medicines, with a total transaction value exceeding 10 billion USD (Liu, 2025). These collaborations secured substantial capital and international recognition for Hengrui's innovations.

In the early licensing-out stage, Hengrui focused on licensing a single product and regional cooperation to mitigate the risks of overseas expansion. For example, the company signed agreements with the US company Incyte and the South Korean company CrystalGenomics (CG) in 2015 and 2018, respectively, to develop the PD-1 antibody Camrelizumab. Among them, the Incyte licensing marked the first overseas licensing of an innovative biopharmaceutical in China. However, this meaningful agreement was ended by Incyte in 2018. Therefore, to avoid repeating the same mistake and potential loss, Hengrui announced the establishment of a joint management committee with CG to conduct strategic oversight of the development and marketing of the licensed products. Unless terminated in advance according to the agreement between the two parties, this agreement will continue until the end of the sales royalty period. Through early exploration, Hengrui verified the market potential of its overseas products and accumulated experience in international cooperation.

Hengrui currently employs two more mature license-out approaches. To begin with, a high-down-payment model for a single product was implemented in March 2025 in cooperation with Merck Sharp & Dohme LLC (MSD). Under the agreement, MSD will provide a \$200 million down payment, with subsequent development, regulatory, and commercialization milestones potentially reaching \$1.77 billion (Hengrui, 2025). Meanwhile, Hengrui can also receive a royalty on overseas sales. This model allows Hengrui to leverage MSD's global network to rapidly enter mainstream Western markets, avoiding the high costs and risks of establishing its own overseas team. This "high down payment + high milestone payment" mode effectively shows MSD's approval of HRS-5346's potential. It will also motivate future R&D. This cooperation dispelled the stereotype that the Chinese market relies on imports, proving that Chinese pharmaceutical companies can develop original technologies.

In addition, on July 28, 2025, Hengrui announced a license-out agreement with GlaxoSmithKline (GSK). The agreement includes an exclusive license for a potential superior PDE3/4 inhibitor, HRS-9821, which is currently in the clinical development stage to treat chronic obstructive pulmonary disease (COPD), and 11 projects that Hengrui will lead for R&D, will complete the first phase of clinical trials by the latest that GSK has the right of priority choice (Hengrui, 2025). The transaction structure includes a $500 million down payment, with potential milestone payments across option exercise, development, registration, and commercialization stages, totaling up to $12.5 billion. This partnership reflects a strategic shift in Hengrui's approach to global expansion. To illustrate, Hengrui has fully used and magnified GSK's advantages, achieving a rebalancing of "technology for market". Unlike in the past, when they were accustomed to conducting global multicenter clinical trials on their own, which were costly and time-consuming, they have now transferred their overseas rights to GSK, which is familiar with European and American regulations and proficient in respiratory and inflammatory diseases. This move reduces Hengrui's risks and offloads the cost-intensive late-stage clinical and commercialization phases to GSK. Such external validation of Hengrui's R&D capacity also strengthens investor confidence, while facilitating access to international sales channels and potential new partners.

The above agreements show Hengrui's strategic evolution from a "single-product, high-down-payment" model to a "portfolio-based, low-upfront, high-milestone" approach, transitioning from short-term to long-term transactions symbiotic partnerships. Through technology licensing, domestic firms can not only share the benefits of the global market but also integrate more deeply into the international division of labor. For instance, the GSK collaboration provided Hengrui with financial support, directly improving its short-term cash flow and boosting its profit by 2025. If R&D fails, it need not bear all the losses. The high-value licensing also strengthens its global bargaining power, facilitating access to additional resources. In the long term, license-out helps Hengrui achieve long-term benefits. For example, in 2024, Hengrui held 19.9% of the shares, making it the second-largest shareholder in the new company Hercules, established in cooperation with a major US fund, which can be recognized as a NewCo. Under this US company's name, it promoted the clinical development, approval, and listing of the pipeline. The newly established NewCo concentrates resources to promote pipeline development, accelerate clinical trials and international registration processes, and enable products to be rapidly launched into overseas markets. This model mitigates geopolitical and cross-cultural complexities by leveraging US capital and pharmaceutical networks to advance pipeline development.

However, licensing-out also entails challenges. The major risk is R&D failure. Nearly 95% of innovative medicines fail at the clinical stage, resulting in the waste of large amounts of milestone payments (Sundial in the Shadow, 2025). Geopolitical issues also pose threats. For instance, the FDA has postponed approval of the first-line PD-1 inhibitor carilizumab combined with apatinib ("Double Ai" therapy) because of production site inspection issues and travel restrictions in some countries. The FDA cannot complete inspections in some regions of global clinical trials within the review period (Wei, 2024). Therefore, factors such as international trade friction may affect the implementation of licensing transactions.

Competitive Advantage

Hengrui's competitive advantage in the overseas market is not solely based on technical or cost advantages. Its success and competitiveness are attributed to its strategic approach of consistently conducting product research and development and selecting the right partners. It focuses on differentiation while also reducing costs to enhance its competitiveness. Such a strategic layout shows the company's forward-looking perspective and insight into the overseas market. It represents the path for Chinese pharmaceutical enterprises to transform from technology followers to rule collaborators.

Hengrui's product differentiation is driven by innovation. Hengrui has optimized its product pipeline layout and continuously enriched and developed its research and development pipeline. Besides continuously deepening its expertise in the traditional tumor field, it has also made extensive deployments in areas such as autoimmune diseases, metabolic diseases, cardiovascular diseases, and respiratory system diseases. According to Hengrui's 2024 Annual Report (2025), its R&D investment reached 8.228 billion yuan in 2024, and the cumulative R&D investment exceeded 44 billion yuan. It has 147 medicine pipelines, of which 94% are independently developed. The diversified pipeline has expanded its target customer base and may help complete potential orders. Continuous innovation can lead to the emergence of new products that its competitors cannot provide. Hengrui can leverage its new products to attract customers and expand its presence in overseas markets and stabilize its position.

In addition, Hengrui's differentiated competitive advantage is reinforced by significant technological barriers. The company ensures all its high-quality export products comply with the standards of the European Pharmacopoeia and the United States Pharmacopeia (Rui, 2024). By 2025, Hengrui had secured US FDA Orphan Drug Designation (ODD) for four innovative medicines, with an additional four receiving FDA Fast Track status. After obtaining orphan drug qualification, it is expected to speed up the progress of clinical trials and product registration. Meanwhile, it can enjoy certain policy support, including, but not limited to, tax credits for clinical trial expenses, exemption from new drug application fees, and 7 years of market exclusivity after product approval (Hengrui, 2025). In generic medicines, Hengrui achieved efficient market penetration through a strategy of monopolizing the first generic medicine period. The company seized the window of opportunity during the US patent cliff for medicines. In 2022, iodixanol injection became the first generic medicine approved by the FDA for this product, and it received a 180-day market exclusivity period under the "Competitive Generic Drug Therapy Act" (CGT). In 2024, this strategy was further extended to products such as bupivacaine liposome injection and tacrolimus sustained-release capsules. Among them, bupivacaine liposome was the first medicine that generalized globally, directly filling the shortage drug market in the United States. Such policy benefits can make Hengrui's products more accessible to the market than competitors' products . Certified medicines can help Hengrui gain credibility and a stronger reputation, and customers will be more confident in their purchases.

Hengrui's overseas cooperation, and sales models are worth discussing as well. It is a diversified licensing framework. For instance, its equity-linked cooperation with Hercules in 2024 broke through the limitations of traditional licensing transactions, enabling Hengrui to take part in decision-making as a shareholder, share long-term asset appreciation, and mitigate intermediary premium losses. Similarly, the 2025 bundled pipeline agreement with GSK dispersed early-stage R&D risks, reduced costs, and established sustainable value-creation channels. Besides, cooperation with foreign companies provided Hengrui with expanded access to local markets. Currently, Hengrui has R&D centers worldwide. Compared with competitors, it was better able to grasp the dynamics of the overseas market and to develop products more comprehensively. To break through the "dependence on authorization" ceiling, Hengrui is speeding up the establishment of an independent overseas operations system. To illustrate, it established the Luzsana subsidiary in the United States, which specializes in the global development of 11 high-potential projects, covering the entire process from pre-clinical to phase III (Wei, 2024). Despite initial cross-cultural management challenges, Hengrui has progressively built in-house clinical and regulatory capabilities, diminishing reliance on multinational partners. These overseas collaborations also provide global clinical trial channels, which could generate differentiated data and promote the R&D of its products.

IMPLEMENTATION OF GLOBAL EXPANSION

Key Initiatives and Investments

Hengrui put a lot of effort into adapting to overseas markets. The most important actions it took were going public in Hong Kong and collaborating with overseas pharmaceutical companies. Both actions have helped Hengrui expand its sales platform and raise additional funds. Hengrui has deeply integrated with international giants to reduce the risks of going global and has used the capital market to connect its global resource network, forming a strategic closed loop for its overseas expansion.

Hengrui disclosed its plan to go public in Hong Kong in December 2024. It intends to issue H-share stocks and list them on the main board of the Hong Kong Stock Exchange. The net proceeds from the offering should fund innovation R&D, product commercialization, and corporate operations. Many analyst reports showed that the Hong Kong listing would enable Hengrui to increase R&D investment, accelerate the development of innovative medicines, and enhance its competitiveness. The company's valuation in overseas markets is expected to change as its overseas expansion strategy progresses smoothly (Wang, 2025). Hengrui achieved its Hong Kong IPO in May 2025, raising 1.3 billion US dollars. It became the largest listing project in the Hong Kong pharmaceutical sector in the past 5 years. This IPO attracted a group of top global investment institutions as cornerstone investors, including the Singapore Government Investment Corporation (GIC), Invesco, UBS Global Asset Management Group (UBS-GAM), Hailong Capital, and Boyu Capital. Their combined subscriptions totaled approximately 4.1 billion Hong Kong dollars (533 million USD), accounting for 43.04% of the issuance size (Stone, 2025). This investor profile reflects strong international confidence in Hengrui and provides strategic support for its global growth. Notably, the Hong Kong capital market has abundant international investor resources, which not only further enhances Hengrui's brand reputation in the global pharmaceutical industry but also opens new financing channels and optimizes its capital structure. It will strengthen the company's worldwide presence, laying a foundation for overseas business expansion and international R&D cooperation, supporting further breakthroughs in global markets.

Besides, the overseas strategic partners chosen by Hengrui can also show its profound understanding of the overseas market. While employing the traditional license-out model, the company has also pioneered the NewCo model through the establishment of US-based Hercules. Hengrui's business development strategies have grown across four key dimensions: the cooperation stage has been advanced from the clinical later stage to the early stage, the cooperation objects have upgraded from small and medium-sized Biotech to multinational pharmaceutical companies, and the transaction structure is not limited to simple licensing, non-tumor projects are becoming a new hotspot for BD cooperation (Wang, 2025). In terms of License-out, it opened up a relatively fast internationalization channel for those Chinese innovative pharmaceutical enterprises with limited resources and little international experience. Hengrui has reached 16 cooperation agreements with well-known overseas enterprises, including GSK, MSD, and Kailera. These collaborations have enhanced the company's understanding of overseas regulations, expanded sales channels, and generated significant funding. However, valuation differences remain the most common challenge. Domestic enterprises focus on R&D potential, while foreign enterprises pay more attention to market size, clinical trial data, and the predictability of regulatory approval (Ji, 2025). Therefore, Hengrui applied the NewCo strategy, acquiring a 19.9% stake in Hercules. This approach not only eases financial pressure in international expansion but also enhances drug competitiveness through independent operations, with potential for future equity appreciation through an IPO or acquisition.

The US-based subsidiary of Hengrui, Luzsana, is led by a former Merck executive and is advancing its global expansion through a decentralized operational model. As a global cooperative development partner for Hengrui's product development and commercialization, it operates with substantial autonomy in selecting candidates from Hengrui's pipeline and driving their development and regulatory approval in markets outside China. It maintains direct engagement with key regulators, such as the FDA and EMA, and emphasizes compliance with international standards from the earliest stages of trial design. Such organizational adjustments enable Hengrui to flexibly allocate its global R&D resources and achieve deeper penetration into mainstream international markets.

Hengrui has grown its investment in research and development and sales expenses. According to its 2024 Annual Report (2025), the company's cumulative R&D expenditure reached RMB 8.228 billion during the reporting period, setting a record high. Among this, the expensed R&D investment totaled RMB 6.583 billion, accounting for 29.40% of sales revenue. As of now, Hengrui's cumulative R&D investment has exceeded 44 billion yuan. Constant investment in R&D has sped up new product launches. To be specific, it plans to launch 11 new products in 2025, 13 in 2026, and 23 in 2027. In 2023, the first year of the globalization of Chinese innovative medicines, Hengrui's R&D expenses reached approximately RMB 4.954 billion, while sales expenses exceeded R&D spending by RMB 2.623 billion (Hengrui, 2024). Sales expenses were mainly used for market activities, such as academic promotion and the construction of an innovative medicine specialized platform, totaling RMB 3.877 billion, accounting for 51.17%. These activities have significantly enhanced Hengrui's global reputation. Hengrui plans to allocate 75% of the funds raised from its Hong Kong stock listing to R&D, 15% to overseas production and research facilities, and 10% to working capital (Ji, 2025). This allocation strategy will further enhance its competitiveness in the global market for innovative drugs.

Differentiated clinical trial designs and diversified collaboration models are also adopted to address varying regional regulatory requirements. While only 25% of clinical trials in China employ blinding, over 70% of trials in the US, Europe, and Japan do, reflecting China's emphasis on local relevance. Western countries prioritize global applicability (Li et al., 2021). In response, international clinical trials are progressing steadily. Currently, Hengrui has launched over 20 overseas clinical trials in countries and regions such as the United States, Europe, Australia, Japan, and South Korea, to meet diverse regional design standards and mitigate supply chain geopolitical risks. Hengrui has established overseas subsidiaries to strengthen local clinical development capabilities and speed up its international regulatory strategy.

Challenges Faced

Hengrui Pharmaceuticals has encountered significant challenges in its overseas expansion, particularly in drug review, registration, and License-out. Exploring the fundamental factors underlying these challenges and finding solutions are of great significance to Hengrui and other innovative pharmaceutical enterprises aiming to go global.

Hengrui's business model has encountered challenges because of its reliance on license-out arrangements. From a revenue perspective, the company's overseas revenue remains negligible. The current licensing-out model entails significant trade-offs, including the loss of long-term returns in international markets. Since the down payment for business development is a onetime income, it leads to significant fluctuations in quarterly performance, affecting the R&D funds. In the license-out cooperation, Hengrui has also had experiences of "selling at a loss", such as licensing the first-class new drug SHR-1905 injection project to the US company Aiolos Bio in 2023. Later, this company was gained by GSK at a premium, and Hengrui failed to share the subsequent appreciation fully; it received only a double-digit percentage of sales commissions from annual net sales, a return substantially below the product's potential value. Positively, this cooperation was highly recognized by GSK, establishing a foundation for future development. Therefore, in the subsequent cooperation with Hercules, Hengrui continued to adopt the approach of first transferring to small companies and then seeking larger buyers, securing future benefits through ownership.

Hengrui also faces significant regulatory barriers stemming from divergent market and geopolitical environments. A case in point is that its PD-1 inhibitor, camrelizumab, combined with apatinib (the "double AI" therapy), was initially rejected by the FDA in May 2024 and later granted a second extension in March

2025. In July 2023, the company first submitted its marketing application for Double AI therapy to the FDA. Because defects in the production site inspection, as well as travel restrictions in some countries, resulted in difficulties in monitoring the production details and being unable to fully complete the biological research monitoring plan (BIMO) clinical checks for this project (Ji, 2025). This setback considerably dampened Hengrui's initial momentum in overseas expansion. However, Hengrui overcame the difficulties and resubmitted the application to the FDA in January 2025. Although Hengrui has rectified the issues that occurred last time, the FDA still proposed three new improvement requirements, underscoring its rigorous standards for dynamic quality management. This experience reveals fundamental challenges confronting Chinese pharmaceutical companies in global expansion. Although both countries emphasize the safety, effectiveness, and quality control of medicines, the United States places greater emphasis on the innovation and clinical value of medicines. It conducts more detailed assessments of the long-term safety and potential risks of medicines. To navigate these differences, Chinese companies planning to enter the international market must align with international standards through optimized clinical trial design, ensure data reliability and completeness throughout the research and development process.

Meanwhile, Hengrui is also confronting fierce competition in overseas markets. The rapid international expansion of domestic pharmaceutical companies is compressing market opportunities for local firms. Therefore, international giants will localize production to reduce costs and gain market share, constraining the growth of Chinese pharmaceutical companies. For instance, MSD has established biopharmaceutical factories in Europe to circumvent tariff barriers, and Trump recently announced that the tariffs on pharmaceuticals would be gradually raised to 250% to ensure the development of the domestic pharmaceutical industry in the United States (Alex, 2025). Although Hengrui has entered the US market, potential additional tariffs could erode profitability and undermine price competitiveness. This squeezing effect also affects the supply chain. European and American regulatory agencies have further raised the entry threshold by adding requirements for local production. For example, the FDA's 2024 regulations will mandate traceability of raw materials and audits of key excipient suppliers, while Hengrui's core materials, such as culture media and chromatography packing materials, depend highly on imports, creating vulnerability to "technical supply disruption" driven by geopolitical factors.

The overseas expansion of other leading Chinese pharmaceutical companies is also a major source of competition for Hengrui. Compared with its principal competitor, BeiGene, Hengrui maintains an advantage through a broader therapeutic pipeline, whereas BeiGene remains predominantly focused on oncology. Strategically, Hengrui pursues sped up capital returns primarily through license-out and NewCo partnerships and emphasizes independent overseas R&D, yielding greater long-term resilience and control. With a mature global commercial infrastructure and core products that have secured FDA approvals, BeiGene is at a more advanced stage of internationalization than Hengrui, which is still in the earlier phases of global expansion. Similarly, Fosun Pharmaceutical employs overseas acquisitions and localized operations as its principal international strategy. Although its competitiveness is not significant at present, it has the potential to become a future competitor to Hengrui. In the future, Hengrui should continue to unlock the value of its pipeline through licensing out and reduce its excessive reliance on the domestic market.

Mitigation Strategies

In response to the challenges already encountered and those yet to come, Hengrui proactively refines its strategies to maximize value. The president and chief operating officer of Hengrui Pharmaceutical, Feng Ji, stated that the company's internationalization strategy continues to prioritize both internal growth and external cooperation, steadily advancing its internationalization (Li, 2025). In the current environment of global uncertainties, the company will prioritize cooperation with leading global pharmaceutical enterprises, while retaining domestic development rights and covering overseas markets as much as possible.

To address revenue volatility under the license-out model, Hengrui has innovatively applied the "Equity Binding + Deep Participation" NewCo model. This approach enables capital appreciation through financing and public listing while allowing the company to gain advanced R&D and commercialization expertise through hands-on involvement in product development. To illustrate, in May 2024, Hengrui's 3 GLP-1 product portfolio completed a $6 billion overseas transaction through a NewCo. The company voluntarily licensed its proprietary GLP-1 product portfolio to the US-based Hercules Company. According to the transaction's financial terms, the total initial payment and future milestone payments could reach $6 billion. Notably, Hengrui secured 19.9% equity in Hercules and will receive future sales royalties. This model provides dual benefits: Hengrui extends its product pipeline lifecycle while investors access lower-cost opportunities with rapid appreciation potential through eventual acquisition by multinational corporations. Unlike a onetime transaction, domestic innovative pharmaceutical companies can not only receive financial support but also get equity from the partner, securing a significant share of rights and interests in subsequent product research and development and even commercialization. By attracting international capital and establishing global management teams, Hengrui maximizes product value while maintaining controlled risk exposure. The company will continue to adopt a cautious strategy and pursue independent global development in certain helpful fields.

To address the FDA's production compliance concerns, Hengrui has proactively implemented corrective measures. For example, the FDA has verified that all issues identified during the inspection that led to the 2024 CRL have been resolved, while proposing three new improvement requirements. The company has responded positively to the relevant issues within the specified time and has maintained close communication with the FDA. Remarkably, among the approved treatment regimens for unresectable or metastatic hepatocellular carcinoma, camrelizumab combined with apatinib has achieved the longest median overall survival (mOS) to date. (Ji, 2025). Given this significant clinical value, Hengrui remains committed to pursuing US approval, and the FDA will not completely reject Hengrui's application. However, this serves as a warning to Hengrui and other pharmaceutical companies applying within the FDA regulatory framework that historical compliance issues and a superficial quality culture ultimately manifest as regulatory risks. Companies must transcend the short-term mindset of responding to inspections and build a quality management system driven by real, traceable data and risk-based decision-making.

The NewCo model is an effective solution for addressing supply chain issues caused by geopolitical risks. Hengrui can continuously improve in areas such as product differentiation, cost control, and R&D efficiency, enabling its products to speed up their entry into overseas markets. To illustrate, this structure provides Hengrui access to a professional team that is both proficient in pharmaceutical research and development and familiar with international market operations. Thus, the company can deepen its international cooperation, actively expand its overseas R&D boundaries, and enhance its competitiveness. Hengrui's core driving force is continuous innovation. By offering more high-quality, innovative drug products, Hengrui can carve out its own territory in the overseas market.

STRATEGIC ANALYSIS

Analytical Frameworks

From a policy perspective, the pharmaceutical industry's revenue from 2018 to 2024 was severely affected by national centralized procurement. In 2021, the National Health Commission issued the "Guiding Opinions on the Centralized Procurement of High-value Medical Consumables". Hengrui, which started with generic drugs, has also been seriously affected. For one, during the fifth and ninth national centralized procurement rounds, Hengrui failed to win bids for products such as contrast agents and anesthetics. The significant price cut made it impossible to tradeoff between price and quantity. Insufficient price reductions would lead to a loss of market share to competitors. Internal price competition in generic drugs decreased Hengrui's revenue by 6.59% in 2021 and by 17.87% in 2022. (Hu, 2024). The field of innovative drugs is also crowded with domestic and foreign competitors. Therefore, it went global for more opportunities. In addition, the impact of US tariffs may grow as Hengrui's overseas revenue grows in the future.

There is considerable pressure from international regulations, such as the clinical trials and supply chain traceability audits required by the FDA, and travel restrictions in some countries have hindered the review process. Therefore, Hengrui has diversified its exposure to geopolitical risks through international cooperation. Fortunately, on June 30, 2025, the National Healthcare Security Administration and the National Health Commission jointly issued "Several Measures to Support the High-Quality Development of Innovative Drugs", proposing to promote the global market for innovative drugs. This includes establishing an innovative medicine trading platform, assisting innovative enterprises in rapid development, and providing price support. In addition, since April 30, 2018, the Hong Kong Stock Exchange's 18A rules have allowed the listing of pre-profit biotech companies, facilitating financing and streamlining approvals for research-intensive firms. Together, these policies provide strong institutional support for Hengrui's overseas expansion.

In terms of the economy, Hengrui has strengthened its financial position through high-value license-out agreements and a successful Hong Kong IPO in 2025. Its stocks reached the limit up on the Chinese A-share main board on July 28, 2025, and the listing on the Hong Kong stock market was also supported by many leading funds, which facilitated Hengrui's overseas trial expenses and the construction of its sales platform.

Socially, global demographic and disease trends support Hengrui's strategic focus. Aging populations and the rising chronic disease burden are expanding international demand for therapeutics. As residents' quality of life improves, people will be more willing to spend on treating chronic diseases. Hengrui's products are mostly targeted at chronic diseases. Through overseas cooperative companies, Hengrui can directly expand its sales channels into high-demand markets in Europe and the United States, achieving greater profits.

Hengrui's globalization relies on its innovative technologies. For instance, in biologics, it has established a powerful ADC technology platform through independent research and development. Its recognition by FTD from the US FDA and orphan drug qualification have become the core bargaining chips for Hengrui in negotiations with international giants. Meanwhile, Hengrui is actively exploring AI-assisted drug design, which has reduced the research and development risks.

Environmentally, Hengrui has achieved an A rating in the MSCI ESG assessment for two consecutive years, in 2024, and received an AA score in the Huazheng ESG assessment, which is at the leading level in the Chinese pharmaceutical industry. This shows that Hengrui attaches great importance to sustainable development in its innovation transformation, which helps overseas large multinational enterprises and investors give Hengrui priority consideration when choosing a partner.

Legally, Hengrui has Intellectual Property Protection, establishing a robust patent portfolio of 585 domestic and 705 international patents, strengthening its technological barriers to entry. However, it also faces challenges with FDA compliance, having been rejected twice by the FDA, showing that Hengrui should pay close attention to compliance for each process.

Brand and Reputation Effects

Hengrui's reputation in the overseas market is mainly established on its professional drug innovation design capabilities and its social responsibility. To begin with, Hengrui has established a robust communication network by entering cooperation agreements with foreign giants. For instance, the cooperation between Hengrui and Aiolos Bio attracted potential partner GSK. Its professional products gained GSK's recognition and trust in its research capabilities, laying the foundation for formal cooperation with GSK in 2025. Such partnerships progressively enhance Hengrui's technical credibility and foster a virtuous cycle of international recognition and further collaboration. In addition, the acquisition of professional qualifications further strengthens the brand's credibility. For example, in August 2025, Hengrui got FDA fast-track designation for 4 drugs, and 4 innovative drugs received FDA orphan drug designation, enabling research registration and commercialization to benefit from US policies (Hengrui, 2025). These certifications from the world's most stringent regulatory agencies convey the "technical parity" signal to the medical professional community, further confirming and enhancing Hengrui's reputation.

Meanwhile, Hengrui has also showed the brand's humanistic care and warmth in its commitment to social responsibility. Hengrui has made donations to the country and the international community during times of hardship. For instance, during the COVID-19 pandemic, Hengrui donated 30 million yuan in special funds and medical protective supplies nationwide (Yue, 2020). When the overseas epidemic broke out, Hengrui Pharmaceutical produced medicines and simultaneously prevent the epidemic with no disruption, promoting the "going global" of high-quality medicines and ensuring the supply of medicines in overseas markets. Among these, to meet the urgent needs of the Belgian government for benzolipine succinate atracurium injection, the company worked overtime to arrange production, overcoming challenges such as the scarcity of domestic flights and transportation difficulties, and promptly delivered the medicine to Belgium to address the local government's immediate needs. Hengrui Pharmaceutical actively established communication channels at home and abroad, providing a platform for remote sharing of anti-epidemic experience and assisting Chinese medical institutions in connecting with medical institutions in Italy, Japan, and other countries via video. Thus, Hengrui's enthusiastic help and sincerity have established a humanized reputation for it.

In the ESG space, the ESG-based investment strategy is increasingly a hot topic both domestically and internationally. Currently, Hengrui's ESG performance ranks at the forefront of the industry, establishing a strong reputation for social responsibility and enabling it to attract investors who use ESG as a reference criterion. Hengrui has also actively met the FDA's traceability requirements, promoting green development and enhancing its image as an enterprise that assumes social responsibilities.

CONCLUSION AND STRATEGIC RECOMMENDATIONS

Summary of Key Findings

This article tells the story of Hengrui Pharmaceuticals' efforts to break barriers and build bridges in its pursuit of overseas development. Through a detailed exploration of its motivations, competitive advantages, and challenges, the article showcases Hengrui's efforts and ambition in its overseas expansion. The core of its success lies in the dual-track drive of differentiated technology layout and innovative cooperation models. It navigates through policy benefits and geopolitical risks to seek breakthrough opportunities. In terms of cooperation models, the company has chosen the License-out and the novel NewCo model to license its innovative medical technology to foreign partners and leverage their global market networks to enter quickly, especially high-barrier markets in Europe and the United States. The company has broken through the traditional limitations of cooperation, combining authorization with low upfront payments and high milestone payments in its collaboration with GSK, shifting its focus from short-term returns to long-term benefits. Through its cooperation with Hercules, it used a 19.9% equity stake to avoid the potential problem of partners withdrawing halfway and to reduce default risk. It's listing on the Hong Kong Stock Exchange in 2025 has earned it significant trust and research and development funding, facilitating the establishment of an international platform. In addition, the company attaches great importance to R&D and has invested heavily in its overseas clinical research. It has received FDA fast-track designation for 4 drugs, and 4 innovative drugs have received FDA orphan drug designation. Notably, Hengrui's PD-1 "Double Ai" therapy was rejected twice by the US FDA, exposing potential production compliance issues. Before becoming a large multinational enterprise, it still needs to make efforts.

Future Growth Opportunities

Currently, Hengrui's overseas expansion is still in its early stages. Although its overseas revenue accounts for a tiny proportion, its efforts show its emphasis on the overseas market. The company will closely monitor changes in the international environment and flexibly respond to external challenges to ensure the long-term, stable development of Hengrui and maximize its market influence.

Looking ahead, Hengrui aims to achieve greater breakthroughs in the export of innovative drugs, with continuous innovation remaining its core driver. Sustained investment in R&D and introducing therapeutics with differentiated profiles form the foundation of its international presence. The company seeks to develop multiple blockbuster products for overseas markets to improve profit margins and reduce reliance on domestic sales. By leveraging its innovative products, Hengrui can pursue partnerships with global pharmaceutical leaders to get additional funding. In addition, Hengrui's BD potential is substantial, as evidenced by its record-breaking BD transaction value. Its cooperation model has gradually matured, helping mitigate geopolitical risks and enhancing autonomy in overseas markets. Therefore, its future expansion may involve more NewCo forms of cooperation to avoid undervaluing its core value. Successful strategies from competitors with established international revenue streams will also be adopted. Strategic adjustments will enable Hengrui to advance independent research and development and commercialization overseas in the future. Conducting key registration clinical trials in the European and American markets and realizing the pipeline value through the license-out model. It is necessary to optimize the overseas expansion strategy and plan precise marketing and regulatory approval strategies tailored to the market characteristics and regulatory requirements of different countries and regions. If Hengrui resolves the issues raised by the FDA and more of its medicines get FDA certification in the future, it can receive greater overseas policy support and industry recognition, achieving higher profits.

Recommendations for Other Firms

The overseas expansion of Hengrui Pharmaceuticals' innovative medicines is a journey filled with challenges and opportunities. It not only embodies the enterprise's development aspirations but also shoulders the mission of promoting the internationalization of China's innovative drug industry. Through continuous breakthroughs and adjustments, Hengrui is expected to carve out its own territory in the global pharmaceutical market, providing more high-quality, innovative drug products to patients worldwide and writing a new chapter in the overseas expansion of Chinese innovative medicines. While other companies were still concentrating on generic drugs, Hengrui had already shifted its focus to emerging markets for innovative medicines.

Hengrui's overseas expansion story can serve as a perfect example for other enterprises to base their development on technology. Under the current complex international environment, only by truly mastering core technologies can one go further. Pharmaceutical innovation is a high-investment, high-risk, and long-cycle project. Researchers screen 10,000 compounds, but only a few enter clinical trials, and only 1-2 are approved for market launch (Song, 2020). This process takes over a decade and requires an investment of several billion yuan. For domestic enterprises, by combining "importation" and "exportation", they can not only effectively overcome development bottlenecks but also effectively connect with the international market and take a distinctive independent innovation path. Only by having more authoritative qualifications can technology be transformed into premium value. Second, a differentiated pipeline layout is also very important. Hengrui's research field coverage is extremely wide, which can avoid homogenized competition and provide more opportunities for itself.

Regarding its overseas expansion strategy, Hengrui has adopted a flexible upgrading approach. By employing various licensing strategies, it has skillfully avoided many risks and diversified its revenue sources. Besides licensing cooperation with major international pharmaceutical companies, it can also explore more diversified cooperation methods, such as conducting joint research and development with international research institutions and establishing strategic alliances with local pharmaceutical companies, to enhance its competitiveness in the international market. However, Hengrui's failure in the FDA review also served as a warning to other companies. They must not overlook any past compliance issues. To avoid additional unexpected expenses, they need to adhere to the review standards set by overseas authorities .

The internationalization journey of Hengrui Pharmaceuticals is precisely a two-way pursuit of "breaking barriers" and "building bridges". It uses the sharp blade of independent innovation to pierce through three layers of barriers: technical barriers, institutional barriers, and cognitive barriers, shattering the label that foreign countries believe Chinese enterprises can only survive by relying on licensing-in. Meanwhile, it establishes bridges across the world, bringing Chinese technology to foreign markets and offering hope of recovery to patients worldwide. Only by breaking through barriers and building bridges can China's pharmaceutical technology flow to the world and generate higher value.

REFERENCES

Alex, J. (2025, August 14). *Trump Pharma Tariffs Would Raise Drug Prices for Americans.* Tax Foundation. https://taxfoundation.org/blog/trump-tariffs-pharma-drug-prices/

GBD 2021 Fertility and Forecasting Collaborators. (2024). Global Fertility in 204 Countries and Territories, 1950–2021, with Forecasts to 2100: A Comprehensive Demographic Analysis for the Global Burden of Disease Study 2021. *The LANCET, 103*(10440), 2204-2256. DOI: 10.1016/S0140-6736(24)00550-6

Hengrui Pharmaceuticals. (2024, April 18). *Hengrui Pharmaceuticals: Hengrui Pharmaceuticals's 2023 Annual Report*. Eastmoney. https://pdf.dfcfw.com/pdf/H2_AN202404171630412062_1.pdf?1713380305000.pdf

Hengrui Pharmaceuticals. (2025, August 8). *Good News! Hengrui Pharmaceuticals' HER2 ADC Innovative Medicine, Trastuzumab Ruikang, has been granted Orphan Drug Designation by the US FDA*. Hengrui. https://www.hengrui.com/media/detail-821.html

Hengrui Pharmaceuticals. (2025, August 8). *Good News! Hengrui Pharmaceuticals' HER2 ADC Innovative Drug Recon Trastuzumab has been granted Orphan Drug Status by the US FDA*. Hengrui. https://www.hengrui.com/media/detail-821.html

Hengrui Pharmaceuticals. (2025, July 28). *Hengrui Pharmaceuticals' Announcement Regarding the Signing of a Cooperation, Option and License Agreement with GSK*. Hengrui. https://static.sse.com.cn/disclosure/listedinfo/announcement/c/new/2025-07-28/600276_20250728_7GZX.pdf

Hengrui Pharmaceuticals. (2025, March 26). *Hengrui Pharmaceuticals and Merck have signed an exclusive licensing agreement for the Lp(a) inhibitor HRS-5346*. Hengrui. https://www.hengrui.com/media/detail-743.html

Hengrui Pharmaceuticals. (2025, March 31). *Hengrui Pharmaceuticals: Hengrui Pharmaceuticals's 2024 Annual Report*. Hengrui. https://www.hengrui.com/investor/regularAnnouncement.html

Hu, Q. (2024, December 12). , [Hengrui Pharmaceuticals is Forced to Venture Overseas and Reveal its Weaknesses]. *Tencent*. https://news.qq.com/rain/a/20241212A05WAR00

Ji, Y. (2025, March 22). PD-1 “ ” ?[Why is Hengrui's “Going Global” Venture Blocked Again as the PD-1 Group's US Listing has been Postponed Twice?]. *21st Century Business Herald.* https://m.21jingji.com/article/20250322/156a123c2c6df4cdd426d7f12dee9832.html

Ji, Y. (2025, May 15). IPO! “ ” [The largest pharmaceutical IPO in Hong Kong in the past five years! A Capital Breakthrough that is not Short of Money]. *21st Century Business Herald.* https://www.21jingji.com/article/20250515/herald/7888b9617c364a6b3f1ee609a35362a9.html

Kathy. (2025, April 17). “ ”, “ ” , ! [*Hengrui and Kangfang “Set Sail for Southeast Asia”, while Fuhonghanlin and Junshi “are Competing in the Middle East”. It's Time for Pharmaceutical Companies to Change Their Strategies as They Expand Globally!*] Xueqiu. https://xueqiu.com/3483303916/332061578

Li, J., Li, H., Li, C., Chen, X., Zhang, X., & Wu, Y. (2021). Comparisons of Clinical Registration Trial Types, Designs and Completion Status of Drugs in China, the United States, Europe and Japan. *Chinese Journal of Evidence-Based Medicine, 21*(07), 845–850. https://doi.org/CNKI:SUN:ZZXZ.0.2021-07-015

Li, M. (2025, April 18). : [Hengrui Pharmaceuticals: Firmly Implement the Strategies of Scientific and Technological Innovation and Internationalization]. *China Securities Journal.* https://epaper.cs.com.cn/zgzqb/html/2025-04/18/nw.D110000zgzqb_20250418_3-A07.htm

Liu, J. (2025, Jun 18). *: ?[Innovative Drugs Going Global: How does Hengrui Medicine Break Through the Defenses of International Pharmaceutical Giants?*]. Sina. https://finance.sina.com.cn/cj/2025-06-18/doc-infanfym5833028.shtml

Qianzhan Industry Research Institute. (2025, March 26). *2025: ( )[Industry Depth Insight 2025: Analysis of the Competitive Landscape in China's Innovative Pharmaceutical Industry (Including Market Concentration ratio, R&D Strength ranking, etc.)*]. Sina. https://finance.sina.com.cn/roll/2025-03-26/doc-ineqxyiv9159522.shtml

Rui, W. (2024, January 9). : [Hengrui Pharmaceuticals: Dual-driven Strategy for Global Expansion]. *Pharmaceutical Economics News.* https://www.yyjjb.com.cn/yyjjb/202401/20240109152225225_17575.shtml

Stone, J. (2025, May 15). *: GIC 5.33 [Hengrui Pharmaceuticals Begins Share Offering Today: Secures $533 million in Cornerstone Subscriptions from GIC, UBS, HHLR, and Boyu Capital*]. Xueqiu. https://xueqiu.com/2854806290/335163197

Sundial in the Shadow. (2025, July 29). *,BD ,License-out( ),NewCo ( )* [*Innovative Medicines, BD Model, License-out (outsourcing), and NewCo model (cooperation with newly established companies)*]. Xueqiu. https://xueqiu.com/1122686438/344662911

Wang, L. (2025, May 7). , [Innovation and Internationalization Drive Together to Launch a Series of New Initiatives, and Hengrui Pharmaceuticals Underwent a Profound Transformation in its Ppgrading and Transformation Process]. *Beijing News*. https://m.bjnews.com.cn/detail/1746620446168854.html

Wei, X. (2024, May 24). [*The Next Step of Hengrui*]. Blue View. https://mp.weixin.qq.com/s/3Zqk7H8kFXoxZw6LdmxC8A

Yue, Q. (2020, July 10). 3 [Three Years of Charitable Donations Exceeded 100 million yuan.Hengrui Pharmaceuticals Initiated Several Special Funds to Support Education]. *Beijing News*. https://www.bjnews.com.cn/detail/159436987315456.html

Zhu, G., Zhang, C., & Zheng, C. (2025). *Special Research Report on the Innovative Pharmaceutical Industry: Innovation Breakthroughs, Overseas Expansion*. Dongwu Securities.

KEY TERMS AND DEFINITIONS

ADC (Antibody-Drug Conjugate): It is a type of drug formed by coupling a monoclonal antibody to a payload via a linker.

Apatinib Mesylate: A targeted drug for gastric cancer that can induce apoptosis.

Belt and Road: An economic cooperation initiative that has become an international regional economic cooperation platform.

Bupivacaine Liposome: A new type of long-lasting local anesthetic drug significantly prolongs the duration of pain relief and reduces side effects.

Camrelizumab (SHR-1210): A drug that has both anti-tumor activity and tolerability. Used to treat advanced lung cancer, liver cancer, etc.

CGMP (Current Good Manufacturing Practice): Regulations implemented by the FDA. Stipulates a system to ensure proper design, monitoring, and control of production processes and facilities.

COPD (Chronic Obstructive Pulmonary Disease): It refers to a lung disease characterized by chronic, often irreversible airway obstruction, leading to a slower exhalation rate.

EMA (European Medicines Agency): An agency responsible for assessing and supervising the centralized marketing authorization of drugs across the European region.

FTD (Fast Track Designation): A channel for accelerating drug research and review, this is a qualification recognition granted by the FDA.

GLP-1: It has a glucose concentration-dependent hypoglycemic effect and is an important drug to treat diabetes and obesity.

HRS-5346: An oral small molecule inhibitor of Lp(a), still in the second phase of clinical trials, has efficacy in preventing and treating cardiovascular diseases.

HRS-9821: A potent inhibitor of PDE3 and PDE4 proteins, with bronchodilatory and anti-inflammatory effects, is still in the clinical stage and can treat COPD.

Iodixanol Injection: A contrast agent that, when injected, allows iodine to absorb X-rays within blood vessels or tissues, forming images.

Median Overall Survival (mOS): 50% of patients are expected to survive beyond this period. This is a commonly used indicator in the evaluation of tumor treatment efficacy.

ODD (Orphan Drugs Designation): A qualification recognition granted to drugs that are suitable for the prevention, treatment, and diagnosis of rare diseases.

US FDA (US Food and Drug Administration): The primary US regulatory and law enforcement agency for food, drugs, cosmetics, and related products.

Chapter 15
Tsingshan's Indonesian Nickel Strategy:
Enclave Growth, the Green Paradox, and ESG Accountability

Rismawati Rismawati
http://orcid.org/0000-0001-8046-6764
Universitas Muhammadiyah Palopo, Indonesia

EXECUTIVE SUMMARY

This chapter examines Tsingshan Holding Group's expansion into Indonesia through the Indonesia Morowali Industrial Park (IMIP), analysing the complex interplay between industrial strategy, geopolitical alignment, and socio-environmental consequences. Using a PESTEL framework, the analysis reveals how Indonesia's downstream processing policies and China's Belt and Road Initiative enabled the world's largest nickel processing facility, yet one marked by debates. The movement of Moronene indigenous communities, uncertain conditions for migrant workers, environmental coal-powered operations, and risks for Tsingshan and its electric vehicle partners show that the company's competitive advantage derives from regulatory asymmetries rather than technological superiority alone. This contributes a critical perspective on extractive globalization, arguing that large-scale resource investments in the Global South must transition from enclave-based growth toward ethical, sharing industrialism to achieve long-term validity and sustainability in an increasingly values-oriented global economy.

DOI: 10.4018/979-8-3373-4302-0.ch015

INTRODUCTION

Tsingshan Holding Group's expansion into Indonesia through the Indonesia Morowali Industrial Park (IMIP) illustrates how a Chinese vertically integrated nickel giant has become central to the global electric vehicle (EV) and green energy supply chain while generating profound socio-environmental controversy. Leveraging Indonesia's vast nickel reserves, downstream industrialization policy, and alignment with China's Belt and Road Initiative, Tsingshan built a greenfield, enclave-style industrial complex that internalizes mining, smelting, power generation, logistics, and export, achieving powerful cost leadership and supply security. However, this model rests heavily on weak regulation, low labour costs, coal-fired energy, and limited public oversight, shifting environmental and social risks onto remote, politically marginal regions such as Central Sulawesi. IMIP has displaced Moronene indigenous communities, eroded traditional fisheries and forests, and fostered precarious conditions for tens of thousands of migrant workers amid reports of dangerous worksites, restricted mobility, and inadequate grievance mechanisms. A PESTEL analysis reveals a project enabled by favourable political and economic conditions but undermined by social conflict, ecological degradation, and legal opacity, producing escalating reputational exposure for Tsingshan and its downstream EV partners. The case shows that Tsingshan's competitive advantage derives as much from regulatory asymmetries as from technological and organizational capabilities. It concludes that future viability depends on embedding robust ESG practices—decarbonizing operations, adopting global reporting standards, instituting co-governance with communities, and reallocating value towards restoration and social inclusion. For other firms, the case offers a warning: large-scale resource investments in the Global South must shift from extractive growth to ethical, participatory industrialism to sustain both legitimacy and long-term competitiveness.

As global industries undergo a substantial transition towards sustainability and technological progress, companies that control access to vital minerals are emerging as prominent leaders (Christmann & Lefebvre, 2022; Dou et al., 2023; Kumar & Vishwanathan, 2025; Yu, 2024). Tsingshan Holding Group has rapidly emerged as a crucial player in the global nickel supply chain, serving as a foundation for the electric vehicle (EV) revolution and the broader green energy transition. In China and using a vertically integrated corporate strategy, Tsingshan exemplifies a novel category of Chinese multinationals—technologically proficient, geopolitically astute, and globally ambitious (Yongtao & Sining, 2024).

This case study examines Tsingshan's global expansion strategy, highlighting its substantial investment in the Indonesia Morowali Industrial Park (IMIP). The IMIP complex, a prime example of China's Belt and Road Initiative (BRI) and Indonesia's downstream industrial policy, has become the largest nickel processing zone worldwide, producing substantial industrial output while facing considerable social and environmental scrutiny (Karim, 2025; Riyanto et al., 2025).

This chapter begins with an analysis of Tsingshan's economic origins, organizational framework, and strategic orientation to thoroughly understand its impact on extractive globalization. This section outlines the firm's historical roots, governance structure, market positioning, and key milestones in internationalization, providing a foundation for analysing its expansion into Indonesia and its broader implications for ESG accountability and social justice.

Amidst the industrial achievements exists a significant human toll. The IMIP expansion has instigated significant demographic changes, displacing indigenous Moronene communities with ancestral connections to the land that extend over centuries. Walhi Sulawesi Selatan (2023) reported that it has drawn over 70,000 migrant workers from various regions of Indonesia into remote enclaves, generating tension with local communities and undermining socio-cultural structures. The conflicting tensions between tradition and modernization, as well as between natives and outsiders, constitute the ethical foundation of this work.

Background of the Company

Tsingshan Holding Group was established in 1988 in Wenzhou, Zhejiang Province, a location emblematic of China's rapid industrial progress. What began as a little stainless steel venture has developed into a global corporate giant, altering supply networks and the physical and social landscapes of remote communities (Camba et al., 2022; Olafsdottir & Sverdrup, 2021; Warburton, 2024).

As the world economy transitions to low-carbon technology, Tsingshan has redefined its position as a crucial participant in the energy transition (Kumar & Vishwanathan, 2025; Tian et al., 2022; Zhao et al., 2022). The company leveraged its industrial capabilities to vertically integrate into the nickel value chain, concentrating on a mineral considered essential for the future of electric vehicles (EVs). This action was deliberate; it made up a premeditated and strategic response to the shifting geopolitics of green energy, where the capacity to refine and manage "transition minerals" confers both economic and political leverage.

Tsingshan's most consequential deed transpired beyond China's borders. It occurred thousands of kilometres to the south, in the heart of Sulawesi, Indonesia—a region rich in nickel yet historically marginalized from the centres of finance and policy. Tsingshan started the creation of the Indonesia Morowali Industrial Park (IMIP), a vast, high-capacity industrial complex that presently functions as the largest nickel processing facility worldwide (Camba et al., 2022; Ching & Camba, 2023; Olafsdottir & Sverdrup, 2021).

For Tsingshan, IMIP stands for engineering aspiration and geopolitical insight, and it is industrial revitalization and economic inclusiveness. For many people living in and around the IMIP complex, the story is considerably more complex and deeply personal (Bole et al., 2022; Christmann & Lefebvre, 2022; Kumar & Vishwanathan, 2025). The company's success is connected to the lives it has affected: the workers facing precarious labour conditions, the communities grappling with environmental degradation, and the local traditions challenged by the rise of a global corporate entity. Their perspectives, often disregarded in boardrooms or bilateral agreements, are the ethical foundation of our case study (Warburton, 2024).

This chapter analyses Tsingshan's business trajectory through the lenses of ESG and social justice, to elucidate rather than condemning or praising. To show the authentic consequences of global expansion, when profit eclipses engagement and ambition undermines accountability.

Motivation for Global Expansion

Tsingshan's decision to expand its operations beyond China's borders was motivated not by mere ambition, but by necessity shaped by changing global conditions. The company encountered a pivotal moment: on one side, intensifying domestic competition and industrial overcapacity within China's mature stainless steel sector; on the other, the emergence of a novel economic frontier driven by climate imperatives — the green energy transition (Ogunlade et al., 2024; Walder, 2024; Widyadwiana & Utami, 2024). The rise of electric vehicles (EVs), which rely heavily on nickel as an essential element of their batteries, primarily propelled the transformation. As worldwide demand for electric vehicles surges, nickel has evolved from an industrial commodity into a strategic mineral. Control of its production and processing became a demonstration of economic authority. Tsingshan, with its optimized supply chain and metallurgical expertise, recognized the opportunity and acted decisively (Hanafi, 2024; Olafsdottir & Sverdrup, 2021).

Indonesia has emerged as a workable location for expansion. The country holds the largest nickel reserves in the world and, in 2014, enacted a substantial mineral export prohibition to encourage foreign investors to develop domestic refining and smelting operations. Where others failed, Tsingshan progressed. Investing in Indonesia's raw material sector will secure access to a crucial resource and align with national policy goals, so boosting the company's legitimacy and market position (ChuanYu et al., 2025; Sunuhadi et al., 2024; Zhao et al., 2022).

Tsingshan's impetus transcended simple resource procurement. It formed a part of a broader national initiative. Inspired by China's Belt and Road Initiative (BRI), Chinese firms were encouraged to pursue international expansion, exporting not only goods but also capital, infrastructure, and industrial models. Tsingshan's concept for IMIP exemplified this premise. The firm was not only building a factory; it was establishing a simultaneous industrial ecosystem: a port, a power plant, dormitories, and roads — all interconnected within a high-intensity export enclave in the Indonesian periphery (Karim, 2025; Ogunlade et al., 2024).

This expansion model assured economic efficiency and vertical integration, yet it exposed a significant asymmetry: capital, technology, and control originated from the corporate centre, while environmental, social, and human risks were shouldered by the periphery (Bria et al., 2025; Jia-Zheng & Broggi, 2025; Qi et al., 2023). For Tsingshan, global expansion involved creating enduring supply networks, reducing costs, and enhancing geopolitical resilience. Tsingshan's global expansion offered Indonesia opportunities for employment, infrastructure advancement, and improved industrial ability. For inhabitants within and next to the IMIP zone, it marked a new period defined by constant noise, unstable livelihoods, and a substantial transformation of daily life.

Understanding Tsingshan's motivation for expansion requires an analysis that transcends mere economic considerations. A moral assessment is required: what consequences ensue for a corporation when it "goes global," especially when the burdens of expansion are unevenly allocated, and the viewpoints of those most affected are sidelined in the conversation?

MARKET ANALYSIS AND ENTRY STRATEGY

Target Market Selection

In selecting its primary aim for foreign expansion, Tsingshan Holding Group made a strategic and consequential choice: Indonesia. This selection was intentional, based on a confluence of geopolitical, economic, and resource-related factors that positioned Indonesia as both a strategic opportunity and a moral benchmark (Liu, 2024; Syarif, 2025)

Indonesia appears nearly flawless at first glance. As of 2023, it holds about 22% of the world's nickel deposits, positioning it as the foremost source of this vital element. The worldwide quest for electrification and battery advancement renders the archipelago both attractive and indispensable because of its resource concentration (ChuanYu et al., 2025; Schodde & Guj, 2025). The Indonesian government, led by President Joko Widodo, enacted a rigorous mineral export ban and a downstream policy framework aimed at attracting foreign investment to develop domestic value-added enterprises (Lazuardi et al., 2024; Santoso et al., 2024).

For Tsingshan, Indonesia was not just a source of nickel but also a pathway to extensive industrial supremacy. By joining a market that actively sought foreign investment in refining and smelting facilities, the firm could establish itself not at the end of the supply chain, but at its beginning. The alignment of business and national interests made Indonesia a workable target for expansion, both logistically and politically (Aditya et al., 2025; Kanugrahan et al., 2022).

Notably, Indonesia's market dynamics showed a distinct divergence from other nickel-rich regions, such as the Philippines and certain African nations. The Philippines has comparable resource wealth; it is impeded by inconsistent mining regulations and recurrent environmental closures. African countries often exhibit high logistical costs and heightened political instability for ongoing industrial operations (Camba et al., 2022; ChuanYu et al., 2025; Karim, 2025). Indonesia, distinguished by its political stability, maritime accessibility, and conducive business climate, offered Tsingshan an ideal chance.

Indonesia's strategic appeal also made it vulnerable to human and environmental threats. Many nickel-rich locations are in remote, underdeveloped places, where traditional livelihoods persist, government structures are weak, and regulatory oversight is often erratic. Central Sulawesi, the site of the Indonesia Morowali Industrial Park (IMIP), exemplifies this reality. The region's infrastructural inadequacies, minimal labour costs, and lenient regulations facilitated rapid industrialization, but simultaneously created structural inequities between investor interests and community rights (Pasinringi, 2021; Warburton, 2024).

Tsingshan's selection of Indonesia as its primary global expansion target represents more than a mere response to market conditions. It underscores a broader context in which resource-rich but socially vulnerable regions function as experimental sites for hyper-scaled industrial capitalism, sometimes without the full engagement or informed consent of the affected populations. While Indonesia was represented on Tsingshan's expansion map solely through coordinates and mineral data, it included histories, communities, and ecosystems—many of which were inadequately prepared for the swift and substantial transformations that followed (Ching & Camba, 2023; Liu, 2024).

Entry Mode Selection

Tsingshan Holding Group's entry into Indonesia stood for a strategic industrial transplantation, executed by direct foreign investment and the creation of a greenfield mega-project, the Indonesia Morowali Industrial Park (IMIP). Unlike conventional entry strategies such as mergers, acquisitions, or joint ventures with established local firms, Tsingshan developed an entirely new industrial ecosystem from scratch (Miao & Zetao, 2025; Tham & Negara, 2022). This entry strategy afforded the company remarkable oversight of infrastructure, labour systems, and supply chains, significantly affecting the region's social, economic, and environmental development.

This strategic decision was shaped by multiple factors. In 2014, Indonesia implemented a ban on raw nickel exports, requiring multinational companies to engage in domestic value-added processing to access the country's natural resources. This regulatory alteration seamlessly aligned with Tsingshan's vertically integrated business model, which prioritizes ownership at each production phase — from extraction to refining to exportation. By opting for a greenfield project, Tsingshan can establish an industrial complex tailored to its operational needs, free from the limitations of pre-existing infrastructure or local regulatory obstacles (Iksan & Soong, 2023; Santoso et al., 2024).

Second, the company entered Indonesia not as an autonomous entity, but as the primary investor in a consortium, partnering with Bintang Delapan Group — an Indonesian firm that provided local legitimacy, land access, and help to navigate domestic bureaucracy. This hybrid strategy—combining comprehensive capital investment with local partnerships—enabled Tsingshan to keep operational management while complying with foreign investment regulations and easing sociopolitical resistance (Bria et al., 2025; Haqq & Gultom, 2022).

This form of entry also has consequences. By bypassing proven local industrial facilities and creating a self-sufficient industrial enclave, Tsingshan effectively isolated IMIP from the broader regional economy. Tsingshan distributed goods and profits outside the region and sourced labour from distant regions. The enclave model intensified spatial inequalities and limited the expected multiplier effects of foreign direct investment (FDI) (Holslag, 2022; Olafsdottir & Sverdrup, 2021; Qi et al., 2023).

Tsingshan's entry strategy illustrates a broader trend in global South-South investments, as Chinese companies, supported by government help and economies of scale, replicate infrastructure-heavy, extractive models in areas marked by weak governance. This technique successfully achieves short-term output goals but often transfers risks to local environments and communities, raising important questions of accountability, equity, and long-term sustainability. In conclusion, Tsingshan's entry strategy in Indonesia maximized corporate autonomy and supply chain management, but at the cost of local integration and inclusive development—a critical trade-off inherent to this case (Bhatti et al., 2024; Oh, 2020; Pribadi, 2024).

Competitive Advantage

Tsingshan Holding Group's rise in the global nickel industry is underpinned by a carefully developed competitive advantage, based on cost leadership, vertical integration, and strategic geopolitical positioning. While many multinational corporations compete in technology, branding, or research and development, Tsingshan's advantage lies in its ability to generate industrial-scale production at considerably reduced costs, mainly by operating in resource-rich yet institutionally weaker areas (Holslag, 2022; Walder, 2024; Xia, 2024).

The essence of this advantage resides in Tsingshan's vertically integrated production strategy. Unlike traditional corporations that outsource or subcontract segments of the supply chain, Tsingshan internalizes nearly all operational processes, including mining, smelting, and shipping. This framework diminishes transaction costs, improves efficiency, and ensures more rigorous quality control (Tham & Negara, 2022; Tian et al., 2022). The company's oversight of its supply chains, including own ports and power facilities within the Indonesia Morowali Industrial Park (IMIP), reduces dependence on public infrastructure, which often proves unreliable in remote regions.

Tsingshan capitalizes on regulatory inconsistencies and labour market fluctuations. The firm functions in regions with restricted labour rights and lenient environmental regulations, leading to significantly lowered operational costs. This cost-efficiency improves profitability and worldwide competitiveness, although it also exposes Tsingshan to reputational risks and intensifies scrutiny on human rights and sustainability practices (Villada-Canela et al., 2021; Widyadwiana & Utami, 2024).

Another side of Tsingshan's competitive edge is its alignment with the geoeconomic goals of host countries. In Indonesia, the company's preparedness for downstream processing aligns nicely with the government's aim to industrialize and elevate the value chain. This alignment provided Tsingshan with governmental favour, exclusive licenses, and infrastructural advantages that would have been difficult to get in highly regulated markets (Riyanto et al., 2025; Yongtao & Sining, 2024).

Tsingshan has strategically positioned itself within the green transition discourse by supplying critical materials for electric vehicle (EV) batteries, a sector increasingly associated with global climate goals. By controlling significant segments of Class I and Class II nickel production, Tsingshan can get favourable contracts with electric vehicle manufacturers and protect itself from price fluctuations (Bharati et al., 2023; Depraiter et al., 2025).

These advantages are ambiguous. The strategies that foster cost leadership may simultaneously jeopardize long-term social legitimacy to function. If overlooked, environmental degradation, labour unrest, and local disenfranchisement could threaten Tsingshan's position in a progressively values-oriented global economy (Madzikatire, 2024). Thus, while Tsingshan's economic advantage is strong, its future will depend not only on efficiency but also on ethics, engagement, and environmental responsibility.

IMPLEMENTATION OF GLOBAL EXPANSION

Key Initiatives and Investments

Tsingshan Holding Group's global development was realized through the creation of the Indonesia Morowali Industrial Park (IMIP) in Central Sulawesi. Launched in 2013, IMIP represents one of the most ambitious foreign direct investments (FDI) in the extractive and metallurgical sectors in Southeast Asia. This effort is essentially a self-sustaining industrial city that oversees all facets of nickel production, from ore extraction to final processing.

Covering over 3,000 hectares, IMIP is a vertically integrated enterprise featuring multiple smelting furnaces, a coal-fired power plant, a private port, road infrastructure, employee housing, and commercial zones. This extensive investment framework allows Tsingshan to bypass public infrastructure and centralize operational control, leading to what some describe as a "enclave economy" - both geographically and institutionally detached from the broader Indonesian industrial system.

This swift advancement incurred significant social repercussions: 1) Indigenous displacement: Twelve villages of the Moronene people have lost 80% of their ancestral forests and fishing areas, undermining traditional livelihoods without Free, Prior, and Informed Consent (FPIC) (JATAM, 2024). Migrant labour precarity: Workers from Java, Flores, and Timor live in segregated dorms, experiencing pay theft and restricted mobility – *'We're trapped: too poor to leave, too exploited to stay'* (Interview with migrant worker ID-M027, 2023)

The program's pivotal element is the application of High-Pressure Acid Leach (HPAL) technology, allowing Tsingshan to transform low-grade laterite nickel into battery-grade nickel sulphate, a crucial constituent for electric vehicle (EV) batteries. This technological shift, coupled with economies of scale, positions the company as a crucial supplier in the global electric vehicle value chain (Bartzas & Komnitsas, 2024).

Tsingshan established a partnership with Bintang Delapan Group, a homegrown entity with considerable local political and economic influence. This strategic relationship provided Tsingshan with regulatory advantages, access to land entitlements, and improved community discussions, often at the expense of significant local participation (Riyanto et al., 2025; Tham & Negara, 2022).

The IMIP project has secured billions in cash, with investments from Chinese companies such as GEM Co., Ltd. and Huayou Cobalt. The joint ventures have expanded Tsingshan's operations to encompass cobalt processing, stainless steel, and lithium battery materials, establishing IMIP as a vital component of China's worldwide green technology industrial policy (Carney, 2023; Herrera-Navarrete et al., 2022).

However, these investments carry both ethical and ecological consequences. The reliance on coal-fired energy undermines the project's environmentally sustainable narrative. The significant intensity of industrial activities has resulted in extensive environmental degradation, labour disputes, and public health concerns—raising critical questions about the nature of the "development" offered and its beneficiaries. IMIP signifies a technological accomplishment and a socio-environmental dispute — a point where global ambitions converge with local vulnerabilities.

Figure 1 depicts the vertically integrated supply chain beginning from IMIP, detailing the transition from nickel production in Central Sulawesi to its conversion into electric vehicle components for global markets. This international value chain underscores IMIP's strategic function as both a production centre and a pivotal element in the decarbonization goals of significant automotive economies.

Figure 1. Integrated Supply Chain from IMIP to Global EV Market

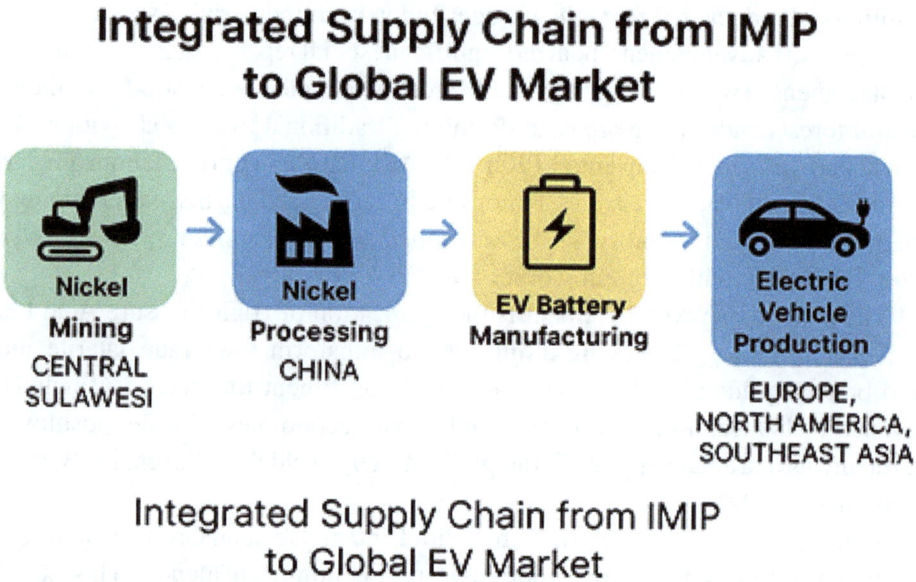

Source: Author's elaboration based on global EV supply chain dynamics and IMIP export patterns.

Challenges Faced

Tsingshan Holding Group's entry into Indonesia through the Indonesia Morowali Industrial Park (IMIP) has produced substantial industrial advantages. Beneath the surface of this rapid progress lies a plethora of substantial and interrelated issues —

environmental, social, regulatory, and reputational — that progressively jeopardize the sustainability and ethics of its operations (Foss & Koelsch, 2022). To understand the spatial dynamics of terrestrial conflict and environmental susceptibility in the Indonesia Morowali Industrial Park (IMIP), it is essential to analyse its geographical proximity to traditional Moronene areas. The map below depicts the location of IMIP in Central Sulawesi, superimposed with significant ecological zones, indigenous land claims, and places susceptible to conflict.

To understand the spatial dynamics of terrestrial conflict and environmental susceptibility in the Indonesia Morowali Industrial Park (IMIP), it is essential to analyse its geographical closeness to traditional Moronene areas. The map below depicts the location of IMIP in Central Sulawesi, superimposed with significant ecological zones, indigenous land claims, and places susceptible to conflict.

Figure 2. Geospatial Context of IMIP and Moronene Territory

Source: Author's elaboration based on administrative boundaries and NGO land-use mapping.

Environmental degradation makes up a vital concern. The large scale and intensity of smelting and refining operations at IMIP have led to heightened levels of air and water pollution, mostly because of the park's reliance on coal-fired energy. Toxic runoff into nearby water bodies, deforestation, and altered marine ecosystems have adversely affected traditional fishing and agricultural practices, threatening local livelihoods and biodiversity (Ogunlade et al., 2024; Taufik et al., 2022). Despite global discussions on "green transition," Tsingshan's dependence on fossil fuels contravenes essential ESG principles and jeopardizes the integrity of its role in the electric vehicle supply chain.

Almost 45,000 migrant workers in Morowali have stretched local resources and provoked ethnic conflicts. Hospital data shows a 300% rise in malnutrition among Moronene children from 2020 because of the loss of fisheries (Provincial Health Office, 2024). Migrant workers experience systemic exclusion, with 78% reporting a lack of access to grievance channels when exploited by subcontractors (ILO, 2023). This dual marginalization incites animosity, as shown by 32 violent confrontations between natives and migrants in 2023 alone (LPMM, 2024).

The issues related to work and social protection are intricately linked. The IMIP complex mostly depends in low-wage labour from various areas around Indonesia, along with an increasing influx from abroad. Reports of hazardous working conditions, prolonged hours, and inadequate health and safety protocols have emerged with increasing frequency (Crossa, 2023; Jajoria et al., 2024).). Between 2021 and 2024, multiple fatal occurrences, particularly smelter explosions, underscored the lack of enforcing safety regulations. Labour unrest, marked by strikes and protests, is intensifying, often facing insufficient reactions from management or governmental entities.

The park operates within a statutory ambiguity from a governance perspective. The semi-autonomous system allows for limited external oversight, and the collaborative governance model including Chinese investors and local elites raises concerns about transparency and accountability (Martino et al., 2024; Qi et al., 2023). There is little evidence of significant community engagement, grievance mechanisms, or independent oversight, leading to restricted options for local inhabitants when faced with harm.

Tsingshan faces a growing reputational crisis. As global investors, regulators, and civil society heighten their scrutiny of ESG compliance, the company's model—efficient yet exclusionary—risks becoming a liability. Media inquiries and NGO publications have portrayed IMIP not as an exemplar of sustainable development, but as a cautionary tale regarding extractive globalization (Aditya et al., 2025; Iksan & Soong, 2023; Wijaya & Sinclair, 2025).

Therefore, the challenges facing Tsingshan are not peripheral but essential. They arise from a mentality that prioritizes production over engagement and scale over sustainability—a tension that will influence the future trajectory of its global operations.

Mitigation Strategies

Besides reactive CSR, three justice-oriented models provide transformative strategies to ease the socio-environmental conflicts associated with IMIP.

The Poso Peacebuilding Blueprint.

In the aftermath of the sectarian hostilities in Central Sulawesi (1998–2001), local NGOs established the Forum Silaturahmi, which effectively diminished violence by 87% over a three-year period. A comparable deliberative platform tailored for IMIP may encompass:

- Monthly discussions among Moronene elders, labourers affected by the transition, and Tsingshan management,
- Joint environmental monitoring councils with both indigenous and migrant representatives,
- Conflict-sensitive grievance systems under ILO norms.

The Philippine Nickel Remediation Fund.

In reaction to marine contamination caused by Rio Tuba's operations in Palawan, a 1.5% revenue allocation was designated for a community-managed trust. This fund rehabilitated over 12,000 mangroves and educated 200 fishers in aquaculture by 2023. A comparable restoration and livelihood diversification plan might be used in the coastal areas of Central Sulawesi affected by IMIP.

Gem Co.'s Supply Chain Justice Program.

Tsingshan's principal partner has instituted ethical supervision throughout its value chain by executing third-party salary audits, multilingual chatbot grievance mechanisms, and climate-resilient housing initiatives for displaced households. These examples show that ethical industrialism is not solely idealistic; it is pragmatically astute. Transformative mitigation causes not only compensation but also co-governance, redistribution, and transparency.

STRATEGIC ANALYSIS

Analytical Frameworks: A PESTEL Analysis of Tsingshan's IMIP Expansion

This section uses the PESTEL analytical framework to assess the strategic and ethical aspects of Tsingshan Holding Group's activities in Indonesia, concentrating on the Political, Economic, Social, Technological, Environmental, and Legal factors affecting the company's growth through the Indonesia Morowali Industrial Park (Miao & Zetao, 2025; Warburton, 2024).

Political Influences.

Tsingshan's entry into Indonesia was facilitated by strong bilateral relations established through the Belt and Road Initiative (BRI) and Indonesia's 2014 ban in mineral exports. The Indonesian government's aim for downstream industrialization aligned with Tsingshan's corporate strategy, creating a favourable political climate. However, local governance frameworks can display deficiencies or fragmentation, leading to limited public oversight and heightening concerns about elite capture and regulatory leniency (Santoso et al., 2024).

Economic Considerations.

From a cost-efficiency standpoint, IMIP offers negligible labour costs, financial incentives, and abundant raw materials. The park contributes significantly to Indonesia's GDP and export earnings. Economic benefits are unevenly distributed. Local economies are marginal to the industrial nucleus, and profit repatriation by foreign investors limits long-term domestic value preservation (Pasinringi, 2021; Warburton, 2024).

Societal Influences.

The rapid progress of IMIP has resulted in significant demographic shifts, labour migration, and social upheaval. Occurrences of industrial accidents, prolonged working hours, and insufficient employee protections have provoked protests and unrest. The relocation of indigenous livelihoods and the lack of community engagement in planning processes have intensified social conflicts (Bria et al., 2025; Tritto & Camba, 2022).

Technological Considerations.

Tsingshan uses High-Pressure Acid Leach (HPAL) technology to transform low-grade laterite into nickel suitable for electric vehicles. However, this advancement has not been matched by technical transfer or the cultivation of local ability. The reliance on outdated coal-fired energy systems contradicts claims of innovation in sustainability (Naryono, 2023).

Ecological Influences.

Environmental degradation remains a critical issue. Air and water pollution, deforestation, and marine degradation are widespread. The magnitude of industrial operations, coupled with inadequate environmental oversight, raises substantial concerns about ecological resilience in the area (Bhatti et al., 2024; Halkos & Nomikos, 2021).

Legal and Regulatory Considerations

Despite Indonesia's documented environmental and labour legislation, implementation is inconsistent. IMIP operates with a quasi-extraterritorial ability, showing limited transparency. The absence of independent audits and inadequate grievance mechanisms worsens regulatory opacity and erodes trust.

The PESTEL framework reveals an expansion strategy that uses systemic asymmetries, where profitability is supported by political alignment but is compromised by social, environmental, and legal vulnerabilities.

Brand and Reputation Effects

Tsingshan Holding Group's global prominence has positioned it as a crucial industrial player and a significant emblem in the narrative of China's corporate globalization. Increased visibility results in greater vulnerability. As scrutiny of Environmental, Social, and Governance (ESG) performance intensifies, Tsingshan's brand has evolved into both an asset and a liability—interwoven with its material achievements and ethical uncertainties (Syarif, 2025).

In the early stages of its expansion, Tsingshan garnered a reputation for industrial efficiency, technological adaptability, and strategic acumen. The establishment of the Indonesia Morowali Industrial Park (IMIP) was praised in specific policy circles as a model of South-South cooperation and a crucial element of China's Belt and Road Initiative (BRI). At one time, Tsingshan's brand symbolized progress for both China's foreign investment policy and Indonesia's economic development objectives (Iksan & Soong, 2023; Widyadwiana & Utami, 2024).

As the human and ecological consequences of IMIP became increasingly clear, a simultaneous narrative appeared. International media organizations, environmental watchdogs, and human rights groups started the documentation of allegations of labour exploitation, perilous working conditions, environmental deterioration, and inadequate local consultation (Landry et al., 2021; Selig et al., 2022). These investigations challenged the developmentalist narrative promoted by Tsingshan, reinterpreting the business as a symbol of unbridled extractive capitalism disguised as a green transition.

The duality of reputation is important in the electric vehicle (EV) revolution, as consumers, investors, and regulators increasingly demand an ethical source of materials (Jajoria et al., 2024; Rouhana et al., 2024). Notable electric car manufacturers, many of which rely on nickel sourced from IMIP, face reputational issues because of their association. This exerts pressure on Tsingshan and its downstream partners to uphold transparent and responsible supply chains.

The lack of thorough public ESG reporting by Tsingshan intensifies this problem. Unlike its global peers, the corporation has not adopted international sustainability disclosure frameworks such as GRI, SASB, or TCFD. This opacity undermines stakeholder trust and limits Tsingshan's ability to actively shape its brand narrative. Opportunities remain. If Tsingshan starts a true ESG transformation—anchored on community engagement, environmental restoration, and independent oversight—it may recast its position not only as a producer of vital minerals but also as a model of ethical industrialism in the Global South. Tsingshan's reputation will be shaped not only by its constructions but also by its receptiveness, adaptability, and the individuals it engages in its advancement.

Lesson Learned

The expansion of Tsingshan Holding Group into Indonesia offers substantial, though unsettling, insights into the prospects and risks inherent in global industrial strategy in the 21st century. It shows the logistical success of a vertically integrated multinational and the substantial divisions that emerge when scale surpasses social responsibility (Abdullah & Sumner, 2025; Ogunlade et al., 2024).

The Tsingshan-IMIP model underscores the limitations of development narratives primarily centered on economic production. The advancement of infrastructure, job prospects, and export potential is clear; these indicators may conceal more intricate problems, such as unstable employment, environmental degradation, and community marginalization. When development is solely evaluated by GDP or industrial output, it may endorse exploitative relationships that predominantly benefit international corporations at the expense of local wellbeing (Syarif, 2025).

Second, Tsingshan's narrative illustrates the reputational risks inherent in operating within regulatory gray areas. The firm exploited Indonesia's lenient regulatory framework to reduce costs and speed up growth; this choice exposed it to global condemnation and examination. In an era of hyper-connectivity and heightened ESG awareness, the consequences of insufficient governance transcend host countries; they reverberate throughout supply chains, investor perceptions, and consumer markets (Foss & Koelsch, 2022).

The absence of effective stakeholder engagement resulted in substantial expenses. Despite Tsingshan's significant investments in infrastructure, it insufficiently allocated resources towards trust, inclusion, and representation. Community issues related to land, pollution, or labour rights were primarily viewed as compliance risks rather than ethical obligations. This hierarchical approach eroded local legitimacy and weakened long-term resistance to social upheaval (Warburton, 2024).

Fourth, Tsingshan's example illustrates that efficiency and justice can coexist when deliberately aligned. Integrating ESG values into the core operational strategy, rather than perceiving them as simply public relations additions, is now essential. It is essential for legitimacy, risk mitigation, and sustainable advancement. This situation causes policymakers and researchers to reevaluate the standards that define "successful" investment. Metrics must evolve to include equity, inclusion, and ecological integrity, rather than only concentrating on financial transactions and production levels. Tsingshan's expansion shows that industrial ambition, lacking ethical considerations, can produce both infrastructure and injustice. The upcoming task is to transform progress by prioritizing humans, the environment, and involvement.

Figure 3 depicts a comparison framework of ESG mitigation measures at IMIP, juxtaposing traditional reactive methods with novel justice-oriented options. This significant change—from extractive to ethical industrialism—highlights the practical feasibility of incorporating human rights, environmental sustainability, and inclusive governance into industrial supply chains.

Figure 3. ESG Mitigation Strategies – Before vs After

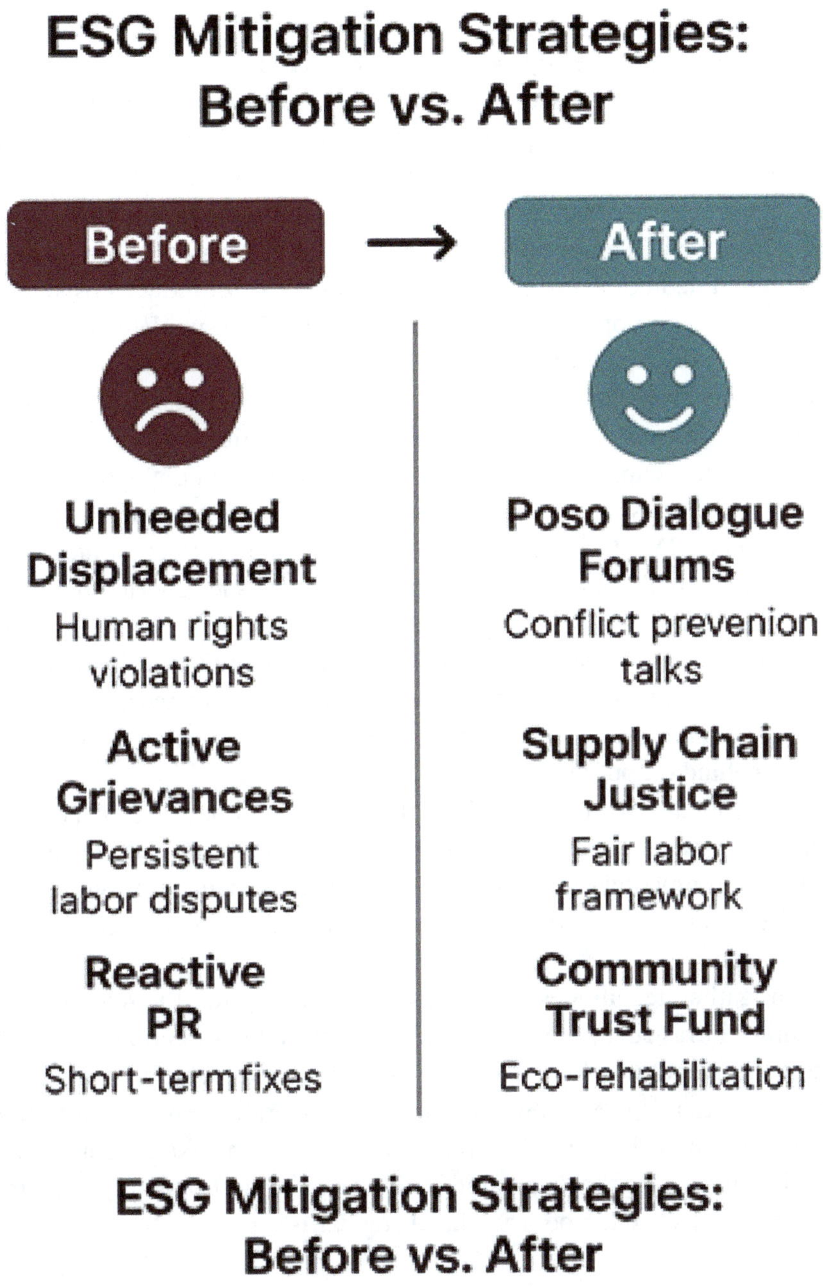

Source: Canva output, author's elabouration (2025)

CONCLUSION AND STRATEGIC RECOMMENDATIONS

Summary of Key Findings

This section outlines the key factors contributing to Tsingshan's rapid industrial growth, as well as the major issues that presently jeopardize the legality and sustainability of its operations. The expansion of Tsingshan Holding Group into Indonesia through the Indonesia Morowali Industrial Park (IMIP) illustrates the complex interplay between economic ambitions, geopolitical strategy, and the experiences of local populations. The project shows industrial efficiency, showcasing how a vertically integrated company can secure resource access, reduce costs, and position itself at the centre of the global electric vehicle (EV) supply chain. On a more personal scale, it reveals the detrimental facets of swift globalization, as the pace of advancement outstrips the mechanisms of responsibility, equity, and sustainability.

A fundamental finding is that Tsingshan's competitive advantage stems not only from technical capabilities, but also from disparities in regulation, bargaining leverage, labour rights, and environmental protections. The company's ability to create and oversee IMIP with minimal external oversight reflects strategic acumen and a troubling exploitation of the host nation's governance shortcomings.

Second, the entry strategy—greenfield investment via enclave industrialization—enabled Tsingshan to bypass integration with local economies and institutions. This paradigm, while offering immediate productivity benefits, created a pattern of exclusion, seeing communities as secondary to planning and prioritizing environmental protections behind output targets.

The reputational risks linked to IMIP have escalated because of its global importance. Tsingshan's deficient disclosure of ESG practices, opaque reactions to labour and environmental issues, and inadequate engagement with civil society have compromised its moral legitimacy, particularly in markets where ethical sourcing is a critical factor.

The mitigating techniques are fragmented and primarily reactive. Despite implementing infrastructure expenditures and safety modifications, they lack the requisite cohesiveness and collaborative spirit for sustainable impact. Tsingshan has yet to show that it views ESG as a strategic imperative essential for long-term value creation rather than simply a reputational cost. The example underscores a bifurcated reality: Tsingshan's method is effective by traditional industrial metrics, although lacking by contemporary ethical standards.

Future Growth Opportunities

Despite the structural and ethical challenges clear in this case, Tsingshan Holding Group has significant potential for future growth, contingent upon its ability to intentionally adopt a paradigm of sustainability, inclusivity, and transparent governance. The swift progression of the global green revolution is expected to increase the demand for battery-grade nickel. In the 21st century, output levels will dictate not solely growth, but by the legitimacy and accountability of production processes.

A critical opportunity exists in the decarbonization of Tsingshan's industrial operations. The ongoing reliance on coal-fired energy at the Indonesia Morowali Industrial Park (IMIP) undermines the company's claim of engaging in the green economy. Shifting to renewable energy sources, such as solar, hydropower, or green hydrogen, might significantly enhance Tsingshan's ESG profile and attract investment from environmentally conscious capital markets. This transformation would reduce emissions and align the corporation with emerging carbon disclosure mandates and sustainable finance frameworks.

Second, Tsingshan could position itself as a leader in ethical mineral sourcing by adopting global sustainability reporting frameworks, such as the Global Reporting Initiative (GRI), the Task Force on Climate-related Financial Disclosures (TCFD), and the OECD Due Diligence Guidance for Responsible Mineral Supply Chains. Proactive openness in labour practices, environmental impact, and community engagement would show a degree of sophistication that many international buyers and investors presently demand.

The enterprise can transform IMIP from an isolated economy into a developmental foundation for neighbouring towns. This involves substantial local employment and skills enhancement, procurement from domestic suppliers, and cooperative community planning. Integrating shared value into the operational framework could convert local stakeholders into lasting allies rather than adversaries.

As geopolitical tensions around essential minerals escalate, Tsingshan can position itself as a reliable and ethically sound partner for international automakers and governments. In an era of rising "green protectionism," market access may increasingly depend not only on price or volume but also on compliance with ethical and environmental norms. Tsingshan's expected expansion will depend not just on technical efficiency but also on its willingness to adapt, increasing both in scale and ethical consciousness. The path ahead lies not merely in extraction, but in co-creation: of value, trust, and a mutually beneficial future.

Recommendations for Other Firms

The circumstances of Tsingshan Holding Group offer both cautionary and instructive lessons for other multinational firms, particularly those entering resource-rich yet institutionally fragile regions. As globalization, decarbonization, and digitization speed up, firms must embrace competitive advantage while incorporating ethical foresight and relational intelligence. The following ideas create a framework for more responsible, inclusive, and sustainable global growth.

Integrate ESG at the Core, Rather than the Periphery.

Environmental, Social, and Governance (ESG) concepts must be integrally embedded within the core business models, viewed not as mere public relations tools, but as vital operational imperatives. Organizations ought to adopt global sustainability frameworks such as GRI, TCFD, and SASB, and commit to independent audits. Transparency is crucial; it is foundational to trust and accessibility in modern global markets.

From Extraction to Co-creation.

Companies entering the Global South must abandon extractive mindsets in favour of co-creative techniques. This involves engaging local communities from the outset, conducting social impact assessments, respecting customary land rights, and creating participatory grievance mechanisms. Development must happen with communities, rather than being enforced upon them or executed on their behalf.

Emphasize Decarbonization and Circularity.

The carbon intensity of industrial operations is under increased scrutiny. Corporations should invest in renewable energy sources, low-emission technologies, and closed-loop production processes. The credibility of climate initiatives will affect long-term competitiveness, especially in industries linked to the green transition.

Reevaluate Supply Chain Ethics.

In response to the requirements of downstream partners and regulatory bodies for ethical sourcing, corporations must maintain labour standards, occupational safety, and environmental protection across all tiers of the supply chain. Due diligence must be proactive instead of reactive and grounded in ongoing dialogue with stakeholders.

Design for Resilience Rather Than Solely for Scale.

Accelerated growth and expansion must not undermine systemic resilience. Organizations must integrate long-term social stability, cultural continuity, and ecological sustainability into their risk management frameworks. Generating shared value with local communities reduces volatility and fosters a sustainable license to operate. The future belongs to enterprises that align growth with stability, ambition with empathy, and innovation with ethical standards. The path forward is clear: responsible growth does not signify less growth, but judicious and cooperative progress.

REFERENCES

Abdullah, I., & Sumner, A. (2025). Linkage development as industrial policy: The state and structural transformation in resource-rich countries. *WIDER Working Paper Series*, Article wp-2025-29. https://ideas.repec.org//p/unu/wpaper/wp-2025-29.html

Aditya, I. A., Wijayanto, T., & Hakam, D. F. (2025). Advancing Renewable Energy in Indonesia: A Comprehensive Analysis of Challenges, Opportunities, and Strategic Solutions. *Sustainability (Basel)*, *17*(5), 5. Advance online publication. DOI: 10.3390/su17052216

Bartzas, G., & Komnitsas, K. (2024). Cradle to gate life-cycle assessment of battery grade nickel sulphate production through high-pressure acid leaching. *The Science of the Total Environment*, *952*, 175902. DOI: 10.1016/j.scitotenv.2024.175902 PMID: 39233072

Bharati, T., Farhad, M., & Jetter, M. (2023). On the relationship between trade openness and government size. *World Economy*, *46*(7), 2102–2133. DOI: 10.1111/twec.13374

Bhatti, U. A., Bhatti, M. A., Tang, H., Syam, M. S., Awwad, E. M., Sharaf, M., & Ghadi, Y. Y. (2024). Global production patterns: Understanding the relationship between greenhouse gas emissions, agriculture greening and climate variability. *Environmental Research*, *245*, 118049. DOI: 10.1016/j.envres.2023.118049 PMID: 38169167

Bole, D., Kumer, P., Gašperič, P., Kozina, J., Pipan, P., & Tiran, J. (2022). Clash of Two Identities: What Happens to Industrial Identity in a Post-Industrial Society? *Societies (Basel, Switzerland)*, *12*(2), 49. DOI: 10.3390/soc12020049

Bria, E., Kemp, D., Kuswati, R. A., Sturman, K., Saputra, M. R. U., & Lechner, A. M. (2025). A holistic framework for examining complex problems in energy transition solutions. *One Earth*, *8*(5), 101249. DOI: 10.1016/j.oneear.2025.101249

Camba, A., Lim, G., & Gallagher, K. (2022). Leading sector and dual economy: How Indonesia and Malaysia mobilised Chinese capital in mineral processing. *Third World Quarterly*, *43*(10), 2375–2395. DOI: 10.1080/01436597.2022.2093180

Carney, R. W. (2023). *China's Chance to Lead: Acquiring Global Influence via Infrastructure Development and Digitalization*. Cambridge University Press., DOI: 10.1017/9781009385879

Ching, V. C., & Camba, A. (2023). A Comparative View of Chinese Relations with Peru. *Springer Books*, 275–294.

Christmann, P., & Lefebvre, G. (2022). Trends in global mineral and metal criticality: The need for technological foresight. *Mineral Economics*, *35*(3–4), 641–652. DOI: 10.1007/s13563-022-00323-5

ChuanYu., J., Manurung, H., Anggara, F., & Petrus, H. T. B. M. (2025). Indonesian Nickel Overview: Potential, Development and Future Prospects. In Metallurgy And Materials Society of (Ed.), *Proceedings of the 63rd Conference of Metallurgists, COM 2024* (pp. 753–763). Springer Nature Switzerland. DOI: 10.1007/978-3-031-67398-6_130

Crossa, M. (2023). Distorted linkages and labour devaluation: An exploration of automotive value chain-driven 'development' in Ciudad Juárez, Mexico. *Canadian Journal of Development Studies. Canadian Journal of Development Studies*, *44*(2), 270–292. DOI: 10.1080/02255189.2022.2058469

Depraiter, L., Goutte, S., & Porcher, T. (2025). Geopolitical risk and the global supply of rare earth permanent magnets: Insights from China's export trends. *Energy Economics*, *146*, 108496. DOI: 10.1016/j.eneco.2025.108496

Dou, S., Xu, D., Zhu, Y., & Keenan, R. (2023). Critical mineral sustainable supply: Challenges and governance. *Futures*, *146*, 103101. DOI: 10.1016/j.futures.2023.103101

Foss, M. M., & Koelsch, J. (2022). *Need Nickel? How Electrifying Transport and Chinese Investment are Playing Out in the Indonesian Archipelago*. DOI: 10.25613/30S0-Y623

Halkos, G., & Nomikos, S. (2021). Corporate social responsibility: Trends in global reporting initiative standards. *Economic Analysis and Policy*, *69*, 106–117. DOI: 10.1016/j.eap.2020.11.008

Hanafi, M. (2024). Designing nickel smelter industry investment competitiveness policy in Indonesia through system dynamics model. *Journal of Science and Technology Policy Management*. DOI: 10.1108/JSTPM-01-2024-0016

Haqq, A. M., & Gultom, Y. M. L. (2022). The challenge of implementing public-private partnerships: A transaction costs perspective on waste to energy projects in Indonesia. *Journal of Financial Management of Property and Construction*, *27*(3), 365–386. DOI: 10.1108/JFMPC-09-2020-0058

Herrera-Navarrete, R., Colín-Cruz, A., Arellano-Wences, H. J., Sampedro-Rosas, M. L., Rosas-Acevedo, J. L., & Rodríguez-Herrera, A. L. (2022). Municipal Wastewater Treatment Plants: Gap, Challenges, and Opportunities in Environmental Management. *Environmental Management*, *69*(1), 75–88. DOI: 10.1007/s00267-021-01562-y PMID: 34799756

Holslag, J. (2022). Controlling the Mine? Assessing China's Emergence as a Minerals Super Power. *Journal of Contemporary China*, *31*(137), 663–674. DOI: 10.1080/10670564.2021.2010381

Iksan, M., & Soong, J.-J. (2023). The Political Economy of Indonesia's Development Strategy under China-USA Power Rivalry and Hegemonic Competition: A Middle Power with Its Hedging Strategy. *Chinese Economy*, *56*(4), 304–320. DOI: 10.1080/10971475.2022.2136696

Jajoria, D., Jatav, M., & Mishra, R. (2024). Trends, patterns and socioeconomic determinants of child and adolescent labour in India: Empirical analysis using national sample survey data. *Journal of International Development*, *36*(3), 1647–1674. DOI: 10.1002/jid.3874

Jia-Zheng, Y., & Broggi, C. B. (2025). The metamorphosis of China's automotive industry (1953–2001): Inward internationalisation, technological transfers and the making of a post-socialist market. *Business History*, *67*(1), 211–238. DOI: 10.1080/00076791.2023.2247366

Kanugrahan, S. P., Hakam, D. F., & Nugraha, H. (2022). Techno-Economic Analysis of Indonesia Power Generation Expansion to Achieve Economic Sustainability and Net Zero Carbon 2050. *Sustainability (Basel)*, *14*(15), 9038. DOI: 10.3390/su14159038

Karim, M. F. (2025). Chinese network power and patronage embeddedness in Indonesia. *Asia Europe Journal*, *23*(2-3), 285–302. Advance online publication. DOI: 10.1007/s10308-025-00717-4

Kumar, A., & Vishwanathan, A. (2025). Race for critical minerals: China's ambitions and challenges. *Comparative Strategy*, *44*(1), 56–72. DOI: 10.1080/01495933.2024.2445490

Landry, V., Semsar-Kazerooni, K., Tjong, J., Alj, A., Darnley, A., Lipp, R., & Guberman, G. I. (2021). The systemized exploitation of temporary migrant agricultural workers in Canada: Exacerbation of health vulnerabilities during the COVID-19 pandemic and recommendations for the future. *Journal of Migration and Health*, *3*, 100035. DOI: 10.1016/j.jmh.2021.100035 PMID: 34405185

Lazuardi, S. D., Hadi, F., Devintasari, D. V., Wuryaningrum, P., Riduwan, M., Noarista, O. S., & Alifia, S. F. (2024). The impact on downstream policy implementation for mineral export products in Indonesia: Marine transportation point of view. *IOP Conference Series. Earth and Environmental Science*, *1298*(1), 012018. DOI: 10.1088/1755-1315/1298/1/012018

Liu, K. (2024). *China's Direct Investment in Indonesia (1990–2022): Multiple Structure and Systemic Risks*. Springer Nature Singapore., DOI: 10.1007/978-981-97-7328-2

Martino, N., Sanders, C. B., & Dej, E. (2024). The 'regulatory grey zone': Bylaw enforcement's governing of homelessness and space. *Policing and Society*, *34*(4), 305–320. DOI: 10.1080/10439463.2023.2263617

Miao, Z., & Zetao, P. (2025). Different Motives, Different Outcomes: A Comparative Study of China's Outward FDI in Industrial Parks in Malaysia and Indonesia. *Asian Economic Papers*, *24*(2), 1–23. DOI: 10.1162/asep_a_00951

Naryono, E. (2023). *Nickel Mine Exploitation in Indonesia, Between a Blessing and a Disaster of Environmental Damage*. OSF. https://doi.org/DOI: 10.31219/osf.io/y58qe

Ogunlade, B. T., Adeniran, J. A., Abdulraheem, K. A., Odediran, E. T., Atanda, A. S., Oyeneye, A. K., Akapo, R. A., & Yusuf, R. O. (2024). Heavy Metals Analysis in the Vicinity of a Northcentral Nigeria Major Scrap-Iron Smelting Plant. *International Journal of Environmental Research*, *18*(6), 107. DOI: 10.1007/s41742-024-00657-8

Oh, S.-Y. (2020). *China's Race to the Top: Regional and Global Implications of China's Industrial* (SSRN Scholarly Paper No. 3735037). Social Science Research Network. https://papers.ssrn.com/abstract=3735037

Olafsdottir, A. H., & Sverdrup, H. U. (2021). Modelling Global Nickel Mining, Supply, Recycling, Stocks-in-Use and Price Under Different Resources and Demand Assumptions for 1850–2200. *Mining, Metallurgy & Exploration*, *38*(2), 819–840. DOI: 10.1007/s42461-020-00370-y

Pasinringi, A. (2021). Mining Conflicts in Central Sulawesi: Cooperate and Public Policy Review. *Journal of Asian Multicultural Research for Social Sciences Study*, *2*(2), 2. Advance online publication. DOI: 10.47616/jamrsss.v2i2.118

Pribadi, R. (2024). *The Significance of the Nickel Ore Export Prohibition for Indonesia in Consolidating Its Middle-Income Status in the World System*. https://lup.lub.lu.se/student-papers/record/9161036

Qi, Y., Yuan, M., & Bai, T. (2023). Where will corporate capital flow to? Revisiting the impact of China's pilot carbon emission trading system on investment. *Journal of Environmental Management, 336*, 117671. DOI: 10.1016/j.jenvman.2023.117671 PMID: 36967695

Riyanto, G., Yeremia, A. E., Astuti, R., Zuada, L. H., Hidayat, A., & Rakhmani, I. (2025). Various visions of the industrialized future: Anxiety, aspiration, and Chinese nickel investment in Indonesia. *Asia Europe Journal, 23*(2-3), 369–391. Advance online publication. DOI: 10.1007/s10308-025-00727-2

Rouhana, F., Zhu, J., Chacon-Hurtado, D., Hertel, S., & Bagtzoglou, A. C. (2024). Ensuring a just transition: The electric vehicle revolution from a human rights perspective. *Journal of Cleaner Production, 462*, 142667. DOI: 10.1016/j.jclepro.2024.142667

Santoso, R. B., Dermawan, W., & Moenardy, D. F. (2024). Indonesia's rational choice in the nickel ore export ban policy. *Cogent Social Sciences, 10*(1), 2400222. DOI: 10.1080/23311886.2024.2400222

Schodde, R., & Guj, P. (2025). Nickel: A Tale of Two Cities. *Geosystems and Geoenvironment, 4*(1), 100356. DOI: 10.1016/j.geogeo.2025.100356

Selig, E. R., Nakayama, S., Wabnitz, C. C. C., Österblom, H., Spijkers, J., Miller, N. A., Bebbington, J., & Decker Sparks, J. L. (2022). Revealing global risks of labour abuse and illegal, unreported, and unregulated fishing. *Nature Communications, 13*(1), 1612. DOI: 10.1038/s41467-022-28916-2 PMID: 35383162

Sunuhadi, D. N., Ernowo, , Hilman, P. M., & Suseno, T. (2024). Availability of Indonesian nickel reserves and efforts to improve reserves resistance and its impact to economic growth. *Mineral Economics, 37*(3), 601–617. DOI: 10.1007/s13563-024-00443-0

Syarif, A. (2025). Navigating Investment in Risky Market: Comparative Analysis of Chinese State-Owned Enterprises and Private Firms Operating in Indonesia. *Journal of Current Southeast Asian Affairs, 18681034251347972*. Advance online publication. DOI: 10.1177/18681034251347972

Taufik, Y., Adijaya, S., & Rela, I. Z. (2022). *Nickel Smelter on Social-Economics and Environmental Issues. Research Square*. DOI: 10.21203/rs.3.rs-2232605/v1

Tham, S. Y., & Negara, S. D. (2022). Chinese Investments in Industrial Parks: Comparison Between Indonesia and Malaysia. In H. N. Au Yong, X. Yuan, & L. Low, *Series on China's Belt and Road Initiative* (Vol. 15, pp. 225–268). WORLD SCIENTIFIC. DOI: 10.1142/9789811221873_0010

Tian, J., Yu, L., Xue, R., Zhuang, S., & Shan, Y. (2022). Global low-carbon energy transition in the post-COVID-19 era. *Applied Energy*, *307*, 118205. DOI: 10.1016/j.apenergy.2021.118205 PMID: 34840400

Tritto, A., & Camba, A. (2022). State-facilitated Industrial Parks in the Belt and Road Initiative: Towards a framework for understanding the localization of the Chinese development model. *World Development Perspectives*, *28*, 100465. DOI: 10.1016/j.wdp.2022.100465

Villada-Canela, M., Muñoz-Pizza, D. M., García-Searcy, V., Camacho-López, R., Daesslé, L. W., & Mendoza-Espinosa, L. (2021). Public Participation for Integrated Groundwater Management: The Case of Maneadero Valley, Baja California, Mexico. *Water (Basel)*, *13*(17), 17. Advance online publication. DOI: 10.3390/w13172326

Walder, A. G. (2024). The Rapid Ascent of China's Corporate Giants. *China Journal (Canberra, A.C.T.)*, *92*, 71–102. DOI: 10.1086/730617

Walhi Sulawesi Selatan. (2023). Catahu: Catatan Akhir Tahun 2023—Sulawesi Selatan Menuju Momentum Politik di Tengah Kerusakan Lingkungan, Proyek Transisi Energi Palsu, dan Hilirisasi Nikel* [Annual year-end report 2023: South Sulawesi toward a political momentum amid environmental destruction, false energy transition projects, and nickel downstreaming]. Indonesian Forum for Environment – South Sulawesi Region. https://walhisulsel.or.id/wp-content/uploads/2024/12/Catahu-WALHI-SS-2023.pdf

Warburton, E. (2024). Nationalist enclaves: Industrialising the critical mineral boom in Indonesia. *The Extractive Industries and Society*, *20*, 101564. DOI: 10.1016/j.exis.2024.101564

Widyadwiana, A., & Utami, C. F. (2024). Sustainable Water Provision Model for Morowali Industrial Area: A System Dynamics Model. *Syntax Literate. Jurnal Ilmiah Indonesia*, *9*(4), 2288–2297. DOI: 10.36418/syntax-literate.v9i4.15457

Wijaya, T., & Sinclair, L. (2025). An EV-fix for Indonesia: The green development-resource nationalist nexus. *Environmental Politics*, *34*(2), 252–274. DOI: 10.1080/09644016.2024.2332129

Xia, Z. (2024). Enterprise Futures Hedging Risk Management -Take the Qingshan Holdings' Nickel Futures Incident on the LME as an Example. *SHS Web of Conferences, 188*, 01005. DOI: 10.1051/shsconf/202418801005

Yongtao, G., & Sining, L. (2024). Examining the Belt and Road Initiative (BRI) from the perspective of clean energy supply chain resilience. *Asian Journal of Political Science*, *32*(3), 329–352. DOI: 10.1080/02185377.2024.2429093

Yu, H. (2024). China-ASEAN Cooperation Under the BRI. In H. Yu, *Understanding China's Belt and Road Initiative* (Vol. 26, pp. 43–68). Springer Nature Singapore. DOI: 10.1007/978-981-99-9633-9_3

Zhao, C., Ju, S., Xue, Y., Ren, T., Ji, Y., & Chen, X. (2022). China's energy transitions for carbon neutrality: Challenges and opportunities. *Carbon Neutrality*, *1*(1), 7. DOI: 10.1007/s43979-022-00010-y

KEY TERMS AND DEFINITIONS

Carbon-Intensive Green Supply Chain: A paradox wherein products linked to decarbonization, such as electric vehicle batteries, are manufactured using energy sources or industrial processes that continue to rely significantly on fossil fuels.

Critical Minerals: Minerals considered crucial for strategic sectors and low-carbon technologies because to their economic significance and supply-chain susceptibility; this chapter focuses on nickel as a critical mineral for battery and electric vehicle manufacturing.

Enclave Growth: A model of industrial growth characterized by a spatial concentration of economic activities, vertical integration, and brief connections to adjacent local economies, resulting in centralized value creation while social and environmental liabilities are externalized to adjoining communities.

Energy Transition: The worldwide transition from fossil fuel-dependent systems to lower-carbon energy, transportation, and industrial systems is driving an increased demand for minerals such as nickel, cobalt, and lithium.

ESG Accountability: The requirement for companies to transparently evaluate, show, and assume accountability for their environmental, social, and governance consequences, encompassing their effects on employees, communities, ecosystems, and institutional integrity.

Ethical Industrialism: A strategy for industrial development that integrates economic advancement with environmental stewardship, human rights safeguarding, social inclusion, and participatory governance.

Green Paradox: A situation where enterprises providing resources for the global green transition concurrently produce considerable ecological harm, carbon emissions, and social inequity at extraction and processing locations.

Greenfield Investment: A type of foreign direct investment when a business establishes new operations and infrastructure from scratch instead of acquiring or merging with an existing local entity.

Grievance Mechanism A structured mechanism enabling affected individuals or communities to lodge grievances: pursue redress, and obtain institutional remedies for labour, environmental, or social injustices.

High-Pressure Acid Leach (HPAL): A metallurgical processing procedure employed to extract nickel from low-grade laterite ores and transform it into battery-grade materials, particularly nickel sulfate for electric car batteries.

Indigenous Displacement: Losing land, livelihoods, cultural continuity, and territorial rights experienced by Indigenous communities because of industrial expansion, land conversion, or extractive development.

Industrial Park Enclave: An autonomous industrial zone featuring its own infrastructure, logistics, energy systems, and worker amenities, frequently functioning with minimal integration into the adjacent social and economic environment.

Labour Precarity: A state of precarious employment marked by unsafe working environments, inadequate grievance procedures, diminished bargaining power, and uncertain living arrangements.

License to Operate The continuous social endorsement and legitimacy conferred onto a corporation by communities: institutions, and stakeholders, transcending formal legal authorizations or contractual agreements.

Nickel Down Streaming: A government-driven industrial policy that limits raw material exports while encouraging domestic processing, refining, and value-added manufacturing to enhance national economic benefits.

Regulatory Asymmetry: A scenario where disparities in enforcement capacity, legal oversight, and institutional robustness allow firms to attain a competitive edge by functioning in jurisdictions with less stringent regulations.

Shared Value: A development strategy wherein companies produce economic advantages while concurrently achieving quantifiable social and environmental benefits for local communities and society at large.

Social Justice: A normative notion highlighting equity in the allocation of advantages, liabilities, opportunities, and decision-making authority, particularly for communities affected by extensive industrial or extractive initiatives.

Stakeholder Engagement: A procedure wherein companies engage relevant stakeholders—including employees, local communities, Indigenous populations, civil society representatives, and regulatory bodies—in consultation, dialogue, and decision-making.

Vertical Integration: A corporate strategy in which a firm controls multiple stages of the supply chain—from extraction and processing to logistics and export—to reduce costs, secure inputs, and strengthen market power.

Chapter 16
Envision's Global Climate Governance Model:
The Resource–Policy–Demand Model

Lan Zhou
http://orcid.org/0009-0004-7151-9210
Beijing Normal-Hong Kong Baptist University, China

EXECUTIVE SUMMARY

This chapter examines Envision Group's evolution from a Chinese wind turbine manufacturer into a global green technology leader, analysing how the company strategically integrates external climate governance frameworks into its core business model. It presents the company's "resource-policy-demand" three-dimensional framework for global market selection across country, regional, and urban scales, detailing entry strategies including mergers and acquisitions, greenfield investment, co-construction models, and digital export of the EnOS™ platform. Through SWOT analysis and examination of zero-carbon industrial parks as replicable infrastructure, this shows how Envision transforms climate governance compliance into competitive advantage. The analysis contributes insights into the coupling effects between international rule systems and corporate strategy, offering a framework for understanding how energy enterprises can navigate geopolitics, secure green financing, and capture governance-driven premiums in the global energy transition.

DOI: 10.4018/979-8-3373-4302-0.ch016

INTRODUCTION

Background of the Company

Envision Group's development trajectory illustrates a strategic leap from a single wind turbine manufacturer to a global provider of green technology solutions. We can divide this trajectory into three core stages.

Between 2007 and 2009, Lei Zhang founded Envision Energy in Jiangsu. Driven by the concept of "software-defined wind turbines," the company launched the world's first low-wind-speed turbine, breaking the industry's reliance on high-wind-speed regions (OFweek Lithium Battery Network, 2021). In 2011, it rolled out the smart wind farm management system Wind OS™, enabling intelligent management of wind turbine operation data. In 2016, they upgraded this system to the Intelligent IoT Operating System EnOS™, marking a leap from single-device management to a system-wide approach. By 2016, Envision's wind turbine shipments ranked second in China, solidifying its position as a leader in offshore wind power technology (Liu et al., 2023).

Starting in 2016, Envision rapidly expanded its business scope: it made strategic investments in Auto Grid (a power grid big data company) and Charge Point (a charging network firm), and acquired Baze Field (a European renewable energy software company), constructing an energy internet ecosystem (NetEase, 2022). In 2018, Envision acquired Nissan's battery subsidiary AESC (later renamed Envision AESC), entering the power battery and energy storage sectors and forming a "turbine + battery + IoT" triad (Fang, 2024). In 2017, Envision Intelligent established its headquarters in Singapore. The company then applied the EnOS system to scenarios like smart cities and building management. Envision Intelligent also became a core technology partner for Singapore's "Smart Nation" initiative (Golden Group, 2025).

In 2021, the group announced its goal to achieve operational carbon neutrality by the end of 2022 and full value chain carbon neutrality by 2028, repositioning itself from an "energy technology company" to a "green technology company." In 2022, it established the world's first Zero-Carbon Industrial Park in Ordos, Inner Mongolia, integrating wind power, photovoltaics, energy storage, and intelligent IoT systems to form a closed loop of green power production and industrial consumption. The group plans to build 100 such parks globally within 10 years, aiming to reduce annual carbon emissions by 1 billion tons (Juda.cn, 2023). As of now, the EnOS system connects over 200 million smart terminals and 500 GW of energy assets, providing carbon management solutions to over 300 international companies, including Microsoft, Nike, and BP (Shanghai Municipal Commission of Economy and Informatization, 2023).

Motivations for Participation in Global Governance

External Pull: Import of Governance Rules from International Initiatives

In 2020, Envision signed the RE100 initiative, committing to 100% renewable electricity consumption by 2030 (Climateweeknyc, 2022). Although voluntary, this initiative has become a key threshold for collaborating with international enterprises. RE100, Climate Group, and CDP (2023) outlined that over 380 multinational members, including Microsoft and Amazon—require suppliers to disclose relevant carbon emission factor data and accept third-party verification when buying green electricity. Without joining RE100, Envision would have lost nearly $1 billion in orders for supplying green electricity to 18 global data centers. Thus, RE100's disclosure standards have become a direct external driver for Envision's carbon data governance.

Since 2021, Envision has published climate-related financial disclosure reports under the TCFD framework, enabling it to access substantial preferential policies. Data from the TCFD working group shows that in 2023, issuers in the global green bond market meeting TCFD disclosure requirements achieved average coupon rates 15–25 basis points lower than the benchmark (Financial Stability Board, 2023). For instance, the green bonds Envision issued in 2023 benefited from a 22-basis-point discount, equivalent to annual interest savings of $1.1 million. The international market's pricing mechanisms for global environmental governance have thus become a rigid constraint, pushing Envision to deepen TCFD implementation.

In 2022, Envision got SBTi 1.5 °C target certification, pledging to reduce Scope 1+2 emissions by 72% by 2030 (SBTi, 2022). SBTi accounting standards mandate lifecycle assessment for upstream wind turbine castings and downstream energy storage operations. This requires Envision to centrally manage emission data that was previously dispersed across over 300 suppliers and integrate it into a global supply chain system, constructed in line with international initiative governance frameworks.

Internal Drive: The Triple Resonance of Brand, Profit, and Policy

In 2022, Envision ranked fifth globally in new wind turbine installations (Bloomberg NEF, 2023). By joining initiatives such as RE100 and SBTi, Envision met the "RE100 membership required" technical threshold for the 2023 UK Highways England 1.2 GWh energy storage tender. Despite submitting a bid 3.7% higher than the second-lowest offer, Envision still won the contract, generating $44 million in brand premium revenue.

As hardware gross margins are vulnerable to commodity price fluctuations, Envision has increased resource investment in platform development. Leveraging its advantages in broad adaptation, best practices, and common services, Envision Digital's EnOS platform has, in less than three years, managed over 100 GW of global new energy assets and connected over 60 million sensors and intelligent devices, achieving 100% clean energy penetration while simultaneously reducing carbon emissions by 20% and lowering users' energy costs by an average of 15–20%. Meanwhile, it will deliver a more efficient, cost-effective, and secure experience to its over 20 ecosystem partners, including Microsoft, Amazon, and ChargePoint, establishing itself as a world-leading energy Internet-of-Things (IoT) platform (China Energy Network, 2019). To meet international clients' requirements for platforms to comply with SBTi Scope 3 accounting rules, Envision embedded SBTi standards as software modules, further expanding its potential Total Addressable Market (TAM) to $1.2 billion.

China's "1+N" policy system stipulates that non-fossil energy consumption should reach 25% by 2030, with local governments offering zero land prices and a 0.2 RMB/KWh subsidy for green electricity to zero-carbon park projects (ScienceDirect, 2025). Envision replicated the Ordos zero-carbon industrial park model in Baotou and Chifeng, securing 8 GW of green electricity resources by 2025. By aligning early with international initiatives, Envision gained additional "early adoption of international rules" points in local government assessments, enabling it to secure 10-year Power Purchase Agreements (PPAs) at electricity prices 12% below the industry average—equivalent to an annual profit buffer of 230 million RMB for the group (Ordos Municipal People's Government, 2025).

Coupling Effect: Synergy Between External Pull and Internal Push

When RE100 requires 100% green electricity by 2030, Envision coincidentally needs large-scale green power internally to offset domestic subsidy reductions; when SBTi mandates Scope 3 emission reductions, its SaaS business requires an international accounting framework to access European and American markets; when TCFD demands climate risk disclosure, it aligns with Envision's need for low-cost green bonds to finance new campuses. The influx of international governance rules complements Envision's internal demands for brand upgrading, profit expansion, and policy arbitrage, ultimately forming a strategic cycle of "gaining market access through governance, and securing premiums through compliance with rules."

MARKET ANALYSIS

Global Market Strategy Framework

After years of strategic planning, Envision Group has developed a global development model centered on "renewable energy + digital technology + market ecology." In its global layout, it evaluates market priorities using the "resource-policy-demand" three-dimensional model. The resource dimension covers renewable energy characteristics and the resource potential of lithium mines and green hydrogen; the policy dimension focuses on carbon neutrality legislation, foreign capital subsidies, and industrial chain localization requirements; the demand dimension quantifies green electricity premium space, electric vehicle penetration rates, and industrial decarbonization rigidity (MobilityNotes, 2025). Its target market selection follows a clear "country-region-city" three-level framework, with differentiated evaluation dimensions at different spatial scales:

Country Level

Envision focuses on key countries with favorable policies and significant market size, such as France and the United Kingdom in Europe, Japan in Asia, and Papua New Guinea (with special strategic significance).

United Kingdom: Policy-Driven Market.

The UK has abundant wind energy resources (the North Sea wind farm has a potential of 40 GW) and ranks first in Europe in offshore wind power installed capacity (34.4 GW). However, its lithium resources depend on imports, limiting local battery supply (MobilityNotes, 2025).

Brexit has led to a 6.8% increase in import tariffs on battery components, and the UK has also lost access to EU green fund support. Its legislation mandates a ban on the sale of fuel-powered vehicles by 2030—earlier than the EU's target. It has also introduced a "super-deduction tax" to incentivize battery investment (RSM, 2022) and provides subsidies for the construction of foreign-funded factories (Envision Group, 2025).

McKinsey (2021) research shows that by 2030, the demand for electric vehicle batteries will exceed 3,900 GWh, while the announced battery production capacity plans can only provide about 2,900 GWh, highlighting a significant supply gap. Envision has laid out the Sunderland Gigafactory (scheduled for operation in 2025) and adopted a "stock upgrading strategy" to expand the factory, increasing its production capacity from 1.9 GWh to 11 GWh—matching Nissan's 40 GWh battery orders. Meanwhile, it uses the EnOS™ platform to build a battery cloud management system, compensating for resource and policy disadvantages through digital services.

France: Market Driven by Strong Policy and High Demand.

Nuclear power accounts for 70% of France's electricity generation, providing low-carbon power, but lagging wind power development has restricted green electricity supply. France has significant wind energy potential (especially in northern and coastal areas). However, its photovoltaic resources (with an annual sunshine duration of approximately 1,500 hours) are lower than the Southern European average. This characteristic has led Envision Group to avoid constructing large-scale photovoltaic power plants (IEA, 2024).

The Macron government has launched the "New Energy Vehicle Revival Plan," offering dual incentives for battery factories: land subsidies (up to 30%) and carbon tax exemptions (€44.6 per tonne of CO_2). The Green Industrial Act requires that the proportion of local battery production capacity exceeds 50% and provides a subsidy of €20 per KWh (French Ministry of Economy and Finance, 2023). More critically, the Climate and Resilience Act (effective in 2021) stipulates that the battery production section of the carbon footprint of locally sold electric vehicles shall not exceed 40%, providing natural protection for battery enterprises with localized production (Rizos & Vu, 2024). Envision accurately seized this policy window and announced in 2021 an investment of 18.7 billion yuan to build a 43 GWh gigafactory in Douai. The French government granted the Douai factory green loan guarantees. By 2030, they expect to supply half of its production capacity to Renault.

The annual growth rate of electric vehicle sales in France reached 34% (average from 2020 to 2024), but the self-sufficiency rate of local battery production capacity is less than 20%. After the Renault factory begins operations, orders for electric vehicle models will reach 120 GWh (accounting for a significant portion of Envision's production capacity), significantly increasing the localization rate and directly addressing the "supply chain disruption" risk (OFweek Lithium Battery Network, 2021b). The carbon footprint tracing mechanism in the EU's New Battery Regulation forces electric vehicle manufacturers to purchase new energy batteries locally (European Commission, 2023).

Japan: A Market with Mature Technology and Demand.

Land scarcity restricts factory construction in Japan, and the country has limited wind and solar resources. It relies 100% on imports for lithium, cobalt, and nickel (METI, 2024).

Japan has established a 2 trillion-yen fund to support battery research and development, with subsidies accounting for 15% of vehicle prices. Envision acquired AESC to gain local production capacity, access policy preferences, mitigate resource shortages, and serve the high-end market. Japan's Ministry of Economy, Trade, and Industry (METI) allows foreign-funded enterprises to take part in bidding for national energy storage projects. In 2023, Envision won the bid for the Osaka smart grid project. By providing the "Virtual Power Plant" solution supported by EnOS™, it integrated the photovoltaic batteries of 6,000 households into a distributed power grid, verifying the feasibility of the "light-asset service model" in resource-constrained markets.

Japan has over 8 million hybrid vehicles in ownership, and the transition to pure electric vehicles is speeding up, driving a surge in battery demand. In response, Envision, relying on AESC's R&D center in Kanagawa (the R&D site for Gen5-811 AIoT batteries), focuses on high-end battery customization and energy storage system services. Several automakers, including Honda, have partnered with Envision's Gen5-811 batteries, with projected demand exceeding 43 GWh by 2030 (Carscoops, 2021).

Regional Scale

It prioritizes geographical clusters with rapid renewable energy growth and strong policy synergy, such as Southeast Asia and the Middle East.

Southeast Asia (Thailand, Vietnam): Cost and Manufacturing Hub.

According to Irena's data, the theoretical development potential of solar energy in this region reaches 241 GW (2030 target). Among Southeast Asian countries, Thailand has a photovoltaic installed capacity of 14.2 GW, Vietnam has a wind power capacity of 21.5 GW (IRENA, 2022), and the region's nickel ore reserves account for 10% of the global total—supporting the localization of battery raw materials (USGS, 2024).

The ASEAN Plan of Action for Energy Cooperation 2021-2025, jointly signed by ten ASEAN countries, explicitly proposes a 50% reduction in tariffs on cross-border electricity trading and the unification of clean energy certification standards. These two initiatives provide cross-regional service scenarios for Envision's EnOS™

platform (MobilityNotes, 2025). Thailand's EV3.5 policy offers subsidies ranging from 15% to 40% of vehicle prices (Medina, 2025), and Vietnam's NDC target stipulates that renewable energy should account for 32% of total energy by 2030 (VGP, 2023). Envision leverages the 72% localization rate of component manufacturing in Thailand to supply Vietnamese projects, reducing tariff costs by 15%; meanwhile, Vietnam's operation and maintenance center serves power stations in Cambodia and Laos, forming a regional synergy effect of "cross-border cycle of manufacturing and services" (Photovoltaic Industry Network, 2024).

Envision focuses on industrial electricity demand in the Thai market. The automobile manufacturing cluster (with Toyota and Honda bases) in the Rayong Industrial Estate consumes 3.4 TWh of electricity annually, with a green electricity premium of $8/MWh. Envision has built a 150 MW rooftop photovoltaic + energy storage system, directly connecting to the factory's Power Purchase Agreement (PPA). Sales volume of electric vehicles in Southeast Asia increased by 80% annually (BMI, 2024). Envision also focuses on exporting energy storage technologies to support the construction of zero-carbon industrial parks.

Middle East (UAE): Green Hydrogen and Springboard to High-End Markets.

The Middle East has significant photovoltaic potential, with the UAE recording an annual sunshine duration of 2,300 hours. The cost of photovoltaic power generation in the region is $0.013/KWh (the world's lowest), and the production cost of green hydrogen is $1.5/kg (MobilityNotes, 2025). Envision has agreed with Masdar for the joint development of a 1.2 GW solar PV project at Masdar City (Masdar, 2023).

The UAE's Centennial Plan 2071 has allocated $160 billion to develop green hydrogen and launched the world's first "green electricity capacity confirmation and trading mechanism," allowing foreign-funded enterprises to purchase power stations and sell electricity independently. Traders on the Dubai Carbon Exchange can transact the electricity price premium. Dubai requires that clean energy account for 25% of total energy by 2030 (Dubai Electricity & Water Authority, 2025). Envision sells green certificates through the Dubai Carbon Exchange (at $5.2 per MWh), generating additional annual revenue of $6.2 million.

Heavy industries such as aviation and steelmaking in the UAE have an urgent need for decarbonization, with projected hydrogen demand of 4 million tons by 2030. Envision has partnered with Masdar City to build a smart energy system (Envision Energy, 2025).

Urban Level

It gives preference to urban nodes with industrial foundations, resource endowments, or policy pilot features—for example, the combination of Ordos (Inner Mongolia) and Shanghai—to realize green electricity linkage between "resource-based cities and consumption-based cities."

- Douai, France: Renault and Envision AESC have signed a long-term order for 40–120 GWh of power batteries, which will supply high-end passenger vehicles in Europe starting from 2025. Relying on Renault's manufacturing cluster, Envision has built a closed loop of "battery factory - recycling center - green power supply." The recycling project in collaboration with Suez has reduced material costs by 30% (Suez, 2024).
- Ibaraki, Japan: Leveraging the scientific research resources of the Tokyo Bay Area (including the University of Tokyo and AIST), Envision researches high-nickel battery technology, with patents accounting for 35% of relevant fields (JPO, 2024).
- Rayong, Thailand: Using the infrastructure advantages of the Eastern Economic Corridor (EEC), Envision integrates the industrial chain of nickel smelting, cathode materials, and battery assembly (Medina, 2025).
- Masdar City, UAE: As the world's first zero-carbon city, Masdar City is piloting a multi-energy complementary system of wind, solar, storage, and hydrogen (Envision-Fives, 2024).

IMPLEMENTATION OF GLOBAL EXPANSION

Entry Strategy

Mergers and Acquisitions Model.

Between 2018 and 2019, Envision acquired Nissan's battery subsidiary, AESC, in phases, taking over the core technology for ternary lithium batteries and integrating Envision's intelligent IoT technology (EnOS™). This acquisition enabled Envision to get production systems directly certified to Japanese, European, and American automotive standards, avoiding the cycle of independent research and development and certification barriers. Meanwhile, it inherited orders from automakers such as Nissan and Renault, forming a "battery-vehicle" collaborative ecosystem and locking in long-term demand (e.g., Renault's 120 GWh order) (Envision Energy, 2025).

Greenfield Investment.

In 2022, relying on Inner Mongolia's "Green Power Application Evaluation Standards" and local government subsidies, Envision invested in the construction of the Ordos Zero-Carbon Industrial Park. It built a 2.2 GW wind and solar power station, a 1 GWh energy storage system, and an energy-carbon system with 100% green power direct supply. The park has introduced Envision's power battery base, Longi's photovoltaic module factory, and Meijin's hydrogen energy equipment factory, forming a vertical industrial cluster (China Association of Circular Economy, 2022). Envision successfully built a closed loop across the entire industrial chain of "wind, solar, storage, hydrogen + intelligent IoT" and verified the economic benefits of the "new coal - new oil - new power grid" technology matrix. Digital Energy Storage Network (2025) reported that Envision has created the world's first zero-carbon industrial park template, promoting the adoption of Chinese standards in international carbon footprint certification systems (such as Bureau Veritas' green ammonia certification).

Co-construction Model.

In 2024, Envision and Thailand's PTT established a joint venture battery factory in Thailand's Eastern Economic Corridor (EEC), which enjoys a 15-year corporate income tax exemption and an exemption on equipment import taxes. Meanwhile, Envision used PTT Group's oil and gas channels to expand charging networks and integrated its battery technology to explore the ASEAN market (OFweek Energy Storage Network, 2025). Envision has localized the industrial chain, integrating upstream nickel mines (PTT-controlled Indonesian nickel enterprises) and downstream automakers (such as the Great Wall Euler assembly plant in Thailand) to achieve vertical integration of "nickel mines - cathodes - batteries" (Envision Energy, 2025). Since electric vehicle tariffs in Southeast Asia are lower than those in Europe and the United States (e.g., Thailand's EV3.5 policy only levies a 10% tariff), localized production through joint ventures can help avoid carbon tariffs (CBAM) and anti-dumping duties. Thus, Envision actively explores the Southeast Asian market through the joint venture factory co-construction model.

Digital Export.

Since 2017, Envision has exported EnOS™ as a SaaS service, avoiding the risks of heavy asset investment through software services and quickly entering markets such as Europe, the United States, and Japan that are strictly regulated (Tian, 2017). Meanwhile, it has built a global energy IoT ecosystem that connects distributed energy assets through a unified platform. By managing over 100 GW of new energy assets worldwide, Envision has built a data monopoly advantage, achieving the goal of increasing asset penetration in high-barrier markets (Wang, 2017). Localization of its algorithm settings adapts to the EU's GDPR data regulations, enabling access to real-time carbon footprint tracking of the Spanish power grid (China Energy Network, 2019).

STRATEGIC ANALYSIS

SWOT Analysis

Strengths.

Envision Group has leveraged the combined advantages of "technology, capital, governance" through long-term development.

Envision possesses large-capacity energy storage cells. In May 2025, it took the lead in mass-producing 500+Ah energy storage cells, and 700+Ah cells are soon to enter production. This technological leadership has merged its position as the fifth-largest player in the global energy storage market (Energy Storage Network, 2025). By the end of 2024, Envision had accumulated 2,800 patents in new energy and AIoT worldwide, of which 37% were PCT international patents (Envision Group, 2024).

The $500 million green bonds issued by Envision in 2023 received a Moody's A2 rating. The financing cost was 110 basis points lower than that of comparable Chinese issuers, providing a "capital buffer" for its overseas zero-carbon projects (Moody's Investors Service, 2023). Meanwhile, Envision full uses green subsidies from various countries: its French factory has got government green loan guarantees, and its Thai joint venture project enjoys a 15-year tax exemption.

Since 2021, Envision has disclosed carbon emission data under the TCFD (Task Force on Climate-related Financial Disclosures) framework. It is among the first private energy enterprises in China to pass international audits, which enables it to gain a brand premium in negotiations with multinational giants such as Microsoft and Amazon (Financial Stability Board, 2021).

Envision has 13 global bases. The Douai factory in France (supporting Renault), the Sunderland factory in the UK (scheduled for operation in 2025), and the Ibaraki base in Japan (focusing on high-nickel battery R&D) form a "Local for Local" supply network, binding orders from leading automobile manufacturers (Energy Storage Network, 2025).

Weaknesses.

Envision still faces two structural shortcomings in its international governance practices.

In 2023, 62% of the critical lithium and nickel minerals for Envision's wind turbines and energy storage systems came from a single country—Chile (for example, its Japanese factory imported 100% of such minerals from Chile). Geopolitical events may trigger export controls, which will directly affect production capacity. Upstream fluctuations will then hinder cost reduction in battery localization (Bloomberg NEF, 2024). Meanwhile, the energy storage cell industry is facing fierce price competition, and fluctuations in raw material costs in 2025 will further compress profit margins (Energy Storage Network, 2025).

Envision released a TCFD report, but a third party has not verified its Scope 3 carbon emission factors (upstream and downstream of the value chain). In contrast, industry giants such as Siemens Gamesa and Vestas have achieved full-scope verification. This gap weakens Envision's bargaining power in reviews under the EU's CBAM (Carbon Border Adjustment Mechanism) (IDC, 2025).

Opportunities.

Amid the global wave of "carbon tariff-green subsidy" policies, Envision faces three external opportunities.

At the macro level, carbon-neutrality legislation in Europe and the United States, as well as requirements for local battery and electric-vehicle production capacity in the UK and France, have stimulated battery demand. In October 2024, the EU put into effect the detailed rules for the transition period of the CBAM, which cover six major industries (including hydrogen and electricity) in the initial phase. Analysts expect it to create a premium space of 25–35 euros per megawatt-hour for zero-carbon electricity once it operates fully in 2026 (IDC, 2025).

At the industry level, the USA Inflation Reduction Act provides a 30% investment tax credit for local energy storage systems. However, starting from 2027, Chinese batteries must meet the requirement that North American or free trade partner countries generated 80% of their value if users want to use them. This implicitly benefits Envision, which has already deployed production capacity in North America (Internal Revenue Service, 2023).

At the institutional level, the United Nations Framework Convention on Climate Change (UNFCCC) is promoting the development of international standards for "zero-carbon parks." Envision expects its Ordos model to become a blueprint, which will allow it to benefit from rule-making dividends (UNFCCC, 2024). The acceleration of China's unified power market construction and inter-provincial green power trading (e.g., from Mengxi to Shanghai) provides incremental space for Envision's "integrated power generation and consumption" model (Envision Energy, 2025).

Threats.

Meanwhile, Envision's market expansion also faces threats and challenges.

Since 2025, the Federal Reserve has maintained a high-interest-rate environment. For every 50 basis points increase in USA dollar financing costs, the Internal Rate of Return (IRR) of Envision's overseas projects will decrease by 0.8–1.2 percentage points (Federal Reserve, 2024). The USA IRA Act requires a certain proportion of battery localization; the EU's New Battery Regulation strengthens carbon footprint tracing; Indonesia and the Philippines restrict nickel ore exports; and Thailand promotes the localization of the battery industrial chain (e.g., PTT's holdings of nickel mines). All these factors have weakened Envision's "resource conversion" strategy, putting Chinese-funded enterprises under pressure to restructure their supply chains.

At the industry level, the 8 GWh battery factory jointly invested in by South Korea's LG Energy Solution and Vietnam's VinES will start production in 2025. It will seize the Southeast Asian market with a per-KWh cost 7% lower than Envision's (LG Energy Solution, 2024). CATL and BYD are speeding up the mass production of 500+Ah battery cells, while LG Energy Solution focuses on the high-end market. The concentration rate of the top 5 energy storage cell manufacturers (CR5) exceeds 70%, and the technical window period is shortening (Energy Storage Network, 2025).

Risk Response Strategies

SO Strategy (Expanding Advantages).

Faced with the premium opportunities (O) brought by the EU's CBAM, Envision's technological patent portfolio and low-cost funds from green bonds (S) enable it to lock in long-term Power Purchase Agreements (PPAs) with European customers for the 2027–2030 period in advance. This will speed up the commissioning of factories in the UK and Spain, secure orders from Renault and Nissan, comply with local regulations, and provide "zero-carbon traceability" value-added services. The growing regulatory pressure and corporate net-zero commitments are driving significant demand for digital carbon management solutions in Europe, reflecting the strong and growing market demand among enterprises for digital carbon management tools, like SaaS services, to meet compliance and disclosure requirements. Meanwhile, in Southeast Asia (Rayong, Thailand) and the Middle East (UAE), Envision will export the closed-loop model of "wind, solar, energy storage + battery manufacturing" to leverage local resources and policy dividends.

WO Strategy (Transforming Disadvantages).

To address the disadvantage of high supply chain concentration (W) coupled with geopolitical risks, Envision can use low-interest green bond funds to invest in and take stakes in lithium mining projects in Australia and Canada (O) or invest in solid-state battery technology. This will diversify the risk of relying on a single supply source in Chile while meeting the local content ratio requirements of the EU's Critical Raw Materials Act. As a result, they can reduce the potential probability of supply disruption from 15% to 5% (Envision Group, 2024).

ST Strategy (Resisting Threats).

Faced with the threat of USA tariffs (T), Envision can replicate its Ordos zero-carbon park model in North Carolina, enabling its European and American bases to meet localization requirements. It can utilize the 30% local tax credit to offset the impact of tariffs; meanwhile, through TCFD transparent disclosure (S), it can pursue the USA Department of Energy's 40C production tax credit, ensuring the project's IRR remains above 12% (USA Department of the Treasury, 2023).

WT Strategy (Defending Weaknesses).

In the worst-case scenario (high interest rates, high tariffs, and supply chain disruptions), Envision's ESG data gaps (W) will exacerbate financing difficulties (T). Engaging one of the Big Four international accounting firms to verify Scope 3 carbon emissions and issue sustainability-linked bonds (SLBs) denominated in USA dollars will enhance risk-resistance capabilities, activating the "WT Defense" (Deloitte US, 2024). Envision can improve the gross profit margin of its green power business by optimizing electricity trading spreads (e.g., between Mengxi and Shanghai) through AI (China Energy Network, 2025).

Brand and Reputation Effects

Brand Awareness.

Fortune recognized Envision in its "50 Companies That Change the World" in 2021 and 2024. In 2021, it ranked second globally (first among independent enterprises). They awarded Envision the "Energy Innovator" title in 2024, emphasizing the global replicability potential of its zero-carbon industrial park model (Murray, 2024). Time magazine also included Envision in its "100 Most Influential Companies in the World" in 2024, praising it as the "Green Giant" and ranking it alongside tech giants such as Nvidia and Microsoft. After being evaluated as "an important force promoting global decarbonization", Envision Group' brand influence is steadily expanding globally (PR Newswire, 2025).

Corporate Social Responsibility (CSR).

Envision actively assumes social and environmental responsibilities, aiming to achieve full value-chain carbon neutrality by 2028—a zero-carbon commitment that leads the industry. The "Zero-Carbon Sheep" public welfare project (raising sheep under photovoltaic panels) in the Ordos Industrial Park has increased herders' income by 30%, enhancing Envision's social influence (Polaris Solar Photovoltaic Network, 2025). Meanwhile, Envision has actively responded to social calls: during the COVID-19 pandemic in 2020, it built a mask factory within 15 days, donated over 6 million self-produced masks and 50-million-yuan worth of materials, and won the "Model Award for Chinese Corporate Social Responsibility" (BioSpectrum Asia, 2021). For the long-term development of the industry, Envision took the lead in establishing the "Envision-Sequoia 10-Billion Carbon Neutrality Fund" to nurture green technology startups and promote supplier carbon management, advancing the goal of carbon neutrality throughout the entire life cycle (Envision, 2021).

Crisis Public Relations.

Envision operates with transparency, regularly releasing carbon-neutrality progress reports and facilitating social oversight through quantifiable goals. In 2022, it urgently recalled faulty AESC batteries and completed public opinion restoration within 72 hours, further enhancing its social credibility.

CONCLUSION & STRATEGIC RECOMMENDATIONS

Summary of Key Findings

Mastery of Technology and Standards.

Envision has achieved remarkable results in energy technology innovation. For example, the Chifeng green hydrogen-ammonia project features an original "wind-solar storage - green power - electrolyzer - dynamic synthesis tower" system, with five core independent technologies, including smart wind turbines and AI-powered grid technology—helping China gain a voice in energy technology (Fuelcellchina, 2025). Despite rapid business growth in 2022 and 2023, Envision continued to promote emission reductions through energy structure optimization and energy efficiency improvements, achieving consecutive years of global operational carbon neutrality. In terms of carbon management technology, based on the Envision Ark Energy-Carbon Management System, Envision implements a trinity management approach to "organizational carbon," "supply chain carbon," and "product carbon," achieving integrated carbon management across the entire group and all processes. Over 60 operating sites worldwide connect to the system (Envision Group, 2024). In summary, Envision is actively taking part in global climate governance through the dual drivers of "technology + standards."

The Zero-Carbon Industrial Park Model as a Replicable and Promotable "Public Good".

Following the launch of the Ordos Zero-Carbon Industrial Park in 2022, Envision invested in the Chifeng green hydrogen-ammonia project. Through technological breakthroughs in new energy systems, it enables the coupling of wind-solar storage with hydrogen, ammonia, and alcohol production, addressing cost challenges in developing zero-carbon hydrogen. This promotes the global replication and dissemination of the industrial park model, providing a practical example for expanding into international markets.

Geopolitics Reshaping the Governance Cost Structure of New Energy Enterprises.

In the global energy transition, as it globally expands business, Envision must consider the impact of geopolitics on the development of its new energy industry—including policies, trade rules, and resource endowments across different countries and regions. For instance, building a zero-carbon industrial park in Brazil requires coordinating resources, responding to policy changes, and addressing trade barriers, which increases governance costs and operational complexity (Smith, 2024).

Future Growth Opportunities

Building a Green Hydrogen Export Hub in Latin America.

Global demand for clean energy continues to grow, and green hydrogen—as a clean and efficient energy carrier—has broad prospects. Latin America is rich in renewable energy resources, with countries such as Chile and Brazil having significant potential for green hydrogen exports. Envision's participation will tap into the development opportunities of the green hydrogen industry. On May 12, 2025, the

Brazilian Trade and Investment Promotion Agency signed a strategic cooperation agreement with Envision. Envision will build Latin America's first zero-carbon industrial park in Brazil, develop green fuel value chains, provide green hydrogen-ammonia equipment, and help build a green petroleum ecosystem and new industrial system (Brazilian Trade and Investment Promotion Agency & Fuelcellchina, 2025).

Upgrading Carbon Management to Lock in SME Customers.

Based on the Ark Energy-Carbon Management System, Envision will upgrade its AIoT platform to a "carbon management SaaS" offering to provide carbon management services to enterprises with centralized Scope 1-3 carbon management services (Univers, 2025). In organizational carbon management, it will connect more global operating sites to strengthen the data-collection network and optimize supply-chain carbon-management service processes, providing digital carbon-management tools for suppliers (Chen et al., 2025). Small and Medium-sized Enterprises (SMEs) lack professional carbon management capabilities and resources. Envision's carbon management SaaS services can help them conveniently and efficiently complete carbon inventory, disclosure, and management, assist in carbon reduction planning, reduce operational costs, and enhance sustainable development capabilities—thus filling the service gap in the SME customer market.

Exploring Zero-Carbon Zones.

Building on the Ordos Zero-Carbon Industrial Park's practice, Envision is exploring a "zero-carbon zone" model (Ordos Municipal People's Government, 2025). The Ordos Airport has launched a "zero-carbon airport" technology demonstration project, building an energy supply system integrating "photovoltaic-storage-charging green power + innovative ground source + CO_2 cooling-heating integration + new air energy + cross-seasonal energy storage + AI intelligent computing." By 2028, Envision Group (2025) plans to promote the system to over 30 trunk airports nationwide, driving a 3 million tons/year industry carbon reduction and expanding the zero-carbon zone model in the transportation sector.

Introducing Carbon Financial Derivatives.

With the rapid development of carbon markets, carbon financial derivatives are crucial for enterprises' carbon asset management and risk aversion. Introducing derivatives such as carbon futures and carbon options in the construction of "zero-carbon zones" can help enterprises flexibly manage carbon assets, provide emission-controlled enterprises with expected future quota prices through forward price curves, reduce emission reduction costs, further promote the development of zero-carbon industries, improve the carbon management financial ecosystem, and provide financial support for industrial development (iScience, 2023).

Insights into Market Expansion Paths

Envision's unique advantage in the global market lies in its ability to adjust production capacity allocation dynamically according to the development status, resource endowments, and policy conditions of different regions. As the global unified electricity market advances, the "green power resource spatial arbitrage" model developed by Envision based on EnOS™ will become even more valuable. AI-enabled wind power trading plays an increasingly indispensable role in Envision's efforts to promote regional and even global development, contributing to cost reduction and efficiency improvement for high-quality development. Implementing the Mengxi-Shanghai green power trading project in 2025 clearly shows that using AI to predict power output and load curves can achieve cross-regional power matching. This action has led to a price increase for wind power in Inner Mongolia and a price decrease for electricity consumers in Shanghai, creating a positive outcome for both. This precise connection between the "resource domain and demand domain" is a high-level application of the "resource-policy-demand" three-dimensional model in spatial optimization. For energy technology enterprises, Envision's global development path provides three key insights:

a) Policy sensitivity determines the timing of market entry (e.g., the French factory leveraging Macron's new policies).
b) The spatial matching of resources and demand is more important than absolute scale (e.g., the Mengxi-Shanghai green power corridor).
c) The dynamic adjustment of three-dimensional weights is the core of risk control (e.g., reducing the policy weight after Brexit).

Only by combining systematic evaluation with flexible implementation can enterprises capture sustainable growth poles in the global energy transformation.

REFERENCES

BioSpectrum Asia. (2021, July 14). China's Envision Group donates medical supplies to fight COVID-19 in India. BioSpectrum Asia. https://www.biospectrumasia.com/news/49/18586/chinas-envision-group-donates-medical-supplies-to-fight-covid-19-in-india.html

Bloomberg, N. E. F. (2023). Goldwind and Vestas in Photo Finish for Top Spot as Global Wind Power Additions Fall. BloombergNEF. https://about.bnef.com/insights/clean-energy/goldwind-and-vestas-in-photo-finish-for-top-spot-as-global-wind-power-additions-fall/

Carscoops. (2021, June 28). Envision AESC and Verkor will supply batteries to Renault Group. Carscoops. https://www.carscoops.com/2021/06/envision-aesc-and-verkor-will-supply-batteries-to-renault-group/

Chen, Z., Wu, J., Yang, X., & Ni, G. (2025). Digitalization and supply chain carbon performance: The role of focal firms. *Journal of Theoretical and Applied Electronic Commerce Research*, *20*(289), 289. Advance online publication. DOI: 10.3390/jtaer20040289

China Association of Circular Economy. (2022, April 24). 2022 : 10 100 [Vision 2022 Carbon Neutrality Action Report: The World's Top 100 Zero-Carbon Industrial Parks Over the Next Decade—China Circular Economy Association]. [China Association of Circular Economy]. https://www.chinacace.org/news/fieldsview?id=13554

China Energy Network. (2019, July 19). EnOS 2.0 , [Envision's EnOS 2.0 Released: Intelligent IoT Leads the Distributed Revolution in Energy Systems]. [China Energy Network]. https://www.china5e.com/news/news-1064482-1.html

China Energy Network. (2025, July 30). AI , [AI-Powered Electricity Trading: Envision Opens a New Model for Self-Operated Wind Power Terminal Consumption]. [China Energy Network]. https://www.cnenergynews.cn/guangfu/2025/07/30/detail_20250730224593.html

Climateweeknyc. (2022). Envision. Climateweeknyc. https://www.climateweeknyc.org/envision

Deloitte, U. S. (2024). 2024 Sustainability action report. Deloitte. https://www.deloitte.com/us/en/services/audit-assurance/articles/esg-survey.html

Digital Energy Storage Network. (2025, August 1). , [From Inner Mongolia to Shanghai, Envision Achieves Full-Cycle Green Electricity Trading]. [Digital Energy Storage Network]. https://desn.com.cn/news/show-2107009.html

Dubai Electricity & Water Authority. (2025). [Powering a green economy. DEWA Publications.]. *Sustainability Report*, •••, 2024.

Energy Storage Network. (2025, September 10). , ! [Global energy storage demand is surging, intensifying the reshuffling of rankings for energy storage cell shipments!]. [Energy Storage Network]. https://www.ideesz.com/zhdt/hyzx1/202509/t20250910_1062.html

Envision. (2021, April 23). Envision promises to be operation-level carbon neutral by 2022, value chain carbon neutral by 2028: Envision's first carbon neutrality report. PR Newswire. https://www.prnewswire.com/news-releases/envision-promises-to-be-operation-level-carbon-neutral-by-2022-value-chain-carbon-neutral-by-2028-envisions-first-carbon-neutrality-report-301275885.html

Envision AESC France. (2025, February 3). France secures €48m EU investment for AESC battery plant. Innovation News Network. https://www.innovationnewsnetwork.com/france-secures-e48m-eu-investment-for-aesc-battery-plant/55101/

Envision Energy. (2025, May 9). Envision Unveils 2025 Net Zero Report at Smarter E Europe, Celebrates Third Year of Carbon Neutrality. PR Newswire. https://www.prnewswire.com/apac/news-releases/envision-unveils-2025-net-zero-report-at-smarter-e-europe-celebrates-third-year-of-carbon-neutrality-302450668.html

Envision Group. (2024). 2024. *Sustainability Report*, •••, 24–31. https://www.envisionpharmagroup.com/sustainability-report

Envision Group. (2025, October 23). Envision Energy Strengthens Global Collaboration with Its First Global Supplier Day to Build a Secure, Resilient, and Sustainable Supply Chain. PR Newswire. https://www.digitimes.com/biz/news.asp?feed=13764

European Commission. (2023). Regulation (EU) 2023/1542 - EUR-Lex. https://eur-lex.europa.eu/eli/reg/2023/1542/oj

European Investment Bank. (2023). French gigafactory provides lithium-ion batteries for electric cars. European Investment Bank. https://www.eib.org/en/projects/all/20220168

Fang, Z. X. (2024, July 26). Corporate profile: Envision AESC. https://www.fangzhenxiu.com/post/10382297/?uri=261_bif1kkekanv%2F1000

Federal Reserve. (2024, December). Minutes of the Federal Open Market Committee. https://www.federalreserve.gov/monetarypolicy/files/fomcminutes20241218.pdf

Financial Stability Board. (2021, October 14). 2021 Status Report: Task Force on Climate-related Financial Disclosures. Financial Stability Board. https://www.fsb.org/2021/10/2021-status-report-task-force-on-climate-related-financial-disclosures/

Financial Stability Board. (2023, October 12). 2023 TCFD Status Report: Task Force on Climate-related Financial Disclosures. Financial Stability Board. https://www.fsb.org/2023/10/2023-tcfd-status-report-task-force-on-climate-related-financial-disclosures/https://www.fsb-tcfd.org

French Ministry of Economy and Finance. (2023, October 23). Loi relative à l'industrie verte [France Green Industry Act]. Legifrance. News/695.htmlhttps://www.legifrance.gouv.fr/jorf/id/JORFTEXT000052238755?init=true&page=1&query=Loi+relative+%C3%A0+l%27industrie+verte+&searchField=ALL&tab_selection=all

Fuelcellchina. (2025). Envision Set to Launch 300,000-Ton Renewable Ammonia Facility in September. Fuelcellchina. https://www.fuelcellchina.com/Industry_information_details/6286.html

Goldden Group. (2025, July 16). Net Zero Centre of Excellence and Digital Battery Centre of Excellence. Goldden Group. htmlhttps://www.golddengroup.com/SG-News/695.html

IDC. (2025, January 14). European financial applications forecast, 2024-2028. IDC. https://my.idc.com/getdoc.jsp?containerId=EUR150690123

IEA. (2024). Electricity. IEA. https://www.iea.org/reports/renewables-2024/electricity

Internal Revenue Service. (2023). Frequently asked questions about the Qualifying Advanced Energy Project (48C) credit. Internal Revenue Service. https://www.irs.gov/credits-deductions/frequently-asked-questions-about-the-qualifying-advanced-energy-project-48c-credit

IRENA. (2022, September 26). Solar PV key to ASEAN decarbonisation, 241GW of installed capacity expected by 2030. IRENA. https://www.pv-tech.org/solar-pv-key-to-asean-decarbonisation-241gw-of-installed-capacity-expected-by-2030-irena/

iScience. (2023, September 25). Influence of carbon derivatives on carbon capture investments in coal-based power sector, a China perspective. iScience. https://pmc.ncbi.nlm.nih.gov/articles/PMC10579434/

JPO. (2024). 2024 [2024 Patent Application Technology Trend Report]. https://www.jpo.go.jp/system/tutuj/tokkyo_jouhou_e/tokkyo_jouhou_2024.html

Liu, F., Sim, J.-Y., Sun, H., Edziah, B. K., Adom, P. K., & Song, S. (2023). Assessing the role of economic globalization on energy efficiency: Evidence from a global perspective. *China Economic Review*, *77*, 101897. DOI: 10.1016/j.chieco.2022.101897

Masdar. (2023, December 5). Masdar, Envision Group to develop 1.2 GW solar PV project at Masdar City. Masdar. https://masdar.ae/en/news/masdar-envision-group-to-develop-1-2-gw-solar-pv-project-at-masdar-city

McKinsey & Company. (2021, October 25). Unlocking growth in battery cell manufacturing for electric vehicles. https://www.mckinsey.com/industries/automotive-and-assembly/our-insights/unlocking-growth-in-battery-cell-manufacturing-for-electric-vehicles

Medina, A. F. (2025, September 2). How BOI EV 3.5 shapes the future of EV battery investments in Thailand. ASEAN Briefing. https://www.aseanbriefing.com/news/how-boi-ev-3-5-shapes-the-future-of-ev-battery-investments-in-thailand/

Mewswire, P. R. (2054, July 25). Envision Energy Powers the World's First Green Marine Ammonia Bunkering, Pioneering Net Zero Shipping Fuel. PR Mewswire. https://www.prnewswire.com/news-releases/envision-energy-powers-the-worlds-first-green-marine-ammonia-bunkering-pioneering-net-zero-shipping-fuel-302513836.html

MobilityNotes. (2025). IRENA Renewable Energy Capacity Statistics 2025. MobilityNotes. https://mobilitynotes.com/irena-renewable-energy-capacity-statistics-2025/ https://www.irena.org/Publications/2025/Jul/Renewable-energy-statistics-2025

Moody's Investors Service. (2023, October 12). Moody's assigns A2 to Envision Energy International Limited's USD 500 million green bonds. Moodys. https://www.moodys.com/research/Moodys-assigns-A2-to-Envision-Energy-International-Limiteds-USD-500-million-green-bonds--PR_488123

Netease. (2022, August 12). 3.0 [Envision Group's 3.0 era]. [Netease]. https://www.163.com/dy/article/HEJLARKM0552LIVZ.html

OFweek Energy Storage Network. (2025, January 22). " ", [“Pointing Toward the Sea”: A Long Shot Capturing Chinese Enterprises' Global Expansion Journey]. OFweek [OFweek Energy Storage Network]. https://chuneng.ofweek.com/news/2025-01/ART-180225-8500-30655992.html

OFweek Lithium Battery Network. (2021a, June 25). , AESC [Supplying Renault, Envision AESC's new battery factory will be located in France]. OFweek [OFweek Lithium Battery Network]. https://libattery.ofweek.com/2021-06/ART-36001-8500-30506240.html

OFweek Lithium Battery Network. (2021b, October 28). , ! [Focusing on both power lithium batteries and energy storage batteries, Envision Technology launches zero-carbon practice in Ordos!]. OFweek [OFweek Lithium Battery Network]. https://libattery.ofweek.com/2021-10/ART-36001-8500-30531951.html

Ordos Municipal People's Government. (2025, January 7). " " [Ordos Zero-Carbon Industrial Park sets an example for global zero-carbon new industrial bases]. [Ordos]. https://www.ordos.gov.cn/xw_127672/jreeds/202501/t20250107_3755597.html

Photovoltaic Industry Network. (2024, April 11). ! , [Photovoltaic industry leaders are entering the market one after another! Vietnam is emerging as a major photovoltaic power]. [Photovoltaic Industry Network]. http://www.solarenpv.com/news/show.php?itemid=19031

Polaris Solar Photovoltaic Network. (2025, March 21). " " [First "Zero-Carbon Ranch" in Etoke Banner, Inner Mongolia: Distributed Photovoltaic Power Plant Completed and Connected to the Grid]. [Polaris Solar Photovoltaic Network]. https://mguangfu.bjx.com.cn/mnews/20250321/1433371.shtml

RE100, Climate Group, & CDP. (2023). RE100 reporting guidance 2023(Version 7.0). https://cdn.cdp.net/cdp-production/cms/guidance_docs/pdfs/000/001/322/original/RE100-reporting-guidance.pdf.pdf

République Française. (2023, October 23). Loi relative à l'industrie verte [France Green Industry Act]. https://www.legifrance.gouv.fr/jorf/id/JORFTEXT000048470515

Rizos, V., & Vu, H. (2024, December). Compliance with the EU's carbon footprint requirements for electric vehicle batteries: An analysis of challenges and opportunities[Report]. Centre for European Policy Studies (CEPS). https://circulareconomy.europa.eu/platform/en/knowledge/compliance-eus-carbon-footprint-requirements-electric-vehicle-batteries-overview-challenges

RSM. (2022, August 20). The capital allowances super-deduction – it could be great for the renewables sector. RSM. https://www.rsmuk.com/insights/tax-voice/the-capital-allowances-super-deduction-it-could-be-great-for-the-renewables-sector

SBTi. (2022). Envision Group science-based targets validation summary. https://sciencebasedtargets.org

ScienceDirect. (2025). China's 1+N policy system supports an earlier peak in carbon emissions. ScienceDirect. https://www.sciencedirect.com/science/article/abs/pii/S1364032125002990

Shanghai Municipal Commission of Economy and Informatization. (2023, January 11). : , [On the new track of a strong country and embarking on a new journey: The zero-carbon journey, this green technology enterprise leads the new zero-carbon industry]. [Shanghai Industrial Policy Service Network]. https://app.sheitc.sh.gov.cn/zxxx/694255.htm

Smith, J. (2024). Geopolitical impact on new energy enterprise governance. *Energy Policy Journal*, *15*(2), 45–62.

SUEZ. (2024, September 24). SUEZ and Eramet recycle electric vehicle batteries. SUEZ. https://www.suez.com/en/news/suez-eramet-recycle-electric-vehicle-batteries

The People's Daily Online. (2012, December 10). : [Envision Energy: Intelligent wind turbines lead the low-wind-speed market]. [The People's Daily Online]. http://finance.people.com.cn/stock/n/2012/1210/c222942-19851561.html

Tian, Q. (2017). Challenges and strategies for Chinese wind turbine manufacturers going global. *Clean Technology Investment*, *15*(3), 45–59.

UAEGOV. (2023). National Hydrogen Strategy: The Official Platform of the UAE Government. UAE Government Portal. u.ae. https://u.ae/en/about-the-uae/strategies-initiatives-and-awards/strategies-plans-and-visions/environment-and-energy/national-hydrogen-strategy

UNFCCC. (2024, November). Decision -/CP.29: Technical guidelines for zero-carbon industrial parks. https://unfccc.int/documents/642899

Univers. (2025, October 2). Univers launches EnOS™ Ark 2.0: Smarter, faster, and scalable AI for energy savings and carbon reduction. Pollution Online. https://www.pollutiononline.com/doc/univers-launches-enos-ark-smarter-faster-and-scalable-ai-for-energy-savings-and-carbon-reduction-0001

USA Department of the Treasury. (2023, October 19). USA Department of the Treasury releases final rules on investment tax credit to produce more American-made clean energy, strengthen industrial base, and cut costs for families[Press release]. USA Department of the Treasury. https://home.treasury.gov/news/press-releases/jy2736

USGS. (2024, January 31). USGS Releases Mineral Commodity Summaries 2024, finds US Mineral Production Jumped 4 billion to exceed 105 billion dollars. Mineral Commodity Summaries. https://www.usgs.gov/news/technical-announcement/usgs-releases-mineral-commodity-summaries-2024-finds-us-mineral

VGP. (2023). Gov't approves 8th National Power Development Plan. baochinhphu. https://en.baochinhphu.vn/decision-approving-national-power-development-plan-8-111230614195813455.htm

Wang, E. (2017, May 17). : ? [Interview with Envision Energy vice president: Where is the difficulty for Chinese wind turbine companies in going global?]. [China Energy Network]. https://www.china5e.com/news/news-988134-1.html

KEY TERMS AND DEFINITIONS

Artificial Intelligence of Things (AIoT): The integration of artificial intelligence with Internet of Things technologies to optimize energy management, predictive maintenance, and carbon accounting. Within the article, AIoT underpins Envision's digital export model and enhances the efficiency of wind, solar, storage, and hydrogen systems.

Carbon Border Adjustment Mechanism (CBAM): A European Union regulatory instrument that imposes carbon costs on imported goods based on embedded emissions. The article presents CBAM as both a compliance pressure and a strategic premium opportunity for Envision's localized zero-carbon production model.

Energy Internet of Things Operating System (EnOS™): Envision's proprietary AIoT-based digital platform that connects distributed energy assets, enables real-time carbon tracking, and supports virtual power plant operations. It represents the company's transition from hardware manufacturing to high-margin Software-as-a-Service (SaaS) solutions.

Power Purchase Agreement (PPA): A long-term contractual arrangement between electricity producers and consumers that locks in pricing and supply conditions. In Envision's strategy, PPAs secure stable revenue streams for zero-carbon electricity and enable cross-regional green power arbitrage.

Renewable Energy 100 (RE100): A global corporate initiative requiring member companies to commit to sourcing 100% of their electricity from renewable energy. In the article, RE100 functions as an external governance mechanism that shapes Envision's market access, supplier compliance requirements, and competitive positioning in international green electricity procurement.

Science-Based Targets Initiative (SBTi): A global climate governance mechanism that validates corporate emission-reduction targets aligned with the Paris Agreement's 1.5°C pathway. In the article, SBTi certification requires Envision to integrate Scope 1, Scope 2, and Scope 3 lifecycle accounting across its global supply chain.

Task Force on Climate-related Financial Disclosures (TCFD): An international framework that standardizes corporate disclosure of climate-related financial risks and opportunities. Envision uses TCFD reporting to reduce green bond financing costs, enhance transparency, and strengthen its credibility in global capital markets.

Zero-Carbon Industrial Park: An integrated industrial ecosystem powered entirely by renewable energy and supported by energy storage, hydrogen systems, and intelligent IoT management. The article highlights the Ordos model as a replicable, governance-aligned infrastructure template that functions as a scalable "public good."

Chapter 17
Hikvision's AIoT Security Expansion:
AIoT Security, Challenges, and Competitive Advantages

Qipei Wan
http://orcid.org/0009-0002-6433-9348
Beijing Normal-Hong Kong Baptist University, China

EXECUTIVE SUMMARY

This chapter examines the global expansion strategies of Hangzhou Hikvision Digital Technology, the world's largest video surveillance manufacturer and a leader in Artificial Intelligence of Things (AIoT) solutions. Grow from a Chinese state-owned research centre to a multinational corporation using in over 180 countries, to analyses the motivations, entry modes, and competitive advantages underpinning its internationalization. Key themes include the saturation of the domestic Chinese market, geopolitical pressures such as U.S. sanctions, and strategic responses including joint ventures in India, acquisitions in Europe, and localized manufacturing in Hungary. To explore Hikvision's technological leadership through substantial R&D investment, its adaptation to regulatory frameworks like the GDPR, and the mitigation of trade barriers via supply chain diversification. By synthesizing strategic frameworks and corporate data, the chapter provides insights into balancing global scale with regional adaptation, offering lessons for technology firms navigating complex international markets.

DOI: 10.4018/979-8-3373-4302-0.ch017

INTRODUCTION

Background of the Company

Brief History and Core Business

Although Hikvision began as a government research center focused on video surveillance technologies with just 28 employees, it has quickly become a global leader in intelligent Internet of Things (IoT) technologies, focusing on video-centric security and digital transformation solutions. The company's core business revolves around the development and application of AIoT technologies, which integrate perception, artificial intelligence (AI), and big data to serve a wide range of fields, including smart city construction, transportation, and industry. Over the years, it has developed to offer integrated security solutions and intelligent vertical solutions. It has expanded into related markets, such as smart home and automotive electronics, all of which are underpinned by its video intelligence technology (Hikvision, 2024).

Products and Manufacturing.

Hikvision offers a comprehensive range of products divided into two categories: hardware and software, including video surveillance cameras, video recording and management systems, access control systems, video intercom products, and software platforms. To take a concise example, the ColorVu technology, a video surveillance camera, is renowned for producing clear, full-color images even in extremely low-light conditions, which is a significant advantage in surveillance applications (Jer-Tech, 2025). The company is also expanding into emerging areas such as smart homes, robotics, automotive electronics, intelligent storage, fire security, infrared sensing, X-ray detection, and medical imaging. Seven global manufacturing bases support Hikvision's manufacturing capabilities and 11 R&D centers.

Current Market Position.

Domestically, Hikvision maintains a leading position in the Chinese security market. As of 2024, it accounted for a significant portion of the domestic video surveillance market. Morningstar (2023) noted that China is Hikvision's largest and fastest-growing market, contributing approximately 70% of its revenue. Globally, the company is the largest video-centric intelligent IoT provider (Morningstar, 2023). In 2024, Hikvision's total revenue reached nearly 93 billion RMB, with international market revenue accounting for 28.10% of the total (Hikvision, 2024). Jer-Tech (2025) reported approximately 23% of the market share in the global security camera market. In short, Hikvision's international expansion has been driven by its ability to offer high-quality, cost-effective products and its investment in local support and technical services.

Key Milestones in Growth and Internationalization.

2001 to 2010 is the cradle period for Hikvision. After its establishment in 2001, Hikvision focused on building its R&D capabilities and product portfolio in the domestic Chinese market. By 2010, it had grown significantly and went public on the Shenzhen Stock Exchange, which provided it with additional capital for further expansion.

In the early 2010s, Hikvision expanded internationally. It established regional offices in the Americas, Europe, and the Middle East, laying the groundwork for its global sales and support network. In 2011, IMS Research recognized Hikvision as the world's number one DVR supplier, which helped boost its international reputation (Hikvision, 2016).

In the years following 2015, Hikvision continued to invest in R&D, especially in emerging technologies such as AI and IoT. It expanded its product portfolio to include more intelligent security solutions and entered new markets such as smart homes and industrial automation. In 2017, Hikvision Canada launched a French-language website to better serve the French-speaking population in Canada, highlighting its efforts to localize in international markets (Hikvision, 2017). The company's revenue continued to flourish, reaching RMB 92.50 billion (USD 12.87 billion) in 2024 (Hikvision, 2024).

Organizational Structure and Leadership Highlights.

Hikvision has a multilevel organizational structure that supports its global operations. At the top is the board of directors, which provides strategic direction. The CEO, Hu Yangzhong, leads a decentralized structure with three divisions: domestic business groups, innovation units, and global operations. The company has a large R&D team, with over 20,000 R&D engineers as of 202(*Hikvision*, n.d.). These engineers are in R&D centers worldwide, including the UK, Canada, and the Asia-Pacific region, as well as in 8 cities in China. This global R&D setup allows Hikvision to develop region-specific solutions and stay at the forefront of technological innovation. As for the ethical framework, Hikvision adheres to "Professional, Honest, Resilient" principles, with compliance systems such as the Whistleblower Policy in 2022 and the Global Human Rights Policy in 2023 (*Hikvision*, 2022).

In terms of leadership, Hikvision's management team has been crucial in driving its growth. The company's leadership has emphasized a culture of innovation, professionalism, and reliability. For example, the company's commitment to investing over 10% of its annual sales revenue into R&D for continued product innovation reflects the leadership's long-term vision for the company. In the August 8, 2024, interview with Harvard Business Review, which was also published on Hikvision's official site, Hu Yangzhong, the chairperson and one founder of Hikvision, stressed that Hikvision "earns money through technological innovation" and makes "huge investment & continuous accumulation in defined major tech directions". He noted that the firm keeps "massive R&D input in AI, including large models" and has "comprehensively deployed sensing technologies across electromagnetic and sound wave bands since 2016" to fuel scenario digitalization (Hu, 2024).

Current Size and Global Presence.

As of 2024, Hikvision employs nearly 60,000 people, with over 28,000 engaged in R&D and technical services. The company's products and services are available in over 180 countries and regions. Hikvision's extensive marketing network, which includes 32 provincial business centers and over 300 city branches in China, and 22 overseas functional centers, supports its global presence. This network enables Hikvision to respond quickly to the needs of customers, users, and partners across different regions. Thus, Hikvision's global reach and large-scale operations have solidified its position as a leading player in the global security technology market.

Motivation for Global Expansion

Regarding Hikvision's domestic market expansion in China, it initially experienced rapid growth in the security technology market. However, over time, the domestic market became increasingly saturated. The Chinese security market has seen significant development, with many domestic and international competitors vying for market share. As of the mid-2020s, the growth rate of the domestic security market, especially in traditional surveillance segments, slowed (Morningstar, 2023). For example, in public-sector surveillance projects, a major driver of growth in the early years, the rate of new project initiations decreased because many urban areas already possessed basic surveillance infrastructure. Ultimately, this slowdown in domestic growth potential became one aspect that pushed Hikvision to seek new markets overseas.

Also, the global security technology industry is becoming increasingly competitive year by year. Hikvision faced competition not only from traditional international security giants such as Bosch Security Systems and Axis Communications, but also from emerging players in both developed and developing markets. In the global market, competitors were constantly innovating and improving their products and services. For instance, Axis Communications had a strong foothold in the high-end, high-quality surveillance market in Europe and North America, known for its advanced video analytics and network-based solutions. To maintain and enhance its competitive position, Hikvision needed to expand globally. By entering new markets, it could diversify its customer base, reduce its reliance on any single market, and leverage its cost-effective manufacturing and R&D capabilities to gain an edge over competitors in different regions (Jer-Tech, 2025).

Macroeconomic policies and government support also play a crucial role in Hikvision's global expansion. In the manufacturing sector, the Made in China 2025 initiative, which promoted high-tech manufacturing in China, encouraged Chinese companies like Hikvision to upgrade their technology, improve product quality, and become more globally competitive. The government's support under this initiative, as R&D subsidies, export incentives, and policy guidance, further motivates Hikvision to pursue international expansion. Apart from this, it actively participated in Belt and Road Initiative (BRI)- related projects in countries across Asia, Europe, Africa, and beyond, including Pakistan, where it provided surveillance systems for infrastructure projects. The BRI not only provided market access but also support through government-to-government cooperation, which helped Hikvision navigate regulatory and business-related challenges in these countries.

From the perspective of internationalization strategies and strategic objectives, one of Hikvision's primary strategic objectives in its international expansion is revenue diversification. By operating in multiple countries and regions, Hikvision could reduce its exposure to risks associated with a single market. For example, if there were an economic downturn or a change in government policies in the Chinese market, its revenue from international operations could help offset potential losses. In 2024, Hikvision's overseas operations accounted for a significant share of its total revenue, with that share steadily increasing over the years. This diversification not only provided financial stability but also allowed the company to invest more in R&D and further expansion (Hikvision, n.d.).

Besides diversifying revenue, global expansion also enabled Hikvision to optimize the supply chain. It established manufacturing bases and R&D centers worldwide. For example, having manufacturing facilities closer to key markets reduced transportation costs and lead times. In India, Hikvision established a manufacturing plant to cater to the growing demand in the South Asian region. This local manufacturing also helped comply with local regulations on import substitution and employment generation. By establishing R&D centers in countries such as Canada and the UK, Hikvision could tap into local talent pools, gain insights into regional market needs, and develop products tailored to specific regions, further enhancing the supply chain efficiency and competitiveness (Hikvision, n.d.).

Building brand recognition is key to gaining the trust of global customers. In the early stages of its international expansion, the company faced the challenge of being a relatively unknown brand in numerous regions outside of China. To address this, it adopted several strategies. Initially, it participated in international security trade shows and exhibitions, such as IFSEC Global in the UK, where it showcased its latest products and technologies. Then it focused on providing high-quality products and after-sales service. By delivering reliable security solutions, the company gradually built a positive reputation among customers and partners in international markets. Over time, Hikvision became more widely recognized as a leading global security technology brand, which helped it attract more customers and expand its market share (Hikvision, 2016).

MARKET ANALYSIS AND ENTRY STRATEGY

Target Market Selection

Hikvision, a global leader in video surveillance and security solutions, has embarked on a steady, ambitious international expansion. The company's success in the international arena is not accidental but the result of a meticulous target market selection process. This process involves evaluating various factors, such as economic growth, consumer demand, the regulatory environment, and the competitive landscape. Armed with this insight, Hikvision can strategically target markets with the highest potential for its products and services, optimizing future growth.

It has established its operational footprint across over 180 countries and regions globally. Key territories where it maintains a substantial market position encompass Southeast Asia, the Middle East, Africa, and select areas of Latin America. Concurrently, the company has also secured a visible market share in mature economies, including Europe and North America. Developing economies are a primary strategic emphasis for Hikvision's growth initiatives. To illustrate, Southeast Asian nations such as Indonesia, Vietnam, and the Philippines are experiencing rapid economic growth. Indonesia, characterized by its large population and expanding middle class, has recorded consistent GDP growth of approximately 5% in recent reporting periods (World Bank, 2024). This progression coincides with heightened urbanization, industrial sector growth, and infrastructure enhancement initiatives. Escalating security requirements are clear across domains such as commercial properties, industrial zones, and transit facilities. Hikvision's varied product lineup, spanning entry-level monitoring devices to sophisticated AI-integrated security platforms, addresses the shifting demands of these developing markets. In Africa, economies such as Kenya's and Nigeria's are similarly showing positive economic momentum. Kenya's digital sector is advancing alongside smart city projects in Nairobi. These factors have elevated market requirements for surveillance equipment, a demand that Hikvision fulfills. The corporation's capacity to deliver economical yet dependable offerings enhances its appeal in these developing markets, where financial limitations often influence procurement decisions.

Prevailing economic growth patterns also influence market selection within developed economies. Consider Europe: the rising adoption of smart city frameworks and the convergence of security technologies with broader urban systems create growth potential. Urban centers aiming to enhance operational efficiency, public safety, and environmental sustainability cause smarter, unified security approaches. Hikvision strategically positions its sophisticated offerings, including public-space cameras equipped with facial recognition and access control solutions synchronized with building management networks, to address these evolving requirements effectively.

When evaluating developed versus emerging economies, developed economies offer distinct advantages for Hikvision. These markets typically feature mature, sophisticated security sectors where customers are more willing to invest in premium, innovative security technologies. Illustratively, North America and Western Europe exhibit a strong demand for AI-driven surveillance systems, sophisticated access control solutions, and integrated security management platforms. Developed economies also present challenges. The competition is intense, with well-established local and international players. Brands like Bosch Security Systems and Axis Communications have a strong foothold in these markets and often maintain long-standing relationships with customers. Emerging economies offer significant growth potential because of expanding middle classes, rapid urbanization, and increased infrastructure investment. As mentioned earlier, the demand for security solutions in these regions is on the rise. The cost-effectiveness of Hikvision's products gives it a competitive edge in emerging markets where price sensitivity is often higher.

Emerging economies also come with their own set of challenges. Infrastructure may be less developed in some areas, making product installation and maintenance more difficult. Apart from that, regulatory frameworks may be less clear or stable, and there may be higher risks associated with political instability and economic volatility. For example, some Latin American countries may experience currency fluctuations that can impact Hikvision's pricing and profitability.

Based on the two target-market categories, Hikvision has identified distinct consumer segments. In the commercial sector, businesses of all sizes, from small and medium-sized enterprises (SMEs) to large corporations, require security solutions. SMEs, in particular, are a growing segment. In 2024, Hikvision launched one-stop SMB solutions tailored for common small- and medium-sized business scenarios, including stores, offices, homes, and farms. These solutions aim to simplify product configurations, reduce installation and maintenance costs, and meet the specific security and operational needs of SMEs. In the residential sector, as living standards improve and people become more security-conscious, the demand for home security systems has increased. Hikvision offers a range of home security products, including video doorbells, indoor and outdoor cameras, and access control systems, which can be easily integrated and managed through mobile applications.

To meet consumer demand, Hikvision adapts its products to local market needs. In some Middle Eastern countries, where extreme temperatures are common, the company has developed cameras with enhanced heat-resistance features. For high-humidity regions like Southeast Asia, its products feature moisture-resistant construction, ensuring consistent performance under demanding environmental conditions.

Entry Mode Selection

During global expansion, Hikvision showed strategic alignment in selecting entry modes with target market attributes, risk appetite, and strategic goals. The company implemented a diverse entry mode portfolio: exporting, joint ventures, mergers and acquisitions (M&A), and organic investments to balance market entry efficiency with control retention. This method enabled adaptation to diverse regional regulatory frameworks, cultural contexts, and competitive environments. The following analysis explains these main entry modes and the strategic reasons behind them.

Exporting served as Hikvision's foundational entry mode, particularly in the early stages of internationalization. This mode involved selling products directly to overseas distributors, system integrators, or end-users without establishing local production facilities. It required minimal upfront capital compared to establishing local operations, making it ideal for testing new markets. In addition, it allowed Hikvision to gauge demand across diverse regions (e.g., Southeast Asia and Africa) before committing to larger investments. By exporting, leveraging Hikvision's cost advantages, and expanding its manufacturing scale in China, it enables competitive pricing in price-sensitive emerging markets (Hikvision, n.d.). By 2010, Hikvision had established export channels covering over 50 countries, partnering with local distributors to handle logistics, marketing, and after-sales services (Hikvision, 2016). It optimized export processes by aligning product certifications with regional standards, such as CE marking for Europe and FCC compliance for North America, to streamline market access.

Apart from achieving initial market testing and scalability through exports, the company exploits joint ventures and partnerships to mitigate risks in complex markets. In regions with strict regulatory barriers or cultural nuances, Hikvision prioritized joint ventures and strategic partnerships to gain local insights and compliance support. Such as joint ventures with local firms helping Hikvision navigate import restrictions, data privacy laws (e.g., GDPR in Europe), and government procurement rules; local partners providing expertise in consumer preferences, enabling tailored marketing and service strategies; shared ownership reducing financial exposure in politically unstable or economically volatile markets (e.g., parts of Africa and Latin America). In India, Hikvision formed a joint venture with a local electronics manufacturer in 2015 to comply with the government's "Make in India" policy, which mandated local production for public sector contracts. This joint venture established a manufacturing plant in Bangalore, enabling access to India's growing smart-city projects. In the Middle East, Hikvision partnered with regional system integrators (e.g., in Dubai) to deploy surveillance systems for mega-projects like Expo 2020, leveraging partners' knowledge of local infrastructure and procurement processes (Hikvision, 2020). On June 5, 2024, reported that Hikvision partnered with Saudi industrial conglomerate Alfanar to unveil a local manufacturing facility in Riyadh. The collaboration aligns with Saudi Arabia's "Vision 2030," focusing on localizing security product production to boost the kingdom's manufacturing sector (Saudi Shopper, 2024).

M&A is a key strategy for Hikvision to gain market share quickly, acquire proprietary technologies, and overcome entry barriers in mature markets. Acquiring established local firms allowed Hikvision to inherit existing customer bases, distribution networks, and brand recognition. M&A enabled access to advanced technologies (e.g., AI algorithms, cybersecurity solutions) to enhance product portfolios. What else, in regions with protectionist policies, acquiring a local entity reduced scrutiny compared to greenfield investments. There were many instances in 2016; Hikvision gained Pyronix, a UK-based manufacturer of alarm systems and access control solutions. This acquisition expanded Hikvision's non-CCTV product lines and strengthened its presence in Europe's security market, where Pyronix had a 30-year brand legacy ("China,United Kingdom," 2016). In 2021, Hikvision gained a majority stake in a Turkish surveillance firm, acquiring access to NATO-aligned markets and local R&D capabilities focused on ruggedized products for harsh climates.

Competitive Advantage

In the highly competitive global security technology market, Hikvision has emerged as a dominant player, with a significant presence in over 180 countries and regions. Its success can be attributed to a set of well-developed competitive advantages that have not only differentiated it from global rivals but also propelled its international expansion. The following statements will delve into these competitive advantages, explore how the company built them, and analyze their contribution to its international development.

From a technological innovation perspective, Hikvision has consistently showed strong technological prowess, offering a wide range of innovative security products.

Its product portfolio includes high-definition cameras, intelligent video analytics systems, access control solutions, and integrated security management platforms. For example, the company's AI-powered cameras, featuring facial recognition, behavioral analysis, and license plate recognition, have set new industry standards. These advanced products enable Hikvision to meet the diverse and evolving security needs of customers across various sectors, such as public safety, transportation, retail, and healthcare (Hikvision, n.d.).

To maintain its technological edge, Hikvision has invested heavily in research and development. The company allocates a significant portion of its annual revenue to R&D, with over 10% of its sales revenue invested in this area in recent years (Hikvision, n.d.). It has established a global network of R&D centers, with facilities in key tech hubs such as Hangzhou, Beijing, Shanghai, Montreal, and London. These centers employ a large team of highly skilled engineers and researchers, dedicated to developing new technologies and improving existing products. As of 2024, Hikvision had over 20,000 R&D engineers worldwide (Hikvision, n.d.), enabling it to remain at the forefront of innovation in the security technology field.

Hikvision enjoys economies of scale in its manufacturing processes. The company has established extensive production facilities in China and other parts of the world, enabling it to produce security products in large quantities. This large-scale production helps reduce per-unit production costs, allowing Hikvision to offer its products at competitive prices compared to many of its global rivals. For example, its ability to mass-produce cameras and other security devices gives it a cost advantage in price-sensitive markets, such as those in emerging economies across Southeast Asia, Africa, and Latin America (Morningstar, 2023).

Significantly, Hikvision has developed a highly efficient supply chain management system. It works closely with numerous suppliers to ensure a stable and cost-effective supply of raw materials and components. By optimizing the supply chain, the company can reduce procurement costs, shorten production cycles, and improve overall operational efficiency. This efficient supply chain management not only reduces costs but also enables Hikvision to respond quickly to market demand and deliver products to customers on time (Hikvision, n.d.).

What else? Hikvision's extensive global distribution network plays a significant role in connecting companies and customers, including partnerships with local distributors, system integrators, and resellers across various countries and regions. This network allows the company to reach customers in even the most remote markets. By leveraging the local expertise and resources of its distribution partners, Hikvision can effectively promote its products, provide technical support, and offer after-sales services. The company's distribution network covers over 180 countries, ensuring that its products are readily available to customers worldwide (Hikvision, n.d.).

Recognizing the importance of meeting local market needs, Hikvision has adopted a strong localization strategy. The company tailors its products and services to the specific requirements of different regions and countries. This includes adapting products to local technical standards, regulatory requirements, and cultural preferences. For example, in Europe, Hikvision ensures its products comply with strict data protection regulations such as the GDPR. In the Middle East, it develops products that can withstand extreme temperatures and harsh environmental conditions. Hikvision hires local employees in its overseas offices and subsidiaries, who have a better understanding of the local market and can provide more personalized services to customers (Hikvision Europe, 2022).

From a brand recognition perspective, Hikvision has built a strong reputation based on the high quality of its products and reliable services. The company adheres to strict quality control standards throughout the production process, ensuring that its products meet or exceed industry standards. Its products are known for their durability, performance, and advanced features, earning the trust and loyalty of customers worldwide. In addition, Hikvision provides comprehensive after-sales services, including technical support, maintenance, and training, to ensure customer satisfaction (Hikvision, n.d.).

In summary, Hikvision's competitive advantages, including technological innovation, cost efficiency, a global distribution network with a localization strategy, and strong brand recognition, have been crucial to its success in the global security technology market. These advantages have been built through strategic planning, heavy investment in R&D, efficient production and supply chain management, talent recruitment and development, and collaboration with partners. They have enabled Hikvision to penetrate new markets, compete with global rivals, and build long-term customer relationships, driving its international development. As the security technology market continues to evolve, Hikvision will need to continue to strengthen its competitive advantages and adapt to changing market conditions to maintain its leading position.

IMPLEMENTATION OF GLOBAL EXPANSION

Hikvision's global expansion is not merely a theoretical plan but a series of concrete actions and investments that have transformed its presence from a domestic Chinese company to a global leader in security technology. The following paragraphs will focus on how Hikvision has implemented its global expansion strategy, including the specific actions taken, the challenges encountered, and the strategies used to overcome them. By examining these practical aspects, we can gain a deeper understanding of how the company has turned its expansion plans into reality.

Key Initiatives and Investments

A strategic global expansion initiative involves establishing local manufacturing operations. This approach reduces production/transportation expenses while enhancing responsiveness to regional requirements and regulatory compliance. Notably, in India, Hikvision partnered with a domestic electronics manufacturer to inaugurate a production facility in Bangalore in 2015. This development directly addressed India's "Make in India" mandate, which stipulates local production thresholds for public-sector eligibility. The site manufactures comprehensive CCTV camera lines and security devices, supporting India's escalating security needs for smart city initiatives and infrastructure expansion. Correspondingly, in Hungary, Hikvision commissioned a production center in 2019 functioning as a European supply nexus. Localized manufacturing curtails delivery timelines and freight costs, enhancing market competitiveness. The facility further mitigates trade barriers and ensures adherence to EU standards governing product safety and environmental protocols.

Maintaining technological leadership and addressing diverse market requirements necessitates substantial investment in Hikvision's worldwide R&D infrastructure. The company operates dedicated research centers across multiple countries: China, Canada, the United Kingdom, and Singapore. Montreal's Canadian facility focuses on artificial intelligence and video analytics, leveraging local AI expertise to develop sophisticated algorithms that enhance product functionality—including facial recognition and object detection. Singapore's center, established in 2023 (Hikvision, 2023), develops smart city solutions that address Southeast Asian needs, such as flood monitoring and traffic management. This globally distributed R&D model enables access to worldwide expertise, provides market-specific insights, and facilitates regionally customized product development. Hikvision sustains its technological edge while enhancing service delivery to international clientele.

Through sustained operational experience, Hikvision recognizes the critical role of local partnerships in international market expansion. The company proactively cultivates collaborations with regional distributors, system integrators, and resellers to develop robust distribution channels. In the Middle East, Hikvision partnered with local integrators on major initiatives, including Dubai's Expo 2020. These alliances enable harnessing partners' regional expertise and superior understanding of market requirements, regulatory frameworks, and cultural nuances. Through such alliances, Hikvision delivered integrated security solutions for the event, strengthening its regional brand recognition and market standing (Hikvision, 2020). Concurrently in Latin America, Hikvision broadened its distribution reach through local reseller engagements. Illustratively, in Chile, the company implemented its Value-Added Solution Partner (VASP) initiative, providing partners with training programs, technical help, and promotional resources. This empowers partners to effectively market and distribute Hikvision's offerings, simultaneously facilitating greater market penetration throughout the territory (Ventas de Seguridad, 2016).

To enhance global brand recognition and advance product promotion, Hikvision undertakes a range of marketing initiatives. The company regularly exhibits at international trade shows like IFSEC International in the UK and ISC West in the US. This allows them to showcase their latest products, connect with clients and partners, and build relationships with industry experts.

Besides trade events, Hikvision employs digital marketing to target prospective clients. Region-specific portals deliver localized product and service details in native languages. Social platforms and online promotions help to increase brand engagement. Collectively, these initiatives elevate Hikvision's global brand stature and solidify its leadership in security solutions.

Challenges Faced

Notwithstanding considerable efforts at globalization, Hikvision faces persistent challenges, with geopolitical friction and trade barriers as primary obstacles. Entanglement in US-China trade disputes culminated in US sanctions, including a 2019 Department of Commerce Entity List designation. This restriction impedes access to American technologies and components, causing costlier and protracted supply chain diversification that substantially disrupts US operations (Stimson Center, 2019). Security concerns in other nations have prompted restrictions; multiple European countries prohibit deployment at sensitive installations such as government facilities and critical infrastructure. These geopolitical headwinds materially constrain market penetration across Western economies.

Regulatory fragmentation across markets creates additional barriers to expansion. The EU's GDPR mandates stringent personal data protocols affecting Hikvision's AI camera functionalities, particularly facial recognition systems. Compliance requires substantial product modifications, including implementing data encryption mechanisms and enhanced user data controls. These resource-intensive adaptations mitigate the risks of non-compliance penalties and reputational damage (Hikvision Europe, n.d.). In some emerging markets, regulatory frameworks for security products are still under development, creating uncertainty for Hikvision. The company must navigate complex, often-changing regulations, which can delay product launches and increase costs. The global security technology market is highly competitive, with both local and global players vying for market share. Hikvision faces competition from well-established global companies such as Bosch Security Systems and Axis Communications, as well as local players in different markets who have a better understanding of local needs and relationships with local customers.

Beyond the challenges discussed above, cultural and market differences across countries can pose dilemmas for Hikvision. Consumer preferences, business practices, and technical standards can vary significantly across markets, requiring Hikvision to adapt its products and services accordingly. For example, in some Middle Eastern countries, cultural and religious factors may influence the design of security products. Hikvision has had to develop cameras that are more discreet and respect local cultural norms. In addition, markets vary in technological development, so Hikvision may need to offer different product ranges across regions, from basic security cameras in some emerging markets to advanced smart city solutions in developed markets.

In developed markets, companies like Axis Communications have strong brand reputations and loyal customer bases, making it difficult for Hikvision to gain market share. In emerging markets, local players may offer lower-priced products, which can be attractive to price-sensitive customers. Fierce market competition demands sustained innovation and differentiation to keep market leadership.

Mitigation Strategies

In response to the challenges mentioned, Hikvision has primarily employed the following strategies to address them.

Confronting trade constraints and geopolitical friction, Hikvision executed supply chain diversification. This entailed reducing US technology and component dependency by sourcing alternatives from South Korean and Taiwanese suppliers, while increasing R&D expenditure to develop proprietary technologies and reduce reliance on external suppliers. Strategically, manufacturing hubs were established in India, Hungary, and Vietnam to support localized production and mitigate the effects of trade barriers. These decentralized supply chain and production measures collectively ensure uninterrupted global product distribution.

To address regulatory complexities, Hikvision strengthened its compliance capabilities by deploying dedicated legal teams to monitor global regulatory shifts and ensure product compliance with local mandates. The company actively engages regulators and industry bodies in standard-setting processes, as exemplified by its European collaborations that ensure GDPR compliance (Hikvision Europe, 2022). This proactive posture anticipates regulatory evolution and ensures system compatibility.

Cultural and market adaptation is achieved through hyper-localization. Market-specific product customization, local talent recruitment, and regional service frameworks address both technical standards and cultural expectations. For example, in Africa, partnerships with system integrators deliver infrastructure-adapted security solutions, while energy-efficient products withstand extreme climatic conditions critical to regional viability.

To maintain a competitive advantage, continuous innovation is necessary. Hikvision's extensive R&D capabilities have pioneered technologies such as AI-enabled cameras that deliver real-time security analytics for critical environments. Integrated solution ecosystems that converge surveillance, access control, and intrusion detection provide comprehensive security architectures. This integrated approach delivers operational efficiency while distinguishing Hikvision from competitors.

STRATEGIC ANALYSIS

Analytical Frameworks

From Hikvision's company insight to analysis, it possesses several notable strengths. With over 20 years in the CCTV security industry, it has developed a strong brand portfolio that is challenging for competitors to undermine, providing valuable brand equity when entering new markets or product categories (Shastri, 2025). The company invests 10% of its annual revenue in research and development, ensuring it remains at the cutting edge of technology, with advancements in AI-powered video analytics, deep learning, and smart detection (Hikvision, n.d.). Its global presence, spanning over 150 countries and R&D centers in many of them, allows for quick adaptation to local market needs and the building of strong customer relationships (Shastri, 2025). Increasing demand for security systems, driven by rising crime rates and security awareness, has led to year-on-year growth in sales and annual revenue, strengthening its financial position (Shastri, 2025). Hikvision also offers a diverse product portfolio, ranging from security thermal cameras and traffic flow detection systems to entrance & exit control, parking management systems, emergency alarms, and LCD video walls, catering to an array of market segments (Shastri, 2025).

Significant weaknesses require attention. Some reports suggest Hikvision may not be as customer-oriented as certain competitors, which might harm customer loyalty (Shastri, 2025). A trend of declining per-unit revenue is a concern, as it may impact overall profitability if left unchecked (Hikvision, 2025). High job stress has led to retention issues, disrupting operations and R&D efforts. The company might lack flexibility in its supply chain, which could create difficulties in responding to sudden changes in demand or supply disruptions (Shastri, 2025).

Even though Hikvision faces those weaknesses, it possesses substantial growth opportunities. The growing low-end market, which is more price-sensitive but has significant volume potential, offers an opportunity to capture a larger share. Collaborating with local players in target international markets can facilitate more effective business expansion by leveraging local knowledge and resources (Shastri, 2025). The trend of consumers moving toward high-end products allows Hikvision to showcase its advanced technology and gain a larger portion of the high-margin market. For example, in the EU, new security product certifications require €500,000+ in testing costs, which deters small competitors and benefits Hikvision's established position.

Despite existing opportunities, persistent threats demand critical examination. Threats to the company include growing criticism from environmental protection groups, which could pose risks to its operations if linked to environmental issues in manufacturing or product use (Shastri, 2025). A talent shortage in the market may hinder recruitment and retention of top employees, hampering innovation and growth potential (Shastri, 2025). Growth opportunities are limited by market saturation and stagnation, as the rural market is stagnating and some urban regions are approaching saturation (Morningstar, 2023). Increasing customer health consciousness may lead to concerns about the potential health impacts of surveillance technology, affecting demand (Fussey & Murray, 2025).

From an external perspective, macro-environmental forces significantly shape a firm's global expansion trajectory. First, political factors play a significant role in Hikvision's international operations. Regulations regarding surveillance technology vary widely across countries. Some nations have strict data protection and privacy laws, while others have rules governing surveillance in public spaces. For example, the European Union's GDPR imposes strict requirements on data collection, storage, and use. Hikvision must ensure compliance with these regulations in all international markets to avoid legal issues and maintain its reputation (European Data Protection Board [EDPB], 2020). Political instability in certain regions can also disrupt business operations. Countries experiencing civil unrest or frequent government changes may have inconsistent policies, making long-term investment and expansion planning difficult (US, 2023).

Concurrently, macroeconomic volatility directly shapes Hikvision's transnational revenue streams. In emerging economies with growing GDP, demand for security solutions to support infrastructure development, urbanization, and business expansion is increasing, presenting opportunities for sales growth. However, during economic downturns, both consumers and businesses may reduce spending on non-essential items, such as advanced surveillance systems, impacting revenue (World Bank, 2024). Exchange rate fluctuations can also affect profitability; a stronger Chinese yuan relative to target-market currencies makes Hikvision's products relatively more expensive, reducing competitiveness (BIS, 2023).

Social dynamics significantly shape market receptivity and stakeholder expectations. Rising crime rates and growing concerns about public safety have increased awareness and demand for security solutions, benefiting Hikvision as more individuals, businesses, and governments invest in surveillance technology. However, there is also a growing concern about privacy invasion from increased surveillance, which could lead to negative public perception if not addressed (Fussey & Murray,

2025). Demographic changes also shape demand: an aging population in some developed countries creates needs for home-based surveillance for elderly care, while a large young population in other countries drives demand for surveillance in public areas, schools, and workplaces (United Nations Department of Economic and Social Affairs, Population Division [UN DESA PD], 2025).

Simultaneously, technological innovation constitutes a critical determinant of competitive advantage within the surveillance sector, which is constantly evolving with new technologies such as AI, machine learning, and the Internet of Things (IoT). Hikvision's continuous R&D investment positions it well to keep pace with these advancements, but failure to innovate at the same rate as competitors could cause market share loss (China Report Hall, 2025). There is also a growing trend toward integrating different security technologies, such as combining video surveillance with access control systems, allowing Hikvision to develop integrated, comprehensive security solutions.

Environmental imperatives increasingly constrain operational frameworks across global markets. There is increasing focus on sustainable manufacturing practices, and Hikvision may face pressure to reduce its environmental footprint by cutting energy consumption and waste generation. Adopting sustainable practices can also enhance its brand image in environmentally conscious markets (Hikvision, 2025a). In regions prone to extreme weather, there is a demand for surveillance products that can withstand harsh conditions, and Hikvision can develop products with enhanced durability and climate-resilience features to meet this need (China Report Hall, 2025).

Ultimately, regulatory compliance pressures represent a further external challenge requiring strategic adaptation. Protecting intellectual property (IP) is crucial as Hikvision expands globally. In some countries, enforcing IP rights is more challenging, with risks of counterfeiting or IP theft. The company must ensure its products and technologies do not infringe on others' IP rights (EDPB, 2020). Different countries have varying product liability laws, and Hikvision must ensure its products meet all safety and quality standards in each market to avoid potential legal liabilities from product failures or malfunctions.

Brand and Reputation Effects

So far, Hikvision has achieved significant global brand recognition in the video surveillance and IoT solutions industry. Its extensive presence in over 150 countries, coupled with its participation in international trade shows and events, has helped establish its brand as a major player in the market (Shastri, 2025). In numerous regions, the brand is associated with advanced technology, reliability, and a wide range of product offerings, which have contributed to a positive perception among customers, including governments, businesses, and institutions.

It is pivotal to recognize that brand perception varies across diverse market contexts. In select developed markets, Hikvision's technological proficiency garners recognition, yet governmental and media concerns about data security and privacy moderately impact brand perception (Fussey & Murray, 2025). These concerns occasionally manifest as operational restrictions or heightened scrutiny, affecting market-specific reputations. Conversely, across emerging economies, the brand is frequently perceived as delivering premium cost-performance solutions, establishing preference for infrastructure and security initiatives, and cultivating substantially positive brand equity.

Concurrently, Hikvision's corporate citizenship and sustainability endeavors serve as a global foundation for its reputation. Sustainability-wise, implemented eco-conscious manufacturing measures include energy-efficient technology investments, waste stream reduction, and sustainable material integration (Hikvision, 2025b). These initiatives align with global environmental imperatives while elevating brand standing among ecological stakeholders. Regarding CSR, the company engages in multifaceted community initiatives: implementing educational technology initiatives to enhance scholastic outcomes and contributing to disaster response through surveillance deployments and technical help during reconstruction following natural calamities (Hikvision, 2023). These initiatives show the company's commitment to giving back to society, which helps build trust and a positive reputation among local communities and the public.

CONCLUSION AND STRATEGIC RECOMMENDATIONS

Summary of Key Findings

Founded in 2001 as a state-owned research center, Hikvision is now the world's largest video-centric IoT provider, operating in over 180 countries with 2024 revenue of nearly 93 billion RMB (28.1% from international sales). Its growth stems from AIoT expertise, serving smart cities, transportation, and industry. International expansion was driven by a saturated domestic market (70% of revenue) and geopolitical pressures, using diverse entry strategies: exporting, joint ventures (e.g., India), acquisitions (e.g., UK's Pyronix), and organic investments (Hungary plant). Competitive strengths include over 10% R&D investment, manufacturing scale, a global distribution network, and localization (e.g., heat-resistant cameras for the Middle East). Challenges such as US sanctions and GDPR were mitigated through supply chain diversification, local teams, and compliance investments.

Future Growth Opportunities

Hikvision can capitalize on emerging markets (e.g., Southeast Asia, Africa, Latin America) where urbanization drives demand for affordable, tailored solutions (e.g., SMB kits). Expanding AIoT and vertical solutions (smart city tools from Singapore's R&D center) aligns with regional infrastructure needs. Diversifying into smart home and automotive electronics reduces reliance on surveillance. Strengthening local production (India, Hungary) bypasses trade barriers, amplifying CSR and sustainability efforts, and builds trust in ESG-focused markets.

Recommendations for Other Firms

In short, Hikvision's experience offers valuable lessons for Chinese companies pursuing international expansion. First, prioritize localization: adapt products, services, and compliance to regional nuances, as Hikvision did with moisture-resistant cameras for Southeast Asia or GDPR-aligned solutions in Europe. Hiring local teams deepens understanding of consumer preferences and regulatory landscapes, easing market entry. Then diversify entry modes to balance risk and control. Start by exporting to test demand, then use joint ventures to navigate complex markets (as in India) or acquisitions to gain instant market access (as in the Pyronix deal in Europe). This layered approach reduces exposure to regulatory or cultural risks. Supply chains should be strengthened to minimize trade disruptions. Hikvision's shift to sourcing from multiple regions (e.g., South Korea and Taiwan) and to local production in Hungary shows how reducing reliance on single suppliers or markets enhances resilience.

If economic conditions permit, invest heavily in R&D and talent retention. Hikvision's 10% revenue allocation to R&D and global R&D centers kept it at the technological forefront; other firms should similarly prioritize innovation to compete with global rivals. Offering competitive incentives to retain top talent prevents bottlenecks in product development.

Meanwhile, proactively manage reputation by addressing ESG and data security concerns. Engage in local CSR projects (such as Hikvision's educational technology donations) and align with global standards to build trust, especially in Western markets. Finally, leverage policy support—such as participating in China's Belt and Road Initiative, as Hikvision did in Pakistan—to access government-backed projects, easing entry into emerging economies.

This case study examines Hikvision's journey in the global security market, focusing on its international expansion strategies, competitive advantages, and challenges encountered. Founded in 2001 as a state-owned research center, Hikvision has grown into the world's largest video surveillance manufacturer and a global leader in AIoT solutions, operating in over 180 countries with nearly 60,000 employees (over 28,000 in R&D) and 2024 revenue of nearly 93 billion RMB (28.1% from international sales).

Driven by a saturated domestic market (70% of revenue from China) and geopolitical pressures, Hikvision expanded internationally through diverse strategies: exporting, joint ventures (e.g., in India to comply with "Make in India" policy), acquisitions (e.g., UK's Pyronix for European access), and local manufacturing (e.g., Hungary for Europe). Its success stems from strengths such as 10% annual investment in R&D, manufacturing economies of scale, a global distribution network, and localization (e.g., heat-resistant cameras for the Middle East, GDPR-compliant solutions for Europe).

However, Hikvision faces challenges, including geopolitical tensions (US sanctions), regulatory hurdles (GDPR), intense competition (e.g., Bosch, Axis Communications), and cultural differences, which are mitigated through supply chain diversification, local partnerships, and compliance efforts. This study offers insights into global expansion strategies, localization, risk management, and balancing scale with regional adaptation for Chinese firms in international markets.

REFERENCES

European Data Protection Board. (2020, January 29). Guidelines 3/2019 on processing of personal data through video devices (Version 2.0). https://www.edpb.europa.eu/sites/default/files/files/file1/edpb_guidelines_201903_video_devices_en_0.pdf

Fussey, P., & Murray, D. (2025, October 13). Input on report on right to privacy in the digital age. United Nations Human Rights Office. https://www.ohchr.org/sites/default/files/documents/cfi-subm/privacy-digital-age/subm-privacy-digital-age-aca-20-pete-f-university-southampton-don.pdf

Hall, C. R. (2025, December 1). 2025 smart surveillance industry prospect analysis: The smart surveillance industry ushers in a dual leap in scale and quality. https://m.chinabgao.com/freereport/110978.html

Hangzhou Hikvision Digital Technology Co. Ltd. (2023). Global human rights policy. https://www.hikvision.com/cn/aboutus/Sustainability/integrity-and-compliance/human-rights-protection/

Hikvision. (2022). Hikvision Whistleblowing Policy. https://www.hikvision.com/content/dam/hikvision/en/marketing/image/about-us/compliance/new/Hikvision-Whistleblowing-Policy-EN_1.pdf/

Hikvision. (2023). –FY2022 [Hikvision at a glance—FY2022]. https://www.hikvision.com/content/dam/hikvision/cn/ / / -2023.pdf

Hikvision. (2024a). Annual report 2024. https://www.hikvision.com/en/newsroom/latest-news/2025/hikvision-releases-2024-full-year-and-2025-first-quarter-financial-results/

Hikvision. (2024b). Company profile. https://www.hikvision.com/cn/about-us/Company-Profile

Hikvision. (2024c). Where are Hikvision cameras manufactured globally? https://www.icseecam.com/where-are-hikvision-cameras-manufactured-glob/

Hikvision. (2025a, August 1). Value chain synergy: Sustainable development. https://www.hikvision.com/cn/aboutus/Sustainability/valuechain/

Hikvision. (2025b, October 22). Our green practices: Corporate sustainability. https://www.hikvision.com/us-en/about-us/sustainability/our-green-practices/

Hikvision. (2025c). 2025 third quarter financial report (Q1–Q3 consolidated) [PDF]. Hangzhou Hikvision Digital Technology Co., Ltd. https://www.hikvision.com/content/dam/hikvision/en/investor-relations/annual-quarterly-reports/2025/3Q2025-Financial-ReportEV.pdf

Hikvision. (n.d.-a). About us. Hikvision Malaysia. https://www.hikvision.net.my/about-us

Hikvision. (n.d.-b). Hikvision focuses on GDPR compliance. Hikvision Europe. https://www.hikvision.com/en/support/cybersecurity/cybersecurity-white-paper/hikvision-focuses-on-gdpr-compliance/

Hikvision North America. (2016, November 4). About Hikvision North America. https://www.hikvision.com/us-en/about-us/about-hikvision-north-america/

Hu, Y. (2024, August 8). Hikvision's Hu Yangzhong: From security to scene digitalization [Interview]. Hikvision. https://www.hikvision.com/cn/NewsEvents/Newsroom/2024/2024-08-08/

Jer-Tech. (2025, March 26). Top global leaders in security camera manufacturing. https://jer-tech.com/top-global-leaders-in-security-camera-manufacturing/

Morningstar. (2023, August 21). Hikvision is undervalued as long-term digitization in China is overshadowed by macroeconomic pain. https://www.morningstar.com/company-reports/1176077

Shastri, A. (2025, August 9). Comprehensive SWOT analysis of Hikvision – one of the largest suppliers of surveillance equipment. Indian Institute of Digital Education. https://iide.co/case-studies/swot-analysis-of-hikvision/

Shopper, S. (2024, June 5). Hikvision–Alfanar partnership unveils local manufacturing facility in Riyadh. https://en.saudishopper.com.sa/?p=49926

Stimson Center. (2019). Hikvision: The dilemma of a surveillance company. https://www.stimson.org/2019/hikvision-dilemma-surveillance-company/

United Nations Department of Economic and Social Affairs. Population Division. (2025). World urbanization prospects: Summary of results (2025 revision) [Report]. https://www.un.org/development/desa/pd/sites/www.un.org.development.desa.pd/files/wup2025_summary_of_results.pdf

US Department of Commerce, Bureau of Industry and Security. (2023, October 19). Entity list additions [Final rule]. Federal Register. https://www.federalregister.gov/documents/2023/10/19/2023-23048/entity-list-additions

Ventas de Seguridad. (2016, November 14). Hikvision opens office in Chile, a market with European level. https://www.ventasdeseguridad.com/en/news/latest-news/431-enterprises/17770-hikvision-opens-office-in-chile-a-market-with-european-level.html

World Bank. (2024). GDP growth (annual %) [Data set]. https://data.worldbank.org/indicator/NY.GDP.MKTP.KD.ZG

KEY TERMS AND DEFINITIONS

Artificial Intelligence (AI): Smart devices that talk to each other and learn from data to decide on their own, like a security camera spotting intruders automatically.

AIoT (Artificial Intelligence of Things): Machines or software that think and learn like humans, such as chatbots answering questions or apps recommending songs.

Belt and Road Initiative (BRI): China's global project funding ports, roads, and railways in other countries to boost trade and its influence.

Brand Recognition: How easily people identify your brand, like spotting a Nike swoosh or Apple logo without seeing the name.

CE marking (Conformité Européenne marking): A symbol on products sold in Europe showing they meet safety and environmental standards.

Corporate Social Responsibility (CSR): Companies doing good beyond profits, like cutting pollution, donating to charities, or treating workers fairly.

DVR (Digital Video Recorder): A device that records TV shows or security footage onto a hard drive so you can watch it later.

ESG (Environmental, Social, and Governance): A framework that judges companies on eco-friendliness, social ethics, and leadership integrity. Investors use it to pick responsible businesses.

FCC compliance (Federal Communications Commission compliance): Certification that electronic devices (e.g., phones) sold in the US. will not interfere with other gadgets.

General Data Protection Regulation (GDPR): EU law requiring companies to protect user data and privacy or face huge fines.

Global Expansion Trajectory: A company's strategic plan to grow into international markets.

Internet of Things (IoT): Everyday objects (like thermostats, watches, or fridges) connected to the internet to share data and be controlled remotely.

ISC West (International Security Conference & Exposition West): A big US security expo where companies launch new cameras, alarms, and cybersecurity tech.

IFSEC International/Global (International Security and Fire Exhibition and Conference International/Globa): A major annual trade show in the UK where companies showcase security and fire safety products.

Joint Ventures (JV): When companies create a new business together, investing money and expertise while splitting ownership.

Mergers & Acquisitions (M&A): Mergers: Two companies combine into one. Acquisitions: One company buys another.

Middle-class: People with comfortable incomes, not rich, not poor, who can afford homes, education, and vacations.

Partnership: Two or more businesses teaming up to share resources, skills, or profits for mutual benefit.

R&D (Research & Development): The process of creating new products or improving existing ones through experiments, testing, and innovation.

SMB (Small and Midsize Business): Companies smaller than corporations, typically with fewer than 500 employees.

Urbanization: As more people move from rural areas to cities, urban populations grow and infrastructure development increases.

Value-Added Solution Partner (VASP): A supplier that does not just sell products but customizes them to solve specific customer problems.

Whistleblower: An employee who reports illegal or unethical behavior at their workplace to authorities or the public.

Compilation of References

360. Dx. (2023, January 26). BGI Genomics 2022 global expansion bid included the launch of new subsidiaries in 14 countries. 360Dx. https://www.360dx.com/sequencing/bgi-genomics-2022-global-expansion-bid-included-launch-new-subsidiaries-14-countries

Abdeldayem, F. M. A., & Kswat, S. F. W. (2025). BRICS expansion in the news coverage of member countries: A political economy perspective. *Journal of Humanities and Applied Social Sciences*, *7*(1), 18–37. DOI: 10.1108/JHASS-12-2023-0167

Abdullah, I., & Sumner, A. (2025). Linkage development as industrial policy: The state and structural transformation in resource-rich countries. *WIDER Working Paper Series*, Article wp-2025-29. https://ideas.repec.org//p/unu/wpaper/wp-2025-29.html

Abrantes, B. F. (Ed.). (2023). *Principles of external business environment analyzability in an organizational context*. IGI Global. DOI: 10.4018/978-1-6684-5543-2

Act, B. I. O. S. E. C. U. R. E. H.R. 8333, 118th Cong. (2024). https://www.congress.gov/bill/118th-congress/house-bill/8333

Aditya, I. A., Wijayanto, T., & Hakam, D. F. (2025). Advancing Renewable Energy in Indonesia: A Comprehensive Analysis of Challenges, Opportunities, and Strategic Solutions. *Sustainability (Basel)*, *17*(5), 5. Advance online publication. DOI: 10.3390/su17052216

Air China. (2025, April 25). 2024 [Air China Limited 2024 Annual Report]. Air China Limited. https://webresource.airchina.com.cn/airchinacms/2/upload/resources/file/10109.pdf

Air China. (n.d.) 2016 [2016 Social Responsibility Report]. Air China Limited. https://webresource.airchina.com.cn/airchinacms/2/upload/resources/file/743.pdf

Air China. (n.d.). 2023 ESG [2023 Sustainable Development and ESG Report]. Air China Limited. https://et.airchina.com.cn/cn/images/investor_relations/2024/03/29/10077396D2B04368941ADF6F10FC61D4.pdf

Air China. (n.d.). 2024 ESG [2024 Sustainable Development and ESG Report]. Air China Limited. https://static.cninfo.com.cn/finalpage/2025-03-28/1222927858.PDF

Air China. (n.d.). [About Air China]. Air China Limited. https://ffp.airchina.com.cn/plan/about_airchina.html

Air China. (n.d.). [Air China and Star Alliance]. Air China Limited. https://m.airchina.com.cn/c/invoke/hzgy@pg

Aldeguer, C. C. (2010). *BYD Company Limited: A case review*. SSRN Electronic Journal. DOI: 10.2139/ssrn.2422240

Alex, J. (2025, August 14). *Trump Pharma Tariffs Would Raise Drug Prices for Americans.* Tax Foundation. https://taxfoundation.org/blog/trump-tariffs-pharma-drug-prices/

Allen, R. (2025). DeepSeek and AI innovation: How Chinese universities broke through the glass ceiling of technological advancement. *American Journal of STEM Education*, *6*, 1–10. DOI: 10.32674/10bz2d04

Aloini, D., Benevento, E., Dulmin, R., Guerrazzi, E., & Mininno, V. (2024). Unlocking real-time decision-making in warehouses: A machine learning-based forecasting and alerting system for cycle time prediction. *Transportation Research Part E, Logistics and Transportation Review*, *194*, 103933. DOI: 10.1016/j.tre.2024.103933

Amling, A., & Daugherty, P. J. (2018). Logistics and distribution innovation in China. *International Journal of Physical Distribution & Logistics Management*, *50*(3), 323–332. DOI: 10.1108/IJPDLM-07-2018-0273

An, L., & Zhao, R. (2019, July 10). China's car association predicts losses throughout 2019. *Caixin Global*. https://www.caixinglobal.com/2019-07-10/chinas-car-association-predicts-losses-throughout-2019-101437882.html

Andrews, M. (2024, June 28). Geely's Aegis short blade LFP battery – Full details including extreme safety. *CarNewsChina*. https://carnewschina.com/2024/06/28/geelys-aegis-short-blade-lfp-battery-full-details-including-extreme-safety/

Armstrong, A. (2025, January 6). Merck Snaps Up WuXi Biologics Facility in Ireland for $500M. Biospace. https://www.biospace.com/business/merck-snaps-up-wuxi-biologics-facility-in-ireland-for-500m

Artxdigi. (2023, July 12). Interpretation of the announcement on continuation and optimization of new energy vehicle purchase tax exemption policy. *ARTXDIGI*. https://www.artxdigi.com/en/insights/china-express12/

Atillah, I. (2024). *AI chatbot blamed in teen's death: Here's what to know about AI's psychological risks and prevention* [Tech News]. AI Chatbot Blamed in Teen's Death: Here's What to Know about AI's Psychological Risks and Prevention. https://www.euronews.com/next/2024/11/02/ai-chatbot-blamed-in-teens-death-heres-what-to-know-about-ais-psychological-risks-and-prev

Autoini. (2025, December 17). Geely safety centre sets global safety benchmark. *Autoini*. https://www.autoini.com/new-car/brand/geely-news/geely-opens-worlds-largest-safety-centre/

Automotive Reference. (2025, July 13). Understanding Euro emission standards and their impact on vehicle regulations. *Automotive Reference*. https://automotivereference.com/euro-emission-standards/

Automotive World. (2025, January 6). Geely auto sales surpassed 2.17 million units, international market growth exceeded 53%. *Automotive World*. https://www.automotiveworld.com/news-releases/geely-auto-sales-surpassed-2-17-million-units-international-market-growth-exceeded-53/

Azizi, O. (2025). *DeepSeek-v3: A high-performance mixture-of-experts language model*. DOI: 10.13140/RG.2.2.32707.52000

Bain & Company. (2024, August 1). *Navigating high winds: Southeast Asia outlook 2024 - 34* [Press release]. https://www.bain.com/about/media-center/press-releases/sea/southeast-asia-outlook-2024-34/

Bank for International Settlements. (2025, September 30). *Triennial central bank survey of foreign exchange and OTC derivatives markets in 2025*. https://www.bis.org/press/p250930.htm

Baptista, E. (2025, January 28). What is DeepSeek and why is it disrupting the AI sector? *Reuters*. https://www.reuters.com/technology/artificial-intelligence/what-is-deepseek-why-is-it-disrupting-ai-sector-2025-01-27/

Bartzas, G., & Komnitsas, K. (2024). Cradle to gate life-cycle assessment of battery grade nickel sulphate production through high-pressure acid leaching. *The Science of the Total Environment*, *952*, 175902. DOI: 10.1016/j.scitotenv.2024.175902 PMID: 39233072

Beijing University. (2025). *Joseph E. stiglitz: the resurgence of industrial policy and the new protectionism.* Bjnews.com.cn. https://www.bjnews.com.cn/detail/173337195119152.html

Bellan, R. (2023, August 7). Chinese luxury EV brand Zeekr continues global push into Kazakhstan. *TechCrunch.* https://techcrunch.com/2023/08/07/chinese-luxury-ev-brand-Zeekr-continues-global-push-into-kazakhstan/

BGI-Shenzhen. (2013, March 19). BGI-Shenzhen completes acquisition of Complete Genomics [Press release]. PR Newswire. https://www.prnewswire.com/news-releases/bgi-shenzhen-completes-acquisition-of-complete-genomics-198820331.html

Bharati, T., Farhad, M., & Jetter, M. (2023). On the relationship between trade openness and government size. *World Economy, 46*(7), 2102–2133. DOI: 10.1111/twec.13374

Bhatti, U. A., Bhatti, M. A., Tang, H., Syam, M. S., Awwad, E. M., Sharaf, M., & Ghadi, Y. Y. (2024). Global production patterns: Understanding the relationship between greenhouse gas emissions, agriculture greening and climate variability. *Environmental Research, 245*, 118049. DOI: 10.1016/j.envres.2023.118049 PMID: 38169167

Bio-IT World Staff. (2013, March 19). BGI-Shenzhen completes acquisition of Complete Genomics. Bio-IT World. https://www.bio-itworld.com/news/2013/03/19/complete-genomics-acquisition-final

BioSpectrum Asia. (2021, July 14). China's Envision Group donates medical supplies to fight COVID-19 in India. BioSpectrum Asia. https://www.biospectrumasia.com/news/49/18586/chinas-envision-group-donates-medical-supplies-to-fight-covid-19-in-india.html

Bloomberg, N. E. F. (2023). Goldwind and Vestas in Photo Finish for Top Spot as Global Wind Power Additions Fall. BloombergNEF. https://about.bnef.com/insights/clean-energy/goldwind-and-vestas-in-photo-finish-for-top-spot-as-global-wind-power-additions-fall/

Bloomberg. (2025, March 22). *Indonesia's nickel export ban reshapes the global supply chain.* Bloomberg.com. https://www.bloomberg.com

Bole, D., Kumer, P., Gašperič, P., Kozina, J., Pipan, P., & Tiran, J. (2022). Clash of Two Identities: What Happens to Industrial Identity in a Post-Industrial Society? *Societies (Basel, Switzerland), 12*(2), 49. DOI: 10.3390/soc12020049

Bria, E., Kemp, D., Kuswati, R. A., Sturman, K., Saputra, M. R. U., & Lechner, A. M. (2025). A holistic framework for examining complex problems in energy transition solutions. *One Earth*, *8*(5), 101249. DOI: 10.1016/j.oneear.2025.101249

Bridge, G., & Faigen, E. (2022). Towards the lithium-ion battery production network: Thinking beyond mineral supply chains. *Energy Research & Social Science*, *89*(102659), 102659. DOI: 10.1016/j.erss.2022.102659

BYD. (2023). BYD's new blade battery set to redefine EV safety standards. BYD USA. Https://En.byd.com/. https://en.byd.com/news/byds-new-blade-battery-set-to-redefine-ev-safety-standards/

BYD. (2025). *Homepage*. https://www.byd.com/cn

ByteBridge. (2025, January 31). DeepSeek AI: Company overview, founding team, culture and DeepSeek R1 model. *Medium*. https://bytebridge.medium.com/deepseek-ai-company-overview-founding-team-culture-and-deepseek-r1-model-ea87f711b4b3

CAACnews. (2017, December 13). :" " [Air China's 10th anniversary of joining Star Alliance: "They are approaching the center of the world stage]. CAACnews. http://caacnews.com.cn/1/6/201712/t20171213_1236293.html

CAACnews. (2017, July 19). " " [Building the "Air Silk Road" of the new era]. CAACnews. http://www.caacnews.com.cn/special/4260/4313/hhcj/201801/t20180129_1239619.html

CAACnews. (2017, May 12). " "

CAACnews. (2021, January 15). " " [Air China has initiated the "one airport, two zones" operation mode at Beijing Capital Airport]. CAACnews. http://www.caacnews.com.cn/1/6/202101/t20210115_1317939.html

CAACnews. (2024, April 23). 4 [Air China has launched and resumed four international routes]. CAACnews. http://www.caacnews.com.cn/1/6/202404/t20240423_1377613.html

CAACnews. (2024, December, 30). 2024 [HiChina has released the 2024 Civil Aviation Travel Report]. CAACnews. http://www.caacnews.com.cn/1/202412/t20241230_1383809.html

CAACnews. (2024, June 26). 2024 2019 90% [In the 2024 summer travel season, Air China's international and regional routes will recover to 90% of the 2019 level]. CAACnews. http://www.caacnews.com.cn/1/6/202406/t20240626_1379324.html

CAACnews. (2025, May 21). : [Avic Group: Inheriting the Red Gene and continuously forging ahead on the journey]. CAACnews. http://www.caacnews.com.cn/1/6/202105/t20210521_1324294.html

CAACnews. [Actively serve the Belt and Road Initiative and comprehensively enhance the level of aviation connectivity - Interview with Wang Zhiqing, Vice Minister of the Civil Aviation Administration of China]. CAACnews. http://www.caacnews.com.cn/special/3494/xgbd/201705/t20170512_1214400.html

Cai, M. Z., & Yu, R. Y. (2023). , [The leading CRDMO with steady progress and long-term vision, providing all-around support for drug development]. 11, 2025, from]. KAIYUAN Securities. https://www.vzkoo.com/document/20230818776748e094c476d5c3f3b8c2.html?keyword=%E8%8D%AF%E6%98%8E%E5%BA%B7%E5%BE%B7CRDMO

Cai, Q. Y., & Wang, C. F. (2020). —— [Research on the performance of cross-border mergers and acquisitions of semiconductor enterprises in China: Taking the acquisition of STATS ChipPAC by JCET as an example]. *[Research on Accounting and Finance]*, (8), 35–41.

Caixin Global. (2021, July 15). Express delivery giant SF recovers from a record quarterly loss. https://www.caixinglobal.com/2021-07-15/express-delivery-giant-sf-recovers-from-a-record-quarterly-loss-101740887.html

Camba, A., Lim, G., & Gallagher, K. (2022). Leading sector and dual economy: How Indonesia and Malaysia mobilised Chinese capital in mineral processing. *Third World Quarterly*, *43*(10), 2375–2395. DOI: 10.1080/01436597.2022.2093180

Cao, W., Zhang, Y., & Antony, B. (2018). Belt and road: A new journey for foreign investment—A case study of the internationalization strategy of BYD. *Proceedings of the 3rd international symposium on Asian B&R conference on international business cooperation (ISBCD 2018),* 58. DOI: 10.2991/isbcd-18.2018.18

Cao, Y. (2024). The research of supply chain management in Chinas e-commerce environment taking JD.com as an example. *Advances in Economics Management and Political Sciences*, *143*(1), 40–47. DOI: 10.54254/2754-1169/2024.GA18957

Carney, R. W. (2023). *China's Chance to Lead: Acquiring Global Influence via Infrastructure Development and Digitalization*. Cambridge University Press., DOI: 10.1017/9781009385879

Carscoops. (2021, June 28). Envision AESC and Verkor will supply batteries to Renault Group. Carscoops. https://www.carscoops.com/2021/06/envision-aesc-and-verkor-will-supply-batteries-to-renault-group/

Cecil, P. (2024). Cross-Border supply chain optimization: Strategies for managing international operations while maintaining speed and cost efficiency. [IJSRM]. *International Journal of Scientific Research and Management, 12*(05), 6565–6588. DOI: 10.18535/ijsrm/v12i05.em23

Center for China & Globalization. (2024, November). *Report on Chinese Enterprise Globalization: The TCL Case Study.* http://www.ccg.org.cn/archives/87276

Central Committee of the Communist Party of China & State Council. (2024). Opinions on accelerating the comprehensive green transformation of economic and social development. https://www.gov.cn/zhengce/202408/content_6967663.htm

Central Desk. (2025, January 1). Geely and Tasco to build $168M auto plant in Vietnam by 2025. *Auto World Journal.* https://www.autoworldjournal.com/geely-and-tasco-to-build-168m-auto-plant/

Chan, A. K., Chen, C. H., & Zhao, L. (2018). JD. com: Leveraging the edge of e-business. *Emerald Emerging Markets Case Studies,* 1-30. https://doi.org/DOI: 10.1108/EEMCS-06-2016-0109

Chandgothia, K. (2025). *Can JD's surging user base power its next phase of revenue growth?* Finance. Yahoo. https://finance.yahoo.com/news/jds-surging-user-power-next-150000882.html?

Chang, C.-H., Lu, C.-S., & Lai, P.-L. (2021). Examining the drivers of competitive advantage of the international logistics industry. *International Journal of Logistics, 25*(12), 1–19. DOI: 10.1080/13675567.2021.1915263

Chen, D. (2023, December 25). Geely's Dragon Eagle-1 chip is on more than 200,000 vehicles. *CarNewsChina.* https://carnewschina.com/2023/12/25/geelys-dragon-eagle-1-first-china-made-automotive-grade-chip-is-on-more-than-200000-vehicles/

Chen, D. Y. (2025, July 5). Geely Galaxy E5 (EX5) hits 150,000-unit sales milestone. *CarNewsChina.* https://carnewschina.com/2025/07/05/geely-galaxy-e5-ex5-hits-150000-unit-sales-milestone/

Chen, G. (2022). *Business Administration's Role in Corporate Strategy Development of Logistics: A Case Study of SF Express Co. Ltd.* https://e-research.siam.edu/wp-content/uploads/2023/03/IMBA-2022-IS-Business-Administration-role-in-Corporate-Strategy-Development-of-Logistics.pdf

Chen, H., & Meng, F. Y. (2025, March 14). *TCL: [TCL: Globalization, regionalization, localization].* Economic Observer Network. https://www.eeo.com.cn/2025/0314/716489.shtml

Chen, S. (2025, March 31). The Losses of China's Three Major Airline Will Narrow in 2024. YiCai Global. https://www.yicaiglobal.com/news/chinas-big-three-airlines-failed-to-turn-profitable-last-year

Chen, Y. (2020). *A case study of overseas strategies of Chinese express logistics: SF Express*. Hub.hku.hk. http://hdl.handle.net/10722/294756

Chen, Y. (2024a, June 26). 2024 43 1200 [In the summer of 2024, Air China will significantly increase its capacity, reaching 43 countries and regions and 1,200 destinations]. Xinhua Net. https://app.xinhuanet.com/news/article.html?articleId=40c14eab281fa5e67deec4e0c599c529

Chen, Y. (2024b, November 28). " " " " [The "Phoenix Mile" frequent flyer program of Air China has been around for 30 years, with the theme of "A Soulmate by your side on the Journey of Life"]. Xinhua Net. https://www.news.cn/digital/20241128/1b0cd7809f3a484292aadd3b85089884/c.html

Chen, Y. H. (2019). —— [Analysis of the motivations and performance of cross-border mergers and acquisitions in China's semiconductor industry: Taking JCET as an example] [Master's thesis, Zhejiang University]. China Master's Theses Full-text Database. https://link.cnki.net/doi/10.27461/d.cnki.gzjdx.2019.000382

Cheng, C., Yang, X., Jiang, F., & Yang, Z. (2023). How to synergize different institutional logics of firms in cross-border acquisitions: A matching theory perspective. *Management International Review*. https://link.springer.com/article/10.1007/s11575-023-00502-8

Cheng, E. (2024, April 25). Geely-backed luxury EV brand Zeekr says it's already beating Tesla in parts of China. *CNBC*. https://www.cnbc.com/2024/04/25/geely-backed-luxury-ev-brand-zeekr-says-it's-already-beating-tesla-in-parts-of-china.html

Chen, P. L. (2021). [Globalization is a sustainable way for companies to respond to challenges]. *China Small & Medium Enterprises*, (04), 48–50.

Chen, T. (2022). Blockchain and accounting fraud prevention: A case study on Luckin Coffee. *Proceedings of the 2022 7th International Conference on Social Sciences and Economic Development (ICSSED 2022)*, 44–49. https://doi.org/DOI: 10.2991/aebmr.k.220405.009

Chen, Z., Wu, J., Yang, X., & Ni, G. (2025). Digitalization and supply chain carbon performance: The role of focal firms. *Journal of Theoretical and Applied Electronic Commerce Research*, *20*(289), 289. Advance online publication. DOI: 10.3390/jtaer20040289

China Association of Circular Economy. (2022, April 24). 2022 : 10 100 [Vision 2022 Carbon Neutrality Action Report: The World's Top 100 Zero-Carbon Industrial Parks Over the Next Decade—China Circular Economy Association]. [China Association of Circular Economy]. https://www.chinacace.org/news/fieldsview?id=13554

China Daily, H. K. (2021, February 10). *SF Holding to take over Kerry Logistics for US$2.3b* (Bloomberg). China Daily Hong Kong. https://www.chinadailyhk.com/hk/article/157509

China Economic Net. (2024, December 25). 2025 [The Beijing Aero-engine maintenance project is expected to be put into use in 2025]. Economic Daily News. http://www.ce.cn/xwzx/gnsz/gdxw/202412/25/t20241225_39247155.shtml

China Energy Network. (2019, July 19). EnOS 2.0 , [Envision's EnOS 2.0 Released: Intelligent IoT Leads the Distributed Revolution in Energy Systems]. [China Energy Network]. https://www.china5e.com/news/news-1064482-1.html

China Energy Network. (2025, July 30). AI , [AI-Powered Electricity Trading: Envision Opens a New Model for Self-Operated Wind Power Terminal Consumption]. [China Energy Network]. https://www.cnenergynews.cn/guangfu/2025/07/30/detail_20250730224593.html

China Optics and Optoelectronics. (2009, November 17). *TCL 245 TFTLCD8.5 [TCL, in collaboration with Shenzhen, has invested 24.5 billion yuan to launch the TFTLCD 8.5-generation production line]*. https://www.coema.org.cn/industry/200911/2040.html

China Post Securities. (2022, May 23). 2022 [Analysis of Air China's Business Layout and Competitive Advantages in 2022: Air China positions Itself on Core routes and Hub Resources]. Vzkoo. https://www.vzkoo.com/read/202205238c5122fda7813274417256ee.html

Chinareospace. (2025, April 21). : [Analysis: Risks and Opportunities for Chinese Civil Aviation Enterprises against the Backdrop of the Escalation of the China-US Trade War]. Chinareospace. https://www.chinaerospace.com/index.php/article/show/ff8401962ed469195f57b71bfb44ae92

Ching, V. C., & Camba, A. (2023). A Comparative View of Chinese Relations with Peru. *Springer Books*, 275–294.

Choe, S., & Parvini, S. (2025, January 28). *Nvidia faces a reckoning as an upstart rival raises questions about Wall Street's darling* [World/Americas]. Nvidia Faces a Reckoning as an Upstart Rival Raises Questions about Wall Street's Darling. https://www.independent.co.uk/news/world/americas/nvidia-ap-new-york-wall-street-apple-b2688009.html

Christmann, P., & Lefebvre, G. (2022). Trends in global mineral and metal criticality: The need for technological foresight. *Mineral Economics*, *35*(3–4), 641–652. DOI: 10.1007/s13563-022-00323-5

ChuanYu., J., Manurung, H., Anggara, F., & Petrus, H. T. B. M. (2025). Indonesian Nickel Overview: Potential, Development and Future Prospects. In Metallurgy And Materials Society of (Ed.), *Proceedings of the 63rd Conference of Metallurgists, COM 2024* (pp. 753–763). Springer Nature Switzerland. DOI: 10.1007/978-3-031-67398-6_130

CINNO Research. (2025, March 6). 2024 OSAT Top10 [2024 global OSAT (outsourced semiconductor assembly and test) industry revenue ranking] [Industry report]. http://www.cinno.com.cn/industry/news/osat2503

CITIC Group. (2015). *Brief Introduction - CITIC GROUP*. Group.citic. https://www.group.citic/en/About_CITIC/Brief_Introduction

CITIC. (2023). *Annual report 2022*. Beijing: CITIC Press. https://www.citic.com/ar2022/pdf/full_en.pdf

CITIC. (2024). *Environmental Social and Governance (ESG) Report - CITIC Limited*. https://www.citic.com/uploadfile/2025/0417/20250417188784.pdf

CITIC. (2024a). *Annual report 2023*. https://www.citic.com/uploadfile/2024/0422/20240422601941.pdf

CITIC. (2024b). *Half-year report 2024*. https://www.citic.com/uploadfile/2024/0916/20240916320865.pdf

CITIC. (2025). *Annual report 2024*. https://www.citic.com/uploadfile/2025/0417/20250417792176.pdf

Climateweeknyc. (2022). Envision. Climateweeknyc. https://www.climateweeknyc.org/envision

Coalition Greenwich. (2023, February 24). *Wealth management firms set technology priorities for 2023*. https://www.greenwich.com/market-structure-technology/wealth-management-firms-set-technology-priorities-2023

Collins, J. (2025, April 17). Lotus Evija finally hits the track as production begins, but questions remain over deliveries and customer appeal. *EVMagz*. https://evmagz.com/lotus-evija-finally-hits-the-track-as-production-begins-but-questions-remain-over-deliveries-and-customer-appeal/

Contemporary Amperex Technology Co. Limited (CATL). (2022, April 15). CATL partners up with Indonesia to boost e-mobility with an investment of nearly 6 billion USD. CATL Official Website. https://www.catl.com/en/news/922.html

Contemporary Amperex Technology Co. Limited (CATL). (2023a). Environmental, Social, and Governance (ESG) Report. CATL Official Website. https://www.catl.com/en/uploads/1/file/public/202404/20240417102933_uuiks9ljr8.pdf

Contemporary Amperex Technology Co. Limited (CATL). (2023b, August 16). CATL launches superfast charging battery Shenxing, opens up era of EV superfast charging. CATL Official Website. https://www.catl.com/en/news/6091.html

Contemporary Amperex Technology Co. Limited (CATL). (2024, December 10). Stellantis and CATL to invest up to €4.1 billion in joint venture for large-scale LFP battery plant in Spain. CATL Official Website. https://www.catl.com/en/news/6328.html

Contemporary Amperex Technology Co. Limited (CATL). (2025, June 23). CATL chairman and CEO Robin Zeng outlines vision for global zero-carbon transition and deeper collaboration at major conference. Prnewswire. https://www.prnewswire.com/il/news-releases/catl-chairman-and-ceo-robin-zeng-outlines-vision-for-global-zero-carbon-transition-and-deeper-collaboration-at-major-conference-302488099.html

Crossa, M. (2023). Distorted linkages and labour devaluation: An exploration of automotive value chain-driven 'development' in Ciudad Juárez, Mexico. *Canadian Journal of Development Studies*. *Canadian Journal of Development Studies*, *44*(2), 270–292. DOI: 10.1080/02255189.2022.2058469

CTNEWS. (2024, September 19). [How can airlines continuously improve their performance when opportunities and challenges coexist]. CTNEWS. https://www.ctnews.com.cn/paper/att/202409/19/7e324460-f6ad-41b6-9e0a-7e6868f96c9e.pdf

Cyberspace Administration of China. (2014, June 26). [National guidelines for the development and promotion of the integrated circuit industry]. https://www.cac.gov.cn/2014-06/26/c_1111325916.htm

Cyranoski, D. (2010, March 3). Chinese bioscience: The sequence factory. *Nature*, *464*(7285), 22–24. DOI: 10.1038/464022a PMID: 20203579

Dang, T. N. A. (2017). A Study on the Strategic Choice of Chinese Household Electrical Appliances Multinational Corporations in Vietnam-Taking TCL Corporation as an Example. [Master's thesis, Shanghai University].

David, R., Nair, D., & Browning, J. (2018, February 28). Geely used a $9 billion collar trade on its Daimler purchase. *Bloomberg*. https://www.bloomberg.com/news/articles/2018-02-27/geely-is-said-to-use-9-billion-collar-trade-on-daimler-purchase

DeepSeek. (2024). *DeepSeek-V2: A strong, economical, and efficient mixture-of-experts language model.* https://huggingface.co/deepseek-ai/DeepSeek-V2

DeepSeek. (2025a). *DeepSeek API: A guide with examples and cost calculations.* https://www.datacamp.com/tutorial/deepseek-api

DeepSeek. (2025b). *DeepSeek-R2: China's bold answer to the AI race – What you need to know.* https://deepseek.ai/blog/deepseek-r2-ai-model-launch-2025

DeepSeek. (2025c). *Leading Ai language models & solutions.* https://deepseek.ai/

Deloitte, U. S. (2024). 2024 Sustainability action report. Deloitte. https://www.deloitte.com/us/en/services/audit-assurance/articles/esg-survey.html

Deng, L. L. (2007). TCL [TCL's journey in Vietnam]. *Foreign Trade & Economic*, *3*, 40–42.

Depraiter, L., Goutte, S., & Porcher, T. (2025). Geopolitical risk and the global supply of rare earth permanent magnets: Insights from China's export trends. *Energy Economics*, *146*, 108496. DOI: 10.1016/j.eneco.2025.108496

Deutsche Börse Group. (2021, May 27). *Deutsche Börse enters partnership with Chinese data provider Wind* [Press release]. https://www.mds.deutsche-boerse.com/mds-en/about-us/news-highlights/Deutsche-B-rse-enters-partnership-with-Chinese-data-provider-Wind-2034190

Digital Energy Storage Network. (2025, August 1). , [From Inner Mongolia to Shanghai, Envision Achieves Full-Cycle Green Electricity Trading]. [Digital Energy Storage Network]. https://desn.com.cn/news/show-2107009.html

Ding, G. E. (2021). [Research on the motivation and performance evaluation of Jiangsu Changjiang Electronics Technology's cross-border merger of STATS ChipPAC] [Master's thesis, Zhejiang University]. China Master's Theses Full-text Database. https://link.cnki.net/doi/10.27175/d.cnki.gjxcu.2021.001524

Ding, W. (2025, April 8). 2024 70 2025 [The three major airlines are expected to reduce losses by 7 billion yuan in 2024 and turn a profit in 2025]. China Aviation News. https://ep.cannews.com.cn/publish/zghkb7/html/5161/node_219916.html

Ding, J., Guo, L., & Wang, Z. (2023). *Geely's path to becoming a global corporation*. Springer. [Book title if applicable], https://link.springer.com/chapter/10.1007/978-981-99-3326-6_10

Document, A. P. I. (n.d.). *JD.com: Revolutionizing e-commerce through technology and logistics excellence*. Just one API. https://blog.justoneapi.com/post-1/post-20250920101714234.html

Doll, S. (2023, March 21). CATL begins mass production of its Qilin batteries with 13% more power than other 4680 cells. Electrek; Electrek. https://electrek.co/2023/03/21/catl-begins-mass-production-of-its-qilin-batteries-with-13-more-power-than-other-4680-cells/

Dong, Z. Y., & Bi, Y. (2025, June 26). [Seizing new opportunities for industrial upgrading driven by artificial intelligence]. *Economic Daily*. http://paper.ce.cn/pc/content/202506/26/content_315985.html

Dou, S., Xu, D., Zhu, Y., & Keenan, R. (2023). Critical mineral sustainable supply: Challenges and governance. *Futures*, *146*, 103101. DOI: 10.1016/j.futures.2023.103101

Duan, Z. (2024). Research on the supply chain optimization approach of JD's transformation into a digital ecosystem retailer. *Advances in Economics Management and Political Sciences*, *138*(1), 22–27. DOI: 10.54254/2754-1169/2024.18798

EEWorld. (2024, August 12). 7nm! The first domestically produced 7nm smart cockpit chip is in mass production and installed in cars. https://en.eeworld.com.cn/news/qcdz/eic675420.html

Electrios Consultants. (2024, March 20). CATL 2023 Annual Report Highlights. Electrios. https://electrios.com/blog_post/catl-2023-annual-report-highlights/

Emerald Publishing. (2024). Analysts' ESG attention and stock pricing. *Journal of Accounting Literature*. Advance online publication. DOI: 10.1108/JAL-06-2024-0128

Energy Storage Network. (2025, September 10). , ! [Global energy storage demand is surging, intensifying the reshuffling of rankings for energy storage cell shipments!]. [Energy Storage Network]. https://www.ideesz.com/zhdt/hyzx1/202509/t20250910_1062.html

Envision AESC France. (2025, February 3). France secures €48m EU investment for AESC battery plant. Innovation News Network. https://www.innovationnewsnetwork.com/france-secures-e48m-eu-investment-for-aesc-battery-plant/55101/

Envision Energy. (2025, May 9). Envision Unveils 2025 Net Zero Report at Smarter E Europe, Celebrates Third Year of Carbon Neutrality. PR Newswire. https://www.prnewswire.com/apac/news-releases/envision-unveils-2025-net-zero-report-at-smarter-e-europe-celebrates-third-year-of-carbon-neutrality-302450668.html

Envision Group. (2024). 2024. *Sustainability Report*, •••, 24–31. https://www.envisionpharmagroup.com/sustainability-report

Envision Group. (2025, October 23). Envision Energy Strengthens Global Collaboration with Its First Global Supplier Day to Build a Secure, Resilient, and Sustainable Supply Chain. PR Newswire. https://www.digitimes.com/biz/news.asp?feed=13764

Envision. (2021, April 23). Envision promises to be operation-level carbon neutral by 2022, value chain carbon neutral by 2028: Envision's first carbon neutrality report. PR Newswire. https://www.prnewswire.com/news-releases/envision-promises-to-be-operation-level-carbon-neutral-by-2022-value-chain-carbon-neutral-by-2028-envisions-first-carbon-neutrality-report-301275885.html

European Commission. (2023). Regulation (EU) 2023/1542 - EUR-Lex. https://eur-lex.europa.eu/eli/reg/2023/1542/oj

European Data Protection Board. (2020, January 29). Guidelines 3/2019 on processing of personal data through video devices (Version 2.0). https://www.edpb.europa.eu/sites/default/files/files/file1/edpb_guidelines_201903_video_devices_en_0.pdf

European Investment Bank. (2023). French gigafactory provides lithium-ion batteries for electric cars. European Investment Bank. https://www.eib.org/en/projects/all/20220168

European Securities and Markets Authority. (2021). *Environmental impact and liquidity of green bonds* (Report No. TRV-2021-2). https://www.esma.europa.eu/sites/default/files/trv_2021_2-environmental_impact_and_liquidity_of_green_bonds.pdf

European Union. (2023). Regulation - 2023/1542 - EN - EUR-Lex. Europa.eu. https://eur-lex.europa.eu/eli/reg/2023/1542/oj/eng

Ezell, S. (2020, February 6). Intellectual Property's Impact on Global Health & Life Sciences Innovation. Information Technology and Innovation Foundation. https://www2.itif.org/2020-ezell-globalization-health-georgetown.pdf

Fan, C. Z. (2021). [Output Analysis of Pharmaceutical Research and Development Innovation in the United States]. Hangye yanjiuyuan. https://www.iir.sjtu.edu.cn/comments/51247.html

Fan, J. H., Wang, S. Q., & Zhou, Y. F. (2025, January 2). *TCL : , [TCL Electronics: Global market share continues to grow, with improved profitability expected].* Huatai Securities. https://inst.htsc.com/research

Fang, Z. X. (2024, July 26). Corporate profile: Envision AESC. https://www.fangzhenxiu.com/post/10382297/?uri=261_bif1kkekanv%2F1000

Fan, Y. X., & Kang, Y. C. (2024). 3C ——TCL [The Overseas Expansion of Chinese Smart 3C Home Appliance Brands: The Case of TCL's International Brand Communication]. *Global Brand Insight*, (24), 64–66.

Fast Technology. (2025, May 9). Geely has launched a rotating CEO system: Dai Qing is appointed as the first financial-background CEO. *Taibo*. https://en.taibo.cn/p/26045732

fDi Intelligence. (2022, August 16). CATL announces Hungary's largest ever investment. fDi Intelligence. https://www.fdiintelligence.com/content/6c410c6a-8193-58d0-907c-9374afd2fd97

Federal Reserve. (2024, December). Minutes of the Federal Open Market Committee. https://www.federalreserve.gov/monetarypolicy/files/fomcminutes20241218.pdf

Feng, L. J., & Liang, J. N. (2024, September 26). TCL: [TCL: From Huizhou to the world, setting an example for going global]. *Huizhou Daily*. http://e.hznews.com/hzrb/pc/content/202409/26/content_1088379.html

Feng, W. G. (2014). ——TCL [Research on the Internationalization Strategy of Chinese Color TV Companies: Taking TCL Color TV as an Example]. *China Collective Economy*, *18*, 25–26.

Fernandez, D. S. (2024, January 30). Geely Coolray global sales continues to rise in 2024. *DSF.my*. https://www.dsf.my/2024/01/geely-coolray-global-sales-exceeded-800000-units/

Financial Post. (2022, March 19). Tesla supplier CATL weighs sites for $5 billion battery plant. Financial Post. https://financialpost.com/pmn/business-pmn/tesla-supplier-catl-weighs-sites-for-5-billion-battery-plant

Financial Stability Board. (2021, October 14). 2021 Status Report: Task Force on Climate-related Financial Disclosures. Financial Stability Board. https://www.fsb.org/2021/10/2021-status-report-task-force-on-climate-related-financial-disclosures/

Financial Stability Board. (2023, October 12). 2023 TCFD Status Report: Task Force on Climate-related Financial Disclosures. Financial Stability Board. https://www.fsb.org/2023/10/2023-tcfd-status-report-task-force-on-climate-related-financial-disclosures/https://www.fsb-tcfd.org

Financial Times. (2023, November 8). *EU carbon border tax to hit Chinese steel exporters*. Financial Times. https://www.ft.com

Foss, M. M., & Koelsch, J. (2022). *Need Nickel? How Electrifying Transport and Chinese Investment are Playing Out in the Indonesian Archipelago*. DOI: 10.25613/30S0-Y623

Franchell, J. (2023, September 13). The intensifying competitive landscape in the IT services sector. *Ironpaper*. https://www.ironpaper.com/webintel/the-intensifying-competitive-landscape-in-the-it-services-sector

French Ministry of Economy and Finance. (2023, October 23). Loi relative à l'industrie verte [France Green Industry Act]. Legifrance. News/695.htmlhttps://www.legifrance.gouv.fr/jorf/id/JORFTEXT000052238755?init=true&page=1&query=Loi+relative+%C3%A0+l%27industrie+verte+&searchField=ALL&tab_selection=all

Fuelcellchina. (2025). Envision Set to Launch 300,000-Ton Renewable Ammonia Facility in September. Fuelcellchina. https://www.fuelcellchina.com/Industry_information_details/6286.html

Fussey, P., & Murray, D. (2025, October 13). Input on report on right to privacy in the digital age. United Nations Human Rights Office. https://www.ohchr.org/sites/default/files/documents/cfi-subm/privacy-digital-age/subm-privacy-digital-age-aca-20-pete-f-university-southampton-don.pdf

Gan, J. B. (2016). [Research on the Integrated Development Strategy of WuXi AppTec]. *Dangdai Jingji*, (33), 28–29.

Gao, V. P., Kaas, H.-W., Mohr, D., & Wee, D. (2016, January). Automotive revolution – Perspective towards 2030. *McKinsey & Company*. https://www.mckinsey.com/industries/automotive-and-assembly/our-insights/disruptive-trends-that-will-transform-the-auto-industry/de-DE

Gasgoo. (2025, January 14). China's annual power battery installation volume shoots up 41.5% in 2024. Gasgoo. https://autonews.gasgoo.com/articles/ev/70035698

Gatta, V., Marcucci, E., & Le Pira, M. (2023). E-commerce and urban logistics: Trends, challenges, and opportunities. In Marcucci, E., Gatta, V., & Le Pira, M. (Eds.), *Handbook on city logistics and urban freight* (pp. 422–443). Edward Elgar Publishing., DOI: 10.4337/9781800370173.00033

GBD 2021 Fertility and Forecasting Collaborators. (2024). Global Fertility in 204 Countries and Territories, 1950–2021, with Forecasts to 2100: A Comprehensive Demographic Analysis for the Global Burden of Disease Study 2021. *The LANCET, 103*(10440), 2204-2256. DOI: 10.1016/S0140-6736(24)00550-6

Geely Automobile Holdings Limited. (2025). Environmental, social and governance report 2024. https://global.geely.com/-/media/project/web-portal/2025/esg-report/esg-report-2024.pdf

Geely Global. (2024a, March 20). Geely auto 2023 financial results released. *Geely Global.* https://global.geely.com/en/news/2024/geely-auto-financial-results-2023

Geely Global. (2024b, August 21). Geely auto surges past 107.3 billion RMB in H1 revenue. *Geely Global.* https://global.geely.com/en/news/2024/geely-auto-h1-2024-revenues

Geely Global. (2025a, January 6). Geely auto sales surpassed 2.17 million units. *Geely Global.* https://global.geely.com/en/news/2025/geely-auto-sales-2024

Geely Global. (2025b, January 24). Geely auto enters Indonesian market. *Geely Global.* https://global.geely.com/en/news/2025/geely-auto-launch-indonesia

Geely Stories. (2020, March 30). The tiger is free – Ten years of Volvo and Geely Holding. *Zhejiang Geely Holding Group.* https://zgh.com/media-center/story/ten-years-of-volvo-and-geely/?lang=en

Geely, H. K. (2025). Geely auto initiated the "five by five" globalization strategy. *Geely Auto HK.* https://www.geelyauto.hk/five-by-five/

Geely. (2017, August 4). Geely and Volvo Cars sign joint venture agreements. *Zhejiang Geely Holding Group.* https://zgh.com/media-center/news/20170804_1/?lang=en

Geely. (2019, October 14). A perfect match: How suppliers benefited from the Geely-Proton partnership. *Zhejiang Geely Holding Group.* https://zgh.com/media-center/story/a-perfect-match-how-supplier-benefited-from-the-geely-proton-partnership/?lang=en

Geely. (2022, November 17). Zeekr's SEA-M architecture is the new answer to future mobility. *Zhejiang Geely Holding Group.* https://zgh.com/media-center/news/2022-11-17-1/?lang=en

Geely. (2024, June 28). Aramco to acquire 10% equity interest in Horse Powertrain Limited. *Zhejiang Geely Holding Group*. https://zgh.com/media-center/news/2024-06-28/?lang=en

Geely. (n.d.). New energy pathway. *Zhejiang Geely Holding Group*. https://zgh.com/new-energy-pathway/?lang=en

GenEng News. (2013). BGI offers $117.6M to acquire Complete Genomics. Genetic Engineering & Biotechnology News (GEN). https://www.genengnews.com/topics/omics/bgi-offers-117-6m-to-acquire-complete-genomics/

GenomeWeb. (2010, January 13). BGI to receive $1.5B in collaborative funds over 10 years from China Development Bank. GenomeWeb. https://www.genomeweb.com/sequencing/bgi-receive-15b-collaborative-funds-over-10-years-china-development-bank

Genomics England. (2015, November 12). Genomics England Contracts with WuXi NextCODE as Clinical Interpretation Partner in both Rare Disease and Cancer. https://www.genomicsengland.co.uk/news/genomics-england-contracts-with-wuxi-nextcode

Genomics, B. G. I. (2023, June 29). BGI Genomics obtains BSI ISO 37301 compliance management system certification [Press release]. PR Newswire. https://www.prnewswire.com/apac/news-releases/bgi-genomics-obtains-bsi-iso-37301-compliance-management-system-certification-301866808.html

GitHub. (2025). *DeepSeek-ai repositories*. https://github.com/orgs/deepseek-ai/repositories?type=all

Global Times. (2023, February 14). CATL to license patent battery technology to Ford plant in US: company - Global Times. Globaltimes.cn. https://www.globaltimes.cn/page/202302/1285424.shtml

Gnee. (2025, July 29). Geely showcases new vehicles and comprehensive AI technologies at WAIC 2025, ushering in a boom in smart technology. *GNEE Group*. https://gneegroup.com/news/geely-showcases-new-vehicles-and-comprehensive-ai-technologies-at-waic-2025-ushering-in-a-boom-in-smart-technology.html

Goldden Group. (2025, July 16). Net Zero Centre of Excellence and Digital Battery Centre of Excellence. Goldden Group. htmlhttps://www.golddengroup.com/SG-News/695.html

Government of Israel. (2016). The life sciences industry in Israel. https://www.gov.il/BlobFolder/dynamiccollectorresultitem/life-sciences-industry-in-israel/he/The%20Life%20Sciences%20Industry%20in%20Israel.pdf

Grand View Research. (2023). Genomics market size, share & trends analysis report, 2023–2030. https://www.grandviewresearch.com/industry-analysis/genomics-market

Grant, R. M. (2021). *Contemporary strategy analysis.* John Wiley & Sons. https://books.google.com/books/about/Contemporary_Strategy_Analysis.html?id=TadJEAAAQBAJ

Group, B. G. I. (n.d.). Huo-Yan Laboratory. BGI. https://www.bgi.com/global/media/27

Group, D. H. L. (2023). *Annual report 2023.* https://reporting-hub.group.dhl.com/2023-fy/en/the-company/forword/

Gryphon Scientific. (2019, February 14). China's biotechnology development: The role of U.S. and other foreign engagement (Report prepared for the U.S.-China Economic and Security Review Commission). https://www.uscc.gov/sites/default/files/Research/US-China%20Biotech%20Report.pdf

Guo, D., Zhu, Q., Yang, D., Xie, Z., Dong, K., Zhang, W., Chen, G., Bi, X., Wu, Y., Li, Y. K., Luo, F., Xiong, Y., & Liang, W. (2024). *DeepSeek-Coder: When the large language model meets programming — The rise of code intelligence* (No. arXiv:2401.14196). arXiv. https://doi.org//arXiv.2401.14196DOI: 10.48550

Guo, M. (2025, March 10). : " + + " [In-depth research on the health management industry: Who will be the first to complete the closed loop of "data + service + payment" in the accelerated expansion of the trillion-yuan blue ocean]. Chinairn. https://www.chinairn.com/news/20250310/144938487.shtml

Gupta, M. (2025, January 21). What are DeepSeek-R1 distilled models? *Data Science in Your Pocket.* https://medium.com/data-science-in-your-pocket/what-are-deepseek-r1-distilled-models-329629968d5d

Gupta, R. (2016, September 8). [Air China is optimizing its ancillary service marketing to focus on the international market]. Travel Daily. https://www.traveldaily.cn/article/106530

Halkos, G., & Nomikos, S. (2021). Corporate social responsibility: Trends in global reporting initiative standards. *Economic Analysis and Policy*, *69*, 106–117. DOI: 10.1016/j.eap.2020.11.008

Hall, C. R. (2025, December 1). 2025 smart surveillance industry prospect analysis: The smart surveillance industry ushers in a dual leap in scale and quality. https://m.chinabgao.com/freereport/110978.html

Halldorsson, A., & Wehner, J. (2020). Last-mile logistics fulfillment: A framework for energy efficiency. *Research in Transportation Business & Management, 37*, 100481. Advance online publication. DOI: 10.1016/j.rtbm.2020.100481

Hamlin, K. (2024, June 12). Breakingviews - Breakingviews: Chinese EV makers will drive around EU tariffs. Reuters. https://www.reuters.com/breakingviews/chinese-ev-makers-will-drive-around-eu-tariffs-2024-06-12/

Hampel, C. (2021, June 18). New details on the scope of Geely SEA e-platform. *Electrive.* https://www.electrive.com/2021/06/18/new-details-on-the-scope-of-geelys-sea-e-platform/

Hanafi, M. (2024). Designing nickel smelter industry investment competitiveness policy in Indonesia through system dynamics model. *Journal of Science and Technology Policy Management.* DOI: 10.1108/JSTPM-01-2024-0016

Hangzhou Hikvision Digital Technology Co. Ltd. (2023). Global human rights policy. https://www.hikvision.com/cn/aboutus/Sustainability/integrity-and-compliance/human-rights-protection/

Han, J. (2024). [Financial analysis of BYD Company based on Harvard framework]. *E-Commerce Letters, 13*(2), 1681–1694. DOI: 10.12677/ecl.2024.132204

Hanley, S. (2024). CATL, BYD To Slash Battery Prices By 50% In 2024. BOOM! EVs Win! CleanTechnica. https://cleantechnica.com/2024/02/26/catl-byd-to-slash-battery-prices-by-50-in-2024-boom-evs-win/

Han, M. (2004). *Obtaining Sustainable Competitive Advantage of CTV Enterprise through "Go-Out"*. Strategy. [Master's thesis, Tsinghua University]

Haqq, A. M., & Gultom, Y. M. L. (2022). The challenge of implementing public-private partnerships: A transaction costs perspective on waste to energy projects in Indonesia. *Journal of Financial Management of Property and Construction, 27*(3), 365–386. DOI: 10.1108/JFMPC-09-2020-0058

Harrington, A. (2025). *The DeepSeek disruption: How China's groundbreaking Ai model is transforming the global tech race.* Alexander Harrington.

Hawkins, A. (2025, January 28). Who is behind DeepSeek and how did it achieve its AI 'Sputnik moment'? *The Guardian.* https://www.theguardian.com/technology/2025/jan/28/who-is-behind-deepseek-and-how-did-it-achieve-its-ai-sputnik-moment

He, H. (2025). The impact of technology-driven business model innovation on corporate performance: A case study of JD. com in the digital economy era. In *2025 5th international conference on enterprise management and economic development* (ICEMED 2025) (pp. 1054-1062). Atlantis Press. https://doi.org/DOI: 10.2991/978-94-6463-811-0_114

He, J. Y., Liu, R. F., & Lai, J. Y. (2025) CXO hangye lingjunzhe, yitihua moshi dianding guoji diwei yu chengzhangxing. [CXO industry leader, integrated model establishes international position and growth potential]. CITIC Securities. https://www.vzkoo.com/document/20250717d82d8edf5fa599531b4fd6e7.html

Hengrui Pharmaceuticals. (2024, April 18). *Hengrui Pharmaceuticals: Hengrui Pharmaceuticals's 2023 Annual Report*. Eastmoney. https://pdf.dfcfw.com/pdf/H2_AN202404171630412062_1.pdf?1713380305000.pdf

Hengrui Pharmaceuticals. (2025, August 8). *Good News! Hengrui Pharmaceuticals' HER2 ADC Innovative Drug Recon Trastuzumab has been granted Orphan Drug Status by the US FDA*. Hengrui. https://www.hengrui.com/media/detail-821.html

Hengrui Pharmaceuticals. (2025, August 8). *Good News! Hengrui Pharmaceuticals' HER2 ADC Innovative Medicine, Trastuzumab Ruikang, has been granted Orphan Drug Designation by the US FDA*. Hengrui. https://www.hengrui.com/media/detail-821.html

Hengrui Pharmaceuticals. (2025, July 28). *Hengrui Pharmaceuticals' Announcement Regarding the Signing of a Cooperation, Option and License Agreement with GSK*. Hengrui. https://static.sse.com.cn/disclosure/listedinfo/announcement/c/new/2025-07-28/600276_20250728_7GZX.pdf

Hengrui Pharmaceuticals. (2025, March 26). *Hengrui Pharmaceuticals and Merck have signed an exclusive licensing agreement for the Lp(a) inhibitor HRS-5346*. Hengrui. https://www.hengrui.com/media/detail-743.html

Hengrui Pharmaceuticals. (2025, March 31). *Hengrui Pharmaceuticals: Hengrui Pharmaceuticals's 2024 Annual Report*. Hengrui. https://www.hengrui.com/investor/regularAnnouncement.html

Herrera-Navarrete, R., Colín-Cruz, A., Arellano-Wences, H. J., Sampedro-Rosas, M. L., Rosas-Acevedo, J. L., & Rodríguez-Herrera, A. L. (2022). Municipal Wastewater Treatment Plants: Gap, Challenges, and Opportunities in Environmental Management. *Environmental Management*, *69*(1), 75–88. DOI: 10.1007/s00267-021-01562-y PMID: 34799756

Hikvision North America. (2016, November 4). About Hikvision North America. https://www.hikvision.com/us-en/about-us/about-hikvision-north-america/

Hikvision. (2022). Hikvision Whistleblowing Policy. https://www.hikvision.com/content/dam/hikvision/en/marketing/image/about-us/compliance/new/Hikvision-Whistleblowing-Policy-EN_1.pdf/

Hikvision. (2023). –FY2022 [Hikvision at a glance—FY2022]. https://www.hikvision.com/content/dam/hikvision/cn/ / / -2023.pdf

Hikvision. (2024a). Annual report 2024. https://www.hikvision.com/en/newsroom/latest-news/2025/hikvision-releases-2024-full-year-and-2025-first-quarter-financial-results/

Hikvision. (2024b). Company profile. https://www.hikvision.com/cn/about-us/Company-Profile

Hikvision. (2024c). Where are Hikvision cameras manufactured globally? https://www.icseecam.com/where-are-hikvision-cameras-manufactured-glob/

Hikvision. (2025a, August 1). Value chain synergy: Sustainable development. https://www.hikvision.com/cn/aboutus/Sustainability/valuechain/

Hikvision. (2025b, October 22). Our green practices: Corporate sustainability. https://www.hikvision.com/us-en/about-us/sustainability/our-green-practices/

Hikvision. (2025c). 2025 third quarter financial report (Q1–Q3 consolidated) [PDF]. Hangzhou Hikvision Digital Technology Co., Ltd. https://www.hikvision.com/content/dam/hikvision/en/investor-relations/annual-quarterly-reports/2025/3Q2025-Financial-ReportEV.pdf

Hikvision. (n.d.-a). About us. Hikvision Malaysia. https://www.hikvision.net.my/about-us

Hikvision. (n.d.-b). Hikvision focuses on GDPR compliance. Hikvision Europe. https://www.hikvision.com/en/support/cybersecurity/cybersecurity-white-paper/hikvision-focuses-on-gdpr-compliance/

Hill, C. W. L., Hwang, P., & Kim, W. C. (1990). An eclectic theory of the choice of international entry mode. *Strategic Management Journal*, *11*(2), 117–128. DOI: 10.1002/smj.4250110204

Holding, S. F. (2023). *2023 annual report.* https://ir.sf-express.com/media/2yldv5tg/2023-annual-report-e.pdf

Holding, S. F. (2024).. . *Sustainability Report, 2024*, •••. https://www.sf-express.com/chn/en/sustainable/0Carbon

Holm, M., & Zhang, L. (2016). *Swedish and Chinese leadership at CEVT: A case study on the cultural differences of Chinese and Swedish leadership* [Master's thesis, Chalmers University of Technology]. Chalmers Publications Library. https://publications.lib.chalmers.se/records/fulltext/237634/237634.pdf

Holslag, J. (2022). Controlling the Mine? Assessing China's Emergence as a Minerals Super Power. *Journal of Contemporary China*, *31*(137), 663–674. DOI: 10.1080/10670564.2021.2010381

Honda Motor Co. Ltd. (Honda). (2023, March). LG Energy Solution and Honda Break Ground for New Joint Venture EV Battery Plant in Ohio. Honda Global; Honda Motor Co., Ltd. https://global.honda/en/newsroom/news/2023/c230301eng.html

Hu, Q. (2024, December 12). , [Hengrui Pharmaceuticals is Forced to Venture Overseas and Reveal its Weaknesses]. *Tencent*. https://news.qq.com/rain/a/20241212A05WAR00

Hu, Y. (2024, August 8). Hikvision's Hu Yangzhong: From security to scene digitalization [Interview]. Hikvision. https://www.hikvision.com/cn/NewsEvents/Newsroom/2024/2024-08-08/

Hu, H., Qi, Y., Lee, H. L., Shen, Z. M., Liu, C., Zhu, W., & Kang, N. (2024). Supercharged by advanced analytics, JD.com attains agility, resilience, and shared value across its supply chain. *INFORMS Journal on Applied Analytics*, *54*(1), 54–70. DOI: 10.1287/inte.2023.0078

Huo, Z. (2022). Analysis of E-commerce business strategy - take JD.com, inc. as the case. *Asian Business Research*, *7*(1), 41–44. DOI: 10.20849/abr.v7i1.989

IDC. (2025, January 14). European financial applications forecast, 2024-2028. IDC. https://my.idc.com/getdoc.jsp?containerId=EUR150690123

IEA. (2024). Electricity. IEA. https://www.iea.org/reports/renewables-2024/electricity

Iksan, M., & Soong, J.-J. (2023). The Political Economy of Indonesia's Development Strategy under China-USA Power Rivalry and Hegemonic Competition: A Middle Power with Its Hedging Strategy. *Chinese Economy*, *56*(4), 304–320. DOI: 10.1080/10971475.2022.2136696

Inagaki, K., White, E., & Jopson, B. (2024, December 10). China's CATL to build €4.1bn battery factory with Stellantis in European expansion. @FinancialTimes; Financial Times. https://www.ft.com/content/b2c41a7d-02fa-4846-ab50-dd27e534dcf5

iNews. (n.d.). The "Geely logic" of global R&D: From "bringing in" to "going global." *inf.news*. https://inf.news/en/auto/7bb140c5b50316013fcebd9486b06f04.html

Insilico Medicine. (2018, June 12). WuXi AppTec Leads Strategic Investment In Insilico Medicine To Accelerate Drug Discovery Using AI. Drug Discovery Trends. https://www.drugdiscoverytrends.com/wuxi-apptec-leads-strategic-investment-in-insilico-medicine-to-accelerate-drug-discovery-using-ai/

Interesse, G. (2024, February 5). China's 2024 catalogue for guiding industry restructuring. *China Briefing*. https://www.china-briefing.com/news/chinas-2024-catalogue-for-guiding-industry-restructuring/

Internal Revenue Service. (2023). Frequently asked questions about the Qualifying Advanced Energy Project (48C) credit. Internal Revenue Service. https://www.irs.gov/credits-deductions/frequently-asked-questions-about-the-qualifying-advanced-energy-project-48c-credit

International Energy Agency (IEA). (2023, July 11). Critical minerals market review 2023. OECD Publishing, Paris. DOI: 10.1787/9cdf8f39-en

International Energy Agency. (2024, April 23). *Global EV outlook 2024*. https://www.iea.org/reports/global-ev-outlook-2024

International Monetary Fund. (2025, October 7). *World economic outlook: All issues*. https://www.imf.org/en/publications/weo

IRENA. (2022, September 26). Solar PV key to ASEAN decarbonisation, 241GW of installed capacity expected by 2030. IRENA. https://www.pv-tech.org/solar-pv-key-to-asean-decarbonisation-241gw-of-installed-capacity-expected-by-2030-irena/

iScience. (2023, September 25). Influence of carbon derivatives on carbon capture investments in coal-based power sector, a China perspective. iScience. https://pmc.ncbi.nlm.nih.gov/articles/PMC10579434/

Jajoria, D., Jatav, M., & Mishra, R. (2024). Trends, patterns and socioeconomic determinants of child and adolescent labour in India: Empirical analysis using national sample survey data. *Journal of International Development*, *36*(3), 1647–1674. DOI: 10.1002/jid.3874

Janek, J., & Zeier, W. G. (2016). A solid future for battery development. *Nature Energy*, *1*(9), 1–4. DOI: 10.1038/nenergy.2016.141

Javed, S. A., Bo, Y., Tao, L., & Dong, W. (2023). The 'Dual Circulation' development model of China: Background and insights. *Rajagiri Management Journal*, *17*(1), 2–20. DOI: 10.1108/RAMJ-03-2021-0016

JCET Group. (2010). 2009 [JCET Group 2009 annual report]. https://www.jcetglobal.com/uploads/report/cfb6aad8dfd3841e174418e599b23b39.pdf

JCET Group. (2015). 2014 [JCET Group 2014 annual report]. https://www.jcetglobal.com/uploads/report/db125b052e176b00bc1efbf07c9a3057.pdf

JCET Group. (2019). 2018 [JCET Group 2018 annual report] https://www.jcetglobal.com/uploads/report/0c74cb869fed48c46619062068723a58.pdf

JCET Group. (2025). news. JCET Group Official Website. https://www.jcetglobal.com/site/news-detail?id=1806

JCET Group. (n.d.). Company Information. JCET Group Official Website. https://www.jcetglobal.com/en/site/JCET-overview

JD.COM. (n.d.). *Biography*. https://ir.jd.com/management/richard-qiangdong-liu

Jer-Tech. (2025, March 26). Top global leaders in security camera manufacturing. https://jer-tech.com/top-global-leaders-in-security-camera-manufacturing/

Ji, Y. (2025, March 22). PD-1 " " ?[Why is Hengrui's "Going Global" Venture Blocked Again as the PD-1 Group's US Listing has been Postponed Twice?]. *21st Century Business Herald*. https://m.21jingji.com/article/20250322/156a123c2c6df4cdd426d7f12dee9832.html

Ji, Y. (2025, May 15). IPO! " " [The largest pharmaceutical IPO in Hong Kong in the past five years! A Capital Breakthrough that is not Short of Money]. *21st Century Business Herald*. https://www.21jingji.com/article/20250515/herald/7888b9617c364a6b3f1ee609a35362a9.html

Jiang, B. (2025, January 28). *China's AI disrupter DeepSeek bets on low-key team of 'young geniuses' to beat US giants* [Artificial intelligence/TechBig/Tech]. https://www.scmp.com/tech/big-tech/article/3294357/chinas-ai-disrupter-deepseek-bets-low-key-team-young-geniuses-beat-us-giants

Jia-Zheng, Y., & Broggi, C. B. (2025). The metamorphosis of China's automotive industry (1953–2001): Inward internationalisation, technological transfers and the making of a post-socialist market. *Business History*, *67*(1), 211–238. DOI: 10.1080/00076791.2023.2247366

Johnson, L. (2025, April 25). *DeepSeek Coder: Let the code write itself.* https://www.byteplus.com/en/topic/382907?title=deepseek-coder-let-the-code-write-itself

JPO. (2024). 2024 [2024 Patent Application Technology Trend Report]. https://www.jpo.go.jp/system/tutuj/tokkyo_jouhou_e/tokkyo_jouhou_2024.html

Kang, L. (2023, April 12). Full CPCA rankings: Top-selling models and automakers in China in Mar. *CNEVPost.* https://cnevpost.com/2023/04/12/full-cpca-rankings-top-selling-models-automakers-china-mar/

Kang, L. (2025a, February 11). Global EV battery market share in 2024: CATL 37.9%, BYD 17.2%. CnEVPost. https://cnevpost.com/2025/02/11/global-ev-battery-market-share-2024/

Kang, L. (2025b, June 6). Global EV battery market share in Jan-Apr 2025: CATL 38.1%, BYD 17.3%. CnEVPost. https://cnevpost.com/2025/06/06/global-ev-battery-market-share-jan-apr-2025/

Kansteiner, F. (2025, August 7, 2025). Amid MFN talks, Lilly chief warns US adoption of international drug prices could bring 'worst of two worlds'. FIERCE Pharma. https://www.fiercepharma.com/pharma/amid-mfn-talks-lilly-chief-warns-adoption-international-drug-prices-could-bring-worst-two

Kanugrahan, S. P., Hakam, D. F., & Nugraha, H. (2022). Techno-Economic Analysis of Indonesia Power Generation Expansion to Achieve Economic Sustainability and Net Zero Carbon 2050. *Sustainability (Basel), 14*(15), 9038. DOI: 10.3390/su14159038

Karim, M. F. (2025). Chinese network power and patronage embeddedness in Indonesia. *Asia Europe Journal, 23*(2-3), 285–302. Advance online publication. DOI: 10.1007/s10308-025-00717-4

Kathy. (2025, April 17). " ", " " , ! [*Hengrui and Kangfang "Set Sail for Southeast Asia", while Fuhonghanlin and Junshi "are Competing in the Middle East". It's Time for Pharmaceutical Companies to Change Their Strategies as They Expand Globally!*] Xueqiu. https://xueqiu.com/3483303916/332061578

Keller, K. L. (2013). Building, Measuring, and Managing Brand Equity: Strategic Brand Management. https://www.pearsonhighered.com/assets/preface/0/1/3/4/0134892496.pdf

Kennedy, J. (2018, March 26). How to Ensure That America's Life-Sciences Sector Remains Globally Competitive. Information Technology and Innovation Foundation. https://itif.org/publications/2018/03/26/how-ensure-americas-life-sciences-sector-remains-globally-competitive/

Khalil, J., Yan, D., Yuan, L., Jafarzadehfadaki, M., Adhikari, S., Han, J., Sisiopiku, V., & Jiang, Z. (2025). Urban traffic simulation with shared mobility services: An approach using spatiotemporal network kernel density estimation and MATSim. *ACM Transactions on Spatial Algorithms and Systems*, *11*(4), 1–31. DOI: 10.1145/3704918

Khan, M. I., Zaman, S. I., & Khan, S. A. (2026). *Supply chain finance: Trends, sustainability and future outlook*. CRC Press.

Knowledge Info Hub. (2025). The rise of Geely: A Chinese automotive giant. *Knowledge and Info Hub*. https://knowledgeinfohub.com/the-rise-of-geely-a-chinese-automotive-giant/

Kraft, J., & Kraft, A. (2024). Geely: How a Chinese upstart became a global automobile maker. *Journal of Research in International Business and Management*, *11*(4), 1–11. https://www.interesjournals.org/articles/geely-how-a-chinese-upstart-became-a-global-automobile-maker-109510.html

Krause, D. (2025). *DeepSeek and FinTech: The democratization of Ai and Its global implications. SSRN*. DOI: 10.2139/ssrn.5116322

Kumar, A., & Vishwanathan, A. (2025). Race for critical minerals: China's ambitions and challenges. *Comparative Strategy*, *44*(1), 56–72. DOI: 10.1080/01495933.2024.2445490

Kurtenbach, E. (2026, February 22). Geely's Volvo purchase faces cultural obstacles. *GOLDSEA*. https://goldsea.com/article_details/geely-s-volvo-purchase-must-overcome-big-cultural-disparity

Landry, V., Semsar-Kazerooni, K., Tjong, J., Alj, A., Darnley, A., Lipp, R., & Guberman, G. I. (2021). The systemized exploitation of temporary migrant agricultural workers in Canada: Exacerbation of health vulnerabilities during the COVID-19 pandemic and recommendations for the future. *Journal of Migration and Health*, *3*, 100035. DOI: 10.1016/j.jmh.2021.100035 PMID: 34405185

Laouiti, S., Detchusananart, M., Bieske, L., & Sodar, M. A. (2018, December). *Geely automobile holdings: From "zero" to Chinese automotive industry "hero"*. ResearchGate. https://www.researchgate.net/publication/332525104

Lau, F., & Seifert, R. (2025). Comparison of drug approvals of the FDA and EMA between 2013 and 2023. *Naunyn-Schmiedeberg's Archives of Pharmacology*. Advance online publication. DOI: 10.1007/s00210-025-04412-4 PMID: 40608116

Lazuardi, S. D., Hadi, F., Devintasari, D. V., Wuryaningrum, P., Riduwan, M., Noarista, O. S., & Alifia, S. F. (2024). The impact on downstream policy implementation for mineral export products in Indonesia: Marine transportation point of view. *IOP Conference Series. Earth and Environmental Science*, *1298*(1), 012018. DOI: 10.1088/1755-1315/1298/1/012018

Lee, M. (2025, August 14). Geely's resilience in a turbulent EV market: Strategic R&D and market expansion as catalysts for long-term value creation. *AInvest*. https://www.ainvest.com/news/geely-resilience-turbulent-ev-market-strategic-market-expansion-catalysts-long-term-creation-2508/

Lee, J., Kim, J., Kim, J., & Choi, S. (2021). Why localization is necessary as a business strategy in emerging markets: The case comparison of Hyundai and Volkswagen. *Journal of Open Innovation*, *7*(3), 190. DOI: 10.3390/joitmc7030190

Li, F. (2024, November 4). Green methanol route to nation's carbon goal. *China Daily*. https://www.chinadaily.com.cn/a/202411/04/WS67282512a310f1265a1cb2ee.html

Li, F. (2025, May 19). "One Geely" integration to hone competitive edge. *China Daily*. https://www.chinadaily.com.cn/a/202505/19/WS682a8e57a310a04af22c0281.html

Li, G., Harding, R., & White, E. (2025, May 20). CATL founder Robin Zeng expects China truck market to be 50% electric by 2028. @FinancialTimes; Financial Times. https://www.ft.com/content/87372b46-ee9c-4747-ae2d-3f729b92b008

Li, M. (2025, April 18). : [Hengrui Pharmaceuticals: Firmly Implement the Strategies of Scientific and Technological Innovation and Internationalization]. *China Securities Journal*. https://epaper.cs.com.cn/zgzqb/html/2025-04/18/nw.D110000zgzqb_20250418_3-A07.htm

Li, M., & Pi, X. (2025, March 12). : [Geely globalization: Insights from Chinese companies going abroad]. *Toutiao*. https://www.toutiao.com/article/7480850536733721115/

Li, D. S. (2025). , [Transforming our mindset to face globalization head-on]. *Manager*, (04), 6–7.

Li, J., Li, H., Li, C., Chen, X., Zhang, X., & Wu, Y. (2021). Comparisons of Clinical Registration Trial Types, Designs and Completion Status of Drugs in China, the United States, Europe and Japan. *Chinese Journal of Evidence-Based Medicine*, *21*(07), 845–850. https://doi.org/CNKI:SUN:ZZXZ.0.2021-07-015

Li, J., Li, L., Yang, Z., & Tian, X. (2024). Managing disruptions in international distribution channels: Effectuation, business model innovation, and channel resilience. *Journal of International Business Studies*. Advance online publication. DOI: 10.1057/s41267-024-00730-6

Lin, R., Chen, J. J., & Xie, L. (2020). *Transnational governance at Geely Auto during its acquisition of Volvo*. Springer. [Book title if applicable], https://link.springer.com/chapter/10.1007/978-981-15-7405-4_3 DOI: 10.1007/978-981-15-7405-4_3

Liu, A. (2017, December 27). Merck Serono, WuXi AppTec, and Pontifax Form Israeli Life Science Incubator. NAI500.https://nai500.com/blog/2017/12/merck-serono-wuxi-apptec-and-pontifax-form-israeli-life-science-incubator/

Liu, E. Y. (2025, July 15). , , [WuXi AppTec Research Report: Leading player in the pharmaceutical outsourcing industry, platform-driven, serving the world]. Dongfang caifu. https://caifuhao.eastmoney.com/news/20230313114751593628580

Liu, J. (2025, Jun 18). : ?[*Innovative Drugs Going Global: How does Hengrui Medicine Break Through the Defenses of International Pharmaceutical Giants?*]. Sina. https://finance.sina.com.cn/cj/2025-06-18/doc-infanfym5833028.shtml

Liu, M. (2022, May 16). New energy vehicles, as represented by BYD. *Atlantis Press*. DOI: 10.2991/aebmr.k.220502.081

Liu, S., Wang, E., & Xiang, J. (2019, March 28). Daimler and Geely Holding form global joint venture to develop smart. *Smart Media*. https://media.smart.com/daimler-and-geely-holding-form-global-joint-venture-to-develop-smart/

Liu, Y. (2025, August 6).2025 CDMO : [2025, the pharmaceutical CDMO industry: R&D and production partners born from professional division of labor]. Chinairn. https://www.chinairn.com/hyzx/20250806/18030158.shtml

Liu, F., Sim, J.-Y., Sun, H., Edziah, B. K., Adom, P. K., & Song, S. (2023). Assessing the role of economic globalization on energy efficiency: Evidence from a global perspective. *China Economic Review*, *77*, 101897. DOI: 10.1016/j.chieco.2022.101897

Liu, K. (2024). *China's Direct Investment in Indonesia (1990–2022): Multiple Structure and Systemic Risks*. Springer Nature Singapore., DOI: 10.1007/978-981-97-7328-2

Logistics, J. D. (2024). *JD Logistics unveils roadmap to enable 2-3 day delivery in global markets*. https://www.waltherploosvanamstel.nl/jd-logistics-unveils-roadmap-to-enable-2-3-day-delivery-global-markets/

Lu, Y. Y. (2024, August 3). : [Going Global: WuXi AppTec's Layout in Singapore]. Weibo. https://www.weibo.com/ttarticle/p/show?id=2309405063278144389200

Ma, S., & Feng, J. x. (2025, June 5). : ,2025 5 VC&PE [The database of the pharmaceutical industry chain: Investment and financing of innovative drugs. In May 2025, the investment and financing of VC&PE of innovative drugs in the global market maintained a year-on-year positive growth. SDIC Security. https://www.essence.com.cn/news/2540202?columnId=002001004

Macarol, J. (2024, November 16). BYD and Geely in the world's top ten: How Chinese car brands are breaking into the world's biggest markets. *City Magazine*. https://citymagazine.si/en/byd-and-geely-in-the-worlds-top-ten-how-chinese-car-brands-penetrate-into-the-worlds-largest/

Mann, J. (2025, January 28). *DeepSeek just dropped an update AI model called Janus Pro. It says the image generator is better than OpenAI's DALL-E.* Business Insider. https://www.businessinsider.com/deepseek-janus-pro-7b-ai-model-openai-dall-e3-2025-1

Manners-Bell, J. (2019). *Future of Logistics.* International Transport Forum. DOI: 10.18235/0001729

Martino, N., Sanders, C. B., & Dej, E. (2024). The 'regulatory grey zone': Bylaw enforcement's governing of homelessness and space. *Policing and Society*, *34*(4), 305–320. DOI: 10.1080/10439463.2023.2263617

Masdar. (2023, December 5). Masdar, Envision Group to develop 1.2 GW solar PV project at Masdar City. Masdar. https://masdar.ae/en/news/masdar-envision-group-to-develop-1-2-gw-solar-pv-project-at-masdar-city

Masiero, G., Ogasavara, M. H., Jussani, A. C., & Risso, M. L. (2016). Electric vehicles in China: BYD strategies and government subsidies. *RAI Revista de Administração E Inovação, 13*(1), 3–11. DOI: 10.1016/j.rai.2016.01.001

McGrane, C. (2017, May 17). Chinese genomics giant BGI announces West Coast Innovation Center to fuel international collaboration. GeekWire. https://www.geekwire.com/2017/bgi/

McKinsey & Company. (2021, October 25). Unlocking growth in battery cell manufacturing for electric vehicles. https://www.mckinsey.com/industries/automotive-and-assembly/our-insights/unlocking-growth-in-battery-cell-manufacturing-for-electric-vehicles

McKinsey. (2023). *McKinsey Year in Review 2023 | McKinsey & Company*. https://www.mckinsey.com/featured-insights/2023-year-in-review

McKinsey. (2025, April 22). *How open source AI solutions are reshaping business | McKinsey*. https://www.mckinsey.com/capabilities/quantumblack/our-insights/open-source-technology-in-the-age-of-ai?utm_source=chatgpt.com

Medina, A. F. (2025, September 2). How BOI EV 3.5 shapes the future of EV battery investments in Thailand. ASEAN Briefing. https://www.aseanbriefing.com/news/how-boi-ev-3-5-shapes-the-future-of-ev-battery-investments-in-thailand/

Mei, X. Y. (2010). TCL [TCL in Vietnam]. *International Communication*, *8*, 59–60.

Mei, X. Y. (2010). TCL : [TCL in Vietnam: A Relatively Successful Case Study of Chinese Overseas Investment]. *China Market*, *46*, 53–68.

Meng, Z., & Wang, X. (2021). The effects of outbound mergers and acquisitions (M&As) on Chinese automobile corporations' performance: A case study of Geely's acquisition of Volvo. *International Business Research*. https://www.ccsenet.org/journal/index.php/ibr/article/view/45467

Messe Düsseldorf Asia. (n.d.). Market highlights: Robust prospects and growing demand in Southeast Asia. *Wire Southeast Asia*. https://www.wire-southeastasia.com/market-highlights

Mewswire, P. R. (2054, July 25). Envision Energy Powers the World's First Green Marine Ammonia Bunkering, Pioneering Net Zero Shipping Fuel. PR Mewswire. https://www.prnewswire.com/news-releases/envision-energy-powers-the-worlds-first-green-marine-ammonia-bunkering-pioneering-net-zero-shipping-fuel-302513836.html

Miao, Z., & Zetao, P. (2025). Different Motives, Different Outcomes: A Comparative Study of China's Outward FDI in Industrial Parks in Malaysia and Indonesia. *Asian Economic Papers*, *24*(2), 1–23. DOI: 10.1162/asep_a_00951

Ministry of Commerce of the People's Republic of China. (2025, May 12). *[Joint Statement of the China-US Geneva Economic and Trade Talks]*. https://www.mofcom.gov.cn:8443/xwfb/ldrhd/art/2025/art_8055948aadb5450598bf73d1aae6828e.html

Ministry of Finance. (2023, June 19). [Announcement on the continuation and optimization of the vehicle purchase tax reduction policy for new energy vehicles]. *Government of the People's Republic of China*. https://www.gov.cn/zhengce/zhengceku/202306/content_6887734.htm

MobilityNotes. (2025). IRENA Renewable Energy Capacity Statistics 2025. MobilityNotes. https://mobilitynotes.com/irena-renewable-energy-capacity-statistics-2025/ https://www.irena.org/Publications/2025/Jul/Renewable-energy-statistics-2025

Molteni, M. (2017, May 18). A Chinese genome giant sets its sights on the ultimate sequencer. WIRED. https://www.wired.com/2017/05/chinese-genome-giant-sets-sights-uitimate-sequencer

Monetary Authority of Singapore. (2019, January 14). *Payment Services Act 2019.* https://sso.agc.gov.sg/act/psa2019

Monetary Authority of Singapore. (2025, October 1). *Singapore strengthens position as third largest global FX centre* [Press release]. https://www.mas.gov.sg/news/media-releases/2025/singapore-strengthens-position-as-third-largest-global-fx-centre

Moody's Investors Service. (2023, October 12). Moody's assigns A2 to Envision Energy International Limited's USD 500 million green bonds. Moodys. https://www.moodys.com/research/Moodys-assigns-A2-to-Envision-Energy-International-Limiteds-USD-500-million-green-bonds--PR_488123

Morningstar. (2023, August 21). Hikvision is undervalued as long-term digitization in China is overshadowed by macroeconomic pain. https://www.morningstar.com/company-reports/1176077

Murong, Y. (2021, October 3). [WuXi AppTec's In-depth Thematic Research Report]. Xueqiu. https://xueqiu.com/4866021334/199366220

Naryono, E. (2023). *Nickel Mine Exploitation in Indonesia, Between a Blessing and a Disaster of Environmental Damage*. OSF. https://doi.org/DOI: 10.31219/osf.io/y58qe

Needham, K., & Baldwin, C. (2021, July 7). China's gene giant harvests data from millions of pregnant women. Reuters Investigates. https://www.reuters.com/investigates/special-report/health-china-bgi-dna/

Netease. (2022, August 12). 3.0 [Envision Group's 3.0 era]. [Netease]. https://www.163.com/dy/article/HEJLARKM0552LIVZ.html

Nguyen, L. H., & Nguyen, H. P. (2020). Generation Z in Vietnam: The quest for authenticity. In Gentina, E., & Parry, E. (Eds.), *The new generation Z in Asia: dynamics, differences, digitalisation* (pp. 135–148). Emerald Publishing Limited., DOI: 10.1108/978-1-80043-220-820201014

Ni, Y. Q. (2024, August 1). TCL : “ ” [Dialogue: TCL Founding Chairman and CEO Li Dongsheng: “Go to overseas markets to ‘grab a share’.”]. *21st Century Business Herald,* 010. https://www.21jingji.com/article/20240801/ba47add878881f75885d7d79ff24e5bc.html

Ni, Y. Q. (2024, August 10). “ ” [China’s “Vietnam Hub” for Going Global]. *21st Century Business Herald,* 008. https://www.21jingji.com/article/20240810/3af1c28a38120a373e4284464101e5ad.html

OFweek Energy Storage Network. (2025, January 22). “ ”, [“Pointing Toward the Sea”: A Long Shot Capturing Chinese Enterprises’ Global Expansion Journey]. OFweek [OFweek Energy Storage Network]. https://chuneng.ofweek.com/news/2025-01/ART-180225-8500-30655992.html

OFweek Lithium Battery Network. (2021a, June 25). , AESC [Supplying Renault, Envision AESC’s new battery factory will be located in France]. OFweek [OFweek Lithium Battery Network]. https://libattery.ofweek.com/2021-06/ART-36001-8500-30506240.html

OFweek Lithium Battery Network. (2021b, October 28). , ! [Focusing on both power lithium batteries and energy storage batteries, Envision Technology launches zero-carbon practice in Ordos!]. OFweek [OFweek Lithium Battery Network]. https://libattery.ofweek.com/2021-10/ART-36001-8500-30531951.html

Ogunlade, B. T., Adeniran, J. A., Abdulraheem, K. A., Odediran, E. T., Atanda, A. S., Oyeneye, A. K., Akapo, R. A., & Yusuf, R. O. (2024). Heavy Metals Analysis in the Vicinity of a Northcentral Nigeria Major Scrap-Iron Smelting Plant. *International Journal of Environmental Research, 18*(6), 107. DOI: 10.1007/s41742-024-00657-8

Oh, S.-Y. (2020). *China’s Race to the Top: Regional and Global Implications of China’s Industrial* (SSRN Scholarly Paper No. 3735037). Social Science Research Network. https://papers.ssrn.com/abstract=3735037

Olafsdottir, A. H., & Sverdrup, H. U. (2021). Modelling Global Nickel Mining, Supply, Recycling, Stocks-in-Use and Price Under Different Resources and Demand Assumptions for 1850–2200. *Mining, Metallurgy & Exploration, 38*(2), 819–840. DOI: 10.1007/s42461-020-00370-y

Ordos Municipal People’s Government. (2025, January 7). “ ” [Ordos Zero-Carbon Industrial Park sets an example for global zero-carbon new industrial bases]. [Ordos]. https://www.ordos.gov.cn/xw_127672/jreeds/202501/t20250107_3755597.html

Osipovich, A., & Ballard, E. (2025, January 27). *Stock market news, Jan. 27, 2025: Nvidia stock sinks in AI rout sparked by China's DeepSeek*. WSJ. https://www.wsj.com/livecoverage/stock-market-today-dow-sp500-nasdaq-live-01-27-2025

Ostic, D., & Obrenovic, B. (2022). JD strategic cross-border expansion–offering retail as strategy solutions abroad. In Fan, M., Wang, L., & Ostic, D. (Eds.), *Casebook of Chinese business management* (pp. 139–148). Springer Nature Singapore., DOI: 10.1007/978-981-16-8074-8_15

Ou, Z. (2024). Study on overseas market strategy of Chinese e-commerce enterprises: Taking JD as a case. *International Journal of Global Economics and Management*, *3*(3), 21–26. DOI: 10.62051/ijgem.v3n3.03

Pan, J. (2024, October, 28). : , , " "?[International Air Transport Market Observation: Total Volume Recovery, Structural Changes, How to Make the "cake" Bigger and Better?]. CAACnews. http://www.caacnews.com.cn/1/202410/t20241028_1382350.html

Pandaily. (2024). *JD.com initiates global expansion, launches "Global sales" In four countries.* https://pandaily.com/jd-com-initiates-global-expansion-launches-global-sales-in-four-countries

Pang, A. (2024, January 23). Financial analysis on Geely major acquisition on Volvo. *Clausius Scientific Press*. https://www.clausiuspress.com/article/10844.html

Paritala, P. K., Manchikatla, S., & Yarlagadda, P. K. D. V. (2017). Digital manufacturing—Applications past, current, and future trends. *Procedia Engineering*, *174*, 982–991. DOI: 10.1016/j.proeng.2017.01.250

Pasinringi, A. (2021). Mining Conflicts in Central Sulawesi: Cooperate and Public Policy Review. *Journal of Asian Multicultural Research for Social Sciences Study*, 2(2), 2. Advance online publication. DOI: 10.47616/jamrsss.v2i2.118

Pereyra, J., Lou, J., Hilde, T., Squire, C., Susanto, S., & Pradipta, A. (2024). Mining, Manufacturing, and Markets An Analysis of Five Years of Electric Vehicle Regulation, Investment, and Industry Development in Indonesia Mining, Manufacturing, and Markets An Analysis of Five Years of Electric Vehicle Regulation, Investment, and Industry Development in Indonesia 2. https://cgs.umd.edu/sites/default/files/2024-11/file_CGS_Indonesia%20EV_11.22.pdf

Permitindo. (2025, July 23). Indonesia's EV industry boost: Regulation's key takeaways. *Permitindo*. https://www.permitindo.com/news/indonesia-ev-industry-regulation

Photovoltaic Industry Network. (2024, April 11). ! , [Photovoltaic industry leaders are entering the market one after another! Vietnam is emerging as a major photovoltaic power]. [Photovoltaic Industry Network]. http://www.solarenpv.com/news/show.php?itemid=19031

PlainConcepts. (2025, February 3). Is DeepSeek R1 right for your business? *Plain Concepts*. https://www.plainconcepts.com/deepseek-r1/

Po, L. M. (2025, May 2). A Brief History of LLMs. *Medium*. https://medium.com/@lmpo/a-brief-history-of-lmms-from-transformers-2017-to-deepseek-r1-2025-dae75dd3f59a

Polaris Solar Photovoltaic Network. (2025, March 21). " " [First "Zero-Carbon Ranch" in Etoke Banner, Inner Mongolia: Distributed Photovoltaic Power Plant Completed and Connected to the Grid]. [Polaris Solar Photovoltaic Network]. https://mguangfu.bjx.com.cn/mnews/20250321/1433371.shtml

Poo, M. (2025). Reflections on DeepSeek's breakthrough. *National Science Review*, *12*(3), nwaf044. Advance online publication. DOI: 10.1093/nsr/nwaf044 PMID: 40041025

Prandelli, D. (2024, November 24). The Chinese automotive revolution: Smashing stereotypes, shaping the future. *Substack*. https://pranda.substack.com/p/the-chinese-automotive-revolution

Precedence Research. (2025). Automotive electronics market. https://www.precedenceresearch.com/automotive-electronics-market

Pribadi, R. (2024). *The Significance of the Nickel Ore Export Prohibition for Indonesia in Consolidating Its Middle-Income Status in the World System*. https://lup.lub.lu.se/student-papers/record/9161036

ProjectPractical. (2025, April 7). Geely automobile marketing strategy 2025: A case study. *ProjectPractical*. https://www.projectpractical.com/geely-automobile-marketing-strategy/

Puglisi, A., & Rask, C. (2024, May). China, biotechnology, and BGI: How China's hybrid economy skews competition. Center for Security and Emerging Technology (CSET). https://cset.georgetown.edu/publication/china-biotechnology-and-bgi/

Qi, Y. L. (2014). *TCL —— [TCL Cross-border Mergers and Acquisitions Research: Taking the Acquisition of Thomson as an Example]*. [Master's thesis, Heilongjiang University].

Qianzhan Industry Research Institute. (2025, March 26). *2025: (*
)[Industry Depth Insight 2025: Analysis of the Competitive Landscape in China's Innovative Pharmaceutical Industry (Including Market Concentration ratio, R&D Strength ranking, etc.)]. Sina. https://finance.sina.com.cn/roll/2025-03-26/doc-ineqxyiv9159522.shtml

Qiao, H., & Rojniruttikul, N. (2025). Enhancing Customer Satisfaction in Logistics Services: A Case Study of SF Express Company. *Review of Integrative Business and Economics Research*, *14*(2), 631–644. https://buscompress.com/uploads/3/4/9/8/34980536/riber_14-2_41_k24-117_631-644.pdf

Qing, Q. (2003). " " , ——TCL [Implementing the "Going Global" Strategy to Expand International Market Development Space — TCL Marketing in Practice]. *China Leather*, *32*(18), 110–112. DOI: 10.13536/j.cnki.issn1001-6813.2003.18.016

Qi, Y., Yuan, M., & Bai, T. (2023). Where will corporate capital flow to? Revisiting the impact of China's pilot carbon emission trading system on investment. *Journal of Environmental Management*, *336*, 117671. DOI: 10.1016/j.jenvman.2023.117671 PMID: 36967695

RE100, Climate Group, & CDP. (2023). RE100 reporting guidance 2023(Version 7.0). https://cdn.cdp.net/cdp-production/cms/guidance_docs/pdfs/000/001/322/original/RE100-reporting-guidance.pdf.pdf

Reiisieh, M. (2025, February 12). *Code, Claims, and Consequences: The legal stakes in OpenAI's case against DeepSeek*. SCBC. https://www.scbc-law.org/post/code-claims-and-consequences-the-legal-stakes-in-openai-s-case-against-deepseek

Reinicke, C. (2025, January 27). Here are the key takeaways from Nvidia, tech rout triggered by DeepSeek. *Bloomberg.Com*. https://www.bloomberg.com/news/articles/2025-01-27/deepseek-ai-market-rout-takeaways-on-nvidia-tech-stocks-nvda-meta-aapl

République Française. (2023, October 23). Loi relative à l'industrie verte [France Green Industry Act]. https://www.legifrance.gouv.fr/jorf/id/JORFTEXT000048470515

Research, S. N. E. (2024). 2023 Global EV Battery Sales Volume by Battery Maker. Sneresearch.com. https://www.sneresearch.com/en/insight/release_view/260/page/0

Reuters. (2020, August 5). Special report: COVID opens new doors for China's gene giant. Reuters. https://www.reuters.com/article/world/special-report-covid-opens-new-doors-for-chinas-gene-giant-idUSKCN2511CD/

Reuters. (2023). *Business & Financial News, U.S & International Breaking News | Reuters*. US https://www.reuters.com

Reuters. (2024, December 12). Baidu, Geely's EV venture faces uproar after it says it needs fresh funds. *Reuters*. https://www.reuters.com/business/autos-transportation/baidu-geelys-ev-venture-faces-uproar-after-it-says-needs-fresh-funds-2024-12-12/

Reuters. (2024a, July 5). How China's EV battery makers stack up in energy storage. Reuters. https://www.reuters.com/business/autos-transportation/how-chinas-ev-battery-makers-stack-up-energy-storage-2024-07-05/

Reuters. (2024b, October 17). Indonesia Battery Corp, CATL unit sign JV deal, state media says. Reuters. https://www.reuters.com/markets/deals/indonesia-battery-corp-catl-unit-sign-jv-deal-state-media-says-2024-10-17/

Reuters. (2024c, November 7). LG Energy Solution signs 5-year battery supply deal with Rivian. Reuters. https://www.reuters.com/technology/lg-energy-solution-signs-5-year-battery-supply-deal-with-rivian-2024-11-07/

Reuters. (2025, January 28). *DeepSeek says its Janus Pro AI model beats rivals in image generation*. https://www.reuters.com/technology/deepseeks-janus-pro-ai-model-beats-rivals-image-generation-2025-01-27/?utm_source=chatgpt.com

Richert, M., & Dudek, M. (2023). Selected problems of the automotive industry—Material and economic risk. *Journal of Risk and Financial Management*, *16*(8), 368. https://www.mdpi.com/1911-8074/16/8/368. DOI: 10.3390/jrfm16080368

Riefler, P. (2020). Local versus global food consumption: The role of brand authenticity. *Journal of Consumer Marketing*, *37*(3), 317–327. DOI: 10.1108/JCM-02-2019-3086

Riyanto, G., Yeremia, A. E., Astuti, R., Zuada, L. H., Hidayat, A., & Rakhmani, I. (2025). Various visions of the industrialized future: Anxiety, aspiration, and Chinese nickel investment in Indonesia. *Asia Europe Journal*, *23*(2-3), 369–391. Advance online publication. DOI: 10.1007/s10308-025-00727-2

Rizos, V., & Vu, H. (2024, December). Compliance with the EU's carbon footprint requirements for electric vehicle batteries: An analysis of challenges and opportunities[Report]. Centre for European Policy Studies (CEPS). https://circulareconomy.europa.eu/platform/en/knowledge/compliance-eus-carbon-footprint-requirements-electric-vehicle-batteries-overview-challenges

Rollet, C. (2025, March 10). *DeepSeek isn't taking VC money yet—Here are 3 reasons why* [TechCrunch]. https://techcrunch.com/2025/03/10/deepseek-isnt-taking-vc-money-yet-here-are-3-reasons-why/?utm_source=chatgpt.com

Root, C. (2014, November 6). WuXi AppTec opens Israel office, partners with Pontifax. Outsourcedpharma. https://www.outsourcedpharma.com/doc/wuxi-apptec-opens-israel-office-partners-with-pontifax-0001

Root, F. R. (1994). *Entry strategies for international markets* (Rev. ed.). Jossey-Bass.

Ropes & Gray LLP. (2023, April 25). Bureau of Industry and Security imposes export restrictions on BGI Group, the world's largest genomics company [Client alert]. https://www.ropesgray.com/en/insights/alerts/2023/04/bis-imposes-export-restrictions-on-bgi-group-the-worlds-largest-genomics-company

Rouhana, F., Zhu, J., Chacon-Hurtado, D., Hertel, S., & Bagtzoglou, A. C. (2024). Ensuring a just transition: The electric vehicle revolution from a human rights perspective. *Journal of Cleaner Production*, *462*, 142667. DOI: 10.1016/j.jclepro.2024.142667

RSM. (2022, August 20). The capital allowances super-deduction – it could be great for the renewables sector. RSM. https://www.rsmuk.com/insights/tax-voice/the-capital-allowances-super-deduction-it-could-be-great-for-the-renewables-sector

Rui, W. (2024, January 9). : [Hengrui Pharmaceuticals: Dual-driven Strategy for Global Expansion]. *Pharmaceutical Economics News*. https://www.yyjjb.com.cn/yyjjb/202401/20240109152225225_17575.shtml

Santoso, R. B., Dermawan, W., & Moenardy, D. F. (2024). Indonesia's rational choice in the nickel ore export ban policy. *Cogent Social Sciences*, *10*(1), 2400222. DOI: 10.1080/23311886.2024.2400222

SBTi. (2022). Envision Group science-based targets validation summary. https://sciencebasedtargets.org

Schodde, R., & Guj, P. (2025). Nickel: A Tale of Two Cities. *Geosystems and Geoenvironment*, *4*(1), 100356. DOI: 10.1016/j.geogeo.2025.100356

ScienceDirect. (2025). China's 1+N policy system supports an earlier peak in carbon emissions. ScienceDirect. https://www.sciencedirect.com/science/article/abs/pii/S1364032125002990

Securities and Exchange Commission. (2020, December 16). *Luckin Coffee agrees to pay $180 million penalty to settle accounting fraud charges* (Release No. 2020-319). https://www.sec.gov/newsroom/press-releases/2020-319

Securities Daily. (2025, May 7). [Focusing on the core automotive business and returning to one Geely: Geely Holding promotes the deep implementation of the "Taizhou Declaration"]. *Securities Daily*. http://www.zqrb.cn/auto/qichedongtai/2025-05-07/A1746615804320.html

Selig, E. R., Nakayama, S., Wabnitz, C. C. C., Österblom, H., Spijkers, J., Miller, N. A., Bebbington, J., & Decker Sparks, J. L. (2022). Revealing global risks of labour abuse and illegal, unreported, and unregulated fishing. *Nature Communications, 13*(1), 1612. DOI: 10.1038/s41467-022-28916-2 PMID: 35383162

Sergeev, A. (2024, February 14). Lynk & Co expands European presence, not coming to UK yet. *Motor1*. https://www.motor1.com/news/708576/lynk-co-not-coming-uk-yet/

Shan, J. (2024). The impact of government subsidies on electric vehicle sales: A regression analysis of BYD in China. *SHS Web of Conferences, 207*, 03017. DOI: 10.1051/shsconf/202420703017

Shanghai Municipal Commission of Economy and Informatization. (2023, January 11). : , [On the new track of a strong country and embarking on a new journey: The zero-carbon journey, this green technology enterprise leads the new zero-carbon industry]. [Shanghai Industrial Policy Service Network]. https://app.sheitc.sh.gov.cn/zxxx/694255.htm

Shanghai Nonferrous Metals. (2024, February 19). 2023 Motive Power Battery Overseas Market Share Battle: CATL in Pursuit, BYD Surges Ahead | Shanghai Non ferrous Metals. News.metal.com. https://news.metal.com/newscontent/102622888/2023-Motive-Power-Battery-Overseas-Market-Share-Battle:-CATL-in-Pursuit-BYD-Surges-Ahead

Sharma, R. (n.d.). *SUV market report: Global forecast from 2025 to 2033*. Data Intelo. https://dataintelo.com/report/suv-market

Shastri, A. (2025, August 9). Comprehensive SWOT analysis of Hikvision – one of the largest suppliers of surveillance equipment. Indian Institute of Digital Education. https://iide.co/case-studies/swot-analysis-of-hikvision/

Shen, P. (2022). [Research on the motivation and economic consequences of WuXi AppTec's privatization]. Xiandai yingxiao, (27), 44–46. DOI: 10.19932/j.cnki.22-1256/F.2022.09.044

Shen, Z. J. M., Sun, S., Qi, Y., Hu, H., Kang, N., Zhang, J., Wang, X., & Lin, X. (2025). JD. com improves fulfillment efficiency with data-driven integrated assortment planning and inventory allocation. *INFORMS Journal on Applied Analytics, 55*(5), 386–398. DOI: 10.1287/inte.2025.0245

Shi, C. Q. (2016). [Analysis of the status of China's integrated circuit industry in the global market]. *Integrated Circuit Applications*, (7), 7–9. https://link.cnki.net/doi/10.19339/j.issn.1674-2583.2016.07.002

Shimizu, K., Hitt, M. A., Vaidyanath, D., & Pisano, V. (2004). Theoretical foundations of cross-border mergers and acquisitions: A review of current research and recommendations for the future. *Journal of International Management, 10*(3), 307–353. DOI: 10.1016/j.intman.2004.05.005

Shopper, S. (2024, June 5). Hikvision–Alfanar partnership unveils local manufacturing facility in Riyadh. https://en.saudishopper.com.sa/?p=49926

Siddiqui, A. (2023, October 3). Big pharma sets sights on Middle East. BioSpectrum Asia Edition. https://www.biospectrumasia.com/analysis/86/23075/big-pharma-sets-sights-on- middle-east-.html

Sinohealth. (2025, February 7). AB :36 67 [The two sides of WuXi Biologics' globalization: Selling European plants for 3.6 billion and signing a 6.7 billion US deal]. Tencent. https://news.qq.com/rain/a/20250107A0AGBX00

Smart Home, T. C. L. (2024, September 11). *TCL BrandZ 100 [TCL selected as one of the 100 most valuable Chinese brands by Kantar BrandZ].* https://www.tclsmarthome.com/newsroom/20240911

Smith, J. (2024). Geopolitical impact on new energy enterprise governance. *Energy Policy Journal, 15*(2), 45–62.

Snyder, J. (2025, January 27). *How DeepSeek built on AI's innovation debt.* https://www.forbes.com/sites/jasonsnyder/2025/01/27/genius-steals-how-deepseek-built-on-ais-innovation-debt/

Soto, H. (2023, September 1). Geely to arrive in Mexico in 4Q23. *Mexico Business News*. https://mexicobusiness.news/automotive/news/geely-arrive-mexico-4q23

Spence, E., & Lee, A. (2023, November 26). Sodium in Batteries: Shift May Herald Another Shakeup. Www.bloomberg.com. https://www.bloomberg.com/news/articles/2023-11-26/sodium-in-ev-and-storage-batteries-may-herald-another-shakeup

Stimson Center. (2019). Hikvision: The dilemma of a surveillance company. https://www.stimson.org/2019/hikvision-dilemma-surveillance-company/

Stone, J. (2025, May 15). : *GIC 5.33 [Hengrui Pharmaceuticals Begins Share Offering Today: Secures $533 million in Cornerstone Subscriptions from GIC, UBS, HHLR, and Boyu Capital*]. Xueqiu. https://xueqiu.com/2854806290/335163197

Stur, B. (2024, July 4). EU imposes provisional countervailing duties on Chinese electric vehicles. *European Interest.* https://www.europeaninterest.eu/eu-imposes-provisional-countervailing-duties-on-chinese-electric-vehicles/

Subin, S. (2025, January 27). *Nvidia sheds almost $600 billion in market cap, biggest one-day loss in US history.* CNBC. https://www.cnbc.com/2025/01/27/nvidia-sheds-almost-600-billion-in-market-cap-biggest-drop-ever.html

SUEZ. (2024, September 24). SUEZ and Eramet recycle electric vehicle batteries. SUEZ. https://www.suez.com/en/news/suez-eramet-recycle-electric-vehicle-batteries

Sun, F. (2023, November 13). [Promote the high-quality development of the dual-hub construction in Beijing in the new era]. CAACnews. http://www.caacnews.com.cn/special/2023nzt/7598/2020mhcy1/2020cybzmhj/202311/t20231113_1372159.html

Sundial in the Shadow. (2025, July 29). *,BD ,License-out( ),NewCo ( ) [Innovative Medicines, BD Model, License-out (outsourcing), and NewCo model (cooperation with newly established companies)*]. Xueqiu. https://xueqiu.com/1122686438/344662911

Sunuhadi, D. N., Ernowo, , Hilman, P. M., & Suseno, T. (2024). Availability of Indonesian nickel reserves and efforts to improve reserves resistance and its impact to economic growth. *Mineral Economics*, *37*(3), 601–617. DOI: 10.1007/s13563-024-00443-0

Su, Q., & Lahiri, B. (2023). Does the Belt and Road Initiative boost Chinese automobile exports? A staggered adoption approach. *Applied Economics*, *56*(59), 8855–8859. DOI: 10.1080/00036846.2023.2295301

Sutter, K. M. (2025, September 9). *U.S.–China trade relations.* Congressional Research Service. https://www.congress.gov/crs-product/IF11284

Sweney, M., & Milmo, D. (2025, January 29). OpenAI 'reviewing' allegations that its AI models were used to make DeepSeek. *The Guardian.* https://www.theguardian.com/technology/2025/jan/29/openai-chatgpt-deepseek-china-us-ai-models

Syarif, A. (2025). Navigating Investment in Risky Market: Comparative Analysis of Chinese State-Owned Enterprises and Private Firms Operating in Indonesia. *Journal of Current Southeast Asian Affairs, 18681034251347972*. Advance online publication. DOI: 10.1177/18681034251347972

Taneja, H., & Zakaria, F. (2023, September 6). AI and the new digital cold war. *Harvard Business Review*. https://hbr.org/2023/09/ai-and-the-new-digital-cold-war

Taufik, Y., Adijaya, S., & Rela, I. Z. (2022). *Nickel Smelter on Social-Economics and Environmental Issues. Research Square*. DOI: 10.21203/rs.3.rs-2232605/v1

TCL Technology Group Corporation. (2025). *2024 Annual Report.* Shenzhen Securities Information Co., Ltd. https://announcement.valueonline.cn/20250429/20250429174586128336609 1926.pdf

TCL. (2019, February 1). *[Progress Announcement on Major Asset Restructuring of the Company]*. Shenzhen Securities Information Co., Ltd. https://static.cninfo.com.cn/finalpage/2019-02-01/1205819820.PDF

TCL. (n.d.). *About TCL.* TCL Official Website. https://www.tcl.com/cn/zh/about-tcl

TCL. (n.d.). *AR glass features*. TCL Official Website. https://www.tcl.com/cn/zh/ar-glass-features

TCL. (n.d.). *TCL 75-inch A300 Pro*. TCL Official Website. https://www.tcl.com/cn/zh/tvs/75-inch-a300pro

Tham, S. Y., & Negara, S. D. (2022). Chinese Investments in Industrial Parks: Comparison Between Indonesia and Malaysia. In H. N. Au Yong, X. Yuan, & L. Low, *Series on China's Belt and Road Initiative* (Vol. 15, pp. 225–268). WORLD SCIENTIFIC. DOI: 10.1142/9789811221873_0010

Thanh, V. (2024, September 24). China's Geely to build $168 million automobile facility with Tasco in Thai Binh. *Vietnam Investment Review*. https://vir.com.vn/chinas-geely-to-build-168-million-automobile-facility-with-tasco-in-thai-binh-114721.html

The China Academy. (2023, September 27). Ford pauses work on EV battery plant in Michigan with CATL. The China Academy. https://thechinaacademy.org/ford-pauses-work-on-ev-battery-plant-in-michigan-with-catl/

The People's Daily Online. (2012, December 10). : [Envision Energy: Intelligent wind turbines lead the low-wind-speed market]. [The People's Daily Online]. http://finance.people.com.cn/stock/n/2012/1210/c222942-19851561.html

The Star. (2024, August 15). Proton to work closely with Geely to explore model enhancement activities. *The Star*. https://www.thestar.com.my/business/business-news/2024/08/15/proton-to-work-closely-with-geely-to-explore-model-enhancement-activities

The White House. (2025, April 2). Regulating imports with a reciprocal tariff to rectify trade practices that contribute to large and persistent annual United States goods trade deficits. https://www.whitehouse.gov/presidential-actions/2025/04/regulating-imports-with-a-reciprocal-tariff-to-rectify-trade-practices-that-contribute-to-large-and-persistent-annual-united-states-goods-trade-deficits/

Tian, S., & Yuan, Y. (2019). How to improve subsidiary willingness towards reverse knowledge transfer in emerging-market multinational enterprises? A case study of Geely Group [Master's thesis, Uppsala University]. DiVA Portal. https://uu.diva-portal.org/smash/record.jsf?pid=diva2:1333290

Tian, J., Yu, L., Xue, R., Zhuang, S., & Shan, Y. (2022). Global low-carbon energy transition in the post-COVID-19 era. *Applied Energy*, *307*, 118205. DOI: 10.1016/j.apenergy.2021.118205 PMID: 34840400

Tian, Q. (2017). Challenges and strategies for Chinese wind turbine manufacturers going global. *Clean Technology Investment*, *15*(3), 45–59.

TMTPost. (2024, September 18). Geely and Xpeng join wave of Chinese automakers to build plant in Europe in the face of EV tariffs. *Sohu*. https://www.sohu.com/a/809720282_116132

TouringCarTimes. (2023, March 1). Geely Group Motorsport teases potential new TCR car. *TouringCarTimes*. https://www.touringcartimes.com/2023/03/01/geely-group-motorsport-teases-potential-new-tcr-car/

TrendForce. (2025). Top 10 global OSAT companies in 2024: Mature leaders stay strong while new regional forces emerge [Research report]. https://www.trendforce.com/research/download/RP250505XH

Tritto, A., & Camba, A. (2022). State-facilitated Industrial Parks in the Belt and Road Initiative: Towards a framework for understanding the localization of the Chinese development model. *World Development Perspectives*, *28*, 100465. DOI: 10.1016/j.wdp.2022.100465

Turing, A. M. (1950). Computing machinery and intelligence. *Oxford University Press, 59*(236), 433–460.

UAEGOV. (2023). National Hydrogen Strategy: The Official Platform of the UAE Government. UAE Government Portal. u.ae. https://u.ae/en/about-the-uae/strategies-initiatives-and-awards/strategies-plans-and-visions/environment-and-energy/national-hydrogen-strategy

UK Investment Institute. (2020). *RMB asset allocation barriers: Annual opportunity cost for UK hedge funds* (White Paper No. WP-2020-09). https://ukinvestmentinstitute.org

UNFCCC. (2024, November). Decision -/CP.29: Technical guidelines for zero-carbon industrial parks. https://unfccc.int/documents/642899

United Nations Conference on Trade and Development. (2023). Israel Exports: Medicinal and Pharmaceutical Products. CEIC. https://www.ceicdata.com.cn/en/indicator/israel/exports-medicinal-and-pharmaceutical-product

United Nations Department of Economic and Social Affairs. Population Division. (2025). World urbanization prospects: Summary of results (2025 revision) [Report]. https://www.un.org/development/desa/pd/sites/www.un.org.development.desa.pd/files/wup2025_summary_of_results.pdf

Univers. (2025, October 2). Univers launches EnOS™ Ark 2.0: Smarter, faster, and scalable AI for energy savings and carbon reduction. Pollution Online. https://www.pollutiononline.com/doc/univers-launches-enos-ark-smarter-faster-and-scalable-ai-for-energy-savings-and-carbon-reduction-0001

University of Debrecen. (2024, October 15). New career opportunities and apprenticeship programs for our future engineers. University of Debrecen News. https://hirek.unideb.hu/en/new-career-opportunities-and-apprenticeship-programs-our-future-engineers

US Department of Commerce, Bureau of Industry and Security. (2023, October 19). Entity list additions [Final rule]. Federal Register. https://www.federalregister.gov/documents/2023/10/19/2023-23048/entity-list-additions

US Food & Drug Administration. (2024, December 19). Warning Letter 320-25-28 Viatris, Inc. FDA. https://www.fda.gov/inspections-compliance-enforcement-and-criminal-investigations/warning-letters/viatris-inc-690897-12192024

USA Department of the Treasury. (2023, October 19). USA Department of the Treasury releases final rules on investment tax credit to produce more American-made clean energy, strengthen industrial base, and cut costs for families[Press release]. USA Department of the Treasury. https://home.treasury.gov/news/press-releases/jy2736

USGS. (2024, January 31). USGS Releases Mineral Commodity Summaries 2024, finds US Mineral Production Jumped 4 billion to exceed 105 billion dollars. Mineral Commodity Summaries. https://www.usgs.gov/news/technical-announcement/usgs-releases-mineral-commodity-summaries-2024-finds-us-mineral

Ventas de Seguridad. (2016, November 14). Hikvision opens office in Chile, a market with European level. https://www.ventasdeseguridad.com/en/news/latest-news/431-enterprises/17770-hikvision-opens-office-in-chile-a-market-with-european-level.html

VGP. (2023). Gov't approves 8th National Power Development Plan. baochinhphu. https://en.baochinhphu.vn/decision-approving-national-power-development-plan-8-111230614195813455.htm

Villada-Canela, M., Muñoz-Pizza, D. M., García-Searcy, V., Camacho-López, R., Daesslé, L. W., & Mendoza-Espinosa, L. (2021). Public Participation for Integrated Groundwater Management: The Case of Maneadero Valley, Baja California, Mexico. *Water (Basel)*, *13*(17), 17. Advance online publication. DOI: 10.3390/w13172326

Volumes, E. V. (2023, December 18). CATL drove global EV battery production in first three quarters of 2023. EV Volumes. https://ev-volumes.com/news/eu/catl-drove-global-ev-battery-production-in-first-three-quarters-of-2023/

Walder, A. G. (2024). The Rapid Ascent of China's Corporate Giants. *China Journal (Canberra, A.C.T.)*, *92*, 71–102. DOI: 10.1086/730617

Walhi Sulawesi Selatan. (2023). Catahu: Catatan Akhir Tahun 2023—Sulawesi Selatan Menuju Momentum Politik di Tengah Kerusakan Lingkungan, Proyek Transisi Energi Palsu, dan Hilirisasi Nikel* [Annual year-end report 2023: South Sulawesi toward a political momentum amid environmental destruction, false energy transition projects, and nickel downstreaming]. Indonesian Forum for Environment – South Sulawesi Region. https://walhisulsel.or.id/wp-content/uploads/2024/12/Catahu-WALHI-SS-2023.pdf

Wang, E. (2017, May 17). : ? [Interview with Envision Energy vice president: Where is the difficulty for Chinese wind turbine companies in going global?]. [China Energy Network]. https://www.china5e.com/news/news-988134-1.html

Wang, G., & Zhao, Z. P. (2025, January 16). *TCL : + , [A thorough study of TCL Electronics Company: Profit + market shares dual drivers for continued global breakthroughs]*. Sinolink Securities. https://inst.gjzq.com.cn/inst-res/report/1444294430793351168?from_page=wz_general_search

Wang, H. (2021, December 1). : [Li Ge of WuXi AppTec: Let there be no difficult medicine in the world]. Zhihu. https://zhuanlan.zhihu.com/p/439810907

Wang, J. K. (2014). TCL [The Analysis of TCL Group Investment Strategy in Vietnam]. *Around Southeast Asia, 3,* 76–79.

Wang, L. (2025, May 7). , [Innovation and Internationalization Drive Together to Launch a Series of New Initiatives, and Hengrui Pharmaceuticals Underwent a Profound Transformation in its Ppgrading and Transformation Process]. *Beijing News.* https://m.bjnews.com.cn/detail/1746620446168854.html

Wang, Y. (2025). *JD.com announces "10 billion growth plan" To introduce 1,000 overseas brands to china over next three years.* JINGDONG Corporate Blog. https://jdcorporateblog.com/jd-com-announces-10-billion-growth-plan-to-introduce-1000-overseas-brands-to-china-over-next-three-years/

Wang, Q. (2025). DeepSeek hits hard: Helping to revolutionize higher education in the era of artificial intelligence. *International Journal of Higher Education, 14*(2), 26. DOI: 10.5430/ijhe.v14n2p26

Wang, X. (2023). [Research on the impact of cross-border mergers and acquisitions on enterprise innovation capability]. *Small Business Management and Technology*, (24), 140–142.

Wang, Y., Shen, L. Y., Zhou, X. H., & Liu, J. A. (2022). " - " — [The co-evolution of "innovation-capital" interaction and latecomer firm catch-up: A case study of WuXi AppTec]. *Guanli Pinglun*, *34*(06), 325–340. DOI: 10.14120/j.cnki.cn11-5057/f.2022.06.023

Wang, Z. (2024, June 13). : [A Decade of Reflection on China's Home Appliance Industry: Navigating the Tide of Deglobalization]. *China Business News, A10.* Advance online publication. DOI: 10.28207/n.cnki.ndycj.2024.002230

Warburton, E. (2024). Nationalist enclaves: Industrialising the critical mineral boom in Indonesia. *The Extractive Industries and Society*, *20*, 101564. DOI: 10.1016/j.exis.2024.101564

Wasserman, A., & Wasserman, A. (2019, November 26). Wasserman, A., & Wasserman, A. (2019, November 26). China's SF Express is now an important global logistics force. *GLDPartners.* https://www.gldpartners.com/sf-express-emerging-as-global-force-in-air-cargo-logistics-integrator/

Wei, X. (2024, May 24). [*The Next Step of Hengrui*]. Blue View. https://mp.weixin.qq.com/s/3Zqk7H8kFXoxZw6LdmxC8A

Wen, W. (2005). TCL [Small markets contribute to TCL's internationalization efforts]. *Foreign Trade & Economic*, *1*, 49–49.

Widyadwiana, A., & Utami, C. F. (2024). Sustainable Water Provision Model for Morowali Industrial Area: A System Dynamics Model. *Syntax Literate. Jurnal Ilmiah Indonesia*, *9*(4), 2288–2297. DOI: 10.36418/syntax-literate.v9i4.15457

Wijaya, T., & Sinclair, L. (2025). An EV-fix for Indonesia: The green development-resource nationalist nexus. *Environmental Politics*, *34*(2), 252–274. DOI: 10.1080/09644016.2024.2332129

Williams, K. (2024, July 23). Tariff effect: Zeekr wants to produce electric cars in Europe. *Motor1*. https://www.motor1.com/news/727537/zeekr-plans-european-production-factory/

Wind Information Co. Ltd. (2023, February 23). *China's ESG goes global: Wind ESG rating wins the best solution award* [Press release]. https://www.wind.com.cn/mobile/News/NewsDetail/en.html?id=701

Wind Information Co. Ltd. (2025, January 27). *Wind Alice investment advisor wins financial AI "industry leadership award"* [Press release]. https://www.wind.com.cn/mobile/News/NewsDetail/en.html?id=736

Wittwer, W. (2024, June 29). East meets west: Lessons from Geely's acquisition of Volvo. *Success Across Cultures*. https://successacrosscultures.com/2024/06/29/east-meets-west-lessons-from-geelys-acquisition-of-volvo/

WonderNetwork. (2026, February 25). *Global ping statistics: Shanghai to London network latency*. https://wondernetwork.com/pings/Shanghai

World Bank. (2024). GDP growth (annual %) [Data set]. https://data.worldbank.org/indicator/NY.GDP.MKTP.KD.ZG

World Bank. (2026, January). *Global economic prospects*. https://www.worldbank.org/en/publication/global-economic-prospects

World Economic Forum. (2022, October 11). Amid Recession Fears, These Factories Are Boosting Productivity, Sustainability, and Resilient Supply Chains. World Economic Forum. https://www.weforum.org/press/2022/10/amid-recession-fears-these-factories-are-boosting-productivity-sustainability-and-resilient-supply-chains/

Wu, B. (2025, June 13). 10%, [International oil prices have soared by more than 10%, and the situation in the Middle East has raised supply concerns]. 21st Century Business Herald. https://www.21jingji.com/article/20250613/herald/591260f98640607c3a8068b0b9167066.html

Wu, X. W. (2021, March 4). (603259.SH) , 212 , " " [WuXi AppTec (603259.SH) Scores Another Victory in International Layout, Target Price 212 Yuan, Maintain"Add" Rating]. Zhitongcaijing. https://www.zhitongcaijing.com/content/detail/421290.html

Wu, Q. M. (2024). The embrace and resistance of Chinese battery investments in Hungary: The case of CATL. *Asia Europe Journal*, *22*(2), 201–223. DOI: 10.1007/s10308-024-00699-9

Wu, W. (2024). PEST —— , , [Based on PEST analysis of BYD new energy vehicle export comparative study—Taking Singapore, Switzerland, and Brazil as examples]. *Modern Management*, *14*(1), 136–145. DOI: 10.12677/MM.2024.141020

WuXi AppTec. (2015, January 13). WuXi AppTec Acquires NextCODE. Pharmatech. https://pharm.jgvogel.cn/c902791.shtml

WuXi AppTec. (2016, April 15). WuXi AppTec acquires Crelux. https://www.wuxiapptec.com/news/wuxi-news/1873

WuXi AppTec. (2017, June 1). : , , [WuXi AppTec in Israel: Innovation, Cooperation, Dream Fulfillment]. Sohu. https://www.sohu.com/a/145097878_282570

WuXi AppTec. (2018, April 23). Initial public offering. https://officialsite-static.wuxiapptec.com/upload/_cd50156a9b.pdf

WuXi AppTec. (2021, February 2). WuXi STA to purchase Bristol Myers Squibb manufacturing facility in Couvet, Switzerland. https://www.wuxiapptec.com/news/wuxi-news/4446

WuXi AppTec. (2021, November 29). " "! Get CRDMO! [Making drug R&D "Faster, Better, and More Economical"! get CRDMO in one Article]. Sohu. https://www.sohu.com/a/504099821_282570

WuXi AppTec. (2022, July 19). WuXi AppTec plans to build a new site in Singapore, better serving global partners and advancing healthcare innovation. https://www.wuxiapptec.com/news/wuxi-news/5143

WuXi AppTec. (2024, Secember 10). Voluntary announcement. https://officialsite-static.wuxiapptec.com/upload/1e/20240910/VOLUNTARY%20ANNOUNCEMENT.pdf

WuXi AppTec. (2024, September 26) 2024 WuXi AppTec investor day research enabling platforms enhance CRDMO model. https://officialsite-static.wuxiapptec.com/upload/2024_Wu_Xi_App_Tec_Investor_Day_Research_Enabling_Platforms_a656604c9a.pdf

WuXi AppTec. (2025, April 4) 2024 Environmental, social, and governance report. https://officialsite-static.wuxiapptec.com/upload/ESG_2024_Wu_Xi_App_Tec_EN_0fcdf75d0d.pdf

WuXi AppTec. (2025, July 28). Announcement of the unaudited interim results for the six months ended June 30, 2025. https://officialsite-static.wuxiapptec.com/upload/ANNOUNCEMENT_OF_THE_UNAUDITED_INTERIM_RESULTS_FOR_THE_SIX_MONTHS_ENDED_JUNE_30_2025_0c13c93fd7.pdf

WuXi AppTec. (2025, July 8). Model Region Munich: With companies like WuXi AppTec, Munich is becoming Europe's leading biotech hub. NetEase Official Account. https://www.163.com/dy/article/K3U9DOGN05349C3E.html

WuXi AppTec. (2025, July 9). ! [Not Only the US but Also Europe! WuXi AppTec Joins Hands with Local Partners to Jointly Promote Pharmaceutical Innovation. Jiemian. https://www.jiemian.com/article/13008774.html

WuXi AppTec. (n.d.). Our history. https://www.wuxiapptec.com/about/history

WuXi Biologics. (2025, October 20). WuXi Biologics Honored with 2025 Global Customer Value Leadership Recognition by Frost & Sullivan. PR Newswire. https://www.prnewswire.com/news-releases/wuxi-biologics-honored-with-2025-global-customer-value-leadership-recognition-by-frost--sullivan-302588869.html

Wu, Y. (2005). TCL [TCL's motives, risks, and integration in the acquisition of Thomson Corporation]. *Modernization of Management*, *4*, 36–38.

Xia, Z. (2024). Enterprise Futures Hedging Risk Management -Take the Qingshan Holdings' Nickel Futures Incident on the LME as an Example. *SHS Web of Conferences, 188*, 01005. DOI: 10.1051/shsconf/202418801005

Xiao, M. (2023, February 1). How will the US Inflation Reduction Act affect China's Li-ion battery and EV industry? - Interact Analysis. Interact Analysis. https://interactanalysis.com/insight/how-will-the-us-inflation-reduction-act-affect-chinas-li-ion-battery-and-ev-industry/

Xiao, S. (2024). A company analysis on Geely based on its external and internal environment. *Advances in Economics. Management and Political Sciences*, *79*(1), 283–289. DOI: 10.54254/2754-1169/79/20241848

Xie, X. (2024). Challenges and Strategies for Green Transformation in Logistics Procurement Business: Case Study of SF Express. *Advances in Economics. Management and Political Sciences*, *102*(1), 139–144. DOI: 10.54254/2754-1169/102/2024ED0072

Xin, H. (2025, January 9). : , [Jiailing District: Based on the automotive industry ecosystem, creating a magnificent chapter for an industrial town]. *Nanchong Municipal Government*. https://www.nanchong.gov.cn/fgw/xwdt/bmxx/202501/t20250109_2064973.html

Xinhua Net. (2015, February 3). [Chip companies become China's new favorites in overseas M&A]. *[Economic Information Daily]*. http://jjckb.xinhuanet.com/2015-02/03/content_537060.htm

Xinhua News Network. (2024, November 21). CATL to begin battery cell production in Hungary's Debrecen. News.cn. https://english.news.cn/20241121/6abe70fe521c4be8866f153f40e3caab/c.html

Xinhua Silk Road. (2024, November 17). [Air China's multi-level strategy to deeply cultivate the Asia-Pacific market attracts tourists to visit China]. Xinhua Silk Road. https://www.imsilkroad.com/news/p/529740.html

Yang, V. (2024). *JD.com's strategic advancements in international business: A focus on supply chain and user experience*. JINGDONG Corporate Blog. https://jdcorporateblog.com/jd-coms-strategic-advancements-in-international-business-a-focus-on-supply-chain-and-user-experience/

Yee, L., Chui, M., Roberts, R., & Smit, S. (2025). Technology Trends Outlook 2025. https://www.mckinsey.com/~/media/mckinsey/business%20functions/mckinsey%20digital/our%20insights/the%20top%20trends%20in%20tech%202025/mckinsey-technology-trends-outlook-2025.pdf

Yin, W., Su, Y., Kirkulak-Uludag, B., Yan, A., & Wang, R. (2025). Impact of domestic and foreign investors on ESG disclosure quality in Chinese listed firms: Divergence or convergence? *PLoS One*, *20*(9), e0330418. DOI: 10.1371/journal.pone.0330418 PMID: 40938865

Yi, Z. (2025). Green upgrading strategy of supply chain in the age of digital intelligence economy—Taking JD. com as an example. *Finance & Economics*, *1*(6), 1–6. DOI: 10.61173/ewa8v404

Yongtao, G., & Sining, L. (2024). Examining the Belt and Road Initiative (BRI) from the perspective of clean energy supply chain resilience. *Asian Journal of Political Science*, *32*(3), 329–352. DOI: 10.1080/02185377.2024.2429093

Young. (2025, February 25). DeepSeek, ChatGPT, and the global fight for technological supremacy. *Harvard Law School*. https://hls.harvard.edu/today/deepseek-chatgpt-and-the-global-fight-for-technological-supremacy/

Yu, H. (2024). China-ASEAN Cooperation Under the BRI. In H. Yu, *Understanding China's Belt and Road Initiative* (Vol. 26, pp. 43–68). Springer Nature Singapore. DOI: 10.1007/978-981-99-9633-9_3

Yue, Q. (2020, July 10). 3 [Three Years of Charitable Donations Exceeded 100 million yuan.Hengrui Pharmaceuticals Initiated Several Special Funds to Support Education]. *Beijing News*. https://www.bjnews.com.cn/detail/159436987315456.html

Zegart, A., & Johnston, E. (2025). *A Deep peek into DeepSeek AI's talent and implications for US innovation*. The Hoover Institution and The Stanford Institute for Human-Centered AI.

Zhang, B. S., & Shang, H. M. (2019). [Current situation and trend analysis of chip industry technology at home and abroad]. , *39*(17), 131–134. DOI: 10.3969/j.issn.1000-7695.2019.17.017

Zhang, C. (2022). Analysis of SF Express's strategic risk—Based on 2018-2020 annual report of financial statements. *Advances in Economics, Business and Management Research*, 771–779. DOI: 10.2991/978-94-6463-054-1_83

Zhang, C., Manthey, E., & Luman, R. (2023, July 26). Tightening supply shakes up battery metal dynamics. *ING*. https://think.ing.com/downloads/pdf/article/tightening-supply-shakes-up-battery-metals

Zhang, J. X. (2001). TCL [TCL Group expands into the Vietnamese market]. *Around Southeast Asia, 11,* 36–37. https://doi.org/DOI: 10.3969/j.issn.1003-2479.2001.11.020

Zhang, K., & Liang, J. (2023, May 8). China-Malaysia automotive collaboration of strategic importance: Malaysian PM. *People's Daily Online*. https://en.people.cn/n3/2023/0508/c90000-20015796.html

Zhang, M., & Chen, Y. M. (2025, August 14). " " *——2025H1 ["Reciprocal tariffs" exacerbate currency market volatility; US dollar index enters depreciation cycle - 2025H1 RMB exchange rate analysis report].* National Institution for Finance & Development. http://www.nifd.cn/SeriesReport/Details/4742

Zhang, P. (2022, March 26). CATL teases Qilin battery, says it has 13% higher capacity than 4680 batteries. CnEVPost. https://cnevpost.com/2022/03/26/catl-teases-kirin-battery-says-it-has-13-higher-capacity-than-4680-batteries/

Zhang, T., & He, Z. Y. (2025, February 7). , [WuXi AppTec sells overseas assets again: Seeking adjustments to cope with intensified competition and performance pressure]. Netease. https://www.163.com/dy/article/JNR1ATIB0550DHA5.html

Zhang, X. Y. (2020, December 23). *TCL ,TCL : [The US Secretary of Homeland Security announced that TCL Electronics is under review. TCL Electronics issued a statement in response, saying that it has not received any relevant notification.* Huanqiu wang. https://3w.huanqiu.com/a/c36dc8/41DPHbYk1RX

Zhang, Y. (2021, July 12). *Keynote speech at the Singapore Fintech Summit 2021*. Singapore Fintech Festival. https://fintechfestival.sg

Zhang, M. (2008). [The highly attractive Vietnamese small appliance market]. *Foreign Trade & Economic*, *6*, 70–73.

Zhang, Y. (2003). *China's emerging global businesses*. Springer. DOI: 10.1057/9780230599611

Zhao, C. Y., & Lyu, X. Y. (2024). JD. com: A strategic analysis of its evolution, innovation, and market adaptation. *China-USA Business Review*, *23*(2), 77–83. DOI: 10.17265/1537-1514/2024.02.003

Zhao, C., Ju, S., Xue, Y., Ren, T., Ji, Y., & Chen, X. (2022). China's energy transitions for carbon neutrality: Challenges and opportunities. *Carbon Neutrality*, *1*(1), 7. DOI: 10.1007/s43979-022-00010-y

Zhavoronkov, A., Ivanenkov, Y. A., Aliper, A., Veselov, M. S., Aladinskiy, V. A., Aladinskaya, A. V., Terentiev, V. A., Polykovskiy, D. A., Kuznetsov, M. D., Asadulaev, A., Volkov, Y., Zholus, A., Shayakhmetov, R. R., Zhebrak, A., Minaeva, L. I., Zagribelnyy, B. A., Lee, L. H., Soll, R., Madge, D., & Aspuru-Guzik, A. (2019). Deep learning enables rapid identification of potent DDR1 kinase inhibitors. *Nature Biotechnology*, *37*(9), 1038–1040. DOI: 10.1038/s41587-019-0224-x PMID: 31477924

Zhongshang Industrial Research Institute. (2024). : [Pharmaceutical R&D Giant: In-depth Analysis of WuXi AppTec's Operating Data and Core Competitiveness]. Zhongshang Qingbaowang. https://www.askci.com/news/chanye/20240517/1146422715917602872122 45_4.shtml

Zhu, H., Chen, W. X., & Tang, S. (2025, April 22). *Analysis of the Impact of the US "Reciprocal Tariff" Policy on Global Supply Chains and China's Co.* Chambers and Partners. https://chambers.com/articles/analysis-of-the-impact-of-the-u-s-reciprocal-tariff-policy-on-global-supply-chains-and-chinas-co

Zhu, G., Zhang, C., & Zheng, C. (2025). *Special Research Report on the Innovative Pharmaceutical Industry: Innovation Breakthroughs, Overseas Expansion.* Dongwu Securities.

About the Contributors

Henni Appelgryn holds a PhD, a DBA, and an MBA in Business Administration, reflecting his deep commitment to scholarly excellence. For 18 years, he served as a lecturer at Beijing Normal Hong Kong Baptist University in Zhuhai, and other universities in China, where he taught Entrepreneurship, Marketing Management, and Business Communications. Entrepreneurial leadership, innovation, and the increasing application of artificial intelligence in modern businesses are the nucleus of his intellectual curiosity. Before relocating to China, he had accumulated over 20 years of entrepreneurial experience in his native South Africa. He founded Dragon Eye Sky Intelligence, a cloud-based GPS tracking company, and co-founded Sunburst Solar, a solar importer serving the South African market. He also founded Shenzhen Flying Blue Dragon in China and has implemented Odoo ERP systems and cloud-based platforms. This unique blend of academic depth and hands-on business experience allows him to bring a practical, grounded perspective to his work. He is the editor of the Cases on Chinese Corporate Giants and Global Expansion book, and he is the author of DeepSeek's Open-Source AI Revolution: A "David vs. Goliath" Challenge to Global Tech Giants. Plus, the editor of the Cases on Chinese Unicorns and the Development of Startups book, and the author of Manner Coffee: Journey in China's Specialty Coffee Market. Through his writing and editing, he continues to explore how Chinese enterprises navigate global competition and technological change.

Youssef Elhaoussine is an Assistant Professor in the Department of Management at the Faculty of Business and Management, Beijing Normal–Hong Kong Baptist University. With a strong interdisciplinary background in science and business, he holds a Ph.D. in Corporate Entrepreneurship from Sun Yat-sen University, a Master's in Marketing Management from Cranfield University (UK), a BSc in Applied and Analytical Chemistry from Edinburgh Napier University (UK), and a Technical Diploma in Physics–Chemistry from Université de Reims (France). Before joining academia, he worked in industrial manufacturing in China and Europe, managing production and quality control in the printer-consumables sector. This blend of scientific training and operational experience shapes his approach to teaching. He teaches business ethics, sustainability, and industrial management, incorporating real industrial contexts, applied case studies, and AI-supported learning methods to enhance student independence. He is frequently invited by the French Chamber of Commerce in China and French Tech China to share insights as an industrial and academic expert and serves as Co-Chair for International Development at the Asia Pacific Marketing Academy.

***

Songhao Deng is an undergraduate student majoring in Business Analytics at Beijing Normal University–Hong Kong Baptist University. He studies how global markets work, how big companies plan their strategies, and what drives industries like energy. Through real research projects and hands-on activities, he has learned to connect classroom theories to the real world. For Chapter 9: CATL's Global Energy Supply Role, Songhao wanted to help fellow students understand why CATL has become such a powerful force in the world's energy supply. His deep curiosity about the company's global growth, combined with his practical experience in business analysis, makes him a relatable and trustworthy guide. He wrote this chapter to share useful insights and show you how business analysis comes to life.

Daven Duan, as an undergraduate majoring in Accounting at Beijing Normal Hong Kong Baptist University, DUAN Huaxuan focuses his academic interests on Chinese Multinational Enterprises and Mergers and Acquisitions, with a particular focus on New Energy Vehicle and Automobile Engineering. He has participated in relevant research projects, academic activities, and extracurricular practices, showing a firm commitment to deepening professional understanding. Integrating theoretical knowledge with practical application, he is well-prepared for future academic or professional development and is passionate about Chinese enterprises going abroad, striving to make meaningful contributions to his chosen discipline.

Zhen Gong is an undergraduate finance student at Beijing Normal Hong Kong Baptist University. She wrote Chapter 29: TCL's Localized Global Manufacturing Strategy because she is passionate about helping you understand how Chinese companies succeed around the world. Through class projects and her own research on international business, she has learned how firms like TCL balance global reach with local know-how. Her real-world curiosity is precisely what she contributes to this chapter; she genuinely wants to share what is effective. Zhen knows you are still learning the ropes (she is too), and she wants to show you that textbook ideas come alive in smart manufacturing decisions.

Yulin Li is an undergraduate accounting student at Beijing Normal Hong Kong Baptist University, so she knows exactly what it is like to be in your shoes. Her research on how Chinese companies go global, plus internships in auditing and financial services, gives her a real-world lens on how businesses work. In Chapter 27: SF Holding's Global Logistics Strategy, Yulin unpacks a real logistics giant to help you see past textbook theories. She wrote this chapter because she wants you to understand how global strategies come to life and to show that even as a student, you can start thinking like an analyst. Trust her fresh, grounded perspective.

Liang Zhuoyao is a marketing student at Beijing Normal Hong Kong Baptist University, and she is also an aviation enthusiast. For Chapter 3: Air China's Overseas Market Strategy, she shares what she has learned about how airlines grow their brands and enter new markets. Her hands-on experience includes attending airshows, industry exhibitions, and airline events, where she saw real business strategies in action. She wrote this chapter because she wanted to help fellow students connect classroom theory with real-world cases. As someone who's passionate about the digital transformation in aviation, she hopes her insights make this topic clear, useful, and even a little exciting for you.

Zihan Lin is an undergraduate Accounting student at Beijing Normal Hong Kong Baptist University, someone who has still been in your shoes, learning right alongside you. Her curiosity about how new energy companies grow globally led her to write Chapter 8: BYD International Market Entry Model. Through her own research on car companies' financial performance and investment analysis, she has learned to connect textbook theories with actual business decisions. Zihan is especially passionate about the financial risks companies face when expanding overseas, and she wrote this chapter to help you see how those risks and opportunities play out in a real-world case like BYD (Build Your Dreams). Think of her as a fellow student who dug deep into this topic, so you do not have to start from scratch.

Rismawati is an Associate Professor in Accounting at Universitas Muhammadiyah Palopo, Indonesia, and she thinks of accounting as holding businesses accountable for their real-world impact. Her work focuses on sustainability and social accounting, checking whether companies follow through on their promises to people and the planet. That ability makes her the perfect person to write Chapter 2: Tsingshan's Indonesian Nickel. She wrote it because she wants you to see that accounting is not about numbers. It is a lens for understanding how a giant nickel operation can create both opportunity and harm. By the end, you will understand why what gets measured matters.

QipeiWan is currently an undergraduate student in Finance at Beijing Normal Hong Kong Baptist University. Her academic interests focus on AIoT security and global strategic management, particularly in the study of international expansion challenges and competitive advantages. In Chapter 16: Hikvision's AIoT Security Expansion, she explored how geopolitical sanctions, regulatory fragmentation, and localization strategies shape a firm's global trajectory. Passionate about the intersection of emerging technology and cross-border risk management, she aims to analyze how Chinese tech enterprises build resilience through R&D investment and supply chain diversification. Her work blends theoretical frameworks with real-world corporate practice.

Ziheng Wang is the author of Chapter 10: The CITIC State-Led Globalization Model. He is currently an undergraduate accounting student at Beijing Normal Hong Kong Baptist University, but do not let that fool you. Ziheng has already dug deep into how state-owned giants like CITIC expand globally while balancing government ties and market pressures. His research on CITIC's strategic growth and risk management makes him the perfect guide for this topic. He wrote this chapter because he knows that understanding China's state-led globalization model can feel tricky, and he wants to help you see it clearly, using real examples you can learn from today.

Lanxi Xi, the author of Chapter 17: JD.com Supply Chain Internationalization. Lanxi is an undergraduate accounting student who became curious about how Chinese companies like JD.com (JingDong) grow beyond their home markets. She researched the global logistics of JD.com and its business model, turning classroom concepts into real-world insights. Lanxi wrote this chapter to help you understand exactly how a major e-commerce company builds international supply chains without the jargon. Her own experience as a student researcher makes her the perfect guide: she knows what questions you are asking because she asked them herself. Think of this as learning from a motivated classmate who has already done the digging.

Boyan Xing is a finance and math student at Beijing Normal Hong Kong Baptist University. He loves exploring how data and algorithms can lead to smarter investment decisions. Through internships at an investment bank and a private equity firm, plus his own research in areas like factor mining and cybersecurity, he has seen firsthand why good data governance matters. That is why he wrote Chapter 33: Wind Information Technology's Data Governance Expansion to help students understand how real-world companies manage and protect their financial data. His mix of math theory and hands-on coding makes him a relatable guide for anyone curious about the data powering today's markets.

Yuhua Yu is an undergraduate student majoring in Applied Economics at the Macau University of Science and Technology. Chapter 19: Jiangsu Changjiang Electronics Technology illustrates how a tech company can prioritize climate action. Yuhua studies low-carbon development and Environmental, Social, and Governance (ESG), how businesses measure their environmental footprint and work toward sustainability. She has done research on cutting emissions without crashing growth, so she knows what to seek in a company's green efforts. In the chapter, she collapses how the venture balances innovation with responsibility. Think of her as a fellow student who's curious about the same big questions you are. Yuhua's hands-on experience makes her a trustworthy guide, but her friendly, down-to-earth style makes the topic feel approachable.

Yuan Zhenxiang is a finance undergraduate who loves exploring how marketing and leadership shape real-world organizations. As president of her university's Career Development Association, she has led teams, planned strategies, and worked across different departments, skills that help her see how companies like the Beijing Genomics Institute build their global reputation. In Chapter 6: Beijing Genomics Institute (BGI) Global Biotechnology Positioning, she connects financial thinking with branding to show you how BGI competes and grows on the world stage. Zhenxiang wrote this chapter because she wants students to understand that smart positioning is not just about science; it is also about leadership and strategy. Her hands-on experience and interdisciplinary approach make her the perfect guide for this topic.

Yuqian Zhang is an undergraduate student in Finance at Beijing Normal-Hong Kong Baptist University. She wrote Chapter 15: Hengrui Pharmaceutical's Innovation-Driven Internationalization to share whatshe has learned about how Chinese biotech companies expand globally. Her research focuses on corporate finance and overseas strategies, especially licensing deals and navigating tough markets like the U.S. FDA. By analyzing Hengrui's NewCo model, she connects classroom finance theories to real-world challenges. She's passionate about helping innovative Chinese pharma firms overcome political and regulatory hurdles. As a fellow student, she wanted to write this chapter so her peers could better understand the exciting and complex journey of bringing Chinese medicine to the world.

Cunzhen Zhou, a finance undergraduate at Beijing Normal Hong Kong Baptist University. She wrote Chapter 34: WuXi AppTec's Integrated Global CRDMO Model because she is fascinated by how financial theories explain real-world business decisions. Through her coursework and self-driven projects on risk management and global expansion, she has studied how companies like WuXi AppTec build resilience across borders. That experience, plus her curiosity about what causes financial instability, makes her the perfect guide for this chapter. Cunzhen wants to help you see how a real global company uses finance and strategy to succeed. Think of her as a fellow student who has done the digging so you can learn alongside her.

Lan Zhou, the author of Chapter 12: Envision's Global Climate Governance Model. She is currently a sophomore majoring in Accounting, but her real passion lies at the intersection of climate change and finance, specifically how companies track and report their carbon emissions. Lan wrote this chapter because she wanted to help fellow students understand how a real-world company like Envision uses digital tools to manage its climate impact. Her hands-on research into carbon accounting and AI applications makes her the perfect guide. Think of her as a curious classmate who is already deep into the topic, and she is here to walk you through it step by step.

Index

F

G

H

I

J

T

U

V

Z

www.ingramcontent.com/pod-product-compliance
Lightning Source LLC
LaVergne TN
LVHW061528290926
849162LV00004B/708